DATE DUE

AP 22 '99			
MY 1 2 00			

DEMCO 38-296

THE COLUMBIA ANTHOLOGY OF
BRITISH POETRY

The Columbia Anthology of

BRITISH
POETRY

EDITED BY

CARL WOODRING
and JAMES SHAPIRO

COLUMBIA UNIVERSITY PRESS

NEW YORK

Columbia University Press

New York   Chichester, West Sussex

Copyright © 1995 Columbia University Press

PR 1175 .C6416 1995

taloging-in-Publication Data

poetry /   edited by Carl Woodring and

The Columbia anthology of
British poetry

ing, Carl, 1919–   .   II. Shapiro,
James S., 1955–   .
PR1175.C6416   1995   94-46333   821.008—dc20
                                                                  CIP

Printed in the United States of America

c 10 9 8 7 6 5 4 3 2 1

CONTENTS

Mary Sidney Herbert, Countess of Pembroke   (1561–1621)

Samuel Daniel   (1562/63–1619)

Michael Drayton   (1563–1631)

Christopher Marlowe   (1564–1593)

William Shakespeare   (1564–1616)

INTRODUCTION

Poetry from the British Isles, with its extraordinary range and expressive power, presents a formidable challenge to all who attempt to select from it. In response to this infinite variety, anthologies have been in circulation for nearly as long as British poetry has been in print. By the time that the Gravedigger in *Hamlet* cheerfully recited verse from that most popular of Elizabethan collections, *Tottel's Miscellany*, Shakespeare's own poetry was already being anthologized in such collections as *England's Helicon* and *England's Parnassus*. The impulse to anthologize has continued unabated for the ensuing four centuries, as each generation of readers has discovered that tastes change, some poems grow stale, other poems are exciting to encounter for the first time, and still others are a pleasure to rediscover. Indeed, the continued vitality of British verse is confirmed by the need to anthologize yet again, in the process reorienting the trajectory that British poetry has taken over the course of the past twelve centuries.

The past two decades in particular have seen an explosion of interest in poets and literary traditions that have long lingered in obscurity, as scholars have broadened the canon of "British" poetry to include works by a good many overlooked Irish, Welsh, and Scottish poets. An even more significant change has been the restoration to prominence of women poets, whose work, while celebrated in their own day, has been for various reasons long out of print and unavailable. Recent and forthcoming scholarly editions, along with specialized anthologies such as *Kissing the Rod: An Anthology of Seventeenth-Century Women's Verse*, *The Penguin Book of Renaissance Verse*, *Eighteenth-Century Women Poets*, *The Field Day Anthology of Irish Literature*, *An Anthology of Poetry from Wales*, and *An Anthology of Scottish Women Poets* (to name but a few of the very best) have irrevocably extended the horizons of British poetry and have made available once again a number of these important voices. But as long as these voices remain scattered in narrowly defined and often expensive volumes, few general readers will have a chance to come into contact with much of this poetry.

These specialized anthologies have as yet made little impact on which poets and poems are included in one-volume anthologies of British poetry, the collections general readers have long depended on. The most famous of these, Palgrave's *Golden Treasury of the Best Songs and Lyrical Poems in the English Language*, first published in 1861 and periodically revised since then, has put a firm stamp on what anthologists covering the whole of British poetry have subsequently considered worth including. Palgrave was quite candid about his principles of exclusion: any poem that was too long, unrhymed (or written in heroic couplets), narrative, descriptive, didactic, humorous, erotic, religious, occasional, or overly personal was deemed inappropriate and "foreign" to the nature of the enterprise. That left brief lyrics or songs, in rhyme, possessed of the proper "lyric unity" (which sometimes meant lopping off an offending stanza or two). Palgrave was not particularly interested in poetry written before the mid-sixteenth century, nor did he find space for women poets before the eighteenth century. The result was a collection of first-rate lyric poems, although their range of emotions remained constrained: suffering and exultation, religious illumination and despair, political outrage and triumph, sensuality and sexual loathing, were pushed to the margins or carefully avoided.

The two most influential one-volume anthologies that have appeared since Palgrave—Arthur Quiller-Couch's *Oxford Book of English Verse, 1250–1900*, which appeared at the turn of the century, and Helen Gardner's *Oxford Book of English Verse, 1250–1950*, which superseded her predecessor's volume in 1972—have not greatly changed the parameters established in *The Golden Treasury*. While both included medieval lyrics, and while Gardner also extended her canon to include historical, political, satiric, and religious verse (as well as a number of significant longer poems), women poets were still badly underrepresented and the assumptions underlying what constitutes "English" poetry remained largely unexamined (for example, Gardner made room for what she described as poems in "the Scottish dialect" but not for Irish or Welsh verse).

The Columbia Anthology of British Poetry does its best to redress some of these omissions while not losing sight of the main purpose of any good anthology: to offer poems of the very highest aesthetic merit. Thus, while deeply indebted to recent revisionary work that has enriched the canon of important poetry, we also offer a rich array of time-honored poems that warrant inclusion in any collection that aspires to offer the best that has been written in the British Isles. These favorites take their place beside celebrated longer poems often condemned to exclusion by their length, poems such as Marston's "A Cynic Satire," Pope's "The Rape of the Lock," Coleridge's "The Rime of the Ancient Mariner, and Keats's "The Eve of St. Agnes."

This is also the first general anthology to restore major British women poets of the sixteenth, seventeenth, eighteenth, and nineteenth centuries to the wide readership they enjoyed in their own day. The poems of Queen Elizabeth I, Anne Locke, the Countess of Pembroke, Aemilia Lanyer, Mary Sidney Wroth, Margaret Cavendish, Katherine Philips, Aphra Behn, Anne Killigrew, Anne Finch, Mary Barber, Mary Leapor, Anna Barbauld, Charlotte Turner Smith, Joanna Baillie, Felicia Hemans, and a score of others reveal not only that women were writing verse of the highest merit but that there was a long poetic dialogue, barely acknowledged by modern critics intent on either protecting an old canon or substituting a new one, between men and women poets writing in English. We have tried to bring this dialogue to life by including poems like

Anne Ingram's "On Mr. Pope's Characters of Women," and John Dryden's ode to the memory of Anne Killigrew, as well as by juxtaposing poems (such as Jonson's famous country house poem, "To Penshurst," with Aemilia Lanyer's "Description of Cookham").

Considerable effort has been made to ensure that an anthology of British poetry include more than a token example or two of poems by Scottish, Irish, or Welsh poets. We have also taken the unusual step of including poems written in languages foreign to modern English readers. Dafydd ap Gwilym, the finest medieval Welsh poet and one of the greatest Welsh poets of all time, is included, along with Eochaidh Ó Heóghusa, a contemporary of Shakespeare and one of the great Irish bards. Translations of their poems by poets writing centuries later are also included here and testify to the continuing influence of their work. Following similar principles, we have also chosen to begin the anthology with a number of Anglo-Saxon poems that give a sense of the origins of British poetry and have engaged poets up through this century. Ezra Pound, whose translation of "The Seafarer" we have included, was surely correct when he wrote that "one does not need to learn a whole language in order to understand some one or some dozen poems." A poem by Nuala Ní Dhomhnaill, with her own translation, demonstrates the enduring vitality of Irish Gaelic.

Above all, we have tried in this anthology to restore a sense of the lively conversations that have taken place among the poets—male, female, rich, poor, Irish, Welsh, Scottish, and English—working in these poetic traditions for the past twelve centuries. Their dialogue has taken various forms: imitation, translation, satiric attack, parody, collaboration, and posthumous tribute; all of these have found a place in the pages that follow.

EDITORIAL PRINCIPLES

Our overriding interest is in making poetry accessible. We have modernized unconventional spelling, capitalization, and contractions. We have also modernized punctuation to bring it into line with modern expectations and usage, although here we have been more conservative, since for many poets punctuation has been as much a rhetorical as a grammatical device. We have avoided a procrustean editing policy and have tried instead to be flexible when dealing with the idiosyncrasies of particular poets. For example, the poems of Dunbar and Skelton have been left for the most part unchanged, because to modernize these surprisingly accessible poems would be to translate rather than update. We have also tried to avoid excerpting longer poems.

In general, each poem appears in the form that has been traditional for that poem. These are texts for reading. In editing these poems we have consulted early printed texts or manuscripts of the poems and have also drawn on the insights and expertise of modern scholars. The anthology is arranged along chronological lines, by date of a poet's birth rather than the date of composition or publication of each poem.

For the past few decades readers (usually students) have first approached poetry in such anthologies as the widely used *Norton Anthology of English Poetry* through a veil of extended introductory material and a vast array of footnotes and glosses. The result is as often confusion and alienation as clarity; the message seems to be that readers are ill equipped to deal with the riches of British poetry. But even with unusually difficult poetry, extensive glossing can go beyond the explanation of unfamiliar words and historical details only by choosing one interpretation rather than another. Rhythm, the play of sound and sense, that which makes a poem resonant and memorable, cannot be explained. Nor can the larger literary, historic, or generic feature be adequately set forth in such short space.

In retrospect, one of the great merits of the great general anthologies in this century is that they were unencumbered by this critical commentary and simply trusted readers to discover poems for themselves. Our own policy is closer to this practice. We have included brief biographical introductions to each poet and have only glossed words that do not appear in a standard collegiate diction-ary or whose meanings have changed dramatically over time and would there-fore mislead modern readers. Those interested in learning more about the poetic conventions and literary history of the poetry contained in this volume are urged to consult our companion volume, *The Columbia History of British Poetry*, a collection of essays by leading scholars that explore at length specific periods and authors; the *History* also includes suggestions for further reading, brief biographies, and a list of standard editions.

While this entire enterprise has been collaborative, James Shapiro has taken initial responsibility for poetry from *Beowulf* to Alexander Pope, and Carl Woodring for poetry after Pope.

ACKNOWLEDGMENTS

We are indebted to a number of institutions for providing access to early editions or manuscripts of poetry: the Columbia University Libraries, The Henry E. Huntington Library, The British Library, The Folger Shakespeare Library, and especially the Harry Ransom Humanities Research Center and other libraries at the University of Texas. We would also like to thank a number of friends and colleagues for their help and suggestions: Annette Wheeler Cafarelli, Mary Cregan, Juana Green, Robert Griffin, David Scott Kastan, Brian McHale, James Mirollo, Laura O'Connor, and Edward Tayler. We are no less indebted to the dedicated contributors to the companion volume, *The Columbia History of British Poetry*, for their advice. We are grateful as well to Franz Peter Hugdahl. Finally, this anthology could not have been completed without the support of James Raimes and the superb editing of Edith Hazen of Columbia University Press.

James Shapiro
Carl Woodring

THE COLUMBIA ANTHOLOGY OF
BRITISH POETRY

OLD ENGLISH POETRY

Perhaps thirty thousand lines of Old English poetry, transcribed in a hundred or
so manuscripts, have survived to give us a sense of the rich poetic legacy of the
seventh through eleventh centuries in England. This alliterative verse covers a
range of genres, including wisdom poetry (represented here by an excerpt from
"The Seafarer"), dream vision, and most notably, epic (of which two examples
follow, lines from the beginning of "Beowulf" and from "Battle of Brunan-
burh"). "Beowulf" is generally regarded as the first great masterpiece of English
poetry. Although infrequently read today in the original, and even less fre-
quently anthologized, Old English verse influenced subsequent English poetry,
especially in the late nineteenth and early twentieth centuries. W. H. Auden
writes of being "spellbound" by his first exposure to Old English poetry, while
Gerard Manley Hopkins wrote to Robert Bridges that this poetic language "is a
vastly superior thing to what we have now." A number of poets have been
inspired to translate these poems into modern English; two of the most famous
of these efforts—by Alfred Tennyson and Ezra Pound—are included here,
along with a helpful, literal rendering of the opening lines of "Beowulf" by Ruth
P. M. Lehmann.

From BEOWULF (c. 8th century)

 Hwæt, wē gār-dena in gēardagum,
þēodcyninga þrym gefrūnon,
hū ðā æþelingas ellen fremedon!
 Oft Scyld Scēfing sceaþena þrēatum,
monegum mǣgþum meodosetla oftēah,
egsode eorl[as], syððan ǣrest wearð
fēasceaft funden; hē þæs frōfre gebād
wēox under wolcnum weorðmyndum þāh,
oð þæt him æghwylc ymbsittendra
ofer hronrāde hȳran scolde,   10
gomban gyldan; þæt wæs gōd cyning!
Ðǣm eafera wæs æfter cenned
geong in geardum, þone God sende
folce tō frōfre; fyrenðearfe ongeat,
þē hīe ǣr drugon aldor(lē)ase

1

lange hwīle;   him þæs Līffrêa,
wuldres Wealdend   woroldāre forgeaf,
Bēowulf wæs brēme   —blǣd wīde sprang—
Scyldes eafera   Scedelandum in.
Swā sceal (geong g)uma   gōde gewyrcean,   20
fromum feohgiftum   on fæder (bea)rme,
þæt hine on ylde   eft gewunigen
wilgesīþas,   þonne wīg cume,
lēode gelǣsten;   lofdǣdum sceal
in mǣgþa gehwǣre   man geþéon.

Translated by Ruth P. M. Lehmann (1912–   )

Now we have heard stories of high valor
in times long past   of tribal monarchs,
lords of Denmark,   how those leaders strove.
    Often Scyld Scefing   by the shock of war
kept both troops and tribes   from treasured meadbench,
filled foes with dread   after first being
discovered uncared for;   a cure for that followed:
he grew hale under heaven,   high in honor,
until no nation   near the borders,
beyond teeming seas   but was taught to obey,   10
giving tribute.   He was a good ruler.
    To him a boy was born,   a baby in the homestead,
whom God grants us   as gift and comfort
to ease the people.   He apprehended
dire trouble dogged   those destitute people.
But the Lord of life,   Leader of heaven,
offered them honor,   earthly requital.
Beow was famous—   abroad well renowned—
throughout south Sweden,   the successor to Scyld.
Thus should a fine young man   on his father's throne   20
give generously,   and do good to all
so that when aging,   old companions
stand by him steady   at the stroke of war,
his people serve him.   By praiseworthy deeds
each must prosper   in every tribe.

From BATTLE OF BRUNANBURH

(c. 10th century)

Hēr Æðelstān cyning,   eorla drihten,
beorna bēahgifa,   and his brōðor ēac,
Ēadmund æðeling,   ealdorlangne tīr
geslōgon æt sæcce   sweorda ęcgum
ymbe Brunanburh: bordweall clufon,
hēowon heaðolinde   hamora lāfum,
eaforan Ēadweardes;   swā him geæðele wæs
fram cnēomāgum,   ðæt hī æt campe oft
wið lāðra gehwæne   land ealgodon,
hord and hāmas.   Hęttend crungon,   10
Scotta lēode   and scipflotan,
fæge fēollon: feld dennode
sęcga swāte,   siþþan sunne ūpp
on morgentīd,   mære tungol,
glād ofer grundas,   Godes candel beorht,
ēces Drihtnes,   oð sīo æðele gesceaft
sāh tō sctlc.

Translated by Alfred, Lord Tennyson (1809–1892)

Athelstan King,
Lord among Earls,
Bracelet-bestower and
Baron of Barons,
He with his brother,
Edmund Atheling,
Gaining a lifelong
Glory in battle,
Slew with the sword-edge
There by Brunanburh,   10
Brake the shield-wall,
Hew'd the linden-wood,
Hack'd the battle-shield,
Sons of Edward with hammer'd brands.

Theirs was a greatness
Got from their grandsires—
Theirs that so often in

Strife with their enemies
Struck for their hoards and their hearts and their homes.

    Bow'd the spoiler,   20
    Bent the Scotsman,
    Fell the ship-crews
    Doom'd to the death.
All the field with blood of the fighters
    Flow'd, from when first the great
    Sun-star of morning-tide,
    Lamp of the Lord God
    Lord everlasting,
Glode over earth till the glorious creature
    Sank to his setting.   30

    There lay many a man
    Marr'd by the javelin,
    Men of the Northland
    Shot over shield.
    There was the Scotsman
    Weary of war.

    We the West-Saxons,
    Long as the daylight
    Lasted, in companies
Troubled the track of the host that we hated;   40
Grimly with swords that were sharp from the grindstone,
Fiercely we hack'd at the flyers before us.

    Mighty the Mercian,
    Hard was his hand-play,
    Sparing not any of
    Those that with Anlaf,
    Warriors over the
    Weltering waters
    Borne in the bark's-bosom,
    Drew to this island—   50
    Doom'd to the death.

Five young kings put asleep by the sword-stroke,
Seven strong earls of the army of Anlaf
Fell on the war-field, numberless numbers,
Shipmen and Scotsmen.

Then the Norse leader—
Dire was his need of it,
Few were his following—
Fled to his war-ship;
Fleeted his vessel to sea with the king in it,   60
Saving his life on the fallow flood.

Also the crafty one,
Constantinus,
Crept to his North again,
Hoar-headed hero!

Slender warrant had
He to be proud of
The welcome of war-knives—
He that was reft of his
Folk and his friends that had   70
Fallen in conflict,
Leaving his son too
Lost in the carnage,
Mangled to morsels,
A youngster in war!

Slender reason had
He to be glad of
The clash of the war-glaive—
Traitor and trickster
And spurner of treaties—   80
He nor had Anlaf
With armies so broken
A reason for bragging
That they had the better
In perils of battle
On places of slaughter—
The struggle of standards,
The rush of the javelins,
The crash of the charges,
The wielding of weapons—   90
The play that they play'd with
The children of Edward.

Then with their nail'd prows
Parted the Norsemen, a

Blood-redden'd relic of
Javelins over
The jarring breaker, the deep-sea billow,
Shaping their way toward Dyflen again,
　　Shamed in their souls.

　　Also the brethren,　　　　　　　　　　　　　　100
　　King and Atheling,
　　Each in his glory,
Went to his own in his own West-Saxon-land,
　　Glad of the war.

Many a carcase they left to be carrion,
Many a livid one, many a sallow-skin—
Left for the white-tail'd eagle to tear it, and
Left for the horny-nibb'd raven to rend it, and
Gave to the garbaging war-hawk to gorge it, and
That gray beast, the wolf of the weald.　　　　　110

　　Never had huger
　　Slaughter of heroes
　　Slain by the sword-edge—
　　Such as old writers
　　Have writ of in histories—
　　Hapt in this isle, since
　　Up from the East hither
　　Saxon and Angle from
　　Over the broad billow
　　Broke into Britain with　　　　　　　　　　　120
　　Haughty war-workers who
　　Harried the Welshman, when
　　Earls that were lured by the
　　Hunger of glory gat
　　Hold of the land.

From THE SEAFARER (c. 10th century)

Mæg ic be me sylfum　soðgied wrecan,
siþas secgan,　hu ic geswincdagum
earfoðhwile　oft þrowade,
bitre breostceare　gebiden hæbbe,

gecunnad in ceole   cearselda fela,
atol yþa gewealc,   þær mec oft bigeat
nearo nihtwaco   æt nacan stefnan,
þonne he be clifum cnossað.   Calde geþrungen
wæron mine fet,   forste gebunden,
caldum clommum,   þær þa ceare seofedun   10
hat ymb heortan;   hungor innan slat
merewerges mod.   þæt se mon ne wat
þe him on foldan   fægrost limpeð,
hu ic earmcearig   iscealdne sæ
winter wunade   wræccan lastum,
winemægum bidroren,
bihongen hrimgicelum;   hægl scurum fleag.

Translated by Ezra Pound (1885–1972)

May I for my own self song's truth reckon,
Journey's jargon, how I in harsh days
Hardship endured oft.
Bitter breast-cares have I abided,
Known on my keel many a care's hold,
And dire sea-surge, and there I oft spent
Narrow nightwatch nigh the ship's head
While she tossed close to cliffs. Coldly afflicted,
My feet were by frost benumbed.
Chill its chains are; chafing sighs   10
Hew my heart round and hunger begot
Mere-weary mood. Lest man know not
That he on dry land loveliest liveth,
List how I, care-wretched, on ice-cold sea,
Weathered the winter, wretched outcast
Deprived of my kinsmen;
Hung with hard ice-flakes, where hail-scur flew,
There I heard naught save the harsh sea
And ice-cold wave, at whiles the swan cries,
Did for my games the gannet's clamour,   20
Sea-fowls' loudness was for me laughter,
The mews' singing all my mead-drink.
Storms, on the stone-cliffs beaten, fell on the stern
In icy feathers; full oft the eagle screamed
With spray on his pinion.
                    Not any protector

May make merry man faring needy.
This he little believes, who aye in winsome life
Abides 'mid burghers some heavy business,
Wealthy and wine-flushed, how I weary oft   30
Must bide above brine.
Neareth nightshade, snoweth from north,
Frost froze the land, hail fell on earth then
Corn of the coldest. Nathless there knocketh now
The heart's thought that I on high streams
The salt-wavy tumult traverse alone.
Moaneth alway my mind's lust
That I fare forth, that I afar hence
Seek out a foreign fastness.
For this there's no mood-lofty man over earth's midst,   40
Not though he be given his good, but will have in his youth greed;
Nor his deed to the daring, nor his king to the faithful
But shall have his sorrow for sea-fare
Whatever his lord will.
He hath not heart for harping, nor in ring-having
Nor winsomeness to wife, nor world's delight
Nor any whit else save the wave's slash,
Yet longing comes upon him to fare forth on the water.
Bosque taketh blossom, cometh beauty of berries,
Fields to fairness, land fares brisker,   50
All this admonisheth man eager of mood,
The heart turns to travel so that he then thinks
On flood-ways to be far departing.
Cuckoo calleth with gloomy crying,
He singeth summerward, bodeth sorrow,
The bitter heart's blood. Burgher knows not—
He the prosperous man—what some perform
Where wandering them widest draweth.
So that but now my heart burst from my breast-lock,
My mood 'mid the mere-flood,   60
Over the whale's acre, would wander wide.
On earth's shelter cometh often to me,
Eager and ready, the crying lone-flyer,
Whets for the whale-path the heart irresistibly,
O'er tracks of ocean; seeing that anyhow
My lord deems to me this dead life
On loan and on land, I believe not
That any earth-weal eternal standeth
Save there be somewhat calamitous

That, ere a man's tide go, turn it to twain.   70
Disease or oldness or sword-hate
Beats out the breath from doom-gripped body.
And for this, every earl whatever, for those speaking after—
Laud of the living, boasteth some last word,
That he will work ere he pass onward,
Frame on the fair earth 'gainst foes his malice,
Daring ado, . . .
So that all men shall honour him after
And his laud beyond them remain 'mid the English,
Aye, for ever, a lasting life's-blast,   80
Delight mid the doughty.
                         Days little durable,
And all arrogance of earthen riches,
There come now no kings nor Cæsars
Nor gold-giving lords like those gone.
Howe'er in mirth most magnified,
Whoe'er lived in life most lordliest,
Drear all this excellence, delights undurable!
Wancth the watch, but the world holdeth.
Tomb hideth trouble. The blade is layed low.   90
Earthly glory ageth and seareth.
No man at all going the earth's gait,
But age fares against him, his face paleth,
Grey-haired he groaneth, knows gone companions,
Lordly men are to earth o'ergiven,
Nor may he then the flesh-cover, whose life ceaseth,
Nor eat the sweet nor feel the sorry,
Nor stir hand nor think in mid heart,
And though he strew the grave with gold,
His born brothers, their buried bodies   100
Be an unlikely treasure hoard.

Dafydd ap Gwilym

(*c. 1 3 2 0 – c. 1 3 8 0*)

Dafydd ap Gwilym is generally recognized as the finest medieval Welsh poet and one of the most important of all Welsh poets. Roughly a contemporary of Chaucer, Dafydd, a native of Ceredigion (near Aberystwyth), was born into a prominent Welsh family less than half a century after England had conquered Wales. Much of what we know about Dafydd's life, travels, and career comes from his poetry. The verse form he employed was extremely complex and demanding, especially the requirements of combining rhyme with alliteration in couplets of seven-syllable lines while using a dense poetic syntax punctuated with interjections and interpolations. Dafydd's poetry is also characterized by its use of foreign loanwords (such as "Ffloringod" or "florins" in line 13 of "Mis Mai"). His subject matter is quite broad, encompassing not only religious and elegiac verse but also the love poetry and poems about nature for which he is most celebrated. Throughout his work, Dafydd displays a remarkable capacity to integrate long-standing native traditions with Ovidian and Continental literary models. Some 350 poems have been attributed to him in scores of surviving manuscripts that give some indication of his contemporary reputation; scholars currently accept about 150 as unquestionably Dafydd's own composition. His works were first collected and published in 1789 in London by Owen Jones and William Owen in *Barddoniaeth Dafydd ab Gwilym* and have continued to attract the interest of critics and poets and translators. One of the earliest of these translators was the nineteenth-century writer and lawyer Arthur James Johnes, who published his translations of Dafydd while in his twenties under the pseudonym "Maelog." Johnes was a staunch advocate of Welsh culture and wrote against those who maintained the inferiority of the Celtic people.

From MIS MAI

Duw gwyddiad mai da y gweddai
Dechreuad mwyn dyfiad Mai.
Difeth irgyrs a dyfai
Dyw Calan mis mwynlan Mai.
Digrinflaen goed a'm oedai,
Duw mawr a roes doe y Mai.

Dillyn beirdd ni'm rhydwyllai,
Da fyd ym oedd dyfod Mai.

Harddwas teg a'm anrhegai,
Hylaw ŵr mawr hael yw'r Mai. 10
Anfones ym iawn fwnai,
Glas defyll glân mwyngyll Mai.
Ffloringod brig ni'm digiai,
F'Hŵr-dy-lis gyfoeth mis Mai.
Diongl rhag brad y'm cadwai,
Dan esgyll dail mentyll Mai.
Llawn wyf o ddig na thrigai
(Beth yw i mi?) byth y Mai.

Translated by Arthur James Johnes (1809–1871)

MAY

Many a poet in his lay
Told me May would come again;
Truly sang the bards—for May
Yesterday began to reign!
She is like a bounteous lord,
Gold enough she gives to me;
Gold—such as we poets hoard—
"Florins" of the mead and tree,
Hazel flowers and "fleurs-de-lis,"
Underneath her leafy wings, 10
I am safe from treason's stings:
I am full of wrath with May,
That she will not always stay!
Maidens never hear of love,
But when she has plumed the grove,—
Give of the gift of song
To the poet's heart and tongue.
May! Majestic child of heaven,
To the earth in glory given!
Verdant hills, days long and clear, 20
Come when she is hov'ring near.
Stars, ye cannot journey on
Joyously when she is gone!

Ye are not so glossy bright,
Blackbirds, when she takes her flight.
Sweetest art thou, nightingale;
Poet, thou canst tell thy tale
With a lighter heart, when May
Rules with all her bright array.

Geoffrey Chaucer

(c. 1343 – 1400)

Venerated by contemporaries and successors as the first great English poet, Chaucer was the son of a prosperous London wine merchant. In 1359 he served in France with the forces of Edward III, was taken prisoner, and then ransomed. His wife Philippa Roet, whom he married around 1366, was the sister of John of Gaunt's third wife, and Chaucer would benefit from Gaunt's patronage for the rest of his life. For the next two decades Chaucer was active at court and as a diplomat, traveling to France, Genoa, and Florence (where some have speculated he may have met Petrarch and Boccaccio). He also held a number of lucrative public offices, including Controller of the Custom and Clerk of the King's Work. A strong French and Italian influence is recognizable in Chaucer's early works, *The Book of the Duchess* (c.1370), *The House of Fame* (1370s), and *Troilus and Cressida* (c.1385). Chaucer's range and interests were extraordinary. He composed a scientific *Treatise on the Astrolabe* (1391) for his son Lewis, and he translated Boethius's *Consolation of Philosophy* as well as part of the great French allegorical poem *Le Roman de la Rose*. His masterpiece, *The Canterbury Tales*, was probably begun sometime around 1387; its great popularity is attested to by its survival in eighty-two manuscripts.

From THE CANTERBURY TALES

From THE GENERAL PROLOGUE

Whan that Aprill with his shoures soote
The droghte of March hath perced to the roote,
And bathed every veyne in swich licour
Of which vertu engendred is the flour;
Whan Zephirus eek with his sweete breeth
Inspired hath in every holt and heeth
The tendre croppes, and the yonge sonne
Hath in the Ram his halve cours yronne,
And smale foweles maken melodye,
That slepen al the nyght with open ye   10
(So priketh hem nature in hir corages);
Thanne longen folk to goon on pilgrimages,
And palmeres for to seken straunge strondes,

13

To ferne halwes, kowthe in sondry londes;
And specially from every shires ende
Of Engelond to Caunterbury they wende,
The hooly blisful martir for to seke,
That hem hath holpen whan that they were seeke.
   Bifil that in that seson on a day,
In Southwerk at the Tabard as I lay   20
Redy to wenden on my pilgrymage
To Caunterbury with ful devout corage,
At nyght was come into that hostelrye
Wel nyne and twenty in a compaignye,
Of sondry folk, by aventure yfalle
In felaweshipe, and pilgrimes were they alle,
That toward Caunterbury wolden ryde.
The chambres and the stables weren wyde,
And wel we weren esed atte beste.
And shortly, whan the sonne was to reste,   30
So hadde I spoken with hem everichon
That I was of hir felaweshipe anon,
And made forward erly for to ryse,
To take oure wey ther as I yow devyse.
   But nathelees, whil I have tyme and space,
Er that I ferther in this tale pace,
Me thynketh it acordaunt to resoun
To telle yow al the condicioun
Of ech of hem, so as it semed me,
And whiche they weren, and of what degree,   40
And eek in what array that they were inne;
And at a knyght than wol I first bigynne.

WORDS UNTO ADAM, HIS
OWN SCRIVEYN

Adam scriveyn, if ever it thee bifalle
Boece or Troylus for to wryten newe,
Under thy long lokkes thou most have the scalle,
But after my makyng thou wryte more trewe;
So ofte a-daye I mot thy werk renewe,
It to correcte and eek to rubbe and scrape;
And al is through thy negligence and rape.

1 l. scriveyn = scribe, copyist

ANONYMOUS LYRICS AND BALLADS OF THE FOURTEENTH AND FIFTEENTH CENTURIES

Medieval English lyrics and ballads were above all popular works of art. As such, they owe more in style and tone to native and folk traditions than to the more sophisticated troubadour poetry of the Continent. While these lyrics were intended to be recited or sung, they were occasionally committed to paper· these written versions often survive in only a single copy found in the odd songbook, choir repertory, devotional manual, or commonplace book and occasionally in the margins of a manuscript intended for other purposes. The textual status of ballads is even shakier: most of the ballads attributed to this period were transcribed only centuries later, having passed in an oral tradition from generation to generation. Their authors are unknown and their dates of origin difficult to establish. The subject matter of these lyrics and ballads ranges from love ("The Unquiet Grave" and "Western Wind"), to social criticism ("Money, Money"), to satire ("The Blacksmiths"), to more spiritual and religious concerns ("I Sing of a Maiden"), and to poems that defy easy categorization ("Alone Walking").

MONEY, MONEY

Money, money, now hay goode day!
    Money, where haste thow be?
Money, money, thou gost away
    And wilt not bide with me.

Above all thing thow arte a king,
    And rulest the world over all;
Who lakethe the, all joy, parde,
    Will sone then frome him fall.

In every place thou makeste solas,
    Gret joye, spoorte, and welfare;   10
When money is gone, comfort is none,
    But thought, sorowe, and care.

15

In kinges corte, wher money dothe route,
    It maketh the galandes to jett,
And for to were gorgeouse ther gere,
    Ther cappes a-wry to sett.

In the hey-weyes ther joly palfreys
    It makeght to lepe and praunce,
It maket justinges, pleys, disguisinges,
    Ladys to singe and daunce.   20

For he that alway wanteth money
    Stondeth a mated chere,
Can never wel sing, land daunce nor springe,
    Nor make no lusty chere.

At cardes and dice it bereth the price,
    At king and emperoure;
At tables, tennes, and al othere games,
    Money hathe ever the floure.

Withe squier and knight and every wighte
    Money maketh men faine;   30
And causeth many in sume compeney
    Their felowes to disdaine.

In marchandis who can devise
    So good a ware, I say?
At al times the best ware is
    Ever redy money.

Money to incresse, marchandis never to cease
    Wyth many a sotell wile;
Men say the wolde for silver and golde
    Ther owne faders begile.   40

Women, I trowe, love money also
    To buy them joly gere;
For that helpethe and oft causethe
    Women to loke full faire.

In Westminster Hall the criers call;
    The sargeauntes plede a-pace;

Attorneys apperc, now here, now there,
    Renning in every place.

Whate-so-ever he be, and if that he
    Whante money to plede the lawe,   50
Do whate he came in is mater than
    Shale prove not worthe a strawe.

I know it not, but well I wotte
    I have harde often-times tell,
Prestes usc this guise, ther benefice
    For money to bey and sell.

Craftes-men, that be in every cite,
    They worke and never blinne;
Sum cutte, sume shave, sume knoke, sum grave,
    Only money to winne.   60

The plowman him-selfe doth dige and delve
    In storme, snowe, frost, and raine,
Money to get with laboure and swete,
    Yet small geines and muche peine.

And sume for money lie by the wey
    Another mannes purse to gett;
But they that long use it amonge
    Be hanged by the neke.

The beggars eke in every strete
    Ly walowinge by the wey;   70
They begge, they cryc, of them cume by,
    And all is but for money.

In every coste men love it moste,
    In Ingelonde, Spaine, and Francs,
For every man lacking it than
    Is clene owte of countenaunce.

Of whate degre so ever he be,
    Of vertuouse coning he have,
And want mone, yet men will sey,
    That he is but a knave.   80

Where in-dede, so God me spede,
        Sey all men whate they can;
It is all-wayes sene now-a-dayes
        That money makethe the man.

THE UNQUIET GRAVE

"The wind doth blow today, my love,
        And a few small drops of rain;
I never had but one true-love,
        In cold grave she was lain.

I'll do as much for my true-love
        As any young man may;
I'll sit and mourn all at her grave
        For twelvemonth and a day."

The twelvemonth and a day being up,
        The dead began to speak: 10
"Oh who sits weeping on my grave,
        And will not let me sleep?"

"'Tis I my love, sits on your grave,
        And will not let you sleep;
For I crave one kiss of your clay-cold lips,
        And that is all I seek."

"You crave one kiss of my clay-cold lips;
        But my breath smells earthy strong;
If you have one kiss of my clay-cold lips,
        Your time will not be long.   20

'Tis down in yonder garden green,
        Love, where we used to walk,
The finest flower that ere was seen
        Is withered to a stalk.

The stalk is withered dry, my love,
        So will our hearts decay;
So make yourself content, my love,
        Till God calls you away."

THE BLACKSMITHS

Swarte-smeked smethes, smatered with smoke,
Drive me to deth with den of here dintes;
Swich nois on nightes ne herd men never,
What knavene cry and clatering of knockes,
The cammede kongons cryen after "Col! Col!"
And blowen here bellewes that al here brain brestes.
"Huf, puf," seith that on, "Haf, paf," that other;
They spitten and sprawlen and spellen many spelles,
They gnawen and gnacchen, they grones to-gidere,
And holden hem hote with here hard hamers.   10
Of a bole hide ben here barm-felles,
Here shankes ben shakeled for the fere-flunderes;
Hevy hameres they han that hard ben handled,
Stark strokes they striken on a steled stokke.
"Lus, bus, las, das," rowten by rowe.
Swiche dolful a dreme the Devil it to-drive.
The maister longeth a litel and lasheth a lesse,
Twineth hem twein and toucheth a treble;
"Tik, tak, hic, hac, tiket, taket, tik, tak,
Lus, bus, las, das." Swich lif they leden,   20
Alle clothe-meres, Christ hem give sorwe.
May no man for brenwaters on night han his rest.

I SING OF A MAIDEN

I sing of a maiden
    That is makeles:
King of all kinges
    To her sone she ches.
He cam also stille
    There his moder was,
As dew in Aprille
    That falleth on the grass.
He came stille
    To his moderes bower,   10
As dew in Aprille
    That falleth on the flowr.

He cam also stille
    There his moder lay,
As dew in Aprille
That falleth on the spray.
Moder and maiden
    Was never non but she;
Well may swich a lady
    Godes moder be.   20

ALONE WALKING

Alone walking,
In thought pleyning,
And sore sighing,
    All desolate;
Me remembring
Of my living,
My deth wishing
    Bothe early and late.

Infortunate   10
Is so my fate,
That—wote ye whate?—
    Oute of mesure
My life I hate,
Thus desperate,
In suche pore estate
    Do I endure.

Of other cure
Am I nat sure.   20
Thus to endure
    Is hard, certain.
Suche is my ure,
I yow ensure.
What creature
    May have more pain?

My trouth so pleyn
Is take in vein,
And gret disdein

In remembraunce;   30
Yet I full feine
Wold me compleine
Me to absteine
　　From this penaunce.

But in substaunce
Noon allegeaunce
Of my grevance
　　Can I nat finde.
Right so my chaunce   40
With displesaunce
Doth me avaunce;
　　And thus an ende.

WESTERN WIND

Westron winde when wille thou blow
The small raine downe can raine;
Christ, if my love were in my armes,
And I in my bed againe.

William Dunbar

(1 4 6 0 ? – 1 5 1 3 ?)

Dunbar, a Scot, was probably born in East Lothian, the English-speaking Lowlands of Scotland (rather than the Gaelic-speaking Highlands). Little is known for sure about Dunbar's life, and it would be dangerous to give too much credence as some early biographers have to what rival poets—who were engaged in flytings, or poetic duels, with Dunbar—claimed about his life. Dunbar's repeated admiration for Chaucer led an earlier generation of critics to label him a "Scottish Chaucerian." More recent admirers have preferred to stress his great originality, particularly his gift for a stylistic diversity that included sharp satire, abusive flytings, devotional verse, dream visions, and court poetry. Dunbar's work is also characterized by his inventive use of persona and voices in the eighty or so of his poems that survive. Walter Scott, a great admirer of Dunbar, spoke of him as "unrivalled by any which Scotland ever produced."

MEDITATION IN WINTER

In to thir dirk and drublie dayis
Quhone sabill all the hevin arrayis,
   With mystie vapouris, cluddis, and skyis,
   Nature all curage me denyis
Off sangis, ballattis and of playis.

Quhone that the nycht dois lenthin houris,
With wind, with haill, and havy schouris,
   My dule spreit dois lurk for schoir,
   My hairt for langour dois forloir
For laik of Symmer with his flouris.   10

I walk, I turne, sleip may I nocht,
I vexit am with havie thocht;
   This warld all ovir I cast about,
   And ay the mair I am in dout
The mair that I remeid have socht.

I am assayit on everie syde:
Despair sayis ay, "In tyme provyde
   And get sum thing quhairon to leif,
   Or with grit trouble and mischeif
Thow sall in to this court abyd."   20

Than Patience sayis, "Be not agast;
Hald Hoip and Treuthe within the fast
   And lat Fortoun wirk furthe hir rage,
   Quhone that no rasoun may assuage
Quhill that hir glas be run and past."

And Prudence in my eir sayis ay,
"Quhy wald thow hald that will away?
   Or craif that thow may have mo space,
   Thow tending to ane uther place
A journay going everie day?"   30

And than sayis Age, "My freind, cum neir
And be not strange, I the requeir;
   Cum brodir, by the hand me tak;
   Remember thow hes compt to mak
Off all thi tyme thow spendit heir."

Syne Deid castis upe his yettis wyd
Saying, "Thir oppin sall the abyd;
   Albeid that thow wer never sa stout,
   Undir this lyntall sall thow lowt:
Thair is nane uther way besyde."   40

For feir of this all day I drowp:
No gold in kist nor wyne in cowp,
   No ladeis bewtie nor luiffis blys
   May lat me to remember this,
How glaid that ever I dyne or sowp.

Yit quhone the nycht begynnis to schort
It dois my spreit sum pairt confort
   Off thocht oppressit with the schowris;

Cum lustie Symmer with thi flowris,
That I may leif in sum disport.   50

l.   1. drublie = gloomy
l.   4. curage = inclination for
l.   8. dule spreit = doleful spirit
l. 36. yettis = gates
l. 44. lat = prevent

IN PRAISE OF WOMEN

Now of wemen this I say for me,
Off erthly thingis nane may bettir be;
Thay suld haif wirschep and grit honoring
Off men aboif all uthir erthly thing;
Rycht grit dishonour upoun him self he takkis
In word or deid quha evir wemen lakkis;
Sen that of wemen cumin all ar we;
Wemen ar wemen and sa will end and de.
Wo wirth the fruct wald put the tre to nocht,
And wo wirth him rycht so that sayis ocht   10
Off womanheid that may be ony lak,
Or sic grit schame upone him for to tak.
Thay us consaif with pane, and be thame fed
Within thair breistis thair we be boun to bed;
Grit pane and wo and murnyng mervellus
Into thair birth thay suffir sair for us;
Than meit and drynk to feid us get we nane,
Bot that we sowk out of thair breistis bane.
Thay ar the confort that we all haif heir,
Thair may no man be till us half so deir;   20
Thay ar our verry nest of nurissing;
In lak of thame quha can say ony thing,
That fowll his nest he fylis, and for thy
Exylit he suld be of all gud cumpany;
Thair suld na wyis man gif audience
To sic ane without intelligence.
Chryst to his fader he had nocht ane man;
Se quhat wirschep wemen suld haif than.
That Sone is Lord, that Sone is King of Kingis,
In hevin and erth his majestie ay ringis.   30
Sen scho hes borne him in hir halines,
And he is well and grund of all gudnes,
All wemen of us suld haif honoring,
Service and luve, aboif all uthir thing.

John Skelton

(1 4 6 3 ? – 1 5 2 9)

The first major Tudor poet and dramatist, Skelton had a poetic career that spanned the reigns of Richard III, Henry VII, and Henry VIII, whom he tutored. Little is known for sure about Skelton's early years. He was apparently educated at both Oxford and Cambridge and was created poet laureate at both universities in the late fifteenth century. Among his important early poems are the dream vision *The Bouge of Court* and *The Garland of Laurel.* In 1498 Skelton took holy orders, and a number of religious poems survive from this period. Skelton remained closely connected to the court of Henry VIII, where he was appointed court poet. Many of his works—including the allegorical play *Magnificence* as well as such audacious poems as "Speak, Parrot" (1521) and "Colin Clout" (1522)—directly concern court politics, although their allegorical import is still subject to dispute. While the thrust of Skelton's allegorical satires may be lost to us (although they were extremely popular in his time and frequently reprinted after his death), his poetic innovations, especially the breathless and rattling rhymed "skeltonics," have won modern admirers, including W. H. Auden and Robert Graves.

UPON A DEAD MAN'S HEAD, THAT WAS SENT TO HIM FROM AN HONORABLE GENTLEWOMAN FOR A TOKEN

Youre ugly tokyn
My mynd hath brokyn
From worldly lust;
For I have dyscust
We ar but dust,
And dy we must.
   It is generall
To be mortall:
I have well espyde
No man may hym hyde   10
From Deth holow eyed,

With synnews wyderyd,
With bonys shyderyd,
With hys worme etyn maw,
And his gastly jaw
Gaspyng asyde,
Nakyd of hyde,
Neyther flesh nor fell.
　　Then, by my councell,
Loke that ye spell   20
Well thys gospell:
For wher so we dwell
Deth wyll us qwell,
And with us mell.
　　For all oure pamperde paunchys,
Ther may no fraunchys,
Nor worldly blys,
Redeme us from this:
Oure days be datyd,
To be chekmatyd   30
With drawttys of deth,
Stoppyng oure breth;
Oure eyen synkyng,
Oure bodys stynkyng,
Oure gummys grynnyng,
Oure soulys brynnyng.
To whom, then, shall we sew,
For to have rescew,
But to swete Jesu,
On us then for to rew?   40
　　O goodly chyld
Of Mary mylde,
Then be oure shylde!
That we be not exylyd
To the dyne dale
Of boteles bale,
Nor to the lake
Of fendys blake.
　　But graunt us grace
To se thy face,   50
And to purchace
Thyne hevenly place,
And thy palace,
Full of solace,

Above the sky,
That is so hy;
Eternally
To beholde and se
The Trynyte!
   Amen.   60
Myrres vous y.

l. 13. shyderyd = shattered
l. 18. fell = skin
l. 24. mell = interfere
l. 26. fraunchys = immunity
l. 31. drawttys = draughts, chess pieces
l. 45. dyne = gloomy
l. 61. *Myrres vous y* = Behold yourself therein

KNOWLEDGE, ACQUAINTANCE, RESORT, FAVOUR, WITH GRACE

Knolege, aquayntance, resort, favour, with grace;
Delyte, desyre, respyte, wyth lyberte;
Corage wyth lust, convenient tyme and space;
Dysdayns, dystres, exylyd cruelte;
Wordys well set with good habylyte;
Demure demenaunce, womanly of porte;
Transendyng plesure, surmountyng all dysporte;

Allectuary arrectyd to redres
These feverous axys, the dedely wo and payne
Of thoughtfull hertys plungyd in dystres;   10
Refresshyng myndys the Aprell shoure of rayne;
Condute of comforte and well most soverayne;
Herber enverduryd, contynuall fressh and grene;
Of lusty somer the passyng goodly quene;

The topas rych and precyouse in vertew;
Your ruddys wyth ruddy rubys may compare;
Saphyre of sadnes, envayned wyth Indy blew;
The pullyshed perle youre whytenes doth declare;
Dyamand poyntyd to rase oute hartly care
Geyne surfetous suspecte the emeraud comendable;   20
Relucent smaragd, objecte imcomperable;

Encleryd myrroure and perspectyve most bryght,
Illumynyd wyth feturys far passyng my reporte;
Radyent Esperus, star of the clowdy nyght,
Lodestar to lyght these lovers to theyr porte,
Gayne dangerous stormys theyr anker of supporte,
Theyr sayll of solace most comfortably clad,
Whych to behold makyth hevy hartys glad;

Remorse have I of youre most goodlyhod,
Of youre behavoure curtes and benynge,   30
Of your bownte and of youre womanhod,
Which makyth my hart oft to lepe and sprynge
And to remember many a praty thynge;
But absens, alas, wyth tremelyng fere and drede,
Abashyth me, albeit I have no nede.

You I assure, absens is my fo,
My dedely wo, my paynfull hevynes.
And if ye lyst to know the cause why so,
Open myne hart, beholde my mynde expres.
I wold you coud! Then shuld ye se, mastres,   40
How there nys thynge that I covet so fayne
As to enbrace you in myne armys twayne.

Nothynge yerthly to me more desyrous
Than to beholde youre bewteouse countenaunce:
But hatefull absens, to me so envyous,
Though thou withdraw me from her by long dystaunce,
Yet shall she never oute of remembraunce,
For I have gravyd her wythin the secret wall
Of my trew hart, to love her best of all!

l.   8. Allectuary arrectyd = medicine designed
l.   9. axys = attacks
l. 13. Herber = arbor
l. 21. smaragd = a kind of precious stone
l. 33. praty = pleasant

Sir Thomas Wyatt

(1503–1542)

The son of a Privy Counsellor to Henry VII and Henry VIII, Wyatt himself entered royal service under Henry VIII, and his life and poetry were profoundly intertwined in the affairs of court. The greatest crisis in his fortunes occurred in 1536, when Wyatt was arrested and imprisoned over his suspected relationship to Queen Anne Boleyn, who was put to death, along with her reputed lovers, by Henry VIII. Most scholars believe the Queen to be the subject of Wyatt's "Whoso List to Hunt," and there has been much speculation, then and since, that Wyatt was the Queen's lover. Wyatt was set free and he returned to his activities as diplomat and courtier during extraordinarily volatile political times. He remained active in these capacities until his death in 1542. While Wyatt's verse circulated in manuscript in courtly circles, his poetry reached a much wider audience when about a third of it was anthologized in one of the first and most influential Elizabethan poetry collections, Richard Tottel's *Miscellany*, which went through many editions before the end of the sixteenth century. Problems of dating, order, versification, occasion, and textual variants are still debated by editors of Wyatt's verse, as is the extent to which his poetry is informed by events and personalities at court. Less in dispute is Wyatt's great contribution to sixteenth-century poetry through his complex adaptation into English of the Petrarchan sonnet. Less celebrated but no less powerful verse forms are Wyatt's epistolary satires and penitential psalms. For fellow poet Henry Howard, Earl of Surrey, Wyatt "taught what might be said in rime; / That reft Chaucer the glory of his wit."

WHOSO LIST TO HUNT

Whoso list to hunt, I know where is an hind,
    But as for me, helas, I may no more.
    The vain travail hath wearied me so sore,
I am of them that farthest cometh behind.
Yet may I by no means my wearied mind
    Draw from the deer, but as she fleeth afore
    Fainting I follow. I leave off therefore
Sithens in a net I seek to hold the wind.

Who list her hunt, I put him out of doubt,
  As well as I may spend his time in vain.
  And graven with diamonds in letters plain
There is written her fair neck round about:
  "*Noli me tangere,* for Caesar's I am,
  And wild for to hold though I seem tame."

l.   1. list = cares
l. 13. *Noli me tangere* = *Touch me not*

THEY FLEE FROM ME, THAT SOMETIME DID ME SEEK

They flee from me, that sometime did me seek
With naked foot stalking in my chamber.
I have seen them gentle, tame, and meek
That now are wild, and do not remember
That sometime they put themself in danger
To take bread at my hand; and now they range,
Busily seeking with a continual change.

Thanked be fortune, it hath been otherwise
Twenty times better; but once in special,
In thin array after a pleasant guise   10
When her loose gown from her shoulders did fall,
And she me caught in her arms long and small,
Therewithal sweetly did me kiss,
And softly said, "Dear heart, how like you this?"

It was no dream: I lay broad waking.
But all is turned thorough my gentleness
Into a strange fashion of forsaking,
And I have leave to go of her goodness,
And she also to use newfangleness.
But since that I so kindely am served,   20
I would fain know what she hath deserved

IS IT POSSIBLE

Is it possible
That so high debate,
So sharp, so sore, and of such rate,
Should end so soon and was begun so late?
Is it possible?

Is it possible
So cruel intent,
So hasty heat and so soon spent,
From love to hate and thence for to relent?
Is it possible?   10

Is it possible
That any may find
Within one heart so diverse mind
To change or turn as weather and wind?
Is it possible?

Is it possible
To spy it in an eye
That turns as oft as chance on die?
The truth whereof can any try?
Is it possible?   20

It is possible
For to turn so oft,
To bring that lowest that was most aloft,
And to fall highest yet to light soft:
It is possible.

All is possible
Whoso list believe.
Trust therefore first and after preve,
As men wed ladies by licence and leave,
All is possible.   30

l. 28. preve = prove

Henry Howard, Earl of Surrey

(1517?–1547)

Born into a leading Tudor family, Surrey was educated at the Tudor and French courts and in 1532 married Frances Vere, daughter of the Earl of Oxford. He had a brief and intense career as a courtier, distinguishing himself as a soldier and suffering brief imprisonments for various offences at court. He was wounded at the siege of Montreuil in 1545 and was subsequently given command of Boulogne. After losing a battle the following year, he was recalled to England, condemned on the frivolous charge of treasonably quartering the royal arms, and put to death shortly after he turned thirty. Along with Thomas Wyatt (fourteen years his senior) he is best remembered for introducing the Petrarchan sonnet into English poetry; his sonnet scheme would be adopted by Shakespeare. Forty of his poems appeared in Richard Tottel's influential *Miscellany* in 1557, and his was the only poet's name to appear on its title page. Surrey is also valued for his influential translation into English blank verse of Books II and IV of Virgil's *Aeneid*.

LAID IN MY QUIET BED

Laid in my quiet bed, in study as I were,
I saw within my troubled head a heap of thoughts appear;
And every thought did show so lively in mine eyes,
That now I sigh'd, and then I smiled, as cause of thought did rise.
I saw the little boy, in thought how oft that he
Did wish of God to 'scape the rod, a tall young man to be;
The young man eke that feels his bones with paines opprest,
How he would be a rich old man, to live and lie at rest;
The rich old man, that sees his end draw on so sore,
How he would be a boy again, to live so much the more.   10
Whereat full oft I smiled, to see how all these three,
From boy to man, from man to boy, would chop and change degree;
And musing thus, I thinke the case is very strange,
That man from wealth, to live in woe, doth ever seek to change.
Thus thoughtful as I lay, I saw my wither'd skin,
How it doth show my dinted jaws, the flesh was worn so thin,

And eke my toothless chaps, the gates of my right way,
That opes and shuts as I do speak, do thus unto me say:
"Thy white and hoarish hairs, the messengers of age,
That show like lines of true belief that this life doth assuage,   20
Bids thee lay hand, and feel them hanging on thy chin;
The which do write two ages past, the third now coming in.
Hang up therefore the bit of thy young wanton time,
And thou that there in beaten art, the happiest life define."
Whereat I sigh'd, and said, "Farewell, my wonted joy;
Truss up thy pack, and trudge from me to every little boy,
And tell them thus from me, their time most happy is,
If, to their time, they reason had to know the truth of this."

WHEN WINDSOR WALLS

When Windsor walls sustain'd my wearied arm,
My hand my chin, to ease my restless head,
Ech pleasant plot revested green with warm,
The blossom'd boughs with lusty vere yspred,
The flower'd meads, the wedded birds so late
Mine eyes discover'd. Then did to mind resort
The jolly woes, the hateless short debate,
The rakehell life that longs to love's disport.
Wherewith, alas, mine heavy charge of care
Heap'd in my breast brake forth against my will,
And smoky sighs that overcast the air.
My vapored eyes such dreary tears distill
The tender spring to quicken where they fall,
And I half bent to throw me down withall.

l. 4. vere = Spring

SO CRUEL PRISON

So cruel prison how could betide, alas,
As proud Windsor? Where I in lust and joy
With a king's son my childish years did pass
In greater feast than Priam's sons of Troy;

Where each sweet place returns a taste full sour:
The large green courts where we were wont to hove,
With eyes cast up unto the maidens' tower,
And easy sighs, such as folk draw in love.

The stately sales, the ladies bright of hue,
The dances short, long tales of great delight;   10
With words and looks that tigers could but rue,
Where each of us did plead the other's right.

The palm play, where, despoiled for the game,
With dazed eyes oft we by gleams of love
Have missed the ball and got sight of our dame,
To bait her eyes, which kept the leads above,

The gravel'd ground, with sleeves tied on the helm,
On foaming horse, with swords and friendly hearts,
With cheer, as though the one should overwhelm;
Where we have fought, and chaséd oft with darts.   20

With silver drops the meads yet spread for ruth,
In active games of nimbleness and strength,
Where we did strain, trailéd by swarms of youth,
Our tender limbs that yet shot up in length.

The secret groves which oft we made resound
Of pleasant plaint and of our ladies' praise,
Recording soft what grace each one had found,
What hope of speed, what dread of long delays.

The wild forest, the clothéd holt with green,
With reins avaled, and swift ybreathed horse,   30
With cry of hounds and merry blasts between,
Where we did chase the fearful hart aforce.

The void walls eke that harbored us each night,
Wherewith, alas, revive within my breast
The sweet accord; such sleeps as yet delight,
The pleasant dreams, the quiet bed of rest.

The secret thoughts imparted with such trust,
The wanton talk, the divers change of play,

The friendship sworn, each promise kept so just,
Wherewith we passed the winter nights away.   40

And with this thought the blood forsakes my face,
The tears berain my cheeks of deadly hue,
The which as soon as sobbing sighs, alas,
Upsupped have, thus I my plaint renew:

O place of bliss, renewer of my woes,
Give me accompt—where is my noble fere?
Whom in thy walls thou didst each night enclose,
To other lief, but unto me most dear

Echo, alas, that doth my sorrow rue,
Returns thereto a hollow sound of plaint.   50
Thus I, alone, where all my freedom grew,
In prison pine with bondage and restraint,

And with remembrance of the greater grief
To banish the less, I find my chief relief.

l.   6. hove = linger
l. 30. avaled = slackened

Anne Askew

(c. 1521 – 1546)

Much of what we know of Anne Askew, including the text of "The Ballad Which Anne Askew Made and Sang When She Was in Newgate," derives from John Bale's editions of *The First Examinacyon of Anne Askewe*, published surreptitiously in 1546, and from *The Lattre Examinacyon of Anne Askewe*, which appeared a year later. Bale, who apparently got hold of a manuscript smuggled out of prison, reports that Askew "wrote this in her own hand and I illustrate it with prefaces and notes." On the 16th of July, 1546, Askew was publicly burned as a heretic following her imprisonment and torture in Newgate for her Protestant beliefs. Bale, and after him John Foxe in his *Acts and Monuments*, seized on the example of Askew as a great Protestant martyr. Born into a landed Lincolnshire family, Askew was forced to marry Thomas Kyme (reportedly "to save the money") after her sister Martha, betrothed to Thomas, died. Before her arrest she was a member of the Protestant Reformist circle identified with Queen Catherine Parr. The examinations of Askew reveal her to have been strong, brave, devout, and loyal to her associates, whom she did not betray, although racked until she "was nigh dead." John Foxe's influential reprinting of Askew's testimony is accompanied by a vivid woodcut depicting her execution.

THE BALLAD WHICH ANNE ASKEW MADE AND SANG WHEN SHE WAS IN NEWGATE

Like as the armed knight
   Appointed to the field,
With this world will I fight,
   And faith shall be my shield.

Faith is that weapon strong
   Which will not fail at need;
My foes therefore among
   Therewith will I proceed.

As it is had in strength
   And force of Christes way,
It will prevail at length   10
   Though all the devils say nay.

Faith in the Fathers old
   Obtained righteousness,
Which makes me very bold
   To fear no world's distress.

I now rejoice in heart,
   And hope bid me do so,
For Christ will take my part
   And ease me of my woe.   20

Thou say'st, Lord, who so knock
   To them wilt thou attend.
Undo therefore the lock
   And thy strong power send.

More en'mies now I have
   Than hairs upon my head;
Let them not me deprave,
   But fight thou in my stead.

On thee my care I cast,
   For all their cruel spite;   30
I set not by their haste,
   For thou art my delight.

I am not she that list
   My anchor to let fall,
For every drizzling mist
   My ship substantial.

Not oft use I to write
   In prose nor yet in rhyme,
Yet will I show one sight
   That I saw in my time.   40

I saw a royal throne
   Where Justice should have sit,

But in her stead was one
  Of moody cruel wit.

Absorb'd was righteousness
  As of the raging flood;
Satan in his excess
  Suck'd up the guiltless blood.

Then thought I, Jesus Lord,
  When thou shalt judge us all,   50
Hard is it to record
  On these men what will fall.

Yet, Lord, I thee desire
  For that they do to me,
Let them not taste the hire
  Of their iniquity.

Anne Vaughan Locke

(c. 1530 – c. 1590)

Anne Vaughan Locke was the eldest daughter of Stephen Vaughan, a London merchant, and his first wife, a "witty and housewifely woman." In the 1550s she married Henry Locke and began a friendship and correspondence with the leading Scottish Calvinist, John Knox, who persuaded her to leave England with her children and join the Marian exiles in Geneva. Part of her time abroad was spent translating Calvin's sermons on the song of Hezekiah from Isaiah 38. Locke published her translation in 1560 after her return to England and appended to it *A Meditation of a Penitent Sinner*, comprised of twenty-six sonnets (five "prefatory") that constitute the first published English sonnet sequence. While Locke speaks of having been given this *Meditation* by "a friend," scholars are inclined to believe this to be a literary convention, since the poems are quite similar in style to the language of her sermon translation. These remarkably visceral poems follow the rhyme scheme introduced by Surrey that has come to be called "Shakespearean": ababcdcdefefgg. They anticipate by many decades the religious sonnets of Donne and Herbert. In other ways, too, Locke was "mother" to the devotional sonnet sequence in England: her son Henry Lok became one of the most prolific of Elizabethan writers of religious sonnets.

SO FOUL IS SIN AND LOATHSOME IN THY SIGHT

So foul is sin and loathsome in thy sight,
So foul with sin I see myself to be,
That till from sin I may be washèd white,
So foul I dare not, Lord, approach to thee.
Oft hath thy mercy washèd me before,
Thou madest me clean: but I am foul again.
Yet wash me Lord, again, and wash me more;
Wash me, O Lord, and do away the stain
Of ugly sin that in my soul appear.
Let flow thy plenteous streams of cleansing grace.
Wash me again, yea, wash me everywhere,

39

Both leprous body and defiled face.
Yea, wash me all, for I am all unclean;
And from my sin, Lord, cleanse me once again.

SIN AND DESPAIR HAVE
SO POSSESS'D MY HEART

Sin and despair have so possess'd my heart,
And hold my captive soul in such restraint,
As of thy mercies I can feel no part,
But still in languor do I lie and faint.
Create a new pure heart within my breast:
Mine old can hold no liquor of thy grace.
My feeble faith with heavy load opprest,
Stagg'ring doth scarcely creep a reeling pace,
And fallen it is too faint to rise again.
Renew, O Lord, in me a constant sprite,
That stay'd with mercy may my soul sustain,
A sprite so settled and so firmly pight
Within my bowels, that it never move,
But still uphold th'assurance of thy love.

l. 10. sprite = spirit
l. 12. pight = pitched

Queen Elizabeth I

(1533–1603)

Better known as an object of poetic address by Shakespeare, Spenser, and others than as a poet in her own right, Elizabeth was an accomplished writer of epistles and orations as well as of lyric poetry, devotions, and translations from Plutarch, Seneca, Petrarch, Horace, Boethius's *Consolation of Philosophy*, and *A Godly Meditacyon* and *The Mirror of the Sinful Soul* by Margaret of Navarre. A number of these survive in her own hand. The daughter of Henry VIII and Anne Boleyn, Elizabeth received an outstanding humanist education by such leading scholars as Roger Ascham, John Cheke, and William Grindall. Upon the death of her sister Mary in 1558, Elizabeth succeeded to the throne and reigned until her death in 1603. Her poems on love and marriage—including "On Monsieur's Departure"—take on political weight when set in the context of Elizabeth's decision not to marry.

WRITTEN ON A WALL AT WOODSTOCK

Oh Fortune, thy wresting wavering state,
Hath fraught with cares my troubled wit,
Whose witness this present prison late
Could bear, where once was joy's loan quit.
Thou causedst the guilty to be loosed
From bands where innocents were inclosed,
And caused the guiltless to be reserved,
And freed these that death had well deserved.
But all herein can be nothing wrought,
So God send to my foes all they have thought.

ON MONSIEUR'S DEPARTURE

I grieve and dare not show my discontent,
I love and yet am forced to seem to hate,
I do, yet dare not say I ever meant,
I seem stark mute yet inwardly do prate.

41

I am and not, I freeze and yet am burned,
Since from myself my other self I turned.

My care is like my shadow in the sun,
Follows me flying, flies when I pursue it,
Stands and lies by me, doth what I have done.
His too familiar care doth make me rue it.   10
   No means I find to rid him from my breast,
   Till by the end of things it be supprest.

Some gentler passions slide into my mind,
For I am soft and made of melting snow;
Or be more cruel, love, and so be kind.
Let me or float or sink, be high or low.
   Or let me live with some more sweet content,
   Or die and so forget what love ere meant.

George Gascoigne

(c . 1 5 3 9 – 1 5 7 7)

Gascoigne's literary output covered a tremendous range. An accomplished poet, dramatist, verse theorist, novelist, and satirist, he was deservedly praised by contemporaries for his contribution to English letters. Thomas Nashe describes Gascoigne as one "who first beat the path to that perfection which our best poets have aspired to since his departure," while the gloss to Edmund Spenser's *Shepheardes Calender* describes Gascoigne as "the very chief of our late rhymers." In the two poems anthologized here, Gascoigne explores some of his early forays and failures as scholar, courtier, soldier, and lawyer. In 1573 he published A *Hundred Sundry Flowers*, ostensibly an anthology of many poets' writings, but in fact all composed by Gascoigne himself. Gascoigne revised and republished this controversial volume in 1575 as *The Poesies of George Gascoigne*. While the collection failed to gain the kind of patronage Gascoigne sought, it displayed his remarkable rhetorical and literary brilliance.

GASCOIGNE'S GOOD MORROW

You that have spent the silent night
In sleep and quiet rest,
And joy to see the cheerful light
That riseth in the east:
Now clear your voice, now cheer your heart,
Come help me now to sing:
Each willing wight come bear a part,
To praise the heavenly King.

And you whom care in prison keeps,
Or sickness doth suppress,   10
Or secret sorrow breaks your sleeps,
Or dolours do distress:
Yet bear a part in doleful wise,
Yea think it good accord,
And acceptable sacrifice,
Each sprite to praise the Lord.

The dreadful night with darksome storms
Had overspread the light,
And sluggish sleep with drowsiness
Had overpressèd our might: 20
A glass wherein we may behold
Each storm that stays our breath,
Our bed the grave, our clothes like mould,
And sleep like dreadful death.

Yet as this deadly night did last,
But for a little space,
And heavenly day, now night is past,
Doth show his pleasant face:
So must we hope to see God's face,
At last in heaven on high,   30
When we have changed this mortal place
For immortality.

And of such haps and heavenly joys,
As then we hope to hold,
All earthly sights, all worldly toys,
Are tokens to behold:
The day is like the day of doom,
The sun, the Son of Man,
The skies the heavens, the earth the tomb
Wherein we rest till than.   40

The rainbow bending in the sky,
Bedeckèd with sundry hues,
Is like the seat of God on high,
And seems to tell these news:
That as thereby he promised
To drown the world no more,
So by the blood which Christ hath shed,
He will our health restore.

The misty clouds that fall sometime,
And overcast the skies,   50
Are like to troubles of our time,
Which do but dim our eyes:
But as such dews are dried up quite,
When Phoebus shows his face,

So are such fancies put to flight,
Where God doth guide by grace.

The carrion crow, that loathsome beast,
Which cries against the rain,
Both for her hue and for the rest,
The Devil resembleth plain: 60
And as with guns we kill the crow,
For spoiling our relief,
The Devil so must we overthrow,
With gunshot of belief.

The little birds which sing so sweet,
Are like the angel's voice,
Which render God his praises meet,
And teach us to rejoice:
And as they more esteem that mirth,
Then dread the night's annoy,   70
So must we deem our days on earth
But hell to heavenly joy.

Unto which joys for to attain,
God grant us all his grace,
And send us after worldly pain,
In heaven to have a place.
Where we may still enjoy that light,
Which never shall decay:
Lord for thy mercy lend us might
To see that joyful day.   80

GASCOIGNE'S WOODMANSHIP

My worthy Lord, I pray you wonder not
To see your woodman shoot so oft awry,
Nor that he stands amazed like a sot,
And lets the harmless deer (unhurt) go by.
Or if he strike a doe which is but carren,
Laugh not good Lord, but favour such a fault,
Take will in worth, he would fain hit the barren,
But though his heart be good, his hap is naught.

And therefore now I crave your Lordship's leave,
To tell you plain what is the cause of this.　　　　10
First if it please your honour to perceive,
What makes your woodman shoot so oft amiss,
Believe me, Lord, the case is nothing strange,
He shoots awry almost at every mark,
His eyes have been so used for to range,
That now God knows they be both dim and dark.
For proof he bears the note of folly now,
Who shot sometimes to hit Philosophy,
And ask you why? forsooth I make avow,
Because his wanton wits went all awry.　　　　20
Next that, he shot to be a man of law,
And spent some time with learned Littleton,
Yet in the end, he proved but a daw,
For law was dark and he had quickly done.
Then could he wish Fitzherbert such a brain
As Tully had, to write the law by art,
So that with pleasure, or with little pain,
He might perhaps, have caught a truant's part.
But all too late, he most mislik'd the thing,
Which most might help to guide his arrow straight;　　　　30
He winked wrong, and so let slip the string,
Which cast him wide, for all his quaint conceit.
From thence he shot to catch a courtly grace,
And thought even there to wield the world at will,
But out, alas, he much mistook the place,
And shot awry at every rover still.
The blazing baits which draw the gazing eye,
Unfeather'd there his first affection;
No wonder then although he shot awry,
Wanting the feathers of discretion.　　　　40
Yet more than them, the marks of dignity
He much mistook, and shot the wronger way,
Thinking the purse of prodigality
Had been best mean to purchase such a prey.
He thought the flattering face which fleereth still,
Had been full fraught with all fidelity,
And that such words as courtiers use at will,
Could not have varied from the verity.
But when his bonnet buttoned with gold,
His comely cap beguarded all with gay,　　　　50
His bumbast hose, with linings manifold,

His knit silk stocks and all his quaint array,
Had pick'd his purse of all the Peter-pence,
Which might have paid for his promotion,
Then (all too late) he found that light expense
Had quite quench'd out the court's devotion.
So that since then the taste of misery
Hath been always full bitter in his bit,
And why? forsooth because he shot awry,
Mistaking still the marks which others hit.   60
But now behold what mark the man doth find:
He shoots to be a soldier in his age;
Mistrusting all the virtues of the mind,
He trusts the power of his personage.
As though long limbs led by a lusty heart,
Might yet suffice to make him rich again,
But Flushing frays have taught him such a part
That now he thinks the wars yield no such gain.
And sure I fear, unless your lordship deign
To train him yet into some better trade,   70
It will be long before he hit the vein
Whereby he may a richer man be made.
He cannot climb as other catchers can,
To lead a charge before himself be led.
He cannot spoil the simple sakeless man,
Which is content to feed him with his bread.
He cannot pinch the painful soldier's pay,
And shear him out his share in ragged sheets,
He cannot stoop to take a greedy prey
Upon his fellows grovelling in the streets.   80
He cannot pull the spoil from such as pill,
And seem full angry at such foul offence,
Although the gain content his greedy will,
Under the cloak of contrary pretence:
And nowadays, the man that shoots not so,
May shoot amiss, even as your woodman doth:
But then you marvel why I let them go,
And never shoot, but say farewell forsooth:
Alas my Lord, while I do muse hereon,
And call to mind my youthful years mis-spent,   90
They give me such a bone to gnaw upon,
That all my senses are in silence pent.
My mind is rapt in contemplation,
Wherein my dazzled eyes only behold

The black hour of my constellation
Which framed me so luckless on the mould.
Yet therewithal I cannot but confess,
That vain presumption makes my heart to swell,
For thus I think, not all the world (I guess)
Shoots bet than I, nay some shoots not so well.   100
In Aristotle somewhat did I learn,
To guide my manners all by comeliness.
And Tully taught me somewhat to discern,
Between sweet speech and barbarous rudeness.
Old Parkins, Rastell, and Dan Bracton's books,
Did lend me somewhat of the lawless law;
The crafty courtiers with their guileful looks,
Must needs put some experience in my maw:
Yet cannot these with many mast'ries moe
Make me shoot straight at any gainful prick,   110
Where some that never handled such a bow
Can hit the white or touch it near the quick,
Who can nor speak, nor write in pleasant wise,
Nor lead their life by Aristotle's rule,
Nor argue well on questions that arise,
Nor plead a case more than my Lord Mayor's mule,
Yet can they hit the marks that I do miss,
And win the mean which may the man maintain.
Now when my mind doth mumble upon this,
No wonder then although I pine for pain: 120
And whiles mine eyes behold this mirror thus,
The herd goeth by, and farewell gentle does:
So that your lordship quickly may discuss
What blinds mine eyes so oft (as I suppose).
But since my Muse can to my Lord rehearse
What makes me miss, and why I do not shoot,
Let me imagine in this worthless verse,
If right before me, at my standing's foot
There stood a doe, and I should strike her dead,
And then she prove a carrion carcase too,   130
What figure might I find within my head,
To scuse the rage which ruled me so to do?
Some might interpret with plain paraphrase,
That lack of skill or fortune led the chance,
But I must otherwise expound the case;
I say Jehovah did this doe advance,
And made her bold to stand before me so,

Till I had thrust mine arrow to her heart,
That by the sudden of her overthrow,
I might endeavour to amend my part,   140
And turn mine eyes that they no more behold
Such guileful marks as seem more than they be:
And though they glister outwardly like gold,
Are inwardly like brass, as men may see:
And when I see the milk hang in her teat,
Methinks it saith, old babe now learn to suck,
Who in thy youth couldst never learn the feat
To hit the whites which live with all good luck.
Thus have I told my Lord (God grant in season),
A tedious tale in rhyme, but little reason.   150

Edmund Spenser

(1552? – 1599)

Spenser was born in London and educated at the Merchant Taylors' School before attending Pembroke Hall, Cambridge, where he began writing and publishing his poetry. By the late 1570s, and through the help of literary friends at Cambridge, he had secured a place in the Earl of Leicester's household. In 1580 he was appointed secretary to Lord Grey, Lord Deputy of Ireland, and thereafter, except for visits to London, remained in Ireland to serve in a number of government posts. Spenser was virulently anti-Catholic and supported the policy of brutally suppressing the Irish in his *View of the Present State of Ireland*. In 1579 he published his first major poetic work, *The Shepheardes Calendar*, and began one of the most remarkable poems in English, the allegorical epic *The Faerie Queene* (the first three books of which were published in 1590, the next three in 1596). In 1594 he married Elizabeth Boyle, and their courtship formed the backdrop to his *Amoretti*; he published these poems, along with *Epithalamion*, a celebration of their marriage, in 1595. Spenser's home was burned down by Irish rebels in 1598, and he returned in distressed circumstances to London, where he died a year later and was buried in Westminster Abbey, near Chaucer. His monument describes him as "the prince of poets in his time." Beloved by such poets as Milton and Keats, Spenser remains, in the words of Charles Lamb, "the poet's poet."

EPITHALAMION

Ye learned sisters which have oftentimes
Been to me aiding, others to adorn:
Whom ye thought worthy of your graceful rimes,
That even the greatest did not greatly scorn
To hear their names sung in your simple lays,
But joyed in their praise.
And when ye list your own mishaps to mourn,
Which death, or love, or fortune's wreck did raise,
Your string could soon to sadder tenor turn,
And teach the woods and waters to lament   10
Your doleful dreariment;
Now lay those sorrowful complaints aside,

And having all your heads with garland crowned,
Help me mine own love's praises to resound,
Ne let the same of any be envied:
So Orpheus did for his own bride,
So I unto myself alone will sing,
The woods shall to me answer and my echo ring.

Early before the world's light-giving lamp
His golden beam upon the hills doth spread,   20
Having dispersed the night's uncheerful damp,
Do ye awake, and with fresh lustihead,
Go to the bower of my beloved love,
My truest turtle dove;
Bid her awake; for Hymen is awake,
And long since ready forth his mask to move,
With his bright tead that flames with many a flake,
And many a bachelor to wait on him,
In their fresh garments trim.
Bid her awake therefore and soon her dight,   30
For lo, the wished day is come at last,
That shall for all the pains and sorrows past,
Pay to her usury of long delight;
And whilst she doth her dight,
Do ye to her of joy and solace sing,
That all the woods may answer and your echo ring.

Bring with you all the Nymphs that you can hear
Both of the rivers and the forests green:
And of the sea that neighbours to her near,
All with gay garlands goodly well beseen.   40
And let them also with them bring in hand
Another gay garland
For my fair love of lilies and of roses,
Bound true-love wise with a blue silk riband.
And let them make great store of bridal posies,
And let them eke bring store of other flowers
To deck the bridal bowers.
And let the ground whereas her foot shall tread,
For fear the stones her tender foot should wrong,
Be strewed with fragrant flowers all along,   50
And diapered like the discolored mead.
Which done, do at her chamber door await,
For she will waken straight,

The whiles do ye this song unto her sing;
The woods shall to you answer and your echo ring.

Ye nymphs of Mulla, which with careful heed,
The silver scaly trouts do tend full well,
And greedy pikes which use therein to feed,
(Those trouts and pikes all others do excel)
And ye likewise which keep the rushy lake,   60
Where none do fishes take,
Bind up the locks the which hang scatter'd light,
And in his waters, which your mirror make,
Behold your faces as the crystal bright,
That when you come whereas my love doth lie,
No blemish she may spy.
And eke ye lightfoot maids which keep the deer,
That on the hoary mountain use to tower,
And the wild wolves, which seek them to devour,
With your steel darts do chase from coming near,   70
Be also present here,
To help to deck her and to help to sing,
That all the woods may answer and your echo ring.

Wake now, my love, awake; for it is time.
The rosy morn long since left Tithones' bed,
All ready to her silver coach to climb,
And Phoebus gins to shew his glorious head.
Hark how the cheerful birds do chant their lays
And carol of love's praise.
The merry lark her matins sings aloft,   80
The thrush replies, the mavis descant plays,
The ouzel shrills, the ruddock warbles soft,
So goodly all agree with sweet consent,
To this day's merriment.
Ah, my dear love, why do ye sleep thus long,
When meeter were that ye should now awake,
T' await the coming of your joyous make,
And harken to the birds' love-learned song,
The dewy leaves among?
For they of joy and pleasance to you sing,   90
That all the woods them answer and their echo ring.

My love is now awake out of her dream,
And her fair eyes, like stars that dimmed were

With darksome cloud, now show their goodly beams
More bright than Hesperus his head doth rear.
Come now ye damsels, daughters of delight,
Help quickly her to dight,
But first come ye, fair hours, which were begot
In Jove's sweet paradise, of day and night,
Which do the seasons of the year allot,   100
And all that ever in this world is fair
Do make and still repair.
And ye three handmaids of the Cyprian queen,
The which do still adorn her beauty's pride,
Help to adorn my beautifullest bride;
And as ye her array, still throw between
Some graces to be seen,
And as ye use to Venus, to her sing,
The whiles the woods shall answer and your echo ring.

Now is my love all ready forth to come;   110
Let all the virgins therefore well await,
And ye fresh boys that tend upon her groom
Prepare yourselves; for he is coming straight.
Set all your things in seemly good array
Fit for so joyful day,
The joyful'st day that ever sun did see.
Fair sun, show forth thy favourable ray,
And let thy lifeful heat not fervent be,
For fear of burning her sunshiny face,
Her beauty to disgrace.   120
O fairest Phoebus, father of the Muse,
If ever I did honour thee aright,
Or sing the thing, that mote thy mind delight,
Do not thy servant's simple boon refuse,
But let this day, let this one day, be mine,
Let all the rest be thine.
Then I thy sovereign praises loud will sing,
That all the woods shall answer and their echo ring.

Hark how the minstrels 'gin to shrill aloud
Their merry music that resounds from far,   130
The pipe, the tabor, and the trembling crowd,
That well agree withouten breach or jar.
But most of all the damsels do delight,
When they their timbrels smite,

And thereunto do dance and carol sweet,
That all the senses they do ravish quite,
The whiles the boys run up and down the street,
Crying aloud with strong confused noise,
As if it were one voice.
Hymen, Io Hymen, Hymen, they do shout,   140
That even to the heavens their shouting shrill
Doth reach, and all the firmament doth fill,
To which the people standing all about,
As in approvance do thereto applaud
And loud advance her laud,
And evermore they Hymen, Hymen, sing,
That all the woods them answer and their echo ring.

Lo, where she comes along with portly pace
Like Phoebe from her chamber of the East,
Arising forth to run her mighty race,   150
Clad all in white, that seems a virgin best.
So well it her beseems that ye would ween
Some angel she had been.
Her long loose yellow locks like golden wire,
Sprinkled with pearl, and pearling flowers a-tween,
Do like a golden mantle her attire,
And being crowned with a garland green,
Seem like some maiden queen.
Her modest eyes abashed to behold
So many gazers, as on her do stare,   160
Upon the lowly ground affixed are.
Ne dare lift up her countenance too bold,
But blush to hear her praises sung so loud,
So far from being proud.
Nathless do ye still loud her praises sing,
That all the woods may answer and your echo ring.

Tell me, ye merchants' daughters, did ye see
So fair a creature in your town before,
So sweet, so lovely, and so mild as she,
Adorned with beauty's grace and virtue's store,   170
Her goodly eyes like sapphires shining bright,
Her forehead ivory white,
Her cheeks like apples which the sun hath rudded,
Her lips like cherries charming men to bite,
Her breast like to a bowl of cream uncrudded,

Her paps like lilies budded,
Her snowy neck like to a marble tower,
And all her body like a palace fair,
Ascending up with many a stately stair,
To honour's seat and chastity's sweet bower.   180
Why stand ye still, ye virgins, in amaze,
Upon her so to gaze,
Whiles ye forget your former lay to sing,
To which the woods did answer and your echo ring.

But if ye saw that which no eyes can see,
The inward beauty of her lively spright,
Garnished with heavenly gifts of high degree,
Much more then would ye wonder at that sight,
And stand astonish'd like to those which read
Medusa's mazeful head.   190
There dwells sweet love and constant chastity,
Unspotted faith and comely womanhood,
Regard of honour and mild modesty;
There virtue reigns as queen in royal throne,
And giveth laws alone,
The which the base affections do obey,
And yield their services unto her will;
Ne thought of thing uncomely ever may
Thereto approach to tempt her mind to ill.
Had ye once seen these her celestial treasures,   200
And unrevealed pleasures,
Then would ye wonder and her praises sing,
That all the woods should answer and your echo ring.

Open the temple gates unto my love,
Open them wide that she may enter in,
And all the posts adorn as doth behove,
And all the pillars deck with garlands trim,
For to receive this saint with honour due,
That cometh in to you.
With trembling steps and humble reverence,   210
She cometh in, before th'Almighty's view.
Of her ye virgins learn obedience,
When so ye come into those holy places,
To humble your proud faces:
Bring her up to th'high altar, that she may
The sacred ceremonies there partake,

The which do endless matrimony make,
And let the roaring organs loudly play
The praises of the Lord in lively notes,
The whiles with hollow throats   220
The choristers the joyous anthem sing,
That all the woods may answer and their echo ring.

Behold whiles she before the altar stands,
Hearing the holy priest that to her speaks
And blesseth her with his two happy hands,
How the red roses flush up in her cheeks,
And the pure snow with goodly vermeil stain,
Like crimson dyed in grain,
That even th'angels which continually
About the sacred altar do remain,   230
Forget their service and about her fly,
Oft peeping in her face that seems more fair,
The more they on it stare.
But her sad eyes, still fastened on the ground,
Are governed with goodly modesty,
That suffers not one look to glance awry,
Which may let in a little thought unsound.
Why blush ye, love, to give to me your hand,
The pledge of all our band?
Sing, ye sweet angels, Alleluia sing,   240
That all the woods may answer and your echo ring.

Now all is done; bring home the bride again,
Bring home the triumph of our victory,
Bring home with you the glory of her gain,
With joyance bring her and with jollity.
Never had man more joyful day than this,
Whom heaven would heap with bliss.
Make feast therefore now all this live-long day,
This day for ever to me holy is;
Pour out the wine without restraint or stay,   250
Pour not by cups, but by the belly full,
Pour out to all that wull,
And sprinkle all the posts and walls with wine,
That they may sweat, and drunken be withal.
Crown ye god Bacchus with a coronal,
And Hymen also crown with wreaths of vine,
And let the Graces dance unto the rest;

For they can do it best:
The whiles the maidens do their carol sing,
To which the woods shall answer and their echo ring.   260

Ring ye the bells, ye young men of the town,
And leave your wonted labors for this day:
This day is holy; do ye write it down,
That ye for ever it remember may.
This day the sun is in his chiefest height,
With Barnaby the bright,
From whence declining daily by degrees,
He somewhat loseth of his heat and light,
When once the Crab behind his back he sees.
But for this time it ill ordained was,   270
To choose the longest day in all the year,
And shortest night, when longest fitter were:
Yet never day so long, but late would pass.
Ring ye the bells, to make it wear away,
And bonfires make all day,
And dance about them, and about them sing,
That all the woods may answer, and your echo ring.

Ah, when will this long weary day have end,
And lend me leave to come unto my love?
How slowly do the hours their numbers spend!   280
How slowly does sad Time his feathers move!
Haste thee, O fairest planet, to thy home
Within the western foam;
Thy tired steeds long since have need of rest.
Long though it be, at last I see it gloom,
And the bright evening star with golden crest
Appear out of the east.
Fair child of beauty, glorious lamp of love,
That all the host of heaven in ranks dost lead,
And guidest lovers through the nightes dread,   290
How cheerfully thou lookest from above,
And seem'st to laugh a-tween thy twinkling light,
As joying in the sight
Of these glad many which for joy do sing,
That all the woods them answer and their echo ring.

Now cease, ye damsels, your delights forepast;
Enough is it, that all the day was yours:

Now day is done, and night is nighing fast;
Now bring the bride into the bridal bowers.
Now night is come, now soon her disarray,   300
And in her bed her lay;
Lay her in lilies and in violets,
And silken curtains over her display,
And odoured sheets, and Arras coverlets.
Behold how goodly my fair love does lie
In proud humility;
Like unto Maia, when as Jove her took,
In Tempe, lying on the flowery grass,
'Twixt sleep and wake, after she weary was,
With bathing in the Acidalian brook.   310
Now it is night, ye damsels may be gone,
And leave my love alone,
And leave likewise your former lay to sing;
The woods no more shall answer, nor your echo ring.

Now welcome, night, thou night so long expected,
That long day's labour dost at last defray,
And all my cares, which cruel love collected,
Hast sum'd in one, and cancelled for aye:
Spread thy broad wing over my love and me,
That no man may us see,   320
And in thy sable mantle us enwrap,
From fear of peril and foul horror free.
Let no false treason seek us to entrap,
Nor any dread disquiet once annoy
The safety of our joy:
But let the night be calm and quietsome,
Without tempestuous storms or sad affray;
Like as when Jove with fair Alcmena lay,
When he begot the great Tirynthian groom;
Or like as when he with thyself did lie,   330
And begot majesty.
And let the maids and young men cease to sing;
Ne let the woods them answer, nor their echo ring.

Let no lamenting cries, nor doleful tears,
Be heard all night within nor yet without:
Ne let false whispers, breeding hidden fears,
Break gentle sleep with misconceived doubt.
Let no deluding dreams, nor dreadful sights

Make sudden sad affrights;
Ne let housefires, nor lightning's helpless harms,   340
Ne let the Puck, nor other evil sprights,
Ne let mischievous witches with their charms,
Ne let hobgoblins, names whose sense we see not,
Fray us with things that be not.
Let not the screech owl, nor the stork be heard;
Nor the night raven that still deadly yells,
Nor damned ghosts called up with mighty spells,
Nor grisly vultures make us once affear'd:
Ne let th'unpleasant quire of frogs still croaking
Make us to wish they're choking.   350
Let none of these their dreary accents sing;
Ne let the woods them answer, nor their echo ring.

But let still silence true night watches keep,
That sacred peace may in assurance reign,
And timely sleep, when it is time to sleep,
May pour his limbs forth on your pleasant plain,
The whiles an hundred little winged loves,
Like divers feathered doves,
Shall fly and flutter round about your bed,
And in the secret dark, that none reproves,   360
Their pretty stealths shall work, and snares shall spread
To filch away sweet snatches of delight,
Concealed through covert night.
Ye sons of Venus, play your sports at will,
For greedy pleasure, careless of your toys,
Thinks more upon her paradise of joys,
Than what ye do, albeit good or ill.
All night therefore attend your merry play,
For it will soon be day:
Now none doth hinder you, that say or sing;   370
Ne will the woods now answer, nor your echo ring.

Who is the same, which at my window peeps,
Or whose is that fair face, that shines so bright?
Is it not Cynthia, she that never sleeps,
But walks about high heaven all the night?
O fairest goddess, do thou not envy
My love with me to spy:
For thou likewise didst love, though now unthought,
And for a fleece of wool, which privily

The Latmian shepherd once unto thee brought, 380
His pleasures with thee wrought.
Therefore to us be favorable now;
And sith of women's labours thou hast charge,
And generation goodly dost enlarge,
Incline thy will t'effect our wishful vow,
And the chaste womb inform with timely seed,
That may our comfort breed:
Till which we cease our hopeful hap to sing;
Ne let the woods us answer, nor our echo ring.

And thou great Juno, which with awful might 390
The laws of wedlock still dost patronize,
And the religion of the faith first plight
With sacred rites hast taught to solemnize:
And eke for comfort often called art
Of women in their smart,
Eternally bind thou this lovely band,
And all thy blessings unto us impart.
And thou glad Genius, in whose gentle hand
The bridal bower and genial bed remain,
Without blemish or stain, 400
And the sweet pleasures of their love's delight
With secret aid dost succour and supply,
Till they bring forth the fruitful progeny,
Send us the timely fruit of this same night.
And thou fair Hebe, and thou Hymen free,
Grant that it may so be.
Till which we cease your further praise to sing;
Ne any woods shall answer, nor your echo ring.

And ye high heavens, the temple of the gods,
In which a thousand torches flaming bright 410
Do burn, that to us wretched earthly clods
In dreadful darkness lend desired light;
And all ye powers which in the same remain,
More than we men can feign,
Pour out your blessing on us plenteously,
And happy influence upon us rain,
That we may raise a large posterity,
Which from the earth, which they may long possess,
With lasting happiness,
Up to your haughty palaces may mount, 420

And for the guerdon of their glorious merit
May heavenly tabernacles there inherit,
Of blessed Saints for to increase the count.
So let us rest, sweet love, in hope of this,
And cease till then our timely joys to sing;
The woods no more us answer, nor our echo ring.

Song made in lieu of many ornaments,
With which my love should duly have been decked,
Which cutting off through hasty accidents,
Ye would not stay your due time to expect,   430
But promis'd both to recompense,
Be unto her a goodly ornament,
And for short time an endless monument.

From AMORETTI

❧ 18 ❧

The rolling wheel, that runneth often round,
The hardest steel in tract of time doth tear;
And drizzling drops, that often do redound,
The firmest flint doth in continuance wear:
Yet cannot I, with many a dropping tear
And long entreaty, soften her hard heart;
That she will once vouchsafe my plaint to hear,
Or look with pity on my painful smart.
But when I plead, she bids me play my part;
And when I weep, she says, tears are but water;
And when I sigh, she says, I know the art;
And when I wail, she turns herself to laughter.
So do I weep, and wail, and plead in vain,
Whiles she as steel and flint doth still remain.

❧ 54 ❧

Of this world's theatre in which we stay,
My love, like the spectator, idly sits,
Beholding me, that all the pageants play,
Disguising diversly my troubled wits.
Sometimes I joy when glad occasion fits

And mask in mirth like to a comedy:
Soon after, when my joy to sorrow flits,
I wail, and make my woes a tragedy.
Yet she, beholding me with constant eye,
Delights not in my mirth, nor rues my smart;
But, when I laugh, she mocks; and, when I cry,
She laughs, and hardens evermore her heart.
What then can move her? If nor mirth, nor moan,
She is no woman, but a senseless stone.

ε 67 ε

Like as a huntsman after weary chase,
Seeing the game from him escap'd away,
Sits down to rest him in some shady place,
With panting hounds beguiled of their prey:
So, after long pursuit and vain assay,
When I all weary had the chase forsook,
The gentle dear return'd the self-same way,
Thinking to quench her thirst at the next brook:
There she, beholding me with milder look,
Sought not to fly, but fearless still did bide;
Till I in hand her yet half-trembling took,
And with her own goodwill her firmly tied.
Strange thing, me seem'd, to see a beast so wild,
So goodly won, with her own will beguil'd.

ε 75 ε

One day I wrote her name upon the strand;
But came the waves, and washed it away:
Again, I wrote it with a second hand;
But came the tide, and made my pains his prey.
Vain man! said she, that doest in vain assay
A mortal thing so to immortalize;
For I myself shall like to this decay,
And eke my name be wiped out likewise.
Not so (quod I); let baser things devise
To die in dust, but you shall live by fame:
My verse your vertues rare shall eternize,
And in the heavens write your glorious name;
Where, when as death shall all the world subdue,
Our love shall live, and later life renew.

⊱ 80 ⊰

After so long a race as I have run
Through Faery land, which those six books compile,
Give leave to rest me, being half fordone,
And gather to myself new breath awhile.
Then, as a steed refreshed after toil,
Out of my prison I will break anew;
And stoutly will that second work assoil,
With strong endeavour and attention due.
Till then give leave to me in pleasant mew
To sport my muse, and sing my love's sweet praise;
The contemplation of whose heavenly hue,
My spirit to an higher pitch will raise.
But let her praises yet be low and mean,
Fit for the handmaid of the Faery Queene.

Sir Philip Sidney

(1 5 5 4 – 1 5 8 6)

Born at Penshurst and educated at Shrewsbury and Christ Church, Oxford, Sidney traveled in the early 1570s to France, Germany, Austria, and Italy, where Veronese painted his portrait. In 1583 he married Frances, the daughter of Sir Francis Walsingham. He composed a number of major works around this period, including the *Arcadia*, a pastoral romance posthumously published and completed by his sister, the Countess of Pembroke (who also completed his unfinished translations of the Psalms), his *Defence of Poesy*, and the Petrarchan *Astrophel and Stella*. A strong advocate of the Protestant cause, Sidney was appointed governor of Flushing in 1585 and was killed the next year at Zutphen during an attack on a Spanish convoy. The many tributes after his death— including Spenser's "Astrophil"—nostalgically represent the fallen Sidney as the embodiment of the Elizabethan chivalric ideal.

From ASTROPHEL AND STELLA

1

Loving in truth, and fain in verse my love to show,
That the dear She might take some pleasure of my pain:
Pleasure might cause her read, reading might make her know,
Knowledge might pity win, and pity grace obtain;
    I sought fit words to paint the blackest face of woe,
Studying inventions fine, her wits to entertain:
Oft turning others' leaves, to see if thence would flow
Some fresh and fruitful showers upon my sunburn't brain.
    But words came halting forth, wanting Invention's stay;
Invention, Nature's child, fled step-dame Study's blows;
And others' feet still seemed but strangers in my way.
Thus great with child to speak, and helpless in my throes,
    Biting my truant pen, beating my self for spite,
    "Fool," said my Muse to me, "look in thy heart and write."

❧ 15 ❧

You that do search for every purling spring,
Which from the ribs of old Parnassus flows;
And every flower, not sweet perhaps, which grows
Near thereabouts, into your Poesy wring;
You that do dictionary's method bring
Into your rhymes, running in rattling rows;
You that poor Petrarch's long-deceased woes,
With new-born sighs and denizened wit do sing;
You take wrong ways, those far-fet helps be such
As do bewray a want of inward touch:
And sure at length stol'n goods do come to light.
But if (both for your love and skill) your name
You seek to nurse at fullest breasts of Fame,
Stella behold, and then begin to endite.

❧ 27 ❧

Because I oft, in dark abstracted guise,
Seem most alone in greatest company,
With dearth of words, or answers quite awry,
To them that would make speech of speech arise,
They deem, and of that doom the rumour flies,
That poison foul of bubbling pride doth lie
So in my dwelling breast, that only I
Fawn on my self, and others do despise:
Yet pride, I think, doth not my soul possess,
Which looks too oft in his unflatt'ring glass:
But one worse fault, Ambition, I confess,
That makes me oft my best friends overpass,
Unseen, unheard, while thought to highest place
Bends all his powers, even unto Stella's grace.

❧ 31 ❧

With how sad steps, O Moon, thou climb'st the skies,
How silently, and with how wan a face,
What may it be, that even in heav'nly place
That busie archer his sharp arrows tries?
Sure, if that long with Love acquainted eyes
Can judge of Love, thou feel'st a Lover's case;

I read it in thy looks, thy languish'd grace
To me that feel the like, thy state descries.
Then ev'n of fellowship, O Moon, tell me
Is constant Love deem'd there but want of wit?
Are Beauties there as proud as here they be?
Do they above love to be lov'd, and yet
Those Lovers scorn whom that Love doth possess?
Do they call Virtue there ungratefulness?

54

Because I breathe not love to ev'ry one,
Nor do not use set colours for to wear,
Nor nourish special locks of vowed hair,
Nor give each speech a full point of a groan.
The courtly Nymphs, acquainted with the moan,
Of them, who in their lips Love's standard bear;
"What he?" say they of me, "now I dare swear,
He cannot love: no, no, let him alone."
And think so still, so Stella know my mind,
Profess in deed I do not Cupid's art;
But you fair maid at length this true shall find,
That his right badge is but worn in the heart:
Dumb Swan, not chatt'ring Pies, do Lovers prove,
They love indeed, who quake to say they love.

Fulke Greville, First Baron Brooke

(1 5 5 4 – 1 6 2 8)

Along with his lifelong friend Philip Sidney, Fulke Greville was educated at Shrewsbury School. After attending Cambridge, Greville arrived at court and began a long career of public service. He was also a member of Gabriel Harvey's literary circle, the "Aereopagus." His collection of lyrics, *Caelica*, begun under Sidney's influence, ranges from conventional love lyrics to the more philosophical and spiritual concerns characteristic of his later years. While his most famous work was *The Life of the Renowned Sir Philip Sidney* (written c.1610–1614, but not published until 1652), Greville also wrote some closet plays and philosophical poems on government and religion. He never married. King James made him a peer in 1621, and he was granted Knowle Park and Warwick Castle, where he was stabbed to death a few years later by his servant, Haywood, under mysterious circumstances.

From CAELICA

➳ 56 ❧

All my senses, like beacon's flame,
Gave alarum to desire
To take arms in Cynthia's name,
And set all my thoughts on fire:
Fury's wit persuaded me,
Happy love was hazard's heir,
Cupid did best shoot and see
In the night where smooth is fair;
Up I start believing well
To see if Cynthia were awake;   10
Wonders I saw, who can tell?
And thus unto myself I spake:
"Sweet God Cupid where am I,
That by pale Diana's light,
Such rich beauties do espy,
As harm our senses with delight?
Am I borne up to the skies?

See where Jove and Venus shine,
Showing in her heavenly eyes
That desire is divine.   20
Look where lies the milken way,
Way unto that dainty throne,
Where while all the gods would play,
Vulcan thinks to dwell alone.
Shadowing it with curious art,
Nets of sullen golden hair.
Mars am I and may not part
Till that I be taken there."
Therewithal I heard a sound,
Made of all the parts of love,   30
Which did sense delight and wound;
Planets with such music move.
Those joys drew desires near,
The heavens blush'd, the white show'd red,
Such red as in skies appear
When Sol parts from Thetis' bed.
Then unto myself I said,
"Surely I Apollo am,
Yonder is the glorious maid
Which men do Aurora name,   40
Who for pride she hath in me
Blushing forth desire and fear,
While she would have no man see,
Makes the world know I am there."
I resolve to play my son
And misguide my chariot fire,
All the sky to overcome
And enflame with my desire.
I gave reins to this conceit,
Hope went on the wheel of lust: 50
Fancy's scales are false of weight,
Thoughts take thought that go of trust.
I stepped forth to touch the sky,
I a god by Cupid dreams,
Cynthia who did naked lie
Runs away like silver streams,
Leaving hollow banks behind,
Who can neither forward move,
Nor, if rivers be unkind,

Turn away or leave to love.   60
There stand I, like Arctic pole,
Where Sol passeth o'er the line,
Mourning my benighted soul,
Which so loseth light divine.
There stand I like men that preach
From the execution place,
At their death content to teach
All the world with their disgrace.
He that lets his Cynthia lie,
Naked on a bed of play,   70
To say prayers ere she die,
Teacheth time to run away.
Let no love-desiring heart,
In the stars go seek his fate,
Love is only Nature's art,
Wonder hinders Love and Hate.
None can well behold with eyes,
But what underneath him lies.

* 87 *

Whenas man's life, the light of human lust,
In socket of his earthly lantern burns,
That all this glory unto ashes must,
And generation to corruption turns;
Then fond desires that only fear their end,
Do vainly wish for life, but to amend.
But when this life is from the body fled,
To see itself in that eternal glass
Where time doth end and thoughts accuse the dead,
Where all to come, is one with all that was;
Then living men ask how he left his breath,
That while he lived never thought of death.

❧ 99 ❧

Down in the depth of mine iniquity,
That ugly centre of infernal spirits,
Where each sin feels her own deformity,
In these peculiar torments she inherits,
Depriv'd of human graces, and divine,
Even there appears this saving God of mine.

And in this fatal mirror of transgression,
Shows man as fruit of his degeneration,
The error's ugly infinite impression,
Which bears the faithless down to desperation;   10
Depriv'd of human graces and divine,
Even there appears this saving God of mine;

In power and truth, Almighty and eternal,
Which on the sin reflects strange desolation,
With glory scourging all the spirits infernal,
And uncreated hell with unprivation;
Depriv'd of human graces, not divine,
Even there appears this saving God of mine.

For on this spiritual cross condemned lying,
To pains infernal by eternal doom,   20
I see my Saviour for the same sins dying,
And from that hell I fear'd, to free me, come;
Depriv'd of human graces, not divine,
Thus hath his death rais'd up this soul of mine.

Sir Walter Ralegh

(1 5 5 4 ? – 1 6 1 8)

Ralegh left Oriel College, Oxford, and embarked on a remarkable career as soldier, explorer, colonizer, courtier, historian, and poet. Among his more famous exploits were his expedition to Guiana to search for gold (described in his *Discovery of Guiana*, 1597) and the sack of Cádiz harbor in 1596. He also served in Ireland, where he met Edmund Spenser (who approved of Ralegh's role in the massacre of six hundred Spanish mercenaries at Smerwick). A favorite of Queen Elizabeth, Ralegh incurred her displeasure in 1592 because of his interest in one of her maids of honor, Elizabeth Throckmorton, whom he married. Ralegh was put on trial by King James I in 1603 on trumped-up charges of high treason and was imprisoned in the Tower of London until 1616, when he was released in order to return to Guiana to search out a gold mine there. Upon his return from this disastrous expedition he was once again charged with treason and soon after executed. During his time in prison Ralegh compiled the ambitious *History of the World* (1614). Much of his poetry is lost, and very little was published during his lifetime, although about thirty short pieces survive that give some indication of his gifts as a lyric poet. Perhaps Ralegh's most famous lyric is his "Nymph's Reply" to Marlowe's "Passionate Shepherd (see p. 89)."

THE NYMPH'S REPLY

If all the world and love were young,
And truth in every shepherd's tongue,
These pretty pleasures might me move,
To live with thee, and be thy love.

Time drives the flocks from field to fold,
When rivers rage and rocks grow cold,
And Philomel becometh dumb;
The rest complains of cares to come.

The flowers do fade, and wanton fields,
To wayward winter reckoning yields;   10
A honey tongue, a heart of gall,
Is fancy's spring, but sorrow's fall.

71

Thy gowns, thy shoes, thy beds of roses,
Thy cap, thy kirtle, and thy posies
Soon break, soon wither, soon forgotten;
In folly ripe, in reason rotten.

Thy belt of straw and ivy buds,
Thy coral clasps and amber studs,
All these in me no means can move,
To come to thee, and be thy love.   20

But could youth last and love still breed,
Had joys no date nor age no need,
Then these delights my mind might move,
To live with thee, and be thy love.

MY BODY IN THE WALLS CAPTIVED

My body in the walls captived,
Feels not the wounds of spiteful envy,
But my thrall'd mind, of liberty deprived,
Fast fetter'd in her ancient memory,
Doth naught behold but sorrow's dying face.
Such prison erst was so delightful
As it desir'd no other dwelling place,
But time's effects, and destinies despiteful,
Have changed both my keeper and my fare.
Love's fire and beauty's light I then had store,
But now close kept, as captives wonted are,
That food, that heat, that light I find no more.
   Despair bolts up my doors, and I alone
   Speak to dead walls, but those hear not my moan.

VERSES MADE THE NIGHT
BEFORE HIS BEHEADING

Even such is Time, which takes in trust
Our youth, our joys, and all we have,
And pays us but with age and dust;

Who in the dark and silent grave,
When we have wandered all our ways,
Shuts up the story of our days:
And from which earth, and grave, and dust,
The Lord shall raise me up, I trust.

Mary Sidney Herbert, Countess of Pembroke

(1 5 6 1 – 1 6 2 1)

The Countess of Pembroke was sister to Sir Philip Sidney and aunt to Lady Mary Wroth. Educated in Latin and Greek, she served as Maid of Honor to Queen Elizabeth and married Henry Herbert, Earl of Pembroke, at the age of fifteen. She was a major patron of the arts and supported, among others, Ben Jonson, Thomas Nashe, John Donne, and Samuel Daniel. The Countess of Pembroke's works include translations of Philippe de Mornay's A *Discourse of Life and Death* and the Senecan tragedy *Antonie*, based on Robert Garnier's *Marc Antonie*. After her brother Philip's death she served as his literary executor, revising and completing his unfinished *Arcadia* and taking over his metrical translation of the Psalms (Philip had gotten only as far as the forty-third Psalm). Her accomplished renderings of the Psalms circulated in manuscript and were praised by John Donne, who wrote of them, "They tell us *why*, and teach us *how* to sing."

PSALM 84

How lovely is thy dwelling,
   Great God, to whom all greatness is belonging!
To view thy courts far, far from any telling,
   My soul doth long, and pine with longing.
     Unto the God that liveth
     The God that all life giveth
   My heart and body both aspire,
   Above delight, beyond desire.

Alas! the sparrow knoweth
   The house where free and fearless she resideth: 10
Directly to the nest the swallow goeth,
   Where with her sons she safe abideth.
     O altars thine, most mighty
     In war, yea most almighty:
   Thy altars, Lord! ah! why should I
   From altars thine excluded lie?

O happy who remaineth
  Thy household-man, and still thy praise unfoldeth;
O happy who himself on thee sustaineth,
  Who to thy house his journey holdeth!   20
    Me seems I see them going
    Where mulberries are growing:
  How wells they dig in thirsty plain,
  And cisterns make, for falling rain.

Me seems I see augmented
  Still troop with troop, till all at length discover
Sion, where to their sight is represented
  The Lord of hosts, the Sion lover.
    O Lord, O God, most mighty
    In war, yea most almighty: 30
  Hear what I beg; hearken, I say,
  O Jacob's God, to what I pray.

Thou art the shield us shieldeth:
  Then, Lord, behold the face of thine anointed.
One day spent in thy courts more comfort yieldeth
  Than thousands otherwise appointed.
    I count it clearer pleasure
    To spend my age's treasure
  Waiting a porter at thy gates,
  Than dwell a lord with wicked mates.   40

Thou art the sun that shineth,
  Thou art the buckler, Lord, that us defendeth:
Glory and grace Jehovah's hand assigneth:
  And good, without refusal, sendeth
    To him who truly treadeth
    The path to pureness leadeth.
  O Lord of might, thrice blessed he,
  Whose confidence is built on thee.

PSALM 100

O all you lands, the treasures of your joy,
  In merry shout upon the Lord bestow:
Your service cheerfully on him employ,

With triumph song into his presence go.
Know first that he is God; and after know
   This God did us, not we our selves create:
We are his flock, for us his feedings grow:
   We are his folk, and he upholds our state.
With thankfulness O enter then his gate:
   Make through each porch of his your praises ring,
All good, all grace, of his high name relate,
   He of all grace and goodness is the spring.
Time in no terms his mercy comprehends,
From age to age his truth it self extends.

TO THE ANGEL SPIRIT OF THE
MOST EXCELLENT
SIR PHILIP SIDNEY

To thee pure sprite, to thee alone's address'd
This coupled work, by double int'rest thine:
First rais'd by thy blest hand, and what is mine
Inspir'd by thee, thy secret power impress'd.
So dar'd my Muse with thine itself combine,
As mortal stuff with that which is divine,
Thy lightning beams give lustre to the rest;

That Heaven's King may deign his own transform'd
In substance no, but superficial 'tire,
By thee put on; to praise, not to aspire   10
To those high tones, so in themselves adorn'd,
Which angels sing in their celestial quire,
And all of tongues with soul and voice admire
These sacred hymns thy kingly prophet form'd.

O, had that soul which honor brought to rest
Too soon not left and reft the world of all
What man could show, which we perfection call,
This half-maim'd piece had sorted with the best.
Deep wounds enlarg'd, long fester'd in their gall
Fresh bleeding smart; not eye but heart tears fall.   20
Ah memory, what needs this new arrest?

Yet here behold (O wert thou to behold!)
This finish'd now, thy matchless Muse begun,
The rest but piec'd, as left by thee undone.
Pardon (O blest soul) presumption too, too bold:
If love and zeal such error ill-become,
'Tis zealous love, love which hath never done,
Nor can enough in world of words unfold.

And sith it hath no further scope to go,
Nor other purpose but to honor thee,   30
Thee in thy works where all the Graces be,
As little streams with all their all do flow
To their great sea, due tribute's grateful fee:
So press my thoughts my burthen'd thoughts in me,
To pay the debt of infinites I owe

To thy great worth; exceeding Nature's store,
Wonder of men, sole born perfection's kind,
Phoenix thou wert, so rare thy fairest mind
Heav'nly adorn'd, Earth justly might adore,
Where truthful praise in highest glory shin'd: 40
For there alone was praise to truth confin'd;
And where but there, to live for evermore?

O! when to this accompt, this cast-up sum,
This reck'ning made, this audit of my woe,
I call my thoughts, whence so strange passions flow;
How works my heart, my senses stricken dumb?
That would thee more, then ever heart could show,
And all too short who knew thee best doth know,
There lives no wit that may thy praise become.

Truth I invoke (who scorne else where to move   50
Or here in ought my blood should partialize)
Truth, sacred Truth, thee sole to solemnize,
Those precious rights well known best minds approve:
And who but doth, hath wisdom's open eyes,
Not owly-blind the fairest light still flies
Confirm no less? At least 'tis seal'd above.

Where thou art fix'd among thy fellow lights:
My day put out, my life in darkness cast,
Thy angel's soul with highest angels plac'd,

There blessed sings enjoying heav'n-delights   60
Thy Maker's praise: as far from earthy taste
As here thy works so worthily embrac'd
By all of worth, where never envy bites.

As goodly buildings to some glorious end
Cut off by fate, before the Graces had
Each wondrous part in all their beauties clad
Yet so much done, as art could not amend;
So thy rare works to which no wit can add,
In all men's eyes, which are not blindly mad,
Beyond compare, above all praise, extend.   70

Immortal monuments of thy fair fame,
Though not complete, nor in the reach of thought,
How on that passing peace-time would have wrought,
Had Heav'n so spar'd the life of life to frame
The rest? But ah! such loss hath this world ought
Can equal it? Or which like grievance brought?
Yet there will live thy ever praised name.

To which these dearest off'rings of my heart
Dissolv'd to ink, while pen's impressions move
The bleeding veins of never-dying love,   80
I render here: these wounding lines of smart
Sad characters indeed of simple love
Not art nor skill which abler wits do prove,
Of my full soul receive the meanest part.

Receive these Hymns, these obsequies receive;
If any mark of thy sweet sprite appear,
Well are they born, no title else shall bear.
I can no more: dear soul, I take my leave;
Sorrow still strives, would mount thy highest sphere,
Presuming so just cause might meet thee there,   90
O happy change! Could I so take my leave.

l. 1. sprite = spirit

Samuel Daniel

(1562/63 – 1619)

Daniel was born in Somerset, the son of a musician. After leaving Magdalen Hall, Oxford, he sought out the patronage first of the Countess of Pembroke and later of Fulke Greville. His sonnet sequence, *Delia* (first published in 1592), made a strong impression upon his contemporaries; Spenser praised Daniel in his *Colin Clout* as the "new shepherd late upsprong." The influential sonnets were quickly imitated and subjected to parody (and even plagiarized by a hapless poetaster in Ben Jonson's *Every Man in His Humour*). He served for a brief time as Licenser to the Children of the Queen's Revels. Daniel was accomplished in several literary genres: he wrote a number of plays and court masques, *A Defence of Rhyme*, and *The Civil Wars*, an important verse epic of England's medieval past.

From DELIA

ɛ• 34 •ɞ

When winter snows upon thy golden hairs,
And frost of age hath nipp'd thy flowers near:
When dark shall seem thy day that never clears,
And all lies wither'd that was held so dear;
Then take this picture which I here present thee,
Limn'd with a pencil not all unworthy:
Here see the gifts that God and nature lent thee;
Here read thy self, and what I suffered for thee.
This may remain thy lasting monument,
Which happily posterity may cherish:
These colours with thy fading are not spent;
These may remain, when thou and I shall perish.
If they remain, then thou shalt live thereby;
They will remain, and so thou canst not die.

ɛ• 39 •ɞ

Read in my face a volume of despairs,
The wailing Iliads of my tragic woe;

Drawn with my blood, and printed with my cares,
Wrought by her hand, that I have honour'd so.
Who whilst I burn, she sings at my soul's wrack,
Looking aloft from turret of her pride:
There my soul's tyrant joys her, in the sack
Of her own seat, whereof I made her guide.
There do these smokes that from affliction rise,
Serve as an incense to a cruel dame:
A sacrifice thrice grateful to her eyes,
Because their power serve to'exact the same.
Thus ruins she, to satisfy her will;
The temple, where her name was honour'd still.

ᴥ 45 ᴥ

Care-charmer sleep, son of the sable night,
Brother to death, in silent darkness born:
Relieve my languish, and restore the light,
With dark forgetting of my cares return.
And let the day be time enough to mourn
The shipwrack of my ill-adventured youth:
Let waking eyes suffice to wail their scorn,
Without the torment of the night's untruth.
Cease dreams, th'imagery of our day desires,
To model forth the passions of the morrow:
Never let rising sun approve you liars,
To add more grief to aggravate my sorrow.
Still let me sleep, embracing clouds in vain;
And never wake, to feel the day's disdain.

ᴥ 46 ᴥ

Let others sing of knights and paladins,
In aged accents, and untimely words;
Paint shadows in imaginary lines,
Which well the reach of their high wits records.
But I must sing of thee and those fair eyes,
Authentic shall my verse in time to come,
When yet th'unborn shall say, lo where she lies,
Whose beauty made him speak that else was dumb.
These are the arks, the trophies I erect,
That fortify thy name against old age,
And these thy sacred virtues must protect,

Against the dark, and Time's consuming rage.
Though th'error of my youth they shall discover,
Suffice they show I liv'd and was thy lover.

Michael Drayton

(1 5 6 3 – 1 6 3 1)

Born of humble origins in Warwickshire, Drayton depended on a variety of sources, from aristocratic patrons to the theatergoing public, for support. His poetry ranges over virtually all of the genres explored in the Elizabethan and Jacobean periods: religious verse translations, the sonnet sequence, the minor epic, pastoral eclogues, heroical epistles, and verse chronicles. He also wrote *Polyolbion*, a remarkable historical and geographical portrait of Britain. His early poems appeared in folio in 1619, and a second collection, *The Muses Elizium*, was published in 1630. His poems display a sharp and often quite critical sense of England's literary and political fortunes.

TO THE VIRGINIAN VOYAGE

You brave heroic minds,
   Worthy your country's name,
   That honour still pursue,
   Go, and subdue,
Whilst loit'ring hinds
Lurk here at home, with shame.

Britans, you stay too long,
Quickly aboard bestow you,
   And with a merry gale
   Swell your stretch'd sail,   10
With vows as strong,
As the winds that blow you.

Your course securely steer,
West and by South forth keep,
   Rocks, lee-shores, nor shoals,
   When Æolus scowls,
You need not fear,
So absolute the deep.

And cheerfully at sea,
Success you still entice,   20

To get the pearl and gold,
  And ours to hold,
Virginia,
Earth's only Paradise.

Where Nature hath in store
Fowl, venison, and fish,
  And the fruitful'st soil,
  Without your toil,
Three harvests more,
All greater than your wish.   30

And the ambitious vine
Crowns with his purple mass,
  The cedar reaching high
  To kiss the sky,
The cypress, pine,
And useful sassafras.

To whom the Golden Age
Still Nature's laws doth give,
  No other cares attend,
  But them to defend   40
From Winter's rage,
That long there doth not live.

When as the luscious smell
Of that delicious land,
  Above the seas that flows,
  The clear wind throws,
Your hearts to swell
Approaching the dear strand.

In kenning of the shore
(Thanks to God first given)   50
  O you the happiest men,
  Be frolic then,
Let cannons roar,
Frighting the wide Heaven.

And in regions far
Such heroes bring ye forth,
  As those from whom we came,

And plant our name,
Under that star
Not known unto our North.   60

And as there plenty grows
Of laurel everywhere,
   Apollo's sacred tree,
   You it may see,
A poet's brows
To crown, that may sing there.

Thy voyages attend,
Industrious Hakluyt,
   Whose reading shall inflame
   Men to seek Fame,   70
And much commend
To after-times thy wit.

TO MY NOBLE FRIEND MASTER
WILLIAM BROWNE:

OF THE EVIL TIME

  Dear friend, be silent and with patience see,
What this mad time's catastrophe will be;
The world's first wisemen certainly mistook
Themselves, and spoke things quite beside the book,
And that which they have said of God, untrue,
Or else expect strange judgement to ensue.
  This Isle is a mere bedlam, and therein,
We all lie raving, mad in every sin,
And him the wisest most men use to call,
Who doth (alone) the maddest thing of all;   10
He whom the master of all wisdom found,
For a mark'd fool, and so did him propound,
The time we live in, to that pass is brought,
That only he a censor now is thought;
And that base villain (not an age yet gone),
Which a good man would not have look'd upon;
Now like a god, with divine worship follow'd,

And all his actions are accounted hollow'd.
   This world of ours, thus runneth upon wheels,
Set on the head, bolt upright with her heels,   20
Which makes me think of what the Ethnics told,
Th'opinion, the Pythagorists uphold,
That the immortal soul doth transmigrate;
Then I suppose by the strong power of fate,
That those which at confused Babel were,
And since that time now many a lingering year
Through fools, and beasts, and lunatics have past,
Are here embodied in this age at last,
And though so long we from that time be gone,
Yet taste we still of that confusion.   30
   For certainly there's scarce one found that now,
Knows what t'approve, or what to disallow,
All arsey varsey, nothing is its own,
But to our proverb, all turn'd upside down;
To do in time, is to do out of season,
And that speeds best, that's done the farth'st from reason,
He's high'st that's low'st, he's surest in that's out,
He hits the next way that goes farth'st about,
He getteth up unlike to rise at all,
He slips to ground as much unlike to fall;   40
Which doth enforce me partly to prefer,
The opinion of that mad philosopher,
Who taught, that those all-framing powers above,
(As 'tis suppos'd) made man not out of love
To him at all, but only as a thing,
To make them sport with, which they use to bring
As men do monkeys, puppets, and such tools
Of laughter: so men are but the gods' fools.
Such are by titles lifted to the sky,
As wherefore no man knows, God scarcely why;   50
The virtuous man depressed like a stone
For that dull sot to raise himself upon;
He who ne'er thing yet worthy man durst do,
Never durst look upon his country's foe,
Nor durst attempt that action which might get
Him fame with men: or higher might him set
Then the base begger (rightly if compar'd)
This drone yet never brave attempt that dar'd,
Yet dares be knighted, and from thence dares grow
To any title empire can bestow;   60

For this believe, that impudence is now
A cardinal virtue, and men it allow
Reverence, nay more, men study and invent
New ways, nay, glory to be impudent.
   Into the clouds the devil lately got,
And by the moisture doubting much the rot,
A medicine took to make him purge and cast;
Which in short time began to work so fast,
That he fell to 't, and from his backside flew,
A rout of rascall a rude ribald crew   70
Of base plebeians, which no sooner light
Upon the earth, but with a sudden flight,
They spread this isle, and as Deucalion once
Over his shoulder back, by throwing stones
They became men, even so these beasts became,
Owners of titles from an obscure name.
   He that by riot, of a mighty rent,
Hath his late goodly patrimony spent,
And into base and wilfull beggery run
This man as he some glorious act had done,   80
With some great pension, or rich gift reliev'd,
When he that hath by industry achiev'd,
Some noble thing, condemned and disgrac'd,
In the forlorn hope of the times is plac'd,
As though that God had carelessly left all
That being hath on this terrestial ball,
To Fortune's guiding, nor would have to do
With man, nor ought that doth belong him to,
Or at the least God having given more
Power to the devil, then he did of yore,   90
Over this world: the fiend as he doth hate
The virtuous man; maligning his estate,
All noble things, and would have by his will,
To be damn'd with him, using all his skill,
By his black hellish ministers to vex
All worthy men, and strangely to perplex
Their constancy, there by them so to fright,
That they should yield them wholly to his might.
But of these things I vainly do but tell,
Where hell is heav'n, and heav'n is now turn'd hell;   100
Where that which lately blasphemy hath bin,
Now godliness, much less accounted sin;
And a long while I greatly marvel'd why

Buffoons and bawds should hourly multiply,
Till that of late I construed it, that they
To present thrift had got the perfect way,
When I concluded by their odious crimes,
It was for us no thriving in these times.
    As men oft laugh at little babes, when they
Hap to behold some strange thing in their play,   110
To see them on the sudden strucken sad,
As in their fancy some strange forms they had,
Which they by pointing with their fingers show,
Angry at our capacities so slow,
That by their countenance we no sooner learn
To see the wonder which they so discern:
So the celestial powers do sit and smile
At innocent and virtuous men the while,
They stand amazed at the world o'ergone,
So far beyond imagination,   120
With slavish baseness, that they silent sit
Pointing like children in describing it.
    Then noble friend the next way to control
These worldly crosses, is to arm thy soul
With constant patience: and with thoughts as high
As these below, and poor, winged to fly
To that exalted stand, whether yet they
Are got with pain, that sit out of the way
Of this ignoble age, which raiseth none
But such as think their black damnation   130
To be a trifle; such, so ill, that when
They are advanc'd, those few poor honest men
That yet are living, into search do run
To find what mischief they have lately done,
Which so prefers them; say thou he doth rise,
That maketh virtue his chief exercise.
And in this base world come what ever shall,
He's worth lamenting, that for her doth fall.

SINCE THERE'S NO HELP

Since there's no help, come, let us kiss and part,
Nay, I have done: you get no more of me,
And I am glad, yea, glad with all my heart,

That thus so cleanly I myself can free;
   Shake hands forever, cancel all our vows,
And when we meet at any time again,
Be it not seen in either of our brows,
That we one jot of former love retain.
   Now at the last gasp of Love's latest breath,
When, his pulse failing, passion speechless lies,
When Faith is kneeling by his bed of Death,
And Innocence is closing up his eyes,
    Now if thou wouldst, when all have given him over,
    From death to life thou mightst him yet recover.

Christopher Marlowe

(1 5 6 4 – 1 5 9 3)

Marlowe's remarkable talent was cut short at the age of twenty-nine when he died violently under mysterious circumstances at an inn at Deptford. His brief life was wrapped in intrigue. Born in Canterbury and educated at Cambridge, he was probably in the employ of the secret service, spying on English Catholics on the Continent. His "monstrous opinions" about religion and sex have sometimes diverted attention from his literary achievement. His poetry was enormously popular in its own day, and what Ben Jonson aptly described as "Marlowe's mighty line" strongly influenced a host of imitators and rivals in dramatic and nondramatic verse, including Shakespeare, John Donne, George Chapman, and Jonson himself. In addition to his accomplishments in the theater, including *Tamburlaine*, *Doctor Faustus*, *Edward II*, and *The Jew of Malta*, Marlowe was also an innovative translator and was the first to render Ovid's *Elegies* and parts of Lucan's *Pharsalia* into English.

THE PASSIONATE
SHEPHERD TO HIS LOVE

Come live with me, and be my love,
And we will all the pleasures prove,
That valleys, groves, hills and fields,
Woods, or steepy mountain yields.

And we will sit upon the rocks,
Seeing the shepherds feed their flocks,
By shallow rivers, to whose falls,
Melodious birds sing madrigals.

And I will make thee beds of roses,
And a thousand fragrant posies,   10
A cap of flowers and a kirtle,
Embroidered all with leaves of myrtle;

A gown made of the finest wool,
Which from our pretty lambs we pull,

Fair lined slippers for the cold,
With buckles of the purest gold;

A belt of straw and ivy-buds,
With coral clasps and amber studs,
And if these pleasures may thee move,
Come live with me, and be my love.   20

The shepherd swains shall dance and sing,
For thy delight each May-morning;
If these delights thy mind may move,
Then live with me, and be my love.

From OVID'S ELEGIES

৪৹ I.iv ৩৹

Thy husband to a banquet goes with me,
Pray God it may his latest supper be.
Shall I sit gazing as a bashful guest,
While others touch the damsel I love best?
Wilt lying under him, his bosom clip?
About thy neck shall he at pleasure skip?
Marvel not, though the fair bride did incite
The drunken Centaurs to a sudden fight;
I am no half-horse, nor in woods I dwell,
Yet scarce my hands from thee contain I well.   10
But how thou shouldst behave thyself now know,
Nor let the winds away my warnings blow.
Before thy husband come, though I not see
What may be done, yet there before him be.
Lie with him gently, when his limbs he spread
Upon the bed, but on my foot first tread.
View me, my becks and speaking countenance;
Take, and receive each secret amorous glance.
Words without voice shall on my eyebrows sit,
Lines thou shalt read in wine by my hand writ.   20
When our lascivious toys come in thy mind,
Thy rosy cheeks be to thy thumb inclined.
If aught of me thou speak'st in inward thought,
Let thy soft finger to thy ear be brought.

When I (my light) do or say aught that please thee,
Turn round thy gold ring, as it were to ease thee.
Strike on the board like them that pray for evil,
When thou dost wish thy husband at the devil.
What wine he fills thee, wisely will him drink;
Ask thou the boy what thou enough dost think.   30
When thou hast tasted, I will take the cup,
And where thou drink'st, on that part I will sup.
If he gives thee what first himself did taste,
Even in his face his offered gobbets cast.
Let not thy neck by his vile arms be pressed,
Nor lean thy soft head on his boist'rous breast.
Thy bosom's roseate buds let him not finger,
Chiefly on thy lips let not his lips linger.
If thou givest kisses, I shall all disclose,
Say they are mine and hands on thee impose.
Yet this I'll see, but if thy gown aught cover,   40
Suspicious fear in all my veins will hover.
Mingle not thighs nor to his leg join thine,
Nor thy soft foot with his hard foot combine.
I have been wanton, therefore am perplexèd,
And with mistrust of the like measure vexed.
I and my wench oft under clothes did lurk,
When pleasure mov'd us to our sweetest work.
Do not thou so, but throw thy mantle hence,
Lest I should think thee guilty of offence.   50
Entreat thy husband drink, but do not kiss,
And while he drinks, to add more do not miss;
If he lies down with wine and sleep oppressed,
The thing and place shall counsel us the rest.
When to go homewards we rise all along,
Have care to walk in middle of the throng;
There will I find thee or be found by thee,
There touch whatever thou canst touch of me.
Aye me, I warn what profits some few hours,
But we must part when heav'n with black night lours.   60
At night thy husband clips thee; I will weep
And to the doors sight of thyself keep.
Then will he kiss thee, and not only kiss,
But force thee give him my stol'n honey bliss.
Constrained against thy will, give it the peasant;
Forbear sweet words, and be your sport unpleasant.
To him I pray it no delight may bring,

Or if it do, to thee no joy thence spring;
But though this night thy fortune be to try it,
To me tomorrow constantly deny it.   70

&» I.v «§

In summer's heat, and mid-time of the day,
To rest my limbs upon a bed I lay;
One window shut, the other open stood,
Which gave such light, as twinkles in a wood,
Like twilight glimpse at setting of the sun,
Or night being past, and yet not day begun.
Such light to shamefast maidens must be shown,
Where they may sport, and seem to be unknown.
Then came Corinna in a long loose gown,
Her white neck hid with tresses hanging down,   10
Resembling fair Semiramis going to bed,
Or Lais of a thousand lovers sped.
I snatched her gown; being thin, the harm was small;
Yet strived she to be covered therewithal;
And striving thus as one that would be cast,
Betrayed herself, and yielded at the last.
Stark naked as she stood before mine eye,
Not one wen in her body could I spy.
What arms and shoulders did I touch and see,
How apt her breasts were to be pressed by me.   20
How smooth a belly under her waist saw I,
How large a leg, and what a lusty thigh.
To leave the rest, all liked me passing well;
I clinged her naked body, down she fell;
Judge you the rest: being tired she bade me kiss.
Jove send me more such afternoons as this.

&» I.xv «§

Envy, why carpest thou my time is spent so ill,
And term'st my works fruits of an idle quill?
Or that unlike the line from whence I come,
War's dusty honours are refus'd, being young?
Nor that I study not the brawling laws,
Nor set my voice to sale in every cause?
Thy scope is mortal; mine, eternal fame,
That all the world may ever chant my name.

Homer shall live while Tenedos stands and Ide,
Or into sea swift Simois doth slide.   10
Ascræus lives while grapes with new wine swell,
Or men with crooked sickles corn down fell.
The world shall of Callimachus ever speak,
His art excelled, although his wit was weak.
For ever lasts high Sophocles' proud vein;
With sun and moon Aratus shall remain.
While bondmen cheat, fathers hoard, bawds whorish,
And strumpets flatter, shall Menander flourish.
Rude Ennius, and Plautus full of wit,
Are both in Fame's eternal legend writ.   20
What age of Varro's name shall not be told,
And Jason's Argos, and the fleece of gold?
Lofty Lucretius shall live that hour
That nature shall dissolve this earthly bower.
Æneas' war, and Tityrus shall be read,
While Rome of all the conquered world is head.
Till Cupid's bow and fiery shafts be broken,
Thy verses, sweet Tibullus, shall be spoken:
And Gallus shall be known from East to West,
So shall Lycoris whom he loved best.   30
Therefore when flint and iron wear away,
Verse is immortal and shall ne'er decay.
Let kings give place to verse and kingly shows,
And banks o'er which gold-bearing Tagus flows.
Let base-conceited wits admire vile things,
Fair Phœbus lead me to the Muses' springs.
About my head be quivering myrtle wound,
And in sad lovers' heads let me be found.
The living, not the dead, can envy bite,
For after death all men receive their right: 40
Then though death rakes my bones in funeral fire,
I'll live, and as he pulls me down, mount higher.

ϟ III.i ϟ

An old wood stands uncut, of long years' space,
'Tis credible some godhead haunts the place.
In midst thereof a stone-pav'd sacred spring,
Where round about small birds most sweetly sing.
Here while I walk, hid close in shady grove,
To find what work my muse might move, I strove.

Elegia came with hairs perfumèd sweet,
And one, I think, was longer, of her feet.
A decent form, thin robe, a lover's look,
By her foot's blemish greater grace she took.   10
Then with huge steps came violent Tragedy:
Stern was her front, her cloak on ground did lie.
Her left hand held abroad a regal sceptre,
The Lydian buskin in fit paces kept her.
And first she said, "When will thy love be spent,
O poet careless of thy argument?
Wine-bibbing banquets tell thy naughtiness,
Each cross-way's corner doth as much express.
Oft some points at the prophet passing by,
And, 'This is he whom fierce love burns,' they cry.   20
A laughing-stock thou art to all the city,
While without shame thou sing'st thy lewdness' ditty.
'Tis time to move grave things in lofty style,
Long hast thou loitered; greater works compile.
The subject hides thy wit; men's acts resound;
This thou wilt say to be a worthy ground.
Thy muse hath played what may mild girls content,
And by those numbers is thy first youth spent.
Now give the Roman Tragedy a name,
To fill my laws thy wanton spirit frame."   30
This said, she moved her buskins gaily varnished,
And seven times shook her head with thick locks garnished.
The other smiled (I wot) with wanton eyes;
Err I? or myrtle in her right hand lies.
"With lofty words, stout Tragedy," she said,
"Why tread'st me down? art thou aye gravely played?
Thou deign'st unequal lines should thee rehearse;
Thou fight'st against me using mine own verse.
Thy lofty style with mine I not compare,
Small doors unfitting for large houses are.   40
Light am I, and with me, my care, light Love,
Not stronger am I than the thing I move.
Venus without me should be rustical;
This goddess' company doth to me befall.
What gate thy stately words cannot unlock,
My flatt'ring speeches soon wide open knock.
And I deserve more than thou canst in verity,
By suff'ring much not borne by thy severity.
By me Corinna learns, cozening her guard,

To get the door with little noise unbarred;   50
And slipped from bed, clothed in a loose nightgown,
To move her feet unheard in setting down.
Ah, how oft on hard doors hung I engraved,
From no man's reading fearing to be saved.
But till the keeper went forth, I forget not,
The maid to hide me in her bosom let not.
What gift with me was on her birthday sent,
But cruelly by her was drowned and rent.
First of thy mind the happy seeds I knew,
Thou hast my gift, which she would from thee sue."   60
She left; I said, "You both I must beseech,
To empty air may go my fearful speech.
With sceptres and high buskins th' one would dress me,
So through the world should bright renown express me.
The other gives my love a conquering name;
Come therefore, and to long verse shorter frame.
Grant, Tragedy, thy poet time's least tittle,
Thy labour ever lasts, she asks but little."
She gave me leave, soft loves in time make haste,
Some greater work will urge me on at last.   70

&&ampp; III.vi &ampp;

Either she was foul, or her attire was bad,
Or she was not the wench I wished t' have had.
Idly I lay with her, as if I loved not,
And like a burden grieved the bed that moved not.
Though both of us performed our true intent,
Yet could I not cast anchor where I meant.
She on my neck her ivory arms did throw,
Her arms far whiter than the Scythian snow,
And eagerly she kissed me with her tongue,
And under mine her wanton thigh she flung.   10
Yea, and she soothed me up, and called me "Sir,"
And used all speech that might provoke and stir.
Yet like as if cold hemlock I had drunk,
It mockèd me, hung down the head, and sunk.
Like a dull cipher or rude block I lay,
Or shade or body was I, who can say?
What will my age do, age I cannot shun,
Seeing my prime my force is spent and done?
I blush, that being youthful, hot, and lusty,

I prove neither youth nor man, but old and rusty.   20
Pure rose she, like a nun to sacrifice,
Or one that with her tender brother lies.
Yet boarded I the golden Chie twice,
And Libas, and the white cheeked Pitho thrice.
Corinna craved it in a summer's night,
And nine sweet bouts had we before daylight.
What, waste my limbs through some Thessalian charms?
May spells and drugs do silly souls such harms?
With virgin wax hath some imbased my joints,
And pierced my liver with sharp needles' points?   30
Charms change corn to grass and make it die;
By charms are running springs and fountains dry.
By charms mast drops from oaks, from vines grapes fall,
And fruit from trees when there's no wind at all.
Why might not then my sinews be enchanted,
And I grow faint as with some spirit haunted?
To this add shame: shame to perform it quailed me,
And was the second cause why vigour failed me.
My idle thoughts delighted her no more
Than did the robe or garment which she wore.   40
Yet might her touch make youthful Pylius fire,
And Tithon livelier than his years require.
Even her I had, and she had me in vain,
What might I crave more, if I ask again?
I think the great gods grieved they had bestowed
This benefit which lewdly I forslowed.
I wished to be received in, in I get me;
To kiss, I kiss; to lie with her she let me.
Why was I blest? why made king to refuse it?
Chuff-like had I not gold and could not use it?   50
So in a spring thrives he that told so much,
And looks upon the fruits he cannot touch.
Hath any rose so from a fresh young maid,
As she might straight have gone to church and prayed?
Well, I believe she kissed not as she should,
Nor used the sleight and cunning which she could.
Huge oaks, hard adamants might she have moved,
And with sweet words cause deaf rocks to have loved.
Worthy she was to move both gods and men,   60
But neither was I man nor livèd then.
Can deaf ear take delight when Phaemius sings,
Or Thamyris in curious painted things?

What sweet thought is there but I had the same?
And one gave place still as another came.
Yet notwithstanding, like one dead it lay,
Drooping more than a rose pulled yesterday.
Now, when he should not jet, he bolts upright,
And craves his task, and seeks to be at fight.
Lie down with shame, and see thou stir no more,
Seeing thou wouldst deceive me as before.   70
Thou cozenest me: by thee surprised am I,
And bide sore loss with endless infamy.
Nay more, the wench did not disdain a whit
To take it in her hand and play with it,
But when she saw it would by no means stand,
But still drooped down, regarding not her hand,
"Why mock'st thou me," she cried, "or being ill,
Who bade thee lie down here against thy will?
Either th' art witch'd with blood of frogs new dead,
Or jaded cam'st thou from some other's bed."   80
With that, her loose gown on, from me she cast her;
In skipping out her naked feet much graced her.
And lest her maid should know of this disgrace,
To cover it, spilt water on the place.

William Shakespeare

(1564–1616)

Shakespeare was born in Stratford-upon-Avon, where he attended grammar school. By the late 1580s he had moved to London, where he quickly established himself as a leading playwright. His reputation as a lyric poet was confirmed with the publication of two long Ovidian narratives, *Venus and Adonis* (1593) and *The Rape of Lucrece* (1594), and he continued to write poetry throughout his productive career as a dramatist. His *The Phoenix and Turtle* appeared in Robert Chester's *Love's Martyr* (1601), a collection of verse on this allegorical subject "by the best and chiefest of our modern writers," including Ben Jonson, George Chapman, and John Marston. In his own day, contemporaries praised Shakespeare's "sugared sonnets," which had first circulated "among his private friends" before they reached a wider public when Thomas Thorpe published them, probably without Shakespeare's authorization, in 1609.

From SONNETS

॰ 18 ॰

Shall I compare thee to a summer's day?
   Thou art more lovely and more temperate:
Rough winds do shake the darling buds of May,
   And summer's lease hath all too short a date:
Sometime too hot the eye of heaven shines,
   And often is his gold complexion dimmed;
And every fair from fair sometime declines,
   By chance, or nature's changing course untrimmed;
But thy eternal summer shall not fade,
   Nor lose possession of that fair thou owest,
Nor shall death brag thou wand'rest in his shade,
   When in eternal lines to time thou growest;
     So long as men can breathe or eyes can see,
     So long lives this, and this gives life to thee.

ɣ 23 ᴈ

As an unperfect actor on the stage,
    Who with his fear is put besides his part,
Or some fierce thing replete with too much rage,
    Whose strength's abundance weakens his own heart;
So I, for fear of trust, forget to say,
    The perfect ceremony of love's rite,
And in mine own love's strength seem to decay,
    O'ercharged with burden of mine own love's might.
O, let my books be then the eloquence,
    And dumb presagers of my speaking breast,
Who plead for love, and look for recompense
        More than that tongue that more hath more express'd.
        O, learn to read what silent love hath writ;
        To hear with eyes belongs to love's fine wit.

ɣ 30 ᴈ

When to the sessions of sweet silent thought,
    I summon up remembrance of things past,
I sigh the lack of many a thing I sought,
    And with old woes new wail my dear time's waste:
Then can I drown an eye, unused to flow,
    For precious friends hid in death's dateless night,
And weep afresh love's long since cancelled woe,
    And moan the expense of many a vanish'd sight,
Then can I grieve at grievances foregone,
    And heavily from woe to woe tell o'er
The sad account of fore-bemoaned moan,
    Which I new pay as if not paid before.
        But if the while I think on thee, dear friend,
        All losses are restored, and sorrows end.

ɣ 55 ᴈ

Not marble, nor the gilded monuments
    Of princes, shall outlive this pow'rful rhyme;
But you shall shine more bright in these contents
    Than unswept stone, besmeared with sluttish time.
When wasteful war shall statues overturn,
    And broils root out the work of masonry,

Nor Mars his sword nor war's quick fire shall burn
   The living record of your memory.
'Gainst death and all oblivious enmity
   Shall you pace forth; your praise shall still find room
Ev'n in the eyes of all posterity
   That wear this world out to the ending doom.
      So, till the judgment that yourself arise,
      You live in this, and dwell in lovers' eyes.

ࣿ 60 ࣿ

Like as the waves make towards the pebbled shore,
   So do our minutes hasten to their end,
Each changing place with that which goes before,
   In sequent toil all forwards do contend.
Nativity, once in the main of light,
   Crawls to maturity, wherewith being crowned,
Crooked eclipses 'gainst his glory fight,
   And Time that gave doth now his gift confound.
Time doth transfix the flourish set on youth
   And delves the parallels in beauty's brow,
Feeds on the rarities of nature's truth,
   And nothing stands but for his scythe to mow.
      And yet to times in hope my verse shall stand,
      Praising thy worth, despite his cruel hand.

ࣿ 66 ࣿ

Tired with all these, for restful death I cry:
   As to behold desert a beggar born,
And needy nothing trimmed in jollity,
   And purest faith unhappily forsworn,
And gilded honor shamefully misplaced,
   And maiden virtue rudely strumpeted,
And right perfection wrongfully disgraced,
   And strength by limping sway disablèd,
And art made tongue-tied by authority,
   And folly, doctor-like, controlling skill,
And simple truth miscalled simplicity,
   And captive good attending captain ill.
      Tired with all these, from these would I be gone,
      Save that, to die, I leave my love alone.

❧ 73 ❧

That time of year thou mayst in me behold,
  When yellow leaves, or none, or few, do hang
Upon those boughs which shake against the cold,
  Bare ruined choirs, where late the sweet birds sang.
In me thou see'st the twilight of such day
  As after sunset fadeth in the west;
Which by and by black night doth take away,
  Death's second self, that seals up all in rest.
In me thou see'st the glowing of such fire,
  That on the ashes of his youth doth lie,
As the death-bed whereon it must expire,
  Consumed with that which it was nourished by.
    This thou perceiv'st, which makes thy love more strong,
    To love that well which thou must leave ere long.

❧ 86 ❧

Was it the proud full sail of his great verse,
  Bound for the prize of all too precious you,
That did my ripe thoughts in my brain inhearse,
  Making their tomb the womb wherein they grew?
Was it his spirit, by spirits taught to write
  Above a mortal pitch, that struck me dead?
No, neither he, nor his compeers by night
  Giving him aid, my verse astonishèd.
He, nor that affable familiar ghost
  Which nightly gulls him with intelligence,
As victors, of my silence cannot boast;
  I was not sick of any fear from thence.
    But when your countenance filled up his line,
    Then lacked I matter, that enfeebled mine.

❧ 94 ❧

They that have pow'r to hurt, and will do none,
  That do not do the thing they most do show,
Who, moving others, are themselves as stone,
  Unmovèd, cold, and to temptation slow:
They rightly do inherit heaven's graces
  And husband nature's riches from expense;
They are the lords and owners of their faces,

Others but stewards of their excellence.
The summer's flow'r is to the summer sweet,
 Though to itself it only live and die;
But if that flow'r with base infection meet,
 The basest weed outbraves his dignity:
  For sweetest things turn sourest by their deeds;
  Lilies that fester smell far worse than weeds.

❧ 116 ❧

Let me not to the marriage of true minds
 Admit impediments. Love is not love
Which alters when it alteration finds,
 Or bends with the remover to remove.
O, no, it is an ever-fixed mark,
 That looks on tempests and is never shaken;
It is the star to every wand'ring bark,
 Whose worth's unknown, although his height be taken.
Love's not Time's fool, though rosy lips and cheeks
 Within his bending sickle's compass come;
Love alters not with his brief hours and weeks,
 But bears it out even to the edge of doom.
  If this be error and upon me proved,
  I never writ, nor no man ever loved.

❧ 129 ❧

Th'expense of spirit in a waste of shame
 Is lust in action, and till action, lust
Is perjured, murd'rous, bloody, full of blame,
 Savage, extreme, rude, cruel, not to trust,
Enjoyed no sooner but despisèd straight,
 Past reason hunted, and no sooner had,
Past reason hated, as a swallowed bait
 On purpose laid to make the taker mad;
Mad in pursuit, and in possession so,
 Had, having, and in quest to have, extreme,
A bliss in proof, and proved, a very woe;
 Before, a joy proposed; behind, a dream.
  All this the world well knows, yet none knows well,
  To shun the heav'n that leads men to this hell.

୬ 130 ୬

My mistress' eyes are nothing like the sun;
   Coral is far more red than her lips' red;
If snow be white, why then her breasts are dun;
   If hairs be wires, black wires grow on her head.
I have seen roses damask'd, red and white,
   But no such roses see I in her cheeks,
And in some perfumes is there more delight
   Than in the breath that from my mistress reeks.
I love to hear her speak, yet well I know
   That music hath a far more pleasing sound.
I grant I never saw a goddess go;
   My mistress when she walks treads on the ground.
    And yet, by heav'n, I think my love as rare
    As any she belied with false compare.

୬ 138 ୬

When my love swears that she is made of truth,
   I do believe her, though I know she lies,
That she might think me some untutored youth,
   Unlearnèd in the world's false subtleties.
Thus vainly thinking that she thinks me young,
   Although she knows my days are past the best,
Simply I credit her false-speaking tongue;
   On both sides thus is simple truth suppressed.
But wherefore says she not she is unjust?
   And wherefore say not I that I am old?
O love's best habit is in seeming trust,
   And age in love loves not to have years told.
    Therefore I lie with her, and she with me,
    And in our faults by lies we flattered be.

THE PHOENIX AND TURTLE

Let the bird of loudest lay,
   On the sole Arabian tree,
   Herald sad and trumpet be,
To whose sound chaste wings obey.

But thou shrieking harbinger,
　　Foul precurrer of the fiend,
　　Augur of the fever's end,
To this troop come thou not near.

From this session interdict
　　Every fowl of tyrant wing,
　　Save the eagle, feather'd king;
Keep the obsequy so strict.

Let the priest in surplice white
　　That defunctive music can,
　　Be the death-divining swan,
Lest the requiem lack his right.

And thou treble-dated crow,
　　That thy sable gender mak'st
　　With the breath thou giv'st and tak'st,
'Mongst our mourners shalt thou go.

Here the anthem doth commence:
　　Love and constancy is dead;
　　Phoenix and the turtle fled
In a mutual flame from hence.

So they loved, as love in twain
　　Had the essence but in one;
　　Two distincts, division none;
Number there in love was slain.

Hearts remote, yet not asunder;
　　Distance, and no space was seen
　　Twixt this turtle and his queen;
But in them it were a wonder.

So between them love did shine,
　　That the turtle saw his right,
　　Flaming in the phoenix' sight;
Either was the other's mine.

Property was thus appalled,
　　That the self was not the same;

10

20

30

Single nature's double name
Neither two nor one was called.   40

Reason, in itself confounded,
   Saw division grow together,
   To themselves yet either neither,
Simple were so well compounded,

That it cried, "How true a twain
   Seemeth this concordant one;
   Love hath reason, reason none,
If what parts can so remain."

Whereupon it made this threne,
   To the phoenix and the dove,   50
   Co-supremes and stars of love,
As chorus to their tragic scene.

THRENOS

Beauty, truth, and rarity,
Grace in all simplicity,
Here enclosed, in cinders lie.

Death is now the phoenix' nest;
And the turtle's loyal breast,
To eternity doth rest.

Leaving no posterity,
'Twas not their infirmity,   60
It was married chastity.

Truth may seem, but cannot be;
Beauty brag, but 'tis not she;
Truth and beauty buried be.

To this urn let those repair,
That are either true or fair,
For these dead birds, sigh a prayer.

l.   6. precurrer = forerunner
l. 49. threne = threnos, funeral song

Thomas Campion

(1 5 6 7 – 1 6 2 0)

Campion's most famous work, *Observations in the Art of English Poesie* (1602)—in which the famous lyric "Rose-cheek'd Laura, come" first appeared— offers a passionate although ultimately futile defence of classical meters in English against the increasingly popular "vulgar and unartificial custom of rhyming." Campion, who was educated at Cambridge and Gray's Inn, subsequently trained as a physician and received a medical degree from the University of Caen in 1605. He was also a talented musician, and his best-remembered poems are his songs, many of which he set to his own music. Five of the songs appeared in 1591 appended to an unauthorized edition of Sidney's *Astrophel and Stella*, and in the early years of the seventeenth century, four *Bookes of Ayres* as well as his *Songs of Mourning* in memory of Prince Henry were published. Campion also created elaborate masques for the court of King James I.

WHEN THOU MUST HOME TO SHADES OF UNDERGROUND

When thou must home to shades of underground,
And there arrived, a new admired guest,
The beauteous spirits do ingirt thee round,
White Iope, blithe Helen, and the rest,
To hear the stories of thy finish'd love,
From that smooth tongue whose music hell can move.

Then wilt thou speak of banqueting delights,
Of masks and revels which sweet youth did make,
Of tourneys and great challenges of knights,
And all these triumphs for thy beauty's sake;   10
When thou has told these honours done to thee,
Then tell, O tell, how thou did'st murther me.

ROSE-CHEEK'D LAURA, COME

Rose-cheek'd Laura, come,
Sing thou smoothly with thy beauties
Silent music, either other
    Sweetly gracing.

Lovely forms do flow
From concent divinely framed;
Heav'n is music, and thy beauty's
    Birth is heavenly.

These dull notes we sing
Discords need for helps to grace them;   10
Only beauty purely loving
    Knows no discord:

But still moves delight,
Like clear springs renew'd by flowing,
Ever perfect, ever in them-
    Selves eternal.

Eochaidh Ó Heóghusa

(c . 1 5 6 8 – c . 1 6 1 2)

Eochaidh Ó Heóghusa (also spelled O hEodhasa) was an important Irish bardic poet of the late sixteenth century. From 1586 to 1602 he served as official poet to the Maguires of Fermanagh. His main patron was Hugh Maguire, the subject of "A Winter Campaign" as well as a number of Ó Heóghusa's other poems. At the same time that Shakespeare was writing in *Henry V* (1599) of his desire to see the Earl of Essex, Elizabeth's commander, "from Ireland coming / Bringing rebellion broached on his sword," Ó Heóghusa's verse celebrated the Irish struggle against these English forces. "A Winter Campaign" recounts the extraordinary hardships experienced by Maguire and the Irish fighting in Munster in 1600 and touches on the fear that his patron might not return from battle. Maguire, described by Sir John Davies as "a valiant rebel and the stoutest that ever was of his name," was killed in this campaign. About fifty of Ó Heóghusa's poems have survived and have influenced such later Irish poets as James Clarence Mangan (1803–1849), whose translation (albeit inexact) appears as "O'Hussey's Ode to the Maguire" (see p. 580).

A WINTER CAMPAIGN

Fúar liom an adhaighsi dh'Aodh,
cúis tuirse truime a ciothbhraon;
mo thrúaighe sein dár seise,
neimh fhúaire na hoidhcheise.

Anocht, is neimh rem chridhe,
fearthar frasa teintidhe
a gcomhdháil na gclá seacdha
mar tá is orghráin aigeanta.

Do hosgladh ós ochtaibh néll
doirse uisgidhe an aiér: 10
tug sé minlinnte 'na muir,
do sgé an fhirminnte a hurbhuidh.

Gémadh fiaidhmhíol a bhfiodhbhaidh,
gémadh éigne ar inbhiormhuir,
gémadh ealta, is doiligh dhi
soighidh ar eachtra an úairsi.

Sáoth leamsa Aodh Mhág Uidhir
anocht a gcrích chomhoidhigh,
fá ghrís ndeirg gcáorshoighnén gceath
fá fheirg bhfáobhoirnél bhfuileach.   20

A gcóigeadh Chloinne Dáire
duisan linn dár leannáinne
idir dhorchladh bhfúairfhliuch bhfeóir
is confadh úaibhreach aieóir.

Fúar liom dá leacain shubhaigh
fráoch na n-iodhlann n-earrchamhail,
ag séideadh síongháoth na reann
fá ríoghláoch ngéigeal nGaileang.

Sáoth linn, do loit ar meanmain,
learg thais a thaoibh míndealbhaigh   30
'gá meilt a ngrúamoidhche ghairbh,
a mbeirt fhúarfhoirfe íairn.

Bos tláith na dtachar n-édtláth,
síon oighridh dá fhúaighealtáth
re crann rionnfhúar gcáol gceise
ionnfhúar dh'Aodh san oidhcheise.

Nárab aithreach leis ná leam
a thurus timcheall Éireann;
go ndeach tharainn—ná ti m'olc—
an ní fá ngabhaim gúasacht.   40

Dá dtí ris an toisg do thríall,
do chur chúarta Chráoi Mhaicniadh—
ní tháirtheamar séd mar soin—
créd acht snáithghearradh sáoghail?

Líonaid re hucht na n-ánrath
brúaigh ísle na n-úaránshroth;

clúana sgor fá sgingbheirt reóidh
dá gcor tar ingheilt d'aimhdheóin.

Folchar a gciomhsa cheana,
nach léir do lucht foirgneamha   50
brúaigh easgadh na ngríanshroth nglan,
seasgadh fíanbhoth ní fédtar.

Eagail dó, díochra an anbhúain,
coill eachraidh is aradhshlúaigh,
sul dighthir tar síothLáoi síar,
a slighthibh míonchráoi Mhaicniadh.

Ní hé budh uireasbhaidh linn,
a thurus an tráth smúainim;
lór do chor chúarta ar gcridhe
gomh fhúachta na haimsire.   60

Gidh eadh, is adhbhar téighthe
dhá ghnúis shúaithnidh shoiléirthe
slios gach múir ghormsháothraigh gil
'na dhlúimh thonngháothmhair theintigh.

Téighidh teannál an adhnaidh
sging reóidh an ruisg shocarghlain,
geimhle chuisne a chorrghlac ndonn,
donnbhrat luisne nos leaghonn.

Seachnóin Mhumhan na múr ngeal
iomdha ó airgtheóir fhuinn Gháoidheal   70
cúirte brúachnochta a mbeirt smóil,
ag ceilt fhúardhochta an aieóir.

Iomdha ó chuairt Aoidh Mhéig Uidhir
feadh íarthair fhóid fhionnfhuinidh
cúirt 'na doighir, ní díoth núa,
críoch gan oighir gan íarmhúa.

Aemilia Bassano Lanyer

(1569–1645)

Aemilia Bassano Lanyer (also spelled Lanier) was the daughter of an Italian court musician of Jewish descent and his common-law wife. Mistress to Lord Hunsdon, Queen Elizabeth's first cousin, she was hastily married to Alfonso Lanyer after it was discovered that she was pregnant. Some time after her husband's death she kept a school in St. Giles-in-the-Field, and she wrote in a lawsuit in 1635 of being "in great misery and having two grandchildren to provide for." Little else is known about her later life. Her only book, *Salve Deus Rex Judaeorum* ["Hail God, King of the Jews"], was published in 1611 and is remarkable in its strong advocacy of the cause of women: Lanyer dedicated the work to the Queen and prominent women at court and addressed it to "all virtuous ladies and gentlewomen of this kingdom." In addition to a number of religious and devotional poems, the collection included "The Description of Cookham," one of the earliest country house poems in English, which celebrates the manor in Berkshire where Lanyer was entertained by her aristocratic patroness, Margaret Clifford.

THE DESCRIPTION OF COOKHAM

Farewell (sweet Cookham) where I first obtain'd
Grace from that grace where perfit grace remain'd;
And where the Muses gave their full consent,
I should have power the virtuous to content:
Where princely palace will'd me to indite,
The sacred story of the soul's delight.
Farewell (sweet place) where virtue then did rest,
And all delights did harbour in her breast:
Never shall my sad eyes again behold
Those pleasures which my thoughts did then unfold: 10
Yet you (great lady) mistress of that place,
From whose desires did spring this work of grace;
Vouchsafe to think upon those pleasures past,
As fleeting worldly joys that could not last:
Or, as dim shadows of celestial pleasures,
Which are desir'd above all earthly treasures.

Oh how (me thought) against you thither came,
Each part did seem some new delight to frame!
The house receiv'd all ornaments to grace it,
And would endure no foulness to deface it. 20
The walks put on their summer liveries,
And all things else did hold like similes:
The trees with leaves, with fruits, with flowers clad,
Embrac'd each other, seeming to be glad,
Turning themselves to beauteous canopies,
To shade the bright sun from your brighter eyes:
The crystal streams with silver spangles graced,
While by the glorious Sun they were embraced:
The little birds in chirping notes did sing,
To entertain both you and that sweet spring. 30
And Philomela with her sundry lays,
Both you and that delightful place did praise.
O how me thought each plant, each flower, each tree
Set forth their beauties then to welcome thee!
The very hills right humbly did descend,
When you to tread upon them did intend.
And as you set your feet, they still did rise,
Glad that they could receive so rich a prize.
The gentle winds did take delight to be
Among those woods that were so grac'd by thee. 40
And in sad murmur utter'd pleasing sound,
That pleasure in that place might more abound.
The swelling banks deliver'd all their pride,
When such a Phoenix once they had espied.
Each arbor, bank, each seat, each stately tree,
Thought themselves honor'd in supporting thee.
The pretty birds would oft come to attend thee,
Yet fly away for fear they should offend thee:
The little creatures in the burrow by
Would come abroad to sport them in your eye; 50
Yet fearful of the bow in your fair hand,
Would run away when you did make a stand.
Now let me come unto that stately tree,
Wherein such goodly prospects you did see;
That oak that did in height his fellows pass,
As much as lofty trees, low growing grass;
Much like a comely cedar, straight and tall,
Whose beauteous stature far exceeded all.
How often did you visit this fair tree,

Which seeming joyful in receiving thee,   60
Would like a palm tree spread his arms abroad,
Desirous that you there should make abode:
Whose fair green leaves much like a comely veil,
Defended Phœbus when he would assail:
Whose pleasing boughs did yield a cool fresh air,
Joying his happiness when you were there.
Where being seated, you might plainly see,
Hills, vales, and woods, as if on bended knee
They had appear'd, your honour to salute,
Or to prefer some strange unlook'd for suit.   70
All interlac'd with brooks and crystal springs,
A prospect fit to please the eyes of kings.
And thirteen shires appear'd all in your sight,
Europe could not afford much more delight.
What was there then but gave you all content,
While you the time in meditation spent,
Of their Creator's power, which there you saw,
In all his creatures held a perfit law;
And in their beauties did you plain descry,
His beauty, wisdom, grace, love, majesty.   80
In these sweet woods how often did you walk,
With Christ and his Apostles there to talk;
Placing his holy Writ in some fair tree,
To meditate what you therein did see:
With Moses you did mount his holy hill,
To know his pleasure, and perform his will.
With lovely David you did often sing,
His holy hymns to Heaven's Eternal King.
And in sweet music did your soul delight,
To sound his praises, morning, noon, and night.   90
With blessed Joseph you did often feed
Your pined brethren, when they stood in need.
And that sweet lady sprung from Clifford's race,
Of noble Bedford's blood, fair steam of grace;
To honourable Dorset now espous'd,
In whose fair breast true virtue then was hous'd:
Oh what delight did my weak spirits find
In those pure parts of her well-framed mind.
And yet it grieves me that I cannot be
Near unto her, whose virtues did agree   100
With those fair ornaments of outward beauty,
Which did enforce from all both love and duty.

Unconstant Fortune, thou art most to blame,
Who casts us down into so low a frame:
Where our great friends we cannot daily see,
So great a diff'rence is there in degree.
Many are placed in those orbs of state,
Parters in honour, so ordain'd by Fate;
Nearer in show, yet farther off in love,
In which, the lowest always are above.   110
But whither am I carried in conceit?
My wit too weak to conster of the great.
Why not? Although we are but born of earth,
We may behold the heavens, despising death;
And loving Heaven that is so far above,
May in the end vouchsafe us entire love.
Therefore sweet memory do thou retain
Those pleasures past, which will not turn again;
Remember beauteous Dorset's former sports,
So far from being touch'd by ill reports;   120
Wherein my self did always bear a part,
While reverend Love presented my true heart:
Those recreations let me bear in mind,
Which her sweet youth and noble thoughts did find:
Whereof depriv'd, I evermore must grieve,
Hating blind Fortune, careless to relieve.
And you sweet Cookham, whom these ladies leave,
I now must tell the grief you did conceive
At their departure. When they went away,
How every thing retain'd a sad dismay: 130
Nay long before, when once an inkling came,
Methought each thing did unto sorrow frame:
The trees that were so glorious in our view,
Forsook both flowers and fruit, when once they knew
Of your depart, their very leaves did wither,
Changing their colours as they grew together.
But when they saw this had no power to stay you,
They often wept, though speechless, could not pray you;
Letting their tears in your fair bosoms fall,
As if they said, "Why will ye leave us all?"   140
This being vain, they cast their leaves away,
Hoping that pity would have made you stay:
Their frozen tops, like Age's hoary hairs,
Show their disasters, languishing in fears:
A swarthy rivel'd rine all over spread,

Their dying bodies half alive, half dead.
But your occasions call'd you so away,
That nothing there had power to make you stay.
Yet did I see a noble grateful mind,
Requiting each according to their kind;   150
Forgetting not to turn and take your leave
Of these sad creatures, powerless to receive
Your favour, when with grief you did depart,
Placing their former pleasures in your heart;
Giving great charge to noble Memory,
There to preserve their love continually:
But specially the love of that fair tree,
That first and last you did vouchsafe to see:
In which it pleas'd you oft to take the air,
With noble Dorset, then a virgin fair: 160
Where many a learned book was read and scann'd
To this fair tree, taking me by the hand,
You did repeat the pleasures which had past,
Seeming to grieve they could no longer last.
And with a chaste yet loving kiss took leave,
Of which sweet kiss I did it soon bereave:
Scorning a senseless creature should possess
So rare a favour, so great happiness.
No other kiss it could receive from me,
For fear to give back what it took of thee: 170
So I ingrateful creature did deceive it,
Of that which you vouchsaf'd in love to leave it.
And though it oft had giv'n me much content,
Yet this great wrong I never could repent:
But of the happiest made it most forlorn,
To show that nothing's free from Fortune's scorn,
While all the rest with this most beauteous tree,
Made their sad consort sorrow's harmony.
The flowers that on the banks and walks did grow,
Crept in the ground, the grass did weep for woe.   180
The winds and waters seem'd to chide together,
Because you went away they knew not wither:
And those sweet brooks that ran so fair and clear,
With grief and trouble wrinkl'd did appear.
Those pretty birds that wonted were to sing,
Now neither sing, or chirp, nor use their wing;
But with their tender feet on some bare spray,
Warble forth sorrow, and their own dismay.

Fair Philomela leaves her mournful ditty,
Drown'd in dead sleep, yet can procure no pity: 190
Each arbour, bank, each seat, each stately tree,
Looks bare and desolate now for want of thee;
Turning green tresses into frosty gray,
While in cold grief they wither all away.
The sun grew weak, his beams no comfort gave,
While all green things did make the earth their grave:
Each brier, each bramble, when you went away,
Caught fast your clothes, thinking to make you stay.
Delightful echo wonted to reply
To our last words, did now for sorrow die: 200
The house cast off each garment that might grace it,
Putting on dust and cobwebs to deface it.
All desolation then there did appear,
When you were going whom they held so dear.
This last farewell to Cookham here I give,
When I am dead thy name in this may live,
Wherein I have perform'd her noble hest,
Whose virtues lodge in my unworthy breast,
And ever shall, so long as life remains,
Tying my heart to her by those rich chains.   210

Ben Jonson

(1 5 7 2 – 1 6 3 7)

Educated for a time at the Westminster School under the tutelage of the famous William Camden, Jonson was taken from his studies to serve in his stepfather's trade as an apprentice bricklayer. He then spent time as a soldier in the Low Countries. Upon his return to England Jonson resumed his studies, and by his early twenties he was involved in the theater, first as an itinerant actor, then as a collaborative playwright. By the time of the accession of King James I, Jonson had emerged as one of the great playwrights of the English stage. But he was also a celebrated and influential poet, with an impressive command of classical forms and contemporary verse styles. Jonson's self-proclaimed role as public poet informs much of his verse, including epigrams, elegies, and the occasional verse directed to aristocratic patrons. Jonson published his poetry along with his plays and court masques in 1616 in an expensive folio; a second folio collection appeared in 1640. In his later years he influenced a generation of younger poets, collectively known as the "Sons of Ben." The topographical poem "To Penshurst" describes the home of the Sidney family in Kent, the birthplace of Sir Philip Sidney.

TO PENSHURST

Thou art not, Penshurst, built to envious show
    Of touch or marble; nor canst boast a row
Of polished pillars, or a roof of gold.
    Thou hast no lantern, whereof tales are told,
Or stair, or courts; but stand'st an ancient pile,
    And these grudged at, art reverenc'd the while.
Thou joy'st in better marks, of soil, of air,
    Of wood, of water; therein thou art fair.
Thou hast thy walks for health as well as sport:
    Thy Mount, to which the dryads do resort,   10
Where Pan and Bacchus their high feasts have made,
    Beneath the broad beech and the chestnut shade;
That taller tree, which of a nut was set
    At his great birth, where all the Muses met.
There, in the writhed bark, are cut the names

Of many a sylvan taken with his flames;
And thence the ruddy satyrs oft provoke
    The lighter fauns to reach thy lady's oak.
Thy copse, too, named of Gamage, thou hast there,
    That never fails to serve thee season'd deer,   20
When thou wouldst feast or exercise thy friends.
    The lower land, that to the river bends,
Thy sheep, thy bullocks, kine and calves do feed;
    The middle grounds thy mares and horses breed.
Each bank doth yield thee conies, and the tops,
    Fertile of wood, Ashour and Sidney's copse,
To crown thy open table, doth provide
    The purpled pheasant with the speckled side;
The painted partridge lies in every field,
    And for thy mess is willing to be killed.   30
And if the high-swoll'n Medway fail thy dish,
    Thou hast thy ponds that pay thee tribute fish:
Fat, aged carps, that run into thy net;
    And pikes, now weary their own kind to eat,
As loath, the second draught or cast to stay,
    Officiously, at first, themselves betray.
Bright eels, that emulate them, and leap on land
    Before the fisher, or into his hand.
Then hath thy orchard fruit, thy garden flowers,
    Fresh as the air and new as are the hours.   40
The early cherry, with the later plum,
    Fig, grape and quince, each in his time doth come:
The blushing apricot and woolly peach
    Hang on thy walls, that every child may reach.
And though thy walls be of the country stone,
    They're reared with no man's ruin, no man's groan;
There's none that dwell about them wish them down,
    But all come in, the farmer and the clown,
And no one empty-handed, to salute
    Thy lord and lady, though they have no suit.   50
Some bring a capon, some a rural cake,
    Some nuts, some apples; some that think they make
The better cheeses, bring 'em; or else send
    By their ripe daughters, whom they would commend
This way to husbands; and whose baskets bear
    An emblem of themselves, in plum or pear.
But what can this (more than express their love)

Add to thy free provisions, far above
The need of such? whose liberal board doth flow
    With all, that hospitality doth know!   60
Where comes no guest but is allow'd to eat
    Without his fear, and of thy lord's own meat;
Where the same beer and bread and self-same wine,
    That is his lordship's, shall be also mine;
And I not fain to sit, as some this day
    At great men's tables, and yet dine away.
Here no man tells my cups; nor, standing by,
    A waiter, doth my gluttony envy:
But gives me what I call, and lets me eat;
    He knows below he shall find plenty of meat,   70
Thy tables hoard not up for the next day.
    Nor, when I take my lodging, need I pray
For fire or lights or livery: all is there,
    As if thou then wert mine, or I reign'd here;
There's nothing I can wish, for which I stay.
    That found King James, when, hunting late this way
With his brave son, the Prince, they saw thy fires
    Shine bright on every hearth as the desires
Of thy Penates had been set on flame,
    To entertain them; or the country came   80
With all their zeal, to warm their welcome here.
    What (great, I will not say, but) sudden cheer
Didst thou then make 'em! and what praise was heap'd
    On thy good lady then! who therein reap'd
The just reward of her high housewifery:
    To have her linen, plate, and all things nigh,
When she was far; and not a room, but dress'd,
    As if it had expected such a guest!
These, Penshurst, are thy praise, and yet not all.
    Thy lady's noble, fruitful, chaste withal;   90
His children thy great lord may call his own;
    A fortune in this age but rarely known.
They are and have been taught religion: thence
    Their gentler spirits have sucked innocence.
Each morn and even they are taught to pray,
    With the whole household, and may, every day,
Read in their virtuous parents' noble parts
    The mysteries of manners, arms and arts.
Now, Penshurst, they that will proportion thee

With other edifices, when they see   100
Those proud, ambitious heaps, and nothing else;
  May say, their lords have built, but thy lord dwells.

l. 2. touch = black marble
l. 4. lantern = glassed-in room

TO THE IMMORTAL MEMORY AND FRIENDSHIP OF THAT NOBLE PAIR, SIR LUCIUS CARY AND SIR HENRY MORISON

THE TURN

Brave infant of Saguntum, clear
Thy coming forth in that great year
When the prodigious Hannibal did crown
His rage with razing your immortal town.
Thou, looking then about,
Ere thou wert half got out,
Wise child, didst hastily return,
And mad'st thy mother's womb thine urn.
How summed a circle didst thou leave mankind
Of deepest lore, could we the center find!   10

THE COUNTER-TURN

Did wiser nature draw thee back
From out the horror of that sack?
Where shame, faith, honour, and regard of right
Lay trampled on; the deeds of death and night,
Urged, hurried forth, and hurled
Upon the affrighted world:
Sword, fire, and famine with fell fury met;
And all on utmost ruin set;
As, could they but life's miseries foresee,
No doubt all infants would return like thee.   20

THE STAND

For what is life, if measured by the space,
  Not by the act?
Or masked man, if valued by his face,
  Above his fact?
    Here's one outlived his peers
    And told forth four-score years;
He vexed time, and busied the whole state;
    Troubled both foes and friends;
    But ever to no ends;
What did this stirrer, but die late?   30
How well at twenty had he fallen or stood!
For three of his four-score he did no good.

THE TURN

He entered well by virtuous parts,
Got up and thrived with honest arts;
He purchas'd friends and fame and honours then,
And had his noble name advanced with men.
    But weary of that flight,
    He stooped in all men's sight
To sordid flatteries, acts of strife,
And sunk in that dead sea of life   40
So deep, as he did then death's waters sup,
But that the cork of title buoy'd him up.

THE COUNTER-TURN

Alas, but Morison fell young.
He never fell, thou fall'st, my tongue.
He stood, a soldier to the last right end,
A perfect patriot, and a noble friend,
    But most, a virtuous son.
    All offices were done
By him, so ample, full, and round,
In weight, in measure, number, sound,   50
As, though his age imperfect might appear,
His life was of humanity the sphere.

The Stand

Go now, and tell out days summ'd up with fears;
  And make them years;
Produce thy mass of miseries on the stage,
  To swell thine age;
Repeat of things a throng,
To show thou hast been long,
Not lived; for life does her great actions spell,
  By what was done and wrought   60
  In season, and so brought
To light: her measures are, how well
Each syllab'e answer'd, and was form'd, how fair;
These make the lines of life, and that's her air.

The Turn

It is not growing like a tree
In bulk, doth make man better be;
Or standing long an oak, three hundred year,
To fall a log at last, dry, bald, and sere:
A lily of a day
Is fairer far, in May,   70
Although it fall and die that night;
It was the plant and flower of light.
In small proportions we just beauty see:
And in short measures life may perfect be.

The Counte-Tun

Call, noble Lucius, then for wine,
And let thy looks with gladness shine.
Accept this garland, plant it on thy head;
And think, nay know, thy Morison's not dead.
He leap'd the present age,
Possessed with holy rage,   80
To see that bright eternal day,
Of which we priests and poets say
Such truths as we expect for happy men;
And there he lives with memory, and Ben

THE STAND

Jonson, who sung this of him, ere he went
Himself to rest,
Or taste a part of that full joy he meant
To have express'd
In this bright asterism;
Where it were friendship's schism   90
(Were not his Lucius long with us to tarry)
To separate these twi-
Lights, the Dioscuri;
And keep the one half from his Harry.
But fate doth so alternate the design,
Whilst that in heav'n, this light on earth must shine.

THE TURN

And shine as you exalted are;
Two names of friendship, but one star:
Of hearts the union. And those not by chance
Made, or indentur'd, or leas'd out t' advance   100
The profits for a time.
No pleasures vain did chime,
Of rhymes, or riots, at your feasts,
Orgies of drink, or feign'd protests:
But simple love of greatness, and of good;
That knits brave minds, and manners, more than blood.

THE COUNTER-TURN

This made you first to know the why
You lik'd; then after to apply
That liking; and approach so one the tother,
Till either grew a portion of the other: 110
Each styled, by his end,
The copy of his friend.
You liv'd to be the great surnames
And titles by which all made claims
Unto the virtue. Nothing perfect done
But as a Cary, or a Morison.

THE STAND

And such a force the fair example had,
As they that saw
The good and durst not practise it, were glad
That such a law   120
Was left yet to mankind;
Where they might read and find
Friendship in deed was written, not in words;
And with the heart, not pen,
Of two so early men
Whose lines her rolls were, and records.
Who, ere the first down bloomed on the chin,
Had sow'd these fruits, and got the harvest in.

ON MY FIRST SON

Farewell, thou child of my right hand, and joy;
   My sin was too much hope of thee, lov'd boy.
Seven years thou'wert lent to me, and I thee pay,
   Exacted by thy fate, on the just day.
O, could I lose all father now! For why
   Will man lament the state he should envy?
To have so soon 'scap'd world's and flesh's rage,
   And, if no other misery, yet age?
Rest in soft peace, and, ask'd, say here doth lie
   Ben Jonson his best piece of poetry.
For whose sake, henceforth, all his vows be such,
   As what he loves may never like too much.

AN ODE TO HIMSELF

  Where dost thou careless lie,
    Buried in ease and sloth?
  Knowledge, that sleeps, doth die;
  And this securitie,
    It is the common moth,
That eats on wits, and arts, and oft destroys them both.

Are all th'Aonian springs
    Dried up? lies Thespia waste?
Doth Clarius' harp want strings,
That not a nymph now sings?   10
    Or droop they as disgrac'd,
To see their seats and bowers by chatt'ring pies defac'd?

If hence thy silence be,
    As 'tis too just a cause;
Let this thought quicken thee:
Minds that are great and free,
    Should not on fortune pause;
'Tis crown enough to virtue still, her own applause.

What though the greedy fry
    Be taken with false baits   20
Of worded balladry,
And think it Poesie?
    They die with their conceits,
And only piteous scorn, upon their folly waits.

Then take in hand thy lyre,
    Strike in thy proper strain,
With Japhet's line, aspire
Sol's chariot for new fire,
    To give the world again:
Who aided him, will thee, the issue of Jove's brain.   30

And since our dainty age,
    Cannot endure reproof,
Make not thyself a page
To that strumpet the stage,
    But sing high and aloof,
Safe from the wolf's black jaw, and the dull ass's hoof.

John Donne

(1 5 7 2 – 1 6 3 1)

Donne was born into a devout Catholic family: his uncle was the leader of a
Jesuit mission in England, and his brother Henry died in prison in 1593 after
his arrest for harboring a Catholic priest. In the early 1590s Donne renounced
Catholicism and turned Anglican. He joined Essex in the famous sacking of
Cádiz in 1596 and Ralegh in search of treasure ships in the Azores a year later,
events commemorated in his poems. Donne's fortunes suffered a setback when
he secretly married Ann More, the niece of Lady Egerton, wife of his patron,
Sir Thomas Egerton, who dismissed Donne from his service. The early years of
the seventeenth century were difficult ones for Donne professionally, and Ann
Donne died in 1617 after the birth of their twelfth child. In 1615 he decided to
pursue a career in the Anglican church, ultimately becoming Dean of St. Paul's
in London, where he was celebrated as a brilliant preacher. He produced much
remarkable writing in forty years of literary activity: songs, sonnets, elegies,
satires, the anniversary poems, verse letters, and in his later years, divine
meditations, sermons, and devotions. His poems, which had circulated in
manuscript, were collected and published posthumously in 1633. Donne's
reputation suffered a precipitous decline in the eighteenth and nineteenth
centuries until a renewed interest in him in the early twentieth century was
given impetus by Yeats and T. S. Eliot.

THE GOOD MORROW

I wonder by my troth, what thou, and I
   Did, till we loved? were we not wean'd till then,
But suck'd on country pleasures, childishly?
   Or snorted we in the seven sleepers' den?
'Twas so; but this, all pleasures fancies be.
   If ever any beauty I did see,
Which I desired, and got, 'twas but a dream of thee.

And now good morrow to our waking souls,
   Which watch not one another out of fear;
For love, all love of other sights controls,   10
   And makes one little room, an everywhere.

Let sea-discoverers to new worlds have gone,
  Let maps to others, worlds on worlds have shown,
Let us possess one world, each hath one, and is one.

  My face in thine eye, thine in mine appears,
    And true plain hearts do in the faces rest,
  Where can we find two better hemispheres
    Without sharp north, without declining west?
  Whatever dies, was not mixed equally;
  If our two loves be one, or, thou and I   20
Love so alike, that none do slacken, none can die.

THE SUN RISING

  Busy old fool, unruly sun,
    Why dost thou thus,
Through windows, and through curtains call on us?
Must to thy motions lovers' seasons run?
    Saucy pedantic wretch, go chide
    Late schoolboys, and sour prentices,
  Go tell court-huntsmen, that the King will ride,
  Call country ants to harvest offices;
Love, all alike, no season knows, nor clime,
Nor hours, days, months, which are the rags of time.   ·   10

  Thy beams, so reverend, and strong
    Why shouldst thou think?
I could eclipse and cloud them with a wink,
But that I would not lose her sight so long:
    If her eyes have not blinded thine,
    Look, and tomorrow late, tell me,
  Whether both th'Indias of spice and mine
  Be where thou left'st them, or lie here with me.
Ask for those kings whom thou saw'st yesterday,
And thou shalt hear, all here in one bed lay.   20

  She'is all states, and all princes, I,
    Nothing else is.
Princes do but play us; compar'd to this,
All honour's mimic; all wealth alchemy;
    Thou sun art half as happy as we,

In that the world's contracted thus,
   Thine age asks ease, and since thy duties be
   To warm the world, that's done in warming us.
Shine here to us, and thou art everywhere;
This bed thy center is, these walls, thy sphere.   30

THE CANONIZATION

For God's sake hold your tongue, and let me love,
   Or chide my palsy, or my gout,
My five gray hairs, or ruined fortune flout,
     With wealth your state, your mind with arts improve,
       Take you a course, get you a place,
       Observe his honour, or his grace,
Or the King's real, or his stamped face
     Contemplate; what you will, approve,
     So you will let me love.

Alas, alas, who's injur'd by my love?   10
   What merchant's ships have my sighs drown'd?
Who says my tears have overflowed his ground?
     When did my colds a forward spring remove?
       When did the heats which my veins fill
       Add one more to the plaguy bill?
Soldiers find wars, and lawyers find out still
     Litigious men, which quarrels move,
     Though she and I do love.

Call us what you will, we are made such by love;
   Call her one, me another fly,   20
We'are tapers too, and at our own cost die,
     And we in us find the eagle and the dove;
       The phoenix riddle hath more wit
       By us; we two being one, are it.
So, to one neutral thing both sexes fit.
     We die and rise the same, and prove
     Mysterious by this love.

We can die by it, if not live by love,
   And if unfit for tombs and hearse

Our legend be, it will be fit for verse;   30
　　And if no piece of chronicle we prove,
　　　　We'll build in sonnets pretty rooms;
　　　　As well a well wrought urn becomes
The greatest ashes, as half-acre tombs,
　　And by these hymns, all shall approve
　　Us Canonized for love.

And thus invoke us; You whom reverend love
　　Made one another's hermitage;
You, to whom love was peace, that now is rage;
　　Who did the whole world's soul extract, and drove,   40
　　　　Into the glasses of your eyes,
　　　　So made such mirrors, and such spies,
That they did all to you epitomize,
　　Countries, towns, courts: beg from above
　　A pattern of your love!

A NOCTURNAL UPON ST. LUCY'S DAY, BEING THE SHORTEST DAY

'Tis the year's midnight, and it is the day's,
Lucy's, who scarce seven hours herself unmasks,
　　The sun is spent, and now his flasks
　　Send forth light squibs, no constant rays;
　　　　The world's whole sap is sunk:
The general balm th' hydroptic earth hath drunk,
Whither, as to the bed's-feet, life is shrunk,
Dead and interr'd; yet all these seem to laugh,
Compar'd with me, who am their epitaph.

Study me then, you who shall lovers be   10
At the next world, that is, at the next spring:
　　For I am every dead thing,
　　In whom love wrought new alchemy.
　　　　For his art did express
A quintessence even from nothingness,
From dull privations, and lean emptiness
He ruin'd me, and I am re-begot
Of absence, darkness, death; things which are not.

All others, from all things, draw all that's good,
Life, soul, form, spirit, whence they being have;   20
   I, by love's limbeck, am the grave
   Of all, that's nothing. Oft a flood
     Have we two wept, and so
Drown'd the whole world, us two; oft did we grow
To be two chaoses, when we did show
Care to aught else; and often absences
Withdrew our souls, and made us carcases.

But I am by her death (which word wrongs her)
Of the first nothing, the elixir grown;
   Were I a man, that I were one,   30
   I needs must know; I should prefer,
     If I were any beast,
Some ends, some means; yea plants, yea stones detest,
And love; all, all some properties invest;
If I an ordinary nothing were,
As shadow, a light, and body must be here.

But I am none; nor will my sun renew.
You lovers, for whose sake, the lesser sun
   At this time to the Goat is run
   To fetch new lust, and give it you,   40
     Enjoy your summer all;
Since she enjoys her long night's festival,
Let me prepare towards her, and let me call
This hour her vigil, and her eve, since this
Both the year's, and the day's deep midnight is.

A VALEDICTION
FORBIDDING MOURNING

As virtuous men pass mildly away,
   And whisper to their souls, to go,
Whilst some of their sad friends do say,
   The breath goes now, and some say, no:

So let us melt, and make no noise,
   No tear-floods, nor sigh-tempests move,

'Twere profanation of our joys
  To tell the laity our love.

Moving of th' earth brings harms and fears,
  Men reckon what it did and meant,   10
But trepidation of the spheres,
  Though greater far, is innocent.

Dull sublunary lovers' love
  (Whose soul is sense) cannot admit
Absence, because it doth remove
  Those things which elemented it.

But we by a love, so much refin'd,
  That ourselves know not what it is,
Inter-assured of the mind,
  Care less, eyes, lips, and hands to miss.   20

Our two souls therefore, which are one,
  Though I must go, endure not yet
A breach, but an expansion,
  Like gold to airy thinness beat.

If they be two, they are two so
  As stiff twin compasses are two,
Thy soul the fixed foot, makes no show
  To move, but doth, if th'other do.

And though it in the centre sit,
  Yet when the other far doth roam,   30
It leans, and hearkens after it,
  And grows erect, as that comes home.

Such wilt thou be to me, who must
  Like th' other foot, obliquely run;
Thy firmness makes my circle just,
  And makes me end, where I begun.

THE ECSTASY

Where, like a pillow on a bed,
  A pregnant bank swelled up, to rest

The violet's reclining head,
    Sat we two, one another's best;

Our hands were firmly cemented
    With a fast balm, which thence did spring,
Our eye-beams twisted, and did thread
    Our eyes, upon one double string;

So to' intergraft our hands, as yet
    Was all the means to make us one,   10
And pictures in our eyes to get
    Was all our propagation.

As 'twixt two equal armies, Fate
    Suspends uncertain victory,
Our souls, (which to advance their state,
    Were gone out), hung 'twixt her, and me.

And whilst our souls negotiate there,
    We like sepulchral statues lay;
All day, the same our postures were,
    And we said nothing, all the day.   20

If any, so by love refined,
    That he soul's language understood,
And by good love were grown all mind,
    Within convenient distance stood,

He (though he knew not which soul spake
    Because both meant, both spake the same)
Might thence a new concoction take,
    And part far purer than he came.

This Ecstasy doth unperplex
    (We said) and tell us what we love,   30
We see by this, it was not sex,
    We see, we saw not what did move:

But as all several souls contain
    Mixture of things, they know not what,
Love, these mixed souls doth mix again,
    And makes both one, each this and that.

A single violet transplant,
    The strength, the colour, and the size,
(All which before was poor, and scant,)
    Redoubles still, and multiplies.   40

When love, with one another so
    Interinanimates two souls,
That abler soul, which thence doth flow,
    Defects of loneliness controls.

We then, who are this new soul, know,
    Of what we are composed, and made,
For, th' atomies of which we grow,
    Are souls, whom no change can invade.

But O alas, so long, so far
    Our bodies why do we forbear?   50
They'are ours, though they'are not we, we are
    The intelligences, they the sphere.

We owe them thanks, because they thus,
    Did us, to us, at first convey,
Yielded their forces, sense, to us,
    Nor are dross to us, but allay.

On man heaven's influence works not so,
    But that it first imprints the air,
So soul into the soul may flow,
    Though it to body first repair.   60

As our blood labours to beget
    Spirits, as like souls as it can,
Because such fingers need to knit
    That subtle knot, which makes us man:

So must pure lovers' souls descend
    T' affections, and to faculties,
Which sense may reach and apprehend,
    Else a great prince in prison lies.

To our bodies turn we then, that so
    Weak men on love revealed may look;   70

Love's mysteries in souls do grow,
    But yet the body is his book.

And if some lover, such as we,
    Have heard this dialogue of one,
Let him still mark us, he shall see
    Small change, when we'are to bodies gone.

ON HIS MISTRESS

By our first strange and fatal interview,
By all desires which thereof did ensue,
By our long starving hopes, by that remorse
Which my words' masculine persuasive force
Begot in thee, and by the memory
Of hurts which spies and rivals threaten'd me,
I calmly beg; but by thy parents' wrath,
By all pains which want and divorcement hath,
I conjure thee; and all those oaths which I
And thou have sworn, to seal joint constancy,   10
Here I unswear, and over-swear them thus:
Thou shalt not love by means so dangerous.
Temper, O fair love, love's impetuous rage,
Be my true mistress still, not my feign'd page.
I'll go, and, by thy kind leave, leave behind
Thee, only worthy to nurse in my mind
Thirst to come back; oh, if thou die before,
From other lands my soul towards thee shall soar,
Thy (else almighty) beauty cannot move
Rage from the seas, nor thy love teach them love,   20
Nor tame wild Boreas' harshness; Thou hast read
How roughly he in pieces shivered
Fair Orithea, whom he swore he lov'd.
Fall ill or good, 'tis madness to have prov'd
Dangers unurg'd; Feed on this flattery,
That absent lovers one in th' other be.
Dissemble nothing, not a boy, nor change
Thy body's habit, nor mind's; be not strange
To thy self only; all will spy in thy face
A blushing womanly discovering grace.   30
Richly cloth'd apes are call'd apes, and as soon

Eclips'd as bright, we call the moon, the moon.
Men of France, changeable chameleons,
Spitals of diseases, shops of fashions,
Love's fuellers, and the rightest company
Of players which upon the world's stage be,
Will quickly know thee, and know thee; and alas
Th' indifferent Italian, as we pass
His warm land, well content to think thee page,
Will haunt thee, with such lust and hideous rage   40
As Lot's fair guests were vexed. But none of these
Nor spongy hydroptic Dutch, shall thee displease,
If thou stay here. Oh stay here, for, for thee
England is only a worthy gallery,
To walk in expectation, till from thence
Our great King call thee into his presence.
When I am gone, dream me some happiness,
Nor let thy looks our long hid love confess,
Nor praise, nor dispraise me, nor bless nor curse
Openly love's force; nor in bed fright thy nurse   50
With midnight's startings, crying out, "O, O
Nurse, O my love is slain; I saw him go
O'er the white Alps, alone; I saw him, I,
Assail'd, fight, taken, stabb'd, bleed, fall, and die."
Augur me better chance, except dread Jove
Think it enough for me, to have had thy love.

DEATH BE NOT PROUD

Death be not proud, though some have called thee
Mighty and dreadful, for, thou art not so,
For, those, whom thou think'st, thou dost overthrow,
Die not, poor death, nor yet canst thou kill me;
From rest and sleep, which but thy pictures be,
Much pleasure, then from thee, much more must flow,
And soonest our best men with thee do go,
Rest of their bones, and soul's delivery.
Thou art slave to fate, chance, kings, and desperate men,
And dost with poison, war, and sickness dwell,
And poppy, or charms can make us sleep as well,
And better than thy stroke; why swell'st thou then?
One short sleep past, we wake eternally,
And death shall be no more, Death thou shalt die.

BATTER MY HEART,
THREE-PERSON'D GOD

Batter my heart, three-person'd God; for, you
As yet but knock, breathe, shine, and seek to mend;
That I may rise, and stand, o'erthrow me, 'and bend
Your force, to break, blow, burn, and make me new.
I, like an usurp'd town, to another due,
Labour to admit you, but O, to no end,
Reason your viceroy in me, me should defend,
But is captiv'd, and proves weak or untrue,
Yet dearly'I love you, 'and would be loved fain,
But am betroth'd unto your enemy,
Divorce me, untie, or break that knot again,
Take me to you, imprison me, for I
Except you'enthral me, never shall be free,
Nor ever chaste, except you ravish me.

Richard Barnfield

(1 5 7 4 – 1 6 2 7)

Educated at Brasenose College, Oxford, Barnfield settled in the early 1590s in London, where he entered the circle of literary patronage of the Countess of Pembroke. He published his first works at the age of twenty, including "The Affectionate Shepherd," but stopped writing poetry at the age of twenty-four. He retired from London in 1606 to his estates at Darlaston, where he lived the rest of his life and where he was buried. Barnfield was praised for his skill in pastoral, as were both Sidney and Spenser, by his contemporary and friend Francis Meres. Later commentators had some difficulty with what Thomas Warton described as Barnfield's "equivocal tendency," no doubt an allusion to the strong homoerotic aspects of "The Affectionate Shepherd." Barnfield defended his poem from such attacks in *Cynthia*, his third book of poetry, where he wrote that "Some there were, that did interpret *The Affectionate Shepherd* otherwise than (in truth) I meant, touching the subject thereof, to wit, the love of a shepherd to a boy; the which I will not excuse, because I never made. Only this, I will unshadow my conceit: being nothing else, but an imitation of Virgil, in the second Eclogues of Alexis." Scholars have recognized in Barnfield's work strong affinities to the poetry of both Marlowe and Shakespeare.

THE TEARS OF AN AFFECTIONATE
SHEPHERD SICK FOR LOVE

Scarce had the morning star hid from the light
   Heaven's crimson canopy with stars bespangled,
But I began to rue th'unhappy sight
   Of that fair boy that had my heart entangled;
     Cursing the time, the place, the sense, the sin;
     I came, I saw, I viewed, I slipped in.

If it be sin to love a sweet-fac'd boy
   (Whose amber locks truss'd up in golden trammels
Dangle adown his lovely cheeks with joy,
   When pearl and flowers his fair hair enamels)   10
     If it be sin to love a lovely lad,
     Oh then sin I, for whom my soul is sad.

His ivory-white and alabaster skin
  Is stain'd throughout with rare vermilion red,
Whose twinkling starry lights do never blin
  To shine on lovely Venus (beauty's bed):
    But as the lily and the blushing rose,
    So white and red on him in order grows.

Upon a time the nymphs bestirr'd themselves
  To try who could his beauty soonest win;   20
But he accounted them but all as elves,
  Except it were the fair Queen Gwendolen;
    Her he embrac'd, of her he was beloved,
    With plaints he proved, and with tears he moved.

But her an old man had been suitor to,
  That in his age began to dote again;
Her would he often pray, and often woo,
  When through old age enfeebled was his brain:
    But she before had loved a lusty youth
    That now was dead, the cause of all her ruth.   30

And thus it happen'd, Death and Cupid met
  Upon a time at swilling Bacchus' house,
Where dainty cates upon the board were set,
  And goblets full of wine to drink carouse:
    Where Love and Death did love the liquor so,
    That out they fall and to the fray they go.

And having both their quivers at their back
  Fill'd full of arrows; th'one of fatal steel,
The other all of gold; Death's shaft was black,
  But Love's was yellow: Fortune turn'd her wheel;   40
    And from Death's quiver fell a fatal shaft,
    That under Cupid by the wind was waft.

And at the same time by ill hap there fell
  Another arrow out of Cupid's quiver;
The which was carried by the wind at will,
  And under Death the amorous shaft did shiver.
    They being parted, Love took up Death's dart,
    And Death took up Love's arrow (for his part).

Thus as they wander'd both about the world,
  At last Death met with one of feeble age;   50
Wherewith he drew a shaft and at him hurled
  The unknown arrow (with a furious rage),
    Thinking to strike him dead with Death's black dart,
    But he (alas) with Love did wound his heart.

This was the doting fool, this was the man
  That lov'd fair Gwendolena Queen of Beauty;
She cannot shake him off, do what she can,
  For he hath vowed to her his soul's last duty,
    Making him trim upon the holy-days,
    And crowns his love with garlands made of bays.   60

Now doth he stroke his beard, and now (again)
  He wipes the drivel from his filthy chin;
Now offers he a kiss; but high Disdain
  Will not permit her heart to pity him:
    Her heart more hard than adamant or steel,
    Her heart more changeable than Fortune's wheel.

But leave we him in love (up to the ears)
  And tell how Love behaved himself abroad;
Who seeing one that mourned still in tears
  (A young man groaning under love's great load)   70
    Thinking to ease his burden, rid his pains:
    For men have grief as long as life remains.

Alas (the while) that unawares he drew
  The fatal shaft that Death had dropped before,
By which deceit great harm did then issue,
  Staining his face with blood and filthy gore.
    His face, that was to Gwendolen more dear
    Than love of lords, of any lordly peer.

This was that fair and beautiful young man
  Whom Gwendolena so lamented for;   80
This is that love whom she doth curse and ban,
  Because she doth that dismal chance abhor;
    And if it were not for his mother's sake,
    Even Ganymede himself she would forsake.

Oh would she would forsake my Ganymede,
　Whose sugar'd love is full of sweet delight,
Upon whose forehead you may plainly read
　Love's pleasure, grav'd in ivory tables bright;
　　In whose fair eye-balls you may clearly see
　　Base love still stained with foul indignity.　　　　90

Oh would to God he would but pity me,
　That love him more than any mortal wight;
Then he and I with love would soon agree,
　That now cannot abide his suitors' sight.
　　O would to God (so I might have my fee)
　　My lips were honey, and thy mouth a bee.

Then shouldst thou suck my sweet and my fair flower
　That now is ripe and full of honey-berries:
Then would I lead thee to my pleasant bower
　Fill'd full of grapes, of mulberries, and cherries;　　　100
　　Then shouldst thou be my wasp or else my bee,
　　I would thy hive, and thou my honey be.

I would put amber bracelets on thy wrests,
　Crownets of pearl about thy naked arms;
And when thou sit'st at swilling Bacchus' feasts,
　My lips with charms should save thee from all harms:
　　And when in sleep thou took'st thy chiefest pleasure,
　　Mine eyes should gaze upon thine eye-lids' treasure.

And every morn by dawning of the day,
　When Phoebus riseth with a blushing face,　　　110
Silvanus' chapel-clerks shall chaunt a lay,
　And play thee hunts-up in thy resting place:
　　My cote thy chamber, my bosom thy bed,
　　Shall be appointed for thy sleepy head.

And when it pleaseth thee to walk abroad
　(Abroad into the fields to take fresh air),
The meads with Flora's treasure should be strowed
　(The mantled meadows and the fields so fair),
　　And by a silver well, with golden sands,
　　I'll sit me down, and wash thine ivory hands.　　　120

And in the sweltering heat of summer time,
  I would make cabinets for thee (my love):
Sweet-smelling arbours made of eglantine
    Should be thy shrine, and I would be thy dove.
      Cool cabinets of fresh green laurel boughs
      Should shadow us, o'er-set with thick-set yews.

Or if thou list to bathe thy naked limbs
  Within the crystal of a pearl-bright brook,
Pav'd with the dainty pebbles to the brims,
    Or clear, wherein thyself thyself mayst look,   130
      We'll go to Ladon, whose still trickling noise
      Will lull thee fast sleep amidst thy joys.

Or if thou'lt go unto the river side
  To angle for the sweet fresh-water fish,
Arm'd with thy implements that will abide
    (Thy rod, hook, line) to take a dainty dish;
      Thy rods shall be of cane, thy lines of silk,
      Thy hooks of silver, and thy baits of milk.

Or if thou lov'st to hear sweet melody,
  Or pipe a round upon an oaten reed,   140
Or make thyself glad with some mirthful glee,
    Or play them music whilst thy flock doth feed;
      To Pan's own pipe I'll help my lovely lad,
      (Pan's golden pipe) which he of Syrinx had.

Or if thou dar'st to climb the highest trees
  For apples, cherries, medlars, pears, or plums,
Nuts, walnuts, filberts, chestnuts, services,
    The hoary peach, when snowy winter comes;
      I have fine orchards full of mellowed fruit,
      Which I will give thee to obtain my suit.   150

Not proud Alcinous himself can vaunt
  Of goodlier orchards or of braver trees
Than I have planted; yet thou wilt not grant
    My simple suit; but like the honey bees
      Thou suck'st the flower till all the sweet be gone,
      And lov'st me for my coin till I have none.

Leave Gwendolen (sweet-heart). Though she is fair
    Yet is she light; not light in virtue shining,
But light in her behaviour, to impair
        Her honour in her chastity's declining;   160
            Trust not her tears, for they can wantonize,
            When tears in pearl are trickling from her eyes.

If thou wilt come and dwell with me at home;
    My sheep-cote shall be strowed with new green rushes:
We'll haunt the trembling prickets as they roam
        About the fields, along the hawthorn bushes;
            I have a piebald cur to hunt the hare:
            So we will live with dainty forest fare.

Nay more than this, I have a garden-plot,
    Wherein there wants nor herbs, nor roots, nor flowers;   170
(Flowers to smell, roots to eat, herbs for the pot),
        And dainty shelters when the welkin lowers:
            Sweet-smelling beds of lilies and roses,
            Which rosemary banks and lavender encloses.

There grows the gillyflower, the mint, the daisy
    Both red and white, the blue-veined violet;
The purple hyacinth, the spike to please thee;
        The scarlet-dyed carnation bleeding yet;
            The sage, the savory, and sweet marjoram,
            Hyssop, thyme, and eye-bright, good for the blind and dumb.   180

The pink, the primrose, cowslip, and daffadilly,
    The harebell blue, the crimson columbine,
Sage, lettuce, parsley, and the milk-white lily,
        The rose, and speckled flowers called sops-in-wine,
            Fine pretty king-cups, and the yellow boots,
            That grows by rivers and by shallow brooks.

And many thousand moe (I cannot name)
    Of herbs and flowers that in gardens grow,
I have for thee; and coneys that be tame,
        Young rabbits, white as swan and black as crow,   190
            Some speckled here and there with dainty spots;
            And more I have two milch and milk-white goats.

All these, and more, I'll give thee for thy love;
  If these, and more, may tice thy love away:
I have a pigeon-house, in it a dove,
    Which I love more than mortal tongue can say:
      And last of all, I'll give thee a little lamb
      To play withal, new-weaned from her dam.

But if thou wilt not pity my complaint,
  My tears, nor vows, nor oaths, made to thy beauty,   200
What shall I do? But languish, die, or faint,
    Since thou dost scorn my tears and my soul's duty;
      And tears contemned, vows and oaths must fail;
      For where tears cannot, nothing cannot prevail.

Compare the love of fair Queen Gwendolen
  With mine, and thou shalt see how she doth love thee:
I love thee for thy qualities divine,
    But she doth love another swain above thee;
      I love thee for thy gifts, she for her pleasure;
      I for thy virtue, she for beauty's treasure.   210

And always (I am sure) it cannot last,
  But sometime Nature will deny those dimples:
Instead of beauty (when thy blossom's past)
    Thy face will be deformed, full of wrinkles;
      Then she that loved thee for thy beauty's sake,
      When age draws on, thy love will soon forsake.

But I that lov'd thee for thy gifts divine,
  In the December of thy beauty's waning,
Will still admire, with joy, those lovely eyne,
    That now behold me with their beauties baning.   220
      Though January will never come again,
      Yet April years will come in showers of rain.

When will my May come, that I may embrace thee?
  When will the hour be of my soul's joying?
Why dost thou seek in mirth still to disgrace me?
    Whose mirth's my health, whose grief's my heart's annoying.
      Thy bane my bale, thy bliss my blessedness,
      Thy ill my hell, thy weal my welfare is.

Thus do I honour thee that love thee so,
   And love thee so, that so do honour thee   230
Much more than any mortal man doth know
     Or can discern by love or jealousy;
        But if that thou disdain'st my loving ever,
        Oh happy I if I had loved never.

l.   15. blin = cease
l. 113. cote = cottage
l. 185. boots = marsh marigold

John Marston

(1576–1634)

In his own time Marston was recognized mainly for his brilliant wit and his "sharp-fanged" satires. In an anonymous Cambridge play, *The Return from Parnassus* (c.1600), Marston the satirist is himself satirized as one who in his literary battles "cuts" and "thrusts" at "whomsoever he meets" and is a "ruffi[an] in his style." Marston's inventive language also came under attack by Ben Jonson in his play *Poetaster*, where a character resembling Marston is forced to take an emetic to purge himself of his difficult and knotty vocabulary. Rather than follow in his father's footsteps as a lawyer, Marston turned to writing plays and poetry. His contribution to the Elizabethan and Jacobean stage was substantial and included such plays as *The Malcontent*, *Antonio's Revenge*, *The Fawn*, and along with Ben Jonson and George Chapman, the controversial *Eastward Ho*. In his earliest published verse, *The Metamorphosis of Pygmalion's Image*, Marston tried his hand at that fading popular genre, the minor epic. But his most influential poetry is to be found in his neo-Stoic *The Scourge of Villainy* (which includes "A Cynic Satire" with its parodic recollection of Shakespeare's *Richard III* in its opening line), first published in 1598 and twice reprinted in 1599 before being consigned to the flames following the Bishops' ban on satire in June 1599.

A CYNIC SATIRE

"A man, a man, a kingdom for a man!"
"Why, how now, currish mad Athenian?
Thou Cynic dog, seest not the streets do swarm
With troops of men?" "No, no, for Circe's charm
Hath turn'd them all to swine. I never shall
Think those same Samian saws authentical,
But rather, I dare swear, the souls of swine
Do live in men; for that same radiant shine,
That lustre wherewith nature's nature decked
Our intellectual part, that gloss, is soil'd   10
With staining spots of vile impiety
And muddy dirt of sensuality.
These are no men but apparitions,

145

Ignes fatui, glow-worms, fictions,
Meteors, rats of Nilus, fantasies,
Colosses, pictures, shades, resemblances.
      "Ho, Linceus!
Seest thou yon gallant in the sumptuous clothes?
How brisk, how spruce, how gorgeously he shows?
Note his French herring-bones, but note no more,   20
Unless thou spy his fair appendant whore
That lackeys him. Mark nothing but his clothes,
His new-stamped complement, his cannon oaths;
Mark those, for nought but such lewd viciousness
E'er gracèd him, save Sodom beastliness.
Is this a man? Nay, an incarnate devil,
That struts in vice and glorieth in evil.
  "A man, a man!" "Peace, Cynic, yon is one,
A complete soul of all perfection."
"What, mean'st thou him that walks all open-breasted,   30
Drawn through the ear with ribbons, plumy-crested?
He that doth snort in fat-fed luxury,
And gapes for some grinding monopoly?
He that in effeminate invention,
In beastly source of all pollution,
In riot, lust, and fleshly seeming-sweetness,
Sleeps sound, secure under the shade of greatness?
Mean'st thou that senseless, sensual epicure,
That sink of filth, that guzzle most impure?
What, he? Linceus, on my word thus presume,   40
He's nought but clothes and scenting sweet perfume.
His very soul, assure thee, Linceus,
Is not so big as is an atomus.
Nay, he is spriteless; sense or soul hath none,
Since last Medusa turned him to a stone.
  "A man, a man! Lo, yonder I espy
The shade of Nestor in sad gravity;
Since old Silenus brake his ass's back,
He now is forc'd his paunch and guts to pack
In a fair tumbrel." "Why, sour satirist,   50
Canst thou unman him? Here I dare insist
And soothly say he is a perfect soul,
Eats nectar, drinks ambrosia, sans control.
An inundation of felicity
Fats him with honour and huge treasury."
"Canst thou not, Linceus, cast thy searching eye,

And spy his imminent catastrophe?
He's but a sponge, and shortly needs must leese
His wrong-got juice, when greatness' fist shall squeeze
His liquor out. Would not some shallow head,   60
That is with seeming shadows only fed,
Swear yon same damask-coat, yon guarded man,
Were some grave sober Cato Utican?
When let him but in judgment's sight uncase,
He's nought but budge, old guards, brown fox-fur face.
He hath no soul the which the Stagirite
Term'd rational; for beastly appetite,
Base dunghill thoughts, and sensual action
Hath made him lose that fair creation;
And now no man, since Circe's magic charm   70
Hath turn'd him to a maggot, that doth swarm
In tainted flesh, whose foul corruption
Is his fair food, whose generation
Another's ruin. Oh, Canaan's dread curse,
To live in people's sins! nay, far more worse,
To muck rank hate. But, sirrah, Linceus,
Seest thou that troop that now affronteth us?
They are nought but eels, that never will appear
Till that tempestuous winds or thunder tear
Their slimy beds. But prithee, stay awhile;   80
Look, yon comes John-a-Noke and John-a-Stile.
They're nought but slow-pac'd dilatory pleas,
Demure demurrers, still striving to appease
Hot zealous love. The language that they speak
Is the pure barb'rous blacksaunt of the Gete;
Their only skill rests in collusions,
Abatements, stopples, inhibitions.
Heavy-pac'd jades, dull-pated jobbernowls!
Quick in delays, checking with vain controls
Fair Justice' course; vile necessary evils,   90
Smooth seem-saints, yet damned incarnate devils!
   "Far be it from my sharp satiric muse
Those grave and reverend legists to abuse
That aid Astraea, that do further right;
But these Megaeras that inflame despite,
That broach deep rancour, that do study still
To ruin right, that they their paunch may fill
With Irus' blood; these Furies I do mean,
These hedgehogs, that disturb Astraea's scene.

"A man, a man!" "Peace, Cynic, yon's a man;   100
Behold yon sprightly dread Mavortian;
With him I stop thy currish barking chops."
"What, mean'st thou him that in his swaggering slops
Wallows unbracèd all along the street?
He that salutes each gallant he doth meet
With 'Farewell, sweet captain; kind heart, adieu!'
He that last night tumbling, thou didst view,
From out the Great Man's Head, and thinking still
He had been sentinel of warlike Brill,
Cries out, 'Que va là? zounds, que?' and out doth draw   110
His transformed poniard to a syringe straw,
And stabs the drawer. What, that ringo-root?
Mean'st thou that wasted leg, puff-bombast boot?
What, he that's drawn and quarterèd with lace?
That Westphalian gammon, clove-stuck face?
Why, he is nought but huge blaspheming oaths,
Swart snout, big looks, misshapen Switzers' clothes.
Weak meagre lust hath now consumèd quite
And wasted clean away his martial sprite;
Enfeebling riot, all vices' confluence,   120
Hath eaten out that sacred influence
Which made him man.
That divine part is soak'd away in sin,
In sensual lust; and midnight bezzling,
Rank inundation of luxuriousness
Have tainted him with such gross beastliness
That now the seat of that celestial essence
Is all possessed with Naples' pestilence.
Fat peace and dissolute impiety
Have lullèd him in such security   130
That now, let whirlwinds and confusion tear
The centre of our state, let giants rear
Hill upon hill, let Western Termagant
Shake heaven's vault: he with his occupant
Are cling'd so close, like dew-worms in the morn,
That he'll not stir till out his guts are torn
With eating filth. Tubrio, snort on, snort on!
Till thou art waked with sad confusion.
     "Now rail no more at my sharp Cynic sound,
Thou brutish world that, in all vileness drown'd,   140
Hast lost thy soul; for nought but shades I see,
Resemblances of men inhabit thee.

"Yon tissue-slop, yon holy-crossèd pane,
Is but a water spaniel that will fawn
And kiss the water whilst it pleasures him,
But being once arrivèd at the brim,
He shakes it off.
    "Yon in the cap'ring cloak, a mimic ape
That only strives to seem another's shape.
    "Yon's Aesop's ass; yon sad civility   150
Is but an ox that with base drudgery
Ears up the land, whilst some gilt ass doth chaw
The golden wheat, he well apaid with straw.
    "Yon's but a muck-hill overspread with snow,
Which with that veil doth even as fairly show
As the green meads, whose native outward fair
Breathes sweet perfumes into the neighbour air.
    "Yon effeminate sanguine Ganymede
Is but a beaver, hunted for the bed."
    "Peace, Cynic, see what yonder doth approach."   160
"A cart? a tumbrel?" "No, a badgèd coach."
"What's in 't? some man?" "No, nor yet womankind,
But a celestial angel fair refined."
"The devil as soon! Her mask so hinders me
I cannot see her beauty's deity.
Now that is off, she is so vizarded,
So steep'd in lemons' juice, so surphuled,
I cannot see her face. Under one hood
Two faces, but I never understood
Or saw one face under two hoods till now: 170
'Tis the right semblance of old Janus' brow.
Her mask, her vizard, her loose-hanging gown
For her loose-lying body, her bright spangled crown,
Her long slit sleeve, stiff busk, puff-farthingale
Is all that makes her thus angelical.
Alas, her soul struts round about her neck,
Her seat of sense is her rebato set,
Her intellectual is a feignèd niceness:
Nothing but clothes and simpering preciseness.
    "Out on these puppets, painted images,   180
Haberdashers' shops, torchlight maskeries,
Perfuming pans, Dutch ancients, glow-worms bright,
That soil our souls and damp our reason's light:
Away, away, hence, coachman! go enshrine
Thy new-glaz'd puppet in Port Esquiline.

Blush, Martia, fear not or look pale—all's one:
Margara keeps thy set complexion.
    "Sure, I ne'er think those axioms to be true,
That souls of men from that great Soul ensue
And of his essence do participate   190
As 'twere by pipes, when so degenerate,
So adverse, is our nature's motion
To his immaculate condition,
That such foul filth from such fair purity,
Such sensual acts from such a Deity,
Can ne'er proceed. But if that dream were so,
Then sure the slime that from our souls do flow
Have stopp'd those pipes by which it was convey'd,
And now no human creatures, once disray'd
Of that fair gem.   200
Beasts' sense, plants' growth, like *being*, as a stone;
But out, alas, our cognizance is gone."

l.   39. guzzle = gutter
l.   62. guarded = elaborately trimmed
l.   85. blacksaunt = black *sanctus*, a noisy burlesque hymn
l.   88. jobbernowls = blockhead
l. 124. bezzling = drunken revelry
l. 167. surphuled = painted with cosmetics
l. 185. Port Esquiline = i.e., a dunghill

Mary Sidney Wroth

(1 5 8 7 ? – 1 6 2 3 ?)

Wroth came from a distinguished literary family: Sir Philip Sidney was her uncle, and the Countess of Pembroke her aunt. An active patroness of the arts, she acted in one of Ben Jonson's court masques and wrote a play, unpublished at the time, called *Love's Victorie*. Her poetry circulated in manuscript and was praised by contemporaries; Ben Jonson, for example, wrote that after reading her sonnets he had "become a better lover and much better poet." Wroth's *Urania*, from which the poems below are taken, was modeled on the Countess of Pembroke's *Arcadia* and was the only work Wroth published in her lifetime. It provoked controversy almost immediately and was withdrawn from sale; Wroth was admonished not to produce "lascivious tales and amorous toys." In her later years she withdrew from court to the country and traveled abroad.

From URANIA

WHEN NIGHT'S BLACK MANTLE

When night's black mantle could most darkness prove,
And sleep, Death's image, did my senses hire
From knowledge of myself; then thoughts did move
Swifter than those most swiftness need require:
In sleep, a chariot drawn by wing'd desire
I saw: where sat bright Venus, Queen of Love,
And at her feet, her son, still adding fire
To burning hearts which she did hold above;
But one heart flaming more than all the rest
The goddess held, and put it to my breast,
"Dear son, now shoot," said she: "thus must we win";
He her obey'd, and martyr'd my poor heart,
I, waking, hop'd as dreams it would depart
Yet since, (O me!), a lover have I been.

AM I THUS CONQUER'D?

Am I thus conquer'd? Have I lost the powers
That to withstand, which joys to ruin me?

Must I be still while it my strength devours
And captive leads me prisoner, bound, unfree?
Love first shall leave men's phant'sies to them free,
Desire shall quench Love's flames, spring hate sweet showers,
Love shall loose all his darts, have sight, and see
His shame, and wishings hinder happy hours;
Why should we not Love's purblind charms resist?
Must we be servile, doing what he list?
No, seek some host to harbour thee: I fly
Thy babish tricks, and freedom do profess;
But oh, my hurt, makes my lost heart confess
I love, and must; so farewell liberty.

YOU BLESSED STARS

You blessed stars which do heav'ns glory show,
And at your brightness makes our eyes admire,
Yet envy not if I on earth below
Enjoy a sight which moves in me more fire.
I do confess such beauty breeds desire,
You shine, and clearest light on us bestow,
Yet doth a sight on earth more warmth inspire
Into my loving soul, his force to know.
Clear, bright, and shining as you are, is this
Light of my joy, fix'd steadfast, nor will move
His light from me, nor I change from his love,
But still increase as th'eith of all my bliss.
His sight gives life unto my love-rul'd eyes
My love content because in his, love lies.

l. 12. th'eith = the height

IN THIS STRANGE LABYRINTH

In this strange labyrinth how shall I turn?
Ways are on all sides while the way I miss:
If to the right hand, there in love I burn;
Let me go forward, therein danger is;
If to the left, suspicion hinders bliss,
Let me turn back, shame cries I ought return
Nor faint though crosses with my fortunes kiss.
Stand still is harder, although sure to mourn;
Thus let me take the right, or left hand way;

Go forward, or stand still, or back retire;
I must these doubts endure without allay
Or help, but travail find for my best hire;
Yet that which most my troubled sense doth move
Is to leave all, and take the thread of love.

Robert Herrick

(1591 – 1674)

Born in London, at sixteen Herrick was apprenticed to his uncle, a goldsmith; after six years, at the advanced age of twenty-two, he decided to abandon the craft and attend Cambridge. After university, Herrick probably moved to London and fell in with Ben Jonson's poetic circle, the "Sons of Ben," of whom Herrick was one of the most devoted. At the age of thirty-two, perhaps unable to find preferment elsewhere, Herrick took holy orders. After his participation as a chaplain in 1627 in a disastrous military adventure, he settled into a quieter life as a country vicar in Devonshire. Much of his subsequent poetry turns on the tension between urban and country life. His quiet existence was disrupted in 1647 when, as a poet with royalist sympathies living in a part of England strongly sympathetic to the Puritan cause, he was expelled from the parish. After the Restoration of 1660 he returned to his post for thirteen more years. Although his poems circulated in manuscript in his day, Herrick is remarkable for the extraordinary care he took in organizing and seeing into print his only collection of verse, *Hesperides* (which even contains a versified table of contents). Published in 1648, at a time when politics had largely displaced poetry in many people's minds, Herrick's book did not attract much attention. It appears that in the quarter-century before his death he wrote no more poetry.

DELIGHT IN DISORDER

A sweet disorder in the dress
Kindles in clothes a wantonness:
A lawn about the shoulders thrown
Into a fine distraction:
An erring lace, which here and there
Enthralls the crimson stomacher:
A cuff neglectful, and thereby
Ribbands to flow confusedly:
A winning wave (deserving note)
In the tempestuous petticoat:
A careless shoestring, in whose tie
I see a wild civility,
Do more bewitch me, then when Art
Is too precise in every part.

ART ABOVE NATURE, TO JULIA

When I behold a forest spread
With silken trees upon thy head;
And when I see that other dress
Of flowers set in comeliness:
When I behold another grace
In the ascent of curious lace,
Which like a pinnacle doth show
The top, and the top-gallant too:
Then, when I see thy tresses bound
Into an oval, square, or round;   10
And knit in knots far more than I
Can tell by tongue, or true-love tie;
Next, when those lawny films I see
Play with a wild civility:
And all those airy silks to flow,
Alluring me, and tempting so:
I must confess, mine eye and heart
Dotes less on Nature, than on Art.

UPON JULIA'S CLOTHES

When as in silks my Julia goes,
Then, then (methinks) how sweetly flows
That liquifaction of her clothes.

Next, when I cast mine eyes and see
That brave vibration each way free;
O how that glittering taketh me!

CORINNA'S GOING A-MAYING

Get up, get up for shame, the blooming morn
Upon her wings presents the god unshorn.
    See how Aurora throws her fair
    Fresh-quilted colours through the air:
    Get up, sweet slug-a-bed, and see

The dew-bespangling herb and tree.
Each flower has wept, and bow'd toward the East,
Above an hour since; yet you not dress'd,
    Nay! not so much as out of bed?
    When all the birds have Matins said,   10
    And sing their thankful hymns: 'tis sin,
    Nay, profanation to keep in,
When as a thousand virgins on this day,
Spring, sooner than the lark, to fetch in May.

Rise; and put on your foliage, and be seen
To come forth, like the spring-time, fresh and green;
    And sweet as Flora. Take no care
    For jewels for your gown, or hair:
    Fear not; the leaves will strew
    Gems in abundance upon you;   20
Besides, the childhood of the day has kept,
Against you come, some orient pearls unwept:
    Come, and receive them while the light
    Hangs on the dew-locks of the night:
    And Titan on the Eastern hill
    Retires himself, or else stands still
Till you come forth. Wash, dress, be brief in praying:
Few beads are best, when once we go a-Maying.

Come, my Corinna, come; and coming, mark
How each field turns a street; each street a park   30
    Made green, and trimm'd with trees: see how
    Devotion gives each house a bough
    Or branch: each porch, each door, ere this,
    An ark, a tabernacle is
Made up of white-thorn neatly interwove;
As if here were those cooler shades of love.
    Can such delights be in the street
    And open fields, and we not see't?
    Come, we'll abroad; and let's obey
    The proclamation made for May: 40
And sin no more, as we have done, by staying;
But my Corinna, come, let's go a-Maying.

There's not a budding boy, or girl, this day,
But is got up, and none to bring in May.
    A deal of youth, ere this, is come

Back, and with white-thorn laden home.
Some have dispatch'd their cakes and cream,
Before that we have left to dream:
And some have wept, and wooed, and plighted troth,
And chose their priest, ere we can cast off sloth.   50
Many a green-gown has been given;
Many a kiss, both odd and even:
Many a glance too has been sent
From out the eye, Love's firmament:
Many a jest told of the keys betraying
This night, and locks pick'd, yet we're not a-Maying.

Come, let us go, while we are in our prime;
And take the harmless folly of the time.
We shall grow old apace, and die
Before we know our liberty.   60
Our life is short; and our days run
As fast away as does the sun.
And as a vapour, or a drop of rain
Once lost, can ne'er be found again:
So, when or you or I are made
A fable, song, or fleeting shade;
All love, all liking, all delight
Lies drown'd with us in endless night.
Then while time serves, and we are but decaying,
Come, my Corinna, come, let's go a-Maying.   70

Henry King

(1 5 9 2 – 1 6 6 9)

Like his friend John Donne, King was essentially a coterie poet: his poems passed from hand to hand in manuscript, rather than circulating in print. They were not published until 1657, and then anonymously and without his permission. Besides his translation of the Psalms (1651), about eighty of his poems survive, including a good number of elegiac and funereal pieces memorializing Donne, Ben Jonson, Sir Walter Ralegh, and others. His most celebrated poem, "An Exequy," was written in memory of his wife Anne Berkeley, who had married King in 1617 and, after bearing five children, died in 1624.

AN EXEQUY, TO HIS MATCHLESS NEVER TO BE FORGOTTEN FRIEND

Accept thou shrine of my dead saint,
Instead of dirges this complaint;
And for sweet flowers to crown thy hearse,
Receive a strew of weeping verse
From thy griev'd friend, whom thou might'st see
Quite melted into tears for thee.
   Dear loss! Since thy untimely fate
My task hath been to meditate
On thee, on thee: thou art the book,
The library whereon I look   10
Though almost blind. For thee (lov'd clay)
I languish out, not live the day,
Using no other exercise
But what I practise with mine eyes:
By which wet glasses I find out
How lazily time creeps about
To one that mourns. This, only this
My exercise and business is;
So I compute the wearing hours
With sighs dissolved into showers.   20

Nor wonder if my time go thus
Backward and most preposterous;
Thou hast benighted me. Thy set
This eve of blackness did beget,
Who was't my day (though overcast)
Before thou had'st thy noon-tide past
And I remember must in tears,
Thou scarce had'st seen so many years
As day tells hours. By the clear sun
My life and fortune first did run;   30
But thou wilt never more appear
Folded within my hemisphere,
Since both thy light and motion
Like a fled star is fall'n and gone,
And twixt me and my soul's dear wish
The earth now interposed is,
Which such a strange eclipse doth make
As ne'er was read in almanac.
     I could allow thee for a time
To darken me and my sad clime,   40
Were it a month, a year, or ten,
I would thy exile live till then;
And all that space my mirth adjourn,
So thou wouldst promise to return;
And putting off thy ashy shroud,
At length disperse this sorrow's cloud.
     But woe is me! The longest date
Too narrow is to calculate
These empty hopes. Never shall I
Be so much blest as to descry   50
A glimpse of thee, till that day come
Which shall the earth to cinders doom,
And a fierce fever must calcine
The body of this world like thine,
(My little world!). That fit of fire
Once off, our bodies shall aspire
To our souls' bliss. Then we shall rise,
And view ourselves with clearer eyes
In that calm region, where no night
Can hide us from each other's sight.   60
     Meantime, thou hast her, Earth; much good
May my harm do thee. Since it stood
With Heaven's will I might not call

Her longer mine, I give thee all
My short-liv'd right and interest
In her, whom living I lov'd best.
With a most free and bounteous grief,
I give thee what I could not keep.
Be kind to her, and prithee look
Thou write into thy Doomsday book   70
Each parcel of this rarity
Which in thy casket shrin'd doth lie.
See that thou make thy reck'ning straight,
And yield her back again by weight.
For thou must audit on thy trust
Each grain and atom of this dust,
As thou wilt answer Him that lent,
Not gave thee, my dear monument.
   So close the ground, and 'bout her shade
Black curtains draw, my bride is laid.   80
   Sleep on, my love, in thy cold bed
Never to be disquieted.
   My last good night! Thou wilt not wake
Till I thy fate shall overtake:
Till age, or grief, or sickness must
Marry my body to that dust
It so much loves; and fill the room
My heart keeps empty in thy tomb.
Stay for me there: I will not fail
To meet thee in that hollow vale.   90
And think not much of my delay,
I am already on the way,
And follow thee with all the speed
Desire can make, or sorrows breed.
Each minute is a short degree,
And ev'ry hour a step towards thee.
At night when I betake to rest,
Next morn I rise nearer my West
Of life, almost by hour's sail,
Then when sleep breath'd his drowsy gale.   100
   Thus from the sun my bottom steers,
And my day's compass downward bears.
Nor labour I to stem the tide
Through which to thee I swiftly glide.
   'Tis true, with shame and grief I yield,
Thou like the van first took'st the field,

And gotten has the victory
In thus adventuring to die
Before me, whose more years might crave
A just precedence in the grave.   110
But hark! My pulse like to a soft drum
Beats my approach, tells thee I come;
And slow howe'er my marches be,
I shall at last sit down by thee.
    The thought of this bids me go on
And wait my dissolution
With hope and comfort. Dear (forgive
The crime) I am content to live
Divided, with but half a heart,
Till we shall meet, and never part.   120

l. 53. calcine = reduce, refine by fire
l. 106. van = vanguard

George Herbert

(1 5 9 3 – 1 6 3 3)

Born in Wales, Herbert was educated at Westminster School, and then at
Trinity College, Cambridge. He began writing poetry at a young age and
published his first verse in 1612 in a commemorative volume for Prince Henry;
much of his poetry was written during his Cambridge years. In the early 1620s
Herbert rejected a life at court or in politics (the expected step for a university
orator) and decided instead to pursue a life in the church. He was ordained a
deacon around 1624, and a year after his marriage in 1629 was ordained a priest
and served as rector of Bemerton until his death a few years later, shortly before
his fortieth birthday. His prose work *The Country Parson* gives some sense of his
spiritual and social commitment as a parish priest. Before his death Herbert
asked fellow clergyman and friend Nicholas Ferrar to publish his collected
poetry, *The Temple,* which Ferrar did in the year of Herbert's death. This
extremely popular collection of spiritual poetry circulated in over a dozen
editions in the next half-century. Herbert's mastery of the devotional lyric drew
a readership that cut across sectarian differences and exercised a decisive influ-
ence on subsequent religious poetry in English.

THE COLLAR

I struck the board, and cried, No more.
           I will abroad.
      What? shall I ever sigh and pine?
My lines and life are free; free as the road,
      Loose as the wind, as large as store.
           Shall I be still in suit?
      Have I no harvest but a thorn
      To let me blood, and not restore
      What I have lost with cordial fruit?
           Sure there was wine   10
Before my sighs did dry it; there was corn
      Before my tears did drown it.
      Is the year only lost to me?
           Have I no bays to crown it?
No flowers, no garlands gay? All blasted?

All wasted?
Not so, my heart: but there is fruit,
And thou hast hands.
Recover all thy sigh-blown age
On double pleasures: leave thy cold dispute   20
Of what is fit, and not. Forsake thy cage,
Thy rope of sands,
Which petty thoughts have made, and made to thee
Good cable, to enforce and draw,
And be thy law,
While thou didst wink and wouldst not see.
Away; take heed,
I will abroad,
Call in thy death's head there; tie up thy fears.
He that forbears   30
To suit and serve his need,
Deserves his load.
But as I rav'd and grew more fierce and wild
At every word,
Methought I heard one calling, *Child*:
And I replied, *My Lord*.

AFFLICTION (IV)

Broken in pieces all asunder,
Lord, hunt me not,
A thing forgot,
Once a poor creature, now a wonder,
A wonder tortur'd in the space
Betwixt this world and that of grace.

My thoughts are all a case of knives,
Wounding my heart
With scatter'd smart,
As wat'ring pots give flowers their lives.   10
Nothing their fury can control,
While they do wound and pink my soul.

All my attendants are at strife,
Quitting their place
Unto my face:

Nothing performs the task of life:
>The elements are let loose to fight,
>And while I live, try out their right.

Oh help, my God! let not their plot
>Kill them and me,   20
>And also thee,
Who art my life: dissolve the knot,
>As the sun scatters by his light
>All the rebellions of the night.

Then shall those powers, which work for grief
>Enter thy pay,
>And day by day
Labour thy praise, and my relief;
>With care and courage building me,
>Till I reach heav'n, and much more, thee.   30

l. 12. pink = pierce

THE ALTAR

A broken ALTAR, Lord, thy servant rears,
Made of a heart, and cemented with tears:
>Whose parts are as thy hand did frame;
>No workman's tool hath touched the same.
>>A   HEART   alone
>>Is   such   a   stone
>>As   nothing   but
>>Thy power doth cut.
>>Wherefore each part
>>Of my hard heart
>>Meets in this frame,
>>To praise thy Name:
>That, if I chance to hold my peace,
>These stones to praise thee may not cease.
O   let   thy   blessed   SACRIFICE   be   mine,
And   sanctify   this   ALTAR   to   be   thine.

REDEMPTION

Having been tenant long to a rich Lord,
   Not thriving, I resolved to be bold,
   And make a suit unto him, to afford
A new small-rented lease, and cancel th'old.
In heaven at his manor I him sought:
   They told me there that he was lately gone
   About some land, which he had dearly bought
Long since on earth, to take possession.
I straight returned, and knowing his great birth,
   Sought him accordingly in great resorts;
   In cities, theatres, gardens, parks, and courts:
At length I heard a ragged noise and mirth
   Of thieves and murderers: there I him espied,
   Who straight, "Your suit is granted," said, and died.

EASTER WINGS

Lord, who createdst man in wealth and store,
   Though foolishly he lost the same,
      Decaying more and more,
         Till he became
          Most poor:
          With thee
        O let me rise
      As larks, harmoniously,
   And sing this day thy victories:
Then shall the fall further the flight in me.   10

My tender age in sorrow did begin:
   And still with sicknesses and shame
      Thou didst so punish sin
         That I became
          Most thin.
          With thee
        Let me combine
      And feel this day thy victory:
   For, if I imp my wing on thine,
Affliction shall advance the flight in me.   20

JORDAN (II)

When first my lines of heav'nly joys made mention,
Such was their lustre, they did so excel,
That I sought out quaint words and trim invention;
My thoughts began to burnish, sprout, and swell,
Curling with metaphors a plain intention,
Decking the sense as if it were to sell.

Thousands of notions in my brain did run,
Offering their service, if I were not sped;
I often blotted what I had begun;
This was not quick enough, and that was dead.   10
Nothing could seem too rich to clothe the sun,
Much less those joys which trample on his head.

As flames do work and wind when they ascend
So did I weave my self into the sense.
But while I bustled, I might hear a friend
Whisper, "How wide is all this long pretence!
There is in love a sweetness ready penn'd:
Copy out only that, and save expense."

THE AGONY

　　　Philosophers have measur'd mountains,
Fathom'd the depths of seas, of states, and kings,
Walk'd with a staff to heav'n, and traced fountains:
　　　But there are two vast, spacious things,
The which to measure it doth more behove:
Yet few there are that sound them; Sin and Love.

　　　Who would know Sin, let him repair
Unto mount Olivet; there shall he see
A man so wrung with pains, that all his hair,
　　　His skin, his garments bloody be.   10
Sin is that press and vice, which forceth pain
To hunt his cruel food through ev'ry vein.

　　　Who knows not Love, let him assay
And taste that juice, which on the cross a pike

Did set again abroach; then let him say
    If ever he did taste the like.
Love is that liquour sweet and most divine,
Which my God feels as blood; but I, as wine.

LOVE (III)

Love bade me welcome: yet my soul drew back,
    Guilty of dust and sin.
But quick-ey'd Love, observing me grow slack
    From my first entrance in,
Drew nearer to me, sweetly questioning,
    If I lack'd any thing.

"A guest," I answer'd, "worthy to be here":
    Love said, "You shall be he."
"I the unkind, ungrateful? Ah my dear,
    I cannot look on thee."   10
Love took my hand, and smiling did reply,
    "Who made the eyes but I?"

"Truth, Lord, but I have marr'd them: let my shame
    Go where it doth deserve."
"And know you not," says Love, "who bore the
    blame?"
    "My dear, then I will serve."
"You must sit down," says Love, "and taste my meat."
    So I did sit and eat.

Thomas Carew

(1594/95 – 1640)

Born in Kent and educated at Merton College, Oxford, Carew was briefly enrolled at the Middle Temple at the Inns of Court before deciding not to become a lawyer like his father. In 1613 he served in Italy under the English ambassador to Venice, Dudley Carleton, and in 1616 accompanied his patron to the Netherlands, where they had a falling out. Back in London and at court, Carew began writing poetry, for the most part distinctive amatory lyrics. His reputation grew in the 1620s, and a contemporary wrote of Carew's verse that "the sharpness of the fancy, and the elegancy of the language, in which that fancy was spread, were at least equal, if not superior to any of that time." His erotic poem of this time, "A Rapture," brought both censure and attention. A posthumous collection of his poetry appeared in 1640 and was reprinted in expanded editions in 1642 and 1651, some indication of the contemporary popularity of Carew's poetry.

AN ELEGY UPON THE DEATH OF THE DEAN OF PAUL'S, DR. JOHN DONNE

Can we not force from widowed poetry,
Now thou art dead, great Donne, one elegy
To crown thy hearse? Why yet did we not trust,
Though with unkneaded dough-bak'd prose, thy dust,
Such as the unscissor'd lect'rer from the flower
Of fading rhetoric, short-lived as his hour,
Dry as the sand that measures it, might lay
Upon the ashes on the funeral day?
Have we nor tune, nor voice? Didst thou dispense
Through all our language both words and sense?   10
'Tis a sad truth. The pulpit may her plain
And sober Christian precepts still retain;
Doctrines it may, and wholesome uses frame,
Grave homilies and lectures; but the flame
Of thy brave soul, that shot such heat and light
As burnt our earth and made our darkness bright,
Committed holy rapes upon our will,

Did through the eye the melting heart distil,
And the deep knowledge of dark truths so teach
As sense might judge what fancy could not reach,   20
Must be desir'd forever. So the fire
That fills with spirit and heat the Delphic choir,
Which, kindled first by thy Promethean breath,
Glow'd here a while, lies quenched now in thy death.
The Muses' garden, with pedantic weeds
O'erspread, was purg'd by thee; the lazy seeds
Of servile imitation thrown away,
And fresh invention planted; thou didst pay
The debts of our penurious bankrupt age:
Licentious thefts, that make poetic rage   30
A mimic fury, when our souls must be
Possess'd, or with Anacreon's ecstasy,
Or Pindar's, not their own. The subtle cheat
Of sly exchanges, and the juggling feat
Of two-edg'd words, or whatsoever wrong
By ours was done the Greek or Latin tongue,
Thou hast redeem'd, and open'd us a mine
Of rich and pregnant fancy, drawn a line
Of masculine expression, which had good
Old Orpheus seen, or all the ancient brood   40
Our superstitious fools admire, and hold
Their lead more precious than thy burnish'd gold,
Thou hadst been their exchequer, and no more
They in each other's dung had raked for ore.
Thou shalt yield no precedence, but of time
And the blind fate of language, whose tuned chime
More charms the outward sense; yet thou mayest claim
From so great disadvantage greater fame,
Since to the awe of thy imperious wit
Our troublesome language bends, made only fit   50
With her tough thick-ribb'd hoops, to gird about
Thy giant fancy, which had prov'd too stout
For their soft melting phrases. As in time
They had the start, so did they cull the prime
Buds of invention many a hundred year,
And left the rifled fields, besides the fear
To touch their harvest; yet from those bare lands
Of what is only thine, thy only hands
(And that their smallest work) have gleaned more
Than all those times and tongues could reap before.   60

But thou art gone, and thy strict laws will be
Too hard for libertines in poetry.
They will repeal the goodly exiled train
Of gods and goddesses, which in thy just reign
Were banish'd nobler poems; now with these
The silenced tales in the *Metamorphoses*
Shall stuff their lines and swell the windy page,
Till verse, refin'd by thee in this last Age,
Turn ballad-rhyme, or those old idols be
Ador'd again with new apostasy.   70
    O pardon me, that break with untun'd verse
The reverend silence that attends thy hearse,
Whose awful solemn murmurs were to thee,
More than these faint lines, a loud elegy,
That did proclaim in a dumb eloquence
The death of all the Arts, whose influence,
Grown feeble, in these panting numbers lies
Gasping short-winded accents, and so dies:
So doth the swiftly turning wheel not stand
In th' instant we withdraw the moving hand,   80
But some small time retain a faint weak course
By virtue of the first impulsive force:
And so whilst I cast on thy funeral pile
Thy crown of bays, oh, let it crack awhile
And spit disdain, till the devouring flashes
Suck all the moisture up, then turn to ashes.
    I will not draw the envy to engross
All thy perfections, or weep all the loss;
Those are too numerous for one elegy,
And this too great to be express'd by me.   90
Let others carve the rest; it shall suffice
I on thy grave this epitaph incise:

    Here lies a king, that rul'd as he thought fit,
    The universal monarchy of wit;
    Here lie two flamens, and both those the best,
    Apollo's first, at last the true God's priest.

A RAPTURE

I will enjoy thee now, my Celia, come
And fly with me to love's Elysium:
The giant, Honor, that keeps cowards out,
Is but a masquer, and the servile rout
Of baser subjects only bend in vain
To the vast idol, whilst the nobler train
Of valiant lovers daily sail between
The huge Colossus' legs, and pass unseen
Unto the blissful shore; be bold and wise,
And we shall enter; the grim Swiss denies   10
Only tame fools a passage, that not know
He is but form and only frights in show
The duller eyes that look from far; draw near,
And thou shalt scorn what we were wont to fear.
We shall see how the stalking pageant goes
With borrowed legs, a heavy load to those
That made and bear him; not as we once thought
The seed of Gods, but a weak model wrought
By greedy men, that seek to enclose the common,
And within private arms empale free woman.   20
    Come then, and mounted on the wings of love,
We'll cut the flitting air and soar above
The monster's head, and in the noblest seats
Of those blessed shades, quench, and renew our heats.
There shall the Queen of Love, and Innocence,
Beauty, and Nature, banish all offense
From our close ivy twines, there I'll behold
Thy baréd snow and thy unbraided gold.
There my enfranchis'd hand on every side
Shall o'er thy naked polished ivory slide.   30
No curtain there, though of transparent lawn,
Shall be before thy virgin-treasure drawn;
But the rich mine to the enquiring eye
Exposed, shall ready still for mintage lie,
And we will coin young Cupids. There a bed
Of roses and fresh myrtles shall be spread
Under the cooler shade of cypress groves;
Our pillows, of the down of Venus' doves,
Whereon our panting limbs we'll gently lay
In the faint respites of our active play,   40

That so our slumbers may in dreams have leisure,
To tell the nimble fancy our past pleasure;
And so our souls that cannot be embraced
Shall the embraces of our bodies taste.
Meanwhile the bubbling stream shall court the shore,
Th' enamor'd chirping wood-choir shall adore
In varied tunes the Deity of Love;
The gentle blasts of western winds shall move
The trembling leaves, and through their close boughs breathe
Still music, while we rest ourselves beneath   50
Their dancing shade; till a soft murmur, sent
From souls entranc'd in amorous languishment
Rouse us, and shoot into our veins fresh fire,
Till we in their sweet ecstasy expire.
    Then, as the empty bee, that lately bore
Into the common treasure all her store,
Flies 'bout the painted field with nimble wing,
Deflow'ring the fresh virgins of the spring,
So will I rifle all the sweets that dwell
In my delicious paradise, and swell   60
My bag with honey, drawn forth by the power
Of fervent kisses from each spicy flower.
I'll seize the rose-buds in their perfum'd bed,
The violet knots, like curious mazes spread
O'er all the garden, taste the ripen'd cherry,
The warm, firm apple, tipped with coral berry.
Then will I visit with a wandering kiss
The vale of lilies and the bower of bliss,
And where the beauteous region both divide
Into two milky ways, my lips shall slide   70
Down those smooth alleys, wearing as I go
A track for lovers on the printed snow.
Thence climbing o'er the swelling Apennine,
Retire into thy grove of eglantine,
Where I will all those ravish'd sweets distill
Through love's alembic, and with chemic skill
From the mixed mass one sovereign balm derive,
Then bring that great elixir to thy hive.
    Now in more subtle wreaths I will entwine
My sinewy thighs, my legs and arms with thine;   80
Thou like a sea of milk shalt lie displayed,
Whilst I the smooth, calm Océan invade
With such a tempest as when Jove of old

Fell down on Danae in a storm of gold.
Yet my tall pine shall in the Cyprian strait
Ride safe at anchor and unlade her freight;
My rudder, with thy bold hand, like a tried
And skillful pilot thou shalt steer, and guide
My bark into love's channel, where it shall
Dance as the bounding waves do rise or fall.   90
Then shall thy circling arms embrace and clip
My willing body, and thy balmy lip
Bathe me in juice of kisses, whose perfume
Like a religious incense shall consume
And send up holy vapors to those powers
That bless our loves, and crown our sportful hours,
That with such halcyon calmness fix our souls
In steadfast peace, as no affright controls.
There, no rude sounds shake us with sudden starts,
No jealous ears, when we unrip our hearts,   100
Suck our discourse in, no observing spies
This blush, that glance traduce; no envious eyes
Watch our close meetings, nor are we betrayed
To rivals, by the bribéd chamber-maid.
No wedlock bonds unwreathe our twisted loves;
We seek no midnight arbor, no dark groves
To hide our kisses; there, the hated name
Of husband, wife, lust, modest, chaste, or shame
Are vain and empty words, whose very sound
Was never heard in the Elysian ground.   110
All things are lawful there, that may delight
Nature or unrestrainéd appetite;
Like and enjoy, to will and act is one,
We only sin when Love's rites are not done.
    The Roman Lucrece there reads the divine
Lectures of love's great master, Aretine,
And knows as well as Laïs, how to move
Her pliant body in the act of love.
To quench the burning ravisher, she hurls
Her limbs into a thousand winding curls,   120
And studies artful postures, such as be
Carved on the bark of every neighboring tree
By learned hands, that so adorned the rind
Of those fair plants, which, as they lay entwined
Have fann'd their glowing fires. The Grecian dame
That in her endless web toil'd for a name

As fruitless as her work doth there display
Herself before the youth of Ithaca,
And th' amorous sport of gamesome nights prefer
Before dull dreams of the lost traveler.   130
Daphne hath broke her bark, and that swift foot
Which th' angry gods had fasten'd with a root
To the fix'd earth, doth now unfetter'd run
To meet th' embraces of the youthful sun:
She hangs upon him like his Delphic lyre,
Her kisses blow the old and breath new fire;
Full of her god, she sings inspired lays,
Sweet odes of love, such as deserve the bays
Which she herself was. Next her, Laura lies
In Petrarch's learnéd arms, drying those eyes   140
That did in such sweet smooth-paced numbers flow,
As made the world enamor'd of his woe.
These and ten thousand beauties more, that died
Slave to the tyrant, now enlarged, deride
His cancell'd laws, and for their time misspent
Pay into love's exchequer double rent.
    Come then, my Celia, we'll no more forbear
To taste our joys, struck with a panic fear,
But will depose from his imperious sway
This proud usurper and walk free as they,   150
With necks unyok'd; nor is it just that he
Should fetter your soft sex with chastity
Which nature made unapt for abstinence;
When yet this false impostor can dispense
With human justice and with sacred right,
And maugre both their laws, command me fight
With rivals or with emulous loves, that dare
Equal with thine their mistress' eyes or hair.
If thou complain of wrong, and call my sword
To carve out thy revenge, upon that word   160
He bids me fight and kill, or else he brands
With marks of infamy my coward hands.
And yet religion bids from bloodshed fly,
And damns me for that act. Then tell me why
This goblin Honor which the world adores
Should make men atheists, and not women whores.

Edmund Waller

(1606–1687)

When Waller was ten years old his father died, leaving him a sizable fortune. After study at Cambridge he gained a parliamentary seat at a young age and was married at age twenty-six. Only after his wife died in 1634 while giving birth to their second child did Waller turn his hand to poetry, especially public panegyrics, love poems, and complimentary verse. Waller's attempts at maintaining a centrist political position failed miserably during the heady political battles of the 1640s, and he was ultimately involved as a conspirator in the infamous Waller's Plot of 1643. Unlike the other conspirators, Waller connived to have his life spared, although he lost considerable honor in doing so. According to his former friend Clarendon, Waller "preserved and won his life from those who were most resolved to take it, and in an occasion in which he ought to have been ambitious to have lost it." After a period of exile in France, Waller returned to England and ingratiated himself first with Cromwell, then, upon the Restoration, with the ruling Stuarts. His reputation as a poet was unsurpassed at the time and would remain so for half a century after his death, when it plummeted drastically. Skilled at heroic couplets and a cool, smooth style, he was highly valued by Aubrey, Congreve, and Pope and even heralded as "the Father of our English Versification." As far as Dryden was concerned, "unless he had written, none of us could write."

TO A FAIR LADY
PLAYING WITH A SNAKE

Strange! that such horror and such grace
Should dwell together in one place;
A Fury's arm, an Angel's face!

'Tis innocence and youth which makes
In Chloris' fancy such mistakes,
To start at love, and play with snakes.

By this and by her coldness barr'd,
Her servants have a task too hard:
The tyrant has a double guard!

Thrice happy snake, that in her sleeve   10
May boldly creep; we dare not give
Our thoughts so unconfin'd a leave.

Contented in that nest of snow
He lies, as he his bliss did know,
And to the wood no more would go.

Take heed, fair Eve, you do not make
Another tempter of this snake:
A marble one, so warmed, would speak.

OF ENGLISH VERSE

Poets may boast, as safely vain,
Their works shall with the world remain:
Both bound together, live, or die,
The verses and the prophecy.

But who can hope his lines should long
Last in a daily-changing tongue?
While they are new, envy prevails;
And as that dies, our language fails.

When architects have done their part,
The matter may betray their art: 10
Time, if we use ill-chosen stone,
Soon brings a well-built palace down.

Poets that lasting marble seek,
Must carve in Latin or in Greek;
We write in sand, our language grows,
And like the tide, our work o'erflows.

Chaucer his sense can only boast;
The glory of his numbers lost;
Years have defaced his matchless strain;
And yet he did not sing in vain.   20

The beauties which adorned that age,
The shining subjects of his rage,

Hoping they should immortal prove,
Rewarded with success his love.

This was the gen'rous poet's scope;
And all an English pen can hope:
To make the fair approve his flame,
That can so far extend their fame.

Verse, thus design'd, has no ill fate,
If it arrive but at the date   30
Of fading beauty; if it prove
But as long-liv'd as present love.

GO LOVELY ROSE

Go lovely Rose,
Tell her that wastes her time and me,
That now she knows
When I resemble her to thee
How sweet and fair she seems to be.

Tell her that's young,
And shuns to have her graces spied
That hadst thou sprung
In deserts where no men abide,
Thou must have uncommended died.   10

Small is the worth
Of beauty from the light retired;
Bid her come forth,
Suffer herself to be desired,
And not blush so to be admired.

Then die that she
The common fate of all things rare
May read in thee
How small a part of time they share,
That are so wondrous sweet and fair.   20

John Milton

(1 6 0 8 – 1 6 7 4)

A Londoner, Milton was educated at St. Paul's School and then at Christ's College, Cambridge, where he began writing both sacred and secular poetry in Latin, Italian, and English (including "On Shakespeare"). After a period of private study at his father's house in the early 1630s, Milton completed "Lycidas" and a masque, "Comus." *Paradise Lost*, the long epic poem in blank verse for which he is best remembered, was probably begun in the early 1640s and finally published in 1667. During the intervening years, the social, political, and religious turmoil that enveloped England dominated Milton's life and work. This period saw the publication of many of Milton's polemical tracts, including ones on divorce, church government, freedom of the press, and republicanism. By 1652 Milton was totally blind, although he continued to write; he also served as Latin Secretary to the Council of State. After the restoration of the monarchy in 1660 Milton was arrested but subsequently freed; his release is usually attributed to Andrew Marvell. His later years saw the publication of *Paradise Regained* with *Samson Agonistes* (1671); a second edition of his *Poems* (first published in 1645) was printed in 1673. Milton's influence upon subsequent writers, especially Blake and the Romantic poets, has been profound.

ON THE LATE MASSACRE
IN PIEDMONT

Avenge O Lord thy slaughter'd saints, whose bones
    Lie scatter'd on the Alpine mountains cold,
    Ev'n them who kept thy truth so pure of old
    When all our fathers worship't stocks and stones,
Forget not: in thy book record their groans
    Who were thy sheep and in their ancient fold
    Slain by the bloody Piedmontese that roll'd
    Mother with infant down the rocks. Their moans
The vales redoubl'd to the hills, and they
    To Heav'n. Their martyr'd blood and ashes sow
    O'er all th'Italian fields where still doth sway
The triple tyrant: that from these may grow

A hundredfold, who having learnt thy way
Early may fly the Babylonian woe.

WHEN I CONSIDER HOW MY
LIGHT IS SPENT

When I consider how my light is spent,
 Ere half my days, in this dark world and wide,
 And that one talent which is death to hide,
 Lodg'd with me useless, though my soul more bent
To serve therewith my Maker, and present
 My true account, lest he returning chide;
 "Doth God exact day-labor, light denied,"
 I fondly ask; but patience to prevent
That murmur, soon replies, "God doth not need
 Either man's work or his own gifts; who best
 Bear his mild yoke, they serve him best; his state
Is kingly. Thousands at his bidding speed
 And post o'er land and ocean without rest:
 They also serve who only stand and wait."

METHOUGHT I SAW MY LATE
ESPOUSÈD SAINT

Methought I saw my late espousèd saint
 Brought to me like Alcestis from the grave,
 Whom Jove's great son to her glad husband gave,
 Rescu'd from death by force though pale and faint.
Mine as whom washt from spot of child-bed taint,
 Purification in the old Law did save,
 And such, as yet once more I trust to have
 Full sight of her in Heaven without restraint,
Came vested all in white, pure as her mind:
 Her face was veil'd, yet to my fancied sight,
 Love, sweetness, goodness, in her person shin'd
So clear, as in no face with more delight.
 But O, as to embrace me she inclin'd,
 I wak'd, she fled, and day brought back my night.

ON SHAKESPEARE

What needs my Shakespeare for his honor'd bones
The labor of an age in piled stones,
Or that his hallow'd relics should be hid
Under a star-ypointing pyramid?
Dear son of memory, great heir of fame,
What need'st thou such weak witness of thy name?
Thou in our wonder and astonishment
Hast built thyself a live-long monument.
For whilst to th'shame of slow-endeavoring art,
Thy easy numbers flow, and that each heart
Hath from the leaves of thy unvalu'd book
Those Delphic lines with deep impression took,
Then thou our fancy of itself bereaving,
Dost make us marble with too much conceiving;
And so sepulcher'd in such pomp dost lie,
That kings for such a tomb would wish to die.

LYCIDAS

Yet once more, O ye laurels, and once more
Ye myrtles brown, with ivy never sere,
I come to pluck your berries harsh and crude,
And with forc'd fingers rude,
Shatter your leaves before the mellowing year.
Bitter constraint, and sad occasion dear,
Compels me to disturb your season due:
For Lycidas is dead, dead ere his prime,
Young Lycidas, and hath not left his peer:
Who would not sing for Lycidas? he knew   10
Himself to sing, and build the lofty rhyme.
He must not float upon his wat'ry bier
Unwept, and welter to the parching wind,
Without the meed of some melodious tear.
  Begin then, Sisters of the sacred well,
That from beneath the seat of Jove doth spring,
Begin, and somewhat loudly sweep the string.
Hence with denial vain, and coy excuse,
So may some gentle Muse

With lucky words favor my destin'd urn, 20
And as he passes turn,
And bid fair peace be to my sable shroud.
For we were nurst upon the self-same hill,
Fed the same flock, by fountain, shade, and rill.
   Together both, ere the high lawns appear'd
Under the opening eyelids of the morn,
We drove afield, and both together heard
What time the gray-fly winds her sultry horn,
Batt'ning our flocks with the fresh dews of night,
Oft till the star that rose, at ev'ning, bright 30
Toward Heav'n's descent had slop'd his westering wheel.
Meanwhile the rural ditties were not mute,
Temper'd to th'oaten flute;
Rough satyrs danc'd, and fauns with clov'n heel
From the glad sound would not be absent long,
And old Damaetas lov'd to hear our song.
   But O the heavy change, now thou art gone,
Now thou art gone, and never must return!
Thee shepherd, thee the woods, and desert caves,
With wild thyme and the gadding vine o'ergrown, 40
And all their echoes mourn.
The willows and the hazel copses green
Shall now no more be seen,
Fanning their joyous leaves to thy soft lays.
As killing as the canker to the rose,
Or taint-worm to the weanling herds that graze,
Or frost to flowers, that their gay wardrobe wear,
When first the whitethorn blows;
Such, Lycidas, thy loss to shepherd's ear.
   Where were ye nymphs when the remorscless deep 50
Clos'd o'er the head of your lov'd Lycidas?
For neither were ye playing on the steep,
Where your old bards, the famous Druids, lie,
Nor on the shaggy top of Mona high,
Nor yet where Deva spreads her wizard stream:
Ay me, I fondly dream!
Had ye been there—for what could that have done?
What could the Muse herself that Orpheus bore,
The Muse herself, for her enchanting son
Whom universal nature did lament, 60
When by the rout that made the hideous roar,
His gory visage down the stream was sent,

Down the swift Hebrus to the Lesbian shore?
   Alas! What boots it with uncessant care
To tend the homely slighted shepherd's trade,
And strictly meditate the thankless Muse?
Were it not better done as others use,
To sport with Amaryllis in the shade,
Or with the tangles of Neaera's hair?
Fame is the spur that the clear spirit doth raise   70
(That last infirmity of noble mind)
To scorn delights, and live laborious days;
But the fair guerdon when we hope to find,
And think to burst out into sudden blaze,
Comes the blind Fury with th'abhorrèd shears,
And slits the thin-spun life. "But not the praise,"
Phoebus repli'd, and touch'd my trembling ears;
"Fame is no plant that grows on mortal soil,
Nor in the glistering foil
Set off to th'world, nor in broad rumor lies,   80
But lives and spreads aloft by those pure eyes
And perfect witness of all-judging Jove;
As he pronounces lastly on each deed,
Of so much fame in Heav'n expect thy meed."
   O fountain Arethuse, and thou honor'd flood,
Smooth-sliding Mincius; crown'd with vocal reeds,
That strain I heard was of a higher mood:
But now my oat proceeds,
And listens to the herald of the sea
That came in Neptune's plea.   90
He ask'd the waves, and ask'd the felon winds,
What hard mishap hath doom'd this gentle swain?
And question'd every gust of rugged wings
That blows from off each beaked promontory.
They knew not of his story,
And sage Hippotades their answer brings,
That not a blast was from his dungeon stray'd,
The air was calm, and on the level brine,
Sleek Panope with all her sisters play'd.
It was that fatal and perfidious bark   100
Built in th'eclipse, and rigg'd with curses dark,
That sunk so low that sacred head of thine.
   Next Camus, reverend sire, went footing slow,
His mantle hairy, and his bonnet sedge,
Inwrought with figures dim, and on the edge

Like to that sanguine flower inscrib'd with woe.
"Ah! Who hath reft" (quoth he) "my dearest pledge?"
Last came, and last did go,
The pilot of the Galilean lake.
Two massy keys he bore of metals twain   110
(The golden opes, the iron shuts amain).
He shook his mitred locks, and stern bespake:
"How well could I have spar'd for thee, young swain,
Enough of such as for their bellies' sake.
Creep and intrude and climb into the fold?
Of other care they little reck'ning make,
Than how to scramble at the shearers' feast,
And shove away the worthy bidden guest;
Blind mouths! that scarce themselves know how to hold
A sheep-hook, or have learn'd aught else the least   120
That to the faithful herdman's art belongs!
What recks it them? What need they? They are sped;
And when they list, their lean and flashy songs
Grate on their scrannel pipes of wretched straw.
The hungry sheep look up, and are not fed,
But swol'n with wind, and the rank mist they draw,
Rot inwardly, and foul contagion spread:
Besides what the grim wolf with privy paw
Daily devours apace, and nothing said;
But that two-handed engine at the door   130
Stands ready to smite once, and smite no more."
    Return Alpheus, the dread voice is past
That shrunk thy streams; return Sicilian Muse,
And call the vales, and bid them hither cast
Their bells and flowrets of a thousand hues.
Ye valleys low where the mild whispers use,
Of shades and wanton winds and gushing brooks,
On whose fresh lap the swart star sparely looks,
Throw hither all your quaint enamell'd eyes,
That on the green turf suck the honied showers,   140
And purple all the ground with vernal flowers.
Bring the rathe primrose that forsaken dies,
The tufted crow-toe, and pale jessamine,
The white pink, and the pansy freakt with jet,
The glowing violet,
The musk-rose, and the well-attir'd woodbine,
With cowslips wan that hang the pensive head,
And every flower that sad embroidery wears:

Bid amaranthus all his beauty shed,
And daffadillies fill their cups with tears,   150
To strew the laureate hearse where Lycid lies.
For so to interpose a little ease,
Let our frail thoughts dally with false surmise.
Ay me! Whilst thee the shores and sounding seas
Wash far away, where'er thy bones are hurl'd,
Whether beyond the stormy Hebrides,
Where thou perhaps under the whelming tide
Visit'st the bottom of the monstrous world;
Or whether thou to our moist vows denied,
Sleep'st by the fable of Bellerus old,   160
Where the great vision of the guarded mount
Looks toward Namancos and Bayona's hold;
Look homeward angel now, and melt with ruth:
And, O ye dolphins, waft the hapless youth.
   Weep no more, woeful shepherds weep no more,
For Lycidas your sorrow is not dead,
Sunk though he be beneath the wat'ry floor,
So sinks the day-star in the ocean bed,
And yet anon repairs his drooping head,
And tricks his beams, and with new-spangled ore,   170
Flames in the forehead of the morning sky:
So Lycidas, sunk low, but mounted high,
Through the dear might of him that walk'd the waves,
Where other groves, and other streams along,
With nectar pure his oozy locks he laves,
And hears the unexpressive nuptial song,
In the blest kingdoms meek of joy and love.
There entertain him all the saints above,
In solemn troops, and sweet societies
That sing, and singing in their glory move,   180
And wipe the tears for ever from his eyes.
Now Lycidas, the shepherds weep no more;
Henceforth thou art the genius of the shore,
In thy large recompense, and shalt be good
To all that wander in that perilous flood.
   Thus sang the uncouth swain to th'oaks and rills,
While the still morn went out with sandals gray;
He touch't the tender stops of various quills,
With eager thought warbling his Doric lay:
And now the sun had stretch't out all the hills,   190
And now was dropt into the western bay;

At last he rose, and twitch't his mantle blue:
Tomorrow to fresh woods, and pastures new.

l. 124. scrannel = meager, thin, harsh
l. 142. rathe = early blooming

Sir John Suckling

(1 6 0 9 – 1 6 4 1 ?)

Born into a prominent Norwich family, Suckling attended Trinity College, Cambridge, and, for a brief period, Gray's Inn at the Inns of Court, before going off to the Continent to fight in the Thirty Years War. According to John Aubrey, Suckling "was the greatest gallant of his time, and the greatest gamester." He is associated with the other "Cavalier" poets Thomas Carew, Richard Lovelace, and Edmund Waller. Suckling's verse, indebted to both Donne and Jonson, also mirrors the libertinism and cynicism that characterized his short life. In 1641 Suckling took part in the Army Plot, an unsuccessful attempt to free the Earl of Strafford, fled to France, and died there not long after. The two contemporary reports of his death—from an infected foot after a servant robbed him and drove a nail into his shoe to prevent the impetuous Suckling from pursuing him or, alternatively, from suicide after taking poison—remain unsubstantiated. His poetry, which circulated in manuscript during his lifetime, was posthumously collected in *Fragmenta Aurea* (1646) and *The Last Remains of Sir John Suckling* (1659).

UPON MY LADY CARLISLE'S WALKING IN HAMPTON COURT GARDEN

DIALOGUE
THOMAS CAREW/JOHN SUCKLING

T.C.

Didst thou not find the place inspir'd,
And flow'rs, as if they had desir'd
No other sun, start from their beds,
And for a sight steal out their heads?
Heardst thou not music when she talk'd?
And didst not find that as she walk'd
She threw rare perfumes all about
Such as bean-blossoms newly out,
Or chafed spices give?———

J . S .

I must confess those perfumes (Tom)   10
I did not smell; nor found that from
Her passing by, ought sprung up new:
The flow'rs had all their birth from you;
For I pass'd o'er the self same walk,
Nor could I find one single stalk
Of any thing that was to bring
This unknown after after-spring.

T . C .

Dull and insensible, could'st see
A thing so near a deity
Move up and down, and feel no change?   20

J . S .

None, and so great, were alike strange;
I had my thoughts, but not your way,
All are not born (Sir) to the bay;
Alas! Tom, I am flesh and blood,
And was consulting how I could
In spite of masks and hoods descry
The parts deni'd unto the eye;
I was undoing all she wore,
And had she walk'd but one turn more,
Eve in her first state had not been   30
More naked, or more plainly seen.

T . C .

'Twas well for thee she left the place,
For there's great danger in that face;
But had'st thou view'd her leg and thigh,
And upon that discovery
Press'd on to parts that are more dear,
(As fancy seldom stops so near)
No time or age had ever seen
A thing so lost as thou hadst been.

J.S.

'Troth in her face I could descry   40
No danger, no divinity.
But since the pillars were so good
On which the lovely fountain stood,
Being once come so near, I think
I should have ventur'd hard to drink.
What ever fool like me had been
If I'd not done as well as seen?
There to be lost why should I doubt,
Where fools with ease go in and out?

A SESSIONS OF THE POETS

A sessions was held the other day,
And Apollo himself was at it (they say);
The laurel that had been so long reserv'd,
Was now to be given to him best deserv'd.
                    And
Therefore the wits of the town came thither,
'Twas strange to see how they flocked together;
Each strongly confident of his own way,
Thought to carry the laurel away that day.

There was Selden, and he sat hard by the chair;
Wenman not far off, which was very fair;   10
Sandys with Townshend, for they kept no order;
Digby and Chillingworth a little further:
                    And
There was Lucan's translator too, and he
That makes God speak so big in's poetry;
Selwin and Waller, and Berkeleys both the brothers;
Jack Vaughan and Porter, with divers others.

The first that broke silence was good old Ben,
Prepar'd before with Canary wine,
And he told them plainly he deserv'd the bays,
For his were call'd Works, where others were but plays;   20
                    And
Bid them remember how he had purg'd the stage

Of errors, that had lasted many an age,
And he hop'd they did think *The Silent Woman*,
The Fox, and *The Alchemist* out done by no man.

Apollo stopp'd him there, and bid him not go on,
'Twas merit, he said, and not presumption
Must carry it; at which Ben turn'd about,
And in great choler offer'd to go out:
                    But
Those that were there thought it not fit
To discontent so ancient a wit;   30
And therefore Apollo call'd him back again,
And made him mine host of his own New Inn.

Tom Carew was next, but he had a fault
That would not well stand with a laureate;
His Muse was hard bound, and th'issue of's brain
Was seldom brought forth but with trouble and pain.
                    And
All that were present there did agree,
A laureate's Muse should be easy and free;
Yet sure 'twas not that, but 'twas thought that his grace
Consider'd he was well he had a cup-bearer's place.   40

Will Davenant asham'd of a foolish mischance
That he had got lately travelling in France,
Modestly hoped the handsomeness of's Muse
Might any deformity about him excuse.
                    And
Surely the company would have been content,
If they could have found any president;
But in all their records either in verse or prose,
There was not one laureate without a nose.

To Will Berkeley sure all the wits meant well,
But first they would see how his snow would sell: 50
Will smil'd and swore in their judgements they went less,
That concluded of merit upon success.
                    So
Sullenly taking his place again,
He gave way to Selwin, that straight stepp'd in;
But alas! he had been so lately a wit,
That Apollo himself hardly knew him yet.

Toby Mathew (pox on't! how came he there?)
Was busily whispering in somebody's ear,
When he had the honour to be nam'd i'the Court:
But Sir, you may thank my Lady Carlisle for't;   60
        For
Had not her character furnish'd you out
With something of handsome, without all doubt
You and your sorry Lady Muse had been
In the number of those that were not to come in.

In haste two or three from the Court came in,
And they brought letters (forsooth) from the Queen;
'Twas discreetly done too, for if they had come
Without them, they had scarce been let into the room.
        This
Made a dispute; for 'twas plain to be seen
Each man had a mind to gratify the Queen: 70
But Apollo himself could not think it fit;
There was difference, he said, 'twixt fooling and wit.

Suckling next was call'd, but did not appear,
And straight one whisper'd Apollo in's ear,
That of all men living he cared not for't,
He lov'd not the Muses so well as his sport;
        And
Prized black eyes, or a lucky hit
At bowls, above all the trophies of wit;
But Apollo was angry, and publicly said
'Twere fit that a fine were set on his head.   80

Wat Montagu now stood forth to his trial,
And did not so much as suspect a denial;
Wise Apollo then asked him first of all
If he understood his own pastoral.
        For
If he could do it, 'twould plainly appear
He understood more than any man there,
And did merit the bays above all the rest,
But the Mounsier was modest, and silence confess'd.

During these troubles, in the crowd was hid
One that Apollo soon miss'd, little Sid;   90

And having spied him, call'd him out of the throng,
And advis'd him in his ear not to write so strong.
                    Then
Murray was summon'd, but 'twas urg'd that he
Was chief already of another company.

Hales set by himself most gravely did smile
To see them about nothing keep such a coil;
Apollo had spied him, but knowing his mind
Past by, and call'd Falkland that sat just behind:
                    But
He was of late so gone with divinity,
That he had almost forgot his poetry,   100
Though to say the truth (and Apollo did know it)
He might have been both his priest and his poet.

At length who but an alderman did appear,
At which Will Davenant began to swear;
But wiser Apollo bid him draw nigher,
And when he was mounted a little higher
                    He
Openly declared that 'twas the best sign
Of good store of wit to have good store of coin,
And without a syllable more or less said,
He put the laurel on the alderman's head.   110

At this all the wits were in such a maze
That for a good while they did nothing but gaze
One upon another, not a man in the place
But had discontent writ in great in his face.
                    Only
The small poets clear'd up again,
Out of hope (as 'twas thought) of borrowing;
But sure they were out, for he forfeits his crown
When he lends any poet about the town.

Richard Crashaw

(1 6 1 2 / 1 3 – 1 6 4 9)

The son of a noted Anglican divine with Puritan sympathies, Crashaw was educated at the rigorous Charterhouse School and then at Cambridge, where he became the friend of Abraham Cowley. Sometime in the early 1640s he converted to Catholicism, perhaps under the influence of High Church and Catholic adherents at Cambridge, from which he was then expelled. Crashaw fled to Paris, where, thanks to Cowley's intervention, he was assisted by Queen Henrietta Maria, who secured him employment in Rome under Cardinal Palotta. He died of fever shortly thereafter, at the age of thirty-six. His *Steps to the Temple* (1646) self-consciously places itself in the tradition of George Herbert's earlier volume of religious poems, *The Temple* (1633). Crashaw's spiritual verse had strong affinities with both metaphysical and baroque styles and influenced many subsequent poets.

THE FLAMING HEART

UPON THE BOOK AND PICTURE OF THE
SERAPHICAL SAINT Teresa, (AS SHE IS
usually EXPRESSED WITH A Seraphim
BESIDE HER)

Well meaning readers! you that come as friends,
And catch the precious name this piece pretends;
Make not too much haste to'admire
That fair-cheek'd fallacy of fire.
That is a Seraphim, they say,
And this the great Teresia.
Readers, be rul'd by me; and make
Here a well-plac'd and wise mistake,
You must transpose the picture quite,
And spell it wrong to read it right;   10
Read *him* for *her*, and *her* for *him*;
And call the Saint the Seraphim.
　　　Painter, what did'st thou understand,
To put her dart into his hand!

See, even the years and size of him
Shows this the mother Seraphim.
This is the mistress-flame; and dutious he
Her happy fire-works, here, comes down to see.
O most poor-spirited of men!
Had thy cold pencil kiss'd her pen   20
Thou couldst not so unkindly err
To show us this faint shade for her.
Why man, this speaks pure mortal frame;
And mocks with female frost love's manly flame.
One would suspect thou mean'st to paint
Some weak, inferiour, woman saint.
But had thy pale-fac'd purple took
Fire from the burning cheeks of that bright book
Thou would'st on her have heap'd up all
That could be found seraphical;   30
What e'er this youth of fire wears fair,
Rosy fingers, radiant hair,
Glowing cheeks, and glist'ring wings,
All those fair and flagrant things,
But before all, that fiery dart
Had fill'd the hand of this great heart.
       Do then as equal right requires,
Since his the blushes be, and hers the fires,
Resume and rectify thy rude design;
Undress thy Seraphim into mine.   40
Redeem this injury of thy art;
Give him the veil, give her the dart.
       Give him the veil; that he may cover
The red cheeks of a rivall'd lover.
Asham'd that our world, now, can show
Nests of new Seraphims here below.
       Give her the dart for it is she
(Fair youth) shoots both thy shaft and thee.
Say, all ye wise and well-pierc'd hearts
That live and die amidst her darts,   50
What is't your tasteful spirits do prove
In that rare life of her, and love?
Say and bear witness. Sends she not
A Seraphim at every shot?
What magazines of immortal arms there shine!
Heav'ns great artillery in each love-spun line.
Give then the dart to her who gives the flame;

Give him the veil, who kindly takes the shame.
  But if it be the frequent fate
Of worst faults to be fortunate;   60
If all's prescription; and proud wrong
Hearkens not to an humble song;
For all the gallantry of him,
Give me the suff'ring Seraphim.
His be the bravery of all those bright things,
The glowing cheeks, the glist'ring wings;
The rosy hand, the radiant dart;
Leave her alone the flaming heart.
  Leave her that; and thou shalt leave her
Not one loose shaft but love's whole quiver. 70
For in love's field was never found
A nobler weapon than a wound.
Love's passives are his activ'st part.
The wounded is the wounding heart.
O heart! the equal poise of love's both parts,
Big alike with wounds and darts.
Live in these conquering leaves; live all the same;
And walk through all tongues one triumphant flame.
Live here, great heart; and love and die and kill;
And bleed and wound; and yield and conquer still. 80
Let this immortal life where'er it comes
Walk in a crowd of loves and martyrdoms.
Let mystic deaths wait on't; and wise souls be
The love-slain witnesses of this life of thee.
O sweet incendiary! show here thy art,
Upon this carcass of a hard, cold, heart;
Let all thy scatter'd shafts of light, that play
Among the leaves of thy large books of day,
Combin'd against this breast at once break in
And take away from me my self and sin, 90
This gracious robbery shall thy bounty be;
And my best fortunes such fair spoils of me.
O thou undaunted daughter of desires!
By all thy dower of lights and fires;
By all the eagle in thee, all the dove;
By all thy lives and deaths of love;
By thy large draughts of intellectual day,
And by thy thirsts of love more large than they;
By all thy brim-fill'd bowls of fierce desire

By thy last morning's draught of liquid fire;   100
By the full kingdom of that final kiss
That seiz'd thy parting soul, and seal'd thee his;
By all the heav'ns thou hast in him
(Fair sister of the Scraphim!)
By all of him we have in thee;
Leave nothing of my self in me.
Let me so read thy life, that I
Unto all life of mine may die.

ON MR. GEORGE HERBERT'S BOOK, *THE TEMPLE*

Know you fair, on what you look?
Divinest love lies in this book:
Expecting fire from your eyes,
To kindle this his sacrifice.
When your hands untie these strings,
Think you have an angel by th' wings.
One that gladly will be nigh,
To wait upon each morning sigh.
To flutter in the balmy air,
Of your well-perfumèd prayer.   10
These white plumes of his he'll lend you,
Which every day to heav'n will send you:
To take acquaintance of the sphere,
And all the smooth-fac'd kindred there.
    And though *Herbert*'s name do owe
    These devotions, fairest; know
    That while I lay them on the shrine
    Of your white hand, they are mine.

ON HOPE

By way of questions and answer,
between Abraham Crowley and
Richard Crashaw

COWLEY

Hope, whose weak being ruin'd is
Alike, if it succeed, and if it miss.
Whom ill and good doth equally confound,
And both the horns of fates dilemma wound.
   Vain shadow! that doth vanish quite
   Both at full noon, and perfect night.
   The fates have not a possibility
     Of blessing thee.
If things then from their ends we happy call,
'Tis hope is the most hopeless thing of all.   10

CRASHAW

Dear Hope! Earth's dowry, and Heav'n's debt,
The entity of things that are not yet.
Subt'lest, but surest being! Thou by whom
Our nothing hath a definition.
   Fair cloud of fire, both shade, and light,
   Our life in death, our day in night.
   Fates cannot find out a capacity
     Of hurting thee.
From thee their thin dilemma with blunt horn
Shrinks, like the sick Moon at the wholesome morn.   20

COWLEY

Hope, thou bold taster of delight,
Who, instead of doing so, devour'st it quite
Thou bring'st us an estate, yet leav'st us poor,
By clogging it with legacies before.
   The joys, which we entire should wed,
   Come deflower'd virgins to our bed.
   Good fortunes without gain imported be,
     So mighty custom's paid to thee.

For joy, like wine kept close, doth better taste:
If it take air before, its spirits waste.   30

CRASHAW

Thou art love's legacy under lock
Of faith: the steward of our growing stock.
Our crown-lands lie above, yet each meal brings
A seemly portion for the sons of kings.
    Nor will the virgin-joys we wed
    Come less unbroken to our bed,
      Because that from the bridal cheek of bliss,
        Thou thus steal'st down a distant kiss,
Hope's chaste kiss wrongs no more joy's maidenhead,
Than spousal rites prejudge the marriage-bed.   40

CRASHAW

Fair Hope! our earlier Heav'n! by thee
Young time is taster to eternity.
Thy gen'rous wine with age grows strong, not sour;
Nor need we kill thy fruit to smell thy flower.
    Thy golden head ne'er hangs down,
    Till in the lap of love's full noon
    It falls, and dies: oh no, it melts away
      As doth the dawn into the day:
As lumps of sugar lose themselves, and twine
Their subtle essence with the soul of wine.   50

COWLEY

Hope, fortune's cheating lottery,
Where for one prize an hundred blanks there be.
Fond archer Hope, who tak'st thine aim so far,
That still, or short, or wide thine arrows are.
    Thin empty cloud, which th'eye deceives
    With shapes that our own fancie gives:
    A cloud, which gilt, and painted now appears,
      But must drop presently in tears.
When thy false beams o'er reason's light prevail,
By *ignes fatui*, not North Stars we sail.   60

CRASHAW

Fortune? alas, above the world's low wars
Hope kicks the curl'd heads of conspiring stars.
Her keel cuts not the waves, where our winds stir,
And fate's whole lottery is one blank to her.
   Her shafts and she fly far above,
   And forage in the fields of light, and love.
   Sweet Hope! kind cheat! fair fallacy! by thee
     We are not where, or what we be,
But what, and where we would be: thus art thou
Our absent presence, and our future now.   70

COWLEY

Brother of fear! more gaily clad
The merrier fool o'th' two, yet quite as mad.
Sire of repentance! Child of fond desire,
That blows the chemic's, and the lover's fire,
   Still leading them insensibly on,
   With the strange witchcraft of anon.
   By thee the one doth changing nature through
     Her endless labyrinths pursue,
And th'other chases woman, while she goes
More ways, and turns, than hunted nature knows.   80

CRASHAW

Faith's sister! Nurse of fair desire!
Fear's antidote! A wise, and well stay'd fire
Temper'd 'twixt cold despair and torrid joy:
Queen Regent in young love's minority.
   Though the vex'd chemic vainly chases
   His fugitive gold through all her faces,
   And love's more fierce, more fruitless fires assay
     One face more fugitive than all they,
True Hope's a glorious huntress, and her chase
The god of nature in the field of grace.   90

Samuel Butler

(1613–1680)

Born near Worcester, where he attended the King's School until the age of fifteen, Butler spent the next thirty years in service as clerk, secretary, and steward in various aristocratic households; he may have had some legal training as well. He took up painting and also provided translations for the noted antiquarian and legal scholar John Selden. Butler's literary career probably began in the late 1650s as a Royalist pamphleteer. He composed some satiric ballads at this time as well. But his great work, and that for which he is best remembered, is the mock-epic *Hudibras* (1662–1663), published shortly after the Restoration and the source for all subsequent hudibrastic verse. Loosely modeled on Cervantes' *Don Quixote*, the poem was an instant success and went through nine editions (four of them pirated) within a year of its publication. With its satirical attacks on misguided pedants and hypocritical Puritans, *Hudibras* was a particular favorite of King Charles II. Butler's final years were spent in bitterness and poverty.

From HUDIBRAS

From CANTO I

When civil dudgeon first grew high,
And men fell out they knew not why;
When hard words, jealousies and fears
Set folks together by the ears,
And made them fight, like mad or drunk,
For dame religion, as for punk,
Whose honesty they all durst swear for,
Tho' not a man of them knew wherefore:
When gospel trumpeter, surrounded
With long-ear'd rout, to battle sounded;   10
And pulpit, drum ecclesiastic,
Was beat with fist, instead of a stick;
Then did Sir Knight abandon dwelling,
And out he rode a-colonelling.
A wight he was, whose very sight would

Entitle him *Mirrour of Knighthood*;
That never bow'd his stubborn knee
To any thing but chivalry;
Nor put up blow, but that which laid
"Right worshipful" on shoulder-blade: 20
Chief of domestic knights, and errant,
Either for chartel, or for warrant;
Great on the bench, great in the saddle,
That could as well bind o'er, as swaddle;
Mighty he was at both of these,
And styl'd of war as well as peace.
(So some rats of amphibious nature,
Are either for the land or water.)
But here our authors make a doubt,
Whether he were more wise or stout.   30
Some hold the one, and some the other;
But howsoe'er they make a pother,
The diff'rence was so small, his brain
Outweigh'd his rage but half a grain;
Which made some take him for a tool
That knaves do work with, call'd a fool.
For't has been held by many, that
As Montaigne, playing with his cat,
Complains she thought him but an ass,
Much more she would Sir Hudibras;   40
(For that's the name our valiant Knight
To all his challenges did write.)
But they're mistaken very much,
'Tis plain enough he was no such;
We grant, although he had much wit,
H'was very shy of using it;
As being loath to wear it out,
And therefore bore it not about;
Unless on holy-days, or so,
As men their best apparel do.   50
Beside, 'tis known he could speak Greek
As naturally as pigs squeak:
That Latin was no more difficile,
'Than to a blackbird 'tis to whistle:
Being rich in both he never scanted
His bounty unto such as wanted;
But much of either would afford
To many, that had not one word.

For Hebrew roots, although they're found
To flourish most in barren ground,   60
He had such plenty, as suffic'd
To make some think him circumcis'd:
And truly so he was, perhaps,
Not as a proselyte, but for claps.
He was in logic a great critic,
Profoundly skill'd in analytic;
He could distinguish, and divide
A hair 'twixt south and south-west side;
On either which he would dispute,
Confute, change hands, and still confute.   70
He'd undertake to prove by force
Of argument a man's no horse;
He'd prove a buzzard is no fowl,
And that a lord may be an owl;
A calf an alderman, a goose a justice,
And rooks committee-men and trustees.
He'd run in debt by disputation,
And pay with ratiocination.
All this by syllogism, true
In mood and figure, he would do.   80
For rhetoric, he could not ope
His mouth, but out there flew a trope;
And when he happen'd to break off
I'th' middle of his speech, or cough,
H' had hard words ready to show why,
And tell what rules he did it by:
Else when with greatest art he spoke,
You'd think he talk'd like other folk.
For all a rhetorician's rules
Teach nothing but to name his tools.   90
But, when he pleas'd to show't, his speech
In loftiness of sound was rich;
A Babylonish dialect,
Which learned pedants much affect;
It was a party-color'd dress
Of patch'd and pye-ball'd languages:
'Twas English cut on Greek and Latin,
Like fustian heretofore on satin.
It had an odd promiscuous tone,
As if h' had talk'd three parts in one;   100
Which made some think, when he did gabble,

Th' had heard three labourers of Babel;
Or Cerberus himself pronounce
A leash of languages at once.
This he as volubly would vent
As if his stock would ne'er be spent;
And truly, to support that charge,
He had supplies as vast and large:
For he could coin or counterfeit
New words, with little or no wit;   110
Words so debas'd and hard, no stone
Was hard enough to touch them on:
And when with hasty noise he spoke 'em,
The ignorant for current took 'em;
That had the orator, who once
Did fill his mouth with pebble stones
When he harangu'd, but known his phrase,
He would have us'd no other ways.
In mathematics he was greater
Than Tycho Brahe, or Erra Pater: 120
For he, by geometric scale,
Could take the size of pots of ale;
Resolve by sines and tangents, straight,
If bread or butter wanted weight;
And wisely tell what hour o' th' day
The clock does strike, by algebra.
Beside, he was a shrewd philosopher,
And had read ev'ry text and gloss over;
Whate'er the crabbed'st author hath,
He understood b' implicit faith: 130
Whatever sceptic could inquire for,
For ev'ry why he had a wherefore:
Knew more than forty of them do,
As far as words and terms could go.
All which he understood by rote,
And, as occasion serv'd, would quote;
No matter whether right or wrong,
They might be either said or Sung.
His notions fitted things so well,
That which was which he could not tell;   140
But oftentimes mistook the one
For th' other, as great clerks have done.
He could reduce all things to acts,
And knew their natures by abstracts;

Where entity and quiddity,
The ghosts of defunct bodies, fly;
Where truth in person does appear,
Like words congeal'd in northern air.
He knew *what's what*, and that's as high
As metaphysic wit can fly.   150
In school-divinity as able
As he that hight *Irrefragable*;
A second Thomas, or at once
To name them all, another dunce:
Profound in all the nominal
And real ways beyond them all;
For he a rope of sand could twist
As tough as learned Sorbonist;
And weave fine cobwebs, fit for skull
That's empty when the moon is full;   160
Such as take lodgings in a head
That's to be let unfurnished.
He could raise scruples dark and nice,
And after solve 'em in a trice,
As if divinity had catch'd
The itch, on purpose to be scratch'd;
Or, like a mountebank, did wound
And stab herself with doubts profound,
Only to show with how small pain
The sores of faith are cur'd again;   170
Although by woeful proof we find,
They always leave a scar behind.
He knew the seat of Paradise,
Could tell in what degree it lies:
And, as he was disposed, could prove it,
Below the moon, or else above it.
What Adam dreamt of, when his bride
Came from her closet in his side:
Whether the Devil tempted her
By a *High Dutch* interpreter: 180
If either of them had a navel:
Who first made music malleable:
Whether the serpent, at the fall,
Had cloven feet, or none at all.
All this, without a gloss or comment,
He could unriddle in a moment,
In proper terms, such as men smatter,

When they throw out and miss the matter.
   For his religion it was fit
To match his learning and his wit: 190
'Twas Presbyterian true blue,
For he was of that stubborn crew
Of errant saints, whom all men grant
To be the true church militant;
Such as do build their faith upon
The holy text of pike and gun;
Decide all controversies by
Infallible artillery;
And prove their doctrine orthodox
By apostolic blows and knocks;   200
Call fire, and sword, and desolation,
A *godly thorough Reformation*,
Which always must be carried on,
And still be doing, never done;
As if religion were intended
For nothing else but to be mended.
A sect whose chief devotion lies
In odd perverse antipathies:
In falling out with that or this,
And finding somewhat still amiss;   210
More peevish, cross, and splenetic,
Than dog distract, or monkey sick.
That with more care keep holy-day
The wrong, than others the right way;
Compound for sins they are inclined to,
By damning those they have no mind to.
Still so perverse and opposite,
As if they worship'd God for spite.
The self-same thing they will abhor
One way, and long another for.   220
Free-will they one way disavow,
Another, nothing else allow.
All piety consists therein
In them, in other men all sin.
Rather than fail, they will defy
That which they love most tenderly;
Quarrel with minc'd-pies, and disparage
Their best and dearest friend, plum-porridge;
Fat pig and goose itself oppose,
And blaspheme custard through the nose.   230

Th' apostles of this fierce religion,
Like Mahomet's, were ass and widgeon.
To whom our Knight, by fast instinct
Of wit and temper, was so linkt,
As if hypocrisy and nonsense
Had got th' advowson of his conscience.
   Thus was he gifted and accouter'd,—
We mean on th' inside, not the outward,
That next of all we shall discuss;
Then listen, Sirs, it follows thus: 240
His tawny beard was th' equal grace
Both of his wisdom and his face;
In cut and dye so like a tile,
A sudden view it would beguile;
The upper part thereof was whey,
The nether, orange mixed with grey.
This hairy meteor did denounce
The fall of sceptres and of crowns;
With grisly type did represent
Declining age of government,   250
And tell with hieroglyphic spade,
Its own grave and the state's were made.
Like Sampson's heart-breakers, it grew
In time to make a nation rue;
Though it contributed its own fall,
To wait upon the public downfall.
It was monastic, and did grow
In holy orders by strict vow:
Of rule as sullen and severe,
As that of rigid Cordeliere;   260
'Twas bound to suffer persecution,
And martyrdom with resolution;
T' oppose itself against the hate
And vengeance of th' incensed state;
In whose defiance it was worn,
Still ready to be pull'd and torn,
With red-hot irons to be tortur'd,
Revil'd, and spit upon, and martyr'd.
Maugre all which, 'twas to stand fast,
As long as monarchy should last;   270
But when the state should hap to reel,
'Twas to submit to fatal steel,
And fall, as it was consecrate,

A sacrifice to fall of state;
Whose thread of life the fatal sisters
Did twist together with its whiskers,
And twine so close, that time should never,
In life or death, their fortunes sever;
But with his rusty sickle mow
Both down together at a blow.   280

l. 152. hight = is called, bears the name

John Denham

(1615 – 1669)

Born in Dublin and educated at Trinity College, Oxford, Denham inherited his father's ancestral estates in Surrey in 1639. A Royalist, his fortunes declined with the outbreak of the Civil War, and he fled England and lived on the Continent from 1648 to 1653. Denham's fortunes turned again with the Restoration, when he was appointed surveyor general by Charles II. In 1665 he married Margaret Brooke, who was less than half his age, and who soon became mistress to the future King James II. This turn of events may have precipitated Denham's brief bout of madness, during which he confronted the King and claimed that he was the Holy Ghost. Denham's most famous poem, and the one upon which his reputation rests, is "Cooper's Hill," published in 1642 and again in 1655, although with extensive revisions that dulled the poem's polemical edge. "Cooper's Hill" exercised an important influence on such eighteenth-century descriptive poems as John Dyer's *Grongar Hill* and Pope's *Windsor Forest*. Pope called Denham "majestic," and Samuel Johnson praised Denham as a poet who "improved our taste and advanced our language." One of Denham's final literary projects was completing Katherine Philips's unfinished translation of Corneille's *Horace*. Denham's *Poems and Translations* remained popular long after his death and was reprinted more than twenty times by the mid-nineteenth century. Since then, his reputation has faded considerably.

COOPER'S HILL

    Sure there are poets which did never dream
Upon Parnassus, nor did taste the stream
Of Helicon, we therefore may suppose
Those made not poets, but the poets those.
And as courts make not kings, but kings the court,
So where the Muses and their train resort,
Parnassus stands; if I can be to thee
A poet, thou Parnassus art to me.
Nor wonder, if (advantag'd in my flight,
By taking wing from thy auspicious height)   10
Through untrac'd ways, and aery paths I fly,
More boundless in my fancy than my eye:

My eye, which swift as thought contracts the space
That lies between, and first salutes the place
Crown'd with that sacred pile, so vast, so high,
That whether 'tis a part of Earth, or sky,
Uncertain seems, and may be thought a proud
Aspiring mountain, or descending cloud,
Paul's, the late theme of such a Muse whose flight
Has bravely reach'd and soar'd above thy height: 20
Now shalt thou stand though sword, or time, or fire,
Or zeal more fierce than they, thy fall conspire,
Secure, whilst thee the best of poets sings,
Preserv'd from ruin by the best of kings.
Under his proud survey the city lies,
And like a mist beneath a hill doth rise;
Whose state and wealth the business and the crowd,
Seems at this distance but a darker cloud:
And is to him who rightly things esteems,
No other in effect than what it seems: 30
Where, with like haste, though several ways, they run
Some to undo, and some to be undone;
While luxury, and wealth, like war and peace,
Are each the others ruin, and increase;
As rivers lost in seas some secret vein
Thence reconveys, there to be lost again.
Oh happiness of sweet retir'd content!
To be at once secure, and innocent.
Windsor the next (where Mars with Venus dwells,
Beauty with strength) above the valley swells   40
Into my eye, and doth it self present
With such an easy and unforc'd ascent,
That no stupendious precipice denies
Access, no horror turns away our eyes:
But such a rise, as doth at once invite
A pleasure, and a reverence from the sight.
Thy mighty master's emblem, in whose face
Sat meekness, heighten'd with majestic grace
Such seems thy gentle height, made only proud
To be the basis of that pompous load,   50
Than which, a nobler weight no mountain bears,
But Atlas only that supports the spheres.
When Nature's hand this ground did thus advance,
'Twas guided by a wiser power than chance;
Mark'd out for such a use, as if 'twere meant

T' invite the builder, and his choice prevent.
Nor can we call it choice, when what we choose,
Folly, or blindness only could refuse.
A crown of such majestic tow'rs doth grace
The gods' great mother, when her heavenly race   60
Do homage to her, yet she cannot boast
Amongst that numerous, and celestial host,
More heroes than can Windsor, nor doth Fame's
Immortal book record more noble names.
Not to look back so far, to whom this Isle
Owes the first glory of so brave a pile,
Whether to Caesar, Albanact, or Brute,
The British Arthur, or the Danish Knute,
(Though this of old no less contest did move,
Then when for Homer's birth seven cities strove)   70
(Like him in birth, thou should'st be like in fame,
As thine his fate, if mine had been his flame)
But whosoere it was, Nature design'd
First a brave place, and then as brave a mind.
Not to recount those several kings, to whom
It gave a cradle, or to whom a tomb,
But thee (great Edward) and thy greater son,
(The lillies which his father wore, he won)
And thy Bellona, who the consort came
Not only to thy bed, but to thy fame,   80
She to thy triumph led one captive king,
And brought that son, which did the second bring.
Then didst thou found that order (whither love
Or victory thy royal thoughts did move)
Each was a noble cause, and nothing less,
Than the design, has been the great success:
Which foreign kings, and emperors esteem
The second honour to their diadem.
Had thy great destiny but given thee skill
To know, as well as power to act her will,   90
That from those kings, who then thy captives were,
In after-times should spring a royal pair
Who should possess all that thy mighty power,
Or thy desires more mighty, did devour;
To whom their better fate reserves what e're
The victor hopes for, or the vanquish'd fear;
That blood, which thou and thy great grandsire shed,
And all that since these sister nations bled,

Had been unspilt, had happy Edward known
That all the blood he spilt, had been his own.   100
When he that patron chose, in whom are join'd
Soldier and martyr, and his arms confin'd
Within the azure circle, he did seem
But to foretell, and prophesy of him,
Who to his realms that azure round hath joyn'd,
Which Nature for their bound at first design'd.
That bound, which to the world's extremest ends,
Endless it self, its liquid arms extends;
Nor doth he need those emblems which we paint,
But is himself the soldier and the saint.   110
Here should my wonder dwell, and here my praise,
But my fix'd thoughts my wand'ring eye betrays,
Viewing a neighbouring hill, whose top of late
A chapel crown'd, till in the common fate,
The adjoining Abbey fell: (may no such storm
Fall on our times, where ruin must reform.)
Tell me (my Muse) what monstrous dire offence,
What crime could any Christian king incense
To such a rage? Was't luxury, or lust?
Was he so temperate, so chast, so just?   120
Were these their crimes? They were his own much more:
But wealth is crime enough to him that's poor,
Who having spent the treasures of his crown,
Condemns their luxury to feed his own.
And yet this act, to varnish o're the shame
Of sacrilege, must bear devotion's name.
No crime so bold, but would be understood
A real, or at least a seeming good.
Who fears not to do ill, yet fears the name,
And free from conscience, is a slave to fame.   130
Thus he the Church at once protects, and spoils:
But princes' swords arc sharper than their stiles.
And thus to th'ages past he makes amends,
Their charity destroys, their faith defends.
Then did Religion in a lazy cell,
In empty, airy contemplations dwell;
And like the block, unmoved lay: but ours,
As much too active, like the stork devours.
Is there no temperate region can be known,
Betwixt their Frigid, and our Torrid Zone?   140
Could we not wake from that lethargic dream,

But to be restless in a worse extreme?
And for that lethargy was there no cure,
But to be cast into a calenture?
Can knowledge have no bound, but must advance
So far, to make us wish for ignorance?
And rather in the dark to grope our way,
Than led by a false guide to err by day?
Who sees these dismal heaps, but would demand
What barbarous Invader sack'd the land?   150
But when he hears, no Goth, no Turk did bring
This desolation, but a Christian king;
When nothing, but the name of zeal, appears
'Twixt our best actions and the worst of theirs,
What does he think our sacrilege would spare,
When such th'effects of our devotions are?
Parting from thence 'twixt anger, shame, and fear,
Those for what's past, and this for what's too near:
My eye descending from the hill, surveys
Where Thames amongst the wanton valleys strays.   160
Thames, the most lov'd of all the Ocean's sons,
By his old sire to his embraces runs,
Hasting to pay his tribute to the sea,
Like mortal life to meet eternity.
Though with those streams he no resemblance hold,
Whose foam is amber, and their gravel gold;
His genuine, and less guilty wealth t' explore,
Search not his bottom, but survey his shore;
O'er which he kindly spreads his spacious wing,
And hatches plenty for th'ensuing Spring.   170
Nor then destroys it with too fond a stay,
Like mothers which their infants overlay.
Nor with a sudden and impetuous wave,
Like profuse kings, resumes the wealth he gave.
No unexpected inundations spoil
The mowers hopes, nor mock the plowmans toil:
But god-like his unwearied bounty flows;
First loves to do, then loves the good he does.
Nor are his blessings to his banks confin'd,
But free, and common, as the sea or wind;   180
When he to boast, or to disperse his stores
Full of the tributes of his grateful shores,
Visits the world, and in his flying towers
Brings home to us, and makes both Indies ours;

Finds wealth where 'tis, bestows it where it wants
Cities in deserts, woods in cities plants.
So that to us no thing, no place is strange,
While his fair bosom is the world's exchange.
O could I flow like thee, and make thy stream
My great example, as it is my theme!   190
Though deep, yet clear, though gentle, yet not dull,
Strong without rage, without o'er-flowing full.
Heaven her Eridanus no more shall boast,
Whose fame in thine, like lesser currents lost,
Thy nobler streams shall visit Jove's abodes,
To shine amongst the stars, and bathe the gods.
Here Nature, whether more intent to please
Us or herself, with strange varieties,
(For things of wonder give no less delight
To the wise maker's, than beholder's sight.   200
Though these delights from several causes move
For so our children, thus our friends we love)
Wisely she knew, the harmony of things,
As well as that of sounds, from discords springs.
Such was the discord, which did first disperse
Form, order, beauty through the universe;
While dryness moisture, coldness heat resists,
All that we have, and that we are, subsists.
While the steep horrid roughness of the wood
Strives with the gentle calmness of the flood.   210
Such huge extremes when Nature doth unite,
Wonder from thence results, from thence delight.
The stream is so transparent, pure, and clear,
That had the self-enamour'd youth gaz'd here,
So fatally deceiv'd he had not been,
While he the bottom, not his face had seen.
But his proud head the aery mountain hides
Among the clouds; his shoulders, and his sides
A shady mantle clothes; his curled brows
Frown on the gentle stream, which calmly flows,   220
While winds and storms his lofty forehead beat:
The common fate of all that's high or great.
Low at his foot a spacious plain is plac'd,
Between the mountain and the stream embrac'd;
Which shade and shelter from the hill derives,
While the kind river wealth and beauty gives;
And in the mixture of all these appears

Variety, which all the rest endears.
This scene had some bold greek, or British bard
Beheld of old, what stories had we heard,   230
Of fairies, satyrs, and the nymphs their dames,
Their feasts, their revels, and their amorous flames:
'Tis still the same, although their aery shape
All but a quick poetic sight escape.
There Faunus and Sylvanus keep their courts,
And thither all the horned host resorts,
To graze the ranker mead, that noble herd
On whose sublime and shady fronts is rear'd
Nature's great masterpiece; to show how soon
Great things are made, but sooner are undone.   240
Here have I seen the King, when great affairs
Give leave to slacken, and unbend his cares,
Attended to the chase by all the flower
Of youth, whose hopes a nobler prey devour:
Pleasure with praise, and danger, they would buy,
And wish a foe that would not only fly.
The stag now conscious of his fatal growth,
At once indulgent to his fear and sloth,
To some dark covert his retreat had made,
Where no man's eye, nor heaven's should invade   250
His soft repose; when th'unexpected sound
Of dogs, and men, his wakeful ear doth wound.
Rous'd with the noise, he scarce believes his ear,
Willing to think th'illusions of his fear
Had given this false alarm, but straight his view
Confirms, that more than all he fears is true.
Betray'd in all his strengths, the wood beset,
All instruments, all arts of ruin met;
He calls to mind his strength, and then his speed,
His winged heels, and then his armèd head;   260
With these t' avoid, with that his fate to meet:
But fear prevails, and bids him trust his feet.
So fast he flies, that his reviewing eye
Has lost the chasers, and his ear the cry;
Exulting, till he finds, their nobler sense
Their disproportion'd speed does recompense.
Then curses his conspiring feet, whose scent
Betrays that safety which their swiftness lent.
Then tries his friends, among the baser herd,
Where he so lately was obey'd, and fear'd,   270

His safety seeks: the herd, unkindly wise,
Or chases him from thence, or from him flies.
Like a declining statesman, left forlorn
To his friends' pity, and pursuers' scorn,
With shame remembers, while himself was one
Of the same herd, himself the same had done.
Thence to the coverts, and the conscious groves,
The scenes of his past triumphs, and his loves;
Sadly surveying where he rang'd alone
Prince of the soil, and all the herd his own;   280
And like a bold knight errant did proclaim
Combat to all, and bore away the dame;
And taught the woods to echo to the stream
His dreadful challenge, and his clashing beam.
Yet faintly now declines the fatal strife;
So much his love was dearer than his life.
Now every leaf, and every moving breath
Presents a foe, and every foe a death.
Wearied, forsaken, and pursu'd, at last
All safety in despair of safety plac'd,   290
Courage he thence resumes, resolv'd to bear
All their assaults, since 'tis in vain to fear.
And now too late he wishes for the fight
That strength he wasted in ignoble flight:
But when he sees the eager chase renew'd,
Himself by dogs, the dogs by men pursu'd;
He straight revokes his bold resolve, and more
Repents his courage, than his fear before;
Finds that uncertain ways unsafest are,
And doubt a greater mischief than despair.   300
Then to the stream, when neither friends, nor force,
Nor speed, nor art avail, he shapes his course;
Thinks not their rage so desperate t'assay
An element more merciless than they.
But fearless they pursue, nor can the flood
Quench their dire thirst; alas, they thirst for blood.
So towards a ship the oar-finn'd galleys ply,
Which wanting sea to ride, or wind to fly,
Stands but to fall reveng'd on those that dare
Tempt the last fury of extreme despair.   310
So fares the stag among th'enraged hounds,
Repels their force, and wounds returns for wounds.

And as a hero, whom his baser foes
In troops surround, now these assails, now those,
Though prodigal of life, disdains to die
By common hands; but if he can descry
Some nobler foes approach, to him he calls,
And begs his fate, and then contented falls.
So when the King a mortal shaft lets fly
From his unerring hand, then glad to die,   320
Proud of the wound, to it resigns his blood,
And stains the crystal with a purple flood.
This a more innocent, and happy chase,
Than when of old, but in the self-same place,
Fair liberty pursu'd, and meant a prey
To lawless power, here turn'd, and stood at bay.
When in that remedy all hope was plac'd
Which was, or should have been at least, the last.
Here was the charter seal'd, wherein the crown
All marks of arbitrary power lays down: 330
Tyrant and slave, those names of hate and fear,
The happier style of king and subject bear:
Happy, when both to the same center move,
When kings give liberty, and subjects love.
Therefore not long in force this charter stood;
Wanting that seal, it must be seal'd in blood.
The subjects arm'd, the more their princes gave,
Th'advantage only took the more to crave.
Till kings by giving, give themselves away,
And even that power, that should deny, betray.   340
Who gives constrain'd, but his own fear reviles
Not thank'd, but scorn'd; nor are they gifts, but spoils.
Thus kings, by grasping more than they could hold,
First made their subjects by oppression bold:
And popular sway, by forcing kings to give
More than was fit for subjects to receive,
Ran to the same extremes; and one excess
Made both, by striving to be greater, less.
When a calm river rais'd with sudden rains,
Or snows dissolv'd, o'erflows th'adjoining plains,   350
The husbandmen with high-rais'd banks secure
Their greedy hopes, and this he can endure.
But if with bays and dams they strive to force
His channel to a new, or narrow course;

No longer then within his banks he dwells,
First to a torrent, then a deluge swells:
Stronger, and fiercer by restraint he roars,
And knows no bound, but makes his power his shores.

Richard Lovelace

(1618–1657)

Educated at the Charterhouse School in London and then at Oxford, Lovelace entered royal service at the age of fifteen. He was devoted to the Royalist cause, fought for it, and was imprisoned by Parliament in 1642 and again in 1648 for his service to King Charles I. Poems like "To Lucasta, Going to the Wars" speak directly to his political idealism and loyalty. Shortly after his second imprisonment, Lovelace published his first volume of poetry, *Lucasta* (1649). On the losing side in the Civil War, Lovelace spent his final decade in financial straits. He died before the age of forty. Three years later a second volume of his verse, *Lucasta: Posthume Poems*, was published. The two volumes of poetry reveal a talented lyricist, skilled in writing about both love and war and possessed of the "careless ease" that befitted the role of gentleman poet.

TO LUCASTA, GOING
TO THE WARS

Tell me not (Sweet) I am unkind,
That from the nunnery
Of thy chaste breast and quiet mind,
To war and arms I fly.

True; a new mistress now I chase,
The first foe in the field;
And with a stronger faith embrace
A sword, a horse, a shield.

Yet this inconstancy is such,
As you too shall adore;   10
I could not love thee (Dear) so much,
Lov'd I not honour more.

THE GRASSHOPPER

Oh, thou that swing'st upon the waving hair
   Of some well-filled oaten beard,
Drunk every night with a delicious tear
   Dropped thee from Heav'n, where now th' art reared,

The joys of earth and air are thine entire,
   That with thy feet and wings dost hop and fly;
And when thy poppy works thou dost retire
   To thy carv'd acorn-bed to lie.

Up with the day, the sun thou welcom'st then,
   Sport'st in the gilt-plats of his beams,   10
And all these merry days mak'st merry men,
   Thyself, and melancholy streams.

But ah, the sickle! golden ears are cropped,
   Ceres and Bacchus bid goodnight;
Sharp frosty fingers all your flow'rs have topped,
   And what scythes spared, winds shave off quite.

Poor verdant fool! and now green ice! thy joys
   Large and as lasting as thy perch of grass,
Bid us lay in 'gainst winter rain, and poise
   Their floods with an o'erflowing glass.   20

Thou best of men and friends! we will create
   A genuine summer in each other's breast;
And spite of this cold Time and frozen Fate
   Thaw us a warm seat to our rest.

Our sacred hearths shall burn eternally
   As vestal flames; the North wind, he
Shall strike his frost-stretched wings, dissolve, and fly
   This Etna in epitome.

Dropping December shall come weeping in,
   Bewail th'usurping of his reign;   30
But when in show'rs of old Greek we begin,
   Shall cry, he hath his crown again!

Night as clear Hesper shall our tapers whip
   From the light casements where we play,
And the dark hag from her black mantle strip,
   And stick there everlasting day.

Thus richer than untempted kings are we,
   That asking nothing, nothing need:
Though lord of all that seas embrace, yet he
   That wants himself, is poor indeed.   40

SONG: TO AMARANTHA,
THAT SHE WOULD DISHEVEL
HER HAIR

   Amarantha sweet and fair,
Ah, braid no more that shining hair!
   As my curious hand or eye,
Hov'ring round thee let it fly.

   Let it fly as unconfin'd
As its calm ravisher, the wind,
   Who hath left his darling th' east,
To wanton o'er that spicy nest.

   Ev'ry tress must be confessed
But neatly tangled at the best;   10
   Like a clue of golden thread
Most excellently ravellèd.

   Do not then wind up that light
In ribands, and o'ercloud in night;
   Like the sun in 's early ray,
But shake your head and scatter day.

   See, 'tis broke! Within this grove,
The bower and the walks of love,
   Weary lie we down and rest,
And fan each other's panting breast.   20

Here we'll strip and cool our fire
In cream below, in milk-baths higher;
    And when all wells are drawn dry,
I'll drink a tear out of thine eye.

    Which our very joys shall leave
That sorrows thus we can deceive;
    Or our very sorrows weep,
That joys so ripe, so little keep.

Abraham Cowley

(1 6 1 8 – 1 6 8 7)

Cowley started writing accomplished poetry at a remarkably young age: he completed the verse romance *Pyramus and Thisbe* by the age of ten and published his first collection of poems, *Poetical Blossoms*, when he was fifteen. Born posthumously to a London bookdealer, Cowley was educated at Westminster and Cambridge (where he first befriended Richard Crashaw, with whom he collaboratively wrote "On Hope"). He was committed to the Royalist cause and wrote in its behalf in his satiric *The Puritan and the Papist* (1643). Along with Crashaw and other Royalists, Cowley left England for France and the court of Henrietta Maria. He continued writing and publishing poetry, including a collection of love lyrics, *The Mistress* (1647), as well as *Poems* (1656), which includes his epic on King David and his influential Pindaric odes, which, although rhymed, retain elements of free verse. He returned to England in 1654, perhaps as a spy, and was briefly imprisoned. Neither side quite trusted him, and after the Restoration, having failed to receive the expected recompense for his services, Cowley retired to the country and wrote on botanical subjects.

WRITTEN IN JUICE OF LEMON

Whilst what I write I do not see,
I dare thus, even to you, write poetry.
Ah foolish Muse, which dost so high aspire,
    And know'st her judgment well
    How much it does thy power excel,
Yet dar'st be read by, thy just doom, the fire.

Alas, thou think'st thy self secure,
Because thy form is innocent and pure:
Like hypocrites, which seem unspotted here;
    But when they sadly come to die,   10
    And the last fire their truth must try,
Scrawl'd o'er like thee, and blotted they appear.

Go then, but reverently go,
And, since thou needs must sin, confess it too:

221

Confess'd, and with humility clothe thy shame,
  For thou, who else must burned be
  An heretic, if she pardon thee,
May'st like a martyr then enjoy the flame.

  But if her wisdom grow severe,
And suffer not her goodness to be there;   20
If her large mercies cruelly it restrain;
  Be not discourag'd, but require
  A more gentle ordeal fire,
And bid her by love's-flames read it again.

  Strange power of heat, thou yet dost show
Like winter earth, naked, or cloth'd with snow,
But, as the quick'ning sun approaching near,
  The plants arise up by degrees,
  A sudden paint adorns the trees,
And all kind Nature's characters appear.   30

  So, nothing yet in thee is seen,
But when a genial heat warms thee within,
A new-born wood of various lines there grows;
  Here buds an A, and there a B,
  Here sprouts a V, and there a T,
And all the flourishing letters stand in rows.

  Still, silly paper, thou wilt think
That all this might as well be writ with ink.
Oh no; there's sense in this, and mystery;
  Thou now may'st change thy author's name,   40
  And to her hand lay noble claim;
For as she reads, she makes the words in thee.

  Yet if thine own unworthiness
Will still, that thou art mine, not hers, confess;
Consume thy self with fire before her eyes,
  And so her grace or pity move;
  The gods, though beasts they do not love,
Yet like them when they're burnt in sacrifice.

THE MUSE

Go, the rich chariot instantly prepare,
    The queen, my Muse, will take the air.
Unruly Fancy with strong Judgment trace,
    Put in nimble-footed Wit,
    Smooth-pac'd Eloquence join with it,
Sound Memory with young Invention place
    Harness all the winged race.
Let the postillion Nature mount, and let
    The coachman Art be set.

And let the airy footmen running all beside,   10
    Make a long row of goodly pride.
Figures, conceits, raptures, and sentences
    In a well-worded dress.
And innocent loves, and pleasant truths, and useful lies,
    In all their gaudy liveries.
    Mount, glorious queen, thy travelling throne,
        And bid it to put on;
    For long, though cheerful, is the way,
And life, alas, allows but one ill winter's day.

Where never foot of man, or hoof of beast,   20
        The passage press'd,
    Where never fish did fly,
And with short silver wings cut the low liquid sky.
    Where bird with painted oars did ne'er
Row through the trackless ocean of the air.
        Where never yet did pry
    The busy morning's curious eye:
The wheel of thy bold coach pass quick and free;
    And all's an open road to thee.
    Whatever God did say,   30
Is all thy plain and smooth, uninterrupted way.
Nay, ev'n beyond His works thy voyages are known,
    Thou hast thousand worlds too of thine own.
Thou speak'st, great queen, in the same style as He,
And a new world leaps forth when thou say'st "Let it be."

Thou fathom'st the deep gulf of ages past,
    And canst pluck up with ease

The years which thou dost please,
Like shipwrack'd treasures by rude tempests cast
    Long since into the sea,   40
Brought up again to light and public use by thee.
    Nor dost thou only dive so low,
        But fly
With an unwearied wing the other way on high,
    Where Fates among the stars do grow;
There into the close nests of Time dost peep,
     And there with piercing eye,
Through the firm shell, and the thick white dost spy,
     Years to come a forming lie,
Close in their sacred secondine sleep,   50
       Till hatch'd by the sun's vital heat
       Which o'er them yet does brooding set
       They life and motion get,
    And ripe at last with vig'rous might
Break through the shell, and take their everlasting flight.

      And sure we may
    The same too of the present say,
If past and future times do thee obey.
    Thou stopp'st this current, and dost make
This running river settle like a lake,   60
Thy certain hand holds fast this slipp'ry snake,
      The fruit which does so quickly waste,
      Men scarce can see it, much less taste,
Thou comfitest in sweets to make it last.
       This shining piece of ice
       Which melts so soon away
        With the sun's ray,
Thy verse does solidate and crystalize,
      Till it a lasting mirror be.
      Nay thy immortal rhyme   70
    Makes this one short point of Time,
To fill up half the orb of round Eternity.

l. 50. secondine = the thin film with which an infant is covered in the womb
l. 64. comfitest = preserve

Henry Vaughan

(1621–1695)

Along with his twin brother Thomas—who became a noted writer on alchemy and mysticism—Vaughan was raised in Brecknock, Wales. He studied at Oxford and the Inns of Court in London before turning to a career in medicine, which he practiced until his death at age seventy-three. Vaughan's *Poems* was published in 1646, about the same time he married. The secular verse contained within his first published works gave no signal of the religious and hermetic impulse for which Vaughan was later celebrated. Scholars have placed this shift in Vaughan's work around the year 1648. Some have suggested that it was prompted by the defeat of the Royalist cause; others, by the death of a younger brother. Vaughan's outpouring of devotional poetry, published in *Silex Scintillans* (1650), *The Mount of Olives* (1652), and *Flores Solitudinis* (1654), followed—work deeply indebted to George Herbert, "whose holy life and verse," Vaughan wrote, "gained many pious converts (of whom I am the least)." Although his reputation flagged in the eighteenth century, the influence of Vaughan's poetry on such nineteenth-century poets as Wordsworth and Tennyson was significant.

TO THE MOST EXCELLENTLY ACCOMPLISHED MRS. KATHERINE PHILIPS

Say witty fair one, from what sphere
Flow these rich numbers you shed here?
For sure such incantations come
From thence, which strike your readers dumb.
A strain, whose measures gently meet
Like virgin lovers, or time's feet,
Where language smiles, and accents rise
As quick, and pleasing as your eyes,
The poem smooth, and in each line
Soft as your self, yet masculine;   10
Where no coarse trifles blot the page
With matter borrow'd from the age,

But thoughts as innocent, and high
As angels have, or saints that die.
   These raptures when I first did see
New miracles in poetry,
And by a hand, their god would miss
His bays and fountains but to kiss,
My weaker genius (cross to fashion)
Slept in a silent admiration,   20
A rescue, by whose grave disguise
Pretenders oft have past for wise,
And yet as pilgrims humbly touch
Those shrines to which they bow so much,
And clouds in courtship flock, and run
To be the mask unto the sun,
So I concluded, It was true
I might at distance worship you
A Persian votary, and say
It was your light show'd me the way.   30
So lodestones guide the duller steel,
And high perfections are the wheel
Which moves the less, for gifts divine
Are strung upon a vital line
Which touch'd by you, excites in all
Affections epidemical
And this made me (a truth most fit)
Add my weak echo to your wit,
Which pardon, Lady, for assays
Obscure as these might blast your bays,   40
As common hands soil flowers, and make
That dew they wear, weep the mistake.
But I'll wash off the stain, and vow
No laurel grows, but for your brow.

THE RETREAT

Happy those early days! when I
Shin'd in my angel infancy.
Before I understood this place
Appointed for my second race,
Or taught my soul to fancy aught
But a white, celestial thought,

When yet I had not walk'd above
A mile or two, from my first love,
And looking back (at that short space)
Could see a glimpse of his bright face;   10
When on some gilded cloud, or flower
My gazing soul would dwell an hour,
And in those weaker glories spy
Some shadows of eternity;
Before I taught my tongue to wound
My conscience with a sinful sound,
Or had the black art to dispense
A sev'ral sin to ev'ry sense,
But felt through all this fleshly dress
Bright shoots of everlastingness.   20
    O how I long to travel back
And tread again that ancient track!
That I might once more reach that plain,
Where first I left my glorious train,
From whence th' enlighten'd spirit sees
That shady city of palm trees;
But (ah!) my soul with too much stay
Is drunk, and staggers in the way.
Some men a forward motion love,
But I by backward steps would move,   30
And when this dust falls to the urn
In that state I came, return.

THEY ARE ALL GONE INTO THE WORLD OF LIGHT

They are all gone into the world of light!
    And I alone sit lingering here;
Their very memory is fair and bright
    And my sad thoughts doth clear.

It grows and glitters in my cloudy breast,
    Like stars upon some gloomy grove,
Or those faint beams in which this hill is dress'd
    After the sun's remove.

I see them walking in an air of glory,
    Whose light doth trample on my days: 10
My days, which are at best but dull and hoary,
    Mere glimmering and decays.

Oh holy hope, and high humility,
    High as the Heavens above!
These are your walks, and you have show'd them me
    To kindle my cold love.

Dear, beauteous death! the jewel of the Just,
    Shining nowhere but in the dark,
What mysteries do lie beyond thy dust,
    Could man outlook that mark!   20

He that hath found some fledg'd bird's nest, may know
    At first sight, if the bird be flown;
But what fair well or grove he sings in now,
    That is to him unknown.

And yet, as angels in some brighter dreams
    Call to the soul when man doth sleep,
So some strange thoughts transcend our wonted themes,
    And into glory peep.

If a star were confined into a tomb,
    Her captive flames must needs burn there;   30
But when the hand that lock'd her up, gives room,
    She'll shine through all the sphere.

Oh Father of eternal life, and all
    Created glories under thee!
Resume thy spirit from this world of thrall
    Into true liberty.

Either disperse these mists, which blot and fill
    My perspective (still) as they pass;
Or else remove me hence unto that hill,
    Where I shall need no glass.   40

Andrew Marvell

(1621 – 1678)

After attending Cambridge, Marvell traveled on the Continent, perhaps as a way of staying outside the entanglements of the English Civil War. After his return to England, Marvell moved in literary circles in London and then was tutor, first to Mary Fairfax, daughter of the parliamentary general, and then to Oliver Cromwell's ward, William Dutton. His "Mower" poems and "Upon Appleton House" probably date from this period, as does "An Horatian Ode upon Cromwell's Return from Ireland," one of the most brilliant and ambivalent political poems in the English language. In 1657 he was appointed Latin Secretary to the Council of State, a post previously held by his friend and sponsor, John Milton. In his later years Marvell again traveled abroad; he also wrote anonymously pamphlets advocating tolerance and attacking court corruption—most notably his *An Account of the Growth of Popery and Arbitrary Government in England* (1677). He was far better known as a satirist in his own day, and it was not until the early twentieth century that Marvell's posthumously published, lyric *Poems* (1681), no less political than his more overt satires, were fully appreciated.

TO HIS COY MISTRESS

Had we but world enough, and time,
This coyness, Lady, were no crime.
We would sit down, and think which way
To walk, and pass our long love's day.
Thou by the Indian Ganges' side
Should'st rubies find: I by the tide
Of Humber would complain. I would
Love you ten years before the Flood:
And you should, if you please, refuse
Till the conversion of the Jews.   10
My vegetable love should grow
Vaster than empires, and more slow.
An hundred years should go to praise
Thine eyes, and on thy forehead gaze.
Two hundred to adore each breast;

But thirty thousand to the rest.
An age at least to every part,
And the last age should show your heart.
For, Lady, you deserve this state;
Nor would I love at lower rate.   20
　　But at my back I always hear
Time's wingèd chariot hurrying near;
And yonder all before us lie
Deserts of vast eternity.
Thy beauty shall no more be found;
Nor, in thy marble vault, shall sound
My echoing song: then worms shall try
That long-preserved virginity:
And your quaint honour turn to dust;
And into ashes all my lust.   30
The grave's a fine and private place,
But none, I think, do there embrace.
　　Now therefore, while the youthful glue
Sits on thy skin like morning dew,
And while thy willing soul transpires
At every pore with instant fires,
Now let us sport us while we may;
And now, like am'rous birds of prey,
Rather at once our time devour,
Than languish in his slow-chapp'd power.   40
Let us roll all our strength, and all
Our sweetness, up into one ball:
And tear our pleasures with rough strife
Thorough the iron grates of life.
Thus, though we cannot make our sun
Stand still, yet we will make him run.

l. 11. vegetable = having the principle of simple life and growth

AN HORATIAN ODE
UPON CROMWELL'S
RETURN FROM IRELAND

The forward youth that would appear
Must now forsake his Muses dear,
　　Nor in the shadows sing

His numbers languishing.
'Tis time to leave the books in dust,
And oil th' unused armour's rust;
    Removing from the wall
    The corslet of the hall.
So restless Cromwell could not cease
In the inglorious arts of peace,   10
    But through adventurous war
    Urgèd his active star.
And, like the three-forked lightning, first
Breaking the clouds where it was nursed,
    Did thorough his own side
    His fiery way divide.
For 'tis all one to courage high
The emulous or enemy;
    And with such to inclose
    Is more than to oppose.   20
Then burning through the air he went,
And palaces and temples rent;
    And Caesar's head at last
    Did through his laurels blast.
'Tis madness to resist or blame
The force of angry Heaven's flame:
    And, if we would speak true,
    Much to the man is due,
Who, from his private gardens, where
He lived reservèd and austere,   30
    As if his highest plot
    To plant the bergamot,
Could by industrious valour climb
To ruin the great work of time,
    And cast the kingdoms old
    Into another mould.
Though justice against fate complain,
And plead the ancient rights in vain:
    But those do hold or break
    As men are strong or weak.   40
Nature, that hateth emptiness,
Allows of penetration less:
    And therefore must make room
    Where greater spirits come.
What field of all the Civil Wars,
Where his were not the deepest scars?

And Hampton shows what part
He had of wiser art,
Where, twining subtile fears with hope,
He wove a net of such a scope,   50
    That Charles himself might chase
    To Carisbrook's narrow case:
That thence the royal actor born
The tragic scaffold might adorn:
    While round the armèd bands
    Did clap their bloody hands.
He nothing common did or mean
Upon that memorable scene;
    But with his keener eye
    The axe's edge did try: 60
Nor called the gods with vulgar spite
To vindicate his helpless right;
    But bowed his comely head
    Down as upon a bed.
This was that memorable hour
Which first assured the forcèd power.
    So when they did design
    The Capitol's first line,
A bleeding head where they begun,
Did fright the architects to run;   70
    And yet in that the State
    Foresaw its happy fate.
And now the Irish are asham'd
To see themselves in one year tam'd:
    So much one man can do,
    That does both act and know.
They can affirm his praises best,
And have, though overcome, confessed
    How good he is, how just,
    And fit for highest trust: 80
Nor yet grown stiffer with command,
But still in the Republic's hand:
    How fit he is to sway
    That can so well obey.
He to the Commons' feet presents
A kingdom, for his first year's rents:
    And, what he may, forbears
    His fame, to make it theirs:
And has his sword and spoils ungirt,

To lay them at the public's skirt.   90
   So when the falcon high
   Falls heavy from the sky,
She, having killed, no more does search
But on the next green bough to perch,
   Where, when he first does lure,
   The falc'ner has her sure.
What may not then our Isle presume
While victory his crest does plume?
   What may not others fear
   If thus he crown each year?   100
A Caesar, he, ere long to Gaul,
To Italy an Hannibal,
   And to all states not free
   Shall climactéric be.
The Pict no shelter now shall find
Within his party-coloured mind,
   But from this valour sad
   Shrink underneath the plaid:
Happy, if in the tufted brake
The English hunter him mistake,   110
   Nor lay his hounds in near
   The Caledonian deer.
But thou, the Wars' and Fortune's son,
March indefatigably on,
   And for the last effect
   Still keep thy sword erect:
Besides the force it has to fright
The spirits of the shady night,
   The same arts that did gain
   A pow'r, must it maintain.   120

l. 32. bergamot = a fine type of pear, also known as a "prince's pear"

ON MR. MILTON'S *PARADISE LOST*

When I beheld the poet blind, yet bold,
In slender book his vast design unfold:
Messiah crowned, God's reconciled decree,
Rebelling Angels, the Forbidden Tree,
Heaven, Hell, Earth, Chaos, all; the argument

Held me a while misdoubting his intent,
That he would ruin (for I saw him strong)
The sacred Truths to fable and old song
(So Sampson groped the temple's posts in spite),
The world o'erwhelming to revenge his sight.   10
    Yet as I read, soon growing less severe,
I lik'd his project, the success did fear;
Through that wide field how he his way should find
O'er which lame Faith leads Understanding blind;
Lest he perplex'd the things he would explain,
And what was easy he should render vain.
    Or if a work so infinite he spanned,
Jealous I was that some less skilful hand
(Such as disquiet always what is well,
And by ill imitating would excel)   20
Might hence presume the whole Creation's day
To change in scenes, and show it in a play.
    Pardon me, mighty poet, nor despise
My causeless, yet not impious, surmise.
But I am now convinced that none will dare
Within thy labours to pretend a share.
Thou hast not miss'd one thought that could be fit,
And all that was improper dost omit;
So that no room is here for writers left,
But to detect their ignorance or theft.   30
    That majesty which through thy work doth reign
Draws the devout, deterring the profane;
And things divine thou treatst of in such state
As them preserves, and thee, inviolate.
At once delight and horror on us seize,
Thou singst with so much gravity and ease;
And above human flight dost soar aloft,
With plume so strong, so equal, and so soft.
The bird nam'd from that Paradise you sing
So never flags, but always keeps on wing.   40
    Where couldst thou words of such a compass find?
Whence furnish such a vast expense of mind?
Just heaven thee, like Tiresias, to requite,
Rewards with prophecy thy loss of sight.
    Well mightst thou scorn thy readers to allure
With tinkling rhyme, of thine own sense secure;
While the Town-Bays writes all the while and spells,
And like a pack-horse tires without his bells.

Their fancies like our bushy points appear,
The poets tag them; we for fashion wear.   50
I too, transported by the mode, offend,
And while I meant to *praise* thee must *commend*.
Thy verse created like thy theme sublime,
In number, weight, and measure, needs not rhyme.

THE MOWER AGAINST GARDENS

Luxurious man, to bring his vice in use,
    Did after him the world seduce,
And from the fields the flowers and plants allure,
    Where Nature was most plain and pure.
He first enclosed within the garden's square
    A dead and standing pool of air,
And a more luscious earth for them did knead,
    Which stupefied them while it fed.
The pink grew then as double as his mind;
    The nutriment did change the kind.   10
With strange perfumes he did the roses taint;
    And flowers themselves were taught to paint.
The tulip, white, did for complexion seek,
    And learned to interline its cheek:
Its onion root they then so high did hold,
    That one was for a meadow sold.
Another world was searched, through oceans new,
    To find the Marvel of Peru.
And yet these rarities might be allowed
    To man, that sovereign thing and proud,   20
Had he not dealt between the bark and tree,
    Forbidden mixtures there to see.
No plant now knew the stock from which it came;
    He grafts upon the wild the tame:
That the uncertain and adulterate fruit
    Might put the palate in dispute.
His green seraglio has its eunuchs too,
    Lest any tyrant him outdo.
And in the cherry he does Nature vex,
    To procreate without a sex.   30
'Tis all enforced, the fountain and the grot,
    While the sweet fields do lie forgot;

Where willing nature does to all dispense
   A wild and fragrant innocence:
And fauns and fairies do the meadows till,
   More by their presence than their skill.
Their statues, polish'd by some ancient hand,
   May to adorn the gardens stand:
But howsoe'er the figures do excel,
   The gods themselves with us do dwell.   40

Margaret Lucas Cavendish, Duchess of Newcastle

(c.1623 – 1674)

Cavendish was the first Englishwoman to publish prolifically: her works include *Poems and Fancies* (1653), *Philosophical Fancies* (1653), *The World's Olio* (1655), *Philosophical and Physical Opinions* (1655), *Natures Pictures Drawn by Fancies Pencil to the Life* (1656), *Playes* (1662), and a half dozen other titles on science, philosophy, romance, and even science fiction. Cavendish justified her prodigious output by explaining that her "ambition is restless and not ordinary, because it would have an extraordinary fame," notwithstanding the fact that "all heroic actions, public employments, powerful governments, and eloquent pleadings are denied our sex in this age." She was fortunate insofar as her husband, the Duke of Newcastle, whom she married in 1645, supported her literary activities and in fact published her *Letters and Poems* shortly after her death. She was buried in Westminster Abbey. Virginia Woolf wrote that "though her philosophies are futile, and her plays intolerable, and her verses mainly dull, the vast bulk of the Duchess is leavened by a vein of authentic fire."

THE POETRESS'S PETITION

Like to a fever's pulse my heart doth beat,
For fear my book some great repulse should meet.
If it be nought, let her in silence lie,
Disturb her not, let her in quiet die;
Let not the bells of your dispraise ring loud,
But wrap her up in silence as a shroud;
Cause black oblivion on her hearse to hang,
Instead of tapers, let dark night there stand;
Instead of flowers to the grave her strow,
Before her hearse, sleepy, dull, poppy throw;   10
Instead of scutcheons, let my tears be hung,
Which grief and sorrow from my eyes outwrung:
Let those that bear her corpse no jesters be,
But sad, and sober, grave mortality.

No satyr poets to her funeral come,
No altars raised to write inscriptions on.
Let dust of all forgetfulness be cast
Upon her corpse, there let them lie and waste;
Not let her rise again; unless some know
At Judgement's some good merits she can show.   20
Then she shall live in heavens of high praise,
And for her glory, garlands of fresh bays.

l. 15. satyr = satiric

John Dryden

(1 6 3 1 – 1 7 0 0)

A leading Restoration dramatist, poet, translator, and critic, Dryden was edu-
cated at Westminster School and Trinity College, Cambridge. He left Cam-
bridge for London, where he married and earned his living as a writer and
dramatist. Dryden's verse was from the outset deeply engaged with the complex
political issues of his day, and he has occasionally been accused by literary
historians of changing his views to suit the prevailing political climate. By 1670
Dryden was Poet Laureate and historiographer royal, and his interest turned
from the theater to polemical and political poetry. His satires—including *Mac-
Flecknoe* (1682), with its humorous (and barely veiled scatological) attack on
"Sh——" (i.e., the dramatist Thomas Shadwell)—were highly valued, as were
the late poems written after his conversion to Roman Catholicism that included
A *Song for St. Cecilia's Day*, 1687. Dryden's translations of Homer, Ovid,
Juvenal, Horace, and especially Virgil were enormously influential, as was his
critical essay *Of Dramatick Poesie* (1668). Deeply influenced by both Shake-
speare and Jonson, Dryden in turn influenced the next generation of dramatists
and poets, holding court for this circle at Will's Coffee House in Covent
Garden. Dr. Johnson recorded that Dryden "found the language brick and left
it marble."

MACFLECKNOE

All human things are subject to decay,
And when fate summons, monarchs must obey.
This Flecknoe found, who, like Augustus, young
Was call'd to empire, and had govern'd long;
In prose and verse, was own'd, without dispute,
Through all the realms of Nonsense, absolute.
This aged prince, now flourishing in peace,
And blest with issue of a large increase,
Worn out with business, did at length debate
To settle the succession of the state: 10
And, pond'ring which of all his sons was fit
To reign, and wage immortal war with wit,
Cried: " 'Tis resolv'd; for Nature pleads, that he

Should only rule, who most resembles me.
Sh—— alone my perfect image bears,
Mature in dullness from his tender years:
Shadwell alone, of all my sons, is he
Who stands confirm'd in full stupidity.
The rest to some faint meaning make pretence,
But Sh—— never deviates into sense.   20
Some beams of wit on other souls may fall,
Strike through, and make a lucid interval;
But Sh——'s genuine night admits no ray;
His rising fogs prevail upon the day.
Besides, his goodly fabric fills the eye,
And seems design'd for thoughtless majesty;
Thoughtless as monarch oaks, that shade the plain,
And, spread in solemn state, supinely reign.
Heywood and Shirley were but types of thee,
Thou last great prophet of tautology.   30
Even I, a dunce of more renown than they,
Was sent before but to prepare thy way.
And, coarsely clad in Norwich drugget, came
To teach the nations in thy greater name.
My warbling lute, the lute I whilom strung,
When to King John of Portugal I sung,
Was but the prelude to that glorious day,
When thou on silver Thames did'st cut thy way,
With well-tim'd oars before the royal barge,
Swelled with the pride of thy celestial charge;   40
And big with hymn, commander of a host,
The like was ne'er in Epsom blankets tossed.
Methinks I see the new Arion sail,
The lute still trembling underneath thy nail.
At thy well-sharpened thumb from shore to shore
The treble squeaks for fear, the basses roar;
Echoes from Pissing Alley 'Sh——' call,
And 'Sh——' they resound from Ashton Hall.
About thy boat the little fishes throng,
As at the morning toast that floats along.   50
Sometimes, as prince of thy harmonious band,
Thou wield'st thy papers in thy threshing hand.
St. André's feet ne'er kept more equal time,
Not e'en the feet of thy own *Psyche's* rhyme;
Though they in number as in sense excel;
So just, so like tautology they fell,

That, pale with envy, Singleton forswore
The lute and sword, which he in triumph bore,
And vowed he ne'er would act Villerius more."
Here stopped the good old sire, and wept for joy   60
In silent raptures of the hopeful boy.
All arguments, but most his plays, persuade,
That for anointed dullness he was made.
　　Close to the walls which fair Augusta bind,
(The fair Augusta much to fears inclin'd)
An ancient fabric raised to inform the sight,
There stood of yore, and Barbican it hight:
A watchtower once; but now, so Fate ordains,
Of all the pile an empty name remains.
From its old ruins brothel-houses rise,   70
Scenes of lewd loves, and of polluted joys,
Where their vast courts the mother-strumpets keep,
And, undisturb'd by watch, in silence sleep.
Near these a nursery erects its head,
Where queens are form'd, and future heroes bred;
Where unfledg'd actors learn to laugh and cry,
Where infant punks their tender voices try,
And little Maximins the gods defy.
Great Fletcher never treads in buskins here,
Nor greater Jonson dares in socks appear;   80
But gentle Simkin just reception finds
Amidst this monument of vanish'd minds:
Pure clenches the suburban muse affords,
And Panton waging harmless war with words.
Here Flecknoe, as a place to fame well known,
Ambitiously designed his Sh——'s throne;
For ancient Dekker prophesi'd long since,
That in this pile should reign a mighty prince,
Born for a scourge of wit, and flail of sense;
To whom true dullness should some *Psyches* owe,   90
But worlds of *Misers* from his pen should flow;
Humourists and *Hypocrites* it should produce,
Whole Raymond families, and tribes of Bruce.
　　Now Empress Fame had publish'd the renown
Of Sh——'s coronation through the town.
Rous'd by report of Fame, the nations meet,
From near Bunhill, and distant Watling Street.
No Persian carpets spread th'imperial way,
But scattered limbs of mangled poets lay.

From dusty shops neglected authors come,   100
Martyrs of pies, and relics of the bum.
Much Heywood, Shirley, Ogilby there lay,
But loads of Sh—— almost chok'd the way.
Bilk'd stationers for yeomen stood prepar'd,
And Herringman was captain of the guard.
The hoary prince in majesty appear'd,
High on a throne of his own labours rear'd.
At his right hand our young Ascanius sate,
Rome's other hope, and pillar of the State.
His brows thick fogs, instead of glories, grace,   110
And lambent dullness play'd around his face.
As Hannibal did to the altars come,
Sworn by his sire a mortal foe to Rome;
So Sh—— swore, nor should his vow be vain,
That he till death true dullness would maintain;
And, in his father's right, and realm's defence,
Ne'er to have peace with wit, nor truce with sense.
The king himself the sacred unction made,
As king by office, and as priest by trade:
In his sinister hand, instead of ball,   120
He placed a mighty mug of potent ale;
Love's Kingdom to his right he did convey,
At once his sceptre, and his rule of sway;
Whose righteous lore the prince had practis'd young,
And from whose loins recorded *Psyche* sprung.
His temples, last, with poppies were o'erspread,
That nodding seemed to consecrate his head.
Just at that point of time, if Fame not lie,
On his left hand twelve reverend owls did fly.
So Romulus, 'tis sung, by Tiber's brook,   130
Presage of sway from twice six vultures took.
The admiring throng loud acclamations make,
And omens of his future empire take.
The sire then shook the honours of his head,
And from his brows damps of oblivion shed
Full on the filial dullness: long he stood,
Repelling from his breast the raging god;
At length burst out in this prophetic mood:
    "Heavens bless my son, from Ireland let him reign
To far Barbadoes on the Western main;   140
Of his dominion may no end be known,
And greater than his father's be his throne;

Beyond *Love's Kingdom* let him stretch his pen!"
He paused, and all the people cried, "Amen."
Then thus continued he: "My son, advance
Still in new impudence, new ignorance.
Success let others teach, learn thou from me
Pangs without birth, and fruitless industry.
Let *Virtuosos* in five years be writ;
Yet not one thought accuse thy toil of wit.   150
Let gentle George in triumph tread the stage,
Make Dorimant betray, and Loveit rage,
Let Cully, Cockwood, Fopling, charm the pit,
And in their folly show the writer's wit.
Yet still thy fools shall stand in thy defence,
And justify their author's want of sense.
Let 'em be all by thy own model made
Of dullness, and desire no foreign aid;
That they to future ages may be known,
Not copies drawn, but issue of thy own.   160
Nay, let thy men of wit too be the same,
All full of thee, and differing but in name;
But let no alien Sedley interpose
To lard with wit thy hungry *Epsom* prose.
And when false flowers of rhetoric thou would'st cull,
Trust nature, do not labour to be dull;
But write thy best, and top; and in each line,
Sir Formal's oratory will be thine.
Sir Formal, though unsought, attends thy quill,
And does thy northern dedications fill.   170
Nor let false friends seduce thy mind to fame,
By arrogating Jonson's hostile name.
Let father Flecknoe fire thy mind with praise,
And uncle Ogilby thy envy raise.
Thou art my blood, where Jonson has no part:
What share have we in Nature, or in Art?
Where did his wit on learning fix a brand,
And rail at arts he did not understand?
Where made he love in Prince Nicander's vein,
Or swept the dust in *Psyche's* humble strain?   180
Where sold he bargains, 'whip-stitch, kiss my arse,'
Promised a play and dwindled to a farce?
When did his muse from Fletcher scenes purloin,
As thou whole Etherege dost transfuse to thine?
But so transfus'd, as oil on water's flow,

His always floats above, thine sinks below.
This is thy province, this thy wondrous way,
New humours to invent for each new play:
This is that boasted bias of thy mind,
By which one way, to dullness, 'tis inclin'd;   190
Which makes thy writings lean on one side still,
And, in all changes, that way bends thy will.
Nor let thy mountain-belly make pretence
Of likeness; thine's a tympany of sense.
A tun of man in thy large bulk is writ,
But sure thou'rt but a kilderkin of wit.
Like mine, thy gentle numbers feebly creep;
Thy Tragic Muse gives smiles, thy Comic sleep.
With whate'er gall thou settst thyself to write,
Thy inoffensive satires never bite.   200
In thy felonious heart though venom lies,
It does but touch thy Irish pen, and dies.
Thy genius calls thee not to purchase fame
In keen iambics, but mild anagram.
Leave writing plays, and choose for thy command
Some peaceful province in acrostic land.
There thou mayst wings display and altars raise,
And torture one poor word ten thousand ways.
Or, if thou would'st thy diff'rent talents suit,
Set thy own songs, and sing them to thy lute."   210
    He said: but his last words were scarcely heard;
For Bruce and Longvil had a trap prepar'd,
And down they sent the yet declaiming bard.
Sinking he left his drugget robe behind,
Borne upwards by a subterranean wind.
The mantle fell to the young prophet's part,
With double portion of his father's art.

l. 33. drugget = course stuff of wool and linen
l. 181. sold bargains = replied coarsely

TO THE PIOUS MEMORY OF THE ACCOMPLISHED YOUNG LADY MRS. ANNE KILLIGREW

An Ode

Thou youngest virgin-daughter of the skies,
Made in the last promotion of the Blest;
Whose palms, new pluck'd from Paradise,
In spreading branches more sublimely rise,
Rich with immortal green above the rest:
Whether, adopted to some neighbouring star,
Thou roll'st above us, in thy wand'ring race,
   Or, in procession fix'd and regular,
   Mov'd with the Heavens' majestic pace;
   Or, call'd to more superior bliss,   10
Thou tread'st, with Seraphims, the vast Abyss:
What ever happy region is thy place,
Cease thy celestial song a little space;
(Thou wilt have time enough for hymns divine,
   Since Heav'ns eternal year is thine.)
Hear then a mortal muse thy praise rehearse,
     In no ignoble verse;
But such as thy own voice did practice here,
When thy first fruits of poesie were giv'n;
To make thy self a welcome inmate there: 20
   While yet a young probationer,
     And candidate of Heav'n.

If by traduction came thy mind,
   Our wonder is the less to find
A soul so charming from a stock so good;
Thy father was transfus'd into thy blood:
So wert thou born into the tuneful strain,
(An early, rich, and inexhausted vein.)
   But if thy pre-existing soul
   Was form'd, at first, with myriads more,   30
It did through all the mighty poets roll,
   Who Greek or Latin laurels wore,
And was that Sappho last, which once it was before.
   If so, then cease thy flight, O Heav'n-born mind!
   Thou hast no dross to purge from thy rich ore:

Nor can thy soul a fairer mansion find,
Than was the beauteous frame she left behind:
Return, to fill or mend the quire, of thy celestial kind.

May we presume to say, that at thy birth,
New joy was sprung in Heav'n, as well as here on Earth.   40
  For sure the milder planets did combine
  On thy auspicious horoscope to shine,
  And ev'n the most malicious were in trine.
    Thy brother-angels at thy birth
    Strung each his lyre, and tun'd it high,
    That all the people of the sky
  Might know a poetess was born on Earth.
    And then if ever, mortal ears
    Had heard the music of the spheres!
    And if no clust'ring swarm of bees   50
  On thy sweet mouth distill'd their golden dew,
    'Twas that, such vulgar miracles,
    Heav'n had not leisure to renew:
  For all the blest fraternity of love
Solemniz'd there thy birth, and kept thy holyday above.

O gracious God! How far have we
Prophan'd thy Heav'nly gift of poesy?
Made prostitute and profligate the Muse,
Debas'd to each obscene and impious use,
Whose harmony was first ordain'd above   60
For tongues of angels, and for hymns of love?
O wretched we! why were we hurried down
  This lubric and adult'rate age,
  (Nay added fat pollutions of our own)
  T' increase the steaming ordures of the stage?
  What can we say t' excuse our Second Fall?
  Let this thy vestal, Heav'n, atone for all!
  Her Arethusian stream remains unsoil'd,
  Unmixt with foreign filth, and undefil'd,
Her wit was more than man, her innocence a child!   70

Art she had none, yet wanted none:
  For Nature did that want supply,
  So rich in treasures of her own,
  She might our boasted stores defy:
  Such noble vigour did her verse adorn,

That it seem'd borrow'd, where 'twas only born.
Her morals too were in her bosom bred
    By great examples daily fed,
What in the best of books, her father's life, she read.
    And to be read herself she need not fear,   80
    Each test, and ev'ry light, her Muse will bear,
    Though Epictetus with his lamp were there.
    Ev'n love (for love sometimes her Muse express'd)
Was but a lambent-flame which play'd about her breast:
    Light as the vapours of a morning dream,
    So cold herself, whilst she such warmth express'd,
    'Twas Cupid bathing in Diana's stream.

    Born to the spacious empire of the Nine,
    One would have thought, she should have been content
    To manage well that mighty government: 90
    But what can young ambitious souls confine?
        To the next realm she strech'd her sway,
        For painture near adjoining lay,
    A plenteous province, and alluring prey.
    A chamber of dependences was fram'd,
    (As conquerors will never want pretence,
        When arm'd, to justify the offence)
And the whole fief, in right of poetry she claim'd.
    The country open lay without defence:
    For poets frequent inroads there had made,   100
        And perfectly could represent
    The shape, the face, with ev'ry lineament;
And all the large demains which the dumb-sister sway'd,
        All bow'd beneath her government,
        Receiv'd in triumph wheresoe'er she went.
    Her pencil drew, what e'er her soul design'd,
And oft the happy draught surpass'd the image in her mind.
    The sylvan scenes of herds and flocks,
    And fruitful plains and barren rocks,
    Of shallow brooks that flow'd so clear,   110
    The bottom did the top appear;
    Of deeper too and ampler floods,
    Which as in mirrors, show'd the woods;
    Of lofty trees with sacred shades,
    And perspectives of pleasant glades,
    Where nymphs of brightest form appear,
    And shaggy satyrs standing near,

Which them at once admire and fear.
The ruins too of some majestic piece,
Boasting the pow'r of ancient Rome or Greece,   120
Whose statues, freezes, columns broken lie,
And though defac'd, the wonder of the eye,
What nature, art, bold fiction e'er durst frame,
Her forming hand gave feature to the name.
So strange a Concourse ne'er was seen before,
But when the peopl'd ark the whole Creation bore.

The scene then chang'd, with bold erected look
Our martial king the sight with reverence strook:
For not content t' express his outward part,
Her hand call'd out the image of his heart,   130
His warlike mind, his soul devoid of fear,
His high-designing thoughts, were figur'd there,
As when, by magic, ghosts are made appear.
    Our phoenix queen was portray'd too so bright,
Beauty alone could beauty take so right:
Her dress, her shape, her matchless grace,
Were all observ'd, as well as heav'nly face.
With such a peerless majesty she stands,
As in that day she took the crown from sacred hands:
Before a train of heroines was seen,   140
In beauty foremost, as in rank, the queen!
    Thus nothing to her genius was denied,
But like a ball of fire the further thrown,
    Still with a greater blaze she shone,
And her bright soul broke out on ev'ry side.
What next she had design'd, Heaven only knows,
To such immod'rate growth her conquest rose,
That fate alone its progress could oppose.

    Now all those charms, that blooming grace,
The well-proportion'd shape, and beauteous face,   150
Shall never more be seen by mortal eyes;
In earth the much lamented virgin lies!
    Not wit, nor piety could fate prevent;
    Nor was the cruel destiny content
    To finish all the murder at a blow,
To sweep at once her life, and beauty too;
But, like a hard'n'd felon, took a pride
    To work more mischievously slow,

And plunder'd first, and then destroy'd.
O double sacrilege on things divine,   160
To rob the relic, and deface the shrine!
    But thus Orinda died:
Heav'n, by the same disease, did both translate,
As equal were their souls, so equal was their fate.

    Meantime her warlike brother on the seas
    His waving streamers to the winds displays,
And vows for his return, with vain devotion, pays.
      Ah, generous youth, that wish forbear,
      The winds too soon will waft thee here!
      Slack all thy sails, and fear to come,   170
Alas, thou know'st not, thou art wreck'd at home!
No more shalt thou behold thy sister's face,
Thou hast already had her last embrace.
But look aloft, and if thou kenn'st from far,
Among the Pleiad's a new-kindl'd star,
If any sparkles, than the rest, more bright,
'Tis she that shines in that propitious light.

When in mid-air, the golden trump shall sound,
    To raise the nations under ground;
    When in the valley of Jehosaphat,   180
The judging God shall close the Book of Fate;
    And there the last assizes keep,
    For those who wake, and those who sleep;
    When rattling bones together fly,
From the four corners of the sky,
When sinews o'er the skeletons are spread,
Those cloth'd with flesh, and life inspires the dead:
The sacred poets first shall hear the sound,
    And foremost from the tomb shall bound:
For they are cover'd with the lightest ground   190
And straight, with in-born vigour, on the wing,
Like mounting larks, to the new morning sing.
There thou, sweet saint, before the quire shalt go,
As harbinger of Heav'n, the way to show,
The way which thou so well hast learn'd below.

l. 63. lubric = smooth and slippery

A SONG FOR ST. CECILIA'S DAY, 1687

From harmony, from heav'nly harmony
  This universal frame began.
  When Nature underneath a heap
    Of jarring atoms lay,
  And could not heave her head,
The tuneful voice was heard from high,
    "Arise ye more than dead."
Then cold, and hot, and moist, and dry,
In order, to their stations leap,
    And music's power obey.   10
From harmony, from heavenly harmony
  This universal frame began:
  From harmony to harmony
Through all the compass of the notes it ran,
The diapason closing full in man.

What passion cannot music raise and quell!
    When Jubal struck the corded shell,
  His list'ning brethren stood around,
    And wond'ring, on their faces fell
To worship that celestial sound.   20
Less than a god they thought there could not dwell
    Within the hollow of that shell
    That spoke so sweetly and so well.
What passion cannot music raise and quell!

  The trumpet's loud clangor
    Excites us to arms
  With shrill notes of anger
    And mortal alarms.
  The double double double beat
    Of the thundering drum   30
  Cries "Hark, the foes come;
Charge, charge, 'tis too late to retreat!"

  The soft complaining flute
  In dying notes discovers
  The woes of hopeless lovers,
Whose dirge is whisper'd by the warbling lute.

Sharp violins proclaim
Their jealous pangs and desperation,
Fury, frantic indignation,
Depth of pains, and height of passion   40
  For the fair, disdainful dame.

  But O! what art can teach
  What human voice can reach
The sacred organ's praise?
Notes inspiring holy love,
Notes that wing their heav'nly ways
  To mend the choirs above.

Orpheus could lead the savage race;
And trees unrooted left their place,
  Sequacious of the lyre;   50
But bright Cecilia rais'd the wonder higher:
When to her organ vocal breath was giv'n,
An angel heard, and straight appear'd
  Mistaking Earth for Heaven.

  Grand Chorus

As from the pow'r of sacred lays
  The spheres began to move,
And sung the great Creator's praise
  To all the bless'd above,
So when the last and dreadful hour
This crumbling pageant shall devour,   60
The trumpet shall be heard on high,
The dead shall live, the living die,
And music shall untune the sky.

Katherine Fowler Philips

(1 6 3 1 – 1 6 6 4)

Born in London, educated at Mrs. Salmon's School for girls (she is reported to have read the Bible through before age four), Philips married at age sixteen and spent much of the rest of her life in southwest Wales. Before her death from smallpox at the age of thirty-three, Philips had achieved a considerable reputation as a poet. About half of her verse was printed in an unauthorized edition in 1664; three years after her death a more substantial edition of a hundred and twenty poems, as well as translations from Corneille's plays *Pompey* and *Horace*, was published. Known by her poetic name of "Orinda," under which she wrote, Philips was a central figure in a small circle of poets, mostly women (known as her "Society of Friendship"), to whom much of her verse is addressed. A later admirer of her verse was John Keats, who in 1817 wrote of Philips to his friend John Hamilton Reynolds, "You must have heard of her, and most likely read her poetry. . . . You will not regret reading them once more."

ON THE WELSH LANGUAGE

If honour to an ancient name be due,
Or riches challenge it for one that's new,
The British language claims in either sense,
Both for its age, and for its opulence.
But all great things must be from us remov'd,
To be with higher reverence belov'd
So landscapes which in prospects distant lie,
With greater wonder draw the pleased eye.
Is not great Troy to one dark ruin hurl'd?
Once the fam'd scene of all the fighting world.   10
Where's Athens now, to whom Rome learning owes,
And the safe laurels that adorn'd her brows?
A strange reverse of fate she did endure,
Never once greater, then she's now obscure.
Ev'n Rome herself can but some footsteps show
Of Scipio's times, or those of Cicero.
And as the Roman and the Grecian state,
The British fell, the spoil of time and fate.

But though the language hath her beauty lost,
Yet she has still some great remains to boast;   20
For 'twas in that, the sacred bards of old,
In deathless numbers did their thoughts unfold.
In groves, by rivers, and on fertile plains,
They civilized and taught the list'ning swains;
Whilst with high raptures, and as great success,
Virtue they cloth'd in music's charming dress.
This Merlin spoke, who in his gloomy cave,
Ev'n destiny herself seem'd to enslave.
For to his sight the future time was known,
Much better than to others is their own: 30
And with such state, predictions from him fell,
As if he did decree, and not foretell.
This spoke King Arthur; who, if fame be true,
Could have compell'd mankind to speak it too.
In this once Boadicea valour taught,
And spoke more nobly then her soldiers fought:
Tell me what hero could do more then she,
Who fell at once for fame and liberty?
Nor could a greater sacrifice belong,
Or to her children's, or her country's wrong.   40
This spoke Caratacus, who was so brave,
That to the Roman fortune check he gave;
And when their yoke he could decline no more,
He it so decently and nobly wore,
That Rome herself with blushes did believe
A Brittan would the law of honour give;
And hastily his chains away she threw,
Least her own captive else should her subdue.

EPITAPH ON HER SON
HECTOR PHILIPS

What on Earth deserves our trust?
Youth and beauty both are dust.
Long we gathering are with pain,
What one moment calls again.
Seven years childless, marriage past,
A son, a son is born at last;

So exactly limb'd and fair,
Full of good spirits, mien, and air,
As a long life promised;
Yet, in less then six weeks, dead.   10
Too promising, too great a mind
In so small room to be confin'd:
Therefore, fit in Heav'n to dwell,
He quickly broke the prison shell.
So the subtle alchemist,
Can't with Hermes' seal resist
The powerful spirit's subtler flight,
But 'twill bid him long good night.
And so the sun, if it arise
Half so glorious as his eyes,   20
Like this infant, takes a shroud,
Buried in a morning cloud.

FRIENDSHIP IN EMBLEM,
OR THE SEAL,
TO MY DEAREST LUCASIA

The hearts thus intermixed speak
A love that no bold shock can break;
For join'd and growing both in one,
Neither can be disturb'd alone.

That means a mutual knowledge too;
For what is't either heart can do,
Which by its panting sentinel
It does not to the other tell?

That friendship hearts so much refines,
It nothing but itself designs: 10
The hearts are free from lower ends,
For each point to the other tends.

They flame, 'tis true, and several ways,
But still those flames do so much raise,
That while to either they incline
They yet are noble and divine.

From smoke or hurt those flames are free,
From grossness or mortality:
The hearts (like Moses' bush presum'd)
Warm'd and enlighten'd, not consum'd.   20

The compasses that stand above
Express this great immortal love;
For friends, like them, can prove this true,
They are, and yet they are not, two.

And in their posture is express'd
Friendship's exalted interest:
Each follows where the other leans,
And what each does, the other means.

And as when one foot does stand fast,
And t'other circles seeks to cast,   30
The steady part does regulate
And make the wand'rer's motion straight:

So friends are only two in this,
T'reclaim each other when they miss;
For whosoe'er will grossly fall,
Can never be a friend at all.

And as that useful instrument
For even lines was ever meant;
So friendship from good angels springs,
To teach the world heroic things.   40

As these are found out in design
To rule and measure every line;
So friendship governs actions best,
Prescribing unto all the rest.

And as in Nature nothing's set
So just as lines and numbers met;
So compasses for these being made,
Do friendship's harmony persuade.

And like to them, so friends may own
Extension, not division: 50

Their points, like bodies, separate;
But head, like souls, knows no such fate.

And as each part so well is knit,
That their embraces ever fit:
So friends are such by destiny,
And no third can the place supply.

There needs no motto to the seal:
But that we may the mind reveal
To the dull eye, it was thought fit
That friendship only should be writ.   60

But as there are degrees of bliss,
So there's no friendship meant by this,
But such as will transmit to fame
Lucasia's and Orinda's name.

Thomas Traherne

(1637? – 1674)

A shoemaker's son from Hereford, on the Welsh border, Traherne attended
Oxford before being assigned a living in a parish near his birthplace. Contempo-
rary accounts describe Traherne as a pious charitable individual, given to
visions. After his death friends brought out two volumes of his devotional prose,
interspersed with poems. But his great body of spiritual poetry (and especially
his explorations of childhood experience) would have been lost to posterity were
it not for William T. Brooke's fortunate discovery of two of Traherne's manu-
scripts in a London bookstall in 1896–1897. Brooke actually thought these
religious poems were by Henry Vaughan; the correct attribution was soon made
by Bertram Dobell, and Traherne's *Centuries* was finally published in the first
decade of the twentieth century. Another manuscript—a commonplace book in
which Traherne wrote prose and verse during his later years—was found in
1967 at a garbage dump in Lancashire by a man looking for spare auto parts.

INNOCENCE

But that which most I wonder at, which most
I did esteem my bliss, which most I boast,
And ever shall enjoy, is that within
    I felt no stain, nor spot of sin.
    No darkness then did overshade,
    But all within was pure and bright;
    No guilt did crush nor fear invade,
    But all my soul was full of light.
    A joyful sense and purity
        Is all I can remember.   10
    The very night to me was bright,
    'Twas summer in December.

A serious meditation did employ
My soul within, which taken up with joy
Did seem no outward thing to note, but fly
    All objects that do feed the eye.
    While it those very objects did

Admire, and prize, and praise, and love,
Which in their glory most are hid,
Which presence only doth remove.   20
Their constant daily presence I
    Rejoicing at, did see;
And that which takes them from the eye
Of others, offer'd them to me.

No inward inclination did I feel
To avarice or pride: my soul did kneel
In admiration all the day. No lust, nor strife,
    Polluted then my infant life.
No fraud nor anger in me mov'd,
No malice, jealousy, or spite;   30
All that I saw I truly lov'd.
Contentment only and delight
Were in my soul. O Heav'n! what bliss
    Did I enjoy and feel!
What powerful delight did this
Inspire! For this I daily kneel.

Whether it be that Nature is so pure,
And Custom only vicious; or that sure
God did by miracle the guilt remove,
    And make my soul to feel his love,   40
    So early: or that 'twas one day
    Wherein this happiness I found;
    Whose strength and brightness so do ray,
    That still it seemeth to surround.
Whate'er it is, it is a light
    So endless unto me
That I a world of true delight
Did then and to this day do see.

That prospect was the gate of Heav'n, that day
The ancient light of Eden did convey   50
Into my soul: I was an Adam there,
    A little Adam in a sphere
    Of joys! O there my ravish'd sense
    Was entertained in Paradise,
    And had a sight of innocence.
All was beyond all bound and price.

An antepast of Heaven sure!
   I on the Earth did reign.
Within, without me, all was pure.
I must become a child again.   60

SHADOWS IN THE WATER

In unexperienc'd infancy
Many a sweet mistake doth lie:
Mistake though false, intending true;
A seeming somewhat more than view;
   That doth instruct the mind
   In things that lie behind,
And many secrets to us show
Which afterwards we come to know.

Thus did I by the water's brink
Another world beneath me think;   10
And while the lofty spacious skies
Reversed there abus'd mine eyes,
   I fancied other feet
   Came mine to touch and meet;
As by some puddle I did play
Another world within it lay.

Beneath the water people drown'd,
Yet with another heaven crown'd,
In spacious regions seemed to go
Freely moving to and fro: 20
   In bright and open space
   I saw their very face;
Eyes, hands, and feet they had like mine;
Another sun did with them shine.

'Twas strange that people there should walk,
And yet I could not hear them talk:
That through a little wat'ry chink,
Which one dry ox or horse might drink,
   We other worlds should see,
   Yet not admitted be;   30

And other confines there behold
Of light and darkness, heat and cold.

I call'd them oft, but call'd in vain;
No speeches we could entertain:
Yet did I there expect to find
Some other world, to please my mind.
   I plainly saw by these
    A new Antipodes,
Whom, though they were so plainly seen,
A film kept off that stood between.   40

By walking men's reversed feet
I chanced another world to meet;
Though it did not to view exceed
A phantasm, 'tis a world indeed,
   Where skies beneath us shine,
    And earth by art divine
Another face presents below,
Where people's feet against ours go.

Within the regions of the air,
Compass'd about with Heav'ns fair,   50
Great tracts of land there may be found
Enriched with fields and fertile ground;
   Where many num'rous hosts,
    In those far distant coasts,
For other great and glorious ends,
Inhabit, my yet unknown friends.

O ye that stand upon the brink,
Whom I so near me, through the chink,
With wonder see: what faces there,
Whose feet, whose bodies, do ye wear?
   I, my companions, see   60
    In you another me.
They seemed others, but are we;
Our second selves those shadows be.

Look how far off those lower skies
Extend themselves! scarce with mine eyes
I can them reach. O ye, my friends,
What secret borders on those ends?

Are lofty heavens hurl'd
  'Bout your inferior world?   70
Are ye the representatives
Of other peoples' distant lives?

Of all the play-mates which I knew
That here I do the image view
In other selves; what can it mean?
But that below the purling stream
  Some unknown joys there be
  Laid up in store for me;
To which I shall, when that thin skin
Is broken, be admitted in.   80

Aphra Behn

(1640 – 1689)

Behn's early years and upbringing remain shrouded in mystery and speculation. More substantiated are her early travels to Surinam and her work as a spy in Holland, undertaken before her return to London and the beginning of her successful career as poet and dramatist in the early 1670s. Best known today for her work in the theater (*The Forced Marriage, The Rover,* and some twenty other plays) and for her fiction (*Oronooko* and *The Fair Jilt*), Behn was in her own day also recognized as a prominent poet, composing prologues and epilogues for the theater, elegies and panegyrics for aristocratic and royal patrons, as well as some translations. A leading figure of the Restoration literary scene, friend of Dryden, Thomas Otway, the Earl of Rochester, Nell Gwynn, Thomas Killigrew, and others, Behn also inspired other women to write poems in her honor and memory. She was honored by burial in Westminster Abbey.

EPITAPH ON THE TOMBSTONE
OF A CHILD, THE LAST OF
SEVEN THAT DIED BEFORE

This little, silent, gloomy monument,
Contains all that was sweet and innocent;
The softest prattler that e'er found a tongue,
His voice was music and his words a song;
Which now each list'ning angel smiling hears,
Such pretty harmonies compose the spheres;
Wanton as unfledg'd cupids, ere their charms
Had learn'd the little arts of doing harms;
Fair as young cherubins, as soft and kind,
And though translated, could not be refin'd;
The seventh dear pledge the nuptial joys had given,
Toil'd here on Earth, retir'd to rest in Heaven;
Where they the shining host of angels fill,
Spread their gay wings before the throne, and smile.

TO THE FAIR CLARINDA, WHO MADE LOVE TO ME, IMAGINED MORE THAN WOMAN

Fair lovely maid, or if that title be
Too weak, too feminine for nobler thee,
Permit a name that more approaches truth:
And let me call thee, lovely charming youth.
This last will justify my soft complaint,
While that may serve to lessen my constraint;
And without blushes I the youth pursue,
When so much beauteous woman is in view.
Against thy charms we struggle but in vain
With thy deluding form thou giv'st us pain,   10
While the bright nymph betrays us to the swain.
In pity to our sex sure thou wert sent,
That we might love, and yet be innocent:
For sure no crime with thee we can commit;
Or if we should—thy form excuses it.
For who, that gathers fairest flowers, believes
A snake lies hid beneath the fragrant leaves.
    Thou beauteous wonder of a different kind,
Soft Cloris with the dear Alexis join'd;
Whene'er the manly part of thee would plead   20
Thou tempts us with the image of the maid,
While we the noblest passions do extend
The love to Hermes, Aphrodite the friend.

THE DISAPPOINTMENT

One day the amorous Lysander,
By an impatient passion sway'd,
Surpris'd fair Cloris, that lov'd maid,
Who could defend herself no longer.
All things did with his love conspire;
The gilded planet of the day,
In his gay chariot drawn by fire,
Was now descending to the sea,

And left no light to guide the world,
But what from Cloris' brighter eyes was hurl'd.   10

In a lone thicket made for love,
Silent as yielding maids' consent,
She with a charming languishment,
Permits his force, yet gently strove;
Her hands his bosom softly meet,
But not to put him back design'd,
Rather to draw 'em on inclin'd:
Whilst he lay trembling at her feet,
Resistance 'tis in vain to show;
She wants the pow'r to say—"Ah! What d'ye do?"   20

Her bright eyes sweet, and yet severe,
Where love and shame confus'dly strive,
Fresh vigor to Lysander give;
And breathing faintly in his ear,
She cry'd—"Cease, cease—your vain desire,
Or I'll call out—What would you do?
My dearer honour ev'n to you
I cannot, must not give—retire,
Or take this life, whose chiefest part
I gave you with the conquest of my heart."   30

But he as much unus'd to fear,
As he was capable of love,
The blessed minutes to improve,
Kisses her mouth, her neck, her hair;
Each touch her new desire alarms,
His burning trembling hand he prest
Upon her swelling snowy breast,
While she lay panting in his arms.
All her unguarded beauties lie
The spoils and trophies of the enemy.   40

And now without respect or fear,
He seeks the object of his vows,
(His love no modesty allows)
By swift degrees advancing—where
His daring hand that altar seiz'd,
Where gods of love do sacrifice:
That awful throne, that paradise

Where rage is calm'd, and anger pleas'd;
That fountain where delight still flows,
And gives the universal world repose.   50

Her balmy lips incount'ring his,
Their bodies, as their souls, are join'd;
Where both in transports unconfin'd
Extend themselves upon the moss.
Cloris half-dead and breathless lay;
Her soft eyes cast a humid light,
Such as divides the day and night;
Or falling stars, whose fires decay:
And now no signs of life she shows,
But what in short-breath'd sighs returns and goes.   60

He saw how at her length she lay;
He saw her rising bosom bare;
Her loose thin robes, through which appear
A shape design'd for love and play;
Abandon'd by her pride and shame.
She does her softest joys dispense,
Off'ring her virgin-innocence
A victim to love's sacred flame;
While the o'er-ravish'd shepherd lies
Unable to perform the sacrifice.   70

Ready to taste a thousand joys,
The too-transported hapless swain
Found the vast pleasure turn'd to pain;
Pleasure which too much love destroys:
The willing garments by he laid,
And heaven all open'd to his view,
Mad to possess, himself he threw
On the defenceless lovely maid.
But O, what envying god conspires
To snatch his power, yet leave him the desire!   80

Nature's support (without whose aid
She can no human being give)
Itself now wants the art to live;
Faintness its slack'ned nerves invade:
In vain th' enraged youth essay'd
To call its fleeting vigor back,

No motion 'twill from motion take;
Excess of love his love betray'd:
In vain he toils, in vain commands;
The insensible fell weeping in his hand.   90

In this so amorous cruel strife,
Where love and fate were too severe,
The poor Lysander in despair
Renounc'd his reason with his life:
Now all the brisk and active fire
That should the nobler part enflame,
Serv'd to increase his rage and shame,
And left no spark for new desire:
Not all her naked charms could move
Or calm that rage that had debauch'd his love.   100

Cloris returning from the trance
Which love and soft desire had bred,
Her timorous hand she gently laid
(Or guided by design or chance)
Upon that fabulous Priapus,
That potent god, as poets feign;
But never did young shepherdess,
Gath'ring of fern upon the plain,
More nimbly draw her fingers back,
Finding beneath the verdant leaves a snake: 110

Than Cloris her fair hand withdrew,
Finding that god of her desires
Disarm'd of all his awful fires,
And cold as flow'rs bath'd in the morning dew.
Who can the nymph's confusion guess?
The blood forsook the hinder place,
And strew'd with blushes all her face,
Which both disdain and shame express'd:
And from Lysander's arms she fled,
Leaving him fainting on the gloomy bed.   120

Like lightning through the grove she hies,
Or Daphne from the Delphic god,
No print upon the grassy road
She leaves, t' instruct pursuing eyes.
The wind that wanton'd in her hair,

And with her ruffled garments play'd,
Discover'd in the flying maid
All that the gods e'er made, if fair.
So Venus, when her love was slain,
With fear and haste flew o'er the fatal plain.   130

The nymph's resentments none but I
Can well imagine or condole:
But none can guess Lysander's soul,
But those who sway'd his destiny.
His silent griefs swell up to storms,
And not one god his fury spares;
He curs'd his birth, his fate, his stars;
But more the shepherdess's charms,
Whose soft bewitching influence
Had damn'd him to the hell of impotence.   140

John Wilmot, Second Earl of Rochester

(1647–1680)

Remembered to posterity as the "wicked Earl," Rochester's brief life began precociously: he had received his B.A. and M.A. from Oxford by the age of fourteen, toured Europe, and had returned to the court of Charles II in 1664. He carried off the young heiress Elizabeth Malet at the age of eighteen, and she married him eighteen months later. Rochester spent his time in the country with Elizabeth (with whom he had four children) and at court, where he had several mistresses, including the actress Elizabeth Barry. Rochester was notorious for his drinking, his wit, his courage, his quarrelsome nature, and his debauchery; Dr. Johnson recorded that Rochester "blazed out his youth in lavish voluptuousness" (although it must be noted that in his final year of life Rochester devoted serious interest to theology and politics). Known in his own day as an atheist and a libertine, he was also highly regarded as a poet, and Andrew Marvell described him as "the only man in England that had the true vein of satire." He is no less heralded for his frank, licentious verse; the Victorian biographer Sidney Lee wrote that Rochester was "the writer of the filthiest verse in the language." Last of the "Cavaliers," Rochester's poetic gifts and legacy were to make a strong impression on the poetry of Dryden, Pope, and Swift.

AGAINST CONSTANCY

Tell me no more of constancy,
   That frivolous pretense,
Of cold age, narrow jealousy,
   Disease and want of sense.

Let duller fools on whom kind chance
   Some easy heart has thrown,
Despairing higher to advance,
   Be kind to one alone.

Old men and weak, whose idle flame,
   Their own defects discovers,
Since changing can but spread their shame,
   Ought to be constant lovers;

10

But we, whose hearts do justly swell,
   With no vainglorious pride,
Who know how we in love excel,
   Long to be often tried.

Then bring my bath, and strew my bed,
   As each kind night returns,
I'll change a mistress till I'm dead,
   And fate change me for worms.   20

A SATIRE AGAINST REASON
AND MANKIND

   Were I (who to my cost already am
One of those strange, prodigious creatures, man)
A spirit free to choose, for my own share,
What case of flesh and blood I pleased to wear,
I'd be a dog, a monkey, or a bear,
Or anything but that vain animal
Who is so proud of being rational.
   The senses are too gross, and he'll contrive
A sixth to contradict the other five;
And before certain instinct will prefer   10
Reason, which fifty times for one does err;
Reason, an *ignis fatuus* in the mind,
Which, leaving light of Nature, sense, behind,
Pathless and dangerous wandering ways it takes
Through error's fenny bogs and thorny brakes;
Whilst the misguided follower climbs with pain
Mountains of whimseys, heaped in his own brain;
Stumbling from thought to thought falls headlong down,
Into doubt's boundless sea, where, like to drown,
Books bear him up a while, and make him try,   20
To swim with bladders of philosophy;
In hopes still to o'ertake the escaping light,
The vapour dances in his dazzling sight
Till, spent, it leaves him to eternal night.
Then old age and experience, hand in hand,
Lead him to death and make him understand,
After a search so painful and so long,

That all his life he has been in the wrong.
Huddled in dirt the reasoning engine lies,
Who was so proud, so witty, and so wise.   30
Pride drew him in, as cheats, their bubbles catch,
And made him venture to be made a wretch.
His wisdom did his happiness destroy,
Aiming to know that world he should enjoy;
And wit was his vain, frivolous pretence,
Of pleasing others at his own expense.
For wits are treated just like common whores:
First they're enjoy'd, and then kick'd out of doors.
The pleasure past, a threat'ning doubt remains
That frights th' enjoyer with succeeding pains.   40
Women and men of wit are dangerous tools,
And ever fatal to admiring fools.
Pleasure allures, and when the fops escape,
'Tis not that they're beloved, but fortunate,
And therefore what they fear at heart, they hate.
    But now, methinks, some formal band and beard
Takes me to task. Come on, sir; I'm prepar'd.
    "Then, by your favour, anything that's writ
Against this gibing, jingling knack called wit
Likes me abundantly; but you take care   50
Upon this point, not to be too severe.
Perhaps my Muse were fitter for this part,
For I profess I can be very smart
On wit, which I abhor with all my heart.
I long to lash it in some sharp essay,
But your grand indiscretion bids me stay,
And turns my tide of ink another way.
    "What rage ferments in your degen'rate mind,
To make you rail at Reason and Mankind?
Blest, glorious man! to whom alone kind Heav'n   60
An everlasting soul has freely giv'n;
Whom his great Maker took such care to make,
That from himself he did the image take;
And this fair frame in shining reason dress'd,
To dignify his nature above beast;
Reason, by whose aspiring influence,
We take a flight beyond material sense,
Dive into mysteries, then soaring pierce,
The flaming limits of the Universe,
Search Heav'n and Hell, find out what's acted there,   70

And give the World true grounds of hope and fear."
    Hold, mighty man, I cry, all this we know
From the pathetic pen of Ingelo,
From Patrick's *Pilgrim*, Sibbes's soliloquies,
And 'tis this very reason I despise.
This supernatural gift that makes a mite
Think he's the image of the Infinite:
Comparing his short life, void of all rest,
To the eternal and the ever blest;
This busy, puzzling stirrer-up of doubt   80
That frames deep mysteries, then finds 'em out;
Filling with frantic crowds of thinking fools
Those reverend bedlams, colleges, and schools;
Borne on whose wings, each heavy sot can pierce
The limits of the boundless Universe;
So charming ointments make an old witch fly,
And bear a crippled carcass through the sky.
'Tis this exalted pow'r, whose bus'ness lies
In nonsense and impossibilities.
This made a whimsical philosopher,   90
Before the spacious world, his tub prefer,
And we have modern cloister'd coxcombs, who
Retire to think, 'cause they have nought to do.
    But thoughts are giv'n for action's government;
Where action ceases, thought's impertinent.
Our sphere of action is life's happiness,
And he who thinks beyond, thinks like an ass.
Thus, whilst against false reas'ning I inveigh,
I own right Reason, which I would obey:
That Reason which distinguishes by sense   100
And gives us rules, of good and ill from thence,
That bounds desires with a reforming will,
To keep 'em more in vigour, not to kill.
Your Reason hinders, mine helps to enjoy,
Renewing appetites yours would destroy.
My Reason is my friend, yours is a cheat;
Hunger calls out, my Reason bids me eat;
Perversely, yours your appetite does mock:
This asks for food, that answers, "What's o'clock?"
This plain distinction, sir, your doubt secures: 110
'Tis not true Reason I despise, but yours.
    Thus I think Reason righted: but for man,
I'll ne'er recant; defend him if you can.

For all his pride and his philosophy,
'Tis evident beasts are, in their degree,
As wise at least and better far than he.
Those creatures are the wisest who attain
By surest means the ends at which they aim.
If therefore Jowler finds and kills his hares,
Better than Meres supplies committee chairs,   120
Though one's a statesman, the other but a hound,
Jowler, in justice, would be wiser found.
    You see how far man's wisdom here extends,
Look next if human nature makes amends,
Whose principles most generous are and just,
And to whose morals you would sooner trust.
Be judge yourself, I'll bring it to the test:
Which is the basest creature, man or beast?
Birds feed on birds, beasts on each other prey,
But savage man alone does man betray.   130
Pressed by necessity, they kill for food;
Man undoes man to do himself no good.
With teeth and claws by Nature arm'd, they hunt
Nature's allowance, to supply their want.
But man, with smiles, embraces, friendship, praise,
Inhumanly his fellow's life betrays;
With voluntary pains works his distress,
Not through necessity, but wantonness.
For hunger or for love they fight and tear,
Whilst wretched man is still in arms for fear.   140
For fear he arms, and is of arms afraid,
By fear to fear successively betray'd;
Base fear, the source whence his best passions came:
His boasted honour, and his dear-bought fame;
That lust of power, to which he's such a slave,
And for the which alone he dares be brave;
To which his various projects are design'd,
Which makes him generous, affable, and kind.
For which he takes such pains to be thought wise,
And screws his actions in a forc'd disguise: 150
Leading a tedious life in misery
Under laborious, mean hypocrisy.
Look to the bottom of his vast design,
Wherein man's wisdom, pow'r, and glory join:
The good he acts, the ill he does endure,
'Tis all from fear, to make himself secure.

Merely for safety, after fame we thirst,
For all men would be cowards if they durst.
And honesty's against all common sense:
Men must be knaves, 'tis in their own defence.   160
Mankind's dishonest; if you think it fair
Amongst known cheats to play upon the square,
You'll be undone—
Nor can weak truth your reputation save:
The knaves will all agree to call you knave.
Wrong'd shall he live, insulted o'er, opprest,
Who dares be less a villain than the rest.
Thus, sir, you see what human nature craves:
Most men are cowards, all men should be knaves.
The difference lies (as far as I can see)   170
Not in the thing itself but the degree,
And all the subject matter of debate
Is only: Who's a knave of the first rate?
    All this with indignation have I hurl'd
At the pretending part of the proud world,
Who, swollen with selfish vanity, devise
False freedoms, holy cheats, and formal lies
Over their fellow slaves to tyrannize.
    But if in court so just a man there be
(In court a just man, yet unknown to me)   180
Who does his needful flattery direct,
Not to oppress and ruin, but protect;
(Since flattery, which way soever laid,
Is still a tax on that unhappy trade).
If so upright a statesman you can find,
Whose passions bend to his unbias'd mind,
Who does his arts and policies apply
To raise his country, not his family;
Nor, while his pride owned avarice withstands,
Receives close bribes through friends' corrupted hands. 190
    Is there a churchman who on God relies?
Whose life his faith and doctrine justifies?
Not one blown up with vain prelatic pride,
Who for reproof of sins does man deride;
Whose envious heart makes preaching a pretence,
With his obstreperous, saucy eloquence,
To chide at kings, and rail at men of sense.
None of that sensual tribe whose talents lie
In Avarice, Pride, Sloth, and Gluttony.

Who hunt good livings but abhor good lives;   200
Whose Lust exalted to that height arrives
They act adultery with their own wives.
And ere a score of years completed be,
Can from the lofty pulpit proudly see,
Half a large parish, their own progeny.
   Nor doting bishop who would be ador'd,
For domineering at the council board,
A greater fop in business at fourscore,
Fonder of serious toys, affected more,
Than the gay, glitt'ring fool at twenty proves   210
With all his noise, his tawdry clothes, and loves.
   But a meek, humble man of honest sense,
Who, preaching peace, does practice continence;
Whose pious life's a proof he does believe
Mysterious truths, which no man can conceive.
If upon earth there dwell such God-like men,
I'll here recant my paradox to them,
Adore those shrines of virtue, homage pay,
And, with the rabble world, their laws obey.
If such there are, yet grant me this at least: 220
Man differs more from man, than man from beast.

l. 12. *ignus fatuus* = "foolish fire," that is, a receding and misleading
light seen flitting over marshy ground

Mary Lee, Lady Chudleigh

(1 6 5 6 – 1 7 1 0)

Married at the age of seventeen, Lady Chudleigh had three children and apparently lived a quiet life in Devon, where she was born. She wrote to a fellow woman poet that "the great part of my time is spent in my closet; there I meet with nothing to disturb me, nothing to render me uneasy; I find my books and my thoughts to be my most agreeable companions." Lady Chudleigh was influenced by the feminist writing of Mary Astell, with whom she corresponded and to whom she addressed a poem. Popular in her own day, she would inspire other woman poets, including Elizabeth Thomas, who corresponded with her and addressed a poem to her. She was best known for *The Ladies Defence*, a sharp rejoinder to a misogynist sermon. She also published *Poems on Several Occasions* and *Essays upon Several Subjects in Verse and Prose* and left unpublished two tragedies, two operas, and some translations.

TO THE LADIES

Wife and servant are the same,
But only differ in the name:
For when that fatal knot is tied,
Which nothing, nothing can divide:
When she the word *obey* has said,
And man by law supreme has made,
Then all that's kind is laid aside,
And nothing left but state and pride.
Fierce as an Eastern prince he grows,
And all his innate rigor shows: 10
Then but to look, to laugh, or speak,
Will the nuptial contract break.
Like mutes, she signs alone must make,
And never any freedom take:
But still be govern'd by a nod,
And fear her husband as her god:
Him still must serve, him still obey,
And nothing act, and nothing say,
But what her haughty lord thinks fit,

Who, with the power, has all the wit.
Then shun, O! shun that wretched state,   20
And all the fawning flatt'rers hate.
Value yourselves, and men despise,
You must be proud, if you'll be wise.

Anne Killigrew

(1660–1685)

Killigrew was born in London and died of smallpox there at the age of twenty-five. Her father, chaplain to the Duke of York, secured for her a place as Maid of Honor to Mary of Modena, alongside another young poet, Anne Finch, the future Countess of Winchilsea. In her brief life Anne Killigrew was celebrated as both a painter and a poet, and an engraving of a self-portrait was prefixed to the edition of her poems published by her father shortly after her death. John Dryden contributed a prefatory poem, "To the Pious Memory of the Accomplished Young Lady, Mrs. Anne Killigrew: An Ode" (see p. 245).

A FAREWELL TO WORLDLY JOYS

Farewell ye unsubstantial joys,
Ye gilded nothings, gaudy toys;
Too long ye have my soul misled,
Too long with aery diet fed.
But now my heart ye shall no more
Deceive, as you have heretofore:
For when I hear such Syrens sing,
Like Ithaca's forewarned king,
With prudent resolution I
Will so my will and fancy tie,
That stronger to the mast not he,
Than I to reason bound will be:
And though your witchcrafts strike my ear,
Unhurt like him, your charms I'll hear.

UPON THE SAYING THAT MY VERSES WERE MADE BY ANOTHER

Next Heav'n, my vows to thee (O sacred Muse!)
I offer'd up, nor did'st thou them refuse.

O Queen of verse, said I, if thou'lt inspire,
And warm my soul with thy poetic fire,
No love of gold shall share with thee my heart,
Or yet ambition in my breast have part,
More rich, more noble I will ever hold
The Muse's laurel, than a crown of gold.
An undivided sacrifice I'll lay
Upon thine altar, soul and body pay;   10
Thou shalt my pleasure, my employment be,
My all I'll make a holocaust to thee.

The deity that ever does attend
Prayers so sincere, to mine did condescend.
I writ, and the judicious prais'd my pen:
Could any doubt ensuing glory then?
What pleasing raptures fill'd my ravish'd sense?
How strong, how sweet, Fame, was thy influence?
And thine, false Hope, that to my flatter'd sight
Did'st glories represent so near, and bright?   20
By thee deceiv'd, methought, each verdant tree,
Apollo's transform'd Daphne seem'd to be;
And ev'ry fresher branch, and ev'ry bough
Appear'd as garlands to empale my brow.
The learn'd in love say, thus the winged boy
Does first approach, dress'd up in welcome joy;
At first he to the cheated lovers' sight
Nought represents, but rapture and delight,
Alluring hopes, soft fears, which stronger bind
Their hearts, than when they more assurance find.   30

Embolden'd thus, to Fame I did commit,
(By some few hands) my most unlucky wit.
But, ah, the sad effects that from it came!
What ought t'have brought me honour, brought me shame!
Like Aesop's painted jay I seem'd to all,
Adorn'd in plumes, I not my own could call:
Rifl'd like her, each one my feathers tore,
And, as they thought, unto the owner bore.
My laurels thus another's brow adorn'd,
My numbers they admir'd, but me they scorn'd: 40
Another's brow, that had so rich a store
Of sacred wreaths, that circled it before;
Where mine quite lost (like a small stream that ran

Into a vast and boundless ocean),
Was swallow'd up, with what it join'd and drown'd,
And this abyss yet no accession found.

    Orinda (Albion's and her sex's grace)
Ow'd not her glory to a beauteous face,
It was her radiant soul that shone within,
Which struck a lustre through her outward skin;   50
That did her lips and cheeks with roses die,
Advanc'd her height, and sparkl'd in her eye.

Anne Kingsmill Finch,
Countess of Winchilsea

(1 6 6 1 – 1 7 2 0)

Born into a prominent Hampshire family, Finch served at court as Maid of Honor to Mary of Modena. She married a strong supporter of the Stuarts, Heneage Finch, and, following the deposition of Stuart monarch James II in 1688, the couple left the court and spent much of the rest of their lives in a country retreat in Kent. This change proved conducive to Finch's poetic activity, and for the rest of her life she produced at a steady rate poems about nature, melancholy, love, marriage, and the place of women in society. She also explored a range of contemporary verse forms and genres and was a skillful imitator and parodist. Finch published a collection of her poetry in 1713, *Miscellany Poems on Several Occasions, Written by a Lady*, and her work was acknowledged in her own lifetime by Pope, Swift, Nicholas Rowe, and others. In the early nineteenth century her nature poetry was immediately recognized by William Wordsworth as a forerunner of the Romantics; he anthologized her poetry and praised "A Nocturnal Reverie" for being the only poem written between Milton's *Paradise Lost* and James Thomson's *The Seasons* that contained "a single new image of external nature." A carefully ordered manuscript of her poetry, which she apparently had hoped to see published posthumously, was not printed until 1903.

A NOCTURNAL REVERIE

In such a night, when every louder wind
Is to its distant cavern safe confin'd;
And only gentle Zephyr fans his wings,
And lonely Philomel, still waking, sings;
Or from some tree, famed for the owl's delight,
She, hollowing clear, directs the wand'rer right:
In such a night, when passing clouds give place,
Or thinly veil the Heav'ns' mysterious face;
When in some river, overhung with green,
The waving moon and trembling leaves are seen;   10
When freshen'd grass now bears itself upright,

And makes cool banks to pleasing rest invite,
Whence springs the woodbine, and the bramble-rose,
And where the sleepy cowslip shelter'd grows;
Whilst now a paler hue the foxglove takes,
Yet chequers still with red the dusky brakes,
When scattered glow-worms, but in twilight fine,
Show trivial beauties watch their hour to shine;
When odours, which declin'd repelling day,
Through temp'rate air uninterrupted stray;   20
When darken'd groves their softest shadows wear,
And falling waters we distinctly hear;
When through the gloom more venerable shows
Some ancient fabric, awful in repose,
While sunburnt hills their swarthy looks conceal,
And swelling haycocks thicken up the vale:
When the loos'd horse now, as his pasture leads,
Comes slowly grazing through th'adjoining meads,
Whose stealing pace, and lengthen'd shade we fear,
Till torn-up forage in his teeth we hear: 30
When nibbling sheep at large pursue their food,
And unmolested kine rechew the cud;
When curlews cry beneath the village walls,
And to her straggling brood the partridge calls;
Their short-liv'd jubilee the creatures keep,
Which but endures while tyrant man does sleep;
When a sedate content the spirit feels,
And no fierce light disturbs, whilst it reveals;
But silent musings urge the mind to seek
Something, too high for syllables to speak;   40
Till the free soul to a compos'dness charm'd,
Finding the elements of rage disarm'd,
O'er all below a solemn quiet grown,
Joys in th'inferior world, and thinks it like her own:
In such a night let me abroad remain,
Till morning breaks, and all's confus'd again;
Our cares, our toils, our clamours are renew'd,
Or pleasures, seldom reach'd, pursu'd.

ARDELIA TO MELANCHOLY

At last, my old inveterate foe,
No opposition shalt thou know.

Since I, by struggling, can obtain
Nothing, but increase of pain
I will at last no more do so,
Though I confess I have applied
Sweet mirth, and music, and have tried
A thousand other arts beside,
To drive thee from my darken'd breast,
Thou, who hast banish'd all my rest.   10
But, though sometimes a short reprieve they gave,
Unable they, and far too weak, to save;
All arts to quell, did but augment thy force,
As rivers check'd, break with a wilder course.
Friendship, I to my heart have laid,
Friendship, th'applauded sov'reign aid,
And thought that charm so strong would prove,
As to compel thee to remove;
And to myself I boasting said,
Now I a conqu'ror sure shall be,   20
The end of all my conflicts see,
And noble triumph wait on me;
My dusky, sullen foe will sure
Ne'er this united charge endure.
But, leaning on this reed, ev'n whilst I spoke,
It pierced my hand, and into pieces broke.
Still some new object, or new int'rest came
And loos'd the bonds, and quite dissolv'd the claim.
These failing, I invok'd a Muse,
And poetry would often use   30
To guard me from thy tyrant power;
And to oppose thee every hour
New troops of fancies did I choose.
Alas! in vain, for all agree
To yield me captive up to thee,
And Heav'n alone can set me free.
Thou through my life wilt with me go,
And make the passage sad, and slow.
All that could e'er thy ill-got rule invade,
Their useless arms before thy feet have laid;   40
The fort is thine, now ruin'd, all within,
Whilst by decays without, thy conquest too is seen.

THE CIRCUIT OF APOLLO

Apollo as lately a circuit he made,
Through the lands of the Muses when Kent he survey'd,
And saw there that poets were not very common,
But most that pretended to verse, were the women,
Resolv'd to encourage the few that he found,
And she that writ best with a wreath should be crown'd.
A summons sent out, was obey'd but by four,
When Phoebus, afflicted, to meet with no more,
And standing, where sadly, he now might descry,
From the banks of the Stoure the desolate Wye,   10
He lamented for Behn o'er that place of her birth,
And said amongst femens was not on the earth
Her superiour in fancy, in language, or wit,
Yet own'd that a little too loosely she writ;
Since the art of the Muse is to stir up soft thoughts.
Yet to make all hearts beat, without blushes, or faults.
But now to proceed, and their merits to know,
Before he on any, the bays would bestow,
He order'd them each in their several way,
To show him their papers, to sing, or to say,   20
What e'er they thought best, their pretentions might prove,
When Alinda, began, with a song upon love.
So easy the verse, yet compos'd with such art,
That not one expression fell short of the heart;
Apollo himself, did their influence obey,
He catch'd up his lyre, and a part he would play,
Declaring, no harmony else, could be found,
Fit to wait upon words, of so moving a sound.
The wreath, he reach'd out, to have plac'd on her head,
If Laura not quickly a paper had read,   30
Wherin she Orinda has praised so high,
He own'd it had reach'd him, while yet in the sky,
That he thought with himself, when it first struck his ear,
Who e'er could write that, ought the laurel to wear.
Betwixt them he stood, in a musing suspense,
Till Valeria withdrew him a little from thence,
And told him, as soon as she'd got him aside,
Her works, by no other, but him should be tried;
Which so often he read, and with still new delight,
That judgment 'twas thought would not pass till 'twas night;   40

Yet at length, he restor'd them, but told her withal
If she kept it still close, he'd the talent recall.
Ardelia came last as expecting least praise,
Who writ for her pleasure and not for the bays,
But yet, as occasion, or fancy should sway,
Would sometimes endeavour to pass a dull day,
In composing a song, or a scene of a play
Not seeking for fame, which so little does last,
That ere we can taste it, the pleasure is past.
But Apollo replied, though so careless she seem'd,   50
Yet the bays, if her share, would be highly esteem'd.
And now, he was going to make an oration,
Had thrown by one lock, with a delicate fashion,
Upon the left foot, most genteelly did stand,
Had drawn back the other, and wav'd his white hand,
When calling to mind, how the prize although given
By Paris, to her, who was fairest in Heaven,
Had pull'd on the rash, inconsiderate boy,
The fall of his house, with the ruin of Troy,
Since in wit, or in beauty, it never was heard,   60
One female could yield t' have another preferr'd,
He changed his design, and divided his praise,
And said that they all had a right to the bays,
And that t'were injustice, one brow to adorn,
With a wreath, which so fitly by each might be worn.
Then smil'd to himself, and applauded his art,
Who thus nicely has acted so subtle a part,
Four women to wheedle, but found 'em too many,
For who would please all, can never please any.
In vain then, he thought it, there longer to stay,   70
But told them, he now must go drive on the day,
Yet the case to Parnassus, should soon be referr'd,
And there in a council of Muses, be heard,
Who of their own sex, best the title might try,
Since no man upon earth, nor himself in the sky,
Would be so imprudent, so dull, or so blind,
To loose three parts in four from amongst womankind.

l. 12. femens = females

Lady Grisell Baillie

(1665–1746)

Lady Grisell Baillie, a Scot, was the eldest daughter of eighteen children. When her father, a friend of the slain Jacobite Robert Baillie (whose son she would later marry), fled Scotland to Utrecht, she managed the household and even made a secret voyage back to Scotland to rescue a sister left behind. Her heroic exploits were later celebrated in Joanna Baillie's *Metrical Legend*. Lady Grisell Baillie kept meticulous *Day Books* after her marriage that provide rich insight into her domestic activities. Sadly, most of her poetry—a manuscript "book of songs" described by her daughter—is lost. Her striking ballad, "Were Na My Heart Licht I Wad Die," is believed to have come from that lost volume and was first printed anonymously in 1726.

WERE NA MY HEART LICHT, I WAD DIE

There was ance a may, and she lo'ed na men;
She biggit her bonny bower down i' yon glen,
But now she cries dool and well-a-day!
Come down the green gait, and come here away.

When bonny young Johnny cam o'er the sea,
He said he saw naething sae lovely as me;
He hecht me baith rings and mony braw things;
And were na my heart licht, I wad die.

He had a wee titty that lo'ed na me,
Because I was twice as bonny as she;   10
She raised such a pother 'twixt him and his mother,
That were na my heart licht, I wad die.

The day it was set, and the bridal to be:
The wife took a dwam, and lay down to dee;
She maned and she graned out o' dolour and pain,
Till he vowed he never wad see me again.

His kin was for ane of a higher degree,
Said, "What had he to do wi' the like of me?"
Albeit I was bonny, I was na for Johnny:
And were na my heart licht, I wad die.   20

They said I had neither cow nor calf,
Nor dribbles o' drink rins through the draff,
Nor pickles o' meal rins through the mill-eye;
And were na my heart licht, I wad die.

His titty she was baith wily and slee,
She spied me as I cam o'er the lea;
And then she cam in and made a loud din;
Believe your ain een, an he trow na me.

His bonnet stood aye fu' round on his brow;
His auld ane looked aye as weel as some's new;   30
But now he lets 't wear ony gait it will hing,
And casts himself dowie upon the corn-bing.

And now he gaes daunerin about the dykes,
And a' he dow dae is to hound the tykes;
The live-lang nicht he ne'er steeks his eye,
And were na my heart licht, I wad die.

Were I young for thee as I hae been
We should hae been gallopin' down on yon green,
And linkin' it on yon lily-white lea;
And wow gin I were but young for thee.   40

l.   1. may = maid
l.   2. biggit = built
l.   3. dool = dole, sorrow
l.   7. hecht = promised
l.   9. titty = sister
l. 14. dwam = swoon
l. 32. dowie = melancholy
l. 34. hound the tykes = set on the dogs
l. 35. steeks = closes

Jonathan Swift

(1 6 6 7 – 1 7 4 5)

Best known today as the author of *Gulliver's Travels* (1726), Swift was born in
Dublin and educated (along with the dramatist William Congreve) at Kilkenny
Grammar School and at Trinity College, Dublin. After a brief period in En-
gland in service to Sir William Temple, Swift returned to Ireland and was
ordained an Anglican priest in 1695. He returned to England and worked for
Temple until the latter's death in 1699. While in Temple's service, Swift first
met "Stella" (Hester Jonson), the love of his life. After returning again to
Ireland, Swift was given a prebend in St. Patrick's, in Dublin, where he became
Dean in 1713. Swift visited London regularly, and by the early years of the
eighteenth century was friends with Addison, Steele, Gay, and Pope and was a
prominent member of the literary circle called the "Scribblerians." Swift ex-
celled at satire and was an extraordinarily prolific writer of both verse and
polemical prose. Among his early successes were *The Battle of the Books* and *A
Tale of a Tub*, published together in 1704, and his poems on London life
published in *The Tatler* in 1709. In his later years Swift produced his unusual
Verses on the Death of Dr. Swift (1721; published 1739) and *A Modest Proposal*
(1729).

MRS. HARRIS'S PETITION

To Their Excellencies the Lords Justices of Ireland.
The Humble Petition of Frances Harris, Who Must
Starve and Die a Maid If It Miscarries

Humbly showeth:
That I went to warm myself in Lady Betty's chamber, because I was cold,
And I had in a purse, seven pound, four shillings and sixpence, besides
    farthings, in money, and gold;
So because I had been buying things for my Lady last night,
I was resolved to tell my money, to see if it was right.
Now you must know, because my trunk has a very bad lock,
Therefore all the money I have, which, God knows, is a very small stock,
I keep in a pocket tied about my middle, next my smock:

So when I went to put up my purse, as God would have it, my smock was
    unripped,
And, instead of putting it into my pocket, down it slipped:
Then the bell rung, and I went down to put my Lady to bed,   10
And, God knows, I thought my money was as safe as my maidenhead.
So when I came up again, I found my pocket feel very light,
But when I searched, and missed my purse, Lord! I thought I should have
    sunk outright.
"Lord! Madam," says Mary, "how d'ye do?"—"Indeed," said I, "never worse;
But pray, Mary, can you tell what I have done with my purse?"
"Lord help me," said Mary, "I never stirred out of this place!"
"Nay," said I, "I had it in Lady Betty's chamber, that's a plain case."
So Mary got me to bed, and covered me up warm,
However, she stole away my garters, that I might do myself no harm.
So I tumbled and tossed all night, as you may very well think,   20
But hardly ever set my eyes together, or slept a wink.
So I was a-dreamed, methought, that we went and searched the folks round,
And in a corner of Mrs. Dukes' box, tied in a rag, the money was found.
So next morning we told Whittle, and he fell a-swearing;
Then my Dame Wadgar came, and she, you know, is thick of hearing;
"Dame," said I, as loud as I could bawl, "do you know what a loss I have had?"
"Nay," said she, "my Lord Collway's folks are all very sad,
For my Lord Dromedary comes a Tuesday without fail";
"Pugh!" said I, "but that's not the business that I ail."
Says Cary, says he, "I have been a servant this five and twenty years, come
    spring,   30
And in all the places I liv'd, I never heard of such a thing."
"Yes," says the steward, "I remember when I was at my Lady Shrewsbury's,
Such a thing as this happened, just about the time of gooseberries.
So I went to the party suspected, and I found her full of grief;
(Now you must know, of all things in the world, I hate a thief)."
However, I was resolv'd to bring the discourse slyly about.
"Mrs. Dukes," said I, "here's an ugly accident has happen'd out;
'Tis not that I value the money three skips of a louse;
But the thing I stand upon, is the credit of the House;
'Tis true, seven pound, four shillings, and sixpence, makes a great hole in
    my wages,   40
Besides, as they say, service is no inheritance in these ages.
Now, Mrs. Dukes, you know, and everybody understands,
That though 'tis hard to judge, yet money can't go without hands."
"The devil take me," said she (blessing herself), "if ever I saw't!"
So she roared like a Bedlam, as though I had called her all to naught;
So you know, what could I say to her any more:

I e'en left her, and came away as wise as I was before.
Well: but then they would have had me gone to the cunning-man;
"No," said I, " 'tis the same thing, the chaplain will be here anon."
So the chaplain came in. Now the servants say he is my sweetheart,   50
Because he's always in my chamber, and I always take his part;
So, as the devil would have it, before I was aware, out I blunder'd,
"Parson," said I, "can you cast a nativity, when a body's plunder'd?"
(Now you must know, he hates to be call'd Parson, like the devil.)
"Truly," says he, "Mrs. Nab, it might become you to be more civil:
If your money be gone, as a learned divine says, d'ye see,
You are no text for my handling, so take that from me:
I was never taken for a conjurer before, I'd have you to know."
"Lord," said I, "don't be angry, I'm sure I never thought you so;
You know I honour the cloth, I design to be a parson's wife,   60
I never took one in your coat for a conjurer in all my life."
With that, he twisted his girdle at me like a rope, as who should say,
"Now you may go hang yourself for me," and so went away.
Well, I thought I should have swooned. "Lord," said I, "what shall I do?
I have lost my money, and I shall lose my true-love too."
Then my Lord called me; "Harry," said my Lord, "don't cry,
I'll give something towards thy loss"; and says my Lady, "so will I."
"Oh but," said I, "what if after all the chaplain won't come to?"
For that, he said (an't please your Excellencies) I must petition you.
The premises tenderly considered, I desire your Excellencies' protection,   70
And that I may have a share in next Sunday's collection:
And over and above, that I may have your Excellencies' letter,
With an order for the chaplain aforesaid; or instead of him, a better;
And then your poor petitioner, both night and day,
Or the chaplain (for 'tis his trade) as in duty bound, shall ever pray."

IN SICKNESS. WRITTEN
SOON AFTER THE
AUTHOR'S COMING TO
LIVE IN IRELAND, UPON
THE QUEEN'S DEATH,
OCTOBER 1714

'Tis true—then why should I repine,
To see my life so fast decline?
But why obscurely here alone?

Where I am neither loved nor known.
My state of health none care to learn;
My life is here no soul's concern.
And, those with whom I now converse
Without a tear will tend my hearse;
Removed from kind Arbuthnot's aid,
Who knows his art but not his trade,   10
Preferring his regard for me
Before his credit or his fee.
Some formal visits, looks, and words,
What mere humanity affords,
I meet perhaps from three or four,
From whom I once expected more;
Which those who tend the sick for pay
Can act as decently as they.
But no obliging, tender friend
To help at my approaching end,   20
My life is now a burthen grown
To others, e'er it be my own.
    Ye formal weepers for the sick,
In your last offices be quick:
And spare my absent friends the grief
To hear, yet give me no relief;
Expired today, entombed tomorrow,
When known, will save a double sorrow.

STELLA'S BIRTHDAY, 1725

As, when a beauteous nymph decays,
We say, she's past her dancing days;
So, poets lose their feet by time,
And can no longer dance in rhyme.
Your annual bard had rather chose
To celebrate your birth in prose;
Yet, merry folks, who want by chance
A pair to make a country dance,
Call the old housekeeper, and get her
To fill a place, for want of better;   10
While Sheridan is off the hooks,
And friend Delany at his books,
That Stella may avoid disgrace,

Once more the Dean supplies their place.
   Beauty and wit, too sad a truth,
Have always been confined to youth;
The god of wit, and beauty's queen,
He twenty-one and she fifteen:
No poet ever sweetly sung,
Unless he were, like Phoebus, young;   20
Nor ever nymph inspir'd to rhyme,
Unless, like Venus, in her prime.
At fifty-six, if this be true,
Am I a poet fit for you?
Or, at the age of forty-three,
Are you a subject fit for me?
Adieu bright wit and radiant eyes;
You must be grave, and I be wise.
Our fate in vain we would oppose,
But I'll be still your friend in prose: 30
Esteem and friendship to express
Will not require poetic dress;
And if the Muse deny her aid
To have them *sung*, they may be *said*.
   But, Stella say, what evil tongue
Reports you are no longer young?
That Time sits with his scythe to mow
Where erst sat Cupid with his bow;
That half your locks are turn'd to grey?
I'll ne'er believe a word they say.   40
'Tis true, but let it not be known,
My eyes are somewhat dimmish grown;
For Nature, always in the right,
To your decays adapts my sight,
And wrinkles undistinguish'd pass,
For I'm ashamed to use a glass;
And till I see them with these eyes,
Whoever says you have them, lies.
   No length of time can make you quit
Honour and virtue, sense and wit;   50
Thus you may still be young to me,
While I can better *hear* than *see*;
O ne'er may Fortune show her spite,
To make me *deaf*, and mend my *sight*.

Sarah Fyge Egerton

(1670–1723)

The daughter of a London physician, Sarah Fyge Egerton was apparently sent away from home by her father after her notorious publication as a teenager of *The Female Advocate* (1686), a repudiation in verse of a misogynist satire, *Love Given O'er*. Fyge married twice, neither time very happily. She sued her second husband for divorce while he in turn accused her of having run off with a married lover. Sometime friend Delarivier Manley retailed these marital scandals in *The New Atalantis* (1709). Known in her own day as "Mrs. Field" or "Clarinda," Sarah Fyge Egerton's work was praised by John Froud for its poetic skill: "Not Behn herself with all her softest art / So well could talk of love, or touch the heart."

THE EMULATION

Say, tyrant custom, why must we obey
The impositions of thy haughty sway;
From the first dawn of life unto the grave,
Poor womankind's in every state a slave.
The nurse, the mistress, parent and the swain,
For love she must, there's none escape that pain;
Then comes the last, the fatal slavery,
The husband with insulting tyranny
Can have ill manners justify'd by law;
For men all join to keep the wife in awe.   10
Moses who first our freedom did rebuke,
Was marry'd when he writ the Pentateuch;
They're wise to keep us slaves, for well they know
If we were loose, we soon should make them so.
We yield like vanquish'd kings whom fetters bind
When chance of war is to usurpers kind;
Submit in form; but they'd our thoughts control,
And lay restraints on the impassive soul:
They fear we should excel their sluggish parts
Should we attempt the sciences and arts;   20
Pretend they were design'd for them alone,

So keep us fools to raise their own renown:
Thus priests of old their grandeur to maintain
Cried vulgar eyes would sacred laws profane.
So kept the mysteries behind a screen,
There homage and the name were lost had they been seen:
But in this blessed age, such freedom's given
That every man explains the will of heaven;
And shall we women now sit tamely by,
Make no excursions in philosophy,   30
Or grace our thoughts in tuneful poetry?
We will our rights in learning's world maintain,
Wit's empire, now, shall know a female reign;
Come all ye fair, the great attempt improve,
Divinely imitate the realms above:
There's ten celestial females govern wit,
And but two gods that dare pretend to it;
And shall these finite males reverse their rules?
No, we'll be wits, and then men must be fools.

THE REPULSE TO ALCANDER

What is't you mean, that I am thus approach'd,
Dare you to hope, that I may be debauch'd?
For your seducing words the same implies,
In begging pity with a soft surprise,
For one who loves, and sighs, and almost dies.
In ev'ry word and action doth appear
Something I hate and blush to see or hear;
At first your love for vast respect was told,
Till your excess of manners grew too bold
And did your base, designing thoughts unfold.   10
When a salute did seem to custom due,
With too much ardour you'd my lips pursue;
My hand, with which you play'd, you'd kiss and press,
Nay ev'ry look had something of address.
Ye gods! I cried, sure he designs to woo,
For thus did amorous Phylaster do,
The youth whose passion none could disapprove,
When Hymen waited to complete his love;
But now, when sacred laws and vows confine
Me to another, what can you design?   20

At first, I could not see the lewd abuse,
But fram'd a thousand things for your excuse.
I knew that Bacchus sometimes did inspire
A sudden transport, though not lasting fire;
For he no less than Cupid can make kind,
And force a fondness which was ne'er design'd;
Or thought you'd travel'd far, and it might chance
To be the foreign mode of complaisance.
Till you so oft your amorous crimes repeat,
That to permit you would make mine as great;   30
Nor stopped you here but languishingly spake
That love which I endeavour'd to mistake:
What saw you in me, that could make you vain,
Or any thing expect, but just disdain?
I must confess I am not quite so nice
To damn all little gallantries for vice
(But I see now my charity's misplac'd,
If none but sullen saints can be thought chaste).
Yet know, base man, I scorn your lewd amours,
Hate them from all, not only 'cause they're yours.   40
Oh sacred Love! let not the world profane
Thy transports, thus to sport, and entertain;
The beau, with some small artifice of's own,
Can make a treat, for all the wanton town:
I thought myself secure, within these shades,
But your rude love, my privacy invades,
Affronts my virtue, hazards my just fame:
Why should I suffer for your lawless flame?
For oft 'tis known, through vanity and pride,
Men boast those favours which they are denied;   50
Or others' malice, which can soon discern,
Perhaps may see in you some kind concern,
So scatter false suggestions of their own
That I love too: Oh! stain to my renown!
No, I'll be wise, avoid your sight in time,
And shun at once the censure and the crime.

Elizabeth Thomas

(1675–1731)

Thomas's father (some forty years older than her mother) died when she was two, and she spent much of the rest of her life with her mother in London. For the most part self-educated, Thomas began writing poetry while fairly young and began a correspondence with the aging John Dryden, who wrote back that her "verses were . . . too good to be a woman's," for "you want neither vigour in your thoughts, nor force in your expressions, nor harmony in your numbers." Thomas was influenced by Mary Astell (who snubbed her for her politics) and corresponded with Lady Chudleigh. She may also have known Sarah Egerton, a fellow contributor to a volume of poetry in memory of Dryden. In her later years Thomas was burdened with financial problems and was confined to the Fleet Prison for debt in 1727. Strapped for funds, she sold off some letters Pope had written to a mutual friend, Henry Cromwell, for which Pope excoriated her in *The Dunciad*. Her poems, publication of which she had initially deferred, were printed in 1722 and reissued in 1726 and 1727. The year before her death, destitute, in London, she published *The Metamorphosis of the Town*.

ON SIR J—— S—— SAYING IN A SARCASTIC MANNER, MY BOOKS WOULD MAKE ME MAD

AN ODE

Unhappy sex! how hard's our fate,
By Custom's tyranny confin'd
To foolish needlework, and chat,
Or such like exercise as that,
But still denied th' improvement of our mind!
"Women!" men cry, "alas, poor fools!
What are they but domestic tools?
On purpose made our toils to share,
And ease the husband's economic care.
To dress, to sing, to work, to play,   10
To watch our looks, our words obey,
And with their little follies drive dull thoughts away.

Thus let them humbly in subjection live;
But learning leave to man, our great prerogative."

Most mighty sov'reigns, we submit,
And own ye monarchs of the realms of Wit:
 But might a slave to her superiors speak,
  And without treason silence break,
  She'd first implore your royal grace,
 Then humbly thus expostulate the case.   20
Those, who to husbands have their power resigned,
 Will in their house a full employment find,
 And little time command to cultivate the mind.
  Had we been made intuitively wise,
  Like angels' vast capacities,
  I would allow we need not use
  Those rules experience does infuse:
 But if born ignorant, though fit for more,
Can you deny we should improve our store?
  Or won't you be so just to grant   30
  That those perfections which we want,
And can't acquire when in a married state,
   Should be attained before?
Believe me, 'tis a truth long understood,
That those who know not why they're so, can ne'er be wise or good.

What surer method can we take
 Than this ye seem to choose?
'Tis books ye write, and books ye use;
 But yet we must a serious judgment make,
  What to elect, and what refuse.   40
 Is't not by books we're taught to know
 The great Creator of this world below?
 The vast dimensions of this earth,
And to what minute particles poor mortals owe their birth?
 By books, th' Almighty's works we learn and prize,
 But those phenomenas, which dazzle vulgar eyes,
  We can as much despise.
 And more than this, well chosen books do show
  What unto God, and what to man we owe.
   Yet, if we enquire for a book,   50
  Beyond a novel or a play,
 Good lord! how soon th' alarm's took,
  How soon your eyes your souls betray,

And with what spite ye look!
How nat'rally ye stare and scowl,
   Like wond'ring birds about an owl,
And with malicious sneer these dismal accents howl.

   "Alas, poor Plato! All thy glory's past:
  What, in a female hand arriv'd at last!"
  "Sure," adds another, " 'tis for something worse;   60
This itch of reading's sent her as a curse."
"No, no," cries good Sir John, "but 'tis as bad,
For if she's not already craz'd, I'm sure she will be mad."
  'Tis thus ye rail to vent your spleen,
  And think your wond'rous wit is seen:
But 'tis the malice of your sex appears.
   What, suffer woman to pretend to sense!
  Oh! how this optic magnifies the offence,
   And aggravates your fears!
  But since the French in all ye ape,   70
Why should not they your morals shape?
   Their women are as gay and fair,
Yet learned ladies are no monsters there.
   What is it from our sex ye fear,
    That thus ye curb our powers?
   D'ye apprehend a bookish war,
Or are your judgments less for raising ours?
   Come, come, the real truth confess
  (A fault acknowledged is the less),
   And own it was an avaricious soul,   80
Which would, with greedy eyes, monopolize the whole:
  And bars us learning on the selfish score;
   That, conscious of our native worth,
    Ye dread to make it more.
Then thanks to Heaven we're English-born and free,
And thank our gracious laws that give such liberty.

John Gay

(1 6 8 5 – 1 7 3 2)

Gay was born into a poor family in Barnstaple, Devonshire. His parents both
died before he was ten. When Gay finished grammar school his uncle arranged
for him to serve as an apprentice to a silk mercer in London, but he soon
abandoned this profession. After struggling on the fringes of the literary world,
Gay began to publish some of his work, and his earliest poems were burlesque
and mock heroic, modeled on the work of Pope. Before long he was befriended
by both Pope and Swift. The financial security he gained from early successes
was squandered in disastrous speculation, and for much of the rest of his life
Gay depended upon various patrons for employment and support. He achieved
a considerable success in the theater in 1728 with *The Beggar's Opera*. Gay was
buried in Westminster Abbey, next to Chaucer's tomb, and the monument to
his memory includes the epitaph he had first published in his collected *Poems*
of 1720.

TO A YOUNG LADY, WITH SOME LAMPREYS

With lovers 'twas of old the fashion
By presents to convey their passion;
No matter what the gift they sent,
The lady saw that love was meant.
Fair Atalanta, as a favour,
Took the boar's head her hero gave her;
Nor could the bristly thing affront her,
'Twas a fit present from a hunter.
When squires send woodcocks to the dame,
It serves to show their absent flame: 10
Some by a snip of woven hair,
In posied lockets bribe the fair;
How many mercenary matches
Have sprung from di'mond-rings and watches!
But hold—a ring, a watch, a locket,
Would drain at once a poet's pocket;
He should send songs that cost him nought,

Nor ev'n be prodigal of thought.
　　Why then send lampreys? fie, for shame!
'Twill set a virgin's blood on flame.   20
This to fifteen a proper gift!
It might lend sixty five a lift.
　　I know your maiden aunt will scold,
And think my present somewhat bold.
I see her lift her hands and eyes:
　　"What, eat it, niece? eat Spanish flies!
Lamprey's a most immodest diet:
You'll neither wake nor sleep in quiet.
Should I tonight eat sago-cream,
'Twould make me blush to tell my dream;   30
If I eat lobster, 'tis so warming,
That ev'ry man I see looks charming;
Wherefore had not the filthy fellow
Laid Rochester upon your pillow?
I vow and swear, I think the present
Had been as modest and as decent.
　　Who has her virtue in her power?
Each day has its unguarded hour;
Always in danger of undoing,
A prawn, a shrimp may prove our ruin!   40
　　The shepherdess, who lives on salad,
To cool her youth controls her palate;
Should Dian's maids turn liqu'rish livers,
And of huge lampreys rob the rivers,
Then all beside each glade and visto,
You'd see nymphs lying like Calisto.
　　The man who meant to heat your blood,
Needs not himself such vicious food—"
　　In this, I own, your aunt is clear,
I sent you what I well might spare: 50
For when I see you (without joking)
Your eyes, lips, breasts, are so provoking,
They set my heart more cock-a-hoop
Than could whole seas of craw-fish soup.

MY OWN EPITAPH

Life is a jest; and all things show it;
I thought so once; but now I know it.

Alexander Pope

(1 6 8 8 – 1 7 4 4)

Born into a Roman Catholic family in 1688—a year that marked the decline of Catholic fortunes following the abdication of King James II—Pope was tutored at home and enrolled for brief periods in small Catholic academies. By the age of twelve he had been stricken with Pott's disease (tuberculosis of the spine), which left him, in the words of the painter Sir Joshua Reynolds, "about four-feet-six high" and "very humpbacked and deformed," though with "a large and very fine eye, and a long handsome nose." His skill as a poet was recognized early by writers like Wycherley and Congreve, and his reputation was secured with the publication of *An Essay on Criticism* and the brilliant mock-epic, *The Rape of the Lock*. His financial stability as a poet was assured with the subscription to and publication of his translation of Homer's *Iliad*, completed in 1720, after which he turned his attention to editing Shakespeare's *Works*. Pope's later years saw no slackening of his poetic talents: he published the seathing *Dunciad*, his *An Essay on Man* (1733–1734), and his satires, *Imitations of Horace* (1733–1738). Swift, a friend and admirer, would speak for many when he wrote: "In Pope, I cannot read a line, / But with a sigh, I wish it mine." Pope's great reputation would be eclipsed by the Romantics, especially Wordsworth, who, although deeply influenced by Pope, needed to define a new poetic movement by repudiating this important precursor. "Of the Characters of Women" (1732–1734), an "Epistle" addressed to a valued friend, Martha Blount, satirizes the "World" of fashion—both by its argument that women embody contradictory traits rather than a single "ruling passion" and by its tone. It elicited several feminist rebuttals, including those by Montagu and Ingram in this volume (see pp. 329, 338).

   In *The Rape of the Lock* (1712–1717), written to reconcile two Catholic families after a lord cut off a lock of a young lady's hair, Pope awarded a card game of ombre the attributes of epic battle. Among the devices with which he created one of the finest mock-epics in any language, he substituted Rosicrucian sylphs and gnomes for the Greco-Roman gods of epic convention and linked high moral values with social trivia in couplet after couplet.

EPISTLE TO A LADY:

Of the Characters of Women

Nothing so true as what you once let fall,
"Most women have no characters at all":
Matter too soft a lasting mark to bear,
And best distinguish'd by black, brown, or fair.
How many pictures of one nymph we view,
And how unlike each other, all how true!
Arcadia's countess here, in ermin'd pride,
Is there, Pastora by a fountain side:
Here Fannia, leering on her own good man,
Is there a naked Leda with a swan.   10
Let then the fair one beautifully cry,
In Magdalen's loose hair and lifted eye,
Or drest in smiles of sweet Cecilia shine,
With simp'ring angels, palms, and harps divine;
Whether the charmer sinner it, or saint it,
If folly grow romantic, I must paint it.
    Come, then, the colours and the ground prepare!
Dip in the rainbow, trick her off in air;
Choose a firm cloud before it fall, and in it
Catch, ere she change, the Cynthia of this minute.   20
    Rufa, whose eye quick-glancing o'er the park,
Attracts each light gay meteor of a Spark,
Agrees as ill with Rufa studying Locke,
As Sappho's diamonds with her dirty smock,
Or Sappho at her toilet's greasy task,
With Sappho fragrant at an ev'ning masque.
So morning insects, that in muck begun,
Shine, buzz, and fly-blow in the setting sun.
    How soft is Silia! fearful to offend;
The frail one's advocate, the weak one's friend: 30
To her Calista prov'd her conduct nice,
And good Simplicius asks of her advice.
Sudden she storms! she raves! you tip the wink,
But spare your censure; Silia does not drink.
All eyes may see from what the change arose,
All eyes may see—a pimple on her nose.
    Papillia, wedded to her doating Spark,
Sighs for the shades—"How charming is a park!"

A park is purchas'd; but the Fair he sees
All bathed in tears—"Oh, odious, odious trees!"   40
    Ladies, like variegated tulips, show;
'Tis to their changes half their charms we owe:
Their happy spots the nice admirer take,
Fine by defect, and delicately weak.
'Twas thus Calypso once each heart alarm'd,
Aw'd without virtue, without beauty charm'd;
Her tongue bewitch'd as oddly as her eyes;
Less Wit than Mimic, more a Wit than wise.
Strange graces still, and stranger flights, she had,
Was just not ugly, and was just not mad;   50
Yet ne'er so sure our passion to create,
As when she touch'd the brink of all we hate.
    Narcissa's nature, tolerably mild,
To make a wash, would hardly stew a child;
Has ev'n been prov'd to grant a lover's prayer,
And paid a tradesman once to make him stare;
Gave alms at Easter, in a Christian trim,
And made a widow happy, for a whim.
Why then declare good-nature is her scorn,
When 'tis by that alone she can be borne?   60
Why pique all mortals, yet affect a name?
A fool to Pleasure, yet a slave to Fame:
Now deep in Taylor and the Book of Martyrs,
Now drinking citron with his Grace and Chartres:
Now Conscience chills her, and now Passion burns,
And atheism and religion take their turns:
A very heathen in the carnal part,
Yet still a sad, good Christian at her heart.
    See Sin in state, majestically drunk,
Proud as a peeress, prouder as a punk;   70
Chaste to her husband, frank to all beside,
A teeming mistress, but a barren bride.
What then? let blood and body bear the fault;
Her head's untouch'd, that noble Seat of Thought:
Such this day's doctrine—in another fit
She sins with poets through pure love of Wit.
What has not fir'd her bosom or her brain?
Caesar and Tall-boy, Charles and Charlemagne.
As Helluo, late dictator of the feast,
The nose of Hautgout, and the tip of Taste,   80

Critiqued your wine, and analyz'd your meat,
Yet on plain pudding deign'd at home to eat:
So Philomedé, lect'ring all mankind
On the soft passion, and the taste refin'd,
The address, the delicacy—stoops at once,
And makes her hearty meal upon a Dunce.
    Flavia's a Wit, has too much sense to pray;
To toast our wants and wishes, is her way;
Nor asks of God, but of her stars, to give
The mighty blessing "while we live, to live."   90
Then all for death, that opiate of the soul!
Lucretia's dagger, Rosamunda's bowl.
Say, what can cause such impotence of mind?
A Spark too fickle, or a Spouse too kind.
Wise wretch! with pleasures too refin'd to please;
With too much spirit to be e'er at ease;
With too much quickness ever to be taught;
With too much Thinking to have common Thought:
Who purchase pain with all that joy can give,
And die of nothing but a rage to live.   100
    Turn then from Wits, and look on Simo's mate,
No ass so meek, no ass so obstinate:
Or her that owns her faults, but never mends,
Because she's honest, and the best of friends:
Or her whose life the church and scandal share,
For ever in a Passion or a Pray'r:
Or her who laughs at Hell, but (like her Grace)
Cries, "Ah! how charming if there's no such place!"
Or who in sweet vicissitude appears
Of Mirth and Opium, Ratifie and Tears;   110
The daily Anodyne, and nightly Draught,
To kill those foes to fair ones, Time and Thought.
Woman and Fool are two hard things to hit;
For true No-meaning puzzles more than Wit.
    But what are these to great Atossa's mind?
Scarce once herself, by turns all womankind!
Who, with herself, or others, from her birth
Finds all her life one warfare upon earth;
Shines in exposing knaves and painting fools,
Yet is whate'er she hates and ridicules;   120
No thought advances, but her eddy brain
Whisks it about, and down it goes again.

Full sixty years the World has been her Trade,
The wisest fool much time has ever made:
From loveless youth to unrespected age,
No passion gratified except her rage:
So much the Fury still outran the Wit,
The Pleasure miss'd her, and the Scandal hit.
Who breaks with her, provokes revenge from Hell,
But he's a bolder man who dares be well.   130
Her ev'ry turn with violence pursued,
Nor more a storm her hate than gratitude:
To that each passion turns or soon or late;
Love, if it makes her yield, must make her hate.
Superiors? death! and equals? what a curse!
But an inferior not dependent? worse.
Offend her, and she knows not to forgive;
Oblige her, and she'll hate you while you live:
But die, and she'll adore you—then the bust
And temple rise—then fall gain to dust.   140
Last night her lord was all that's good and great;
A knave this morning, and his will a cheat.
Strange! by the means defeated of the ends,
By Spirit robb'd of pow'r, by Warmth of friends,
By Wealth of follow'rs! without one distress,
Sick of herself through very selfishness!
Atossa, curs'd with ev'ry granted pray'r,
Childless with all her children, wants an heir:
To heirs unknown descends th'unguarded store,
Or wanders, Heav'n-directed, to the poor.   150
  Pictures like these, dear Madam! to design,
Asks no firm hand and no unerring line;
Some wand'ring touches, some reflected light,
Some flying stroke alone can hit 'em right:
For how should equal colours do the knack?
Chameleons who can paint in white and black?
  "Yet Chloë sure was form'd without a spot."
Nature in her then err'd not, but forgot.
With ev'ry pleasing, ev'ry prudent part,
Say, "What can Chloë want?"—She wants a Heart,   160
She speaks, behaves, and acts just as she ought,
But never, never reach'd one gen'rous thought.
Virtue she finds too painful an endeavour,
Content to dwell in decencies for ever.

So very reasonable, so unmov'd,
As never yet to love, or to be lov'd.
She, while her Lover pants upon her breast,
Can mark the figures on an Indian chest;
And when she sees her friend in deep despair,
Observes how much a chintz exceeds mohair. 170
Forbid it, Heav'n! a favour or a debt
She e'er should cancel!—but she may forget.
Safe is your secret still in Chloë's ear;
But none of Chloë's shall you ever hear.
Of all her Dears she never slander'd one,
But cares not if a thousand are undone.
Would Chloë know if you're alive or dead?
She bids her footman put it in her head.
Chloë is prudent—Would you too be wise?
Then never break your heart when Chloë dies. 180
    One certain portrait may (I grant) be seen,
Which Heav'n has varnish'd out, and made a queen;
The same for ever! and described by all
With Truth and Goodness, as with Crown and Ball.
Poets heap virtues, painters gems, at will,
And show their zeal, and hide their want of skill.
'Tis well—but, artists! who can paint or write,
To draw the naked is your true delight:
That Robe of Quality so struts and swells,
None see what Parts of Nature it conceals: 190
Th'exactest traits of body or of mind,
We owe to models of an humble kind.
If Queensberry to strip there's no compelling,
'Tis from a handmaid we must take a Helen.
From peer or bishop 'tis no easy thing
To draw the man who loves his God, or king.
Alas! I copy (or my draught would fail)
From honest Mah'met or plain parson Hale.
But grant, in public, men sometimes are shown,
A woman's seen in private life alone: 200
Our bolder talents in full light display'd;
Your virtues open fairest in the shade.
Bred to disguise, in public 'tis you hide;
There none distinguish 'twixt your shame or pride,
Weakness or delicacy; all so nice,
That each may seem a Virtue or a Vice.

In men, we various Ruling Passions find;
In women, two almost divide the kind;
Those, only fix'd, they first or last obey,
The love of Pleasure, and the love of Sway.   210
  That, Nature gives; and where the lesson taught
Is but to please, can Pleasure seem a fault?
Experience, this: by man's oppression curst,
They seek the second not to lose the first.
  Men, some to bus'ness, some to pleasure take;
But ev'ry woman is at heart a rake:
Men, some to quiet, some to public strife;
But ev'ry Lady would be Queen for life.
  Yet mark the fate of a whole sex of Queens!
Power all their end, but Beauty all the means.   220
In youth they conquer, with so wild a rage,
As leaves them scarce a subject in their age:
For foreign glory, foreign joy, they roam;
No thought of peace or happiness at home.
But Wisdom's Triumph is well-tim'd Retreat,
As hard a science to the Fair as Great!
Beauties, like tyrants, old and friendless grown,
Yet hate to rest, and dread to be alone,
Worn out in public, weary ev'ry eye,
Nor leave one sigh behind them when they die.   230
  Pleasures the sex, as children birds, pursue,
Still out of reach, yet never out of view;
Sure, if they catch, to spoil the toy at most,
To covet flying, and regret when lost:
At last, to follies youth could scarce defend,
'Tis half their age's prudence to pretend;
Asham'd to own they gave delight before,
Reduc'd to feign it, when they give no more.
As hags hold Sabbaths, less for joy than spite,
So these their merry miserable night;   240
Still round and round the Ghosts of Beauty glide,
And haunt the places where their Honour died.
  See how the World its veterans rewards!
A youth of frolics, an old age of cards;
Fair to no purpose, artful to no end,
Young without lovers, old without a friend;
A Fop their Passion, but their Prize a Sot,
Alive ridiculous, and dead forgot!

Ah friend! to dazzle let the vain design;
To raise the thought and touch the heart be thine!   250
That charm shall grow, while what fatigues the Ring
Flaunts and goes down, an unregarded thing.
So when the sun's broad beam has tir'd the sight,
All mild ascends the moon's more sober light,
Serene in virgin modesty she shines,
And unobserv'd the glaring orb declines.
   O! blest with temper, whose unclouded ray
Can make tomorrow cheerful as today;
She who can love a sister's charms, or hear
Sighs for a daughter with unwounded ear;   260
She who ne'er answers till a husband cools,
Or, if she rules him, never shows she rules;
Charms by accepting, by submitting sways,
Yet has her humour most when she obeys;
Lets Fops or Fortune fly which way they will,
Disdains all loss of Tickets, or Codille;
Spleen, Vapours, or Smallpox, above them all,
And mistress of herself, though China fall.
   And yet, believe me, good as well as ill,
Woman's at best a contradiction still.   270
Heav'n, when it strives to polish all it can
Its last best work, but forms a softer Man;
Picks from each sex to make its fav'rite blest,
Your love of Pleasure, our desire of Rest;
Blends, in exception to all gen'ral rules,
Your taste of Follies, with our scorn of Fools;
Reserve with Frankness, Art with Truth allied,
Courage with Softness, Modesty with Pride;
Fix'd principles, with Fancy ever new:
Shakes all together, and produces—You.   280
   Be this a woman's fame; with this unblest,
Toasts live a scorn, and Queens may die a jest.
This Phoebus promis'd (I forget the year)
When those blue eyes first open'd on the sphere;
Ascendant Phoebus watch'd that hour with care,
Averted half your parents' simple pray'r,
And gave you beauty, but denied the pelf
That buys your sex a tyrant o'er itself.
The gen'rous God, who wit and gold refines,
And ripens spirits as he ripens mines,   290

Kept dross for duchesses, the world shall know it,
To you gave Sense, Good-humour, and a Poet.

l. 63. Taylor = Jeremy Taylor, *Holy Living and Holy Dying*
l. 64. Chartres = Francis Charteris, thief, usurer, rapist
l. 78. Tall-boy = loutish lover in a popular comedy by Brome
l. 110. Ratafie = a brandy
l. 193. Queensberry = a beauty, honored by Pope and Gay
l. 198. Mah'met = servant to George I
l. 198. Hale = Stephen Hales, a physiologist
l. 251. Ring = fashionable rendezvous in Hyde Park
l. 266. tickets = lottery tickets
l. 266. codille = loss at cards in ombre

THE RAPE OF THE LOCK

CANTO 1

What dire offense from amorous causes springs,
What mighty contests rise from trivial things,
I sing—This verse to Caryll, Muse, is due:
This, even Belinda may vouchsafe to view:
Slight is the subject, but not so the praise,
If she inspire, and he approve my lays.
Say what strange motive, Goddess, could compel
A well-bred lord to assault a gentle belle?
O, say what stranger cause, yet unexplored,
Could make a gentle belle reject a lord?   10
In tasks so bold, can little men engage,
And in soft bosoms dwells such mighty rage?
Sol through white curtains shot a timorous ray,
And oped those eyes that must eclipse the day.
Now lapdogs give themselves the rousing shake,
And sleepless lovers, just at twelve, awake:
Thrice rung the bell, the slipper knocked the ground,
And the pressed watch returned a silver sound.
Belinda still her downy pillow pressed,
Her guardian sylph prolonged the balmy rest: 20
'Twas he had summoned to her silent bed
The morning-dream that hovered o'er her head.
A youth more glittering than a birth-night beau
(That even in slumber caused her cheek to glow)
Seemed to her ear his winning lips to lay,
And thus in whispers said, or seemed to say:

"Fairest of mortals, thou distinguished care
Of thousand bright inhabitants of air!
If e'er one vision touched thy infant thought,
Of all the nurse and all the priest have taught,   30
Of airy elves by moonlight shadows seen,
The silver token, and the circled green,
Or virgins visited by angel powers,
With golden crowns and wreaths of heavenly flowers,
Hear and believe! thy own importance know,
Nor bound thy narrow views to things below.
Some secret truths, from learned pride concealed,
To maids alone and children are revealed:
What though no credit doubting wits may give?
The fair and innocent shall still believe.   40
Know, then, unnumbered spirits round thee fly,
The light militia of the lower sky:
These, though unseen, are ever on the wing,
Hang o'er the box, and hover round the Ring.
Think what an equipage thou hast in air,
And view with scorn two pages and a chair.
As now your own, our beings were of old,
And once enclosed in woman's beauteous mould;
Thence, by a soft transition, we repair
From earthly vehicles to these of air.   50
Think not, when woman's transient breath is fled,
That all her vanities at once are dead:
Succeeding vanities she still regards,
And though she plays no more, o'erlooks the cards.
Her joy in gilded chariots, when alive,
And love of ombre, after death survive.
For when the fair in all their pride expire,
To their first elements their souls retire:
The sprites of fiery termagants in flame
Mount up, and take a salamander's name.   60
Soft yielding minds to water glide away,
And sip, with nymphs, their elemental tea.
The graver prude sinks downward to a gnome,
In search of mischief still on earth to roam.
The light coquettes in sylphs aloft repair,
And sport and flutter in the fields of air.
Know further yet; whoever fair and chaste
Rejects mankind, is by some sylph embraced:
For spirits, freed from mortal laws, with ease

Assume what sexes and what shapes they please.   70
What guards the purity of melting maids,
In courtly balls, and midnight masquerades,
Safe from the treacherous friend, and daring spark,
The glance by day, the whisper in the dark,
When kind occasion prompts their warm desires,
When music softens, and when dancing fires?
'Tis but their sylph, the wise celestials know,
Though Honour is the word with men below.
    Some nymphs there are, too conscious of their face,
For life predestined to the gnomes' embrace.   80
These swell their prospects and exalt their pride,
When offers are disdained, and love denied:
Then gay ideas crowd the vacant brain,
While peers and dukes, and all their sweeping train,
And garters, stars, and coronets appear,
And in soft sounds, 'your grace' salutes their ear.
'Tis these that early taint the female soul,
Instruct the eyes of young coquettes to roll,
Teach infant cheeks a bidden blush to know,
And little hearts to flutter at a beau.   90
    Oft, when the world imagine women stray,
The sylphs through mystic mazes guide their way,
Through all the giddy circle they pursue,
And old impertinence expel by new.
What tender maid but must a victim fall
To one man's treat, but for another's ball?
When Florio speaks, what virgin could withstand,
If gentle Damon did not squeeze her hand?
With varying vanities, from every part,
They shift the moving toyshop of their heart;   100
Where wigs with wigs, with sword-knots sword-knots strive,
Beaux banish beaux, and coaches coaches drive.
This erring mortals levity may call;
O, blind to truth! the sylphs contrive it all.
    Of these am I, who thy protection claim,
A watchful sprite, and Ariel is my name.
Late, as I ranged the crystal wilds of air,
In the clear mirror of thy ruling star
I saw, alas! some dread event impend,
Ere to the main this morning sun descend,   110
But Heaven reveals not what, or how, or where:
Warned by the sylph, O pious maid, beware!

This to disclose is all thy guardian can:
Beware of all, but most beware of man!"
    He said; when Shock, who thought she slept too long,
Leapt up, and waked his mistress with his tongue.
'Twas then, Belinda, if report say true,
Thy eyes first opened on a billet-doux;
Wounds, charms, and ardors were no sooner read,
But all the vision vanished from thy head.   120
    And now, unveiled, the toilet stands displayed,
Each silver vase in mystic order laid.
First, robed in white, the nymph intent adores,
With head uncovered, the cosmetic powers.
A heavenly image in the glass appears;
To that she bends, to that her eyes she rears.
The inferior priestess, at her altar's side,
Trembling, begins the sacred rites of pride.
Unnumbered treasures ope at once, and here
The various offerings of the world appear;   130
From each she nicely culls with curious toil,
And decks the goddess with the glittering spoil.
This casket India's glowing gems unlocks,
And all Arabia breathes from yonder box.
The tortoise here and elephant unite,
Transformed to combs, the speckled and the white.
Here files of pins extend their shining rows,
Puffs, powders, patches, bibles, billet-doux.
Now awful Beauty puts on all its arms;
The fair each moment rises in her charms,   140
Repairs her smiles, awakens every grace,
And calls forth all the wonders of her face;
Sees by degrees a purer blush arise,
And keener lightnings quicken in her eyes.
The busy sylphs surround their darling care,
These set the head, and those divide the hair,
Some fold the sleeve, while others plait the gown;
And Betty's praised for labours not her own.

    CANTO 2

    Not with more glories, in the ethereal plain,
The sun first rises o'er the purpled main,
Than, issuing forth, the rival of his beams
Launched on the bosom of the silver Thames.

Fair nymphs and well-dressed youths around her shone,
But every eye was fixed on her alone.
On her white breast a sparkling cross she wore,
Which Jews might kiss, and infidels adore.
Her lively looks a sprightly mind disclose,
Quick as her eyes, and as unfixed as those: 10
Favours to none, to all she smiles extends;
Oft she rejects, but never once offends.
Bright as the sun, her eyes the gazers strike,
And, like the sun, they shine on all alike.
Yet graceful ease, and sweetness void of pride,
Might hide her faults, if belles had faults to hide:
If to her share some female errors fall,
Look on her face, and you'll forget 'em all.
　　This nymph, to the destruction of mankind,
Nourished two locks which graceful hung behind   20
In equal curls, and well conspired to deck
With shining ringlets her smooth ivory neck.
Love in these labyrinths his slaves detains,
And mighty hearts are held in slender chains.
With hairy springes we the birds betray,
Slight lines of hair surprise the finny prey,
Fair tresses man's imperial race ensnare,
And beauty draws us with a single hair.
　　The adventurous baron the bright locks admired,
He saw, he wished, and to the prize aspired: 30
Resolved to win, he meditates the way,
By force to ravish, or by fraud betray;
For when success a lover's toil attends,
Few ask, if fraud or force attained his ends.
　　For this, ere Phoebus rose, he had implored
Propitious Heaven, and every power adored,
But chiefly Love—to Love an altar built,
Of twelve vast French romances, neatly gilt.
There lay three garters, half a pair of gloves,
And all the trophies of his former loves.   40
With tender billet-doux he lights the pyre,
And breathes three amorous sighs to raise the fire.
Then prostrate falls, and begs with ardent eyes
Soon to obtain, and long possess the prize:
The powers gave ear, and granted half his prayer,
The rest the winds dispersed in empty air.
　　But now secure the painted vessel glides,

The sunbeams trembling on the floating tides,
While melting music steals upon the sky,
And softened sounds along the waters die.   50
Smooth flow the waves, the zephyrs gently play,
Belinda smiled, and all the world was gay.
All but the sylph—with careful thoughts opprest,
The impending woe sat heavy on his breast.
He summons straight his denizens of air;
The lucid squadrons round the sails repair:
Soft o'er the shrouds aerial whispers breathe
That seemed but zephyrs to the train beneath.
Some to the sun their insect-wings unfold,
Waft on the breeze, or sink in clouds of gold.   60
Transparent forms, too fine for mortal sight,
Their fluid bodies half dissolved in light,
Loose to the wind their airy garments flew,
Thin glittering textures of the filmy dew,
Dipped in the richest tincture of the skies,
Where light disports in ever-mingling dyes,
While every beam new transient colours flings,
Colours that change whene'er they wave their wings.
Amid the circle, on the gilded mast,
Superior by the head, was Ariel placed;   70
His purple pinions opening to the sun,
He raised his azure wand, and thus begun:
    "Ye sylphs and sylphids, to your chief give ear!
Fays, fairies, genii, elves, and daemons, hear!
Ye know the spheres and various tasks assigned
By laws eternal to the aerial kind.
Some in the fields of purest aether play,
And bask and whiten in the blaze of day.
Some guide the course of wandering orbs on high,
Or roll the planets through the boundless sky.   80
Some less refined, beneath the moon's pale light,
Pursue the stars that shoot athwart the night,
Or suck the mists in grosser air below,
Or dip their pinions in the painted bow,
Or brew fierce tempests on the wintry main,
Or on the glebe distill the kindly rain.
Others on earth o'er human race preside,
Watch all their ways, and all their actions guide:
Of these the chief the care of nations own,
And guard with arms divine the British throne.   90

Our humbler province is to tend the fair,
Not a less pleasing, though less glorious care:
To save the powder from too rude a gale,
Nor let the imprisoned essences exhale;
To draw fresh colours from the vernal flowers;
To steal from rainbows e'er they drop in showers
A brighter wash; to curl their waving hairs,
Assist their blushes, and inspire their airs;
Nay oft, in dreams invention we bestow,
To change a flounce, or add a furbelow.   100
   This day black omens threat the brightest fair,
That e'er deserved a watchful spirit's care;
Some dire disaster, or by force or slight,
But what, or where, the Fates have wrapped in night:
Whether the nymph shall break Diana's law,
Or some frail china jar receive a flaw,
Or stain her honour, or her new brocade,
Forget her prayers, or miss a masquerade,
Or lose her heart, or necklace, at a ball;
Or whether Heaven has doomed that Shock must fall.   110
Haste, then, ye spirits! to your charge repair:
The fluttering fan be Zephyretta's care;
The drops to thee, Brillante, we consign;
And, Momentilla, let the watch be thine;
Do thou, Crispissa, tend her favorite lock;
Ariel himself shall be the guard of Shock.
   To fifty chosen sylphs, of special note,
We trust the important charge, the petticoat;
Oft have we known that sevenfold fence to fail,
Though stiff with hoops, and armed with ribs of whale.   120
Form a strong line about the silver bound,
And guard the wide circumference around.
   Whatever spirit, careless of his charge,
His post neglects, or leaves the fair at large,
Shall feel sharp vengeance soon o'ertake his sins,
Be stopped in vials, or transfixed with pins,
Or plunged in lakes of bitter washes lie,
Or wedged whole ages in a bodkin's eye;
Gums and pomatums shall his flight restrain,
While clogged he beats his silken wings in vain,   130
Or alum styptics with contracting power
Shrink his thin essence like a riveled flower:
Or, as Ixion fixed, the wretch shall feel

The giddy motion of the whirling mill,
In fumes of burning chocolate shall glow,
And tremble at the sea that froths below!"
   He spoke; the spirits from the sails descend;
Some, orb in orb, around the nymph extend;
Some thread the mazy ringlets of her hair;
Some hang upon the pendants of her ear: 140
With beating hearts the dire event they wait,
Anxious, and trembling for the birth of Fate.

CANTO 3

   Close by those meads, forever crowned with flowers,
Where Thames with pride surveys his rising towers,
There stands a structure of majestic frame,
Which from the neighbouring Hampton takes its name.
Here Britain's statesmen oft the fall foredoom
Of foreign tyrants and of nymphs at home;
Here thou, great Anna, whom three realms obey,
Dost sometimes counsel take—and sometimes tea.
   Hither the heroes and the nymphs resort,
To taste awhile the pleasures of a court;   10
In various talk the instructive hours they passed,
Who gave a ball or paid the visit last;
One speaks the glory of the British queen,
And one describes a charming Indian screen;
A third interprets motions, looks, and eyes;
At every word a reputation dies.
Snuff, or the fan, supply each pause of chat,
With singing, laughing, ogling, *and all that*.
   Meanwhile, declining from the noon of day,
The sun obliquely shoots his burning ray;   20
The hungry judges soon the sentence sign,
And wretches hang that jurymen may dine;
The merchant from the Exchange returns in peace,
And the long labours of the toilet cease.
Belinda now, whom thirst of fame invites,
Burns to encounter two adventurous knights,
At ombre singly to decide their doom,
And swells her breast with conquests yet to come.
Straight the three bands prepare in arms to join,
Each band the number of the sacred nine.   30
Soon as she spreads her hand, the aerial guard

Descend, and sit on each important card:
First Ariel perched upon a matadore,
Then each according to the rank they bore;
For sylphs, yet mindful of their ancient race,
Are, as when women, wondrous fond of place.
　　Behold, four kings in majesty revered,
With hoary whiskers and a forky beard;
And four fair queens whose hands sustain a flower,
The expressive emblem of their softer power;　　　　　　　40
Four knaves in garbs succinct, a trusty band,
Caps on their heads, and halberts in their hand;
And parti-coloured troops, a shining train,
Draw forth to combat on the velvet plain.
　　The skillful nymph reviews her force with care;
"Let spades be trumps!" she said, and trumps they were.
Now move to war her sable matadores,
In show like leaders of the swarthy Moors.
Spadillio first, unconquerable lord!
Led off two captive trumps, and swept the board.　　　　　　50
As many more Manillio forced to yield,
And marched a victor from the verdant field.
Him Basto followed, but his fate more hard
Gained but one trump and one plebeian card.
With his broad sabre next, a chief in years,
The hoary Majesty of Spades appears,
Puts forth one manly leg, to sight revealed,
The rest his many-coloured robe concealed.
The rebel knave, who dares his prince engage,
Proves the just victim of his royal rage.　　　　　　60
Even mighty Pam, that kings and queens o'erthrew
And mowed down armies in the fights of loo,
Sad chance of war! now destitute of aid,
Falls undistinguished by the victor spade.
　　Thus far both armies to Belinda yield;
Now to the baron fate inclines the field.
His warlike Amazon her host invades,
The imperial consort of the crown of spades.
The club's black tyrant first her victim died,
Spite of his haughty mien and barbarous pride.　　　　　　70
What boots the regal circle on his head,
His giant limbs, in state unwieldy spread?
That long behind he trails his pompous robe,
And of all monarchs only grasps the globe?

The baron now his diamonds pours apace;
The embroidered king who shows but half his face,
And his refulgent queen, with powers combined
Of broken troops an easy conquest find.
Clubs, diamonds, hearts, in wild disorder seen,
With throngs promiscuous strew the level green.   80
Thus when dispersed a routed army runs,
Of Asia's troops, and Afric's sable sons,
With like confusion different nations fly,
Of various habit, and of various dye,
The pierced battalions disunited fall
In heaps on heaps; one fate o'erwhelms them all.
   The knave of diamonds tries his wily arts,
And wins (oh, shameful chance!) the queen of hearts.
At this, the blood the virgin's cheek forsook,
A livid paleness spreads o'er all her look;   90
She sees, and trembles at the approaching ill,
Just in the jaws of ruin, and Codille,
And now (as oft in some distempered state)
On one nice trick depends the general fate.
An ace of hearts steps forth: the king unseen
Lurked in her hand, and mourned his captive queen.
He springs to vengeance with an eager pace,
And falls like thunder on the prostrate ace.
The nymph exulting fills with shouts the sky,
The walls, the woods, and long canals reply.   100
   O thoughtless mortals, ever blind to fate,
Too soon dejected, and too soon elate!
Sudden these honours shall be snatched away,
And cursed forever this victorious day.
   For lo! The board with cups and spoons is crowned,
The berries crackle, and the mill turns round;
On shining altars of Japan they raise
The silver lamp; the fiery spirits blaze:
From silver spouts the grateful liquors glide,
While China's earth receives the smoking tide.   110
At once they gratify their scent and taste,
And frequent cups prolong the rich repast.
Straight hover round the fair her airy band;
Some, as she sipped, the fuming liquor fanned,
Some o'er her lap their careful plumes displayed,
Trembling, and conscious of the rich brocade.
Coffee (which makes the politician wise,

And see through all things with his half-shut eyes)
Sent up in vapours to the baron's brain
New stratagems, the radiant lock to gain.   120
Ah, cease, rash youth, desist ere 'tis too late,
Fear the just gods, and think of Scylla's fate!
Changed to a bird, and sent to flit in air,
She dearly pays for Nisus' injured hair!
   But when to mischief mortals bend their will,
How soon they find fit instruments of ill!
Just then, Clarissa drew with tempting grace
A two-edged weapon from her shining case:
So ladies in romance assist their knight,
Present the spear, and arm him for the fight.   130
He takes the gift with reverence, and extends
The little engine on his fingers' ends;
This just behind Belinda's neck he spread,
As o'er the fragrant steams she bends her head.
Swift to the lock a thousand sprites repair,
A thousand wings, by turns, blow back the hair,
And thrice they twitched the diamond in her ear,
Thrice she looked back, and thrice the foe drew near.
Just in that instant, anxious Ariel sought
The close recesses of the virgin's thought;   140
As on the nosegay in her breast reclined,
He watched the ideas rising in her mind,
Sudden he viewed, in spite of all her art,
An earthly lover lurking at her heart.
Amazed, confused, he found his power expired,
Resigned to fate, and with a sigh retired.
   The peer now spreads the glittering forfex wide,
To enclose the lock; now joins it, to divide.
Even then, before the fatal engine closed,
A wretched sylph too fondly interposed;   150
Fate urged the shears, and cut the sylph in twain
(But airy substance soon unites again):
The meeting points the sacred hair dissever
From the fair head, for ever, and for ever!
   Then flashed the living lightnings from her eyes,
And screams of horror rend the affrighted skies.
Not louder shrieks to pitying heaven are cast,
When husbands or when lapdogs breathe their last;
Or when rich china vessels, fallen from high,
In glittering dust and painted fragments lie!   160

"Let wreaths of triumph now my temples twine,"
The victor cried, "the glorious prize is mine!
While fish in streams, or birds delight in air,
Or in a coach and six the British fair,
As long as *Atalantis* shall be read,
Or the small pillow grace a lady's bed,
While visits shall be paid on solemn days,
When numerous wax-lights in bright order blaze,
While nymphs take treats, or assignations give,
So long my honour, name, and praise shall live!   170
    What time would spare, from steel receives its date,
And monuments, like men, submit to fate!
Steel could the labour of the gods destroy,
And strike to dust the imperial towers of Troy;
Steel could the works of mortal pride confound,
And hew triumphal arches to the ground.
What wonder then, fair nymph! thy hairs should feel,
The conquering force of unresisted steel?"

CANTO 4

    But anxious cares the pensive nymph opprest,
And secret passions laboured in her breast.
Not youthful kings in battle seized alive,
Not scornful virgins who their charms survive,
Not ardent lovers robbed of all their bliss,
Not ancient ladies when refused a kiss,
Not tyrants fierce that unrepenting die,
Not Cynthia when her manteau's pinned awry,
E'er felt such rage, resentment, and despair,
As thou, sad virgin! for thy ravished hair.   10
    For, that sad moment, when the sylphs withdrew,
And Ariel weeping from Belinda flew,
Umbriel, a dusky, melancholy sprite
As ever sullied the fair face of light,
Down to the central earth, his proper scene,
Repaired to search the gloomy Cave of Spleen.
    Swift on his sooty pinions flits the gnome,
And in a vapour reached the dismal dome.
No cheerful breeze this sullen region knows,
The dreaded east is all the wind that blows.   20
Here in a grotto, sheltered close from air,
And screened in shades from day's detested glare,

She sighs for ever on her pensive bed,
Pain at her side, and megrim at her head.
   Two handmaids wait the throne: alike in place
But differing far in figure and in face.
Here stood Ill-Nature like an ancient maid,
Her wrinkled form in black and white arrayed;
With store of prayers for mornings, nights, and noons,
Her hand is filled; her bosom with lampoons.   30
   There Affectation, with a sickly mien,
Shows in her cheek the roses of eighteen,
Practiced to lisp, and hang the head aside,
Faints into airs, and languishes with pride,
On the rich quilt sinks with becoming woe,
Wrapped in a gown, for sickness and for show.
The fair ones feel such maladies as these,
When each new nightdress gives a new disease.
   A constant vapour o'er the palace flies,
Strange phantoms rising as the mists arise;   40
Dreadful as hermit's dreams in haunted shades,
Or bright as visions of expiring maids.
Now glaring fiends, and snakes on rolling spires,
Pale spectres, gaping tombs, and purple fires;
Now lakes of liquid gold, Elysian scenes,
And crystal domes, and angels in machines.
   Unnumbered throngs on every side are seen
Of bodies changed to various forms by Spleen.
Here living teapots stand, one arm held out,
One bent; the handle this, and that the spout: 50
A pipkin there, like Homer's tripod walks;
Here sighs a jar, and there a goose pie talks;
Men prove with child, as powerful fancy works,
And maids, turned bottles, call aloud for corks.
   Safe passed the gnome through this fantastic band,
A branch of healing spleenwort in his hand.
Then thus addressed the power: "Hail, wayward queen!
Who rule the sex to fifty from fifteen:
Parent of vapours and of female wit,
Who give the hysteric or poetic fit,   60
On various tempers act by various ways,
Make some take physic, others scribble plays;
Who cause the proud their visits to delay,
And send the godly in a pet to pray.
A nymph there is that all your power disdains,

And thousands more in equal mirth maintains.
But oh! If e'er thy gnome could spoil a grace,
Or raise a pimple on a beauteous face,
Like citron-waters matrons' cheeks inflame,
Or change complexions at a losing game;   70
If e'er with airy horns I planted heads,
Or rumpled petticoats, or tumbled beds,
Or caused suspicion when no soul was rude,
Or discomposed the headdress of a prude,
Or e'er to costive lapdog gave disease,
Which not the tears of brightest eyes could ease,
Hear me, and touch Belinda with chagrin:
That single act gives half the world the spleen."
    The goddess with a discontented air
Seems to reject him, though she grants his prayer.   80
A wondrous bag with both her hands she binds,
Like that where once Ulysses held the winds;
There she collects the force of female lungs,
Sighs, sobs, and passions, and the war of tongues.
A vial next she fills with fainting fears,
Soft sorrows, melting griefs, and flowing tears.
The gnome rejoicing bears her gifts away,
Spreads his black wings, and slowly mounts to day.
    Sunk in Thalestris' arms the nymph he found,
Her eyes dejected and her hair unbound.   90
Full o'er their heads the swelling bag he rent,
And all the Furies issued at the vent.
Belinda burns with more than mortal ire,
And fierce Thalestris fans the rising fire.
"O wretched maid!" she spread her hands, and cried,
(While Hampton's echoes, "Wretched maid!" replied),
"Was it for this you took such constant care
The bodkin, comb, and essence to prepare?
For this your locks in paper durance bound,
For this with torturing irons wreathed around?   100
For this with fillets strained your tender head,
And bravely bore the double loads of lead?
Gods! shall the ravisher display your hair,
While the fops envy, and the ladies stare!
Honour forbid! at whose unrivaled shrine
Ease, pleasure, virtue, all our sex resign.
Methinks already I your tears survey,
Already hear the horrid things they say,

Already see you a degraded toast,
And all your honour in a whisper lost!   110
How shall I, then, your helpless fame defend?
'Twill then be infamy to seem your friend!
And shall this prize, the inestimable prize,
Exposed through crystal to the gazing eyes,
And heightened by the diamond's circling rays,
On that rapacious hand forever blaze?
Sooner shall grass in Hyde Park Circus grow,
And wits take lodgings in the sound of Bow;
Sooner let earth, air, sea, to chaos fall,
Men, monkeys, lapdogs, parrots, perish all!"   120
    She said; then raging to Sir Plume repairs,
And bids her beau demand the precious hairs
(Sir Plume of amber snuffbox justly vain,
And the nice conduct of a clouded cane),
With earnest eyes, and round unthinking face,
He first the snuffbox opened, then the case,
And thus broke out—"My Lord, why, what the devil!
Zounds! damn the lock! 'Fore Gad, you must be civil!
Plague on't! 'tis past a jest—nay prithee, pox!
Give her the hair"—he spoke, and rapped his box.   130
    "It grieves me much," replied the peer again,
"Who speaks so well should ever speak in vain.
But by this lock, this sacred lock I swear
(Which never more shall join its parted hair;
Which never more its honours shall renew,
Clipped from the lovely head where late it grew),
That while my nostrils draw the vital air,
This hand, which won it, shall forever wear."
He spoke, and speaking, in proud triumph spread
The long-contended honours of her head.   140
    But Umbriel, hateful gnome, forbears not so;
He breaks the vial whence the sorrows flow.
Then see! The nymph in beauteous grief appears,
Her eyes half languishing, half drowned in tears;
On her heaved bosom hung her drooping head,
Which with a sigh she raised, and thus she said:
    "For ever cursed be this detested day,
Which snatched my best, my favourite curl away!
Happy! ah, ten times happy had I been,
If Hampton Court these eyes had never seen!   150
Yet am not I the first mistaken maid,

By love of courts to numerous ills betrayed.
O, had I rather unadmired remained
In some lone isle, or distant northern land;
Where the gilt chariot never marks the way,
Where none learn ombre, none e'er taste bohea!
There kept my charms concealed from mortal eye,
Like roses that in deserts bloom and die.
What moved my mind with youthful lords to roam?
O, had I stayed, and said my prayers at home!   160
'Twas this the morning omens seemed to tell,
Thrice from my trembling hand the patch-box fell;
The tottering china shook without a wind,
Nay, Poll sat mute, and Shock was most unkind!
A sylph too warned me of the threats of fate,
In mystic visions, now believed too late!
See the poor remnants of these slighted hairs!
My hands shall rend what ev'n thy rapine spares.
These, in two sable ringlets taught to break,
Once gave new beauties to the snowy neck;   170
The sister lock now sits uncouth, alone,
And in its fellow's fate foresees its own;
Uncurled it hangs, the fatal shears demands,
And tempts once more thy sacrilegious hands.
O, hadst thou, cruel! been content to seize
Hairs less in sight, or any hairs but these!"

    CANTO 5

    She said; the pitying audience melt in tears.
But Fate and Jove had stopped the baron's ears.
In vain Thalestris with reproach assails,
For who can move when fair Belinda fails?
Not half so fixed the Trojan could remain,
While Anna begged and Dido raged in vain.
Then grave Clarissa graceful waved her fan;
Silence ensued, and thus the nymph began:
    "Say why are beauties praised and honoured most,
The wise man's passion, and the vain man's toast?   10
Why decked with all that land and sea afford,
Why angels called, and angel-like adored?
Why round our coaches crowd the white-gloved beaux,
Why bows the side-box from its inmost rows?
How vain are all these glories, all our pains,

Unless good sense preserve what beauty gains;
That men may say when we the front-box grace,
'Behold the first in virtue as in face!'
O! if to dance all night, and dress all day,
Charmed the smallpox, or chased old age away,   20
Who would not scorn what housewife's cares produce,
Or who would learn one earthly thing of use?
To patch, nay ogle, might become a saint,
Nor could it sure be such a sin to paint.
But since, alas! frail beauty must decay,
Curled or uncurled, since locks will turn to grey;
Since painted, or not painted, all shall fade,
And she who scorns a man must die a maid;
What then remains but well our power to use,
And keep good humour still whate'er we lose?   30
And trust me, dear, good humour can prevail
When airs, and flights, and screams, and scolding fail.
Beauties in vain their pretty eyes may roll;
Charms strike the sight, but merit wins the soul."
    So spoke the dame, but no applause ensued;
Belinda frowned, Thalestris called her prude.
"To arms, to arms!" the fierce virago cries,
And swift as lightning to the combat flies.
All side in parties, and begin the attack;
Fans clap, silks rustle, and tough whalebones crack;   40
Heroes' and heroines' shouts confusedly rise,
And bass and treble voices strike the skies.
No common weapons in their hands are found,
Like gods they fight, nor dread a mortal wound.
    So when bold Homer makes the gods engage,
And heavenly breasts with human passions rage;
'Gainst Pallas, Mars; Latona, Hermes arms;
And all Olympus rings with loud alarms:
Jove's thunder roars, heaven trembles all around,
Blue Neptune storms, the bellowing deeps resound: 50
Earth shakes her nodding towers, the ground gives way,
And the pale ghosts start at the flash of day!
    Triumphant Umbriel on a sconce's height
Clapped his glad wings, and sat to view the fight:
Propped on the bodkin spears, the sprites survey
The growing combat, or assist the fray.
    While through the press enraged Thalestris flies,
And scatters death around from both her eyes,

A beau and witling perished in the throng,
One died in metaphor, and one in song. 60
"O cruel nymph! a living death I bear,"
Cried Dapperwit, and sunk beside his chair.
A mournful glance Sir Fopling upwards cast,
"Those eyes are made so killing"—was his last.
Thus on Maeander's flowery margin lies
The expiring swan, and as he sings he dies.
    When bold Sir Plume had drawn Clarissa down,
Chloe stepped in, and killed him with a frown;
She smiled to see the doughty hero slain,
But, at her smile, the beau revived again. 70
    Now Jove suspends his golden scales in air,
Weighs the men's wits against the lady's hair;
The doubtful beam long nods from side to side;
At length the wits mount up, the hairs subside.
    See, fierce Belinda on the baron flies,
With more than usual lightning in her eyes;
Nor feared the chief the unequal fight to try,
Who sought no more than on his foe to die.
    But this bold lord, with manly strength endued,
She with one finger and a thumb subdued: 80
Just where the breath of life his nostrils drew,
A charge of snuff the wily virgin threw;
The gnomes direct, to every atom just,
The pungent grains of titillating dust.
Sudden, with starting tears each eye o'erflows,
And the high dome re-echoes to his nose.
    "Now meet thy fate," incensed Belinda cried,
And drew a deadly bodkin from her side.
(The same, his ancient personage to deck,
Her great-great-grandsire wore about his neck, 90
In three seal rings; which after, melted down,
Formed a vast buckle for his widow's gown:
Her infant grandame's whistle next it grew,
The bells she jingled, and the whistle blew;
Then in a bodkin graced her mother's hairs,
Which long she wore, and now Belinda wears).
    "Boast not my fall," he cried, "insulting foe!
Thou by some other shalt be laid as low.
Nor think to die dejects my lofty mind:
All that I dread is leaving you behind! 100
Rather than so, ah, let me still survive,

And burn in Cupid's flames—but burn alive."
    "Restore the lock!" she cries; and all around
"Restore the lock!" the vaulted roofs rebound.
Not fierce Othello in so loud a strain
Roared for the handkerchief that caused his pain.
But see how oft ambitious aims are crossed,
And chiefs contend till all the prize is lost!
The lock, obtained with guilt, and kept with pain,
In every place is sought, but sought in vain: 110
With such a prize no mortal must be blessed,
So Heaven decrees! With Heaven who can contest?
    Some thought it mounted to the lunar sphere,
Since all things lost on earth are treasured there.
There heroes' wits are kept in ponderous vases,
And beaux' in snuffboxes and tweezer cases.
There broken vows and deathbed alms are found,
And lovers' hearts with ends of riband bound,
The courtier's promises, and sick man's prayers,
The smiles of harlots, and the tears of heirs,   120
Cages for gnats, and chains to yoke a flea,
Dried butterflies, and tomes of casuistry.
    But trust the Muse—she saw it upward rise,
Though marked by none but quick, poetic eyes
(So Rome's great founder to the heavens withdrew,
To Proculus alone confessed in view);
A sudden star, it shot through liquid air,
And drew behind a radiant trail of hair.
Not Berenice's locks first rose so bright,
The heavens bespangling with disheveled light.   130
The sylphs behold it kindling as it flies,
And pleased pursue its progress through the skies.
    This the beau monde shall from the Mall survey,
And hail with music its propitious ray.
This the blest lover shall for Venus take,
And send up vows from Rosamonda's lake.
This Partridge soon shall view in cloudless skies,
When next he looks through Galileo's eyes;
And hence the egregious wizard shall foredoom
The fate of Louis, and the fall of Rome.   140
    Then cease, bright nymph! to mourn thy ravished hair,
Which adds new glory to the shining sphere!
Not all the tresses that fair head can boast,
Shall draw such envy as the lock you lost.

For, after all the murders of your eye,
When, after millions slain, yourself shall die:
When those fair suns shall set, as set they must,
And all those tresses shall be laid in dust,
This lock the Muse shall consecrate to fame,
And 'midst the stars inscribe Belinda's name.   150

1:3. Caryll = John Caryll requested the conciliatory light satire
1:44. Ring = place for flirting in Hyde Park [cf. 4:117]
2:105. Diana's law = virginity
  3.7. Anna = Anne, Queen of Great Britain, Ireland, and (by claim)
      France
  3.33. matadore = a card of highest rank in ombre
  3.61. Pam = highest card in loo
3.165. *Atalantis* = book of scandal by Delarivier Manley

Lady Mary Wortley Montagu

(1 6 8 9 – 1 7 6 2)

Mary Pierrepont, eldest daughter of a duke, wrote superbly observant letters during her exotic travels—informed and witty enough to divert attention from her friendship, and her later quarrels, with Pope. In 1712 she secretly married Edward Wortley Montagu, ambassador in 1716–1718 to Constantinople. She separated from Montagu in 1739, but she was never to escape men who deceived and swindled. Pope in 1718, when he was declaring Lady Mary mistress of every grace and every virtue, sent her his reverent stanzas "On Two Lovers Struck Dead by Lightning"; the tetrameter of her answering "Epitaph" signals the intent of satire. A fiercer intent needed no signal in the "Verses" written with the help of Lord Hervey when they thought Pope had ridiculed them in his imitation of Horace, *Satires* II.1. All agreed that Pope directed at her the lines beginning with *Satires* II.2.50: "him you'll call a dog, and her a bitch."

EPITAPH

Here lies John Hughes and Sarah Drew.
Perhaps you'll say, what's that to you?
Believe me, friend, much may be said
On this poor couple that are dead.
On Sunday next they should have married;
But see how oddly things are carried.
On Thursday last it rained and lightened;
Those tender lovers, sadly frightened,
Sheltered beneath the cocking hay,
In hopes to pass the storm away.   10
But the bold thunder found them out
(Commissioned for that end, no doubt)
And seizing on their trembling breath,
Assigned them to the shades of death.
Who knows if 'twas not kindly done?
For had they seen the next year's sun
A beaten wife and cuckold swain

Had jointly cursed the marriage chain.
Now they are happy in their doom
For P[ope] has wrote upon their tomb.   20

VERSES

Addressed to the Imitator of the
First Satire of the Second Book
of Horace

In two large columns on thy motley page,
Where Roman wit is strip'd with English rage;
Where ribaldry to satire makes pretence,
And modern scandal rolls with ancient sense:
Whilst on one side we see how Horace thought,
And on the other how he never wrote;
Who can believe, who view the bad, the good,
That the dull copyist better understood
That spirit he pretends to imitate,
Than heretofore that Greek he did translate?   10
    Thine is just such an image of *his* pen,
As thou thyself art of the sons of men,
Where our own species in burlesque we trace,
A sign-post likeness of the human race,
That is at once resemblance and disgrace.
    Horace can laugh, is delicate, is clear,
You only coarsely rail, or darkly sneer:
His style is elegant, his diction pure,
Whilst none thy crabbed numbers can endure;
Hard as thy heart, and as thy birth obscure.   20
    If *he* has thorns, they all on roses grow;
Thine like thistles, and mean brambles shew;
With this exception, that, though rank the soil,
Weeds as they are, they seem produc'd by toil.
    Satire should, like a polish'd razor, keen,
Wound with a touch, that's scarcely felt or seen;
Thine is an oyster-knife, that hacks and hews;
The rage, but not the talent to abuse;
And is in *hate*, what *love* is in the stews.
'Tis the gross *lust* of hate, that still annoys,   30

Without distinction, as gross love enjoys:
Neither to folly, nor to vice confin'd,
The object of thy spleen is humankind:
It preys on all who yield, or who resist;
To thee 'tis provocation to exist.
   But if thou seest a great and generous heart,
Thy bow is doubly bent to force a dart.
Nor dignity nor innocence is spar'd,
Nor age, nor sex, nor thrones, nor graves, rever'd.
Nor only justice vainly we demand,   40
But even benefits can't rein thy hand;
To this or that alike in vain we trust,
Nor find thee less ungrateful than unjust.
   Not even youth and beauty can control
The universal rancour of thy soul;
Charms that might soften superstition's rage,
Might humble pride, or thaw the ice of age.
But how should'st thou by beauty's force be mov'd,
No more for loving made than to be lov'd?
It was the equity of righteous Heav'n,   50
That such a soul to such a form was giv'n;
And shews the uniformity of fate,
That one so odious should be born to hate.
   When God created thee, one would believe
He said the same as to the snake of Eve;
To human race antipathy declare,
'Twixt them and thee be everlasting war.
But O! the sequel of the sentence dread,
And whilst you *bruise their heel*, beware your head.
Nor think thy weakness shall be thy defence,   60
The female scold's protection in offence.
Sure 'tis as fair to beat who cannot fight,
As 'tis to libel those who cannot write.
And if thou draw'st thy pen to aid the law,
Others a cudgel, or a rod, may draw.
If none with vengeance yet thy crimes pursue,
Or give thy manifold affronts their due;
If limbs unbroken, skin without a stain,
Unwhipt, unblanketed, unkick'd, unslain,
That wretched little carcass you retain,   70
The reason is, not that the world wants eyes,
But thou 'rt so mean, they see, and they despise:
When fretful *porcupine*, with ranc'rous will,

From mounted back shoots forth a harmless quill,
Cool the spectators stand: and all the while
Upon the angry little monster smile.
Thus 'tis with thee:—while impotently safe,
You strike unwounding, we unhurt can laugh.
Who but must laugh, this bully when he sees,
A puny insect shiv'ring at a breeze?   80
One over-match'd by every blast of wind,
Insulting and provoking all mankind.
    Is this the *thing* to keep mankind in awe,
To make those tremble who escape the law?
Is this *the ridicule* to live so long,
The deathless satire, and *immortal song?*
No: like the self-blown praise, thy scandal flies;
And, as we're told of wasps, it stings and dies.
    If none do yet return th' intended blow,
You all your safety to your dulness owe: 90
But whilst that armour thy poor corse defends,
'Twill make thy readers few, as are thy friends:
Those, who thy nature loath'd yet lov'd thy art,
Who lik'd thy head, and yet abhorr'd thy heart:
Chose thee to read, but never to converse,
And scorn'd in prose him whom they priz'd in verse;
Ev'n they shall now their partial error see,
Shall shun thy writings like thy company;
And to thy books shall ope their eyes no more
Than to thy person they would do their door.   100
    Nor thou the justice of the world disown,
That leaves thee thus an outcast and alone;
For though in law to murder be to kill,
In equity the murder 's in the will:
Then whilst with coward-hand you stab a name,
And try at least t' assassinate our fame,
Like the first bold assassin's be thy lot,
Ne'er be thy guilt forgiven, or forgot;
But, as thou hat'st, be hated by mankind,
And with the emblem of thy crooked mind   110
Mark'd on thy back, like Cain by God's own hand
Wander, like him, accursed through the land.

Elizabeth Boyd

(fl. 1727–1745)

What is known of Boyd comes from her own publications—separate and gathered poems, a ballad-opera, a novel, a miscellany, and one surviving number of an abortive periodical that she produced while in poor health and recurrent financial need, although members of the nobility were numbered among her subscribers. The couplets of mourning and expostulation given here formed one of several poems of affliction in *The Humorous Miscellany* (1733).

ON THE DEATH OF AN INFANT OF FIVE DAYS OLD, BEING A BEAUTIFUL BUT ABORTIVE BIRTH

How frail is human life! How fleet our breath,
Born with the symptoms of approaching death!
What dire convulsions rend a mother's breast,
When by a first-born son's decease distressed.
Although an embryo, an abortive boy,
Thy wond'rous beauties give a wond'rous joy:
Still flattering Hope a flattering idea gives,
And, whilst the birth can breathe, we say it lives.
With what kind warmth the dear-loved babe was pressed:
The darling man was with less love caressed!   10
How dear, how innocent, the fond embrace!
The father's form all o'er, the father's face,
The sparkling eye, gay with a cherub smile,
Some flying hours the mother-pangs beguile;
The pretty mouth a Cupid's tale expressed,
In amorous murmurs, to the full-swoll'n breast.
If angel infancy can so endear,
Dear angel-infants must command a tear.
O! could the stern-soul'd sex but know the pain,
Or the soft mother's agonies sustain,   20
With tenderest love the obdurate heart would burn,
And the shock'd father tear for tear return.

332

Mary Barber

(1690? – 1757)

In the preface to her collected *Poems* (1734), printed by the novelist Samuel Richardson, Barber explains that she had begun writing poetry "chiefly to form the minds of my children." She had begun publishing her poems in the 1720s in Dublin, where she lived with her husband, who was a woollen-draper, and their four children. Barber was befriended by Swift, who campaigned in England for a subscription to her poetry and urged literary friends to support her. He also wrote of her that "she seemeth to have a true poetical genius, better cultivated than could well be expected, either from her sex, or the scene she hath acted in, as the wife of a citizen." Barber was loyal to Swift and was arrested in 1733 for smuggling into England some of his politically subversive poetry, although she was released without having to stand trial. After the publication of her volume of poetry, Barber's attempts to settle in England failed, in part because of her failing health, and she suffered from both gout and rheumatism. Her poetry was popular—and anthologized—in her own day but fell out of favor by the late eighteenth century.

THE CONCLUSION OF A LETTER TO THE REV. MR. C——

'Tis time to conclude; for I make it a rule,
To leave off all writing, when Con. comes from school.
He dislikes what I've written, and says, I had better
To send what he calls a *poetical* letter.

To this I replied, you are out of your wits;
A letter in verse would put him in fits:
He thinks it a crime in a woman, to read—
Then, what would he say, should your counsel succeed?

I pity poor Barber, his wife's so romantic:
A letter in rhyme!—Why, the woman is frantic!   10
This reading the poets has quite turn'd her head!
On my life, she should have a dark room, and straw bed.
I often heard say, that St. Patrick took care,

333

No poisonous creature should live in this air:
He only regarded the body, I find;
But Plato consider'd who poison'd the mind.
Would they'd follow his precepts, who sit at the helm,
And drive poetasters from out of the realm!

    Her husband has surely a terrible life;
There's nothing I dread, like a verse-writing wife: 20
Defend me, ye powers, from that fatal curse;
Which must heighten the plagues of, *for better for worse!*

    May I have a wife, that will dust her own floor;
And not the fine minx, recommended by More.
(That he was a dotard, is granted, I hope,
Who died for asserting the rights of the Pope.)
If ever I marry, I'll choose me a spouse,
That shall *serve* and *obey*, as she's bound by her vows;
That shall, when I'm dressing, attend like a valet;
Then go to the kitchen, and study my palate.   30
She has wisdom enough, that keeps out of the dirt,
And can make a good pudding, and cut out a shirt.
What good's in a dame, that will pore on a book?
No!—Give me the wife, that shall save me a cook.

    Thus far I had written—Then turn'd to my son,
To give him advice, ere my letter was done.
My son, should you marry, look out for a wife,
That's fitted to lighten the labours of life.
Be sure, wed a woman you thoroughly know,
And shun, above all things, a *housewifely shrew*;   40
That would fly to your study, with fire in her looks,
And ask what you got by your poring on books;
Think dressing of dinner the height of all science,
And to peace, and good humour bid open defiance.
    Avoid the fine lady, whose beauty's her care;
Who sets a high price on her shape, and her air;
Who in dress, and in visits, employs the whole day;
And longs for the ev'ning, to sit down to play.

    Choose a woman of wisdom, as well as good breeding,
With a turn, or at least no aversion, to reading: 50
In the care of her person, exact and refin'd;
Yet still, let her principal care be her mind:

Who can, when her family cares give her leisure,
Without the dear cards, pass an ev'ning with pleasure;
In forming her children to virtue and knowledge,
Nor trust, for that care, to a school, or a college:
By learning made humble, not thence taking airs,
To despise, or neglect, her domestic affairs:
Nor think her less fitted for doing her duty,
By knowing its reasons, its use, and its beauty.   60

When you gain her affection, take care to preserve it;
Lest others persuade her, you do not deserve it.
Still study to heighten the joys of her life;
Nor treat her the worse, for her being your wife.
If in judgment she errs, set her right, without pride:
'Tis the province of insolent fools, to deride.
A husband's first praise, is a friend and protector:
Then change not these titles, for tyrant and hector.
Let your person be neat, unaffectedly clean,
Tho' alone with your wife the whole day you remain.   70
Choose books, for her study, to fashion her mind,
To emulate those who excell'd of her kind.
Be religion the principal care of your life,
As you hope to be blest in your children and wife:
So you, in your marriage, shall gain its true end;
And find, in your wife, a companion and friend.

l. 2. Con. = her son Constantine

WRITTEN FOR MY SON, AND
SPOKEN BY HIM AT HIS FIRST
PUTTING ON BREECHES

What is it our mammas bewitches,
To plague us little boys with breeches?
To tyrant Custom we must yield,
Whilst vanquish'd Reason flies the field.
Our legs must suffer by ligation,
To keep the blood from circulation;
And then our feet, tho' young and tender,
We to the shoemaker surrender;

Who often makes our shoes so straight
Our growing feet they cramp and fret: 10
Whilst with contrivance most profound,
Across our insteps we are bound;
Which is the cause, I make no doubt,
Why thousands suffer in the gout.
Our wiser ancestors wore brogues,
Before the surgeons brib'd these rogues,
With narrow toes, and heels like pegs,
To help to make us break our legs,

　　Then, ere we know to use our fists,
Our mothers closely bind our wrists;   20
And never think our clothes are neat,
Till they're so tight we cannot eat.
And, to increase our other pains,
The hat-band helps to cramp our brains.
The cravat finishes the work,
Like bow-string sent from the Grand Turk.

　　Thus dress, that should prolong our date,
Is made to hasten on our fate.
Fair privilege of nobler natures,
To be more plagu'd than other creatures!   30
The wild inhabitants of air
Are cloth'd by Heav'n, with wond'rous care;
Their beauteous, well-compacted feathers
Are coats of mail against all weathers;
Enamell'd, to delight the eye,
Gay, as the bow that decks the sky.
The beasts are cloth'd with beauteous skins;
The fishes arm'd with scales and fins;
Whose lustre lends the sailor light,
When all the stars are hid in night.   40

　　O were our dress contriv'd like these,
For use, for ornament and ease!
Man only seems to sorrow born,
Naked, defenceless and forlorn.

　　Yet we have reason, to supply
What Nature did to Man deny:
Weak viceroy! Who thy pow'r will own,

When Custom has usurp'd thy throne?
In vain did I appeal to thee,
Ere I would wear his livery;   50
Who, in defiance to thy rules,
Delights to make us act like fools.
O'er human race the tyrant reigns,
And binds them in eternal chains:
We yield to his despotic sway,
The only monarch all obey.

Anne Ingram, Viscountess Irwin

(1 6 9 6 – 1 7 6 4)

Anne Howard's early years were spent in Castle Howard with her parents, the Earl of Carlisle and his wife, the daughter of the Earl of Essex. Anne became Viscountess Irwin upon marriage in 1717 to Richard Ingram, who died of smallpox in 1721. In 1736 she accompanied the Princess of Wales to Holland as Lady of the Bedchamber. She was married from 1737 until his death in 1748 to Col. William Douglas. During this adventurous life she protested the view of her friend Lady Mary Wortley Montagu that constancy was unreasonable and unnatural.

Upon Pope's publication early in 1735 of the verse essay "Of the Characters of Women" (see p. 300), later to become Epistle II of his *Moral Essays,* Lady Irwin's reply, which anticipates the arguments in 1787 and 1792 of Mary Wollstonecraft, was circulated and frequently reprinted, most effectively, in *The New Foundling Hospital for Wit* (1786).

ON MR. POPE'S CHARACTERS OF WOMEN

> By custom doomed to folly, sloth, and ease,
> No wonder Pope such female triflers sees;
> But, would the satirist confess the truth,
> Nothing so like as male and female youth;
> Nothing so like as man and woman old,
> Their joys, their loves, their hates, if truly told,
> Though different acts seem different sex's growth,
> 'Tis the same principle impels them both.
> View daring man, stung with ambition's fire,
> The conquering hero, or the youthful squire,   10
> By different deeds aspire to deathless fame,
> One murders man, the other murders game.
> View a fair nymph, blessed with superior charms,
> Whose tempting form the coldest bosom warms;
> No eastern monarch more despotic reigns,
> Than this fair tyrant of the Cyprian plains.

Whether a crown or bauble we desire;
Whether to learning, or to dress aspire;
Whether we wait with joy the trumpet's call,
Or wish to shine the fairest at a ball;   20
In either sex the appetite's the same,
For love of power is still the love of fame.
    Women must in a narrow orbit move,
But power, alike, both males and females love.
What makes the difference then, you may enquire,
Between the hero, and the rural squire?
Between the maid bred up with courtly care,
Or she who earns by toil, her daily fare?
Their power is stinted, but not so their will,
Ambitious thoughts the humblest cottage fill;   30
Far as they can, they push their little fame,
And try to leave behind a deathless name.
In education all the difference lies;
Women, if taught, would be as learned and wise
As haughty man, improved by arts and rules;
Where God makes one, Neglect makes many fools;
And though Nugatrixes are daily found,
Fluttering Nugators equally abound.
Such heads are toy-shops, filled with trifling ware,
And can each folly with each female share: 40
A female mind like a rude fallow lies,
No seed is sown, but weeds spontaneous rise.
As well we might expect in winter, spring,
As land untilled a fruitful crop should bring;
As well we might expect Peruvian ore
We would possess, yet dig not for the store.
Culture improves all fruits, all sorts we find,
Wit, judgment, sense, fruits of the human mind.
    Ask the rich merchant, conversant in trade,
How Nature op'rates in the growing blade;   50
Ask the philosopher the price of stocks;
Ask the gay courtier how to manage flocks;
Enquire the dogmas of the learned schools—
From Aristotle down to Newton's rules—
Of a rough soldier, bred to boist'rous war,
Or one still rougher, a true British tar.
They'll all reply, unpractised in such laws,
Th'effect they know, though ign'rant of the cause.
The sailor may, perchance, have equal parts

With him bred up to science and to arts;   60
And he who at the helm or stern is seen,
Philosopher or hero might have been.
The whole in application is comprised,
Reason's not reason, if not exercised.
Use, not possession, real good affords;
No miser's rich, that dares not touch his hoards!
Can female youth, left to weak woman's care,
Misled by Custom, Folly's fruitful heir;
Told that their charms a monarch may enslave,
That beauty, like the gods, can kill, or save;   70
Taught the arcanas, the mysterious arts,
By ambush dress, to catch unwary hearts:
If wealthy born, taught to lisp French, and dance,
Their morals left, Lucretius-like, to chance:
Strangers to reason and reflection made,
Left to their passions, and by them betrayed;
Untaught the nobler end of glorious truth,
Bred to deceive, even from their earliest youth!
Unused to books, nor virtue taught to prize,
Whose mind, a savage waste, unpeopled lies;   80
Which to supply, trifles fill up the void,
And idly busy, to no end employed.
Can these, from such a school, more virtue show?
Or tempting vice treat like a common foe?
Can they resist, when soothing pleasure woos?
Preserve their virtue, when their fame they lose?
Can they on other themes converse or write
Than what they hear all day, or dream all night?
Not so the Roman female fame was spread,
Not so was Clelia, or Lucretia bred: 90
Not so such heroines true glory sought,
Not so was Portia, or Cornelia taught!
Portia, the glory of the female race!
Portia, more lovely by her mind than face!
Early informed, by Truth's unerring beam,
What to reject, what justly to esteem;
Taught by philosophy all moral good,
How to repel in youth th'impetuous blood!
How her most fav'rite passions to subdue,
And Fame, through Virtue's avenues, pursue;   100
She tries herself, and finds, even dolorous pain
Can't the great secret from her breast obtain;

To Cato born, to noble Brutus joined,
She shines invincible in form and mind!
 No more such gen'rous sentiments we trace
In the gay moderns of the female race!
No more, alas! heroic virtue's shown,
Since knowledge ceased, philosophy's unknown.
No more can we expect our modern wives
Heroes should breed, who lead such useless lives.   110
Would you, who know th'arcana of the soul,
The secret springs which move and guide the whole;
Would you, who can instruct as well as please,
Bestow some moments of your darling ease
To rescue woman from this Gothic state,
New passions raise, their minds anew create,
Then for the Spartan virtues we might hope,
For who stands unconvinced by gen'rous Pope?
Then would the British fair perpetual bloom,
And vie in fame with ancient Greece and Rome!   120

l. 90. Clelia = heroine of a feat retold from Livy 2.13 by Made-
  leine de Scudéry in 1656

John Dyer

(1699 – 1757)

After attendance at Westminster School and serious study of painting, Dyer became an itinerant painter in his native Wales. He was ordained and served as Anglican vicar and, with a law degree from Cambridge, as rector in various parishes in England. His "Grongar Hill" (1725), especially in the octosyllabic format of 1726 printed here, set a pattern for topographic description. Wordsworth's sonnet beginning "Bard of the Fleece," in praise of Dyer's long poem on sheep raising and the wool trade, ends in tribute to "Grongar Hill." Dyer's poem satisfied the growing taste for the picturesque, as in line 30 on long vistas reflecting bright light.

GRONGAR HILL

Silent Nymph, with curious eye!
Who, the purple ev'ning, lie
On the mountain's lonely van,
Beyond the noise of busy man,
Painting fair the form of things,
While the yellow linnet sings;
Or the tuneful nightingale
Charms the forest with her tale;
Come with all thy various hues,
Come, and aid the sister Muse;   10
Now while Phoebus riding high
Gives lustre to the land and sky!
Grongar Hill invites my song,
Draw the landskip bright and strong;
Grongar, in whose mossy cells
Sweetly-musing Quiet dwells;
Grongar, in whose silent shade,
For the modest Muses made,
So oft I have, the evening still,
At the fountain of a rill,   20
Sate upon a flow'ry bed,
With my hand beneath my head;

While stray'd my eyes o'er Towy's flood,
Over mead, and over wood,
From house to house, from hill to hill,
'Til Contemplation had her fill.
    About his chequer'd sides I wind,
And leave his brooks and meads behind,
And groves, and grottoes where I lay,
And vistoes shooting beams of day: 30
Wide and wider spreads the vale;
As circles on a smooth canal:
The mountains round, unhappy fate!
Sooner or later, of all height,
Withdraw their summits from the skies,
And lessen as the others rise:
Still the prospect wider spreads,
Adds a thousand woods and meads,
Still it widens, widens still,
And sinks the newly-risen hill.   40
    Now, I gain the mountain's brow,
What a landskip lies below!
No clouds, no vapours intervene,
But the gay, the open scene
Does the face of nature show,
In all the hues of heaven's bow!
And, swelling to embrace the light,
Spreads around beneath the sight.
    Old castles on the cliffs arise,
Proudly tow'ring in the skies!   50
Rushing from the woods, the spires
Seem from hence ascending fires!
Half his beams Apollo sheds
On the yellow mountain-heads!
Gilds the fleeces of the flocks:
And glitters on the broken rocks!
    Below me trees unnumber'd rise,
Beautiful in various dyes:
The gloomy pine, the poplar blue,
The yellow beech, the sable yew,   60
The slender fir, that taper grows,
The sturdy oak with broad-spread boughs.
And beyond the purple grove,
Haunt of Phillis, queen of love!
Gaudy as the op'ning dawn,

Lies a long and level lawn
On which a dark hill, steep and high,
Holds and charms the wand'ring eye!
Deep are his feet in Towy's flood,
His sides are cloth'd with waving wood,   70
And ancient towers crown his brow,
That cast an aweful look below;
Whose ragged walls the ivy creeps,
And with her arms from falling keeps;
So both a safety from the wind
On mutual dependence find.
   'Tis now the raven's bleak abode;
'Tis now th'apartment of the toad;
And there the fox securely feeds;
And there the pois'nous adder breeds   80
Conceal'd in ruins, moss and weeds;
While, ever and anon, there falls
Huge heaps of hoary moulder'd walls.
Yet time has seen, that lifts the low,
And level lays the lofty brow,
Has been this broken pile compleat,
Big with the vanity of state;
But transient is the smile of fate!
A little rule, a little sway,
A sun beam in a winter's day,   90
Is all the proud and mighty have
Between the cradle and the grave.
   And see the rivers how they run,
Through woods and meads, in shade and sun,
Sometimes swift, sometimes slow,
Wave succeeding wave, they go
A various journey to the deep,
Like human life to endless sleep!
Thus is nature's vesture wrought,
To instruct our wand'ring thought;   100
Thus she dresses green and gay,
To disperse our cares away.
   Ever charming, ever new,
When will the landskip tire the view!
The fountain's fall, the river's flow,
The woody valleys, warm and low;
The windy summit, wild and high,
Roughly rushing on the sky!

The pleasant seat, the ruin'd tow'r,
The naked rock, the shady bow'r;   110
The town and village, dome and farm,
Each give each a double charm,
As pearls upon an Æthiop's arm.
   See on the mountain's southern side,
Where the prospect opens wide,
Where the evening gilds the tide;
How close and small the hedges lie!
What streaks of meadows cross the eye!
A step methinks may pass the stream,
So little distant dangers seem;   120
So we mistake the future's face,
Ey'd through hope's deluding glass;
As yon summits soft and fair
Clad in colours of the air,
Which do those who journey near,
Barren, brown, and rough appear;
Still we tread the same coarse way,
The present's still a cloudy day.
   O may I with myself agree,
And never covet what I see: 130
Content me with an humble shade,
My passions tam'd, my wishes laid;
For while our wishes wildly roll,
We banish quiet from the soul:
'Tis thus the busy beat the air;
And misers gather wealth and care.
   Now, ev'n now, my joys run high,
As on the mountain-turf I lie;
While the wanton Zephyr sings,
And in the vale perfumes his wings;   140
While the waters murmur deep;
While the shepherd charms his sheep;
While the birds unbounded fly,
And with music fill the sky,
Now, ev'n now, my joys run high.
   Be full, ye courts, be great who will;
Search for Peace with all your skill:
Open wide the lofty door,
Seek her on the marble floor,
In vain you search, she is not there;   150
In vain ye search the domes of care!

Grass and flowers Quiet treads,
On the meads, and mountain-heads,
Along with Pleasure, close allied,
Ever by each other's side:
And often, by the murm'ring rill,
Hears the thrush, while all is still,
Within the groves of Grongar Hill.

James Thomson

(1700–1748)

Born on the Scottish border, Thomson attended Edinburgh University but moved to London in 1725. *The Seasons* (1726–1730; repeatedly revised until 1746) became *the* poem of nature—including topography, piety, sublimity, science, and husbandry—before faint praise from the Romantics, who thought Thomson's anti-Popeian, Miltonic blank verse unnatural in diction. His "Hymn" appeared in 1730 with "Winter," which was later used as the first book of *The Seasons*.

A HYMN ON THE SEASONS

These, as they change, Almighty Father! these
Are but the varied God. The rolling year
Is full of thee. Forth in the pleasing Spring
Thy beauty walks, thy tenderness and love.
Wide flush the fields; the softening air is balm;
Echo the mountains round; the forest smiles;
And every sense, and every heart, is joy.
Then comes thy glory in the Summer-months,
With light and heat refulgent. Then thy Sun
Shoots full perfection through the swelling year: 10
And oft thy voice in dreadful thunder speaks,
And oft, at dawn, deep noon, or falling eve,
By brooks and groves, in hollow-whispering gales.
Thy bounty shines in Autumn unconfined,
And spreads a common feast for all that lives.
In Winter awful thou! with clouds and storms
Around thee thrown, tempest o'er tempest rolled,
Majestic darkness! On the whirlwind's wing
Riding sublime, thou bidst the world adore,
And humblest nature with thy northern blast.   20

Mysterious round! what skill, what force divine,
Deep-felt in these appear! a simple train,
Yet so delightful mixed, with such kind art,

Such beauty and beneficence combined,
Shade unperceived so softening into shade,
And all so forming an harmonious whole
That, as they still succeed, they ravish still.
But, wandering oft with brute unconscious gaze,
Man marks not thee, marks not the mighty hand
That, ever busy, wheels the silent spheres,   30
Works in the secret deep, shoots steaming thence
The fair profusion that o'erspreads the Spring,
Flings from the sun direct the flaming day,
Feeds every creature, hurls the tempest forth,
And, as on earth this grateful change revolves,
With transport touches all the springs of life.

   Nature, attend! join, every living soul
Beneath the spacious temple of the sky,
In adoration join; and ardent raise
One general song! To him, ye vocal gales,   40
Breathe soft, whose spirit in your freshness breathes:
O! talk of him in solitary glooms,
Where, o'er the rock, the scarcely-waving pine
Fills the brown shade with a religious awe.
And ye, whose bolder note is heard afar,
Who shake the astonished world, lift high to Heaven
The impetuous song, and say from whom you rage.
His praise, ye brooks, attune, ye trembling rills;
And let me catch it as I muse along.
Ye headlong torrents, rapid and profound;   50
Ye softer floods, that lead the humid maze
Along the vale; and thou, majestic main,
A secret world of wonders in thyself,
Sound his stupendous praise, whose greater voice
Or bids you roar or bids your roarings fall.
Soft roll your incense, herbs, and fruits, and flowers,
In mingled clouds to him, whose sun exalts,
Whose breath perfumes you, and whose pencil paints.
Ye forests, bend; ye harvests, wave to him—
Breathe your still song into the reaper's heart   60
As home he goes beneath the joyous moon.
Ye that keep watch in heaven, as earth asleep
Unconscious lies, effuse your mildest beams,
Ye constellations! while your angels strike
Amid the spangled sky the silver lyre.

Great source of day! best image here below
Of thy Creator, ever pouring wide
From world to world the vital ocean round!
On nature write with every beam his praise.
The thunder rolls: be hushed the prostrate world,   70
While cloud to cloud returns the solemn hymn.
Bleat out afresh, ye hills; ye mossy rocks,
Retain the sound; the broad responsive low,
Ye valleys, raise; for the Great Shepherd reigns,
And his unsuffering kingdom yet will come.
Ye woodlands all, awake: a boundless song
Burst from the groves; and, when the restless day,
Expiring, lays the warbling world asleep,
Sweetest of birds, sweet Philomela! charm
The listening shades, and teach the night his praise!   80
Ye, chief, for whom the whole creation smiles,
At once the head, the heart, and tongue of all,
Crown the great hymn! In swarming cities vast,
Assembled men, to the deep organ join
The long-resounding voice, oft breaking clear
At solemn pauses through the swelling bass;
And, as each mingling flame increases each,
In one united ardour rise to heaven.
Or, if you rather choose the rural shade,
And find a fane in every sacred grove,   90
There let the shepherd's flute, the virgin's lay,
The prompting seraph, and the poet's lyre
Still sing the God of Seasons as they roll.
For me, when I forget the darling theme,
Whether the blossom blows, the summer-ray
Russets the plain, inspiring autumn gleams,
Or winter rises in the blackening east,
Be my tongue mute, may fancy paint no more,
And, dead to joy, forget my heart to beat!

Should fate command me to the farthest verge   100
Of the green earth, to distant barbarous climes,
Rivers unknown to song, where first the sun
Gilds Indian mountains, or his setting beam
Flames on the Atlantic isles, 'tis nought to me;
Since God is ever present, ever felt,
In the void waste as in the city full,
And where he vital spreads there must be joy.

When even at last the solemn hour shall come,
And wing my mystic flight to future worlds,
I cheerful will obey; there, with new powers,   110
Will rising wonders sing: I cannot go
Where Universal Love not smiles around,
Sustaining all yon orbs and all their sons;
From seeming evil still educing good,
And better thence again, and better still,
In infinite progression. But I lose
Myself in him, in light ineffable!
Come then, expressive Silence, muse his praise.

l. 58. pencil = small brush

Samuel Johnson

(1709–1784)

From Grub Street hack, after youth in Lichfield, B.A. from Pembroke College, Oxford, and apprenticeship in Birmingham, Johnson became the foremost critic and scholar of English literature and language in his time. He transformed lexicography with his comprehensive *Dictionary of the English Language* (1755) and transformed biography in part with his *Lives of the Poets* (1781) but more by talking to James Boswell. His *London* (1738), based on Juvenal's third satire, was surpassed by the satire of 1749 given here, which directs against human ambitions the scorn of a rational Christian. The lines omitted point to examples of the futility of success in learning (Bodley, Roger Bacon, Galileo, Laud), politics (Wolsey, Villiers, Harley, Wentworth, Hyde), and military action.

From THE VANITY OF HUMAN WISHES

THE TENTH SATIRE OF JUVENAL IMITATED

> Let Observation, with extensive view,
> Survey mankind, from China to Peru;
> Remark each anxious toil, each eager strife,
> And watch the busy scenes of crowded life;
> Then say how hope and fear, desire and hate
> O'erspread with snares the clouded maze of fate,
> Where wavering man, betrayed by venturous pride
> To tread the dreary paths without a guide,
> As treacherous phantoms in the mist delude,
> Shuns fancied ills, or chases airy good;   10
> How rarely Reason guides the stubborn choice,
> Rules the bold hand, or prompts the suppliant voice;
> How nations sink, by darling schemes oppressed,
> When Vengeance listens to the fool's request.
> Fate wings with every wish the afflictive dart,
> Each gift of nature, and each grace of art;
> With fatal heat impetuous courage glows,
> With fatal sweetness elocution flows,
> Impeachment stops the speaker's powerful breath,
> And restless fire precipitates on death.   20

But scarce observed, the knowing and the bold
Fall in the general massacre of gold;
Wide-wasting pest! that rages unconfined,
And crowds with crimes the records of mankind;
For gold his sword the hireling ruffian draws,
For gold the hireling judge distorts the laws;
Wealth heaped on wealth, nor truth nor safety buys,
The dangers gather as the treasures rise.
   Let History tell where rival kings command,
And dubious title shakes the madded land,　　　　　　　　30
When statutes glean the refuse of the sword,
How much more safe the vassal than the lord;
Low skulks the hind beneath the rage of power,
And leaves the wealthy traitor in the Tower,
Untouched his cottage, and his slumbers sound,
Though Confiscation's vultures hover round.
   The needy traveler, serene and gay,
Walks the wild heath, and sings his toil away.
Does envy seize thee? crush the upbraiding joy,
Increase his riches and his peace destroy;　　　　　　　　40
New fears in dire vicissitude invade,
The rustling brake alarms, and quivering shade,
Nor light nor darkness bring his pain relief,
One shows the plunder, and one hides the thief.
   Yet still one general cry the skies assails,
And gain and grandeur load the tainted gales;
Few know the toiling statesman's fear or care,
The insidious rival and the gaping heir.
   Once more, Democritus, arise on earth,
With cheerful wisdom and instructive mirth,　　　　　　　50
See motley life in modern trappings dressed,
And feed with varied fools the eternal jest:
Thou who couldst laugh where Want enchained Caprice,
Toil crushed Conceit, and man was of a piece;
Where Wealth unloved without a mourner died;
And scarce a sycophant was fed by Pride;
Where ne'er was known the form of mock debate,
Or seen a new-made mayor's unwieldy state;
Where change of favorites made no change of laws,
And senates heard before they judged a cause;　　　　　　60
How wouldst thou shake at Britain's modish tribe,
Dart the quick taunt, and edge the piercing gibe?
Attentive truth and nature to descry,

And pierce each scene with philosophic eye,
To thee were solemn toys or empty show
The robes of pleasures and the veils of woe:
All aid the farce, and all thy mirth maintain,
Whose joys arc causeless, or whose griefs are vain.
   Such was the scorn that filled the sage's mind,
Renewed at every glance on human kind;   70
How just that scorn ere yet thy voice declare,
Search every state, and canvass every prayer.
   Unnumbered suppliants crowd Preferment's gate,
Athirst for wealth, and burning to be great;
Delusive Fortune hears the incessant call,
They mount, they shine, evaporate, and fall.
On every stage the foes of peace attend,
Hate dogs their flight, and Insult mocks their end.
Love ends with hope, the sinking statesman's door
Pours in the morning worshiper no more;   80
For growing names the weekly scribbler lies,
To growing wealth the dedicator flies;
From every room descends the painted face,
That hung the bright palladium of the place;
And smoked in kitchens, or in auctions sold,
To better features yields the frame of gold;
For now no more we trace in every line
Heroic worth, benevolence divine:
The form distorted justifies the fall,
And Detestation rids the indignant wall.   90
   But will not Britain hear the last appeal,
Sign her foes' doom, or guard her favorites' zeal?
Through Freedom's sons no more remonstrance rings,
Degrading nobles and controlling kings;
Our supple tribes repress their patriot throats,
And ask no questions but the price of votes,
With weekly libels and septennial ale,
Their wish is full to riot and to rail.

       *   *   *

   Enlarge my life with multitude of days!
In health, in sickness, thus the suppliant prays;
Hides from himself his state, and shuns to know,
That life protracted is protracted woe.
Time hovers o'er, impatient to destroy,
And shuts up all the passages of joy;   260

In vain their gifts the bounteous seasons pour,
The fruit autumnal, and the vernal flower;
With listless eyes the dotard views the store,
He views, and wonders that they please no more;
Now pall the tasteless meats, and joyless wines,
And Luxury with sighs her slave resigns.
Approach, ye minstrels, try the soothing strain,
Diffuse the tuneful lenitives of pain:
No sounds, alas! would touch the impervious ear,
Though dancing mountains witnessed Orpheus near;   270
Nor lute nor lyre his feeble powers attend,
Nor sweeter music of a virtuous friend,
But everlasting dictates crowd his tongue,
Perversely grave, or positively wrong.
The still returning tale, and lingering jest,
Perplex the fawning niece and pampered guest,
While growing hopes scarce awe the gathering sneer,
And scarce a legacy can bribe to hear;
The watchful guests still hint the last offense;
The daughter's petulance, the son's expense,   280
Improve his heady rage with treacherous skill,
And mold his passions till they make his will.
   Unnumbered maladies his joints invade,
Lay siege to life and press the dire blockade;
But unextinguished avarice still remains,
And dreaded losses aggravate his pains;
He turns, with anxious heart and crippled hands,
His bonds of debt, and mortgages of lands;
Or views his coffers with suspicious eyes,
Unlocks his gold, and counts it till he dies.   290
   But grant, the virtues of a temperate prime
Bless with an age exempt from scorn or crime;
An age that melts with unperceived decay,
And glides in modest innocence away;
Whose peaceful day Benevolence endears,
Whose night congratulating Conscience cheers;
The general favorite as the general friend:
Such age there is, and who shall wish its end?
   Yet even on this her load Misfortune flings,
To press the weary minutes' flagging wings;   300
New sorrow rises as the day returns,
A sister sickens, or a daughter mourns.
Now kindred Merit fills the sable bier,

Now lacerated Friendship claims a tear;
Year chases year, decay pursues decay,
Still drops some joy from withering life away;
New forms arise, and different views engage,
Superfluous lags the veteran on the stage,
Till pitying Nature signs the last release,
And bids afflicted Worth retire to peace.   310
    But few there are whom hours like these await,
Who set unclouded in the gulfs of Fate.
From Lydia's monarch should the search descend,
By Solon cautioned to regard his end,
In life's last scene what prodigies surprise,
Fears of the brave, and follies of the wise!
From Marlborough's eyes the streams of dotage flow,
And Swift expires a driveler and a show.
    The teeming mother, anxious for her race,
Begs for each birth the fortune of a face: 320
Yet Vane could tell what ills from beauty spring;
And Sedley cursed the form that pleased a king.
Ye nymphs of rosy lips and radiant eyes,
Whom Pleasure keeps too busy to be wise,
Whom Joys with soft varieties invite,
By day the frolic, and the dance by night;
Who frown with vanity, who smile with art,
And ask the latest fashion of the heart,
What care, what rules your heedless charms shall save,
Each nymph your rival, and each youth your slave?   330
Against your fame with Fondness Hate combines,
The rival batters, and the lover mines.
With distant voice neglected Virtue calls,
Less heard and less, the faint remonstrance falls;
Tired with contempt, she quits the slippery reign,
And Pride and Prudence take her seat in vain.
In crowd at once, where none the pass defend,
The harmless freedom, and the private friend.
The guardians yield, by force superior plied:
To Interest, Prudence; and to Flattery, Pride.   340
Now Beauty falls betrayed, despised, distressed,
And hissing Infamy proclaims the rest.
    Where then shall Hope and Fear their objects find?
Must dull Suspense corrupt the stagnant mind?
Must helpless man, in ignorance sedate,
Roll darkling down the torrent of his fate?

Must no dislike alarm, no wishes rise,
No cries invoke the mercies of the skies?
Inquirer, cease; petitions yet remain,
Which Heaven may hear, nor deem religion vain. 350
Still raise for good the supplicating voice,
But leave to Heaven the measure and the choice,
Safe in His power, whose eyes discern afar
The secret ambush of a specious prayer.
Implore His aid, in His decisions rest,
Secure, whate'er He gives, He gives the best.
Yet when the sense of sacred presence fires,
And strong devotion to the skies aspires,
Pour forth thy fervors for a healthful mind,
Obedient passions, and a will resigned, 360
For love, which scarce collective man can fill;
For patience sovereign o'er transmuted ill;
For faith, that panting for a happier seat,
Counts death kind Nature's signal of retreat;
These goods for man the laws of Heaven ordain,
These goods He grants, who grants the power to gain,
With these celestial Wisdom calms the mind,
And makes the happiness she does not find.

l. 97. septennial ale = provided to win votes
l. 313. Lydia's monarch = wealthy Croesus
l. 321. Vane = royal mistress
l. 322. Sedley = royal mistress

Thomas Gray

(*1716 – 1771*)

A studious don at Cambridge University, with degrees or authority in classics, law, and history, Gray introduced passion to the "Augustan Age" in Pindaric odes that foreshadowed and influenced the Romantics. His famous elegy of 1751 (begun in 1742) unites classical order and introspective sympathy. It includes almost as many memorable phrases as *Hamlet*. Gray's father was a London scrivener and his mother kept a milliner's shop there; their son formed a close friendship with Horace Walpole at Eton.

ELEGY WRITTEN IN A COUNTRY CHURCHYARD

The curfew tolls the knell of parting day,
The lowing herd wind slowly o'er the lea,
The ploughman homeward plods his weary way,
And leaves the world to darkness and to me.

Now fades the glimmering landscape on the sight,
And all the air a solemn stillness holds,
Save where the beetle wheels his droning flight,
And drowsy tinklings lull the distant folds;

Save that from yonder ivy-mantled tow'r
The moping owl does to the moon complain   10
Of such as, wand'ring near her secret bow'r,
Molest her ancient solitary reign.

Beneath those rugged elms, that yew-tree's shade,
Where heaves the turf in many a mould'ring heap,
Each in his narrow cell for ever laid,
The rude forefathers of the hamlet sleep.

The breezy call of incense-breathing morn,
The swallow twitt'ring from the straw-built shed,

The cock's shrill clarion or the echoing horn,
No more shall rouse them from their lowly bed.   20

For them no more the blazing hearth shall burn,
Or busy housewife ply her evening care:
No children run to lisp their sire's return,
Or climb his knees the envied kiss to share.

Oft did the harvest to their sickle yield,
Their furrow oft the stubborn glebe has broke;
How jocund did they drive their team afield!
How bowed the woods beneath their sturdy stroke!

Let not Ambition mock their useful toil,
Their homely joys, and destiny obscure;   30
Nor Grandeur hear, with a disdainful smile,
The short and simple annals of the poor.

The boast of heraldry, the pomp of pow'r,
And all that beauty, all that wealth e'er gave,
Awaits alike th' inevitable hour.
The paths of glory lead but to the grave.

Nor you, ye Proud, impute to these the fault,
If Mem'ry o'er their tomb no trophies raise,
Where through the long-drawn aisle and fretted vault
The pealing anthem swells the note of praise.   40

Can storied urn or animated bust
Back to its mansion call the fleeting breath?
Can Honour's voice provoke the silent dust,
Or Flatt'ry soothe the dull cold ear of Death?

Perhaps in this neglected spot is laid
Some heart once pregnant with celestial fire,
Hands that the rod of empire might have swayed,
Or waked to ecstasy the living lyre.

But Knowledge to their eyes her ample page
Rich with the spoils of time did ne'er unroll;   50
Chill Penury repressed their noble rage,
And froze the genial current of the soul.

Full many a gem of purest ray serene
The dark unfathomed caves of ocean bear:
Full many a flower is born to blush unseen
And waste its sweetness on the desert air.

Some village-Hampden that with dauntless breast
The little tyrant of his fields withstood;
Some mute inglorious Milton here may rest,
Some Cromwell guiltless of his country's blood.   60

Th' applause of list'ning senates to command,
The threats of pain and ruin to despise,
To scatter plenty o'er a smiling land,
And read their hist'ry in a nation's eyes,

Their lot forbade: nor circumscribed alone
Their growing virtues, but their crimes confined;
Forbade to wade through slaughter to a throne,
And shut the gates of mercy on mankind,

The struggling pangs of conscious truth to hide,
To quench the blushes of ingenuous shame,   70
Or heap the shrine of Luxury and Pride
With incense kindled at the Muse's flame.

Far from the madding crowd's ignoble strife
Their sober wishes never learned to stray;
Along the cool sequestered vale of life
They kept the noiseless tenor of their way.

Yet ev'n these bones from insult to protect
Some frail memorial still erected nigh,
With uncouth rhymes and shapeless sculpture decked,
Implores the passing tribute of a sigh.   80

Their name, their years, spelt by th' unlettered muse,
The place of fame and elegy supply:
And many a holy text around she strews,
That teach the rustic moralist to die.

For who to dumb Forgetfulness a prey,
This pleasing anxious being e'er resigned,

Left the warm precincts of the cheerful day,
Nor cast one longing ling'ring look behind?

On some fond breast the parting soul relies,
Some pious drops the closing eye requires; 90
Ev'n from the tomb the voice of Nature cries,
Ev'n in our ashes live their wonted fires.

For thee who, mindful of th' unhonoured dead,
Dost in these lines their artless tale relate;
If chance, by lonely Contemplation led,
Some kindred spirit shall inquire thy fate,

Haply some hoary-headed swain may say,
"Oft have we seen him at the peep of dawn
Brushing with hasty steps the dews away
To meet the sun upon the upland lawn. 100

"There at the foot of yonder nodding beech
That wreathes its old fantastic roots so high,
His listless length at noontide would he stretch,
And pore upon the brook that babbles by.

"Hard by yon wood, now smiling as in scorn,
Muttering his wayward fancies he would rove,
Now drooping, woeful wan, like one forlorn,
Or crazed with care, or crossed in hopeless love.

"One morn I missed him on the customed hill,
Along the heath and near his fav'rite tree; 110
Another came; nor yet beside the rill,
Nor up the lawn, nor at the wood was he;

"The next with dirges due in sad array
Slow through the church-way path we saw him borne.
Approach and read (for thou canst read) the lay,
Graved on the stone beneath yon aged thorn."

THE EPITAPH

Here rests his head upon the lap of earth
A youth to fortune and to fame unknown.

Fair Science frowned not on his humble birth,
And Melancholy marked him for her own.   120

Large was his bounty and his soul sincere,
Heaven did a recompense as largely send:
He gave to Mis'ry all he had, a tear,
He gained from Heav'n ('twas all he wished) a friend.

No farther seek his merits to disclose,
Or draw his frailties from their dread abode
(There they alike in trembling hope repose),
The bosom of his Father and his God.

l. 16. rude = unsophisticated
l. 51. rage = enthusiasm
l. 73. madding = scuffling

Elizabeth Carter

(1717–1806)

Although living in Deal, Kent, Carter was an honored member of the Blue Stocking Circle of London. Translator of Epictetus, she won praise from Samuel Johnson for her Greek and awe from others for her Latin, Hebrew, French, Italian, Portuguese, German, and Arabic. Typically, *Letters from Mrs. Elizabeth Carter to Mrs. Montagu* required three volumes in 1817. Samuel Richardson inserted "Ode to Wisdom," submitted to *Gentleman's Magazine* in 1746, into his *Clarissa* (1747).

A DIALOGUE

Says Body to Mind, " 'Tis amazing to see,
We're so nearly related yet never agree,
But lead a most wrangling strange sort of a life,
As great plagues to each other as husband and wife.
The fault's all your own, who with flagrant oppression,
Encroach every day on my lawful possession.
The best room in my house you have seized for your own,
And turned the whole tenement quite upside down,
While you hourly call in a disorderly crew
Of vagabond rogues, who have nothing to do   10
But to run in and out, hurry scurry, and keep
Such a horrible uproar, I can't get to sleep.
There's my kitchen sometimes is as empty as sound,
I call for my servants, not one's to be found:
They are all sent out on your Ladyship's errand,
To fetch some more riotous guests in, I warrant!
And since things are growing, I see, worse and worse,
I'm determined to force you to alter your course."
    Poor Mind, who heard all with extreme moderation,
Thought it now time to speak, and make her allegation.   20
" 'Tis I that, methinks, have most cause to complain,
Who am crampt and confined like a slave in a chain.
I did but step out, on some weighty affairs,

362

To visit, last night, my good friends in the stars,
When, before I was got half as high as the moon,
You despatched Pain and Languor to hurry me down;
Vi et Armis they seized me, in midst of my flight,
And shut me in caverns as dark as the night."
  " 'Twas no more," replied Body, "than what you deserved;
While you rambled abroad, I at home was half starved: 30
And, unless I had closely confined you in hold,
You had left me to perish with hunger and cold."
  "I've a friend," answers Mind, "who, though slow, is yet sure,
And will rid me, at last, of your insolent power:
Will knock down your mud walls, the whole fabric demolish,
And at once your strong holds and my slavery abolish:
And while in the dust your dull ruins decay,
I shall snap off my chains and fly freely away."

l. 1. Vi et Armis = by force of arms

ODE TO WISDOM

The solitary bird of night
Thro' the pale shades now wings his flight,
   And quits his time-shook tower;
Where, sheltered from the blaze of day,
In philosophic gloom he lay,
   Beneath his ivy bower.

With joy I hear the solemn sound,
Which midnight echoes waft around,
   And sighing gales repeat:
Fav'rite of Pallas! I attend,   10
And faithful to thy summons bend
   At Wisdom's awful seat.

She loves the cool, the silent eve,
Where no false shows of life deceive,
   Beneath the lunar ray:
Here Folly drops each vain disguise,
Nor sport her gaily-coloured dyes,
   As in the glare of day.

O Pallas! Queen of every art
"That glads the sense, or mends the heart,"   20
   Blest source of purer joys:
In every form of beauty bright,
That captivates the mental sight
   With pleasure and surprize!

To thy unspotted shrine I bow,
Assist thy modest suppliant's vow,
   That breathes no wild desires:
But taught by thy unerring rules,
To shun the fruitless wish of fools,
   To nobler views aspires.   30

Not Fortune's gem, Ambition's plume,
Nor Cytheréa's fading bloom,
   Be objects of my prayer:
Let Avarice, Vanity, and Pride,
Those glitt'ring envied toys, divide
   The dull rewards of Care.

To me thy better gifts impart,
Each moral beauty of the heart
   By studious thought refined:
For Wealth, the smiles of glad Content,   40
For Power, its amplest, best extent,
   An empire o'er my mind.

When Fortune drops her gay parade,
When Pleasure's transient roses fade,
   And wither in the tomb,
Unchanged is thy immortal prize;
Thy ever-verdant laurels rise
   In undecaying bloom.

By thee protected, I defy
The coxcomb's sneer, the stupid lie   50
   Of ignorance and spite:
Alike contemn the leaden fool,
And all the pointed ridicule
   Of undiscerning wit.

From envy, hurry, noise, and strife,
The dull impertinence of life,
    In thy retreat I rest:
Pursue thee to the peaceful groves,
Where Plato's sacred spirit roves
    In all thy beauties dressed.   60

He bid Ilyssus' tuneful stream
Convey thy philosophic theme
    Of Perfect, Fair, and Good:
Attentive Athens caught the sound,
And all her listening sons around
    In awful silence stood:

Reclaimed, her wild licentious youth
Confest the potent voice of Truth,
    And felt its just control.
The Passions ceased their loud alarms,   70
And Virtue's soft persuasive charms
    O'er all their senses stole.

Thy breath inspires the Poet's song,
The Patriot's free, unbiass'd tongue,
    The Hero's gen'rous strife;
Thine are Retirement's silent joys,
And all the sweet endearing ties
    Of still, domestic life.

No more to fabled names confined,
To Thee! Supreme all-perfect mind,   80
    My thoughts direct their flight:
Wisdom's thy gift, and all her force
From Thee derived, unchanging source
    Of intellectual light!

O send her sure, her steady ray,
To regulate my doubtful way,
    Thro' Life's perplexing road:
The mists of error to control,
And thro' its gloom direct my soul
    To happiness and good.   90

Beneath her clear discerning eye
The visionary shadows fly
    Of Folly's painted show:
She sees, thro' ev'ry fair disguise,
That all, but Virtue's solid joys
    Is vanity and woe.

William Collins

(1721 – 1759)

Son of a Chichester hatter, Collins advanced through education at Winchester and Oxford and his literary friendships in London to an outward success but with an increasingly profound melancholia—which subsequently added to the reputation of his poems. His *Odes on Several Descriptive and Allegoric Subjects* (1746) included these three poems: the unrhymed *Ode to Evening*, the tribute to British soldiers lost in recent battles, and the song imagined for the sons of Cymbeline.

ODE TO EVENING

If aught of oaten stop, or pastoral song
May hope, chaste Eve, to soothe thy modest ear,
   Like thy own solemn springs,
   Thy springs and dying gales,
O nymph reserved, while now the bright-haired sun
Sits in yon western tent, whose cloudy skirts,
   With brede ethereal wove,
   O'erhang his wavy bed;
Now air is hushed, save where the weak-ey'd bat
With short shrill shriek flits by on leathern wing,   10
   Or where the beetle winds
   His small but sullen horn,
As oft he rises midst the twilight path,
Against the pilgrim borne in heedless hum:
   Now teach me, maid composed,
   To breathe some softened strain,
Whose numbers stealing through thy darkening vale
May not unseemly with its stillness suit;
   As musing slow, I hail
   Thy genial loved return!   20
For when thy folding star arising shows
His paly circlet, at his warning lamp
   The fragrant hours, and elves
   Who slept in flowers the day,
And many a nymph who wreathes her brows with sedge,

And sheds the freshening dew, and, lovelier still,
   The Pensive Pleasures sweet,
   Prepare thy shadowy car.
Then lead, calm votaress, where some sheety lake
Cheers the lone heath, or some time-hallowed pile,   30
   Or upland fallows grey,
   Reflect its last cool gleam.
But when chill blustering winds or driving rain
Forbid my willing feet, be mine the hut
   That from the mountain's side
   Views wilds and swelling floods,
And hamlets brown, and dim-discovered spires,
And hears their simple bell, and marks o'er all
   Thy dewy fingers draw
   The gradual dusky veil.   40
While Spring shall pour his showers, as oft he wont,
And bathe thy breathing tresses, meekest Eve!
   While Summer loves to sport
   Beneath thy lingering light;
While sallow Autumn fills thy lap with leaves,
Or Winter, yelling through the troublous air,
   Affrights thy shrinking train,
   And rudely rends thy robes;
So long, sure-found beneath the sylvan shed,
Shall Fancy, Friendship, Science, rose-lipped Health,   50
   Thy gentlest influence own,
   And hymn thy favourite name!

HOW SLEEP THE BRAVE

How sleep the brave who sink to rest
By all their country's wishes blest!
When Spring, with dewy fingers cold,
Returns to deck their hallowed mold,
She there shall dress a sweeter sod
Than Fancy's feet have ever trod.

By fairy hands their knell is rung,
By forms unseen their dirge is sung;
There Honor comes, a pilgrim gray,

To bless the turf that wraps their clay,   10
And Freedom shall awhile repair,
To dwell a weeping hermit there!

A SONG FROM SHAKESPEARE'S
CYMBELINE

SUNG BY GUIDERUS AND ARVIRAGUS OVER
FIDELE, SUPPOS'D TO BE DEAD

To fair Fidele's grassy tomb
    Soft maids and village hinds shall bring
Each op'ning sweet, of earliest bloom,
    And rifle all the breathing spring.

No wailing ghost shall dare appear,
    To vex with shrieks this quiet grove:
But shepherd lads assemble here,
    And melting virgins own their love.

No wither'd witch shall here be seen,
    No goblins lead their nightly crew: 10
The female fays shall haunt the green,
    And dress thy grave with pearly dew.

The redbreast oft at ev'ning hours
    Shall kindly lend his little aid,
With hoary moss, and gather'd flow'rs,
    To deck the ground where thou art laid.

When howling winds, and beating rain,
    In tempests shake the sylvan cell,
Or midst the chace on ev'ry plain,
    The tender thought on thee shall dwell.   20

Each lonely scene shall thee restore,
    For thee the tear be duly shed:
Belov'd, till life could charm no more;
    And mourn'd, till Pity's self be dead.

Mary Leapor

(1722 – 1746)

Daughter of a Northamptonshire gardener, herself a kitchen maid in precarious health, Leapor read Dryden and Pope carefully enough to find subjects "upstairs" worthy of satire. The two volumes of her *Poems upon Several Occasions* were published posthumously (1748, 1751). "Mira's Will," which imitates a legal document, is given here with the capitalization of nouns conventional in both poetry and prose until the end of the eighteenth century.

MIRA'S WILL

Imprimis—My departed Shade I trust
To Heav'n—My Body to the silent Dust;
My Name to publick Censure I submit,
To be disposed of as the World thinks fit;
My Vice and Folly let Oblivion close,
The World already is o'erstocked with those;
My Wit I give, as Misers give their Store,
To those who think they had enough before.
Bestow my Patience to compose the Lives
Of slighted Virgins and neglected Wives;   10
To modish Lovers I resign my Truth,
My cool Reflexion to unthinking Youth;
And some Good-Nature give ('tis my Desire)
To surly Husbands, as their Needs require;
And first discharge my funeral—and then
To the small Poets I bequeath my Pen.

   Let a small Sprig (true Emblem of my Rhyme)
Of blasted Laurel on my Hearse recline;
Let some grave Wight, that struggles for Renown,
By chanting Dirges through a Market-Town,   20
With gentle Step precede the solemn Train;
A broken Flute upon his Arm shall lean.
Six comick Poets may the Corse surround,
And All Free-holders, if they can be found:

370

Then follow next the melancholy Throng
As shrewd Instructors, who themselves are wrong;
The Virtuoso, rich in sun-dry'd Weeds;
The Politician, whom no Mortal heeds;
The silent Lawyer, chamber'd all the Day;
And the stern Soldier that receives no Pay.   30
But stay—the Mourners should be first our Care:
Let the freed Prentice lead the Miser's Heir;
Let the young Relict wipe her mournful Eye,
And widow'd Husbands o'er their Garlick cry.

    All this let my Executors fulfil,
And rest assur'd that this is *Mira*'s Will,
Who was, when she these Legacies design'd,
In Body healthy, and compos'd in Mind.

AN EPISTLE TO A LADY

In vain, dear Madam, yes, in vain you strive,
Alas! to make your luckless Mira thrive,
For Tycho and Copernicus agree,
No golden planet bent its rays on me.

    'Tis twenty winters, if it is no more,
To speak the truth it may be twenty-four,
As many springs their 'pointed space have run,
Since Mira's eyes first opened on the sun.
'Twas when the flocks on slabby hillocks lie,
And the cold Fishes rule the wat'ry sky: 10
But though these eyes the learnèd page explore,
And turn the ponderous volumes o'er and o'er,
I find no comfort from their systems flow,
But am dejected more as more I know.
Hope shines a while, but like a vapour flies
(The fate of all the curious and the wise),
For, ah! cold Saturn triumphed on that day,
And frowning Sol denied his golden ray.

    You see I'm learnèd, and I shew't the more,
That none may wonder when they find me poor.   20
Yet Mira dreams, as slumb'ring poets may,

And rolls in treasures till the breaking day,
While books and pictures in bright order rise,
And painted parlours swim before her eyes:
Till the shrill clock impertinently rings,
And the soft visions move their shining wings:
Then Mira wakes,—her pictures are no more,
And through her fingers slides the vanished ore.
Convinced too soon, her eye unwilling falls
On the blue curtains and the dusty walls: 30
She wakes, alas! to business and to woes,
To sweep her kitchen, and to mend her clothes.

But see pale Sickness with her languid eyes,
At whose appearance all delusion flies:
The world recedes, its vanities decline,
Clorinda's features seem as faint as mine;
Gay robes no more the aching sight admires,
Wit grates the ear, and melting music tires.
Its wonted pleasures with each sense decay,
Books please no more, and paintings fade away,   40
The sliding joys in misty vapours end:
Yet let me still, ah! let me grasp a friend:
And when each joy, when each loved object flies,
Be you the last that leaves my closing eyes.

But how will this dismantled soul appear,
When stripped of all it lately held so dear,
Forced from its prison of expiring clay,
Afraid and shivering at the doubtful way?

Yet did these eyes a dying parent see,
Loosed from all cares except a thought for me,   50
Without a tear resign her shortening breath,
And dauntless meet the lingering stroke of death.
Then at th' Almighty's sentence shall I mourn,
"Of Dust thou art, to Dust shalt thou return,"
Or shall I wish to stretch the line of fate,
That the dull years may bear a longer date,

To share the follies of succeeding times
With more vexations and with deeper Crimes?
Ah no—though Heav'n brings near the final day,
For such a life I will not, dare not pray;   60

But let the tear for future mercy flow,
And fall resigned beneath the mighty blow.
Nor I alone—for through the spacious ball,
With me will numbers of all ages fall:
And the same day that Mira yields her breath,
Thousands may enter through the gates of death.

Christopher Smart

(1 7 2 2 – 1 7 7 1)

Born in Kent, Smart matriculated at Pembroke Hall, Cambridge, in 1739, won a Craven scholarship and (five times) the Seatonian Prize for poems on the Supreme Being, and remained at Cambridge as Fellow until 1753. Employed by John Newbery as an editor in London (he married a stepdaughter of Newbery), Smart issued poems of the order of "On a Bed of Guernsey Lilies" (1764) almost every year except 1757–1762, when he was confined in various hospitals for the insane. He died in a debtor's prison. *Jubilate Agno* ("Rejoice in the Lamb"), adapting the antiphonal verse of the Psalms and including the passage on his cat Jeoffry, was first published in 1939.

ON A BED OF GUERNSEY LILIES

Ye beauties! O how great the sum
    Of sweetness that ye bring;
On what a charity ye come
    To bless the latter spring!
How kind the visit that ye pay,
Like strangers on a rainy day,
    When heartiness despaired of guests:
No neighbour's praise your pride alarms,
No rival flow'r surveys your charms,
    Or heightens, or contests!   10

Lo, through her works gay nature grieves
    How brief she is and frail,
As ever o'er the falling leaves
    Autumnal winds prevail.
Yet still the philosophic mind
Consolatory food can find,
    And hope her anchorage maintain:
We never are deserted quite;
'Tis by succession of delight
    That love supports his reign.   20

From JUBILATE AGNO

MY CAT JEOFFRY

For I will consider my Cat Jeoffry.

For he is the servant of the Living God duly and daily serving him.

For at the first glance of the glory of God in the East he worships in his way.

For is this done by wreathing his body seven times round with elegant quickness.

For then he leaps up to catch the musk, which is the blessing of God upon his prayer.

For he rolls upon prank to work it in.

For having done duty and received blessing he begins to consider himself.

For this he performs in ten degrees.

For first he looks upon his fore-paws to see if they are clean.

For secondly he kicks up behind to clear away there.   10

For thirdly he works it upon stretch with the fore paws extended.

For fourthly he sharpens his paws by wood.

For fifthly he washes himself.

For Sixthly he rolls upon wash.

For Seventhly he fleas himself, that he may not be interrupted upon the beat.

For Eighthly he rubs himself against a post.

For Ninthly he looks up for his instructions.

For Tenthly he goes in quest of food.

For having considered God and himself he will consider his neighbour.

For if he meets another cat he will kiss her in kindness.   20

For when he takes his prey he plays with it to give it chance.

For one mouse in seven escapes by his dallying.

For when his day's work is done his business more properly begins.

For he keeps the Lord's watch in the night against the adversary.

For he counteracts the powers of darkness by his electrical skin and glaring eyes.

For he counteracts the Devil, who is death, by brisking about the life.

For in his morning orisons he loves the sun and the sun loves him.

For he is of the tribe of Tiger.

For the Cherub Cat is a term of the Angel Tiger.

For he has the subtlety and hissing of a serpent, which in goodness he suppresses.   30

For he will not do destruction, if he is well-fed, neither will he spit without provocation.

For he purrs in thankfulness, when God tells him he's a good Cat.

For he is an instrument for the children to learn benevolence upon.

For every house is incompleat without him and a blessing is lacking in the spirit.

For the Lord commanded Moses concerning the cats at the departure of the Children of Israel from Egypt.

For every family had one cat at least in the bag.

For the English Cats are the best in Europe.

For he is the cleanest in the use of his fore-paws of any quadrupede.

For the dexterity of his defence is an instance of the love of God to him exceedingly.

For he is the quickest to his mark of any creature.   40

For he is tenacious of his point.

For he is a mixture of gravity and waggery.

For he knows that God is his Saviour.

For there is nothing sweeter than his peace when at rest.

For there is nothing brisker than his life when in motion.

For he is of the Lord's poor and so indeed is he called by benevolence perpetually—Poor Jeoffry! poor Jeoffry! the rat has bit thy throat.

For I bless the name of the Lord Jesus that Jeoffry is better.

For the divine spirit comes about his body to sustain it in compleat cat.

For his tongue is exceeding pure so that it has in purity what it wants in music.

For he is docile and can learn certain things.   50

For he can set up with gravity which is patience upon approbation.

For he can fetch and carry, which is patience in employment.

For he can jump over a stick which is patience upon proof positive.

For he can spraggle upon waggle at the word of command.

For he can jump from an eminence into his master's bosom.

For he can catch the cork and toss it again.

For he is hated by the hypocrite and miser.

For the former is affraid of detection.

For the latter refuses the charge.

For he camels his back to bear the first notion of business.   60

For he is good to think on, if a man would express himself neatly.

For he made a great figure in Egypt for his signal services.

For he killed the Icneumon-rat very pernicious by land.

For his ears are so acute that they sting again.

For from this proceeds the passing quickness of his attention.

For by stroaking of him I have found out electricity.

For I perceived God's light about him both wax and fire.

For the Electrical fire is the spiritual substance, which God sends from heaven to sustain the bodies both of man and beast.

For God has blessed him in the variety of his movements.

For, tho he cannot fly, he is an excellent clamberer.   70

For his motions upon the face of the earth are more than any other
    quadrupede.
For he can tread to all the measures upon the music.
For he can swim for life.
For he can creep.

Oliver Goldsmith

(1 7 3 0 ? – 1 7 7 4)

Born and educated in Ireland, Goldsmith studied medicine at Edinburgh and abroad before moving in 1756 to London. There, his reputation as a blundering buffoon contrasted with his skill as essayist, editor, playwright, novelist, and poet of *The Deserted Village* (1770). The sentimentally tragical vision of his song on "lovely woman" (1766) contrasts with the happy ending of Goldsmith's endlessly popular novel of that year, *The Vicar of Wakefield*, and certainly with the vivacity of *She Stoops to Conquer* (1773).

WHEN LOVELY WOMAN STOOPS TO FOLLY

When lovely woman stoops to folly,
   And finds too late that men betray,
What charm can soothe her melancholy,
   What art can wash her guilt away?

The only art her guilt to cover,
   To hide her shame from every eye,
To give repentance to her lover,
   And wring his bosom—is to die.

From THE DESERTED VILLAGE

Sweet Auburn, loveliest village of the plain,
Where health and plenty cheered the labouring swain,
Where smiling spring its earliest visit paid,
And parting summer's lingering blooms delayed;
Dear lovely bowers of innocence and ease,
Seats of my youth, when every sport could please,
How often have I loitered o'er thy green,
Where humble happiness endeared each scene;

How often have I paused on every charm,
The sheltered cot, the cultivated farm,   10
The never-failing brook, the busy mill,
The decent church that topped the neighbouring hill,
The hawthorn bush, with seats beneath the shade,
For talking age and whispering lovers made.
How often have I blessed the coming day,
When toil remitting lent its turn to play,
And all the village train, from labour free,
Led up their sports beneath the spreading tree,
While many a pastime circled in the shade,
The young contending as the old surveyed;   20
And many a gambol frolicked o'er the ground,
And sleights of art and feats of strength went round.
And still as each repeated pleasure tired,
Succeeding sports the mirthful band inspired;
The dancing pair that simply sought renown
By holding out to tire each other down;
The swain mistrustless of his smutted face,
While secret laughter tittered round the place;
The bashful virgin's sidelong looks of love,
The matron's glance that would those looks reprove.   30
These were thy charms, sweet village; sports like these,
With sweet succession, taught even toil to please;
These round thy bowers their cheerful influence shed,
These were thy charms—But all these charms are fled.

Sweet smiling village, loveliest of the lawn,
Thy sports are fled and all thy charms withdrawn;
Amidst thy bowers the tyrant's hand is seen,
And desolation saddens all thy green:
One only master grasps the whole domain,
And half a tillage stints thy smiling plain: 40
No more thy glassy brook reflects the day,
But, choked with sedges, works its weedy way.
Along thy glades, a solitary guest,
The hollow-sounding bittern guards its nest;
Amidst thy desert walks the lapwing flies,
And tires their echoes with unvaried cries.
Sunk are thy bowers in shapeless ruin all,
And the long grass o'ertops the mouldering wall;
And trembling, shrinking from the spoiler's hand,
Far, far away, thy children leave the land.   50

Ill fares the land, to hastening ills a prey,
Where wealth accumulates and men decay:
Princes and lords may flourish or may fade;
A breath can make them, as a breath has made;
But a bold peasantry, their country's pride,
When once destroyed, can never be supplied.

A time there was, ere England's griefs began,
When every rood of ground maintained its man;
For him light labour spread her wholesome store,
Just gave what life required, but gave no more: 60
His best companions, innocence and health;
And his best riches, ignorance of wealth.

But times are altered; trade's unfeeling train
Usurp the land and dispossess the swain;
Along the lawn, where scattered hamlets rose,
Unwieldy wealth and cumbrous pomp repose;
And every want to opulence allied,
And every pang that folly pays to pride.
These gentle hours that plenty bade to bloom,
Those calm desires that asked but little room,   70
Those healthful sports that graced the peaceful scene,
Lived in each look and brightened all the green;
These, far departing, seek a kinder shore,
And rural mirth and manners are no more.

Sweet Auburn! parent of the blissful hour,
Thy glades forlorn confess the tyrant's power.
Here as I take my solitary rounds,
Amidst thy tangling walks and ruined grounds,
And, many a year elapsed, return to view
Where once the cottage stood, the hawthorn grew,   80
Remembrance wakes with all her busy train,
Swells at my breast and turns the past to pain.

In all my wanderings round this world of care,
In all my griefs—and God has given my share—
I still had hopes my latest hours to crown,
Amidst these humble bowers to lay me down;
To husband out life's taper at the close,
And keep the flame from wasting by repose.
I still had hopes, for pride attends us still,

Amidst the swains to show my book-learned skill,   90
Around my fire an evening group to draw,
And tell of all I felt and all I saw;
And, as a hare, whom hounds and horns pursue,
Pants to the place from whence at first she flew,
I still had hopes, my long vexations past,
Here to return—and die at home at last.

    O blest retirement, friend to life's decline,
Retreats from care, that never must be mine,
How happy he who crowns in shades like these
A youth of labour with an age of ease;   100
Who quits a world where strong temptations try
And, since 'tis hard to combat, learns to fly.
For him no wretches, born to work and weep,
Explore the mine or tempt the dangerous deep;
No surly porter stands in guilty state
To spurn imploring famine from the gate;
But on he moves to meet his latter end,
Angels around befriending virtue's friend;
Bends to the grave with unperceived decay,
While resignation gently slopes the way;   110
And, all his prospects brightening to the last,
His Heaven commences ere the world be past!

           *   *   *

    Even now the devastation is begun,
And half the business of destruction done;
Even now, methinks, as pondering here I stand,
I see the rural virtues leave the land.
Down where yon anchoring vessel spreads the sail,
That idly waiting flaps with every gale,   400
Downward they move, a melancholy band,
Pass from the shore and darken all the strand.
Contented toil and hospitable care,
And kind connubial tenderness are there;
And piety, with wishes placed above,
And steady loyalty and faithful love.
And thou, sweet Poetry, thou loveliest maid,
Still first to fly where sensual joys invade;
Unfit, in these degenerate times of shame,
To catch the heart or strike for honest fame;   410
Dear charming nymph, neglected and decried,

My shame in crowds, my solitary pride;
Thou source of all my bliss and all my woe,
That found'st me poor at first and keep'st me so;
Thou guide by which the nobler arts excel,
Thou nurse of every virtue, fare thee well!
Farewell, and oh, where'er thy voice be tried,
On Torno's cliffs or Pambamarca's side,
Whether where equinoctial fervours glow,
Or winter wraps the polar world in snow,   420
Still let thy voice, prevailing over time,
Redress the rigours of the inclement clime;
Aid slighted truth; with thy persuasive strain
Teach erring man to spurn the rage of gain;
Teach him that states of native strength possessed,
Though very poor, may still be very blest;
That trade's proud empire hastes to swift decay,
As ocean sweeps the laboured mole away;
While self-dependent power can time defy,
As rocks resist the billows and the sky.   430

William Cowper

(1 7 3 1 – 1 8 0 0)

Born in a Hertfordshire village, Cowper was educated at Westminster School and the Middle Temple, London. He abandoned law for retirement in a nervous depression relieved by what Coleridge called the "divine chit-chat" of *The Task*, in six books of blank verse (1785), and by the comic narrative "The Diverting History of John Gilpin." "Light Shining out of Darkness" (1773), like all the *Olney Hymns* (with John Newton, 1779), came from the same evangelical faith and conviction as the "Complaint" (1788), which addresses the conscience of England with the poet's own diction and convictions. It was first published in a broadsheet as an anti-slavery ballad set to a popular tune.

LIGHT SHINING OUT OF DARKNESS

God moves in a mysterious way,
    His wonders to perform;
He plants his footsteps in the sea,
    And rides upon the storm.

Deep in unfathomable mines
    Of never-failing skill,
He treasures up his bright designs,
    And works his sovereign will.

Ye fearful saints fresh courage take,
    The clouds ye so much dread   10
Are big with mercy, and shall break
    In blessings on your head.

Judge not the Lord by feeble sense,
    But trust him for his grace;
Behind a frowning providence,
    He hides a smiling face.

His purposes will ripen fast,
    Unfolding ev'ry hour;
The bud may have a bitter taste,
    But sweet will be the flow'r.   20

Blind unbelief is sure to err,
    And scan his work in vain;
God is his own interpreter,
    And he will make it plain.

THE NEGRO'S COMPLAINT

Forc'd from home, and all its pleasures,
    Afric's coast I left forlorn;
To increase a stranger's treasures,
    O'er the raging billows borne.
Men from England bought and sold me,
    Paid my price in paltry gold;
But, though theirs they have enroll'd me,
    Minds are never to be sold.

Still in thought as free as ever,
    What are England's rights, I ask,   10
Me from my delights to sever,
    Me to torture, me to task?
Fleecy locks, and black complexion
    Cannot forfeit nature's claim;
Skins may differ, but affection
    Dwells in white and black the same.

Why did all-creating Nature
    Make the plant for which we toil?
Sighs must fan it, tears must water,
    Sweat of ours must dress the soil.   20
Think, ye masters, iron-hearted,
    Lolling at your jovial boards;
Think how many backs have smarted
    For the sweets your cane affords.

Is there, as ye sometimes tell us,
    Is there one who reigns on high?

Has he bid you buy and sell us,
   Speaking from his throne the sky?
Ask him, if your knotted scourges,
   Matches, blood-extorting screws,   30
Are the means which duty urges
   Agents of his will to use?

Hark! he answers—Wild tornadoes,
   Strewing yonder sea with wrecks;
Wasting towns, plantations, meadows,
   Are the voice with which he speaks.
He, foreseeing what vexations
   Afric's sons should undergo,
Fix'd their tyrants' habitations
   Where his whirlwinds answer—No.   40

By our blood in Afric wasted,
   Ere our necks receiv'd the chain;
By the mis'ries we have tasted,
   Crossing in your barks the main;
By our suff'rings since ye brought us
   To the man-degrading mart;
All sustain'd by patience, taught us
   Only by a broken heart:

Deem our nation brutes no longer
   Till some reason ye shall find   50
Worthier of regard and stronger
   Than the colour of our kind.
Slaves of gold, whose sordid dealings
   Tarnish all your boasted pow'rs,
Prove that you have human feelings,
   Ere you proudly question ours!

Hester Lynch Salusbury Thrale Piozzi

(1 7 4 1 – 1 8 2 1)

An heiress as a child in Hertfordshire, Hester Salusbury suffered financial reversals that made her a writer for money. As Mrs. Thrale, she published "Della Cruscan" poems in the *Florence Miscellany* (1785). Samuel Johnson, Fanny Burney, and other friends had protested her marriage in 1784 to Piozzi, an Italian musician. "A Winter in Wales," published in *Thraliana* (1942), is addressed to her daughter Sophia, wife of the painter William Hoare.

A WINTER IN WALES

Whilst dear Sophia plans some pictured strife
   Where artificial suns through shade appear;
Me, Destiny condemns in fading life
   To sing the sorrows of the fading year.

Now the lone traveller his pathway lost
   Creeps by old ocean's edge, and shuns the vale;
Sees strewed with wreck our billow-beaten coast
   And hears the hoarse gull screaming to the gale.

Now cold caducity—or call it Age
   With chilling palsy blasts each withered bough;   10
While its last leaf, torn by the tempest's rage,
   Leaps undelighted o'er the frozen snow.

Round the wide range far as my sight extends
   No cultured plains or verdant trees I trace,
But the sad Muse o'er the pale prospect bends
   To pore upon dull Nature's dying face.

Yet Thomson, through the thick-wove wintry shroud
   That wraps in solemn white her cold remains,
Could see resuscitation pierce the cloud,
   And hail long-hoped-for spring with sprightlier strains.   20

His was indeed the harp! and his the pow'r,
   Like the famed artists of Bologna's School,
To pick from Nature's wild—Perfection's flow'r,
   And rich Redundancy reduce to Rule.

Nor Cowper's wintry strains, though less refined,
   Can be by pensive reader e'er forgot;
With Gainsbro' he protects their village hind,
   The woodman and his cur's snow-powdered coat.

Various the roads ye took to well-earned fame
   And various were your gifts, ye mighty dead!   30
Of us your feeble followers but the shame,
   Whilst with unequal steps your paths we tread.

Yet some with ardent pow'rs persuade the Muse
   To burst from connoisseur and critic free;
Nor poet's wreath, nor painter's they'll refuse
   Keen author of the Rhymes on Art, to thee.

Blest be your labours all! could less beguile
   The melancholy season? could less cheer
Our hearts? or move a momentary smile
   In days like these, to land and sea severe?   40

The mute magnificence of Snowden's height,
   Heaped to the sky with hoary horrors pale:
The star of evening and the bird of night
   Combine to tell the same sad winter's tale.

The clock that erst to the convivial hall
   Beat with his merry bell time's cheerful round,
Scarce heard amid the storm, now sends his call
   A cold, unechoing, suffocated sound.

And look what's left of my paternal oaks,
   That bore their old time-honoured heads so high,   50
Sad victims to the wind's unpitying strokes,
   In scattered fragments 'mid the forest lie.

Tomorrow's dawn of slowly rising day
   Doomed to discern those paths whence pleasure fled,

Shall see them dragged disgracefully away
    Piled in short pieces near some peasant's shed.

Best consolation! 'Twas to warm the poor
    Perhaps Heav'n struck our disappointed pride
Best disposition of Superfluous Store,
    When modest Want is by such stores supplied.   60

Anna Hunter Seward

(1742 – 1809)

Anna Hunter Seward was born at Eyam in the Peak of Derbyshire, daughter of the rector there, the Rev. Thomas Seward, and his wife Elizabeth Hunter. Resident from the age of ten in Lichfield, Seward was so lavishly praised by Erasmus Darwin and fellow writers in the Midlands that neoclassicists—including Samuel Johnson, whom she had known before he left for London—disparaged her as "the Swan of Lichfield." "Eyam," published in 1792, was written, according to her own note, in August 1788 during a brief escape from care of her senile father, long a Canon of Lichfield Cathedral.

EYAM

For one short week I leave, with anxious heart,
Source of my filial cares, the Full of Days,
Lured by the promise of harmonic art
To breathe her Handel's soul-exalting lays.
Pensive I trace the Derwent's amber wave,
Foaming through umbrag'd banks, or view it lave
The soft, romantic valleys, high o'er-peered,
By hills and rocks, in savage grandeur reared.

Not two short miles from thee, can I refrain
Thy haunts, my native Eyam, long unseen?—   10
Thou and thy lov'd inhabitants, again
Shall meet my transient gaze.—Thy rocky screen,
Thy airy cliffs I mount; and seek thy shade,
Thy roofs, that brow the steep, romantic glade;
But, while on me the eyes of Friendship glow,
Swell my pain'd sighs, my tears spontaneous flow.

In scenes paternal, not beheld through years,
Nor viewed, till now, but by a Father's side,
Well might the tender, tributary tears,
From keen regrets of duteous fondness glide!   20
Its pastor, to this human-flock no more

Shall the long flight of future days restore!
Distant he droops, and that once gladdening eye
Now languid gleams, e'en when his friends are nigh.

Through this known walk, where weedy gravel lies,
Rough, and unsightly;—by the long, coarse grass
Of the once smooth, and vivid green, with sighs
To the deserted rectory I pass;—
Stray through the darken'd chambers' naked bound,
Where childhood's earliest, liveliest bliss I found;   30
How chang'd, since erst, the lightsome walls beneath,
The social joys did their warm comforts breathe!

Ere yet I go, who may return no more,
That sacred pile, 'mid yonder shadowy trees,
Let me revisit!—Ancient, massy door,
Thou gratest hoarse!—my vital spirits freeze,
Passing the vacant pulpit, to the space
Where humble rails the decent altar grace,
And where my infant sister's ashes sleep,
Whose loss I left the childish sport to weep.   40

Now the low beams, with paper garlands hung
In memory of some village youth, or maid,
Draw the soft tear, from thrill'd remembrance sprung,
How oft my childhood mark'd that tribute paid.
The gloves, suspended by the garland's side,
White as its snowy flowers, with ribbons tied;—
Dear village, long these wreaths funereal spread,
Simple memorials of thy early dead!

But O! thou blank, and silent pulpit!—thou,
That with a Father's precepts, just, and bland,   50
Didst win my car, as reason's strength'ning glow
Show'd their full value, now thou seem'st to stand
Before my sad, suffus'd, and trembling gaze,
The dreariest relic of departed days.
Of eloquence paternal, nervous, clear,
Dim Apparition thou—and bitter is my tear!

Hannah Parkhouse Cowley

(1 7 4 3 – 1 8 0 9)

Daughter of a Tiverton bookseller, married about 1768 and a mother, Cowley seemed unperturbed when her husband left in 1783 for India, where he died in 1797. Successful and prolific as a playwright, frequently at odds with other prominent writers, she published poems as "Anna Matilda" in the Della Cruscan circle of Robert Merry. Her work appeared in the weekly *World* and in the *British Album* (1790)—savaged by William Gifford in *The Baviad*. "Departed Youth," probably written soon after her husband's death, was published in her collected *Works* (1813).

DEPARTED YOUTH

What though the rosebuds from my cheek
Have faded all! which once so sleek
Spoke youth, and joy, and careless thought.
By guilt, or fear, or shame uncaught,
My soul, uninjured, still hath youth,
Its lively sense attests the truth!
  Oh! I can wander yet, and taste
The beauties of the flowery waste,
The nightingale's deep swell can feel
Till to the eye a tear doth steal;   10
Rapt! gaze upon the gem-decked night,
Or mark the clear moon's gradual flight,
Whilst the bright river's rippled wave
Repeats the quivering beams she gave.
  Nor yet does Painting strive in vain
To waken from its canvas plain
The lofty passions of the mind,
Or hint the sentiment refined:
To the sweet magic yet I bow,
As when youth decked my polished brow.   20
The chisel's lightest touch to trace
Through the pure form, or softened grace,
Is lent me still; I still admire,

And kindle at the Poet's fire—
   Why Time! since these are left me still,
Of lesser thefts e'en take thy fill.
Yes, take all lustre from my eye,
And let the blithe carnation fly,
My tresses sprinkle o'er with snow,
That boasted once their auburn glow,   30
Break the slim form that was adored
By him so loved, my wedded lord;
But leave me, whilst all these you steal,
The mind to taste, the nerve to feel!

Anna Laetitia Aikin Barbauld

(1 7 4 3 – 1 8 2 5)

Like others in the Aikin family, Barbauld accepted the duty of applying her intellect in prose and verse to raise the moral and spiritual level of children and adults. The two poems in quatrains, on the French in 1792 and on women's rights—neither published before her death in 1825—carry the same message: first defeat the foe and then renounce the power gained. In 1792 the "despots" of Austria and Prussia were allied against France; in August a new Commune suspended Louis XVI as king; the Terror lay ahead. Barbauld's quite different warning to "Mr. C—ge" in 1797 (published in 1799) anticipated by several years Coleridge's own awareness that "the maze of metaphysic lore" threatened to dim his aims of practical service to humanity.

ON THE EXPECTED GENERAL RISING OF THE FRENCH NATION IN 1792

Rise, mighty nation, in thy strength,
And deal thy dreadful vengeance round;
Let thy great spirit, roused at length,
Strike hordes of despots to the ground!

Devoted land! thy mangled breast
Eager the royal vultures tear;
By friends betrayed, by foes oppressed—
And Virtue struggles with Despair.

The tocsin sounds! arise, arise!   10
Stern o'er each breast let Country reign;
Nor virgin's plighted hand, nor sighs,
Must now the ardent youth detain:

Nor must the hind who tills thy soil
The ripened vintage stay to press,

Till Rapture crown the flowing bowl,
And Freedom boast of full success.

Briareus-like extend thy hands,
That every hand may crush a foe;
In millions pour thy generous bands,
And end a warfare by a blow!   20

Then wash with sad repentant tears
Each deed that clouds thy glory's page;
Each frenzied start impelled by fears,
Each transient burst of headlong rage:

Then fold in thy relenting arms
Thy wretched outcasts where they roam;
From pining want and war's alarms,
O call the child of misery home!

Then build the tomb—O not alone
Of him who bled in Freedom's cause;   30
With equal eye the martyr own
Of faith revered and ancient laws.

Then be thy tide of glory stayed;
Then be thy conquering banners furled;
Obey the laws thyself hast made,
And rise the model of the world!

THE RIGHTS OF WOMAN

Yes, injured Woman! rise, assert thy right!
Woman! too long degraded, scorned, oppressed;
O born to rule in partial Law's despite,
Resume thy native empire o'er the breast!

Go forth arrayed in panoply divine,
That angel pureness which admits no stain;
Go, bid proud Man his boasted rule resign
And kiss the golden sceptre of thy reign.

Go, gird thyself with grace, collect thy store
Of bright artillery glancing from afar;   10
Soft melting tones thy thundering cannon's roar,
Blushes and fears thy magazine of war.

Thy rights are empire; urge no meaner claim,—
Felt, not defined, and if debated, lost;
Like sacred mysteries, which withheld from fame,
Shunning discussion, are revered the most.

Try all that wit and art suggest to bend
Of thy imperial foe the stubborn knee;
Make treacherous Man thy subject, not thy friend;
Thou mayst command, but never canst be free.   20

Awe the licentious and restrain the rude;
Soften the sullen, clear the cloudy brow:
Be, more than princes' gifts, thy favours sued;—
She hazards all, who will the least allow.

But hope not, courted idol of mankind,
On this proud eminence secure to stay;
Subduing and subdued, thou soon shalt find
Thy coldness soften, and thy pride give way.

Then, then, abandon each ambitious thought;
Conquest or rule thy heart shall feebly move,   30
In Nature's school, by her soft maxims taught
That separate rights are lost in mutual love.

TO MR. S. T. COLERIDGE

Midway the hill of science, after steep
And rugged paths that tire the unpractised feet,
A grove extends; in tangled mazes wrought,
And filled with strange enchantment:—dubious shapes
Flit through dim glades, and lure the eager foot
Of youthful ardour to eternal chase.
Dreams hang on every leaf: unearthly forms
Glide through the gloom; and mystic visions swim

Before the cheated sense. Athwart the mists,
Far into vacant space, huge shadows stretch   10
And seem realities; while things of life,
Obvious to sight and touch, all glowing round,
Fade to the hue of shadows.—Scruples here,
With filmy net, most like the autumnal webs
Of floating gossamer, arrest the foot
Of generous enterprise; and palsy hope
And fair ambition with the chilling touch
Of sickly hesitation and blank fear.
Nor seldom Indolence these lawns among
Fixes her turf-built seat; and wears the garb   20
Of deep philosophy, and museful sits
In dreamy twilight of the vacant mind,
Soothed by the whispering shade; for soothing soft
The shades; and vistas lengthening into air,
With moonbeam rainbows tinted.—Here each mind
Of finer mould, acute and delicate,
In its high progress to eternal truth
Rests for a space, in fairy bowers entranced;
And loves the softened light and tender gloom;
And, pampered with most unsubstantial food,   30
Looks down indignant on the grosser world,
And matter's cumbrous shapings. Youth beloved
Of Science—of the Muse beloved,—not here,
Not in the maze of metaphysic lore,
Build thou thy place of resting! lightly tread
The dangerous ground, on noble aims intent;
And be this Circe of the studious cell
Enjoyed, but still subservient. Active scenes
Shall soon with healthful spirit brace thy mind;
And fair exertion, for bright fame sustained,   40
For friends, for country, chase each spleen-fed fog
 That blots the wide creation.—
Now heaven conduct thee with a parent's love!

Charlotte Turner Smith

(1749–1806)

For Turner, the several results of arranged marriage to Benjamin Smith in 1765 were twelve children; the writing of novels, stories, verse, histories, and other prose for a livelihood; imprisonment for debt and a year in Normandy to escape creditors; marital separation in 1788; and a subsequent career as novelist. Her *Elegiac Sonnets and Other Essays* were so popular that subsequent editions appeared from 1784 to 1797; the sonnet below appeared in the edition of 1789. At the end of 1806 Byron wrote a poem with the refrain "Friendship is Love without wings!" (with the title in French). Neither Byron nor Smith—in *On Beachy Head, and Other Poems* (1807)—took the adage lightly.

SONNET WRITTEN IN THE CHURCH-YARD AT MIDDLETON IN SUSSEX

Press'd by the Moon, mute arbitress of tides,
  While the loud equinox its power combines,
  The sea no more its swelling surge confines,
But o'er the shrinking land sublimely rides.
The wild blast, rising from the Western cave,
  Drives the huge billows from their heaving bed;
  Tears from their grassy tombs the village dead,
And breaks the silent sabbath of the grave!
With shells and sea-weed mingled, on the shore
  Lo! their bones whiten in the frequent wave;
  But vain to them the winds and waters rave;
They hear the warring elements no more:
While I am doom'd—by life's long storm opprest,
To gaze with envy on their gloomy rest.

ON THE APHORISM
"L'AMITIÉ EST
L'AMOUR SANS AILES"

Friendship, as some sage poet sings,
Is chasten'd Love, depriv'd of wings,
Without all wish or power to wander;
Less volatile, but not less tender:
Yet says the proverb—"Sly and slow
Love creeps, even where he cannot go;"
To clip his pinions then is vain,
His old propensities remain;
And she, who years *beyond fifteen,*
Has counted *twenty,* may have seen
How rarely unplum'd Love will stay;
He flies not—but he coolly walks away.

Robert Fergusson

(1 7 5 0 – 1 7 7 4)

Born in Edinburgh, where he returned as a lawyer's clerk after education in
Dundee and the University of St. Andrews, Fergusson was a contributor to a
leading weekly and performed the surgery of satire, not without affection, on
the manners and shams of Edinburgh ("Auld Reikie"). He revived stanzaic
forms that had been a Scottish glory before the Union of Crowns in 1603. "The
Daft Days" (1771), in the "standart Habby" tail-rhyme stanza, was his first poem
in Scots for Ruddiman's *Weekly*.

THE DAFT DAYS

Now mirk December's dowie face
Glowrs owr the rigs wi' sour grimace,
While, thro' his *minimum* o' space,
         The bleer-ey'd sun,
Wi' blinkin' light and stealin' pace,
         His race doth run.

Frae naked groves nae birdie sings;
To shepherd's pipe nae hillock rings;
The breeze nae od'rous flavour brings
         Frae Borean cave;   10
And dwynin' Nature, droops her wings,
         Wi' visage grave.

Mankind but scanty pleasure glean
Frae snawy hill or barren plain,
Whan Winter, 'midst his nipping train,
         Wi' frozen spear,
Sends drift owr a' his bleak domain,
         And guides the weir.

Auld Reikie! thou'rt the canty hole,
A bield for mony a cauldrife soul,   20

Wha snugly at thine ingle loll,
    Baith warm and couth;
While round they gar the bicker roll
    To weet their mouth.

When merry Yule-day comes I trow,
You'll scantlins find a hungry mou;
Sma' are our cares, our stamacks fou
    O' gusty gear,
And kickshaws, strangers to our view.
    Sin' fairn-year.   30

Ye browster wives! now busk ye bra,
And fling your sorrows far awa';
Then, come and gie's the tither blaw
    Of reaming ale,
Mair precious than the Well of Spa,
    Our hearts to heal.

Then, tho' at odds wi' a' the warl',
Amang oursells we'll never quarrel;
Tho' Discord gie a cankered snarl
    To spoil our glee,   40
As lang's there's pith into the barrel
    We'll drink and 'gree.

Fiddlers! your pins in temper fix,
And roset weel your fiddlesticks,
But banish vile Italian tricks
    From out your quorum,
Nor *fortes* wi' *pianos* mix—
    Gie's *Tullochgorum*.

For nought can cheer the heart sae weel
As can a canty Highland reel;   50
It even vivifies the heel
    To skip and dance:
Lifeless is he wha canna feel
    Its influence.

Let mirth abound; let social cheer
Invest the dawning of the year;

Let blithesome innocence appear
                    To crown our joy;
Nor envy, wi' sarcastic sneer,
                    Our bliss destroy.   60

And thou, great god of *aqua vitæ!*
Wha sways the empire of this city—
When fou we're sometimes capernoity—
                    Be thou prepared
To hedge us frae that black banditti,
                    The City Guard.

l.   1. dowie = dismal
l. 11. dwyning = wasting away
l. 19. canty = lively
l. 20. bield = shelter
l. 20. cauldrife = chilled
l. 23. bicker = wooden cup
l. 30. fairn = past
l. 31. browster = brewer
l. 33. tither blaw = second (other) draft
l. 44. roset = rosin
l. 48. *Tullochgorum* = Tulloch's rant
l. 63. capernoity = capricious

Thomas Chatterton

(1752 – 1770)

Chatterton, the "marvelous boy," was born and lived in Bristol, but in April 1770 he went to London with the poems in archaic language that he attributed to an (imaginary) Bristol poet of the fifteenth century, Thomas Rowley; in August he died of arsenic poisoning. To the Romantics he was a martyr destroyed by unreasonably rational critics. His antiquing required superfluity in spelling. This is the first stanza of the Minstrel's Song, from "Aella: A Tragycal Enterlude" (1769; published in 1777), as modernized by the Old English scholar W. W. Skeat:

> Oh sing unto my roundelay,
> Oh drop the briny tear with me,
> Dance no more on holiday;
> Like a running river be.
> > My love is dead,
> > Gone to his death-bed,
> > All under the willow-tree.

From AELLA

MYNSTRELLES SONGE

O! synge untoe mie roundelaie,
O! droppe the brynie teare wythe mee,
Daunce ne moe atte hallie daie,
Lycke a reynynge ryver bee;
  Mie love ys dedde,
  Gon to hys death-bedde,
  Al under the wyllowe tree.

Blacke hys cryne as the wyntere nyghte,
Whyte hys rode as the ſommer ſnowc,
Rodde hys face as the mornynge lyghte,   10
Cale he lyes ynne the grave belowe;
  Mie love ys dedde,
  Gon to hys deathe-bedde,
  Al under the wyllowe tree.

Swote hys tyngue as the throſtles note,
Quycke ynn daunce as thoughte canne bee,
Deſte hys taboure, codgelle ſtote,
O! hee lyes bie the wyllowe tree:
  Mie love ys dedde,
   Gonne to hys deathe-bedde,   20
  Alle underre the wyllowe tree.

Harke! the ravenne flappes hys wynge,
In the briered delle belowe;
Harke! the dethe-owle loude dothe ſynge,
To the nyghte-mares as heie goe;
  Mie love ys dedde,
   Gonne to hys deathe-bedde,
  Al under the wyllowe tree.

See! the whyte moone ſheenes onne hie;
Whyterre ys mie true loves ſhroude;   30
Whyterre yanne the mornynge ſkie,
Whyterre yanne the evenynge cloude;
  Mie love ys dedde,
   Gon to hys deathe-bedde,
  Al under the wyllowe tree.

Heere, uponne mie true loves grave,
Schalle the baren fleurs be layde,
Nee one hallie Seyncte to ſave
Al the celneſs of a mayde.
  Mie love ys dedde,   40
   Gonne to hys death-bedde,
  Alle under the wyllowe tree.

Wythe mie hondes I'lle dente the brieres
Rounde his hallie corſe to gre,
Ouphante fairie, lyghte youre fyres,
Heere mie boddie ſtylle ſchalle bee.
  Mie love ys dedde,
   Gon to hys death-bedde,
  Al under the wyllowe tree.

Comme, wythe acorne-coppe & thorne,   50
Drayne mie hartys blodde awaie;
Lyfe & all yttes goode I ſcorne,

Daunce bie nete, or feaſte by daie.
    Mie love ys dedde,
    Gon to hys death-bedde,
    Al under the wyllowe tree.

Waterre wytches, crownede wythe reytes,
Bere mee to yer leathalle tyde.
I die; I comme; mie true love waytes.
Thos the damfelle ſpake, and dyed.   60

l. 11. cale = cold
l. 44. gre = grow
l. 45. Ouphante = Elfin
l. 57. reytes = seaweed, water-flags

Jane Cave Winscom

(1 7 5 4 ? – 1 8 1 3)

Little is known of Jane Cave. A working woman who early on was drawn to "books and poetry," she published her *Poems on Various Subjects, Entertaining, Elegiac, and Religious* in Winchester in 1783; the same year she married Thomas Winscom, an exciseman. Cave revised, expanded, and reissued her volume of poems in 1786, 1789, and again in 1794. Several of her poems complain of terrible headaches; others attacked the slave trade. Her most celebrated poem is her elegy upon losing her name and taking that of her husband.

AN ELEGY ON
A MAIDEN NAME

Adieu, dear name which birth and nature gave—
Lo! at the altar I've interred dear CAVE;
For there it fell, expired, and found a grave.

   Forgive, dear spouse, this ill-timed tear or two,
They are not meant in disrespect to you;
I hope the name which you have lately given
Was kindly meant and sent to me by heaven.
But ah! the loss of CAVE I must deplore,
For that dear name the tend'rest mother bore.
With that she passed full forty years of life,   10
Adorned th' important character of wife:
Then meet for bliss from earth to heaven retired,
With holy zeal and true devotion fired.

   In me what blessed my father may you find,
A wife domestic, virtuous, meek and kind.
What blessed my mother may I meet in you,
A friend and husband—faithful, wise, and true.

   Then be our voyage prosperous or adverse,
No keen upbraiding shall our tongues rehearse;
But mutually we'll brave against the storm,   20

Remembering still for helpmates we were born.
Then let rough torrents roar or skies look dark,
If love commands the helm which guides our bark,
No shipwreck will we fear, but to the end
Each find in each a just, unshaken friend.

George Crabbe

(1754 – 1832)

Physician, clergyman, and unromantic poet in his birthplace, Aldeburgh in
Suffolk, after 1781 Crabbe served elsewhere as curate, chaplain, and vicar. He
set about in *The Village* (1783), *The Borough* (1810), and *Tales in Verse* (1812)
to negate Goldsmith's illusioned view of village life. To Crabbe industrial blight
could not deprive rural ways of a charm they never had.

From THE BOROUGH

From LETTER I

"Describe the Borough."—Though our idle tribe
May love description, can we so describe,
That you shall fairly streets and buildings trace,
And all that gives distinction to a place?
This cannot be; yet, moved by your request,
A part I paint—let fancy form the rest.
    Cities and towns, the various haunts of men,
Require the pencil; they defy the pen.
Could he, who sang so well the Grecian fleet,
So well have sung of alley, lane, or street?   10
Can measured lines these various buildings show,
The Town-Hall Turning, or the Prospect Row?
Can I the seats of wealth and want explore,
And lengthen out my lays from door to door?
    Then, let thy fancy aid me.—I repair
From this tall mansion of our last-year's mayor,
Till we the outskirts of the Borough reach,
And these half-buried buildings next the beach;
Where hang at open doors the net and cork,
While squalid sea-dames mend the meshy work;   20
Till comes the hour, when, fishing through the tide,
The weary husband throws his freight aside—
A living mass, which now demands the wife,
Th' alternate labours of their humble life.

407

William Blake

(1757–1827)

Londoner, self-created poet, engraver, and inventor of the method of illuminated printing by which he made available individual copies of his poems with the designs that ideally surround them, Blake is a unique and incomparable figure in literature and art. After study in the drawing school of Henry Pars, he was apprenticed to an engraver and studied at the Royal Academy. His marriage in 1782 lasted through many trials—including an actual trial for treasonous utterance, of which he was acquitted. Little subsequent symbolism is without influence from Blake. Tributes to his worth have been paid notably by D. G. Rossetti, Swinburne, Yeats, Binyon, Auden, and in the twelve lines by James Thomson (see p. 653). "The Lamb" and "The Little Black Boy" belong to *Songs of Innocence* (1789); "The Tyger," "The Sick Rose," and "London," from *Songs of Experience* (1794), were balancing contraries to innocence. *Visions of the Daughters of Albion* bears the date 1793. The poem in four quatrains that Blake etched in the Preface to *Milton* (1804) is popularly known as "Jerusalem."

THE LAMB

Little Lamb who made thee
Dost thou know who made thee
Gave thee life & bid thee feed.
By the stream & o'er the mead;
Gave thee clothing of delight,
Softest clothing wooly bright;
Gave thee such a tender voice,
Making all the vales rejoice!
Little Lamb who made thee
Dost thou know who made thee?   10

Little Lamb I'll tell thee,
Little Lamb I'll tell thee!
He is called by thy name,
For he calls himself a Lamb:
He is meek & he is mild,

He became a little child:
I a child & thou a lamb,
We are called by his name.
   Little Lamb God bless thee.
   Little Lamb God bless thee.   20

THE TYGER

Tyger Tyger, burning bright,
In the forests of the night;
What immortal hand or eye,
Could frame thy fearful symmetry?

In what distant deeps or skies.
Burnt the fire of thine eyes?
On what wings dare he aspire?
What the hand, dare sieze the fire?

And what shoulder, & what art,
Could twist the sinews of thy heart?   10
And when thy heart began to beat,
What dread hand? & what dread feet?

What the hammer? what the chain,
In what furnace was thy brain?
What the anvil? what dread grasp,
Dare its deadly terrors clasp!

When the stars threw down their spears
And water'd heaven with their tears:
Did he smile his work to see?
Did he who made the Lamb make thee?   20

Tyger Tyger burning bright,
In the forests of the night:
What immortal hand or eye,
Dare frame thy fearful symmetry?

THE LITTLE BLACK BOY

My mother bore me in the southern wild,
And I am black, but O! my soul is white;
White as an angel is the English child:
But I am black as if bereav'd of light.

My mother taught me underneath a tree
And sitting down before the heat of day,
She took me on her lap and kissed me,
And pointing to the east began to say.

Look on the rising sun: there God does live
And gives his light, and gives his heat away.   10
And flowers and trees and beasts and men recieve
Comfort in morning joy in the noon day.

And we are put on earth a little space,
That we may learn to bear the beams of love,
And these black bodies and this sun-burnt face
Is but a cloud, and like a shady grove.

For when our souls have learn'd the heat to bear
The cloud will vanish we shall hear his voice.
Saying: come out from the grove my love & care,
And round my golden tent like lambs rejoice.   20

Thus did my mother say and kissed me,
And thus I say to little English boy.
When I from black and he from white cloud free,
And round the tent of God like lambs we joy:

Ill shade him from the heat till he can bear,
To lean in joy upon our fathers knee.
And then I'll stand and stroke his silver hair,
And be like him and he will then love me.

THE SICK ROSE

O Rose thou art sick.
The invisible worm,
That flies in the night
In the howling storm:

Has found out thy bed
Of crimson joy:
And his dark secret love
Does thy life destroy.

LONDON

I wander thro' each charter'd street,
Near where the charter'd Thames does flow.
And mark in every face I meet
Marks of weakness, marks of woe.

In every cry of every Man,
In every Infants cry of fear,
In every voice: in every ban,
The mind-forg'd manacles I hear

How the Chimney-sweepers cry
Every blackning Church appalls,   10
And the hapless Soldiers sigh
Runs in blood down Palace walls

But most thro' midnight streets I hear
How the youthful Harlots curse
Blasts the new-born Infants tear
And blights with plagues the Marriage hearse.

From *MILTON*

From PREFACE

And did those feet in ancient time,
Walk upon Englands mountains green:
And was the holy Lamb of God,
On Englands pleasant pastures seen!

And did the Countenance Divine,
Shine forth upon our clouded hills?
And was Jerusalem builded here,
Among these dark Satanic Mills?

Bring me my Bow of burning gold:
Bring me my Arrows of desire: 10
Bring me my Spear: O clouds unfold!
Bring me my Chariot of fire!

I will not cease from Mental Fight,
Nor shall my Sword sleep in my hand:
Till we have built Jerusalem,
In Englands green & pleasant Land.

VISIONS OF THE
DAUGHTERS
OF ALBION

"The Eye sees more than the Heart knows."

THE ARGUMENT

I loved Theotormon
And I was not ashamed
I trembled in my virgin fears
And I hid in Leutha's vale!

I plucked Leutha's flower,
And I rose up from the vale;
But the terrible thunders tore
My virgin mantle in twain.

VISIONS

Enslav'd, the Daughters of Albion weep: a trembling lamentation
Upon their mountains; in their valleys, sighs toward America.

For the soft soul of America, Oothoon wanderd in woe,
Along the vales of Leutha seeking flowers to comfort her;
And thus she spoke to the bright Marygold of Leutha's vale:

> Art thou a flower! art thou a nymph! I see thee now a flower;
> Now a nymph! I dare not pluck thee from thy dewy bed!

> The Golden nymph replied; pluck thou my flower Oothoon the mild!
> Another flower shall spring, because the soul of sweet delight
> Can never pass away. She ceas'd & clos'd her golden shrine.   10

Then Oothoon pluck'd the flower saying, I pluck thee from thy bed
Sweet flower, and put thee here to glow between my breasts
And thus I turn my face to where my whole soul seeks.

Over the waves she went in wing'd exulting swift delight;
And over Theotormons reign, took her impetuous course.

Bromion rent her with his thunders; on his stormy bed
Lay the faint maid, and soon her woes appalld his thunders hoarse.

Bromion spoke: behold this harlot here on Bromions bed,
And let the jealous dolphins sport around the lovely maid;
Thy soft American plains are mine, and mine thy north & south: 20
Stampt with my signet are the swarthy children of the sun:
They are obedient, they resist not, they obey the scourge:
Their daughters worship terrors and obey the violent.
Now thou maist marry Bromions harlot, and protect the child
Of Bromions rage, that Oothoon shall put forth in nine moons time.

Then storms rent Theotormons limbs; he rolld his waves around
And folded his black jealous waters round the adulterate pair
Bound back to back in Bromions caves terror & meekness dwell:

At entrance Theotormon sits wearing the threshold hard
With secret tears; beneath him sound like waves on a desart shore   30
The voice of slaves beneath the sun, and children bought with money,
That shiver in religious caves beneath the burning fires
Of lust, that belch incessant from the summits of the earth.

Oothoon weeps not: she cannot weep! her tears are locked up;
But she can howl incessant writhing her soft snowy limbs,
And calling Theotormons Eagles to prey upon her flesh.

I call with holy voice! kings of the sounding air,
Rend away this defiled bosom that I may reflect
The image of Theotormon on my pure transparent breast.

The Eagles at her call descend & rend their bleeding prey;   40
Theotormon severely smiles; her soul reflects the smile,
As the clear spring mudded with feet of beasts grows pure & smiles.

The Daughters of Albion hear her woes & eccho back her sighs.

Why does my Theotormon sit weeping upon the threshold;
And Oothoon hovers by his side, perswading him in vain:
I cry arise O Theotormon for the village dog
Barks at the breaking day; the nightingale has done lamenting;
The lark does rustle in the ripe corn, and the Eagle returns
From nightly prey, and lifts his golden beak to the pure east;
Shaking the dust from his immortal pinions to awake   50
The sun that sleeps too long. Arise my Theotormon I am pure:
Because the night is gone that clos'd me in its deadly black.
They told me that the night & day were all that I could see;
They told me that I had five senses to inclose me up.
And they inclos'd my infinite brain into a narrow circle,
And sunk my heart into the Abyss, a red round globe hot burning
Till all from life I was obliterated and erased.
Instead of morn arises a bright shadow, like an eye
In the eastern cloud: instead of night a sickly charnel house;
That Theotormon hears me not! to him the night and morn   60
Are both alike: a night of sighs, a morning of fresh tears;
And none but Bromion can hear my lamentations.

With what sense is it that the chicken shuns the ravenous hawk?
With what sense does the tame pigeon measure out the expanse?
With what sense does the bee form cells? have not the mouse & frog
Eyes and ears and sense of touch? yet are their habitations
And their pursuits, as different as their forms and as their joys:
Ask the wild ass why he refuses burdens: and the meek camel
Why he loves man: is it because of eye ear mouth or skin
Or breathing nostrils? No, for these the wolf and tyger have.   70
Ask the blind worm the secrets of the grave, and why her spires

Love to curl round the bones of death; and ask the rav'nous snake
Where she gets poison: & the wing'd eagle why he loves the sun,
And then tell me the thoughts of man, that have been hid of old.

Silent I hover all the night, and all day could be silent,
If Theotormon once would turn his loved eyes upon me;
How can I be defild when I reflect thy image pure?
Sweetest the fruit that the worm feeds on, & the soul prey'd on by woe,
The new wash'd lamb ting'd with the village smoke & the bright swan
By the red earth of our immortal river: I bathe my wings,   80
And I am white and pure to hover round Theotormons breast.

Then Theotormon broke his silence, and he answered.

Tell me what is the night or day to one o'erflowd with woe?
Tell me what is a thought? & of what substance is it made?
Tell me what is a joy? & in what gardens do joys grow?
And in what rivers swim the sorrows? and upon what mountains
Wave shadows of discontent? and in what houses dwell the wretched
Drunken with woe forgotten, and shut up from cold despair?

Tell me where dwell the thoughts forgotten till thou call them forth!
Tell me where dwell the joys of old! & where the ancient loves?   90
And when will they renew again & the night of oblivion past?
That I might traverse times & spaces far remote and bring
Comforts into a present sorrow and a night of pain.
Where goest thou O thought? to what remote land is thy flight?
If thou returnest to the present moment of affliction
Wilt thou bring comforts on thy wings, and dews and honey and balm;
Or poison from the desart wilds, from the eyes of the envier?

Then Bromion said: and shook the cavern with his lamentation:

Thou knowest that the ancient trees seen by thine eyes have fruit;
But knowest thou that trees and fruits flourish upon the earth   100
To gratify senses unknown? trees beasts and birds unknown:
Unknown, not unpercievd, spread in the infinite microscope,
In places yet unvisited by the voyager, and in worlds
Over another kind of seas, and in atmospheres unknown?
Ah! are there other wars, beside the wars of sword and fire!
And are there other sorrows, beside the sorrows of poverty!
And are there other joys, beside the joys of riches and ease?
And is there not one law for both the lion and the ox?

And is there not eternal fire, and eternal chains?
To bind the phantoms of existence from eternal life?   110

Then Oothoon waited silent all the day, and all the night,
But when the morn arose, her lamentation renewd,
The Daughters of Albion hear her woes, & eccho back her sighs.

O Urizen! Creator of men! mistaken Demon of heaven:
Thy joys are tears! thy labour vain, to form men to thine image.
How can one joy absorb another? are not different joys
Holy, eternal, infinite! and each joy is a Love.

Does not the great mouth laugh at a gift? & the narrow eyelids mock
At the labour that is above payment, and wilt thou take the ape
For thy councellor? or the dog, for a schoolmaster to thy children?   120
Does he who contemns poverty, and he who turns with abhorrence
From usury: feel the same passion or are they moved alike?
How can the giver of gifts experience the delights of the merchant?
How the industrious citizen the pains of the husbandman.
How different far the fat fed hireling with hollow drum,
Who buys whole corn fields into wastes, and sings upon the heath:
How different their eye and ear! how different the world to them!
With what sense does the parson claim the labour of the farmer?
What are his nets & gins & traps & how does he surround him
With cold floods of abstraction, and with forests of solitude,   130
To build him castles and high spires, where kings & priests may dwell.
Till she who burns with youth, and knows no fixed lot, is bound
In spells of law to one she loaths: and must she drag the chain
Of life, in weary lust! must chilling murderous thoughts obscure
The clear heaven of her eternal spring? to bear the wintry rage
Of a harsh terror driv'n to madness, bound to hold a rod
Over her shrinking shoulders all the day; & all the night
To turn the wheel of false desire: and longings that wake her womb
To the abhorred birth of cherubs in the human form
That live a pestilence & die a meteor & are no more.   140
Till the child dwell with one he hates, and do the deed he loaths,
And the impure scourge force his seed into its unripe birth
E'er yet his eyelids can behold the arrows of the day.

Does the whale worship at thy footsteps as the hungry dog?
Or does he scent the mountain prey, because his nostrils wide
Draw in the ocean? does his eye discern the flying cloud
As the ravens eye? or does he measure the expanse like the vulture?

Does the still spider view the cliffs where eagles hide their young?
Or does the fly rejoice, because the harvest is brought in?
Does not the eagle scorn the earth & despise the treasures beneath?   150
But the mole knoweth what is there, & the worm shall tell it thee.
Does not the worm erect a pillar in the mouldering church yard?
And a palace of eternity in the jaws of the hungry grave?
Over his porch these words are written: Take thy bliss O Man!
And sweet shall be thy taste & sweet thy infant joys renew!

Infancy, fearless, lustful, happy! nestling for delight
In laps of pleasure; Innocence! honest, open, seeking
The vigorous joys of morning light; open to virgin bliss,
Who taught thee modesty, subtil modesty! child of night & sleep
When thou awakest, wilt thou dissemble all thy secret joys   160
Or wert thou not awake when all this mystery was disclos'd!
Then com'st thou forth a modest virgin knowing to dissemble
With nets found under thy night pillow, to catch virgin joy,
And brand it with the name of whore; & sell it in the night,
In silence, ev'n without a whisper, and in seeming sleep:
Religious dreams and holy vespers light thy smoky fires:
Once were thy fires lighted by the eyes of honest morn,
And does my Theotormon seek this hypocrite modesty!
This knowing, artful, secret, fearful, cautious, trembling hypocrite.

Then is Oothoon a whore indeed! and all the virgin joys   170
Of life are harlots: and Theotormon is a sick mans dream
And Oothoon is the crafty slave of selfish holiness.

But Oothoon is not so, a virgin fill'd with virgin fancies
Open to joy and to delight where ever beauty appears,
If in the morning sun I find it: there my eyes are fix'd
In happy copulation; if in evening mild, wearied with work;
Sit on a bank and draw the pleasures of this free born joy.

   The moment of desire! the moment of desire! The virgin
That pines for man; shall awaken her womb to enormous joys
In the secret shadows of her chamber; the youth shut up from   180
The lustful joy, shall forget to generate, & create an amorous image
In the shadows of his curtains and in the folds of his silent pillow.
Are not these the places of religion? the rewards of continence?
The self enjoyings of self denial? Why dost thou seek religion?
Is it because acts are not lovely, that thou seekest solitude,
Where the horrible darkness is impressed with reflections of desire.

Father of Jealousy, be thou accursed from the earth!
Why hast thou taught my Theotormon this accursed thing?
Till beauty fades from off my shoulders darken'd and cast out,
A solitary shadow wailing on the margin of non-entity.　　　　　190

I cry, Love! Love! Love! happy happy Love! free as the mountain wind!
Can that be Love, that drinks another as a sponge drinks water?
That clouds with jealousy his nights, with weepings all the day:
To spin a web of age around him, grey and hoary! dark!
Till his eyes sicken at the fruit that hangs before his sight.
Such is self-love that envies all! a creeping skeleton
With lamplike eyes watching around the frozen marriage bed.

But silken nets and traps of adamant will Oothoon spread,
And catch for thee girls of mild silver, or of furious gold;
I'll lie beside thee on a bank & view their wanton play　　　　　200
In lovely copulation bliss on bliss with Theotormon:
Red as the rosy morning, lustful as the first born beam,
Oothoon shall view his dear delight, nor e'er with jealous cloud
Come in the heaven of generous love; nor selfish blightings bring.

Does the sun walk in glorious raiment. On the secret floor
Where the cold miser spreads his gold? or does the bright cloud drop
On his stone threshold? does his eye behold the beam that brings
Expansion to the eye of pity? or will he bind himself
Beside the ox to thy hard furrow? does not that mild beam blot

The bat, the owl, the glowing tyger, and the king of night.　　　　210
The sea fowl takes the wintry blast, for a cov'ring to her limbs:
And the wild snake, the pestilence to adorn him with gems & gold.
And trees, & birds, & beasts, & men, behold their eternal joy.
Arise you little glancing wings, and sing your infant joy!
Arise and drink your bliss, for every thing that lives is holy!

Thus every morning wails Oothoon, but Theotormon sits
Upon the margind ocean conversing with shadows dire.

The Daughters of Albion hear her woes, & eccho back her sighs.

Robert Burns

(1759 – 1796)

Born in Alloway in southwest Scotland, Burns was a farmer, acquainted from childhood with rural ways, balladry, hard work, and hard drink. In such supreme pieces as "Auld Lang Syne" and "John Anderson My Jo" he revised familiar songs and set them to traditional tunes. Father of at least three children besides those with his wife Jean Armour, he was a natural enemy of the Church of Scotland and its Calvinistic doctrine embodied in Holy Willie, pre-elected by God. His *Poems, Chiefly in the Scottish Dialect*, published in Kilmarnock in 1786—which included "To a Mouse"—led to attention from the literati of Edinburgh and achieved successively enlarged editions. The prayer of Holy Willie (an actual "oldish batchelor Elder" who informed against Burns's friend Gavin Hamilton in 1785) was composed in triumph after Hamilton's acquittal, but published posthumously in 1798. The unrepentant narrative of the unrepentant Tam was published in 1791, when Burns enjoyed a degree of financial relief as a tax inspector. He had lost sympathy with the Revolution in France, but not with its principles, when he wrote "For a' that and a' that" (1794).

SONG—FOR A' THAT AND A' THAT

Is there, for honest Poverty
   That hings his head, and a' that;
The coward-slave, we pass him by,
    We dare be poor for a' that!
For a' that, and a' that,
    Our toils obscure, and a' that,
The rank is but the guinea's stamp,
    The Man's the gowd for a' that.—

What though on hamely fare we dine,
    Wear hoddin grey, and a' that.   10
Gie fools their silks, and knaves their wine,
    A Man's a Man for a' that.
For a' that, and a' that,

Their tinsel show, and a' that;
The honest man, though e'er sae poor,
Is king o' men for a' that.—

Ye see yon birkie ca'd, a lord,
    Wha struts, and stares, and a' that,
Though hundreds worship at his word,
    He's but a coof for a' that.   20
    For a' that, and a' that,
        His ribband, star and a' that,
    The man of independant mind,
        He looks and laughs at a' that.—

A prince can mak a belted knight,
    A marquis, duke, and a' that;
But an honest man's aboon his might,
    Gude faith he mauna fa' that!
    For a' that, and a' that,
        Their dignities, and a' that,   30
    The pith o' Sense, and pride o' Worth,
        Are higher rank than a' that.—

Then let us pray that come it may,
    As come it will for a' that,
That Sense and Worth, o'er a' the earth
    Shall bear the gree, and a' that.
    For a' that, and a' that,
        Its comin yet for a' that,
    That Man to Man the warld o'er,
        Shall brothers be for a' that.—   40

l.   8. gowd = gold
l. 20. coof = fool
l. 28. mauna fa' = may not claim
l. 36. gree = highest degree

TO A MOUSE

On Turning Her Nest,
With The Plough,
November, 1785

Wee, sleeket, cowran, tim'rous beastie,
O, what a panic's in thy breastie!
Thou need na start awa sae hasty,
   Wi' bickering brattle!
I wad be laith to rin an' chase thee,
   Wi' murd'ring pattle!

I'm truly sorry man's dominion
Has broken Nature's social union,
An' justifies that ill opinion,
   Which makes thee startle   10
At me, thy poor, earth-born companion,
   An' fellow-mortal!

I doubt na, whyles, but thou may thieve;
What then? poor beastie, thou maun live!
A daimen-icker in a thrave
   'S a sma' request:
I'll get a blessin wi' the lave,
   And never miss't!

Thy wee-bit housie, too, in ruin!
It's silly wa's the winds are strewin!   20
An' naething, now, to big a new ane,
   O' foggage green!
An' bleak December's winds ensuin,
   Baith snell an' keen!

Thou saw the fields laid bare an' wast,
An' weary winter comin fast,
An' cozie here, beneath the blast,
   Thou thought to dwell,
Till crash! the cruel coulter past
   Out thro' thy cell.   30

That wee-bit heap o' leaves an' stibble
Has cost thee monie a weary nibble!

Now thou's turn'd out, for a' thy trouble,
But house or hald,
To thole the winter's sleety dribble,
An' cranreuch cauld!

But Mousie, thou art no thy lane,
In proving foresight may be vain:
The best laid schemes o' mice and men,
Gang aft agley,   40
An' lea'e us nought but grief an' pain,
For promis'd joy!

Still, thou art blest, compar'd wi' me!
The present only toucheth thee:
But och! I backward cast my e'e,
On prospects drear!
An' forward, tho' I canna see,
I guess an' fear!

l.   4. bickering brattle = sudden scurry
l. 15. daimen-icker in a thrave = chance ear in 24 sheaves
l. 17. lave = leavings
l. 21. big = build
l. 24. snell = bitter
l. 34. But house or hald = Without dwelling or refuge
l. 37. no thy lane = not alone
l. 40. agley = awry (joy rhymes as jie)

HOLY WILLIE'S PRAYER

O thou that in the heavens does dwell!
Wha, as it pleases best thysel,
Sends ane to heaven and ten to h–ll,
A' for thy glory!
And no for ony gude or ill
They've done before thee.—

I bless and praise thy matchless might,
When thousands thou has left in night,
That I am here before thy sight,
For gifts and grace,   10

A burning and a shining light
     To a' this place.—

What was I, or my generation,
That I should get such exaltation?
I, wha deserv'd most just damnation,
     For broken laws
Sax thousand years ere my creation,
     Thro' Adam's cause!

When from my mother's womb I fell,
Thou might hae plunged me deep in hell,   20
To gnash my gooms, and weep, and wail,
     In burning lakes,
Where damned devils roar and yell
     Chain'd to their stakes.—

Yet I am here, a chosen sample,
To shew thy grace is great and ample:
I'm here, a pillar o' thy temple
     Strong as a rock,
A guide, a ruler and example
     To a' thy flock.—   30

But yet—O L––d—confess I must—
At times I'm fash'd wi' fleshly lust;
And sometimes too, in warldly trust
     Vile Self gets in;
But thou remembers we are dust,
     Defil'd wi' sin.—

O L––d—yestreen—thou kens—wi' Meg—
Thy pardon I sincerely beg!
O may 't ne'er be a living plague,
     To my dishonor!   40
And I'll ne'er lift a lawless leg
     Again upon her.—

Besides, I farther maun avow,
Wi' Leezie's lass, three times—I trow—
But L––d, that Friday I was fou
     When I cam near her;

Or else, thou kens, thy servant true
      Wad never steer her.—

Maybe thou lets this fleshy thorn
Buffet thy servant e'en and morn,   50
Lest he o'er proud and high should turn,
      That he 's sae gifted;
If sae, thy hand maun e'en be borne
      Untill thou lift it.—

L––d bless thy Chosen in this place,
For here thou has a chosen race:
But G–d, confound their stubborn face,
      And blast their name,
Wha bring thy rulers to disgrace
      And open shame.—   60

L––d mind Gaun Hamilton's deserts!
He drinks, and swears, and plays at cartes,
Yet has sae mony taking arts
      Wi' Great and Sma',
Frae G–d's ain priest the people's hearts
      He steals awa.—

And when we chasten'd him therefore,
Thou kens how he bred sic a splore,
And set the warld in a roar
      O' laughin at us: 70
Curse thou his basket and his store,
      Kail and potatoes.—

L––d hear my earnest cry and prayer
Against that Presbytry of Ayr!
Thy strong right hand, L––d, make it bare
      Upon their heads!
L––d visit them, and dinna spare,
      For their misdeeds!

O L––d my G–d, that glib-tongu'd Aiken!
My very heart and flesh are quaking   80
To think how I sat, sweating, shaking,
      And p–ss'd wi' dread,

While Auld wi' hingin lip gaed sneaking
    And hid his head!

L——d, in thy day o' vengeance try him!
L——d visit him that did employ him!
And pass not in thy mercy by them,
            Nor hear their prayer;
But for thy people's sake destroy them,
            And dinna spare!   90

But L——d, remember me and mine
Wi' mercies temporal and divine!
That I for grace and gear may shine,
            Excell'd by nane!
And a' the glory shall be thine!
            AMEN! AMEN!

TAM O' SHANTER

A TALE

Of Brownyis and of Bogillis full is this Buke.
                    —Gawin Douglas

When chapman billies leave the street,
And drouthy neebors neebors meet,
As market-days are wearing late,
An' folk begin to take the gate;
While we sit bousing at the nappy,
An' gettin fou and unco happy,
We think na on the lang Scots miles,
The mosses, waters, slaps, and stiles,
That lie between us and our hame,
Whare sits our sulky, sullen dame,   10
Gathering her brows like gathering storm,
Nursing her wrath to keep it warm.

This truth fand honest Tam o' Shanter,
As he frae Ayr ae night did canter:
(Auld Ayr, wham ne'er a town surpasses,
For honest men and bonie lasses.)

O Tam! had'st thou but been sae wise
As taen thy ain wife Kate's advice!
She tauld thee weel thou was a skellum,
A bletherin, blusterin, drunken blellum;   20
That frae November till October,
Ae market-day thou was na sober;
That ilka melder wi' the miller,
Thou sat as lang as thou had siller;
That ev'ry naig was ca'd a shoe on,
The smith and thee gat roaring fou on;
That at the Lord's house, even on Sunday,
Thou drank wi' Kirkton Jean till Monday.
She prophesied, that, late or soon,
Thou would be found deep drowned in Doon: 30
Or catched wi' warlocks in the mirk,
By Alloway's auld haunted kirk.

Ah, gentle dames! it gars me greet,
To think how monie counsels sweet,
How monie lengthened sage advices,
The husband frae the wife despises!

But to our tale:—Ae market night,
Tam had got planted unco right,
Fast by an ingle, bleezing finely,
Wi' reaming swats that drank divinely;   40
And at his elbow, Souter Johnie,
His ancient, trusty, drouthy cronie:
Tam lo'ed him like a very brither;
They had been fou for weeks thegither.
The night drave on wi' sangs and clatter;
And ay the ale was growing better:
The landlady and Tam grew gracious
Wi' favours, secret, sweet, and precious:
The souter tauld his queerest stories;
The landlord's laugh was ready chorus: 50
The storm without might rair and rustle,
Tam did na mind the storm a whistle.

Care, mad to see a man sae happy,
E'en drowned himsel amang the nappy:
As bees flee hame wi' lades o' treasure,
The minutes winged their way wi' pleasure;

Kings may be blest, but Tam was glorious,
O'er a' the ills o' life victorious!

But pleasures are like poppies spread,
You seize the flow'r, its bloom is shed;   60
Or like the snow falls in the river,
A moment white—then melts forever;
Or like the borealis race,
That flit ere you can point their place;
Or like the rainbow's lovely form
Evanishing amid the storm.
Nae man can tether time nor tide:
The hour approaches Tam maun ride—
That hour, o' night's black arch the keystane,
That dreary hour Tam mounts his beast in;   70
And sic a night he taks the road in,
As ne'er poor sinner was abroad in.

The wind blew as 'twad blawn its last;
The rattling showers rose on the blast;
The speedy gleams the darkness swallowed;
Loud, deep, and lang the thunder bellowed:
That night, a child might understand,
The Deil had business on his hand.

Weel mounted on his gray mare, Meg—
A better never lifted leg—   80
Tam skelpit on thro' dub and mire,
Despising wind and rain and fire;
Whiles holding fast his guid blue bonnet,
Whiles crooning o'er some auld Scots sonnet,
Whiles glow'ring round wi' prudent cares,
Lest bogles catch him unawares.
Kirk-Alloway was drawing nigh,
Whare ghaists and houlets nightly cry.

By this time he was cross the ford,
Whare in the snaw the chapman smoored;   90
And past the birks and meikle stane,
Whare drunken Charlie brak's neck-bane;
And thro' the whins, and by the cairn,
Whare hunters fand the murdered bairn;
And near the thorn, aboon the well,

Whare Mungo's mither hanged hersel.
Before him Doon pours all his floods;
The doubling storm roars thro' the woods;
The lightnings flash from pole to pole,
Near and more near the thunders roll;   100
When, glimmering thro' the groaning trees,
Kirk-Alloway seemed in a bleeze:
Thro' ilka bore the beams were glancing,
And loud resounded mirth and dancing.

Inspiring bold John Barleycorn!
What dangers thou canst make us scorn!
Wi' tippenny we fear nae evil;
Wi' usquebae we'll face the devil!
The swats sae reamed in Tammie's noddle,
Fair play, he cared na deils a boddle.   110
But Maggie stood right sair astonished,
Till, by the heel and hand admonished,
She ventured forward on the light;
And, vow! Tam saw an unco sight!

Warlocks and witches in a dance;
Nae cotillion brent-new frae France,
But hornpipes, jigs, strathspeys, and reels
Put life and mettle in their heels:
A winnock bunker in the east,
There sat Auld Nick in shape o' beast;   120
A towsie tyke, black, grim, and large,
To gie them music was his charge;
He screwed the pipes and gart them skirl,
Till roof and rafters a' did dirl.
Coffins stood round like open presses,
That shawed the dead in their last dresses;
And by some devilish cantraip sleight
Each in its cauld hand held a light,
By which heroic Tam was able
To note upon the haly table   130
A murderer's banes in gibbet airns;
Twa span-lang, wee, unchristened bairns;
A thief, new-cutted frae a rape—
Wi' his last gasp his gab did gape;
Five tomahawks, wi' bluid red-rusted;
Five scymitars, wi' murder crusted;

A garter, which a babe had strangled;
A knife, a father's throat had mangled,
Whom his ain son o' life bereft—
The gray hairs yet stack to the heft;   140
Wi' mair o' horrible and awfu',
Which even to name wad be unlawfu'.

  As Tammie glowered, amazed and curious,
The mirth and fun grew fast and furious:
The piper loud and louder blew,
The dancers quick and quicker flew;
They reeled, they set, they crossed, they cleekit,
Till ilka carlin swat and reekit,
And coost her duddies to the wark
And linket at it in her sark!   150

  Now Tam, O Tam! had thae been queans,
A' plump and strapping in their teens!
Their sarks, instead o' creeshie flannen,
Been snaw-white seventeen hunder linen!—
Thir breeks o' mine, my only pair,
That ance were plush, o' guid blue hair,
I wad hae gien them aff my hurdies,
For ae blink o' the bonie burdies!

  But wither'd beldams, auld and droll,
Rigwoodie hags wad spean a foal,   160
Louping and flinging on a crummock,
I wonder didna turn thy stomach.

  But Tam kend what was what fu' brawlie;
There was ae winsome wench and wawlie,
That night enlisted in the core
(Lang after kend on Carrick shore
For monie a beast to dead she shot,
An' perished monie a bonie boat,
And shook baith meikle corn and bear,
And kept the countryside in fear).   170
Her cutty sark, o' Paisley harn,
That while a lassie she had worn,
In longitude tho' sorely scanty,
It was her best, and she was vauntie.
Ah! little kend thy reverend grannie,

That sark she coft for her wee Nannie,
Wi' twa pund Scots ('twas a' her riches),
Wad ever graced a dance o' witches!

But here my Muse her wing maun cour,
Sic flights are far beyond her power;   180
To sing how Nannie lap and flang,
(A souple jade she was and strang),
And how Tam stood like ane bewitched,
And thought his very een enriched;
Even Satan glowered and fidged fu' fain,
And hotched and blew wi' might and main:
Till first ae caper, syne anither,
Tam tint his reason a' thegither,
And roars out, "Weel done, Cutty-sark!"
And in an instant all was dark: 190
And scarcely had he Maggie rallied,
When out the hellish legion sallied.

As bees bizz out wi' angry fyke,
When plundering herds assail their byke;
As open pussie's mortal foes,
When, pop! she starts before their nose;
As eager runs the market-crowd,
When "Catch the thief!" resounds aloud;
So Maggie runs, the witches follow,
Wi' monie an eldritch skriech and hollo.   200

Ah, Tam! ah, Tam! thou'll get thy fairin!
In hell they'll roast thee like a herrin!
In vain thy Kate awaits thy comin!
Kate soon will be a woefu' woman!
Now, do thy speedy utmost, Meg,
And win the keystane of the brig:
There at them thou thy tail may toss,
A running stream they dare na cross.
But ere the keystane she could make,
The fient a tail she had to shake!   210
For Nannie, far before the rest,
Hard upon noble Maggie prest,
And flew at Tam wi' furious ettle;
But little wist she Maggie's mettle—
Ae spring brought aff her master hale,

But left behind her ain gray tail:
The carlin claught her by the rump,
And left poor Maggie scarce a stump.

Now, wha this tale o' truth shall read,
Ilk man and mother's son, take heed,   220
Whene'er to drink you are inclined,
Or cutty-sarks run in your mind,
Think, ye may buy the joys o'er dear,
Remember Tam o' Shanter's mare.

l.   1. chapman billies = peddlers
l.   23. ilka medler = every grinding
l.   25. ca'd = hammered
l.   33. gars me greet = makes me weep
l.   40. swats = ale
l. 119. winnock-bunker = window-seat
l. 124. dirl = rattle
l. 147. cleekit = linked arms
l. 149. coost her duddies = cast off her clothes
l. 188. tint = lost
l. 194. byke = hive
l. 195. pussie = hare
l. 210. fient = devil
l. 213. ettle = aim

Joanna Baillie

(1 7 6 2 – 1 8 5 1)

Born in Lanarkshire, educated in Glasgow, later resident in London and Hampstead, Baillie has been continuously admired for *A Series of Plays in Which It Is Attempted to Delineate the Stronger Passions of the Mind* (3 vols., 1798–1812). While best known in her own day as a dramatist, Baillie also wrote and anthologized poetry, including *Metrical Legends* (1821) and *Fugitive Verses* (1840). She was friends with fellow writers Anna Barbauld, Maria Edgeworth, and Walter Scott, who was a strong admirer of her work.

A MOTHER TO HER
WAKING INFANT

Now in thy dazzled half-oped eye,
Thy curlèd nose and lip awry,
Up-hoisted arms and nodding head,
And little chin with crystal spread,
Poor helpless thing! what do I see,
    That I should sing of thee?

From thy poor tongue no accents come,
Which can but rub thy toothless gum:
Small understanding boasts thy face,
Thy shapeless limbs nor step nor grace;   10
A few short words thy feats may tell,
    And yet I love thee well.

When sudden wakes the bitter shriek,
And redder swells thy little cheek;
When rattled keys thy woes beguile,
And through thine eyelids gleams the smile,
Still for thy weakly self is spent
    Thy little silly plaint.

But when thy friends are in distress,
Thou'lt laugh and chuckle ne'ertheless,   20

Nor with kind sympathy be smitten,
Though all are sad but thee and kitten;
Yet puny varlet that thou art,
    Thou twitchest at the heart.

Thy smooth round cheek so soft and warm;
Thy pinky hand and dimpled arm;
Thy silken locks that scantly peep,
With gold-tipped ends, where circles deep,
Around thy neck in harmless grace,
So soft and sleekly hold their place,   30
Might harder hearts with kindness fill,
    And gain our right good will.

Each passing clown bestows his blessing,
Thy mouth is worn with old wives' kissing:
E'en lighter looks the gloomy eye
Of surly sense when thou art by;
And yet, I think, whoe'er they be,
    They love thee not like me.

Perhaps when time shall add a few
Short months to thee, thou'lt love me too.   40
And after that, through life's long way,
Become my sure and cheering stay,
Wilt care for me, and be my hold,
    When I am weak and old.

Thou'lt listen to my lengthened tale,
And pity me when I am frail—
But see, the sweepy spinning fly
Upon the window takes thine eye;
Go to thy little senseless play;
    Thou dost not heed my lay.   50

A CHILD TO HIS SICK
GRANDFATHER

Grand-Dad, they say you're old and frail,
Your stiffen'd legs begin to fail:
Your staff, no more my pony now,

Supports your body bending low,
While back to wall you lean so sad,
  I'm vexed to see you, Dad.

You used to smile and stroke my head,
And tell me how good children did;
But now, I wot not how it be,
You take me seldom on your knee;   10
Yet ne'ertheless I am right glad
  To sit beside you, Dad.

How lank and thin your beard hangs down!
Scant are the white hairs on your crown;
How wan and hollow are your cheeks!
Your brow is cross'd with many streaks;
But yet although his strength be fled,
  I love my own old Dad.

The housewives round their potions brew,
And gossips come to ask for you: 20
And for your weal each neighbour cares,
And good men kneel and say their prayers;
And every body looks so sad,
  When you are ailing, Dad.

You will not die, and leave us then?
Rouse up and be our Dad again.
When you are quiet and laid in bed,
We'll doff our shoes and softly tread;
And when you wake, we'll aye be near,
  To fill old Dad his cheer.   30

When through the house you change your stand,
I'll lead you kindly by the hand;
When dinner's set I'll with you bide,
And aye be serving by your side;
And when the weary fire burns blue,
  I'll sit and talk with you.

I have a tale both long and good,
About a partlet and her brood,
And cunning greedy fox that stole,
By dead of midnight through a hole,   40

Which slyly to the hen-roost led—
    You love a story, Dad?

And then I have a wond'rous tale
Of men all clad in coats of mail,
With glitt'ring swords;—you nod, I think?
Your heavy eyes begin to wink;—
Down on your bosom sinks your head:—
    You do not hear me, Dad.

William Wordsworth

(1770–1850)

Lyrical Ballads, with a Few Other Poems (1798) opened with Coleridge's "Ancient Mariner" and closed with the lines known as "Tintern Abbey." In "She dwelt among the untrodden ways"—one of several elegies in the second volume added in 1800—the Dove is a river in the Lake District of northwest England, where Wordsworth was born, lived, set most of his poems, and died. Hence the surprise to Wordsworthians that the "poet-priest of Nature" should revere London (at sunrise) in the sonnet on Westminster Bridge! The "Intimations Ode," written in two stages, 1802 and 1804, first appeared in *Poems* (1807), as did "The Solitary Reaper," which derived during a walking tour in Scotland from a friend's anecdote about being unable to understand the Gaelic of a singer who "bended over her sickle." From his autobiographical poem *The Prelude*, the poet published in his own lifetime, in 1845, only the lines from Book VI attributed to the experience of crossing the Alps in 1790, "The Simplon Pass."

In 1802 Wordsworth restored dignity to the sonnet, specifically in its Miltonic form: the references to the Greek god Proteus and merman Triton, which close "The World Is Too Much with Us," may be taken in part as tributes to Milton (*Paradise Lost* III.603–4) and Spenser (*Colin Clout*, 1.245). The sonnet on the subjugation of Switzerland, collected in the series called "Dedicated to National Independence and Liberty," provided an opportunity for J. K. Stephen's parody (see p. 696). The sonnet of 1815, "Surprised by Joy," memorializes a daughter who died in 1812 at the age of four.

LINES

COMPOSED A FEW MILES ABOVE TINTERN
ABBEY, ON REVISITING THE BANKS OF THE
WYE DURING A TOUR. JULY 13, 1798

Five years have past; five summers, with the length
Of five long winters! and again I hear
These waters, rolling from their mountain-springs
With a soft inland murmur.—Once again
Do I behold these steep and lofty cliffs,

That on a wild secluded scene impress
Thoughts of more deep seclusion; and connect
The landscape with the quiet of the sky.
The day is come when I again repose
Here, under this dark sycamore, and view   10
These plots of cottage-ground, these orchard-tufts,
Which at this season, with their unripe fruits,
Are clad in one green hue, and lose themselves
'Mid groves and copses. Once again I see
These hedge-rows, hardly hedge-rows, little lines
Of sportive wood run wild: these pastoral farms,
Green to the very door; and wreaths of smoke
Sent up, in silence, from among the trees!
With some uncertain notice, as might seem
Of vagrant dwellers in the houseless woods,   20
Or of some Hermit's cave, where by his fire
The Hermit sits alone.
                              These beauteous forms,
Through a long absence, have not been to me
As is a landscape to a blind man's eye:
But oft, in lonely rooms, and 'mid the din
Of towns and cities, I have owed to them
In hours of weariness, sensations sweet,
Felt in the blood, and felt along the heart;
And passing even into my purer mind,
With tranquil restoration:—feelings too   30
Of unremembered pleasure: such, perhaps,
As have no slight or trivial influence
On that best portion of a good man's life,
His little, nameless, unremembered, acts
Of kindness and of love. Nor less, I trust,
To them I may have owed another gift,
Of aspect more sublime; that blessed mood
In which the burthen of the mystery,
In which the heavy and the weary weight
Of all this unintelligible world,   40
Is lightened:—that serene and blessed mood,
In which the affections gently lead us on,—
Until, the breath of this corporeal frame
And even the motion of our human blood
Almost suspended, we are laid asleep
In body, and become a living soul:

While with an eye made quiet by the power
Of harmony, and the deep power of joy,
We see into the life of things.
                                        If this
Be but a vain belief, yet, oh! how oft—   50
In darkness and amid the many shapes
Of joyless daylight; when the fretful stir
Unprofitable, and the fever of the world,
Have hung upon the beatings of my heart—
How oft, in spirit, have I turned to thee,
O sylvan Wye! thou wanderer thro' the woods,
How often has my spirit turned to thee!

    And now, with gleams of half-extinguished thought,
With many recognitions dim and faint,
And somewhat of a sad perplexity,   60
The picture of the mind revives again:
While here I stand, not only with the sense
Of present pleasure, but with pleasing thoughts
That in this moment there is life and food
For future years. And so I dare to hope,
Though changed, no doubt, from what I was when first
I came among these hills; when like a roe
I bounded o'er the mountains, by the sides
Of the deep rivers, and the lonely streams,
Wherever nature led: more like a man   70
Flying from something that he dreads than one
Who sought the thing he loved. For nature then
(The coarser pleasures of my boyish days,
And their glad animal movements all gone by)
To me was all in all.—I cannot paint
What then I was. The sounding cataract
Haunted me like a passion: the tall rock,
The mountain, and the deep and gloomy wood,
Their colours and their forms, were then to me
An appetite; a feeling and a love,   80
That had no need of a remoter charm,
By thought supplied, nor any interest
Unborrowed from the eye.—That time is past,
And all its aching joys are now no more,
And all its dizzy raptures. Not for this
Faint I, nor mourn nor murmur; other gifts
Have followed; for such loss, I would believe,

Abundant recompense. For I have learned
To look on nature, not as in the hour
Of thoughtless youth, but hearing oftentimes   90
The still, sad music of humanity,
Nor harsh nor grating, though of ample power
To chasten and subdue. And I have felt
A presence that disturbs me with the joy
Of elevated thoughts; a sense sublime
Of something far more deeply interfused,
Whose dwelling is the light of setting suns,
And the round ocean and the living air,
And the blue sky, and in the mind of man:
A motion and a spirit, that impels   100
All thinking things, all objects of all thought,
And rolls through all things. Therefore am I still
A lover of the meadows and the woods,
And mountains; and of all that we behold
From this green earth; of all the mighty world
Of eye, and ear,—both what they half create,
And what perceive; well pleased to recognise
In nature and the language of the sense
The anchor of my purest thoughts, the nurse,
The guide, the guardian of my heart, and soul   110
Of all my moral being.
                          Nor perchance,
If I were not thus taught, should I the more
Suffer my genial spirits to decay:
For thou art with me here upon the banks
Of this fair river; thou my dearest Friend,
My dear, dear Friend; and in thy voice I catch
The language of my former heart, and read
My former pleasures in the shooting lights
Of thy wild eyes. Oh! yet a little while
May I behold in thee what I was once,   120
My dear, dear Sister! and this prayer I make,
Knowing that Nature never did betray
The heart that loved her; 'tis her privilege,
Through all the years of this our life, to lead
From joy to joy: for she can so inform
The mind that is within us, so impress
With quietness and beauty, and so feed
With lofty thoughts, that neither evil tongues,
Rash judgments, nor the sneers of selfish men,

Nor greetings where no kindness is, nor all   130
The dreary intercourse of daily life,
Shall e'er prevail against us, or disturb
Our cheerful faith, that all which we behold
Is full of blessings. Therefore let the moon
Shine on thee in thy solitary walk;
And let the misty mountain-winds be free
To blow against thee: and, in after years,
When these wild ecstasies shall be matured
Into a sober pleasure; when thy mind
Shall be a mansion for all lovely forms,   140
Thy memory be as a dwelling-place
For all sweet sounds and harmonies; oh! then,
If solitude, or fear, or pain, or grief,
Should be thy portion, with what healing thoughts
Of tender joy wilt thou remember me,
And these my exhortations! Nor, perchance—
If I should be where I no more can hear
Thy voice, nor catch from thy wild eyes these gleams
Of past existence—wilt thou then forget
That on the banks of this delightful stream   150
We stood together; and that I, so long
A worshipper of Nature, hither came
Unwearied in that service: rather say
With warmer love—oh! with far deeper zeal
Of holier love. Nor wilt thou then forget,
That after many wanderings, many years
Of absence, these steep woods and lofty cliffs,
And this green pastoral landscape, were to me
More dear, both for themselves and for thy sake!

SHE DWELT AMONG THE
UNTRODDEN WAYS

She dwelt among the untrodden ways
   Beside the springs of Dove,
A Maid whom there were none to praise
   And very few to love:

A violet by a mossy stone
　　Half hidden from the eye!
—Fair as a star, when only one
　　Is shining in the sky.

She lived unknown, and few could know
　　When Lucy ceased to be;　　　　　　　　　　　10
But she is in her grave, and, oh,
　　The difference to me!

I WANDERED LONELY AS
A CLOUD

I wandered lonely as a cloud
That floats on high o'er vales and hills,
When all at once I saw a crowd,
A host, of golden daffodils;
Beside the lake, beneath the trees,
Fluttering and dancing in the breeze.

Continuous as the stars that shine
And twinkle on the milky way,
They stretched in never-ending line
Along the margin of a bay:　　　　　　　　　　　10
Ten thousand saw I at a glance,
Tossing their heads in sprightly dance.

The waves beside them danced; but they
Out-did the sparkling waves in glee:
A poet could not but be gay,
In such a jocund company:
I gazed—and gazed—but little thought
What wealth the show to me had brought:

For oft, when on my couch I lie
In vacant or in pensive mood,　　　　　　　　　　20
They flash upon that inward eye
Which is the bliss of solitude;
And then my heart with pleasure fills,
And dances with the daffodils.

THE SOLITARY
REAPER

Behold her, single in the field,
Yon solitary Highland Lass!
Reaping and singing by herself;
Stop here, or gently pass!
Alone she cuts and binds the grain,
And sings a melancholy strain;
O listen! for the Vale profound
Is overflowing with the sound.

No Nightingale did ever chaunt
More welcome notes to weary bands   10
Of travellers in some shady haunt,
Among Arabian sands:
A voice so thrilling ne'er was heard
In spring-time from the Cuckoo-bird,
Breaking the silence of the seas
Among the farthest Hebrides.

Will no one tell me what she sings?—
Perhaps the plaintive numbers flow
For old, unhappy, far-off things,
And battles long ago: 20
Or is it some more humble lay,
Familiar matter of to-day?
Some natural sorrow, loss, or pain,
That has been, and may be again?

Whate'er the theme, the Maiden sang
As if her song could have no ending;
I saw her singing at her work,
And o'er the sickle bending:—
I listened, motionless and still;
And, as I mounted up the hill,   30
The music in my heart I bore,
Long after it was heard no more.

ODE

INTIMATIONS OF IMMORTALITY FROM RECOLLECTIONS OF EARLY CHILDHOOD

The Child is father of the Man;
And I could wish my days to be
Bound each to each by natural piety.

There was a time when meadow, grove, and stream,
The earth, and every common sight,
    To me did seem
    Apparelled in celestial light,
The glory and the freshness of a dream.
It is not now as it hath been of yore;—
    Turn wheresoe'er I may,
      By night or day,
The things which I have seen I now can see no more.

    The Rainbow comes and goes,   10
    And lovely is the Rose,
    The Moon doth with delight
Look round her when the heavens are bare;
    Waters on a starry night
    Are beautiful and fair;
  The sunshine is a glorious birth;
  But yet I know, where'er I go,
That there hath past away a glory from the earth.

Now, while the birds thus sing a joyous song,
  And while the young lambs bound   20
    As to the tabor's sound,
To me alone there came a thought of grief:
A timely utterance gave that thought relief,
    And I again am strong:
The cataracts blow their trumpets from the steep;
No more shall grief of mine the season wrong;
I hear the Echoes through the mountains throng,
The Winds come to me from the fields of sleep,
    And all the earth is gay;
      Land and sea   30
  Give themselves up to jollity,
    And with the heart of May
Doth every Beast keep holiday;—

Thou Child of Joy,
Shout round me, let me hear thy shouts, thou happy Shepherd-boy!

Ye blessèd Creatures, I have heard the call
   Ye to each other make; I see
The heavens laugh with you in your jubilee;
   My heart is at your festival,
    My head hath its coronal,   40
The fulness of your bliss, I feel—I feel it all.
    Oh evil day! if I were sullen
    While Earth herself is adorning,
     This sweet May-morning,
    And the Children are culling
     On every side,
    In a thousand valleys far and wide,
    Fresh flowers; while the sun shines warm,
And the Babe leaps up on his Mother's arm:—
   I hear, I hear, with joy I hear!   50
   —But there's a Tree, of many, one,
A single Field which I have looked upon,
Both of them speak of something that is gone:
    The Pansy at my feet
    Doth the same tale repeat:
Whither is fled the visionary gleam?
Where is it now, the glory and the dream?

Our birth is but a sleep and a forgetting:
The Soul that rises with us, our life's Star,
    Hath had elsewhere its setting,   60
     And cometh from afar:
    Not in entire forgetfulness,
    And not in utter nakedness,
But trailing clouds of glory do we come
    From God, who is our home:
Heaven lies about us in our infancy!
Shades of the prison-house begin to close
    Upon the growing Boy,
      But He
Beholds the light, and whence it flows,   70
    He sees it in his joy;
The Youth, who daily farther from the east
    Must travel, still is Nature's Priest,
    And by the vision splendid

Is on his way attended;
At length the Man perceives it die away,
And fade into the light of common day.

Earth fills her lap with pleasures of her own;
Yearnings she hath in her own natural kind,
And, even with something of a Mother's mind,   80
    And no unworthy aim,
    The homely Nurse doth all she can
To make her Foster-child, her Inmate Man,
    Forget the glories he hath known,
And that imperial palace whence he came.

Behold the Child among his new-born blisses,
A six years' Darling of a pigmy size!
See, where 'mid work of his own hand he lies,
Frettied by sallies of his mother's kisses,
With light upon him from his father's eyes!   90
See, at his feet, some little plan or chart,
Some fragment from his dream of human life,
Shaped by himself with newly-learned art;
    A wedding or a festival,
    A mourning or a funeral;
      And this hath now his heart,
    And unto this he frames his song:
      Then will he fit his tongue
To dialogues of business, love, or strife;
    But it will not be long   100
    Ere this be thrown aside,
    And with new joy and pride
The little Actor cons another part;
Filling from time to time his "humorous stage"
With all the Persons, down to palsied Age,
That Life brings with her in her equipage;
    As if his whole vocation
    Were endless imitation.

Thou, whose exterior semblance doth belie
    Thy Soul's immensity;   110
Thou best Philosopher, who yet dost keep
Thy heritage, thou Eye among the blind,
That, deaf and silent, read'st the eternal deep,
Haunted for ever by the eternal mind,—

Mighty Prophet! Seer blest!
On whom those truths do rest,
Which we are toiling all our lives to find,
In darkness lost, the darkness of the grave;
Thou, over whom thy Immortality
Broods like the Day, a Master o'er a Slave,   120
A Presence which is not to be put by;
Thou little Child, yet glorious in the might
Of heaven-born freedom on thy being's height,
Why with such earnest pains dost thou provoke
The years to bring the inevitable yoke,
Thus blindly with thy blessedness at strife?
Full soon thy Soul shall have her earthly freight,
And custom lie upon thee with a weight,
Heavy as frost, and deep almost as life!

    Oh joy! that in our embers   130
    Is something that doth live,
    That nature yet remembers
    What was so fugitive!
The thought of our past years in me doth breed
Perpetual benediction: not indeed
For that which is most worthy to be blest;
Delight and liberty, the simple creed
Of Childhood, whether busy or at rest,
With new-fledged hope still fluttering in his breast:—
    Not for these I raise   140
    The song of thanks and praise;
   But for those obstinate questionings
   Of sense and outward things,
   Fallings from us, vanishings;
   Blank misgivings of a Creature
Moving about in worlds not realised,
High instincts before which our mortal Nature
Did tremble like a guilty Thing surprised:
    But for those first affections,
    Those shadowy recollections,   150
   Which, be they what they may,
Are yet the fountain light of all our day,
Are yet a master light of all our seeing;
   Uphold us, cherish, and have power to make
Our noisy years seem moments in the being
Of the eternal Silence: truths that wake,

To perish never;
Which neither listlessness, nor mad endeavour,
   Nor Man nor Boy,
Nor all that is at enmity with joy,   160
Can utterly abolish or destroy!
   Hence in a season of calm weather
   Though inland far we be,
Our Souls have sight of that immortal sea
   Which brought us hither,
  Can in a moment travel thither,
And see the Children sport upon the shore,
And hear the mighty waters rolling evermore.

Then sing, ye Birds, sing, sing a joyous song!
   And let the young Lambs bound   170
   As to the tabor's sound!
We in thought will join your throng,
   Ye that pipe and ye that play,
   Ye that through your hearts to-day
   Feel the gladness of the May!
What though the radiance which was once so bright
Be now for ever taken from my sight,
   Though nothing can bring back the hour
Of splendour in the grass, of glory in the flower;
   We will grieve not, rather find   180
   Strength in what remains behind;
   In the primal sympathy
   Which having been must ever be;
   In the soothing thoughts that spring
   Out of human suffering;
   In the faith that looks through death,
In years that bring the philosophic mind.

And Oh, ye Fountains, Meadows, Hills, and Groves,
Forebode not any severing of our loves!
Yet in my heart of hearts I feel your might;   190
I only have relinquished one delight
To live beneath your more habitual sway.
I love the Brooks which down their channels fret,
Even more than when I tripped lightly as they;
The innocent brightness of a new-born Day
      Is lovely yet;
The Clouds that gather round the setting sun

Do take a sober colouring from an eye
That hath kept watch o'er man's mortality;
Another race hath been, and other palms are won.   200
Thanks to the human heart by which we live,
Thanks to its tenderness, its joys, and fears,
To me the meanest flower that blows can give
Thoughts that do often lie too deep for tears.

THE SIMPLON PASS

——Brook and road
Were fellow-travellers in this gloomy Pass,
And with them did we journey several hours
At a slow step. The immeasurable height
Of woods decaying, never to be decayed,
The stationary blasts of waterfalls,
And in the narrow rent, at every turn,
Winds thwarting winds bewildered and forlorn,
The torrents shooting from the clear blue sky,
The rocks that muttered close upon our ears,   10
Black drizzling crags that spake by the wayside
As if a voice were in them, the sick sight
And giddy prospect of the raving stream,
The unfettered clouds and region of the heavens,
Tumult and peace, the darkness and the light—
Were all like workings of one mind, the features
Of the same face, blossoms upon one tree,
Characters of the great Apocalypse,
The types and symbols of Eternity,
Of first, and last, and midst, and without end.   20

THE WORLD IS TOO MUCH
WITH US

The world is too much with us; late and soon,
Getting and spending, we lay waste our powers:
Little we see in Nature that is ours;
We have given our hearts away, a sordid boon!

This Sea that bares her bosom to the moon;
The winds that will be howling at all hours,
And are up-gathered now like sleeping flowers;
For this, for everything, we are out of tune;
It moves us not.—Great God! I'd rather be
A Pagan suckled in a creed outworn;
So might I, standing on this pleasant lea,
Have glimpses that would make me less forlorn;
Have sight of Proteus rising from the sea;
Or hear old Triton blow his wreathèd horn.

COMPOSED UPON
WESTMINSTER BRIDGE,
SEPTEMBER 3, 1802

Earth has not anything to show more fair:
Dull would he be of soul who could pass by
A sight so touching in its majesty:
This City now doth, like a garment, wear
The beauty of the morning; silent, bare,
Ships, towers, domes, theatres, and temples lie
Open unto the fields, and to the sky;
All bright and glittering in the smokeless air.
Never did sun more beautifully steep
In his first splendour, valley, rock, or hill;
Ne'er saw I, never felt, a calm so deep!
The river glideth at his own sweet will:
Dear God! the very houses seem asleep;
And all that mighty heart is lying still!

THOUGHT OF A BRITON ON
THE SUBJUGATION OF
SWITZERLAND

Two Voices are there; one is of the sea,
One of the mountains; each a mighty Voice:
In both from age to age thou didst rejoice,

They were thy chosen music, Liberty!
There came a Tyrant, and with holy glee
Thou fought'st against him; but hast vainly striven:
Thou from thy Alpine holds at length art driven,
Where not a torrent murmurs heard by thee.
Of one deep bliss thine ear hath been bereft:
Then cleave, O cleave to that which still is left;
For, high-souled Maid, what sorrow would it be
That Mountain floods should thunder as before,
And Ocean bellow from his rocky shore,
And neither awful Voice be heard by thee!

SURPRISED BY JOY

Surprised by joy—impatient as the Wind
I turned to share the transport—O! with whom
But Thee, deep buried in the silent tomb,
That spot which no vicissitude can find?
Love, faithful love, recalled thee to my mind—
But how could I forget thee? Through what power,
Even for the least division of an hour,
Have I been so beguiled as to be blind
To my most grievous loss!—That thought's return
Was the worst pang that sorrow ever bore,
Save one, one only, when I stood forlorn,
Knowing my heart's best treasure was no more;
That neither present time, nor years unborn
Could to my sight that heavenly face restore.

James Hogg

(1 7 7 0 – 1 8 3 5)

Born on his parents' farm in Ettrick, Scotland, "discovered" by Walter Scott, and known to readers of *Blackwood's Edinburgh Magazine* as "the Ettrick Shepherd," Hogg, although skilled and prolific in verse and prose, is admired now largely for his anti-Calvinistic tale, *The Private Memoirs and Confessions of a Justified Sinner*. Admired as a poet of faerie and the supernatural, with some of Burns's instinct for adapting songs ("Maggy" was set by the composer Henry Bishop to an old melody), Hogg is habitually sly: did the priest sin only in calling Maggy "divine"?

WHEN MAGGY
GANGS AWAY

O what will a' the lads do
   When Maggy gangs away?
O what will a' the lads do
   When Maggy gangs away?
There's no a heart in a' the glen
   That disna dread the day.
O what will a' the lads do
   When Maggy gangs away?

Young Jock has ta'en the hill for't—
   A waefu' wight is he;   10
Poor Harry's ta'en the bed for't,
   An' laid him down to dee;
An' Sandy's gane unto the kirk,
   And learnin' fast to pray.
And, O, what will the lads do
   When Maggy gangs away?

The young laird o' the Lang-Shaw
   Has drunk her health in wine;
The priest has said—in confidence—

The lassie was divine—   20
And that is mair in maiden's praise
   Than ony priest should say:
But, O, what will the lads do
   When Maggy gangs away?

The wailing in our green glen
   That day will quaver high,
'Twill draw the redbreast frae the wood,
   The laverock frae the sky;
The fairies frae their beds o' dew
   Will rise an' join the lay: 30
An' hey! what a day will be
   When Maggy gangs away!

Sir Walter Scott

(1 7 7 1 – 1 8 3 2)

Scott was active as lawyer, antiquarian, ballad-collector, poet, novelist, biographer, Scot, royalist, and in the founding of the Tory *Quarterly Review*. After translations from German and his three volumes of *Minstrelsy of the Scottish Border*—ballads modified freely, as Burns had modified Scottish songs—he followed *The Lay of The Last Minstrel* (1805) with other narratives in verse. The greater public appeal of Byron's narratives turned Scott into one of the most popular novelists yet known. The mad, dying Madge Wildfire sings the dirge "Proud Maisie" in *The Heart of Midlothian* (1818).

PROUD MAISIE

Proud Maisie is in the wood,
   Walking so early;
Sweet Robin sits on the bush,
   Singing so rarely.

"Tell me, thou bonny bird,
   When shall I marry me?"
"When six braw gentlemen
   Kirkward shall carry ye."

"Who makes the bridal bed,
   Birdie, say truly?"   10
"The gray-headed sexton
   That delves the grave duly.

"The glow-worm o'er grave and stone
   Shall light thee steady,
The owl from the steeple sing,
   'Welcome, proud lady.' "

Dorothy Wordsworth

(1771–1855)

After a painful childhood as an orphan exiled to various relatives, Dorothy lived from 1795 with her brother William. His poems, and Coleridge's, often reflect perceptions and draw phrases from her precise and spirited journals. The stanzas below, addressed to William's daughter Dora in 1805, appeared in editions of his poetry from 1815 to 1836 as "The Cottager to Her Infant," by "a female friend"; he composed two further stanzas as from the infant's mother; these Dorothy crossed out in her notebook.

TO MY NIECE DOROTHY,
A SLEEPLESS BABY

The days are cold; the nights are long,
The north wind sings a doleful song;
Then hush again upon my breast;
All *merry* things are now at rest
   Save thee my pretty love!

The kitten sleeps upon the hearth;
The crickets long have ceased their mirth;
There's nothing stirring in the house
Save one wee hungry nibbling mouse,
   Then why so busy thou?   10

Nay, start not at that sparkling light
'Tis but the moon that shines so bright
On the window-pane bedropp'd with rain
Then, little Darling, sleep again
   And wake when it is Day.

Samuel Taylor Coleridge

(1 7 7 2 – 1 8 3 4)

Coleridge was journalist, philosopher, critic, public lecturer, talker, secretary to the governor of Malta (1802–1804), experimenter in prosody, poet, friend and promoter of Wordsworth, opium addict, usually absent husband and father, and metaphysical expert in the sublimity of guilt, as illustrated by "The Rime of the Ancient Mariner" that appeared in *Lyrical Ballads* (1798). The addition of the Platonist marginal gloss in 1817 is the most significant of his frequent alterations to that poem.

Delaying the publication of "Kubla Khan" until 1816, he declared it the transcription of an opium dream, forever interrupted by "a person on business from Porlock." In "Frost at Midnight" (1798), one of a series called "conversation poems" to mark casual diction, easy flow of blank verse, and address to someone dear (here a son), the poet promises Hartley, aged 2, a rural life unlike his own years at Christ's Hospital, where he (and his equally lonely classmate Charles Lamb) yearned for the flickering sign that a visitor would arrive—not on business.

THE RIME OF THE ANCIENT MARINER

PART I

An ancient Mariner meeteth three Gallants bidden to a wedding-feast, and detaineth one.

It is an ancient Mariner,
And he stoppeth one of three.
"By thy long grey beard and glittering eye,
Now wherefore stopp'st thou me?

The Bridegroom's doors are opened wide,
And I am next of kin;
The guests are met, the feast is set:
May'st hear the merry din."

He holds him with his skinny hand,
"There was a ship," quoth he.   10
"Hold off! unhand me, grey-beard loon!"
Eftsoons his hand dropt he.

The Wedding-
Guest is spell-
bound by the
eye of the old
seafaring man,
and con-
strained to hear
his tale.
He holds him with his glittering eye—
The Wedding-Guest stood still,
And listens like a three years' child:
The Mariner hath his will.

The Wedding-Guest sat on a stone:
He cannot choose but hear;
And thus spake on that ancient man,
The bright-eyed Mariner.   20

"The ship was cheered, the harbour cleared,
Merrily did we drop
The Mariner
tells how the
ship sailed
southward with
a good wind
and fair
weather, till it
reached the
Line.
Below the kirk, below the hill,
Below the lighthouse top.

The Sun came up upon the left,
Out of the sea came he!
And he shone bright, and on the right
Went down into the sea.

Higher and higher every day,
Till over the mast at noon—"   30
The Wedding-Guest here beat his breast,
For he heard the loud bassoon.

The Wedding-
Guest heareth
the bridal mu-
sic; but the
Mariner con-
tinueth his
tale.
The bride hath paced into the hall,
Red as a rose is she;
Nodding their heads before her goes
The merry minstrelsy.

The Wedding-Guest he beat his breast,
Yet he cannot choose but hear;
And thus spake on that ancient man,
The bright-eyed Mariner.   40

The ship
driven by a
storm toward
the south pole.
"And now the STORM-BLAST came, and he
Was tyrannous and strong:
He struck with his o'ertaking wings,
And chased us south along.

With sloping masts and dipping prow,
As who pursued with yell and blow
Still treads the shadow of his foe,

And forward bends his head,
The ship drove fast, loud roared the blast,
And southward aye we fled.   50

And now there came both mist and snow,
And it grew wondrous cold:
And ice, mast-high, came floating by,
As green as emerald.

The land of
ice, and of fear-
ful sounds
where no living
thing was to be
seen.

And through the drifts the snowy clifts
Did send a dismal sheen:
Nor shapes of men nor beasts we ken—
The ice was all between.

The ice was here, the ice was there,
The ice was all around: 60
It cracked and growled, and roared and howled,
Like noises in a swound!

Till a great sea-
bird, called the
Albatross,
came through
the snow-fog,
and was re-
ceived with
great joy and
hospitality.

At length did cross an Albatross,
Thorough the fog it came;
As if it had been a Christian soul,
We hailed it in God's name.

It ate the food it ne'er had eat,
And round and round it flew.
The ice did split with a thunder-fit;
The helmsman steered us through!   70

And lo! the Al-
batross proveth
a bird of good
omen, and fol-
loweth the ship
as it returned
northward
through fog
and floating
ice.

And a good south wind sprung up behind;
The Albatross did follow,
And every day, for food or play,
Came to the mariner's hollo!

In mist or cloud, on mast or shroud,
It perched for vespers nine;
Whiles all the night, through fog-smoke white,
Glimmered the white Moon-shine."

The ancient
Mariner inhos-
pitably killeth
the pious bird
of good omen.

"God save thee, ancient Mariner!
From the fiends, that plague thee thus!—   80
Why look'st thou so?"—With my cross-bow
I shot the ALBATROSS.

PART II

The Sun now rose upon the right:
Out of the sea came he,
Still hid in mist, and on the left
Went down into the sea.

And the good south wind still blew behind,
But no sweet bird did follow,
Nor any day for food or play
Came to the mariners' hollo!   90

His shipmates
cry out against
the ancient
Mariner, for
killing the bird
of good luck.

And I had done a hellish thing,
And it would work 'em woe:
For all averred, I had killed the bird
That made the breeze to blow.
Ah wretch! said they, the bird to slay,
That made the breeze to blow!

But when the
fog cleared off,
they justify the
same, and thus
make them-
selves accom-
plices in the
crime.

Nor dim nor red, like God's own head,
The glorious Sun uprist:
Then all averred, I had killed the bird
That brought the fog and mist.   100
'Twas right, said they, such birds to slay,
That bring the fog and mist.

The fair breeze
continues; the
ship enters the
Pacific Ocean,
and sails north-
ward, even till
it reaches the
Line.

The fair breeze blew, the white foam flew,
The furrow followed free;
We were the first that ever burst
Into that silent sea.

The ship hath
been suddenly
becalmed.

Down dropt the breeze, the sails dropt down,
'Twas sad as sad could be;
And we did speak only to break
The silence of the sea!   110

All in a hot and copper sky,
The bloody Sun, at noon,
Right up above the mast did stand,
No bigger than the Moon.

Day after day, day after day,
We stuck, nor breath nor motion;

As idle as a painted ship
Upon a painted ocean.

And the Alba-
tross begins to
be avenged.

Water, water, every where,
And all the boards did shrink;   120
Water, water, every where,
Nor any drop to drink.

The very deep did rot: O Christ!
That ever this should be!
Yea, slimy things did crawl with legs
Upon the slimy sea.

About, about, in reel and rout
The death-fires danced at night;
The water, like a witch's oils,
Burnt green, and blue and white.   130

A Spirit had
followed them;
one of the in-
visible inhab-
itants of this
planet, neither
departed souls

And some in dreams assuréd were
Of the Spirit that plagued us so;
Nine fathom deep he had followed us
From the land of mist and snow.

nor angels; concerning whom the learned Jew, Josephus, and the Platonic Constantinopolitan, Michael
Psellus, may be consulted. They are very numerous, and there is no climate or element without one or
more.

And every tongue, through utter drought,
Was withered at the root;
We could not speak, no more than if
We had been choked with soot.

The shipmates,
in their sore
distress, would
fain throw the
whole guilt on
the ancient
Mariner: in

Ah! well a-day! what evil looks
Had I from old and young!   140
Instead of the cross, the Albatross
About my neck was hung.

sign whereof they hang the dead sea-bird round his neck.

PART III

There passed a weary time. Each throat
Was parched, and glazed each eye.
A weary time! a weary time!
How glazed each weary eye,

The ancient
Mariner be-
holdeth a sign
in the element
afar off.

When looking westward, I beheld
A something in the sky.

At first it seemed a little speck,
And then it seemed a mist;   150
It moved and moved, and took at last
A certain shape, I wist.

A speck, a mist, a shape, I wist!
And still it neared and neared:
As if it dodged a water-sprite,
It plunged and tacked and veered.

At its nearer ap-
proach, it
seemeth him to
be a ship; and
at a dear ran-
som he freeth
his speech from
the bonds of
thirst.

With throats unslaked, with black lips baked,
We could nor laugh nor wail;
Through utter drought all dumb we stood!
I bit my arm, I sucked the blood,   160
And cried, A sail! a sail!

With throats unslaked, with black lips baked,
Agape they heard me call:
A flash of joy;
Gramercy! they for joy did grin,
And all at once their breath drew in,
As they were drinking all.

And horror fol-
lows. For can it
be a ship that
comes onward
without wind
or tide?

See! see! (I cried) she tacks no more!
Hither to work us weal;
Without a breeze, without a tide,
She steadies with upright keel!   170

The western wave was all a-flame.
The day was well nigh done!
Almost upon the western wave
Rested the broad bright Sun;
When that strange shape drove suddenly
Betwixt us and the Sun.

It seemeth him
but the skele-
ton of a ship.

And straight the Sun was flecked with bars,
(Heaven's Mother send us grace!)
As if through a dungeon-grate he peered
With broad and burning face.   180

Alas! (thought I, and my heart beat loud)
How fast she nears and nears!
Are those *her* sails that glance in the Sun,
Like restless gossameres?

Are those *her* ribs through which the Sun
Did peer, as through a grate?
And is that Woman all her crew?
Is that a DEATH? and are there two?
Is DEATH that woman's mate?

Her lips were red, *her* looks were free,   190
Her locks were yellow as gold:
Her skin was as white as leprosy,
The Night-mare LIFE-IN-DEATH was she,
Who thicks man's blood with cold.

The naked hulk alongside came,
And the twain were casting dice;
"The game is done! I've won! I've won!"
Quoth she, and whistles thrice.

The Sun's rim dips; the stars rush out:
At one stride comes the dark;   200
With far-heard whisper, o'er the sea,
Off shot the spectre-bark.

We listened and looked sideways up!
Fear at my heart, as at a cup,
My life-blood seemed to sip!
The stars were dim, and thick the night,
The steersman's face by his lamp gleamed white;
From the sails the dew did drip—
Till clomb above the eastern bar
The hornéd Moon, with one bright star   210
Within the nether tip.

One after one, by the star-dogged Moon,
Too quick for groan or sigh,
Each turned his face with a ghastly pang,
And cursed me with his eye.

And its ribs are seen as bars on the face of the setting Sun. The Spectre-Woman and her Death-mate, and no other on board the skeleton ship.

Like vessel, like crew! Death and Life-in-Death have diced for the ship's crew, and she (the latter) winneth the ancient Mariner.

No twilight within the courts of the Sun.

At the rising of the Moon,

One after another,

His shipmates
drop down
dead.

Four times fifty living men,
(And I heard nor sigh nor groan)
With heavy thump, a lifeless lump,
They dropped down one by one.

But Life-in-
Death begins
her work on
the ancient
Mariner.

The souls did from their bodies fly,—   220
They fled to bliss or woe!
And every soul, it passed me by,
Like the whizz of my cross-bow!

PART IV

The Wedding-
Guest feareth
that a Spirit is
talking to him;

"I fear thee, ancient Mariner!
I fear thy skinny hand!
And thou art long, and lank, and brown,
As is the ribbed sea-sand.

I fear thee and thy glittering eye,
And thy skinny hand, so brown."—

But the ancient
Mariner as-
sureth him of
his bodily life,
and pro-
ceedeth to re-
late his horrible
penance.

Fear not, fear not, thou Wedding-Guest!
This body dropt not down.

Alone, alone, all, all alone,
Alone on a wide wide sea!
And never a saint took pity on
My soul in agony.

He despiseth
the creatures of
the calm,

The many men, so beautiful!
And they all dead did lie:
And a thousand thousand slimy things
Lived on; and so did I.

And envieth
that *they*
should live,
and so many
lie dead.

I looked upon the rotting sea,   240
And drew my eyes away;
I looked upon the rotting deck,
And there the dead men lay.

I looked to heaven, and tried to pray;
But or ever a prayer had gusht,
A wicked whisper came, and made
My heart as dry as dust.

I closed my lids, and kept them close,
And the balls like pulses beat;
For the sky and the sea, and the sea and the sky   250
Lay like a load on my weary eye,
And the dead were at my feet.

But the curse
liveth for him
in the eye of
the dead men.

The cold sweat melted from their limbs,
Nor rot nor reek did they:
The look with which they looked on me
Had never passed away.

An orphan's curse would drag to hell
A spirit from on high;
But oh! more horrible than that
Is the curse in a dead man's eye!   260
Seven days, seven nights, I saw that curse,
And yet I could not die.

In his loneli-
ness and
fixedness he
yearneth to-
wards the jour-
neying Moon,
and the stars
that still so-
journ, yet still
move onward;
and every
where the blue
sky belongs to
them, and is
their ap-
pointed rest,
and their native

The moving Moon went up the sky,
And no where did abide:
Softly she was going up,
And a star or two beside—

Her beams bemocked the sultry main,
Like April hoar-frost spread;
But where the ship's huge shadow lay,
The charméd water burnt alway   270
A still and awful red.

country and their own natural homes, which they enter unannounced, as lords that are certainly expected
and yet there is a silent joy at their arrival.

By the light of
the Moon he
beholdeth
God's crea-
tures of the
great calm.

Beyond the shadow of the ship,
I watched the water-snakes:
They moved in tracks of shining white,
And when they reared, the elfish light
Fell off in hoary flakes.

Within the shadow of the ship
I watched their rich attire:
Blue, glossy green, and velvet black,
They coiled and swam; and every track   280
Was a flash of golden fire.

Their beauty
and their hap-
piness.

O happy living things! no tongue
Their beauty might declare:
A spring of love gushed from my heart,

He blesseth
them in his
heart.

And I blessed them unaware:
Sure my kind saint took pity on me,
And I blessed them unaware.

The spell be-
gins to break.

The self-same moment I could pray;
And from my neck so free
The Albatross fell off, and sank   290
Like lead into the sea.

PART V

Oh sleep! it is a gentle thing,
Beloved from pole to pole!
To Mary Queen the praise be given!
She sent the gentle sleep from Heaven,
That slid into my soul.

By grace of the
holy Mother,
the ancient
Mariner is re-
freshed with
rain.

The silly buckets on the deck,
That had so long remained,
I dreamt that they were filled with dew;
And when I awoke, it rained.   300

My lips were wet, my throat was cold,
My garments all were dank;
Sure I had drunken in my dreams,
And still my body drank.

I moved, and could not feel my limbs:
I was so light—almost
I thought that I had died in sleep,
And was a blessèd ghost.

He heareth
sounds and
seeth strange
sights and com-
motions in the
sky and the el-
ement.

And soon I heard a roaring wind:
It did not come anear;   310
But with its sound it shook the sails,
That were so thin and sere.

The upper air burst into life!
And a hundred fire-flags sheen,

To and fro they were hurried about!
And to and fro, and in and out,
The wan stars danced between.

And the coming wind did roar more loud,
And the sails did sigh like sedge;
And the rain poured down from one black cloud;   320
The Moon was at its edge.

The thick black cloud was cleft, and still
The Moon was at its side:
Like waters shot from some high crag,
The lightning fell with never a jag,
A river steep and wide.

The bodies of the ship's crew are inspired [inspirited, *S. L.*] and the ship moves on;

The loud wind never reached the ship,
Yet now the ship moved on!
Beneath the lightning and the Moon
The dead men gave a groan.   330

They groaned, they stirred, they all uprose,
Nor spake, nor moved their eyes;
It had been strange, even in a dream,
To have seen those dead men rise.

The helmsman steered, the ship moved on;
Yet never a breeze up-blew;
The mariners all 'gan work the ropes,
Where they were wont to do;
They raised their limbs like lifeless tools—
We were a ghastly crew.   340

The body of my brother's son
Stood by me, knee to knee:
The body and I pulled at one rope,
But he said nought to me.

But not by the souls of the men, nor by dæmons of earth or middle air, but by a

"I fear thee, ancient Mariner!"
Be calm, thou Wedding-Guest!
'Twas not those souls that fled in pain,
Which to their corses came again,
But a troop of spirits blest:

For when it dawned—they dropped their arms,   350
And clustered round the mast;
Sweet sounds rose slowly through their mouths,
And from their bodies passed.

Around, around, flew each sweet sound,
Then darted to the Sun;
Slowly the sounds came back again,
Now mixed, now one by one.

Sometimes a-dropping from the sky
I heard the sky-lark sing;
Sometimes all little birds that are,   360
How they seemed to fill the sea and air
With their sweet jargoning!

And now 'twas like all instruments,
Now like a lonely flute;
And now it is an angel's song,
That makes the heavens be mute.

It ceased; yet still the sails made on
A pleasant noise till noon,
A noise like of a hidden brook
In the leafy month of June,   370
That to the sleeping woods all night
Singeth a quiet tune.

Till noon we quietly sailed on,
Yet never a breeze did breathe:
Slowly and smoothly went the ship,
Moved onward from beneath.

Under the keel nine fathom deep,
From the land of mist and snow,
The spirit slid: and it was he
That made the ship to go.   380
The sails at noon left off their tune,
And the ship stood still also.

The Sun, right up above the mast,
Had fixed her to the ocean:
But in a minute she 'gan stir,

With a short uneasy motion—
Backwards and forwards half her length
With a short uneasy motion.

Then like a pawing horse let go,
She made a sudden bound: 390
It flung the blood into my head,
And I fell down in a swound.

How long in that same fit I lay,
I have not to declare;
But ere my living life returned,
I heard and in my soul discerned
Two voices in the air.

The Polar Spirit's fellow-dæmons, the invisible inhabitants of the element, take part in his wrong; and two of them relate, one to the other, that penance long and heavy for the ancient Mariner hath been accorded to the Polar Spirit, who returneth southward.

"Is it he?" quoth one, "Is this the man?
By him who died on cross,
With his cruel bow he laid full low   400
The harmless Albatross.

The spirit who bideth by himself
In the land of mist and snow,
He loved the bird that loved the man
Who shot him with his bow."

The other was a softer voice,
As soft as honey-dew:
Quoth he, "The man hath penance done,
And penance more will do."

PART VI
First Voice

"But tell me, tell me! speak again,   410
Thy soft response renewing—
What makes that ship drive on so fast?
What is the ocean doing?"

Second Voice

"Still as a slave before his lord,
The ocean hath no blast;
His great bright eye most silently
Up to the Moon is cast—

If he may know which way to go;
For she guides him smooth or grim.
See, brother, see! how graciously   420
She looketh down on him."

First Voice

"But why drives on that ship so fast,
Without or wave or wind?"

Second Voice

"The air is cut away before,
And closes from behind.

Fly, brother, fly! more high, more high!
Or we shall be belated:
For slow and slow that ship will go,
When the Mariner's trance is abated."

I woke, and we were sailing on   430
As in a gentle weather:
'Twas night, calm night, the moon was high;
The dead men stood together.

All stood together on the deck,
For a charnel-dungeon fitter:
All fixed on me their stony eyes,
That in the Moon did glitter.

The pang, the curse, with which they died,
Had never passed away:
I could not draw my eyes from theirs,   440
Nor turn them up to pray.

And now this spell was snapt: once more
I viewed the ocean green,
And looked far forth, yet little saw
Of what had else been seen—

Like one, that on a lonesome road
Doth walk in fear and dread,
And having once turned round walks on,
And turns no more his head;

Marginal glosses:

The Mariner hath been cast into a trance; for the angelic power causeth the vessel to drive northward faster than human life could endure.

The supernatural motion is retarded; the Mariner awakes, and his penance begins anew.

The curse is finally expiated.

Because he knows, a frightful fiend   450
Doth close behind him tread.

But soon there breathed a wind on me,
Nor sound nor motion made:
Its path was not upon the sea,
In ripple or in shade.

It raised my hair, it fanned my cheek
Like a meadow-gale of spring—
It mingled strangely with my fears,
Yet it felt like a welcoming.

Swiftly, swiftly flew the ship,   460
Yet she sailed softly too:
Sweetly, sweetly blew the breeze—
On me alone it blew.

And the
ancient
Mariner
beholdeth his
native country.

Oh! dream of joy! is this indeed
The light-house top I see?
Is this the hill? is this the kirk?
Is this mine own countree?

We drifted o'er the harbour-bar,
And I with sobs did pray—
O let me be awake, my God!   470
Or let me sleep alway.

The harbour-bay was clear as glass,
So smoothly it was strewn!
And on the bay the moonlight lay,
And the shadow of the Moon.

The rock shone bright, the kirk no less,
That stands above the rock:
The moonlight steeped in silentness
The steady weathercock.

And the bay was white with silent light,   480
Till rising from the same,

The angelic
spirits leave the
dead bodies,

Full many shapes, that shadows were,
In crimson colours came.

And appear in
their own
forms of light.

A little distance from the prow
Those crimson shadows were:
I turned my eyes upon the deck—
Oh, Christ! what saw I there!

Each corse lay flat, lifeless and flat,
And, by the holy rood!
A man all light, a seraph-man,   490
On every corse there stood.

This seraph-band, each waved his hand:
It was a heavenly sight!
They stood as signals to the land,
Each one a lovely light;

This seraph-band, each waved his hand,
No voice did they impart—
No voice; but oh! the silence sank
Like music on my heart.

But soon I heard the dash of oars,   500
I heard the Pilot's cheer;
My head was turned perforce away
And I saw a boat appear.

The Pilot and the Pilot's boy,
I heard them coming fast:
Dear Lord in Heaven! it was a joy
The dead men could not blast.

I saw a third—I heard his voice:
It is the Hermit good!
He singeth loud his godly hymns   510
That he makes in the wood.
He'll shrieve my soul, he'll wash away
The Albatross's blood.

PART VII

The Hermit of
the Wood,

This Hermit good lives in that wood
Which slopes down to the sea.
How loudly his sweet voice he rears!

He loves to talk with marineres
That come from a far countree.

He kneels at morn, and noon, and eve—
He hath a cushion plump: 520
It is the moss that wholly hides
The rotted old oak-stump.

The skiff-boat neared: I heard them talk,
"Why, this is strange, I trow!
Where are those lights so many and fair,
That signal made but now?"

Approacheth
the ship with
wonder.
"Strange, by my faith!" the Hermit said—
"And they answered not our cheer!
The planks looked warped! and see those sails,
How thin they are and sere!   530
I never saw aught like to them,
Unless perchance it were

Brown skeletons of leaves that lag
My forest-brook along;
When the ivy-tod is heavy with snow,
And the owlet whoops to the wolf below,
That eats the she-wolf's young."

"Dear Lord! it hath a fiendish look—
(The Pilot made reply)
I am a-feared"—"Push on, push on!"   540
Said the Hermit cheerily.

The boat came closer to the ship,
But I nor spake nor stirred;
The boat came close beneath the ship,
And straight a sound was heard.

The ship sud-
denly sinketh.
Under the water it rumbled on,
Still louder and more dread:
It reached the ship, it split the bay;
The ship went down like lead.

The ancient
Mariner is
Stunned by that loud and dreadful sound,   550
Which sky and ocean smote,

saved in the Pi-
lot's boat.

Like one that hath been seven days drowned
My body lay afloat;
But swift as dreams, myself I found
Within the Pilot's boat.

Upon the whirl, where sank the ship,
The boat spun round and round;
And all was still, save that the hill
Was telling of the sound.

I moved my lips—the Pilot shrieked   560
And fell down in a fit;
The holy Hermit raised his eyes,
And prayed where he did sit.

I took the oars: the Pilot's boy,
Who now doth crazy go,
Laughed loud and long, and all the while
His eyes went to and fro.
"Ha! ha!" quoth he, "full plain I see,
The Devil knows how to row."

And now, all in my own countree,   570
I stood on the firm land!
The Hermit stepped forth from the boat,
And scarcely he could stand.

The ancient
Mariner ear-
nestly en-
treateth the
Hermit to
shrieve him;
and the pen-
ance of life falls
on him.

"O shrieve me, shrieve me, holy man!"
The Hermit crossed his brow.
"Say quick," quoth he, "I bid thee say—
What manner of man art thou?"

Forthwith this frame of mine was wrenched
With a woful agony,
Which forced me to begin my tale;   580
And then it left me free.

And ever and
anon through
out his future
life an agony
constraineth
him to travel
from land to
land;

Since then, at an uncertain hour,
That agony returns:
And till my ghastly tale is told,
This heart within me burns.

I pass, like night, from land to land;
I have strange power of speech;

That moment that his face I see,
I know the man that must hear me:
To him my tale I teach.   590

What loud uproar bursts from that door!
The wedding-guests are there:
But in the garden-bower the bride
And bride-maids singing are:
And hark the little vesper bell,
Which biddeth me to prayer!

O Wedding-Guest! this soul hath been
Alone on a wide wide sea:
So lonely 'twas, that God himself
Scarce seeméd there to be.   600

O sweeter than the marriage-feast,
'Tis sweeter far to me,
To walk together to the kirk
With a goodly company!—

To walk together to the kirk,
And all together pray,
While each to his great Father bends,
Old men, and babes, and loving friends
And youths and maidens gay!

And to teach,   Farewell, farewell! but this I tell   610
by his own ex-   To thee, thou Wedding-Guest!
ample, love   He prayeth well, who loveth well
and reverence   Both man and bird and beast.
to all things
that God made
and loveth.

He prayeth best, who loveth best
All things both great and small;
For the dear God who loveth us,
He made and loveth all.

The Mariner, whose eye is bright,
Whose beard with age is hoar,
Is gone: and now the Wedding-Guest   620
Turned from the bridegroom's door.

He went like one that hath been stunned,
And is of sense forlorn:
A sadder and a wiser man,
He rose the morrow morn.

KUBLA KHAN

In Xanadu did Kubla Khan
A stately pleasure-dome decree:
Where Alph, the sacred river, ran
Through caverns measureless to man
   Down to a sunless sea.
So twice five miles of fertile ground
With walls and towers were girdled round:
And there were gardens bright with sinuous rills,
Where blossomed many an incense-bearing tree;
And here were forests ancient as the hills,   10
Enfolding sunny spots of greenery.

But oh! that deep romantic chasm which slanted
Down the green hill athwart a cedarn cover!
A savage place! as holy and enchanted
As e'er beneath a waning moon was haunted
By woman wailing for her demon-lover!
   And from this chasm, with ceaseless turmoil seething,
As if this earth in fast thick pants were breathing,
A mighty fountain momently was forced:
Amid whose swift half-intermitted burst   20
Huge fragments vaulted like rebounding hail,
Or chaffy grain beneath the thresher's flail:
And 'mid these dancing rocks at once and ever
It flung up momently the sacred river.
Five miles meandering with a mazy motion
Through wood and dale the sacred river ran,
Then reached the caverns measureless to man,
And sank in tumult to a lifeless ocean:
And 'mid this tumult Kubla heard from far
Ancestral voices prophesying war!   30
   The shadow of the dome of pleasure
   Floated midway on the waves;
   Where was heard the mingled measure

From the fountain and the caves.
It was a miracle of rare device,
A sunny pleasure-dome with caves of ice!

   A damsel with a dulcimer
   In a vision once I saw:
   It was an Abyssinian maid,
   And on her dulcimer she played,   40
   Singing of Mount Abora.
   Could I revive within me
   Her symphony and song,
   To such a deep delight 'twould win me,
That with music loud and long,
I would build that dome in air,
That sunny dome! those caves of ice!
And all who heard should see them there,
And all should cry, Beware! Beware!
His flashing eyes, his floating hair!   50
Weave a circle round him thrice,
And close your eyes with holy dread,
For he on honey-dew hath fed,
And drunk the milk of Paradise.

FROST AT MIDNIGHT

The Frost performs its secret ministry,
Unhelped by any wind. The owlet's cry
Came loud—and hark, again! loud as before.
The inmates of my cottage, all at rest,
Have left me to that solitude, which suits
Abstruser musings: save that at my side
My cradled infant slumbers peacefully.
'Tis calm indeed! so calm, that it disturbs
And vexes meditation with its strange
And extreme silentness. Sea, hill, and wood,   10
This populous village! Sea; and hill, and wood,
With all the numberless goings-on of life,
Inaudible as dreams! the thin blue flame
Lies on my low-burnt fire, and quivers not;
Only that film, which fluttered on the grate,
Still flutters there, the sole unquiet thing.

Methinks, its motion in this hush of nature
Gives it dim sympathies with me who live,
Making it a companionable form,
Whose puny flaps and freaks the idling Spirit   20
By its own moods interprets, every where
Echo or mirror seeking of itself,
And makes a toy of Thought.

                       But O! how oft,
How oft, at school, with most believing mind,
Presageful, have I gazed upon the bars,
To watch that fluttering *stranger!* and as oft
With unclosed lids, already had I dreamt
Of my sweet birth-place, and the old church-tower,
Whose bells, the poor man's only music, rang
From morn to evening, all the hot Fair-day,   30
So sweetly, that they stirred and haunted me
With a wild pleasure, falling on mine ear
Most like articulate sounds of things to come!
So gazed I, till the soothing things, I dreamt,
Lulled me to sleep, and sleep prolonged my dreams!
And so I brooded all the following morn,
Awed by the stern preceptor's face, mine eye
Fixed with mock study on my swimming book:
Save if the door half opened, and I snatched
A hasty glance, and still my heart leaped up,   40
For still I hoped to see the *stranger's* face,
Townsman, or aunt, or sister more beloved,
My play-mate when we both were clothed alike!

   Dear Babe, that sleepest cradled by my side,
Whose gentle breathings, heard in this deep calm,
Fill up the interspersèd vacancies
And momentary pauses of the thought!
My babe so beautiful! it thrills my heart
With tender gladness, thus to look at thee,
And think that thou shalt learn far other lore,   50
And in far other scenes! For I was reared
In the great city, pent 'mid cloisters dim,
And saw nought lovely but the sky and stars.
But *thou*, my babe! shalt wander like a breeze
By lakes and sandy shores, beneath the crags
Of ancient mountain, and beneath the clouds,

Which image in their bulk both lakes and shores
And mountain crags: so shalt thou see and hear
The lovely shapes and sounds intelligible
Of that eternal language, which thy God   60
Utters, who from eternity doth teach
Himself in all, and all things in himself.
Great universal Teacher! he shall mould
Thy spirit, and by giving make it ask.

   Therefore all seasons shall be sweet to thee,
Whether the summer clothe the general earth
With greenness, or the redbreast sit and sing
Betwixt the tufts of snow on the bare branch
Of mossy apple-tree, while the nigh thatch
Smokes in the sun-thaw; whether the eave-drops fall   70
Heard only in the trances of the blast,
Or if the secret ministry of frost
Shall hang them up in silent icicles,
Quietly shining to the quiet Moon.

Robert Southey

(1 7 7 4 – 1 8 4 3)

Brother-in-law of Coleridge and frequent butt of Byron's satire, Southey was a "man of letters," prolific in verse and prose, biographer of Nelson and Wesley, appointed Poet Laureate in 1813. Born in Bristol, expelled from Westminster School but graduated from Oxford, he planned with Coleridge a Utopian community ("Pantisocracy") and in 1803 settled in Wordsworth country, at Keswick, where he was foster parent to Coleridge's children. Although later a Tory patriot, in 1798 he could treat Marlborough's victory of 1704 as parallel in futility to the war then current against revolutionary France.

THE BATTLE OF
BLENHEIM

It was a summer evening,
    Old Kaspar's work was done,
And he before his cottage door
    Was sitting in the sun,
And by him sported on the green
His little grandchild Wilhelmine.

She saw her brother Peterkin
    Roll something large and round,
Which he beside the rivulet
    In playing there had found;   10
He came to ask what he had found,
That was so large, and smooth, and round.

Old Kaspar took it from the boy,
    Who stood expectant by;
And then the old man shook his head,
    And with a natural sigh,
" 'Tis some poor fellow's skull, said he,
"Who fell in the great victory."

"I find them in the garden,
 For there's many here about,
And often when I go to plough,
 The ploughshare turns them out;
For many thousand men," said he,
"Were slain in the great victory."   20

"Now tell us what 'twas all about,"
 Young Peterkin, he cries,
And little Wilhelmine looks up
 With wonder-waiting eyes;
"Now tell us all about the war,
And what they kill'd each other for."   30

"It was the English," Kaspar cried,
 "That put the French to rout;
But what they kill'd each other for,
 I could not well make out;
But every body said," quoth he,
"That 'twas a famous victory.

"My father lived at Blenheim then,
 Yon little stream hard by;
They burnt his dwelling to the ground
 And he was forced to fly;   40
So with his wife and child he fled,
Nor had he where to rest his head.

"With fire and sword the country round
 Was wasted far and wide,
And many a childing mother then,
 And new-born baby died.
But things like that, you know, must be
At every famous victory.

"They say it was a shocking sight
 After the field was won,   50
For many thousand bodies here
 Lay rotting in the sun;
But things like that, you know, must be
After a famous victory.

Great praise the Duke of Marlbro' won,
   And our good Prince Eugene."
"Why 'twas a very wicked thing!"
   Said little Wilhelmine.
"Nay—nay—my little girl," quoth he,
"It was a famous victory.   60

"And every body praised the Duke
   Who this great fight did win."
"But what good came of it at last?"
   Quoth little Peterkin.
"Why that I cannot tell," said he,
"But 'twas a famous victory."

Walter Savage Landor

(1 7 7 5 – 1 8 6 4)

An apocryphal anecdote captures Landor's temperament: at his residence in Fiesole, after shoving a visitor from an upstairs window for lack of chivalry, he cried, "O God, I forgot the flower-bed!" Born in Warwick, educated at Rugby and Oxford, separated from his wife in 1835, he lived well on inherited money. Often a long-winded Hellenist, he did learn understatement from Greek literature, as in his replacing with "night" the expected "life" in a "night of memories."

ROSE AYLMER

Ah what avails the sceptred race!
   Ah what the form divine!
What every virtue, every grace!
   Rose Aylmer, all were thine.
Rose Aylmer, whom these wakeful eyes
   May weep, but never see,
A night of memories and of sighs
   I consecrate to thee.

Thomas Campbell

(1777–1844)

A native of Glasgow who became a literary lion in London, immensely popular not only for "Hohenlinden" and "Ye Mariners of England" but also for ballads and long narrative poems—and immortal for the phrase "distance lends enchantment" in *The Pleasures of Memory*—Campbell's popularity has faded over time. By chance not far from the village in Bavaria where the French army ("Frank") defeated the Austrian ("Hun") in December 1800, he devised for "Hohenlinden" a monosyllabic rhythm to catch the crackle and thud of battle.

HOHENLINDEN

On Linden, when the sun was low,
All bloodless lay th' untrodden snow,
And dark as winter was the flow
Of Iser, rolling rapidly.

But Linden saw another sight,
When the drum beat at dead of night,
Commanding fires of death to light
The darkness of her scenery.

By torch and trumpet fast array'd,
Each horseman drew his battle-blade,   10
And furious every charger neigh'd,
To join the dreadful revelry.

Then shook the hills with thunder riven,
Then rush'd the steed to battle driven,
And louder than the bolts of heaven,
Far flash'd the red artillery.

But redder yet that light shall glow
On Linden's hills of stainèd snow,
And bloodier yet the torrent flow
Of Iser, rolling rapidly.   20

'Tis morn; but scarce yon level sun
Can pierce the war-clouds, rolling dun,
Where furious Frank and fiery Hun,
Shout in their sulphurous canopy.

The combat deepens. On, ye brave,
Who rush to glory, or the grave!
Wave, Munich! all thy banners wave,
And charge with all thy chivalry!

Few, few, shall part where many meet!
The snow shall be their winding-sheet,   30
And every turf beneath their feet
Shall be a soldier's sepulchre.

Thomas Moore

(1 7 7 9 – 1 8 5 2)

Moore's lament for ancient days when the kings of Ireland ruled from the hill of Tara, near Dublin, is one of a dozen or so songs from his *Irish Melodies* (1808–1834) that have kept him without a close rival as the national bard. Son of a Dublin grocer, he attended Trinity College, Dublin, and studied law in London. A partisan satirist in verse—and a tenor—he sang in the houses of Whig noblemen and wrote the official biography of his friend Byron.

THE HARP THAT ONCE THROUGH TARA'S HALLS

The harp that once through Tara's halls
　　The soul of music shed,
Now hangs as mute on Tara's walls
　　As if that soul were fled.
So sleeps the pride of former days,
　　So glory's thrill is o'er,
And hearts that once beat high for praise
　　Now feel that pulse no more!

No more to chiefs and ladies bright
　　The harp of Tara swells;
The chord alone that breaks at night
　　Its tale of ruin tells.
Thus Freedom now so seldom wakes,
　　The only throb she gives
Is when some heart indignant breaks,
　　To show that still she lives.

Charlotte Dacre

(*1 7 8 2 – 1 8 4 1 ?*)

Distinguished by omission from the *Dictionary of National Biography*, Dacre has been known to specialists as the Della Cruscan "Rosa Matilda" and as author of *Zafloya, or The Moor* and other Gothic romances that reached many readers—and influenced lurid works of the young Percy Shelley. She was the daughter of the notorious Jewish money-lender and writer Jacob Rey and his first wife, Deborah. "The Kiss" appeared in her *Hours of Solitude* (1805).

THE KISS

The greatest bliss
Is in a kiss—
A kiss of love refin'd,
When springs the soul
Without controul,
And blends the bliss with mind.

For if desire
Alone inspire,
The kiss not *me* can charm;
The eye must beam   10
With *chasten'd* gleam
That would *my* soul disarm.

What fond delight
Does love excite
When sentiment takes part!
The falt'ring sigh,
Voluptuous eye,
And palpitating heart.

Ye fleet too fast—
Sweet moments, last   20

A little longer mine!
  Like Heaven's bow
  Ye fade—ye go;
Too tremulously fine!

Jane Taylor

(1 7 8 3 – 1 8 2 4)

Taylor's poem, of first magnitude among the myriad poems on stars, appeared in *Rhymes for the Nursery* (1806), one of three often-reprinted volumes of verse by the sisters Ann and Jane. Its supremacy is not diminished by Lewis Carroll's parody, "Twinkle, twinkle, little bat!" Born in London, the Taylors assisted their father, a skilled engraver, and imbibed in Suffolk and Essex his piety as a Nonconformist minister. Jane also mastered light satire for adults.

THE STAR

Twinkle, twinkle, little star,
How I wonder what you are!
Up above the world so high,
Like a diamond in the sky.

When the blazing sun is gone,
When he nothing shines upon,
Then you show your little light,
Twinkle, twinkle, all the night.

James Henry Leigh Hunt

(1 7 8 4 – 1 8 5 9)

Notoriously sentenced in 1813 to imprisonment for a libel on the prince regent in the weekly *Examiner*, the first of several periodicals he edited, Leigh Hunt has remained known less as radical, essayist, and poet than as friend and promoter of Keats and original for at least the sunny side of Skimpole in Dickens's *Bleak House*. But his neat "Rondeau" (1838) would probably have lived even if the original Jenny had not been Jane Welsh, wife of Thomas Carlyle. Hunt borrows from the strict French rondeau form only the repetition of the opening words in a short final line.

RONDEAU

Jenny kissed me when we met,
  Jumping from the chair she sat in;
Time, you thief, who love to get
  Sweets into your list, put that in:

Say I'm weary, say I'm sad,
  Say that health and wealth have missed me,
Say I'm growing old, but add,
    Jenny kissed me.

Thomas Love Peacock

(1785–1866)

Peacock's satiric convivial novels, which have outlived his longer poems and poignant lyrics, include such high-spirited verses as this hymn of victory (in Peacock's words, "sum and substance of all . . . military glory") sung by an ancient Welsh king in *The Misfortunes of Elphin* (1829). An official in the East India Company, Peacock was a friend of Shelley, whom he cheerfully satirized in *Nightmare Abbey*; his "Four Ages of Poetry" elicited a rebuttal in Shelley's *A Defence of Poetry*.

THE WAR SONG OF DINAS VAWR

The mountain sheep are sweeter,
But the valley sheep are fatter;
We therefore deemed it meeter
To carry off the latter.
We made an expedition;
We met a host, and quelled it;
We forced a strong position,
And killed the men who held it.

On Dyfed's richest valley,
Where herds of kine were brousing,   10
We made a mighty sally,
To furnish our carousing.
Fierce warriors rushed to meet us;
We met them, and o'erthrew them:
They struggled hard to beat us;
But we conquered them, and slew them.

As we drove our prize at leisure,
The king marched forth to catch us:
His rage surpassed all measure,
But his people could not match us.   20

He fled to his hall-pillars;
And, ere our force we led off,
Some sacked his house and cellars,
While others cut his head off.

We there, in strife bewild'ring,
Spilt blood enough to swim in:
We orphaned many children,
And widowed many women.
The eagles and the ravens
We glutted with our foemen;   30
The heroes and the cravens,
The spearmen and the bowmen.

We brought away from battle,
And much their land bemoaned them,
Two thousand head of cattle,
And the head of him who owned them:
Ednyfed, king of Dyfed,
His head was borne before us;
His wine and beasts supplied our feasts,
And his overthrow, our chorus.   40

George Gordon Noel Byron, Sixth Baron Byron

(1 7 8 8 – 1 8 2 4)

The excitements of Byron's career are best followed through his poems. Born (in London) to an impoverished naval captain and a savagely determined Scottish mother, he inherited in 1798 a baronage and its manor, Newstead Abbey. With only his club-foot, beauty, genius, wit, and carefree seductions as constants, he went through Harrow and Cambridge, on into the House of Lords, and into London society. The explosive popularity of *Childe Harold's Pilgrimage* (1812–1818) was followed by travels, marriage to his friend Lady Melbourne's prim niece (who denounced him for incest with his half-sister or for homosexuality, or both, and took their daughter, Ada). Then ensued debauchery in Venice, friendship with Shelley and collaboration with Hunt, liaison with Countess Guiccioli of Ravenna, and death at Missolonghi in the cause of Greek independence from Turkey.

Those who complain that Byron fell short of the intensest spirituality achieved by others must grant his tremendous poetic range—from controlled understatement in "She walks in beauty" through the casually resigned "So, we'll go no more a-roving" and the facile celebration of Sennacherib's failure to destroy Jerusalem (in Byron's mostly unsacred *Hebrew Melodies*, 1815, based on Second Kings 18–19) to the somber, last-man apocalypse of "Darkness." Byron's metrical range is demonstrated in the descriptive blank verse of "Darkness," the loping anapests of "Sennacherib," the self-enclosed Spenserian stanzas of *Childe Harold*, and the clenching final couplet in each ottava rima stanza of *Don Juan*.

SHE WALKS IN BEAUTY

> She walks in beauty, like the night
>   Of cloudless climes and starry skies;
> And all that's best of dark and bright
>   Meet in her aspect and her eyes:
> Thus mellow'd to that tender light
>   Which heaven to gaudy day denies.
>
> One shade the more, one ray the less,
>   Had half impair'd the nameless grace

Which waves in every raven tress,
    Or softly lightens o'er her face;   10
Where thoughts serenely sweet express
    How pure, how dear their dwelling-place.

And on that cheek, and o'er that brow,
    So soft, so calm, yet eloquent,
The smiles that win, the tints that glow,
    But tell of days in goodness spent,
A mind at peace with all below,
    A heart whose love is innocent!

DARKNESS

I had a dream, which was not all a dream.
The bright sun was extinguish'd, and the stars
Did wander darkling in the eternal space,
Rayless, and pathless, and the icy earth
Swung blind and blackening in the moonless air;
Morn came and went—and came, and brought no day,
And men forgot their passions in the dread
Of this their desolation; and all hearts
Were chill'd into a selfish prayer for light:
And they did live by watchfires—and the thrones,   10
The palaces of crowned kings—the huts,
The habitations of all things which dwell,
Were burnt for beacons; cities were consumed,
And men were gather'd round their blazing homes
To look once more into each other's face;
Happy were those who dwelt within the eye
Of the volcanos, and their mountain-torch:
A fearful hope was all the world contain'd;
Forests were set on fire—but hour by hour
They fell and faded—and the crackling trunks   20
Extinguish'd with a crash—and all was black.
The brows of men by the despairing light
Wore an unearthly aspect, as by fits
The flashes fell upon them; some lay down
And hid their eyes and wept; and some did rest
Their chins upon their clenched hands, and smiled;
And others hurried to and fro, and fed

Their funeral piles with fuel, and look'd up
With mad disquietude on the dull sky,
The pall of a past world; and then again   30
With curses cast them down upon the dust,
And gnash'd their teeth and howl'd: the wild birds shriek'd
And, terrified, did flutter on the ground,
And flap their useless wings; the wildest brutes
Came tame and tremulous; and vipers crawl'd
And twined themselves among the multitude,
Hissing, but stingless—they were slain for food.
And War, which for a moment was no more,
Did glut himself again:—a meal was bought
With blood, and each sate sullenly apart   40
Gorging himself in gloom: no love was left;
All earth was but one thought—and that was death
Immediate and inglorious; and the pang
Of famine fed upon all entrails—men
Died, and their bones were tombless as their flesh;
The meagre by the meagre were devour'd,
Even dogs assail'd their masters, all save one,
And he was faithful to a corse, and kept
The birds and beasts and famish'd men at bay,
Till hunger clung them, or the dropping dead   50
Lured their lank jaws; himself sought out no food,
But with a piteous and perpetual moan,
And a quick desolate cry, licking the hand
Which answer'd not with a caress—he died.
The crowd was famish'd by degrees; but two
Of an enormous city did survive,
And they were enemies: they met beside
The dying embers of an altar-place
Where had been heap'd a mass of holy things
For an unholy usage; they raked up,   60
And shivering scraped with their cold skeleton hands
The feeble ashes, and their feeble breath
Blew for a little life, and made a flame
Which was a mockery; then they lifted up
Their eyes as it grew lighter, and beheld
Each other's aspects—saw, and shriek'd, and died—
Even of their mutual hideousness they died,
Unknowing who he was upon whose brow
Famine had written Fiend. The world was void,
The populous and the powerful was a lump,   70

Seasonless, herbless, treeless, manless, lifeless,
A lump of death—a chaos of hard clay.
The rivers, lakes, and ocean all stood still,
And nothing stirr'd within their silent depths;
Ships sailorless lay rotting on the sea,
And their masts fell down piecemeal: as they dropp'd
They slept on the abyss without a surge—
The waves were dead; the tides were in their grave,
The moon, their mistress, had expired before;
The winds were wither'd in the stagnant air,   80
And the clouds perish'd; Darkness had no need
Of aid from them—She was the Universe.

SO, WE'LL GO NO
MORE A-ROVING

So, we'll go no more a-roving
    So late into the night,
Though the heart be still as loving,
    And the moon be still as bright.

For the sword outwears its sheath,
    And the soul wears out the breast,
And the heart must pause to breathe,
    And love itself have rest.

Though the night was made for loving,
    And the day returns too soon,   10
Yet we'll go no more a-roving
    By the light of the moon.

THE DESTRUCTION
OF SENNACHERIB

The Assyrian came down like the wolf on the fold,
And his cohorts were gleaming in purple and gold;

And the sheen of their spears was like stars on the sea,
When the blue wave rolls nightly on deep Galilee.

Like the leaves of the forest when Summer is green,
That host with their banners at sunset were seen:
Like the leaves of the forest when Autumn hath blown,
That host on the morrow lay wither'd and strown.

For the Angel of Death spread his wings on the blast,
And breathed in the face of the foe as he pass'd;   10
And the eyes of the sleepers wax'd deadly and chill,
And their hearts but once heaved, and for ever grew still!

And there lay the steed with his nostril all wide,
But through it there roll'd not the breath of his pride;
And the foam of his gasping lay white on the turf,
And cold as the spray of the rock-beating surf.

And there lay the rider distorted and pale,
With the dew on his brow, and the rust on his mail:
And the tents were all silent, the banners alone,
The lances unlifted, the trumpet unblown.   20

And the widows of Ashur are loud in their wail,
And the idols are broke in the temple of Baal;
And the might of the Gentile, unsmote by the sword,
Hath melted like snow in the glance of the Lord!

From CHILDE HAROLD'S PILGRIMAGE

From CANTO III

I

Is thy face like thy mother's, my fair child!
Ada! sole daughter of my house and heart?
When last I saw thy young blue eyes they smiled,
And then we parted,—not as now we part,
But with a hope,—Awaking with a start,
The waters heave around me; and on high
The winds lift up their voices: I depart,
Whither I know not; but the hour's gone by,
When Albion's lessening shores could grieve or glad mine eye.

II

Once more upon the waters! yet once more!   10
And the waves bound beneath me as a steed
That knows his rider. Welcome to their roar!
Swift be their guidance, wheresoe'er it lead!
Though the strain'd mast should quiver as a reed,
And the rent canvas fluttering strew the gale,
Still must I on; for I am as a weed,
Flung from the rock, on Ocean's foam to sail
Where'er the surge may sweep, the tempest's breath prevail.

III

In my youth's summer I did sing of One,
The wandering outlaw of his own dark mind;   20
Again I seize the theme, then but begun,
And bear it with me, as the rushing wind
Bears the cloud onwards: in that Tale I find
The furrows of long thought, and dried-up tears,
Which, ebbing, leave a sterile track behind,
O'er which all heavily the journeying years
Plod the last sands of life,—where not a flower appears.

IV

Since my young days of passion—joy, or pain,
Perchance my heart and harp have lost a string,
And both may jar: it may be, that in vain   30
I would essay as I have sung to sing.
Yet, though a dreary strain, to this I cling;
So that it wean me from the weary dream
Of selfish grief or gladness—so it fling
Forgetfulness around me—it shall seem
To me, though to none else, a not ungrateful theme.

V

He, who grown aged in this world of woe,
In deeds, not years, piercing the depths of life,
So that no wonder waits him; nor below
Can love or sorrow, fame, ambition, strife,   40

Cut to his heart again with the keen knife
Of silent, sharp endurance: he can tell
Why thought seeks refuge in lone caves, yet rife
With airy images, and shapes which dwell
Still unimpair'd, though old, in the soul's haunted cell.

V I

'Tis to create, and in creating live
A being more intense, that we endow
With form our fancy, gaining as we give
The life we image, even as I do now.
What am I? Nothing: but not so art thou,   50
Soul of my thought! with whom I traverse earth,
Invisible but gazing, as I glow
Mix'd with thy spirit, blended with thy birth,
And feeling still with thee in my crush'd feelings' dearth.

V I I

Yet must I think less wildly:—I *have* thought
Too long and darkly, till my brain became,
In its own eddy boiling and o'er-wrought,
A whirling gulf of phantasy and flame:
And thus, untaught in youth my heart to tame,
My springs of life were poison'd. 'Tis too late!   60
Yet am I changed; though still enough the same
In strength to bear what time cannot abate,
And feed on bitter fruits without accusing Fate.

V I I I

Something too much of this:—but now 'tis past,
And the spell closes with its silent seal.
Long absent Harold re-appears at last;
He of the breast which fain no more would feel,
Wrung with the wounds which kill not, but ne'er heal;
Yet Time, who changes all, had alter'd him
In soul and aspect as in age: years steal   70
Fire from the mind as vigour from the limb;
And life's enchanted cup but sparkles near the brim.

IX

His had been quaff'd too quickly, and he found
The dregs were wormwood; but he fill'd again,
And from a purer fount, on holier ground,
And deem'd its spring perpetual; but in vain!
Still round him clung invisibly a chain
Which gall'd for ever, fettering though unseen,
And heavy though it clank'd not; worn with pain,
Which pined although it spoke not, and grew keen,   80
Entering with every step he took through many a scene.

X

Secure in guarded coldness, he had mix'd
Again in fancied safety with his kind,
And deem'd his spirit now so firmly fix'd
And sheath'd with an invulnerable mind,
That, if no joy, no sorrow lurk'd behind;
And he, as one, might 'midst the many stand
Unheeded, searching through the crowd to find
Fit speculation; such as in strange land   90
He found in wonder-works of God and Nature's hand.

XI

But who can view the ripen'd rose, nor seek
To wear it? who can curiously behold
The smoothness and the sheen of beauty's cheek,
Nor feel the heart can never all grow old?
Who can contemplate Fame through clouds unfold
The star which rises o'er her steep, nor climb?
Harold, once more within the vortex, roll'd
On with the giddy circle, chasing Time,
Yet with a nobler aim than in his youth's fond prime.

XII

But soon he knew himself the most unfit   100
Of men to herd with Man; with whom he held
Little in common; untaught to submit
His thoughts to others, though his soul was quell'd

In youth by his own thoughts; still uncompell'd,
He would not yield dominion of his mind
To spirits against whom his own rebell'd;
Proud though in desolation; which could find
A life within itself, to breathe without mankind.

XIII

Where rose the mountains, there to him were friends;
Where roll'd the ocean, thereon was his home;   110
Where a blue sky, and glowing clime, extends,
He had the passion and the power to roam;
The desert, forest, cavern, breaker's foam,
Were unto him companionship; they spake
A mutual language, clearer than the tome
Of his land's tongue, which he would oft forsake
For Nature's pages glass'd by sunbeams on the lake.

XIV

Like the Chaldean, he could watch the stars,
Till he had peopled them with beings bright
As their own beams; and earth, and earthborn jars,   120
And human frailties, were forgotten quite:
Could he have kept his spirit to that flight
He had been happy; but this clay will sink
Its spark immortal, envying it the light
To which it mounts, as if to break the link
That keeps us from yon heaven which woos us to its brink.

XV

But in Man's dwellings he became a thing
Restless and worn, and stern and wearisome,
Droop'd as a wild-born falcon with clipt wing,
To whom the boundless air alone were home: 130
Then came his fit again, which to o'ercome,
As eagerly the barr'd-up bird will beat
His breast and beak against his wiry dome
Till the blood tinge his plumage, so the heat
Of his impeded soul would through his bosom eat.

XVI

Self-exiled Harold wanders forth again,
With nought of hope left, but with less of gloom;
The very knowledge that he lived in vain,
That all was over on this side the tomb,
Had made Despair a smilingness assume,   140
Which, though 'twere wild,—as on the plunder'd wreck
When mariners would madly meet their doom
With draughts intemperate on the sinking deck,—
Did yet inspire a cheer, which he forbore to check.

XVII

Stop!—for thy tread is on an Empire's dust!
An Earthquake's spoil is sepulchred below!
Is the spot mark'd with no colossal bust?
Nor column trophied for triumphal show?
None; but the moral's truth tells simpler so,
As the ground was before, thus let it be;—   150
How that red rain hath made the harvest grow!
And is this all the world has gain'd by thee,
Thou first and last of fields! king-making Victory?

XVIII

And Harold stands upon this place of skulls,
The grave of France, the deadly Waterloo!
How in an hour the power which gave annuls
Its gifts, transferring fame as fleeting too!
In "pride of place" here last the eagle flew,
Then tore with bloody talon the rent plain,
Pierced by the shaft of banded nations through;   160
Ambition's life and labours all were vain;
He wears the shatter'd links of the world's broken chain.

XIX

Fit retribution! Gaul may champ the bit
And foam in fetters;—but is Earth more free?
Did nations combat to make *One* submit;
Or league to teach all kings true sovereignty?

What! shall reviving Thraldom again be
The patch'd-up idol of enlighten'd days?
Shall we, who struck the Lion down, shall we
Pay the Wolf homage? proffering lowly gaze   170
And servile knees to thrones? No; *prove* before ye praise!

XX

If not, o'er one fallen despot boast no more!
In vain fair cheeks were furrow'd with hot tears
For Europe's flowers long rooted up before
The trampler of her vineyards; in vain years
Of death, depopulation, bondage, fears,
Have all been borne, and broken by the accord
Of roused-up millions; all that most endears
Glory, is when the myrtle wreathes a sword
Such as Harmodius drew on Athens' tyrant lord.   180

XXI

There was a sound of revelry by night,
And Belgium's capital had gather'd then
Her Beauty and her Chivalry, and bright
The lamps shone o'er fair women and brave men;
A thousand hearts beat happily; and when
Music arose with its voluptuous swell,
Soft eyes look'd love to eyes which spake again,
And all went merry as a marriage bell;
But hush! hark! a deep sound strikes like a rising knell!

XXII

Did ye not hear it?—No; 'twas but the wind,   190
Or the car rattling o'er the stony street;
On with the dance! let joy be unconfined;
No sleep till morn, when Youth and Pleasure meet
To chase the glowing Hours with flying feet—
But hark!—that heavy sound breaks in once more,
As if the clouds its echo would repeat;
And nearer, clearer, deadlier than before!
Arm! Arm! it is—it is—the cannon's opening roar!

From DON JUAN

From CANTO I

I

I want a hero: an uncommon want,
    When every year and month sends forth a new one,
Till, after cloying the gazettes with cant,
    The age discovers he is not the true one:
Of such as these I should not care to vaunt,
    I'll therefore take our ancient friend Don Juan—
We all have seen him, in the pantomime,
Sent to the devil somewhat ere his time.

II

Vernon, the butcher Cumberland, Wolfe, Hawke,
    Prince Ferdinand, Granby, Burgoyne, Keppel, Howe,   10
Evil and good, have had their tithe of talk,
    And fill'd their sign-posts then, like Wellesley now;
Each in their turn like Banquo's monarchs stalk,
    Followers of fame, "nine farrow" of that sow:
France, too, had Buonaparté and Dumourier
Recorded in the Moniteur and Courier.

III

Barnave, Brissot, Condorcet, Mirabeau,
    Pétion, Clootz, Danton, Marat, La Fayette,
Were French, and famous people, as we know;
    And there were others, scarce forgotten yet,   20
Joubert, Hoche, Marceau, Lannes, Desaix, Moreau,
    With many of the military set,
Exceedingly remarkable at times,
But not at all adapted to my rhymes.

IV

Nelson was once Britannia's god of war,
    And still should be so, but the tide is turn'd;
There's no more to be said of Trafalgar,
    'Tis with our hero quietly inurn'd;

Because the army's grown more popular,
 At which the naval people are concern'd,   30
Besides, the prince is all for the landservice,
Forgetting Duncan, Nelson, Howe, and Jervis.

   V

Brave men were living before Agamemnon
 And since, exceeding valorous and sage,
A good deal like him too, though quite the same none;
 But then they shone not on the poet's page,
And so have been forgotten:—I condemn none,
 But can't find any in the present age
Fit for my poem (that is, for my new one);
So, as I said, I'll take my friend Don Juan.   40

   V I

Most epic poets plunge "in medias res"
 (Horace makes this the heroic turnpike road),
And then your hero tells, whene'er you please,
 What went before—by way of episode,
While seated after dinner at his ease,
 Beside his mistress in some soft abode,
Palace, or garden, paradise, or cavern,
Which serves the happy couple for a tavern.

   V I I

That is the usual method, but not mine—
 My way is to begin with the beginning;   50
The regularity of my design
 Forbids all wandering as the worst of sinning,
And therefore I shall open with a line
 (Although it cost me half an hour in spinning)
Narrating somewhat of Don Juan's father,
And also of his mother, if you'd rather.

   V I I I

In Seville was he born, a pleasant city,
 Famous for oranges and women—he
Who has not seen it will be much to pity,

So says the proverb—and I quite agree;   60
Of all the Spanish towns is none more pretty,
   Cadiz, perhaps—but that you soon may see:—
Don Juan's parents lived beside the river,
A noble stream, and call'd the Guadalquivir.

     I X

His father's name was José—*Don,* of course,
   A true Hidalgo, free from every stain
Of Moor or Hebrew blood, he traced his source
   Through the most Gothic gentlemen of Spain;
A better cavalier ne'er mounted horse,
   Or, being mounted, e'er got down again,   70
Than José, who begot our hero, who
Begot—but that's to come——Well, to renew:

     X

His mother was a learned lady, famed
   For every branch of every science known—
In every Christian language ever named,
   With virtues equall'd by her wit alone:
She made the cleverest people quite ashamed,
   And even the good with inward envy groan,
Finding themselves so very much exceeded
In their own way by all the things that she did.   80

     X I

Her memory was a mine: she knew by heart
   All Calderon and greater part of Lopé,
So that if any actor miss'd his part
   She could have served him for the prompter's copy;
For her Feinagle's were an useless art,
   And he himself obliged to shut up shop—he
Could never make a memory so fine as
That which adorn'd the brain of Donna Inez.

     X I I

Her favourite science was the mathematical,
   Her noblest virtue was her magnanimity;   90

Her wit (she sometimes tried at wit) was Attic all,
   Her serious sayings darken'd to sublimity;
In short, in all things she was fairly what I call
   A prodigy—her morning dress was dimity,
Her evening silk, or, in the summer, muslin,
And other stuffs, with which I won't stay puzzling.

XIII

She knew the Latin—that is, the Lord's prayer,
   And Greek—the alphabet—I'm nearly sure;
She read some French romances here and there,
   Although her mode of speaking was not pure;   100
For native Spanish she had no great care,
   At least her conversation was obscure;
Her thoughts were theorems, her words a problem,
As if she deem'd that mystery would ennoble 'em.

XIV

She liked the English and the Hebrew tongue,
   And said there was analogy between 'em;
She proved it somehow out of sacred song,
   But I must leave the proofs to those who've seen 'em,
But this I heard her say, and can't be wrong,
   And all may think which way their judgments lean 'em,   110
" 'Tis strange—the Hebrew noun which means 'I am,'
The English always use to govern d—n."

XV

Some women use their tongues—she *look'd* a lecture,
   Each eye a sermon, and her brow a homily,
An all-in-all sufficient self-director,
   Like the lamented late Sir Samuel Romilly,
The Law's expounder, and the State's corrector,
   Whose suicide was almost an anomaly—
One sad example more, that "All is vanity,"—
(The jury brought their verdict in "Insanity.")   120

XVI

In short, she was a walking calculation,
   Miss Edgeworth's novels stepping from their covers,

Or Mrs. Trimmer's books on education,
   Or "Cœlebs' Wife" set out in quest of lovers,
Morality's prim personification,
   In which not Envy's self a flaw discovers;
To others' share let "female errors fall,"
For she had not even one—the worst of all.

XVII

Oh! she was perfect past all parallel—
   Of any modern female saint's comparison;   130
So far above the cunning powers of hell,
   Her guardian angel had given up his garrison;
Even her minutest motions went as well
   As those of the best time-piece made by Harrison:
In virtues nothing earthly could surpass her,
Save thine "incomparable oil," Macassar!

XVIII

Perfect she was, but as perfection is
   Insipid in this naughty world of ours,
Where our first parents never learn'd to kiss
   Till they were exiled from their earlier bowers,   140
Where all was peace, and innocence, and bliss
   (I wonder how they got through the twelve hours),
Don José, like a lineal son of Eve,
Went plucking various fruit without her leave.

XIX

He was a mortal of the careless kind,
   With no great love for learning, or the learn'd,
Who chose to go where'er he had a mind,
   And never dream'd his lady was concern'd;
The world, as usual, wickedly inclined
   To see a kingdom or a house o'erturn'd   150
Whisper'd he had a mistress, some said *two*,
But for domestic quarrels *one* will do.

XX

Now Donna Inez had, with all her merit,
   A great opinion of her own good qualities;

Neglect, indeed, requires a saint to bear it,
    And such, indeed, she was in her moralities;
But then she had a devil of a spirit,
    And sometimes mix'd up fancies with realities,
And let few opportunities escape
Of getting her liege lord into a scrape.   160

XXI

This was an easy matter with a man
    Oft in the wrong, and never on his guard;
And even the wisest, do the best they can,
    Have moments, hours, and days, so unprepared,
That you might "brain them with their lady's fan";
    And sometimes ladies hit exceeding hard,
And fans turn into falchions in fair hands,
And why and wherefore no one understands.

XXII

'Tis pity learned virgins ever wed
    With persons of no sort of education,   170
Or gentlemen, who, though well born and bred,
    Grow tired of scientific conversation;
I don't choose to say much upon this head,
    I'm a plain man, and in a single station,
But—Oh! ye lords of ladies intellectual,
Inform us truly, have they not hen-peck'd you all?

XXIII

Don José and his lady quarrell'd—*why*,
    Not any of the many could divine,
Though several thousand people chose to try,
    'Twas surely no concern of theirs nor mine;   180
I loathe that low vice—curiosity;
    But if there's anything in which I shine,
'Tis in arranging all my friends' affairs,
Not having, of my own, domestic cares.

XXIV

And so I interfered, and with the best
    Intentions, but their treatment was not kind;

I think the foolish people were possess'd,
   For neither of them could I ever find,
Although their porter afterwards confess'd—
   But that's no matter, and the worst's behind,   190
For little Juan o'er me threw, down stairs,
A pail of housemaid's water unawares.

XXV

A little curly-headed, good-for-nothing,
   And mischief-making monkey from his birth;
His parents ne'er agreed except in doting
   Upon the most unquiet imp on earth;
Instead of quarrelling, had they been but both in
   Their senses, they'd have sent young master forth
To school, or had him soundly whipp'd at home,
To teach him manners for the time to come.   200

XXVI

Don José and the Donna Inez led
   For some time an unhappy sort of life,
Wishing each other, not divorced, but dead;
   They lived respectably as man and wife,
Their conduct was exceedingly well-bred,
   And gave no outward signs of inward strife,
Until at length the smother'd fire broke out,
And put the business past all kind of doubt.

XXVII

For Inez call'd some druggists and physicians,
   And tried to prove her loving lord was *mad*,   210
But as he had some lucid intermissions,
   She next decided he was only *bad*;
Yet when they ask'd her for her depositions,
   No sort of explanation could be had,
Save that her duty both to man and God
Required this conduct—which seem'd very odd.

XXVIII

She kept a journal, where his faults were noted,
   And open'd certain trunks of books and letters,

All which might, if occasion served, be quoted;
　　And then she had all Seville for abettors,　　　　　　　　220
Besides her good old grandmother (who doted);
　　The hearers of her case became repeaters,
Then advocates, inquisitors, and judges,
Some for amusement, others for old grudges.

XXIX

And then this best and meekest woman bore
　　With such serenity her husband's woes,
Just as the Spartan ladies did of yore,
　　Who saw their spouses kill'd, and nobly chose
Never to say a word about them more—
　　Calmly she heard each calumny that rose,　　　　　　　　230
And saw *his* agonies with such sublimity,
That all the world exclaim'd, "What magnanimity!"

XXX

No doubt this patience, when the world is damning us,
　　Is philosophic in our former friends;
'Tis also pleasant to be deem'd magnanimous,
　　The more so in obtaining our own ends;
And what the lawyers call a *"malus animus"*
　　Conduct like this by no means comprehends:
Revenge in person's certainly no virtue,
But then 'tis not *my* fault, if *others* hurt you.　　　　　　240

XXXI

And if our quarrels should rip up old stories,
　　And help them with a lie or two additional,
I'm not to blame, as you well know—no more is
　　Any one else—they were become traditional;
Besides, their resurrection aids our glories
　　By contrast, which is what we just were wishing all:
And science profits by this resurrection—
Dead scandals form good subjects for dissection.

XXXII

Their friends had tried at reconciliation,
　　Then their relations, who made matters worse,　　　　　　250

('Twere hard to tell upon a like occasion
   To whom it may be best to have recourse—
I can't say much for friend or yet relation):
   The lawyers did their utmost for divorce,
But scarce a fee was paid on either side
Before, unluckily, Don José died.

XXXIII

He died: and most unluckily, because,
   According to all hints I could collect
From counsel learned in those kinds of laws
   (Although their talk's obscure and circumspect),   260
His death contrived to spoil a charming cause;
   A thousand pities also with respect
To public feeling, which on this occasion
Was manifested in a great sensation.

XXXIV

But ah! he died; and buried with him lay
   The public feeling and the lawyers' fees:
His house was sold, his servants sent away,
   A Jew took one of his two mistresses,
A priest the other—at least so they say:
   I ask'd the doctors after his disease—   270
He died of the slow fever called the tertian,
And left his widow to her own aversion.

XXXV

Yet José was an honourable man,
   That I must say, who knew him very well;
Therefore his frailties I'll no further scan,
   Indeed there were not many more to tell:
And if his passions now and then outran
   Discretion, and were not so peaceable
As Numa's (who was also named Pompilius),
He had been ill brought up, and was born bilious.   280

XXXVI

Whate'er might be his worthlessness or worth,
   Poor fellow! he had many things to wound him,

Let's own—since it can do no good on earth—
    It was a trying moment that which found him
Standing alone beside his desolate hearth,
    Where all his household gods lay shiver'd round him:
No choice was left his feelings or his pride,
Save death or Doctors' Commons—so he died.

XXXVII

Dying intestate, Juan was sole heir
    To a chancery suit, and messuages and lands,   290
Which, with a long minority and care,
    Promised to turn out well in proper hands:
Inez became sole guardian, which was fair,
    And answer'd but to nature's just demands;
An only son left with an only mother
Is brought up much more wisely than another.

XXXVIII

Sagest of women, even of widows, she
    Resolved that Juan should be quite a paragon,
And worthy of the noblest pedigree:
    (His sire was of Castile, his dam from Aragon).   300
Then for accomplishments of chivalry,
    In case our lord the king should go to war again,
He learn'd the arts of riding, fencing, gunnery,
And how to scale a fortress—or a nunnery.

XXXIX

But that which Donna Inez most desired,
    And saw into herself each day before all
The learned tutors whom for him she hired,
    Was, that his breeding should be strictly moral:
Much into all his studies she inquired,
    And so they were submitted first to her, all,   310
Arts, sciences, no branch was made a mystery
To Juan's eyes, excepting natural history.

XL

The languages, especially the dead,
    The sciences, and most of all the abstruse,

The arts, at least all such as could be said
    To be the most remote from common use,
In all these he was much and deeply read:
    But not a page of anything that's loose,
Or hints continuation of the species,
Was ever suffer'd, lest he should grow vicious.   320

XLI

His classic studies made a little puzzle,
    Because of filthy loves of gods and goddesses,
Who in the earlier ages raised a bustle,
    But never put on pantaloons or bodices;
His reverend tutors had at times a tussle,
    And for their Æneids, Iliads, and Odysseys,
Were forced to make an odd sort of apology
For Donna Inez dreaded the Mythology.

XLII

Ovid's a rake, as half his verses show him,
    Anacreon's morals are a still worse sample,   330
Catullus scarcely has a decent poem,
    I don't think Sappho's Ode a good example,
Although Longinus tells us there is no hymn
    Where the sublime soars forth on wings more ample;
But Virgil's songs are pure, except that horrid one
Beginning with "Formosum Pastor Corydon."

XLIII

Lucretius' irreligion is too strong
    For early stomachs, to prove wholesome food;
I can't help thinking Juvenal was wrong,
    Although no doubt his real intent was good,   340
For speaking out so plainly in his song,
    So much indeed as to be downright rude;
And then what proper person can be partial
To all those nauseous epigrams of Martial?

XLIV

Juan was taught from out the best edition,
    Expurgated by learned men, who place,

Judiciously, from out the schoolboy's vision,
   The grosser parts; but, fearful to deface
Too much their modest bard by this omission,
   And pitying sore his mutilated case,   350
They only add them all in an appendix,
Which saves, in fact, the trouble of an index;

XLV

For there we have them all "at one fell swoop,"
   Instead of being scatter'd through the pages;
They stand forth marshall'd in a handsome troop,
   To meet the ingenuous youth of future ages,
Till some less rigid editor shall stoop
   To call them back into their separate cages,
Instead of standing staring all together,
Like garden gods—and not so decent either.   360

XLVI

The Missal too (it was the family Missal)
   Was ornamented in a sort of way
Which ancient mass-books often are, and this all
   Kinds of grotesques illumined; and how they,
Who saw those figures on the margin kiss all,
   Could turn their optics to the text and pray,
Is more than I know—But Don Juan's mother
Kept this herself, and gave her son another.

XLVII

Sermons he read, and lectures he endured,
   And homilies, and lives of all the saints;   370
To Jerome and to Chrysostom inured,
   He did not take such studies for restraints;
But how faith is acquired, and then insured,
   So well not one of the aforesaid paints
As Saint Augustine in his fine Confessions,
Which make the reader envy his transgressions.

XLVIII

This, too, was a seal'd book to little Juan—
   I can't but say that his mamma was right,

If such an education was the true one.
   She scarcely trusted him from out her sight;   380
Her maids were old, and if she took a new one,
   You might be sure she was a perfect fright,
She did this during even her husband's life—
I recommend as much to every wife.

XLIX

Young Juan wax'd in godliness and grace;
   At six a charming child, and at eleven
With all the promise of as fine a face
   As e'er to man's maturer growth was given.
He studied steadily and grew apace,
   And seem'd, at least, in the right road to heaven,   390
For half his days were pass'd at church, the other
Between his tutors, confessor, and mother.

L

At six, I said, he was a charming child,
   At twelve he was a fine, but quiet boy;
Although in infancy a little wild,
   They tamed him down amongst them: to destroy
His natural spirit not in vain they toil'd,
   At least it seem'd so; and his mother's joy
Was to declare how sage, and still, and steady,
Her young philosopher was grown already.   400

l.   85. Feinagle's art = mnemonics
l. 279. Numa = peaceable legendary king
l. 288. Doctors' Commons = divorce court

Richard Harris Barham

(1 7 8 8 – 1 8 4 5)

A clergyman, attached in 1821 and again in 1842 to St. Paul's in London, Barham claimed, without expecting to be believed, that the rollicking medieval narratives, published singly in popular periodicals and collected in *The Ingoldsby Legends* (1840, with many subsequent editions), were found by one Thomas Ingoldsby in his ancient family manor. The jackdaw, less suspect than the magpie for pilfering, differs from other species of crow in its affinity for Gothic architecture.

THE JACKDAW OF RHEIMS

The Jackdaw sat on the Cardinal's chair!
Bishop, and abbot, and prior were there;
   Many a monk and many a friar,
   Many a knight and many a squire,
With a great many more of lesser degree,—
In sooth a goodly company;
And they served the Lord Primate on bended knee.
   Never, I ween,
   Was a prouder seen,
Read of in books, or dreamt of in dreams,   10
Than the Cardinal Lord Archbishop of Rheims!

   In and out
   Through the motley rout,
That little Jackdaw kept hopping about;
   Here and there
   Like a dog in a fair,
   Over comfits and cates,
   And dishes and plates,
Cowl and cope, and rochet and pall,
Mitre and crosier! he hopped upon all!   20
   With saucy air,
   He perched on the chair
Where, in state, the great Lord Cardinal sat

In the great Lord Cardinal's great red hat;
    And he peered in the face
    Of his Lordship's Grace,
With a satisfied look, as if he would say,
"We two are the greatest folks here to-day!"
    And the priests with awe,
    As such freaks they saw,   30
Said, "The Devil must be in that little Jackdaw!"

The feast was over, the board was cleared,
The flawns and the custards had all disappeared,
And six little Singing-boys,—dear little souls!
In nice clean faces, and nice white stoles,
    Came in order due,
    Two by two,
Marching that grand refectory through!
A nice little boy held a golden ewer,
Embossed and filled with water, as pure   40
As any that flows between Rheims and Namur,
Which a nice little boy stood ready to catch
In a fine golden hand-basin made to match.
Two nice little boys, rather more grown,
Carried lavender-water, and eau de Cologne;
And a nice little boy had a nice cake of soap,
Worthy of washing the hands of the Pope.
    One little boy more
    A napkin bore,
Of the best white diaper, fringed with pink,   50
And a Cardinal's Hat marked in "permanent ink."

The great Lord Cardinal turns at the sight
Of these nice little boys dressed all in white:
    From his finger he draws
    His costly turquoise;
And, not thinking at all about little Jackdaws,
    Deposits it straight
    By the side of his plate,
While the nice little boys on his Eminence wait;
Till, when nobody's dreaming of any such thing,   60
That little Jackdaw hops off with the ring!

    There's a cry and a shout,
    And a deuce of a rout,

And nobody seems to know what they're about,
But the Monks have their pockets all turned inside out.
    The Friars are kneeling,
    And hunting and feeling
The carpet, the floor, and the walls, and the ceiling.
    The Cardinal drew
    Off each plum-coloured shoe,   70
And left his red stockings exposed to the view;
    He peeps, and he feels
    In the toes and the heels;
They turn up the dishes,—they turn up the plates,—
They take up the poker and poke out the grates,
    They turn up the rugs,
    They examine the mugs:—
    But, no!—no such thing;—
    They can't find THE RING!
And the Abbot declared that, "when nobody twigged it,   80
Some rascal or other had popped in, and prigged it!"

The Cardinal rose with a dignified look,
He called for his candle, his bell, and his book!
    In holy anger, and pious grief
    He solemnly cursed that rascally thief!
    He cursed him at board, he cursed him in bed;
    From the sole of his foot to the crown of his head;
    He cursed him in sleeping, that every night
    He should dream of the devil, and wake in a fright;
    He cursed him in eating, he cursed him in drinking,   90
    He cursed him in coughing, in sneezing, in winking;
    He cursed him in sitting, in standing, in lying;
    He cursed him in walking, in riding, in flying,
    He cursed him in living, he cursed him in dying!—
Never was heard such a terrible curse!!
    But what gave rise
    To no little surprise,
Nobody seemed one penny the worse!

    The day was gone,
    The night came on,   100
The Monks and the Friars they searched till dawn;
    When the Sacristan saw,
    On crumpled claw,
Come limping a poor little lame Jackdaw!

No longer gay,
  As on yesterday;
His feathers all seemed to be turned the wrong way;—
His pinions drooped—he could hardly stand,—
His head was as bald as the palm of your hand;
    His eye so dim,   110
    So wasted each limb,
That, heedless of grammar, they all cried, "THAT'S HIM—
That's the scamp that has done this scandalous thing!
That's the thief that has got my Lord Cardinal's Ring!"
    The poor little Jackdaw,
    When the Monks he saw,
Feebly gave vent to the ghost of a caw;
And turned his bald head, as much as to say,
"Pray, be so good as to walk this way!"
    Slower and slower   120
    He limped on before,
Till they came to the back of the belfry door,
    Where the first thing they saw,
    Midst the sticks and the straw,
Was the RING in the nest of that little Jackdaw!

Then the great Lord Cardinal called for his book,
And off that terrible curse he took;
    The mute expression
    Served in lieu of confession,
And, being thus coupled with full restitution,   130
The Jackdaw got plenary absolution!
    —When these words were heard,
    That poor little bird
Was so changed in a moment, 'twas really absurd.

    He grew sleek, and fat;
    In addition to that,
A fresh crop of feathers came thick as a mat!
    His tail waggled more
    Even than before,
But no longer it wagged with an impudent air,   140
No longer he perched on the Cardinal's chair.
    He hopped now about
    With a gait devout;
At Matins, at Vespers, he never was out;
And, so far from any more pilfering deeds,

He always seemed telling the Confessor's beads.
If any one lied,—or if any one swore,—
Or slumbered in prayer-time and happened to snore,
    That good Jackdaw
    Would give a great "Caw!"   150
As much as to say, "Don't do so any more!"
While many remarked, as his manners they saw,
That they "never had known such a pious Jackdaw."
    He long lived the pride
    Of that country side,
And at last in the odour of sanctity died;
    When, as words were too faint
    His merits to paint,
The Conclave determined to make him a Saint;
And on newly-made Saints and Popes, as you know,   160
It's the custom, at Rome, new names to bestow,
So they canonized him by the name of Jim Crow!

Percy Bysshe Shelley

(1792–1822)

At Eton Shelley learned ways of rebellion against his own privileged class; expelled from Oxford for "atheism," he spoke and wrote as a political malcontent and vegetarian. He eloped to Scotland in 1811 with the daughter of a coffeehouse keeper and to the Continent in 1814 with the daughter of the reformers Mary Wollstonecraft and William Godwin; she wrote *Frankenstein* in Switzerland in 1816 and married Shelley when they learned that the first wife had drowned herself. They lived in Italy—in frequent contact with Byron—until Shelley's death when a squall sank his small schooner, the *Don Juan*, as he returned from a visit with Leigh Hunt and Byron at Pisa and Livorno. (In his humanitarian concern for all except his own children, he could have been a model for Dickens's Mrs. Jellyby.) The idealistic, ethereal Shelley, called by Arnold "a beautiful and ineffectual angel," became for the "New Critics" the essence of tasteless Romantic mush.

Shelley had invited the consumptive Keats to visit him in Italy several months before he learned of Keats's death and burial in the Protestant Cemetery of Rome in February 1821. In the Spenserian stanza employed more pictorially by Keats himself, *Adonais* is sometimes denied and sometimes granted a place beside Milton's *Lycidas* among pastoral elegies. Etherealizing the Greek myth retold in Shakespeare's *Venus and Adonis*, Shelley conflates Aphrodite and Urania (as heavenly love) into lover-and-Madonna. The unnamed mourners have been identified as blind Milton, Byron, Moore, Shelley, and Hunt, ranged against the hostile critics thought responsible for Keats's loss of hope.

OZYMANDIAS

I met a traveller from an antique land
Who said: "Two vast and trunkless legs of stone
Stand in the desert . . . Near them, on the sand,
Half sunk, a shattered visage lies, whose frown,
And wrinkled lip, and sneer of cold command,
Tell that its sculptor well those passions read
Which yet survive, stamped on these lifeless things,
The hand that mocked them, and the heart that fed:
And on the pedestal these words appear:
'My name is Ozymandias, king of kings:

Look on my works, ye Mighty, and despair!'
Nothing beside remains. Round the decay
Of that colossal wreck, boundless and bare
The lone and level sands stretch far away."

ODE TO THE WEST WIND

I

O wild West Wind, thou breath of Autumn's being,
Thou, from whose unseen presence the leaves dead
Are driven, like ghosts from an enchanter fleeing,

Yellow, and black, and pale, and hectic red,
Pestilence-stricken multitudes: O thou,
Who chariotest to their dark wintry bed

The wingèd seeds, where they lie cold and low,
Each like a corpse within its grave, until
Thine azure sister of the Spring shall blow

Her clarion o'er the dreaming earth, and fill   10
(Driving sweet buds like flocks to feed in air)
With living hues and odours plain and hill:

Wild Spirit, which art moving everywhere;
Destroyer and preserver; hear, oh, hear!

I I

Thou on whose stream, mid the steep sky's commotion,
Loose clouds like earth's decaying leaves are shed,
Shook from the tangled boughs of Heaven and Ocean,

Angels of rain and lightning: there are spread
On the blue surface of thine aëry surge,
Like the bright hair uplifted from the head   20

Of some fierce Maenad, even from the dim verge
Of the horizon to the zenith's height,
The locks of the approaching storm. Thou dirge

Of the dying year, to which this closing night
Will be the dome of a vast sepulchre,
Vaulted with all thy congregated might

Of vapours, from whose solid atmosphere
Black rain, and fire, and hail will burst: oh, hear!

III

Thou who didst waken from his summer dreams
The blue Mediterranean, where he lay,   30
Lulled by the coil of his crystàlline streams,

Beside a pumice isle in Baiae's bay,
And saw in sleep old palaces and towers
Quivering within the wave's intenser day,

All overgrown with azure moss and flowers
So sweet, the sense faints picturing them! Thou
For whose path the Atlantic's level powers

Cleave themselves into chasms, while far below
The sea-blooms and the oozy woods which wear
The sapless foliage of the ocean, know   40

Thy voice, and suddenly grow gray with fear,
And tremble and despoil themselves: oh, hear!

IV

If I were a dead leaf thou mightest bear;
If I were a swift cloud to fly with thee;
A wave to pant beneath thy power, and share

The impulse of thy strength, only less free
Than thou, O uncontrollable! If even
I were as in my boyhood, and could be

The comrade of thy wanderings over Heaven,
As then, when to outstrip thy skiey speed   50
Scarce seemed a vision; I would ne'er have striven

As thus with thee in prayer in my sore need.
Oh, lift me as a wave, a leaf, a cloud!
I fall upon the thorns of life! I bleed!

A heavy weight of hours has chained and bowed
One too like thee: tameless, and swift, and proud.

      V

Make me thy lyre, even as the forest is:
What if my leaves are falling like its own!
The tumult of thy mighty harmonies

Will take from both a deep, autumnal tone,   60
Sweet though in sadness. Be thou, Spirit fierce,
My spirit! Be thou me, impetuous one!

Drive my dead thoughts over the universe
Like withered leaves to quicken a new birth!
And, by the incantation of this verse,

Scatter, as from an unextinguished hearth
Ashes and sparks, my words among mankind!
Be through my lips to unawakened earth

The trumpet of a prophecy! O, Wind,
If Winter comes, can Spring be far behind?   70

THE CLOUD

I bring fresh showers for the thirsting flowers,
    From the seas and the streams;
I bear light shade for the leaves when laid
    In their noonday dreams.
From my wings are shaken the dews that waken
    The sweet buds every one,
When rocked to rest on their mother's breast,
    As she dances about the sun.
I wield the flail of the lashing hail,
    And whiten the green plains under,   10

And then again I dissolve it in rain,
    And laugh as I pass in thunder.

I sift the snow on the mountains below,
    And their great pines groan aghast;
And all the night 'tis my pillow white,
    While I sleep in the arms of the blast.
Sublime on the towers of my skiey bowers,
    Lightning my pilot sits;
In a cavern under is fettered the thunder,
    It struggles and howls at fits;   20
Over earth and ocean, with gentle motion,
    This pilot is guiding me,
Lured by the love of the genii that move
    In the depths of the purple sea;
Over the rills, and the crags, and the hills,
    Over the lakes and the plains,
Wherever he dream, under mountain or stream,
    The Spirit he loves remains;
And I all the while bask in Heaven's blue smile,
    Whilst he is dissolving in rains.   30

The sanguine Sunrise, with his meteor eyes,
    And his burning plumes outspread,
Leaps on the back of my sailing rack,
    When the morning star shines dead;
As on the jag of a mountain crag,
    Which an earthquake rocks and swings,
An eagle alit one moment may sit
    In the light of its golden wings.
And when Sunset may breathe, from the lit sea beneath,
    Its ardours of rest and of love,   40
And the crimson pall of eve may fall
    From the depth of Heaven above,
With wings folded I rest, on mine aëry nest,
    As still as a brooding dove.

That orbèd maiden with white fire laden,
    Whom mortals call the Moon,
Glides glimmering o'er my fleece-like floor,
    By the midnight breezes strewn;
And wherever the beat of her unseen feet,

Which only the angels hear,   50
May have broken the woof of my tent's thin roof,
    The stars peep behind her, and peer;
And I laugh to see them whirl and flee,
    Like a swarm of golden bees,
When I widen the rent in my wind-built tent,
    Till the calm rivers, lakes, and seas,
Like strips of the sky fallen through me on high,
    Are each paved with the moon and these.

I bind the Sun's throne with a burning zone,
    And the Moon's with a girdle of pearl;   60
The volcanoes are dim, and the stars reel and swim,
    When the whirlwinds my banner unfurl.
From cape to cape, with a bridge-like shape,
    Over a torrent sea,
Sunbeam-proof, I hang like a roof,—
    The mountains its columns be.
The triumphal arch through which I march
    With hurricane, fire, and snow,
When the Powers of the air are chained to my chair,
    Is the million-coloured bow;   70
The sphere-fire above its soft colours wove
    While the moist Earth was laughing below.

I am the daughter of Earth and Water,
    And the nursling of the Sky;
I pass through the pores of the ocean and shores;
    I change, but I cannot die.
For after the rain when with never a stain
    The pavilion of Heaven is bare,
And the winds and sunbeams with their convex gleams
    Build up the blue dome of air,   80
I silently laugh at my own cenotaph,
    And out of the caverns of rain,
Like a child from the womb, like a ghost from the tomb,
    I arise and unbuild it again.

SONG TO THE MEN
OF ENGLAND

Men of England, wherefore plough
For the lords who lay ye low?
Wherefore weave with toil and care
The rich robes your tyrants wear?

Wherefore feed, and clothe, and save,
From the cradle to the grave,
Those ungrateful drones who would
Drain your sweat—nay, drink your blood?

Wherefore, Bees of England, forge
Many a weapon, chain, and scourge,   10
That these stingless drones may spoil
The forced produce of your toil?

Have ye leisure, comfort, calm,
Shelter, food, love's gentle balm?
Or what is it ye buy so dear
With your pain and with your fear?

The seed ye sow, another reaps;
The wealth ye find, another keeps;
The robes ye weave, another wears;
The arms ye forge, another bears.   20

Sow seed,—but let no tyrant reap;
Find wealth,—let no impostor heap;
Weave robes,—let not the idle wear;
Forge arms,—in your defence to bear.

Shrink to your cellars, holes, and cells;
In halls ye deck another dwells.
Why shake the chains ye wrought? Ye see
The steel ye tempered glance on ye.

With plough and spade, and hoe and loom,
Trace your grave, and build your tomb,   30
And weave your winding-sheet, till fair
England be your sepulchre.

ADONAIS

I

I weep for Adonais—he is dead!
O, weep for Adonais! though our tears
Thaw not the frost which binds so dear a head!
And thou, sad Hour, selected from all years
To mourn our loss, rouse thy obscure compeers,
And teach them thine own sorrow, say: "With me
Died Adonais; till the Future dares
Forget the Past, his fate and fame shall be
An echo and a light unto eternity!"

II

Where wert thou, mighty Mother, when he lay,   10
When thy Son lay, pierced by the shaft which flies
In darkness? where was lorn Urania
When Adonais died? With veilèd eyes,
'Mid listening Echoes, in her Paradise
She sate, while one, with soft enamoured breath,
Rekindled all the fading melodies,
With which, like flowers that mock the corse beneath,
He had adorned and hid the coming bulk of Death.

III

Oh, weep for Adonais—he is dead!
Wake, melancholy Mother, wake and weep!   20
Yet wherefore? Quench within their burning bed
Thy fiery tears, and let thy loud heart keep
Like his, a mute and uncomplaining sleep;
For he is gone, where all things wise and fair
Descend;—oh, dream not that the amorous Deep
Will yet restore him to the vital air;
Death feeds on his mute voice, and laughs at our despair.

IV

Most musical of mourners, weep again!
Lament anew, Urania!—He died,

Who was the Sire of an immortal strain,   30
Blind, old, and lonely, when his country's pride,
The priest, the slave, and the liberticide,
Trampled and mocked with many a loathèd rite
Of lust and blood; he went, unterrified,
Into the gulf of death; but his clear Sprite
Yet reigns o'er earth; the third among the sons of light.

        V

Most musical of mourners, weep anew!
Not all to that bright station dared to climb;
And happier they their happiness who knew,
Whose tapers yet burn through that night of time   40
In which suns perished; others more sublime,
Struck by the envious wrath of man or god,
Have sunk, extinct in their refulgent prime;
And some yet live, treading the thorny road,
Which leads, through toil and hate, to Fame's serene abode.

        V I

But now, thy youngest, dearest one, has perished—
The nursling of thy widowhood, who grew,
Like a pale flower by some sad maiden cherished,
And fed with true-love tears, instead of dew;
Most musical of mourners, weep anew!   50
Thy extreme hope, the loveliest and the last,
The bloom, whose petals nipped before they blew
Died on the promise of the fruit, is waste;
The broken lily lies—the storm is overpast.

        V I I

To that high Capital, where kingly Death
Keeps his pale court in beauty and decay,
He came; and bought, with price of purest breath,
A grave among the eternal.—Come away!
Haste, while the vault of blue Italian day
Is yet his fitting charnel-roof! while still   60
He lies, as if in dewy sleep he lay;
Awake him not! surely he takes his fill
Of deep and liquid rest, forgetful of all ill.

VIII

He will awake no more, oh, never more!—
Within the twilight chamber spreads apace
The shadow of white Death, and at the door
Invisible Corruption waits to trace
His extreme way to her dim dwelling-place;
The eternal Hunger sits, but pity and awe
Soothe her pale rage, nor dares she to deface   70
So fair a prey, till darkness, and the law
Of change, shall o'er his sleep the mortal curtain draw.

IX

Oh, weep for Adonais!—The quick Dreams,
The passion-wingèd Ministers of thought,
Who were his flocks, whom near the living streams
Of his young spirit he fed, and whom he taught
The love which was its music, wander not,—
Wander no more, from kindling brain to brain,
But droop there, whence they sprung; and mourn their lot
Round the cold heart, where, after their sweet pain,   80
They ne'er will gather strength, or find a home again.

X

And one with trembling hands clasps his cold head,
And fans him with her moonlight wings, and cries;
"Our love, our hope, our sorrow, is not dead;
See, on the silken fringe of his faint eyes,
Like dew upon a sleeping flower, there lies
A tear some Dream has loosened from his brain."
Lost Angel of a ruined Paradise!
She knew not 'twas her own; as with no stain
She faded, like a cloud which had outwept its rain.   90

XI

One from a lucid urn of starry dew
Washed his light limbs as if embalming them;
Another clipped her profuse locks, and threw
The wreath upon him, like an anadem,
Which frozen tears instead of pearls begem;

Another in her wilful grief would break
Her bow and wingèd reeds, as if to stem
A greater loss with one which was more weak;
And dull the barbèd fire against his frozen cheek.

XII

Another Splendour on his mouth alit,   100
That mouth, whence it was wont to draw the breath
Which gave it strength to pierce the guarded wit,
And pass into the panting heart beneath
With lightning and with music: the damp death
Quenched its caress upon his icy lips;
And, as a dying meteor stains a wreath
Of moonlight vapour, which the cold night clips,
It flushed through his pale limbs, and passed to its eclipse.

XIII

And others came . . . Desires and Adorations,
Winged Persuasions and veiled Destinies,   110
Splendours, and Glooms, and glimmering Incarnations
Of hopes and fears, and twilight Phantasies;
And Sorrow, with her family of Sighs,
And Pleasure, blind with tears, led by the gleam
Of her own dying smile instead of eyes,
Came in slow pomp;—the moving pomp might seem
Like pageantry of mist on an autumnal stream.

XIV

All he had loved, and moulded into thought,
From shape, and hue, and odour, and sweet sound,
Lamented Adonais. Morning sought   120
Her eastern watch-tower, and her hair unbound,
Wet with the tears which should adorn the ground,
Dimmed the aëreal eyes that kindle day;
Afar the melancholy thunder moaned,
Pale Ocean in unquiet slumber lay,
And the wild Winds flew round, sobbing in their dismay.

XV

Lost Echo sits amid the voiceless mountains,
And feeds her grief with his remembered lay,
And will no more reply to winds or fountains,
Or amorous birds perched on the young green spray,   130
Or herdsman's horn, or bell at closing day;
Since she can mimic not his lips, more dear
Than those for whose disdain she pined away
Into a shadow of all sounds:—a drear
Murmur, between their songs, is all the woodmen hear.

XVI

Grief made the young Spring wild, and she threw down
Her kindling buds, as if she Autumn were,
Or they dead leaves; since her delight is flown,
For whom should she have waked the sullen year?
To Phoebus was not Hyacinth so dear   140
Nor to himself Narcissus, as to both
Thou, Adonais: wan they stand and sere
Amid the faint companions of their youth,
With dew all turned to tears; odour, to sighing ruth.

XVII

Thy spirit's sister, the lorn nightingale
Mourns not her mate with such melodious pain;
Not so the eagle, who like thee could scale
Heaven, and could nourish in the sun's domain
Her mighty youth with morning, doth complain,
Soaring and screaming round her empty nest,   150
As Albion wails for thee: the curse of Cain
Light on his head who pierced thy innocent breast,
And scared the angel soul that was its earthly guest!

XVIII

Ah, woe is me! Winter is come and gone,
But grief returns with the revolving year;
The airs and streams renew their joyous tone;
The ants, the bees, the swallows reappear;
Fresh leaves and flowers deck the dead Seasons' bier;

The amorous birds now pair in every brake,
And build their mossy homes in field and brere;   160
And the green lizard, and the golden snake,
Like unimprisoned flames, out of their trance awake.

XIX

Through wood and stream and field and hill and Ocean
A quickening life from the Earth's heart has burst
As it has ever done, with change and motion,
From the great morning of the world when first
God dawned on Chaos; in its stream immersed,
The lamps of Heaven flash with a softer light;
All baser things pant with life's sacred thirst;
Diffuse themselves; and spend in love's delight,   170
The beauty and the joy of their renewèd might.

XX

The leprous corpse, touched by this spirit tender,
Exhales itself in flowers of gentle breath;
Like incarnations of the stars, when splendour
Is changed to fragrance, they illumine death
And mock the merry worm that wakes beneath;
Nought we know, dies. Shall that alone which knows
Be as a sword consumed before the sheath
By sightless lightning?—the intense atom glows
A moment, then is quenched in a most cold repose.   180

XXI

Alas! that all we loved of him should be,
But for our grief, as if it had not been,
And grief itself be mortal! Woe is me!
Whence are we, and why are we? of what scene
The actors or spectators? Great and mean
Meet massed in death, who lends what life must borrow.
As long as skies are blue, and fields are green,
Evening must usher night, night urge the morrow,
Month follow month with woe, and year wake year to sorrow.

XXII

He will awake no more, oh, never more!   190
"Wake thou," cried Misery, "childless Mother, rise
Out of thy sleep, and slake, in thy heart's core,
A wound more fierce than his, with tears and sighs."
And all the Dreams that watched Urania's eyes,
And all the Echoes whom their sister's song
Had held in holy silence, cried: "Arise!"
Swift as a Thought by the snake Memory stung,
From her ambrosial rest the fading Splendour sprung.

XXIII

She rose like an autumnal Night, that springs
Out of the East, and follows wild and drear   200
The golden Day, which, on eternal wings,
Even as a ghost abandoning a bier,
Had left the Earth a corpse. Sorrow and fear
So struck, so roused, so rapt Urania;
So saddened round her like an atmosphere
Of stormy mist; so swept her on her way
Even to the mournful place where Adonais lay.

XXIV

Out of her secret Paradise she sped,
Through camps and cities rough with stone, and steel,
And human hearts, which to her aery tread   210
Yielding not, wounded the invisible
Palms of her tender feet where'er they fell:
And barbèd tongues, and thoughts more sharp than they,
Rent the soft Form they never could repel,
Whose sacred blood, like the young tears of May,
Paved with eternal flowers that undeserving way.

XXV

In the death-chamber for a moment Death,
Shamed by the presence of that living Might,
Blushed to annihilation, and the breath
Revisited those lips, and Life's pale light   220
Flashed through those limbs, so late her dear delight.

"Leave me not wild and drear and comfortless,
    As silent lightning leaves the starless night!
    Leave me not!" cried Urania: her distress
Roused Death: Death rose and smiled, and met her vain caress.

XXVI

"Stay yet awhile! speak to me once again;
    Kiss me, so long but as a kiss may live;
    And in my heartless breast and burning brain
    That word, that kiss, shall all thoughts else survive
    With food of saddest memory kept alive,   230
    Now thou art dead, as if it were a part
    Of thee, my Adonais! I would give
    All that I am to be as thou now art!
But I am chained to Time, and cannot thence depart!

XXVII

"O gentle child, beautiful as thou wert,
    Why didst thou leave the trodden paths of men
    Too soon, and with weak hands though mighty heart
    Dare the unpastured dragon in his den?
    Defenceless as thou wert, oh, where was then
    Wisdom the mirrored shield, or scorn the spear?   240
    Or hadst thou waited the full cycle, when
    Thy spirit should have filled its crescent sphere,
The monsters of life's waste had fled from thee like deer.

XXVIII

"The herded wolves, bold only to pursue;
    The obscene ravens, clamorous o'er the dead;
    The vultures to the conqueror's banner true
    Who feed where Desolation first has fed,
    And whose wings rain contagion;—how they fled,
    When, like Apollo, from his golden bow
    The Pythian of the age one arrow sped   250
    And smiled!—The spoilers tempt no second blow,
They fawn on the proud feet that spurn them lying low.

XXIX

"The sun comes forth, and many reptiles spawn;
He sets, and each ephemeral insect then
Is gathered into death without a dawn,
And the immortal stars awake again;
So is it in the world of living men:
A godlike mind soars forth, in its delight
Making earth bare and veiling heaven, and when
It sinks, the swarms that dimmed or shared its light   260
Leave to its kindred lamps the spirit's awful night."

XXX

Thus ceased she: and the mountain shepherds came,
Their garlands sere, their magic mantles rent;
The Pilgrim of Eternity, whose fame
Over his living head like Heaven is bent,
An early but enduring monument,
Came, veiling all the lightnings of his song
In sorrow; from her wilds Ierne sent
The sweetest lyrist of her saddest wrong,
And Love taught Grief to fall like music from his tongue.   270

XXXI

Midst others of less note, came one frail Form,
A phantom among men; companionless
As the last cloud of an expiring storm
Whose thunder is its knell; he, as I guess,
Had gazed on Nature's naked loveliness,
Actaeon-like, and now he fled astray
With feeble steps o'er the world's wilderness,
And his own thoughts, along that rugged way,
Pursued, like raging hounds, their father and their prey.

XXXII

A pardlike Spirit beautiful and swift—   280
A Love in desolation masked;—a Power
Girt round with weakness;—it can scarce uplift
The weight of the superincumbent hour;
It is a dying lamp, a falling shower,

A breaking billow;—even whilst we speak
Is it not broken? On the withering flower
The killing sun smiles brightly: on a cheek
The life can burn in blood, even while the heart may break.

XXXIII

His head was bound with pansies overblown,
And faded violets, white, and pied, and blue;   290
And a light spear topped with a cypress cone,
Round whose rude shaft dark ivy-tresses grew
Yet dripping with the forest's noonday dew,
Vibrated, as the ever-beating heart
Shook the weak hand that grasped it; of that crew
He came the last, neglected and apart;
A herd-abandoned deer struck by the hunter's dart.

XXXIV

All stood aloof, and at his partial moan
Smiled through their tears; well knew that gentle band
Who in another's fate now wept his own,   300
As in the accents of an unknown land
He sung new sorrow; sad Urania scanned
The Stranger's mien, and murmured: "Who art thou?"
He answered not, but with a sudden hand
Made bare his branded and ensanguined brow,
Which was like Cain's or Christ's—oh! that it should be so!

XXXV

What softer voice is hushed over the dead?
Athwart what brow is that dark mantle thrown?
What form leans sadly o'er the white death-bed,
In mockery of monumental stone,   310
The heavy heart heaving without a moan?
If it be He, who, gentlest of the wise,
Taught, soothed, loved, honoured the departed one,
Let me not vex, with inharmonious sighs,
The silence of that heart's accepted sacrifice.

XXXVI

Our Adonais has drunk poison—oh!
What deaf and viperous murderer could crown
Life's early cup with such a draught of woe?
The nameless worm would now itself disown:
It felt, yet could escape, the magic tone   320
Whose prelude held all envy, hate, and wrong,
But what was howling in one breast alone,
Silent with expectation of the song,
Whose master's hand is cold, whose silver lyre unstrung.

XXXVII

Live thou, whose infamy is not thy fame!
Live! fear no heavier chastisement from me,
Thou noteless blot on a remembered name!
But be thyself, and know thyself to be!
And ever at thy season be thou free
To spill the venom when thy fangs o'erflow;   330
Remorse and Self-contempt shall cling to thee;
Hot Shame shall burn upon thy secret brow,
And like a beaten hound tremble thou shalt—as now.

XXXVIII

Nor let us weep that our delight is fled
Far from these carrion kites that scream below;
He wakes or sleeps with the enduring dead;
Thou canst not soar where he is sitting now.—
Dust to the dust! but the pure spirit shall flow
Back to the burning fountain whence it came,
A portion of the Eternal, which must glow   340
Through time and change, unquenchably the same,
Whilst thy cold embers choke the sordid hearth of shame.

XXXIX

Peace, peace! he is not dead, he doth not sleep—
He hath awakened from the dream of life—
'Tis we, who lost in stormy visions, keep
With phantoms an unprofitable strife,
And in mad trance, strike with our spirit's knife

Invulnerable nothings.—We decay
Like corpses in a charnel; fear and grief
Convulse us and consume us day by day,   350
And cold hopes swarm like worms within our living clay.

XL

He has outsoared the shadow of our night;
Envy and calumny and hate and pain,
And that unrest which men miscall delight,
Can touch him not and torture not again;
From the contagion of the world's slow stain
He is secure, and now can never mourn
A heart grown cold, a head grown gray in vain;
Nor, when the spirit's self has ceased to burn,
With sparkless ashes load an unlamented urn.   360

XLI

He lives, he wakes—'tis Death is dead, not he;
Mourn not for Adonais.—Thou young Dawn,
Turn all thy dew to splendour, for from thee
The spirit thou lamentest is not gone;
Ye caverns and ye forests, cease to moan!
Cease, ye faint flowers and fountains, and thou Air,
Which like a mourning veil thy scarf hadst thrown
O'er the abandoned Earth, now leave it bare
Even to the joyous stars which smile on its despair!

XLII

He is made one with Nature: there is heard   370
His voice in all her music, from the moan
Of thunder, to the song of night's sweet bird;
He is a presence to be felt and known
In darkness and in light, from herb and stone,
Spreading itself where'er that Power may move
Which has withdrawn his being to its own;
Which wields the world with never-wearied love,
Sustains it from beneath, and kindles it above.

XLIII

He is a portion of the loveliness
Which once he made more lovely: he doth bear   380
His part, while the one Spirit's plastic stress
Sweeps through the dull dense world, compelling there,
All new successions to the forms they wear;
Torturing th' unwilling dross that checks its flight
To its own likeness, as each mass may bear;
And bursting in its beauty and its might
From trees and beasts and men into the Heaven's light.

XLIV

The splendours of the firmament of time
May be eclipsed, but are extinguished not;
Like stars to their appointed height they climb,   390
And death is a low mist which cannot blot
The brightness it may veil. When lofty thought
Lifts a young heart above its mortal lair,
And love and life contend in it, for what
Shall be its earthly doom, the dead live there
And move like winds of light on dark and stormy air.

XLV

The inheritors of unfulfilled renown
Rose from their thrones, built beyond mortal thought,
Far in the Unapparent. Chatterton
Rose pale,—his solemn agony had not   400
Yet faded from him; Sidney, as he fought
And as he fell and as he lived and loved
Sublimely mild, a Spirit without spot,
Arose; and Lucan, by his death approved:
Oblivion as they rose shrank like a thing reproved.

XLVI

And many more, whose names on Earth are dark,
But whose transmitted effluence cannot die
So long as fire outlives the parent spark,
Rose, robed in dazzling immortality.
"Thou art become as one of us," they cry,   410

"It was for thee yon kingless sphere has long
   Swung blind in unascended majesty,
   Silent alone amid an Heaven of Song.
Assume thy wingèd throne, thou Vesper of our throng!"

XLVII

Who mourns for Adonais? Oh, come forth,
   Fond wretch! and know thyself and him aright.
   Clasp with thy panting soul the pendulous Earth;
As from a centre, dart thy spirit's light
Beyond all worlds, until its spacious might
Satiate the void circumference: then shrink   420
   Even to a point within our day and night;
   And keep thy heart light lest it make thee sink
When hope has kindled hope, and lured thee to the brink.

XLVIII

Or go to Rome, which is the sepulchre,
   Oh, not of him, but of our joy: 'tis nought
   That ages, empires, and religions there
Lie buried in the ravage they have wrought;
For such as he can lend,—they borrow not
Glory from those who made the world their prey;
   And he is gathered to the kings of thought   430
   Who waged contention with their time's decay,
And of the past are all that cannot pass away.

XLIX

Go thou to Rome,—at once the Paradise,
   The grave, the city, and the wilderness;
   And where its wrecks like shattered mountains rise,
And flowering weeds, and fragrant copses dress
The bones of Desolation's nakedness
Pass, till the spirit of the spot shall lead
   Thy footsteps to a slope of green access
   Where, like an infant's smile, over the dead   440
A light of laughing flowers along the grass is spread;

L

And gray walls moulder round, on which dull Time
Feeds, like slow fire upon a hoary brand;
And one keen pyramid with wedge sublime,
Pavilioning the dust of him who planned
This refuge for his memory, doth stand
Like flame transformed to marble; and beneath,
A field is spread, on which a newer band
Have pitched in Heaven's smile their camp of death,
Welcoming him we lose with scarce extinguished breath.   450

L I

Here pause: these graves are all too young as yet
To have outgrown the sorrow which consigned
Its charge to each; and if the seal is set,
Here, on one fountain of a mourning mind,
Break it not thou! too surely shalt thou find
Thine own well full, if thou returnest home,
Of tears and gall. From the world's bitter wind
Seek shelter in the shadow of the tomb.
What Adonais is, why fear we to become?

L I I

The One remains, the many change and pass;   460
Heaven's light forever shines, Earth's shadows fly;
Life, like a dome of many-coloured glass,
Stains the white radiance of Eternity,
Until Death tramples it to fragments.—Die,
If thou wouldst be with that which thou dost seek!
Follow where all is fled!—Rome's azure sky,
Flowers, ruins, statues, music, words, are weak
The glory they transfuse with fitting truth to speak.

L I I I

Why linger, why turn back, why shrink, my Heart?
Thy hopes are gone before: from all things here   470
They have departed; thou shouldst now depart!
A light is passed from the revolving year,
And man, and woman; and what still is dear

Attracts to crush, repels to make thee wither.
The soft sky smiles,—the low wind whispers near:
'Tis Adonais calls! oh, hasten thither,
No more let Life divide what Death can join together.

LIV

That Light whose smile kindles the Universe,
That Beauty in which all things work and move,
That Benediction which the eclipsing Curse   480
Of birth can quench not, that sustaining Love
Which through the web of being blindly wove
By man and beast and earth and air and sea,
Burns bright or dim, as each are mirrors of
The fire for which all thirst; now beams on me,
Consuming the last clouds of cold mortality.

LV

The breath whose might I have invoked in song
Descends on me; my spirit's bark is driven,
Far from the shore, far from the trembling throng
Whose sails were never to the tempest given;   490
The massy earth and spherèd skies are riven!
I am borne darkly, fearfully, afar;
Whilst, burning through the inmost veil of Heaven,
The soul of Adonais, like a star,
Beacons from the abode where the Eternal are.

l. 160. brere = briar, bush
l. 268. Ierne = Moore's Ireland
l. 381. plastic = formative

John Clare

(1793 – 1864)

A rural laborer born in a village in Northamptonshire to a thresher and shepherd's daughter, both of whom recited ballads and songs, Clare attended local schools until age twelve, had eight children from his marriage in 1820, and with his *Poems Descriptive of Rural Life and Scenery* (1820) shared with Keats the same publisher and for a few years shared also just about the same amount of attention in literary circles. From 1837 he lived under mental supervision, from 1841 in the Northampton General Lunatic Asylum. His many manuscript poems—descriptive, narrative, lyrical, visionary, or hallucinatory (some under the impression that he was Lord Byron)—have restored and increased his fame, beginning in 1920, when Edmund Blunden and Alan Porter edited a selection in *Poems Chiefly from Manuscript*. "I Am" is part of that collection.

THE SHEPHERD BOY

Pleased in his loneliness, he often lies,
　　Telling glad stories to his dog or e'en
His very shadow, that the loss supplies
　　Of living company. Full oft he'll lean
By pebbled brooks and dream with happy ey
　　Upon the fairy pictures spread below,
Thinking the shadowed prospects real skies
　　And happy heavens where his kindred go.
Oft we may track his haunts, where he hath been
　　To spend the leisure which his toils bestow,
By nine-peg morris nicked upon the green,
　　Or flower-stuck gardens, never meant to grow,
　　Or figures cut on trees, his skill to show,
Where he a prisoner from a shower hath been.

l. 11. morris = a game with pegs (merels) as counters

I AM

I am: yet what I am, none cares or knows;
    My friends forsake me like a memory lost:
I am the self-consumer of my woes—
    They rise and vanish in oblivion's host,
Like shadows in love's frenzied stifled throes:
    And yet I am, and live—like vapours tost

Into the nothingness of scorn and noise,
    Into the living sea of waking dreams,
Where there is neither sense of life or joys,
    But the vast shipwreck of my life's esteems;   10
Even the dearest that I love the best
    Are strange—nay, rather, stranger than the rest.

I long for scenes where man hath never trod,
    A place where woman never smiled or wept—
There to abide with my Creator God
    And sleep as I in childhood sweetly slept,
Untroubling and untroubled where I lie
    The grass below; above, the vaulted sky.

Felicia Dorothea Browne Hemans

(1 7 9 3 – 1 8 3 5)

A prolific and immensely popular poet—Shelley wooed her, Scott and Byron respected her lyric gifts, Wordsworth mourned her death—Browne supported herself and five sons when Captain Hemans left her in 1818. Although her fame was reduced until recently to a few phrases "The stately Homes of England," "The boy stood on the burning deck," and other bits of piety and patriotism—the great variety in her accomplishment has been acclaimed anew by critics who find usable opposition to masculine aggressiveness in her *Records of Woman* (1828), including "The Image in Lava" on the impress of a mother and child in the uncovered ruins of Herculaneum.

THE IMAGE IN LAVA

Thou thing of years departed!
  What ages have gone by,
Since here the mournful seal was set
  By love and agony!

Temple and tower have moulder'd,
  Empires from earth have pass'd,—
And woman's heart hath left a trace
  Those glories to outlast!

And childhood's fragile image,
  Thus fearfully enshrin'd,   10
Survives the proud memorials rear'd
  By conquerors of mankind.

Babe! wert thou brightly slumbering
  Upon thy mother's breast,
When suddenly the fiery tomb
  Shut round each gentle guest?

A strange, dark fate o'ertook you,
  Fair babe and loving heart!

One moment of a thousand pangs—
　　Yet better than to part!   20

Haply of that fond bosom,
　　On ashes here impress'd,
Thou wert the only treasure, child!
　　Whereon a hope might rest.

Perchance all vainly lavish'd
　　Its other love had been,
And where it trusted, nought remain'd
　　But thorns on which to lean.

Far better then to perish,
　　Thy form within its clasp,   30
Than live and lose thee, precious one!
　　From that impassion'd grasp.

Oh! I could pass all relics
　　Left by the pomps of old,
To gaze on this rude monument,
　　Cast in affection's mould.

Love, human love! what art thou?
　　Thy print upon the dust
Outlives the cities of renown
　　Wherein the mighty trust!   40

John Keats

(1795–1821)

If no poems by Keats other than the several odes had survived, he would remain one of the most widely anthologized of English poets. Friends recognized in the Cockney orphan apprenticed to a surgeon, as Keats himself did, poetic powers worth staking his short life on. Besides the intensity of his melding of language and feeling, the selections here display Keats's immersion in masterworks of literature, his awareness that tuberculosis would soon end his creativity, and his fierce, jealous love for a near neighbor, Fanny Brawne; unfortunately, marriage would require financial success, an aim entangled with the goal of lasting fame.

In 1819, he devised a stanza form for the odes that was apparently a combination of rhyme-schemes from Shakespearean and Miltonic sonnets. In "To Autumn" he expanded the rhyme-scheme with an additional line to form a hesitational antepenultimate couplet. "To Autumn" was written in September 1819 and published with the odes in *Lamia, Isabella, The Eve of St. Agnes, and Other Poems* (1820). Of the four sonnets, only the earliest, "On First Looking into Chapman's Homer," was published by Keats (*Poems*, 1817), although two were written in 1818 and "Bright Star" in 1819; these, and the ballad "La Belle Dame," were collected by Richard Monckton Milnes in the volumes that intensified and assured Keats's fame, *Life, Letters, and Literary Remains, of John Keats* (1848). On Keats's death in Rome at age twenty-six, see Shelley's "Adonais" (p. 527).

ON FIRST LOOKING INTO CHAPMAN'S HOMER

Much have I travell'd in the realms of gold,
  And many goodly states and kingdoms seen;
  Round many western islands have I been
Which bards in fealty to Apollo hold.
Oft of one wide expanse had I been told
  That deep-brow'd Homer ruled as his demesne;
  Yet did I never breathe its pure serene
Till I heard Chapman speak out loud and bold:
Then felt I like some watcher of the skies

When a new planet swims into his ken;
Or like stout Cortez when with eagle eyes
　　He star'd at the Pacific—and all his men
Look'd at each other with a wild surmise—
　　Silent, upon a peak in Darien.

WHEN I HAVE FEARS THAT I
MAY CEASE TO BE

When I have fears that I may cease to be
　　Before my pen has glean'd my teeming brain,
Before high-piled books, in charactery,
　　Hold like rich garners the full ripen'd grain;
When I behold, upon the night's starr'd face,
　　Huge cloudy symbols of a high romance,
And think that I may never live to trace
　　Their shadows, with the magic hand of chance;
And when I feel, fair creature of an hour,
　　That I shall never look upon thee more,
Never have relish in the faery power
　　Of unreflecting love;—then on the shore
Of the wide world I stand alone, and think
Till love and fame to nothingness do sink.

ON SITTING DOWN TO READ
KING LEAR ONCE AGAIN

O golden tongued Romance, with serene lute!
　　Fair plumed Syren, Queen of far-away!
　　Leave melodizing on this wintry day,
Shut up thine olden pages, and be mute:
Adieu! for, once again, the fierce dispute
　　Betwixt damnation and impassion'd clay
　　Must I burn through; once more humbly assay
The bitter-sweet of this Shakespearian fruit:
Chief Poet! and ye clouds of Albion,
　　Begetters of our deep eternal theme!

When through the old oak Forest I am gone,
　　Let me not wander in a barren dream,
But, when I am consumed in the fire,
Give me new Phœnix wings to fly at my desire.

BRIGHT STAR

Bright star, would I were stedfast as thou art—
　　Not in lone splendour hung aloft the night
And watching, with eternal lids apart,
　　Like nature's patient, sleepless Eremite,
The moving waters at their priestlike task
　　Of pure ablution round earth's human shores,
Or gazing on the new soft-fallen mask
　　Of snow upon the mountains and the moors—
No—yet still stedfast, still unchangeable,
　　Pillow'd upon my fair love's ripening breast,
To feel for ever its soft fall and swell,
　　Awake for ever in a sweet unrest,
Still, still to hear her tender-taken breath,
And so live ever—or else swoon to death.

ODE ON A GRECIAN URN

Thou still unravish'd bride of quietness,
　　Thou foster-child of silence and slow time,
Sylvan historian, who canst thus express
　　A flowery tale more sweetly than our rhyme:
What leaf-fring'd legend haunts about thy shape
　　Of deities or mortals, or of both,
　　　　In Tempe or the dales of Arcady?
　　What men or gods are these? What maidens loth?
What mad pursuit? What struggle to escape?
　　　　What pipes and timbrels? What wild ecstasy?   10

Heard melodies are sweet, but those unheard
　　Are sweeter; therefore, ye soft pipes, play on;
Not to the sensual ear, but, more endear'd,

Pipe to the spirit ditties of no tone:
Fair youth, beneath the trees, thou canst not leave
   Thy song, nor ever can those trees be bare;
      Bold Lover, never, never canst thou kiss,
Though winning near the goal—yet, do not grieve;
   She cannot fade, though thou hast not thy bliss,
      For ever wilt thou love, and she be fair!   20

Ah, happy, happy boughs! that cannot shed
   Your leaves, nor ever bid the Spring adieu;
And, happy melodist, unwearied,
   For ever piping songs for ever new;
More happy love! more happy, happy love!
   For ever warm and still to be enjoy'd,
      For ever panting, and for ever young;
All breathing human passion far above,
   That leaves a heart high-sorrowful and cloy'd,
      A burning forehead, and a parching tongue.   30

Who are these coming to the sacrifice?
   To what green altar, O mysterious priest,
Lead'st thou that heifer lowing at the skies,
   And all her silken flanks with garlands drest?
What little town by river or sea shore,
   Or mountain-built with peaceful citadel,
      Is emptied of this folk, this pious morn?
And, little town, thy streets for evermore
   Will silent be; and not a soul to tell
      Why thou art desolate, can e'er return.   40

O Attic shape! Fair attitude! with brede
   Of marble men and maidens overwrought,
With forest branches and the trodden weed;
   Thou, silent form, dost tease us out of thought
As doth eternity: Cold Pastoral!
   When old age shall this generation waste,
      Thou shalt remain, in midst of other woe
Than ours, a friend to man, to whom thou say'st,
   "Beauty is truth, truth beauty,"—that is all
      Ye know on earth, and all ye need to know.   50

ODE TO A NIGHTINGALE

My heart aches, and a drowsy numbness pains
   My sense, as though of hemlock I had drunk,
Or emptied some dull opiate to the drains
   One minute past, and Lethe-wards had sunk:
'Tis not through envy of thy happy lot,
   But being too happy in thine happiness,—
      That thou, light-winged Dryad of the trees,
         In some melodious plot
   Of beechen green, and shadows numberless,
      Singest of summer in full-throated ease.   10

O, for a draught of vintage! that hath been
   Cool'd a long age in the deep-delved earth,
Tasting of Flora and the country green,
   Dance, and Provençal song, and sunburnt mirth!
O for a beaker full of the warm South,
   Full of the true, the blushful Hippocrene,
      With beaded bubbles winking at the brim,
         And purple-stained mouth;
   That I might drink, and leave the world unseen,
      And with thee fade away into the forest dim: 20

Fade far away, dissolve, and quite forget
   What thou among the leaves hast never known,
The weariness, the fever, and the fret
   Here, where men sit and hear each other groan;
Where palsy shakes a few, sad, last gray hairs,
   Where youth grows pale, and spectre-thin, and dies;
      Where but to think is to be full of sorrow
         And leaden-eyed despairs,
      Where Beauty cannot keep her lustrous eyes,
         Or new Love pine at them beyond to-morrow.   30

Away! away! for I will fly to thee,
   Not charioted by Bacchus and his pards,
But on the viewless wings of Poesy,
   Though the dull brain perplexes and retards:
Already with thee! tender is the night,
   And haply the Queen-Moon is on her throne,
      Cluster'd around by all her starry Fays;

But here there is no light,
  Save what from heaven is with the breezes blown
    Through verdurous glooms and winding mossy ways.   40

I cannot see what flowers are at my feet,
  Nor what soft incense hangs upon the boughs,
But, in embalmed darkness, guess each sweet
  Wherewith the seasonable month endows
The grass, the thicket, and the fruit-tree wild;
  White hawthorn, and the pastoral eglantine;
    Fast fading violets cover'd up in leaves;
      And mid-May's eldest child,
  The coming musk-rose, full of dewy wine,
    The murmurous haunt of flies on summer eves.   50

Darkling I listen; and, for many a time
  I have been half in love with easeful Death,
Call'd him soft names in many a mused rhyme,
  To take into the air my quiet breath;
Now more than ever seems it rich to die,
  To cease upon the midnight with no pain,
    While thou art pouring forth thy soul abroad
      In such an ecstasy!
  Still wouldst thou sing, and I have ears in vain—
    To thy high requiem become a sod.   60

Thou wast not born for death, immortal Bird!
  No hungry generations tread thee down;
The voice I hear this passing night was heard
  In ancient days by emperor and clown:
Perhaps the self-same song that found a path
  Through the sad heart of Ruth, when, sick for home,
    She stood in tears amid the alien corn;
      The same that oft-times hath
  Charm'd magic casements, opening on the foam
    Of perilous seas, in faery lands forlorn.   70

Forlorn! the very word is like a bell
  To toll me back from thee to my sole self!
Adieu! the fancy cannot cheat so well
  As she is fam'd to do, deceiving elf.
Adieu! adieu! thy plaintive anthem fades

Past the near meadows, over the still stream,
   Up the hill-side; and now 'tis buried deep
     In the next valley-glades:
Was it a vision, or a waking dream?
     Fled is that music:—Do I wake or sleep?   80

ODE ON MELANCHOLY

No, no, go not to Lethe, neither twist
   Wolf's-bane, tight-rooted, for its poisonous wine;
Nor suffer thy pale forehead to be kiss'd
   By nightshade, ruby grape of Proserpine;
Make not your rosary of yew-berries,
   Nor let the beetle, nor the death-moth be
     Your mournful Psyche, nor the downy owl
A partner in your sorrow's mysteries;
   For shade to shade will come too drowsily,
     And drown the wakeful anguish of the soul.   10

But when the melancholy fit shall fall
   Sudden from heaven like a weeping cloud,
That fosters the droop-headed flowers all,
   And hides the green hill in an April shroud;
Then glut thy sorrow on a morning rose,
   Or on the rainbow of the salt sand-wave,
     Or on the wealth of globed peonies;
Or if thy mistress some rich anger shows,
   Emprison her soft hand, and let her rave,
     And feed deep, deep upon her peerless eyes.   20

She dwells with Beauty—Beauty that must die;
   And Joy, whose hand is ever at his lips
Bidding adieu; and aching Pleasure nigh,
   Turning to poison while the bee-mouth sips:
Ay, in the very temple of Delight
   Veil'd Melancholy has her sovran shrine,
     Though seen of none save him whose strenuous tongue
   Can burst Joy's grape against his palate fine;
His soul shall taste the sadness of her might,
     And be among her cloudy trophies hung.   30

TO AUTUMN

Season of mists and mellow fruitfulness,
  Close bosom-friend of the maturing sun;
Conspiring with him how to load and bless
  With fruit the vines that round the thatch-eves run;
To bend with apples the moss'd cottage-trees,
  And fill all fruit with ripeness to the core;
    To swell the gourd, and plump the hazel shells
  With a sweet kernel; to set budding more,
And still more, later flowers for the bees,
Until they think warm days will never cease,   10
    For Summer has o'er-brimm'd their clammy cells.

Who hath not seen thee oft amid thy store?
  Sometimes whoever seeks abroad may find
Thee sitting careless on a granary floor,
  Thy hair soft-lifted by the winnowing wind;
Or on a half-reap'd furrow sound asleep,
  Drows'd with the fume of poppies, while thy hook
    Spares the next swath and all its twined flowers:
And sometimes like a gleaner thou dost keep
  Steady thy laden head across a brook;   20
  Or by a cyder-press, with patient look,
    Thou watchest the last oozings hours by hours.

Where are the songs of Spring? Ay, where are they?
  Think not of them, thou hast thy music too,—
While barred clouds bloom the soft-dying day,
  And touch the stubble-plains with rosy hue;
Then in a wailful choir the small gnats mourn
  Among the river sallows, borne aloft
    Or sinking as the light wind lives or dies;
And full-grown lambs loud bleat from hilly bourn;   30
  Hedge-crickets sing; and now with treble soft
  The red-breast whistles from a garden-croft;
    And gathering swallows twitter in the skies.

LA BELLE DAME
SANS MERCI

A Ballad

O, what can ail thee, knight-at-arms,
    Alone and palely loitering?
The sedge has wither'd from the lake,
    And no birds sing.

O, what can ail thee, knight-at-arms,
    So haggard and so woe-begone?
The squirrel's granary is full,
    And the harvest's done.

I see a lily on thy brow,
    With anguish moist and fever dew,   10
And on thy cheeks a fading rose
    Fast withereth too.

I met a lady in the meads,
    Full beautiful—a faery's child,
Her hair was long, her foot was light,
    And her eyes were wild.

I made a garland for her head,
    And bracelets too, and fragrant zone;
She look'd at me as she did love,
    And made sweet moan.   20

I set her on my pacing steed,
    And nothing else saw all day long;
For sidelong would she bend, and sing
    A faery's song.

She found me roots of relish sweet,
    And honey wild, and manna dew,
And sure in language strange she said—
    "I love thee true."

She took me to her elfin grot,
    And there she wept and sigh'd full sore,   30

And there I shut her wild wild eyes
   With kisses four.

And there she lulled me asleep
   And there I dream'd—Ah! woe betide!
The latest dream I ever dream'd
   On the cold hill side.

I saw pale kings and princes too,
   Pale warriors, death-pale were they all;
They cried—"La Belle Dame sans Merci
   Hath thee in thrall!"   40

I saw their starved lips in the gloam,
   With horrid warning gaped wide,
And I awoke and found me here,
   On the cold hill's side.

And this is why I sojourn here
   Alone and palely loitering,
Though the sedge has wither'd from the lake,
   And no birds sing.

THE EVE OF ST. AGNES

1

St. Agnes' Eve—Ah, bitter chill it was!
The owl, for all his feathers, was a-cold;
The hare limp'd trembling through the frozen grass,
And silent was the flock in woolly fold:
Numb were the Beadsman's fingers, while he told
His rosary, and while his frosted breath,
Like pious incense from a censer old,
Seem'd taking flight for heaven, without a death,
Past the sweet Virgin's picture, while his prayer he saith.

2

His prayer he saith, this patient, holy man;   10
Then takes his lamp, and riseth from his knees,

And back returneth, meagre, barefoot, wan,
Along the chapel aisle by slow degrees:
The sculptur'd dead, on each side, seem to freeze,
Emprison'd in black, purgatorial rails:
Knights, ladies, praying in dumb orat'ries,
He passeth by; and his weak spirit fails
To think how they may ache in icy hoods and mails.

3

Northward he turneth through a little door,
And scarce three steps, ere Music's golden tongue   20
Flatter'd to tears this aged man and poor;
But no—already had his deathbell rung;
The joys of all his life were said and sung:
His was harsh penance on St. Agnes' Eve:
Another way he went, and soon among
Rough ashes sat he for his soul's reprieve,
And all night kept awake, for sinners' sake to grieve.

4

That ancient Beadsman heard the prelude soft;
And so it chanc'd, for many a door was wide,
From hurry to and fro. Soon, up aloft,   30
The silver, snarling trumpets 'gan to chide:
The level chambers, ready with their pride,
Were glowing to receive a thousand guests:
The carved angels, ever eager-eyed,
Star'd, where upon their heads the cornice rests,
With hair blown back, and wings put cross-wise on their breasts.

5

At length burst in the argent revelry,
With plume, tiara, and all rich array,
Numerous as shadows haunting fairily
The brain, new stuff'd, in youth, with triumphs gay   40
Of old romance. These let us wish away,
And turn, sole-thoughted, to one Lady there,
Whose heart had brooded, all that wintry day,
On love, and wing'd St. Agnes' saintly care,
As she had heard old dames full many times declare.

6

They told her how, upon St. Agnes' Eve,
Young virgins might have visions of delight,
And soft adorings from their loves receive
Upon the honey'd middle of the night,
If ceremonies due they did aright;   50
As, supperless to bed they must retire,
And couch supine their beauties, lily white;
Nor look behind, nor sideways, but require
Of heaven with upward eyes for all that they desire.

['Twas said her future lord would there appear
Offering, as sacrifice—all in the dream—
Delicious food, even to her lips brought near,
Viands, and wine, and fruit, and sugar'd cream,
To touch her palate with the fine extreme
Of relish: then soft music heard, and then
More pleasures follow'd in a dizzy stream
Palpable almost: then to wake again
Warm in the virgin morn, no weeping Magdalen.]

7

Full of this whim was thoughtful Madeline:
The music, yearning like a god in pain,
She scarcely heard: her maiden eyes divine,
Fix'd on the floor, saw many a sweeping train
Pass by—she heeded not at all: in vain
Came many a tiptoe, amorous cavalier,   60
And back retir'd, not cool'd by high disdain;
But she saw not: her heart was otherwhere:
She sigh'd for Agnes' dreams, the sweetest of the year.

8

She danc'd along with vague, regardless eyes,
Anxious her lips, her breathing quick and short:
The hallow'd hour was near at hand: she sighs
Amid the timbrels, and the throng'd resort
Of whisperers in anger, or in sport;
'Mid looks of love, defiance, hate, and scorn,
Hoodwink'd with faery fancy; all amort,   70

Save to St. Agnes and her lambs unshorn,
And all the bliss to be before to-morrow morn.

9

So, purposing each moment to retire,
She linger'd still. Meantime, across the moors,
Had come young Porphyro, with heart on fire
For Madeline. Beside the portal doors,
Buttress'd from moonlight, stands he, and implores
All saints to give him sight of Madeline,
But for one moment in the tedious hours,
That he might gaze and worship all unseen;   80
Perchance speak, kneel, touch, kiss—in sooth such things have been.

10

He ventures in: let no buzz'd whisper tell:
All eyes be muffled, or a hundred swords
Will storm his heart, Love's fev'rous citadel:
For him, those chambers held barbarian hordes,
Hyena foemen, and hot-blooded lords,
Whose very dogs would execrations howl
Against his lineage: not one breast affords
Him any mercy, in that mansion foul,
Save one old beldame, weak in body and in soul.   90

11

Ah, happy chance! the aged creature came,
Shuffling along with ivory-headed wand,
To where he stood, hid from the torch's flame,
Behind a broad hall-pillar, far beyond
The sound of merriment and chorus bland:
He startled her; but soon she knew his face,
And grasp'd his fingers in her palsied hand,
Saying, "Mercy, Porphyro! hie thee from this place;
They are all here to-night, the whole blood-thirsty race!

12

"Get hence! get hence! there's dwarfish Hildebrand;   100
He had a fever late, and in the fit

He cursed thee and thine, both house and land:
Then there's that old Lord Maurice, not a whit
More tame for his gray hairs—Alas me! flit!
Flit like a ghost away."—"Ah, Gossip dear,
We're safe enough; here in this arm-chair sit,
And tell me how"—"Good Saints! not here, not here;
Follow me, child, or else these stones will be thy bier."

13

He follow'd through a lowly arched way,
Brushing the cobwebs with his lofty plume,   110
And as she mutter'd "Well-a—well-a-day!"
He found him in a little moonlight room,
Pale, lattic'd, chill, and silent as a tomb.
"Now tell me where is Madeline," said he,
"O tell me, Angela, by the holy loom
Which none but secret sisterhood may see,
When they St. Agnes' wool are weaving piously."

14

"St. Agnes! Ah! it is St. Agnes' Eve—
Yet men will murder upon holy days:
Thou must hold water in a witch's sieve,   120
And be liege-lord of all the Elves and Fays,
To venture so: it fills me with amaze
To see thee, Porphyro!—St. Agnes' Eve!
God's help! my lady fair the conjuror plays
This very night: good angels her deceive!
But let me laugh awhile, I've mickle time to grieve."

15

Feebly she laugheth in the languid moon,
While Porphyro upon her face doth look,
Like puzzled urchin on an aged crone
Who keepeth clos'd a wond'rous riddle-book,   130
As spectacled she sits in chimney nook.
But soon his eyes grew brilliant, when she told
His lady's purpose; and he scarce could brook
Tears, at the thought of those enchantments cold,
And Madeline asleep in lap of legends old.

16

Sudden a thought came like a full-blown rose,
Flushing his brow, and in his pained heart
Made purple riot: then doth he propose
A stratagem, that makes the beldame start:
"A cruel man and impious thou art: 140
Sweet lady, let her pray, and sleep, and dream
Alone with her good angels, far apart
From wicked men like thee. Go, go!—I deem
Thou canst not surely be the same that thou didst seem."

17

"I will not harm her, by all saints I swear,"
Quoth Porphyro: "O may I ne'er find grace
When my weak voice shall whisper its last prayer,
If one of her soft ringlets I displace,
Or look with ruffian passion in her face:
Good Angela, believe me by these tears;   150
Or I will, even in a moment's space,
Awake, with horrid shout, my foemen's ears,
And beard them, though they be more fang'd than wolves and bears."

18

"Ah! why wilt thou affright a feeble soul?
A poor, weak, palsy-stricken, churchyard thing,
Whose passing-bell may ere the midnight toll;
Whose prayers for thee, each morn and evening,
Were never miss'd."—Thus plaining, doth she bring
A gentler speech from burning Porphyro;
So woful, and of such deep sorrowing,   160
That Angela gives promise she will do
Whatever he shall wish, betide her weal or woe.

19

Which was, to lead him, in close secrecy,
Even to Madeline's chamber, and there hide
Him in a closet, of such privacy
That he might see her beauty unespied,
And win perhaps that night a peerless bride,

While legion'd fairies pac'd the coverlet,
And pale enchantment held her sleepy-eyed.
Never on such a night have lovers met,   170
Since Merlin paid his Demon all the monstrous debt.

        20

"It shall be as thou wishest," said the Dame:
"All cates and dainties shall be stored there
Quickly on this feast-night: by the tambour frame
Her own lute thou wilt see: no time to spare,
For I am slow and feeble, and scarce dare
On such a catering trust my dizzy head.
Wait here, my child, with patience; kneel in prayer
The while: Ah! thou must needs the lady wed,
Or may I never leave my grave among the dead."   180

        21

So saying, she hobbled off with busy fear.
The lover's endless minutes slowly pass'd;
The dame return'd, and whisper'd in his ear
To follow her; with aged eyes aghast
From fright of dim espial. Safe at last,
Through many a dusky gallery, they gain
The maiden's chamber, silken, hush'd, and chaste;
Where Porphyro took covert, pleas'd amain.
His poor guide hurried back with agues in her brain.

        22

Her falt'ring hand upon the balustrade,   190
Old Angela was feeling for the stair,
When Madeline, St. Agnes' charmed maid,
Rose, like a mission'd spirit, unaware:
With silver taper's light, and pious care,
She turn'd, and down the aged gossip led
To a safe level matting. Now prepare,
Young Porphyro, for gazing on that bed;
She comes, she comes again, like ring-dove fray'd and fled.

23

Out went the taper as she hurried in;
Its little smoke, in pallid moonshine, died: 200
She clos'd the door, she panted, all akin
To spirits of the air, and visions wide:
No uttered syllable, or, woe betide!
But to her heart, her heart was voluble,
Paining with eloquence her balmy side;
As though a tongueless nightingale should swell
Her throat in vain, and die, heart-stifled, in her dell.

24

A casement high and triple-arch'd there was,
All garlanded with carven imag'ries
Of fruits, and flowers, and bunches of knot-grass,   210
And diamonded with panes of quaint device,
Innumerable of stains and splendid dyes,
As are the tiger-moth's deep-damask'd wings;
And in the midst, 'mong thousand heraldries,
And twilight saints, and dim emblazonings,
A shielded scutcheon blush'd with blood of queens and kings.

25

Full on this casement shone the wintry moon,
And threw warm gules on Madeline's fair breast,
As down she knelt for heaven's grace and boon;
Rose-bloom fell on her hands, together prest,   220
And on her silver cross soft amethyst,
And on her hair a glory, like a saint:
She seem'd a splendid angel, newly drest,
Save wings, for heaven:—Porphyro grew faint:
She knelt, so pure a thing, so free from mortal taint.

26

Anon his heart revives: her vespers done,
Of all its wreathed pearls her hair she frees;
Unclasps her warmed jewels one by one;
Loosens her fragrant boddice; by degrees

Her rich attire creeps rustling to her knees: 230
Half-hidden, like a mermaid in sea-weed,
Pensive awhile she dreams awake, and sees,
    In fancy, fair St. Agnes in her bed,
But dares not look behind, or all the charm is fled.

    27

Soon, trembling in her soft and chilly nest,
In sort of wakeful swoon, perplex'd she lay,
Until the poppied warmth of sleep oppress'd
Her soothed limbs, and soul fatigued away;
Flown, like a thought, until the morrow-day;
Blissfully haven'd both from joy and pain;   240
Clasp'd like a missal where swart Paynims pray;
    Blinded alike from sunshine and from rain,
As though a rose should shut, and be a bud again.

    28

Stol'n to this paradise, and so entranced,
Porphyro gazed upon her empty dress,
And listen'd to her breathing, if it chanced
To wake into a slumberous tenderness;
Which when he heard, that minute did he bless,
And breath'd himself: then from the closet crept,
Noiseless as fear in a wide wilderness,   250
    And over the hush'd carpet, silent, stept,
And 'tween the curtains peep'd, where, lo!—how fast she slept.

    29

Then by the bed-side, where the faded moon
Made a dim, silver twilight, soft he set
A table, and, half anguish'd, threw thereon
A cloth of woven crimson, gold, and jet:—
O for some drowsy Morphean amulet!
The boisterous, midnight, festive clarion,
The kettle-drum, and far-heard clarionet,
    Affray his ears, though but in dying tone:—   260
The hall door shuts again, and all the noise is gone.

30

And still she slept an azure-lidded sleep,
In blanched linen, smooth, and lavender'd,
While he from forth the closet brought a heap
Of candied apple, quince, and plum, and gourd;
With jellies soother than the creamy curd,
And lucent syrops, tinct with cinnamon;
Manna and dates, in argosy transferr'd
From Fez; and spiced dainties, every one,
From silken Samarcand to cedar'd Lebanon.   270

31

These delicates he heap'd with glowing hand
On golden dishes and in baskets bright
Of wreathed silver: sumptuous they stand
In the retired quiet of the night,
Filling the chilly room with perfume light.—
"And now, my love, my seraph fair, awake!
Thou art my heaven, and I thine eremite:
Open thine eyes, for meek St. Agnes' sake,
Or I shall drowse beside thee, so my soul doth ache."

32

Thus whispering, his warm, unnerved arm   280
Sank in her pillow. Shaded was her dream
By the dusk curtains:—'twas a midnight charm
Impossible to melt as iced stream:
The lustrous salvers in the moonlight gleam;
Broad golden fringe upon the carpet lies:
It seem'd he never, never could redeem
From such a stedfast spell his lady's eyes;
So mus'd awhile, entoil'd in woofed phantasies.

33

Awakening up, he took her hollow lute,—
Tumultuous,—and, in chords that tenderest be,   290
He play'd an ancient ditty, long since mute,
In Provence call'd, "La belle dame sans mercy":
Close to her ear touching the melody;—

Wherewith disturb'd, she utter'd a soft moan:
He ceased—she panted quick—and suddenly
Her blue affrayed eyes wide open shone:
Upon his knees he sank, pale as smooth-sculptured stone.

34

Her eyes were open, but she still beheld,
Now wide awake, the vision of her sleep:
There was a painful change, that nigh expell'd   300
The blisses of her dream so pure and deep:
At which fair Madeline began to weep,
And moan forth witless words with many a sigh;
While still her gaze on Porphyro would keep;
Who knelt, with joined hands and piteous eye,
Fearing to move or speak, she look'd so dreamingly.

35

"Ah, Porphyro!" said she, "but even now
Thy voice was at sweet tremble in mine ear,
Made tuneable with every sweetest vow;
And those sad eyes were spiritual and clear: 310
How chang'd thou art! how pallid, chill, and drear!
Give me that voice again, my Porphyro,
Those looks immortal, those complainings dear!
Oh leave me not in this eternal woe,
For if thou diest, my love, I know not where to go."

36

Beyond a mortal man impassion'd far
At these voluptuous accents, he arose,
Ethereal, flush'd, and like a throbbing star
Seen mid the sapphire heaven's deep repose;
Into her dream he melted, as the rose   320
Blendeth its odour with the violet,—
Solution sweet: meantime the frost-wind blows
Like Love's alarum pattering the sharp sleet
Against the window-panes; St. Agnes' moon hath set.

37

'Tis dark: quick pattereth the flaw-blown sleet:
"This is no dream, my bride, my Madeline!"
'Tis dark: the iced gusts still rave and beat:
"No dream, alas! alas! and woe is mine!
Porphyro will leave me here to fade and pine.—
Cruel! what traitor could thee hither bring? 330
I curse not, for my heart is lost in thine,
Though thou forsakest a deceived thing;—
A dove forlorn and lost with sick unpruned wing."

38

"My Madeline! sweet dreamer! lovely bride!
Say, may I be for aye thy vassal blest?
Thy beauty's shield, heart-shap'd and vermeil dyed?
Ah, silver shrine, here will I take my rest
After so many hours of toil and quest,
A famish'd pilgrim,—saved by miracle.
Though I have found, I will not rob thy nest 340
Saving of thy sweet self; if thou think'st well
To trust, fair Madeline, to no rude infidel.

39

"Hark! 'tis an elfin-storm from faery land,
Of haggard seeming, but a boon indeed:
Arise—arise! the morning is at hand;—
The bloated wassaillers will never heed:—
Let us away, my love, with happy speed;
There are no ears to hear, or eyes to see,—
Drown'd all in Rhenish and the sleepy mead:
Awake! arise! my love, and fearless be, 350
For o'er the southern moors I have a home for thee."

40

She hurried at his words, beset with fears,
For there were sleeping dragons all around,
At glaring watch, perhaps, with ready spears—
Down the wide stairs a darkling way they found.—

In all the house was heard no human sound.
A chain-droop'd lamp was flickering by each door;
The arras, rich with horseman, hawk, and hound,
Flutter'd in the besieging wind's uproar;
And the long carpets rose along the gusty floor.   360

41

They glide, like phantoms, into the wide hall;
Like phantoms, to the iron porch, they glide;
Where lay the Porter, in uneasy sprawl,
With a huge empty flaggon by his side:
The wakeful bloodhound rose, and shook his hide,
But his sagacious eye an inmate owns:
By one, and one, the bolts full easy slide:—
The chains lie silent on the footworn stones;—
The key turns, and the door upon its hinges groans.

42

And they are gone: ay, ages long ago   370
These lovers fled away into the storm.
That night the Baron dreamt of many a woe,
And all his warrior-guests, with shade and form
Of witch, and demon, and large coffin-worm,
Were long be-nightmar'd. Angela the old
Died palsy-twitch'd, with meagre face deform;
The Beadsman, after thousand aves told,
For aye unsought for slept among his ashes cold.

stanza 6. The bracketed stanza was dropped from the published version.

Thomas Hood

(1799–1845)

A Londoner except for brief residence in Coblenz and Ostend in the late 1830s, editor of literary, popular, and comic periodicals, Hood published in the 1820s romantic narratives and lyrics (some of them almost paraphrases of Keats), and in the "hungry forties" serious poems of social protest. His forte, however, was comic inversion of romanticism's gothic and supernatural sobrieties. Typically, "Sally Simpkin's Lament" (in *Hood's Own*, 1839) exploits conversational clichés for remorseless puns.

SALLY SIMPKIN'S LAMENT;

OR, JOHN JONES'S KIT-CAT-ASTROPHE

"Oh! what is that comes gliding in,
    And quite in middling haste?
It is the picture of my Jones,
    And painted to the waist.

"It is not painted to the life,
    For where's the trowsers blue?
Oh Jones, my dear!—Oh dear! my Jones,
    What is become of you?"

"Oh! Sally dear, it is too true,—
    The half that you remark   10
Is come to say my other half
    Is bit off by a shark!

"Oh! Sally, sharks do things by halves,
    Yet most completely do!
A bite in one place seems enough,
    But I've been bit in two.

"You know I once was all your own,
    But now a shark must share!
But let that pass—for now, to you
    I'm neither here nor there.   20

"Alas! death has a strange divorce
    Effected in the sea,
It has divided me from you,
    And even me from me!

"Don't fear my ghost will walk o' nights
    To haunt, as people say;
My ghost *can't* walk, for, oh! my legs
    Are many leagues away!

"Lord! think when I am swimming round,
    And looking where the boat is,
A shark just snaps away a *half*,   30
    Without a '*quarter*'s notice.'

"One half is here, the other half
    Is near Columbia placed;
Oh! Sally, I have got the whole
    Atlantic for my waist.

"But now, adieu—a long adieu!
    I've solved death's awful riddle,
And would say more, but I am doomed
    To break off in the middle!"   40

Thomas Babington Macaulay

(1 8 0 0 – 1 8 5 9)

Created Baron Macaulay of Rothley near the end of a hyperactive life in Parliament and public office, barrister and educationist, Macaulay had twice won at Cambridge the Chancellor's medal for English verse. He reached successive generations of readers with his collected essays and *History of England* as well as with his *Lays of Ancient Rome* (1842). "Horatius," first of the four heroic lays, inspired those generations for a century—through 1945— with patriotism.

From HORATIUS

Then out spake brave Horatius,
    The Captain of the Gate: 210
"To every man upon this earth
    Death cometh soon or late.
And how can man die better
    Than facing fearful odds,
For the ashes of his fathers,
    And the temples of his Gods,

"And for the tender mother
    Who dandled him to rest,
And for the wife who nurses
    His baby at her breast,   220
And for the holy maidens
    Who feed the eternal flame,
To save them from false Sextus
    That wrought the deed of shame?

"Hew down the bridge, Sir Consul,
    With all the speed ye may;
I, with two more to help me,
    Will hold the foe in play.
In yon strait path a thousand
    May well be stopped by three.   230
Now who will stand on either hand,
    And keep the bridge with me?"

Then out spake Spurius Lartius;
   A Ramnian proud was he:
"Lo, I will stand at thy right hand,
   And keep the bridge with thee."
And out spake strong Herminius;
   Of Titian blood was he:
"I will abide on thy left side,
   And keep the bridge with thee."   240

"Horatius," quoth the Consul,
   "As thou sayest, so let it be."
And straight against that great array
   Forth went the dauntless Three.
For Romans in Rome's quarrel
   Spared neither land nor gold,
Nor son nor wife, nor limb nor life,
   In the brave days of old.

Then none was for a party;
   Then all were for the state;   250
Then the great man helped the poor,
   And the poor man loved the great.
Then lands were fairly portioned;
   Then spoils were fairly sold:
The Romans were like brothers
   In the brave days of old.

John Henry Newman

(1 8 0 1 – 1 8 9 0)

An intensely intellectual believer in assent to God's will almost from his birth in London, co-leader in the Tractarian or Anglican High Church movement at Oxford from 1833 to 1841, a priest in the Roman Catholic Church from 1847 and Cardinal from 1879, Newman turned from controversy, but not from piety and theology, in his dramatic poem *The Dream of Gerontius* (1866). In lines 533–571, the Angel sent to comfort and prepare the dying old man (Gerontius) greets the soul that has newly lost its body. T. S. Eliot's later sympathy with the rhythms and message of the poem differed greatly from his early response in "Gerontion."

From THE DREAM OF GERONTIUS

ANGEL

Nor touch, nor taste, nor hearing hast thou now;
Thou livest in a world of signs and types,
The presentations of most holy truths,
Living and strong, which now encompass thee.
A disembodied soul, thou hast by right
No converse with aught else beside thyself;
But, lest so stern a solitude should load
And break thy being, in mercy are vouchsafed   540
Some lower measures of perception,
Which seem to thee, as though through channels brought,
Through ear, or nerves, or palate, which are gone.
And thou art wrapped and swathed around in dreams,
Dreams that are true, yet enigmatical;
For the belongings of thy present state,
Save through such symbols, come not home to thee.
And thus thou tell'st of space, and time, and size,
Of fragrant, solid, bitter, musical,
Of fire, and of refreshment after fire;   550
As (let me use similitude of earth,
To aid thee in the knowledge thou dost ask)—

As ice which blisters may be said to burn.
Nor hast thou now extension, with its parts
Correlative,—long habit cozens thee,—
Nor power to move thyself, nor limbs to move.
Hast thou not heard of those, who after loss
Of hand or foot, still cried that they had pains
In hand or foot, as though they had it still?
So is it now with thee, who has not lost   560
Thy hand or foot, but all which made up man.
So will it be, until the joyous day
Of resurrection, when thou wilt regain
All thou hast lost, new-made and glorified.
How, even now, the consummated Saints
See God in heaven, I may not explicate;
Meanwhile, let it suffice thee to possess
Such means of converse as are granted thee,
Though, till that Beatific Vision, thou art blind;
For e'en thy purgatory, which comes like fire,   570
Is fire without its light.

Letitia Elizabeth Landon

(1802 – 1838)

Poems signed "L. E. L." in the gift-book Annuals took on even more glamor from rumors of unseemly alliances, her surprising marriage in 1838 to George Maclean, governor of Cape Coast Castle in West Africa, and her almost immediate death there in mysterious circumstances. "The Enchanted Island, from the Picture by Danby in the British Gallery" was first published in July 1825 in the *Bristol Times and Mirror*. Francis Danby himself relied on literary sources and quoted verses to prove it. One of Landon's specialities was descriptive celebration in verse of exhibited paintings; another—not a negligible accomplishment—was wish fulfillment.

THE ENCHANTED ISLAND

And there the island lay, the waves around
Had never known a storm; for the north wind
Was charm'd from coming, and the only airs
That blew brought sunshine on their azure wings,
Or tones of music from the sparry caves,
Where the sea-maids make lutes of the pink conch.
These were sea breezes,—those that swept the land
Brought other gifts,—sighs from blue violets,
Or from June's sweet Sultana, the bright rose,
Stole odours. On the silver mirror's face   10
Was but a single ripple that was made
By a flamingo's beak, whose scarlet wings
Shone like a meteor on the stream: around,
Upon the golden sands, were coral plants,
And shells of many colours, and sea weeds,
Whose foliage caught and chain'd the Nautilus,
Where lay they as at anchor. On each side
Were grottoes, like fair porticoes with steps
Of the green marble; and a lovely light,
Like the far radiance of a thousand lamps,   20
Half-shine, half-shadow, or the glorious track
Of a departing star but faintly seen

In the dim distance, through those caverns shone,
And play'd o'er the tall trees which seem'd to hide
Gardens, where hyacinths rang their soft bells
To call the bees from the anemone,
Jealous of their bright rivals' golden wealth.
—Amid those arches floated starry shapes,
Just indistinct enough to make the eye
Dream of surpassing beauty; but in front,   30
Borne on a car of pearl, and drawn by swans,
There lay a lovely figure,—she was queen
Of the Enchanted Island, which was raised
From ocean's bosom but to pleasure her:
And spirits, from the stars, and from the sea,
The beautiful mortal had them for her slaves.

    She was the daughter of a king, and loved
By a young Ocean Spirit from her birth,—
He hover'd o'er her in her infancy,
And bade the rose grow near her, that her cheek   40
Might catch its colour,—lighted up her dreams
With fairy wonders, and made harmony
The element in which she moved; at last,
When that she turn'd away from earthly love,
Enamour'd of her visions, he became
Visible with his radiant wings, and bore
His bride to the fair island.

William Mackworth Praed

(1 8 0 2 – 1 8 3 9)

Founder at school of the *Etonian*, later barrister, conservative M.P., and government official declining rapidly from tuberculosis, Praed wrote light *vers de société* that deliberately recalled mildly satirical verse by Matthew Prior (and Swift). Lines headed in manuscript "A Letter from a Lady in London to a Lady in Lausanne" were given the title "The Talented Man" by Derwent Coleridge, a friend from Eton and Cambridge days, in the posthumous edition of Praed's *Poems*.

THE TALENTED MAN

A LETTER FROM A LADY IN LONDON TO A LADY AT LAUSANNE

Dear Alice! you'll laugh when you know it,—
    Last week, at the Duchess's ball,
I danced with the clever new poet,—
    You've heard of him,—Tully St. Paul.
Miss Jonquil was perfectly frantic;
    I wish you had seen Lady Anne!
It really was very romantic,
    He *is* such a talented man!

He came up from Brazenose College,
    Just caught, as they call it, this spring;   10
And his head, love, is stuffed full of knowledge
    Of every conceivable thing.
Of science and logic he chatters,
    As fine and as fast as he can;
Though I am no judge of such matters,
    I'm sure he's a talented man.

His stories and jests are delightful;—
    Not stories, or jests, dear, for you;
The jests are exceedingly spiteful,
    The stories not always *quite* true.   20

Perhaps to be kind and veracious
   May do pretty well at Lausanne;
But it never would answer,—good gracious!
   Chez nous—in a talented man.

He sneers,—how my Alice would scold him!—
   At the bliss of a sigh or a tear;
He laughed—only think!—when I told him
   How we cried o'er Trevelyan last year.
I vow I was quite in a passion;
   I broke all the sticks of my fan;   30
But sentiment's quite out of fashion,
   It seems, in a talented man.

Lady Bab, who is terribly moral,
   Has told me that Tully is vain,
And apt—which is silly—to quarrel,
   And fond—which is sad—of champagne.
I listened, and doubted, dear Alice,
   For I saw, when my Lady began,
It was only the Dowager's malice;—
   She *does* hate a talented man!   40

He's hideous, I own it. But fame, love,
   Is all that these eyes can adore;
He's lame,—but Lord Byron was lame, love,
   And dumpy,—but so is Tom Moore.
Then his voice,—*such* a voice! my sweet creature,
   It's like your Aunt Lucy's toucan:
But oh! what's a tone or a feature,
   When once one's a talented man?

My mother, you know, all the season,
   Has talked of Sir Geoffrey's estate;   50
And truly, to do the fool reason,
   He *has* been less horrid of late.
But today, when we drive in the carriage,
   I'll tell her to lay down her plan;—
If ever I venture on marriage
   It must be a talented man!

P.S.—I have found on reflection,
   One fault in my friend,—*entre nous,*

Without it, he'd just be perfection;—
  Poor fellow, he has not a *sou!*   60
And so, when he comes in September
  To shoot with my uncle, Sir Dan,
I've promised mamma to remember
  He's *only* a talented man!

James Clarence Mangan

(1803–1849)

A Dubliner by birth and choice of residence, Mangan combined various literary activities with modest posts as scrivener, as assistant in the library of Trinity College, Dublin, and as clerk in the office of the Irish ordnance survey. He contributed verse and prose to the *United Irishman* and other periodicals. Ultimately he drank away all chance at steady employment. As a translator of verse from many languages, he appropriated and adapted with a passion that made each work his own. He introduced, in the popular periodicals of the day, new worlds from Sanskrit and Arabic as well as from the Gaelic past and some German poets of his own time. Mangan translated, with typical freedom and fire, "O'Hussey's Ode to the Maguire" from the Gaelic of Eochaidh Ó Heóghusa (see p. 108).

O'HUSSEY'S ODE TO THE MAGUIRE

Where is my Chief, my Master, this bleak night, *mavrone!*
O, cold, cold, miserably cold is this bleak night for Hugh,
It's showery, arrowy, speary sleet pierceth one through and through,
Pierceth one to the very bone!

Rolls real thunder? Or was that red, livid light
Only a meteor? I scarce know; but through the midnight dim
The pitiless ice-wind streams. Except the hate that persecutes *him*
Nothing hath crueller venomy might.

An awful, a tremendous night is this, meseems!
The flood-gates of the rivers of heaven, I think, have been burst wide—   10
Down from the overcharged clouds, like unto headlong ocean's tide,
Descends grey rain in roaring streams.

Though he were even a wolf ranging the round green woods,
Though he were even a pleasant salmon in the unchainable sea,
Though he were a wild mountain eagle, he could scarce bear, he,
This sharp, sore sleet, these howling floods.

O, mournful is my soul this night for Hugh Maguire!
Darkly, as in a dream, he strays! Before him and behind
Triumphs the tyrannous anger of the wounding wind,
The wounding wind, that burns as fire!   20

It is my bitter grief—it cuts me to the heart—
That in the country of Clan Darry this should be his fate!
O, woe is me, where is he? Wandering, houseless, desolate,
Alone, without or guide or chart!

Medreams I see just now his face, the strawberry bright,
Uplifted to the blackened heavens, while the tempestuous winds
Blow fiercely over and round him, and the smiting sleet-shower blinds
The hero of Galang to-night!

Large, large affliction unto me and mine it is,
That one of his majestic bearing, his fair, stately form,   30
Should thus be tortured and o'erborne—that this unsparing storm
Should wreak its wrath on head like his!

That his great hand, so oft the avenger of the oppressed,
Should this chill, churlish night, perchance, be paralysed by frost—
While through some icicle-hung thicket—as one lorn and lost—
He walks and wanders without rest.

The tempest-driven torrent deluges the mead,
It overflows the low banks of the rivulets and ponds—
The lawns and pasture-grounds lie locked in icy bonds
So that the cattle cannot feed.   40

The pale bright margins of the streams are seen by none.
Rushes and sweeps along the untamable flood on every side—
It penetrates and fills the cottagers' dwellings far and wide—
Water and land are blent in one.

Through some dark woods, 'mid bones of monsters, Hugh now strays,
As he confronts the storm with anguished heart, but manly brow—
O! what a sword-wound to that tender heart of his were now
A backward glance at peaceful days.

But other thoughts are his—thoughts that can still inspire
With joy and an onward-bounding hope the bosom of Mac-Nee—   50

Thoughts of his warriors charging like bright billows of the sea,
Borne on the wind's wings, flashing fire!

And though frost glaze to-night the clear dew of his eyes,
And white ice-gauntlets glove his noble fine fair fingers o'er,
A warm dress is to him that lightning-garb he ever wore,
The lightning of the soul, not skies.

Avran

Hugh marched forth to the fight—I grieved to see him so depart;
And lo! to-night he wanders frozen, rain-drenched, sad, betrayed—
But the memory of the lime-white mansions his right hand hath laid
In ashes warms the hero's heart!   60

Elizabeth Barrett Browning

(1 8 0 6 – 1 8 6 1)

When Robert Browning wrote to praise *Poems* (1844) by an invalid in London, Elizabeth Barrett Barrett, the result was elopement in 1846, to Italy—escape from the seclusion imposed by her stern father. In "Sonnets from the Portuguese," forty-four Petrarchan sonnets published in 1850, she traced the court-ship. Her *Casa Guidi Windows* (1851) was the first of several collections devoted to liberal causes in Italian politics; the title refers to the Brownings' villa in Florence. Bold in her range of poetic topics and devices, Browning was a largely self-taught linguist, with a special interest in Greek literature and myth, as shown by her return in "A Musical Instrument" (1860) to the Pan she had celebrated elegiacally in 1844.

From SONNETS FROM THE PORTUGUESE

3

Unlike are we, unlike, O princely Heart!
Unlike our uses and our destinies.
Our ministering two angels look surprise
On one another, as they strike athwart
Their wings in passing. Thou, bethink thee, art
A quest for queens to social pageantries,
With gages from a hundred brighter eyes
Than tears even can make mine, to play thy part
Of chief musician. What hast *thou* to do
With looking from the lattice-lights at me,
A poor, tired, wandering singer, singing through
The dark, and leaning up a cypress tree?
The chrism is on thine head,—on mine, the dew,—
And Death must dig the level where these agree.

l. 13. chrism = consecrated annointing oil

∂ 13 ∞

And wilt thou have me fashion into speech
The love I bear thee, finding words enough,
And hold the torch out, while the winds are rough,
Between our faces, to cast light on each?—
I drop it at thy feet. I cannot teach
My hand to hold my spirit so far off
From myself—me—that I should bring thee proof
In words, of love hid in me out of reach.
Nay, let the silence of my womanhood
Commend my woman-love to thy belief,—
Seeing that I stand unwon, however wooed,
And rend the garment of my life, in brief,
By a most dauntless, voiceless fortitude,
Lest one touch of this heart convey its grief.

∂ 43 ∞

How do I love thee? Let me count the ways.
I love thee to the depth and breadth and height
My soul can reach, when feeling out of sight
For the ends of Being and ideal Grace.
I love thee to the level of everyday's
Most quiet need, by sun and candle-light.
I love thee freely, as men strive for Right;
I love thee purely, as they turn from Praise.
I love thee with the passion put to use
In my old griefs, and with my childhood's faith.
I love thee with a love I seemed to lose
With my lost saints,—I love with the breath,
Smiles, tears, of all my life!—and, if God choose,
I shall but love thee better after death.

A MUSICAL INSTRUMENT

What was he doing, the great god Pan,
   Down in the reeds by the river?
Spreading ruin and scattering ban,
Splashing and paddling with hoofs of a goat,
And breaking the golden lilies afloat
   With the dragon-fly on the river.

He tore out a reed, the great god Pan,
　　From the deep cool bed of the river:
The limpid water turbidly ran,
And the broken lilies a-dying lay,　　　　　　　　　　10
And the dragon-fly had fled away,
　　Ere he brought it out of the river.

High on the shore sate the great god Pan,
　　While turbidly flowed the river;
And hacked and hewed as a great god can,
With his hard bleak steel at the patient reed,
Till there was not a sign of a leaf indeed
　　To prove it fresh from the river.

He cut it short, did the great god Pan
　　(How tall it stood in the river!),　　　　　　　　20
Then drew the pith, like the heart of a man,
Steadily from the outside ring,
And notched the poor dry empty thing
　　In holes, as he sate by the river.

"This is the way," laughed the great god Pan
　　(Laughed while he sate by the river),
"The only way, since gods began
To make sweet music, they could succeed."
Then, dropping his mouth to a hole in the reed,
　　He blew in power by the river.　　　　　　　　30

Sweet, sweet, sweet, O Pan!
　　Piercing sweet by the river!
Blinding sweet, O great god Pan!
The sun on the hill forgot to die,
And the lilies revived, and the dragon-fly
　　Came back to dream on the river.

Yet half a beast is the great god Pan,
　　To laugh as he sits by the river,
Making a poet out of a man:
The true gods sigh for the cost and pain,—　　　　40
For the reed which grows nevermore again,
　　As a reed with the reeds in the river.

Edward FitzGerald

(1 8 0 9 – 1 8 8 3)

In Suffolk except for four years as a student at Cambridge, Edward Purcell took his mother's surname, FitzGerald, and thereby increased his inherited income. His letters to Tennyson and other friends have been more widely read than most of his translations from Spanish, Greek, and Persian, but few works have been as perennially popular as his version (1859–1879) of Persian *rubais* (quatrains) by Omar Khayyám (1050–1132). The hedonistic and deterministic stanzas from Omar that FitzGerald chooses to stress are those most often quoted.

From THE RUBÁIYÁT OF OMAR KHAYYÁM

₰ 12 ₰

A Book of Verses underneath the Bough,
A Jug of Wine, a Loaf of Bread—and Thou
    Beside me singing in the Wilderness—
Oh, Wilderness were Paradise enow!

₰ 13 ₰

Some for the Glories of This World; and some
Sigh for the Prophet's Paradise to come;
    Ah, take the Cash, and let the Credit go,
Nor heed the rumble of a distant Drum!

₰ 19 ₰

I sometimes think that never blows so red
The Rose as where some buried Cæsar bled;
    That every Hyacinth the Garden wears
Dropt in her Lap from some once lovely Head.

ক 27 ৩

Myself when young did eagerly frequent
Doctor and Saint, and heard great argument
   About it and about: but evermore
Came out by the same door where in I went.

ক 68 ৩

We are no other than a moving row
Of Magic Shadow-shapes that come and go
   Round with the Sun-illumined Lantern held
In Midnight by the Master of the Show;

ক 69 ৩

But helpless Pieces of the Game He plays
Upon this Chequer-board of Nights and Days;
   Hither and thither moves, and checks, and slays,
And one by one back in the Closet lays.

ক 70 ৩

The Ball no question makes of Ayes and Noes,
But Here or There as strikes the Player goes;
   And He that toss'd you down into the Field,
He knows about it all—HE knows—HE knows!

ক 71 ৩

The Moving Finger writes; and, having writ,
Moves on: nor all your Piety nor Wit
   Shall lure it back to cancel half a Line,
Nor all your Tears wash out a Word of it.

ক 72 ৩

And that inverted Bowl they call the Sky,
Whereunder crawling coop'd we live and die,
   Lift not your hands to *It* for help—for It
As impotently moves as you or I.

ප 73 ෙ

With Earth's first Clay They did the Last Man knead,
And there of the Last Harvest sow'd the Seed:
  And the first Morning of Creation wrote
What the Last Dawn of Reckoning shall read.

ප 74 ෙ

YESTERDAY *This* Day's Madness did prepare;
TO-MORROW'S Silence, Triumph, or Despair:
  Drink! for you know not whence you came, nor why:
Drink! for you know not why you go, nor where.

Alfred Tennyson, First Baron Tennyson

(1 8 0 9 – 1 8 9 2)

Born into a mentally unstable family in Lincolnshire, Tennyson counted among the earlier pilgrims to his homes on the Isle of Wight and in Surrey his friend FitzGerald as well as Edward Lear, Coventry Patmore, Arthur Hugh Clough, and William Allingham. Temperamentally reclusive but the voice of England in his time, Poet Laureate from 1850, he became in 1884 the first to be created baron for achievement in poetry. Tennyson's literary remains have been attended by his son and grandson with devotion almost equal to that of Coleridge's descendants.

"Ulysses" (1842), a monologue concerned both with individual character and with the contrast of daring and domesticity, draws upon a hint in the *Odyssey*, developed by Dante, that Odysseus would again leave his home and companions. "Tithonus," designed in 1842 as the inverse of "Ulysses," but revised and not published until 1860, is spoken in withered age by the husband of Aurora, who secured immortality for Tithonus, but forgot to request eternal youth. In "The Charge of the Light Brigade" (1854) the Laureate made as much as he quickly could of the muddled loss of all but 198 men (of 673) at Balaklava, in the Crimean War. "The Higher Pantheism" (1870; published 1874) marks a watershed in Christian confidence illustrated by Swinburne's parody (see p. 664). When his dear friend Arthur Henry Hallam died in Vienna in 1833, Tennyson began the brief elegies, "swallow flights of song," later arranged into patterns of memory, doubt, despair, faith, and hope in *In Memoriam* (1850).

ULYSSES

It little profits that an idle king,
By this still hearth, among these barren crags,
Match'd with an aged wife, I mete and dole
Unequal laws unto a savage race,
That hoard, and sleep, and feed, and know not me.
I cannot rest from travel; I will drink
Life to the lees. All times I have enjoy'd
Greatly, have suffer'd greatly, both with those

That loved me, and alone; on shore, and when
Thro' scudding drifts the rainy Hyades   10
Vext the dim sea. I am become a name;
For always roaming with a hungry heart
Much have I seen and known,—cities of men
And manners, climates, councils, governments,
Myself not least, but honor'd of them all,—
And drunk delight of battle with my peers,
Far on the ringing plains of windy Troy.
I am a part of all that I have met;
Yet all experience is an arch wherethro'
Gleams that untravell'd world whose margin fades   20
For ever and for ever when I move.
How dull it is to pause, to make an end,
To rust unburnish'd, not to shine in use!
As tho' to breathe were life. Life piled on life
Were all too little, and of one to me
Little remains: but every hour is saved
From that eternal silence, something more,
A bringer of new things; and vile it were
For some three suns to store and hoard myself,
And this gray spirit yearning in desire   30
To follow knowledge like a sinking star,
Beyond the utmost bound of human thought.
    This is my son, mine own Telemachus,
To whom I leave the sceptre and the isle—
Well-loved of me, discerning to fulfil
This labour, by slow prudence to make mild
A rugged people, and thro' soft degrees
Subdue them to the useful and the good.
Most blameless is he, centred in the sphere
Of common duties, decent not to fail   40
In offices of tenderness, and pay
Meet adoration to my household gods,
When I am gone. He works his work, I mine.

    There lies the port: the vessel puffs her sail:
There gloom the dark broad seas. My mariners,
Souls that have toil'd, and wrought, and thought with me—
That ever with a frolic welcome took
The thunder and the sunshine, and opposed
Free hearts, free foreheads—you and I are old;
Old age hath yet his honour and his toil;   50

Death closes all: but something ere the end,
Some work of noble note, may yet be done,
Not unbecoming men that strove with Gods.
The lights begin to twinkle from the rocks:
The long day wanes: the slow moon climbs: the deep
Moans round with many voices. Come, my friends,
'Tis not too late to seek a newer world.
Push off, and sitting well in order smite
The sounding furrows; for my purpose holds
To sail beyond the sunset, and the baths   60
Of all the western stars, until I die.
It may be that the gulfs will wash us down:
It may be we shall touch the Happy Isles,
And see the great Achilles, whom we knew.
Tho' much is taken, much abides; and tho'
We are not now that strength which in old days
Moved earth and heaven; that which we are, we are;
One equal temper of heroic hearts,
Made weak by time and fate, but strong in will
To strive, to seek, to find, and not to yield.   70

TITHONUS

The woods decay, the woods decay and fall,
The vapours weep their burthen to the ground,
Man comes and tills the field and lies beneath,
And after many a summer dies the swan.
Me only cruel immortality
Consumes: I wither slowly in thine arms,
Here at the quiet limit of the world,
A white-hair'd shadow roaming like a dream
The ever-silent spaces of the East,
Far-folded mists, and gleaming halls of morn.   10

    Alas! for this gray shadow, once a man—
So glorious in his beauty and thy choice,
Who madest him thy chosen, that he seem'd
To his great heart none other than a God!
I ask'd thee, "Give me immortality."
Then didst thou grant mine asking with a smile,
Like wealthy men who care not how they give.

But thy strong Hours indignant work'd their wills,
And beat me down and marr'd and wasted me,
And tho' they could not end me, left me maim'd   20
To dwell in presence of immortal youth,
Immortal age beside immortal youth,
And all I was, in ashes. Can thy love,
Thy beauty, make amends, tho' even now,
Close over us, the silver star, thy guide,
Shines in those tremulous eyes that fill with tears
To hear me? Let me go: take back thy gift:
Why should a man desire in any way
To vary from the kindly race of men,
Or pass beyond the goal of ordinance   30
Where all should pause, as is most meet for all?

   A soft air fans the cloud apart; there comes
A glimpse of that dark world where I was born.
Once more the old mysterious glimmer steals
From thy pure brows, and from thy shoulders pure,
And bosom beating with a heart renew'd.
Thy cheek begins to redden thro' the gloom,
Thy sweet eyes brighten slowly close to mine,
Ere yet they blind the stars, and the wild team
Which love thee, yearning for thy yoke, arise,   40
And shake the darkness from their loosen'd manes,
And beat the twilight into flakes of fire.

   Lo! ever thus thou growest beautiful
In silence, then before thine answer given
Departest, and thy tears are on my cheek.

   Why wilt thou ever scare me with thy tears,
And make me tremble lest a saying learnt,
In days far-off, on that dark earth, be true?
"The Gods themselves cannot recall their gifts."

   Ay, me! ay me! with what another heart   50
In days far-off, and with what other eyes
I used to watch—if I be he that watch'd—
The lucid outline forming round thee; saw
The dim curls kindle into sunny rings;
Changed with thy mystic change, and felt my blood
Glow with the glow that slowly crimson'd all

Thy presence and thy portals, while I lay,
Mouth, forehead, eyelids, growing dewy-warm
With kisses balmier than half-opening buds
Of April, and could hear the lips that kiss'd   60
Whispering I knew not what of wild and sweet,
Like that strange song I heard Apollo sing,
While Ilion like a mist rose into towers.

　　Yet hold me not for ever in thine East:
How can my nature longer mix with thine?
Coldly thy rosy shadows bathe me, cold
Are all thy lights, and cold my wrinkled feet
Upon thy glimmering thresholds, when the steam
Floats up from those dim fields about the homes
Of happy men that have the power to die,   70
And grassy barrows of the happier dead.
Release me, and restore me to the ground;
Thou seëst all things, thou wilt see my grave:
Thou wilt renew thy beauty morn by morn;
I earth in earth forget these empty courts,
And thee returning on thy silver wheels.

l. 29. kindly = akin by nature

THE HIGHER PANTHEISM

The sun, the moon, the stars, the seas, the hills and the plains,—
Are not these, O Soul, the Vision of Him who reigns?

Is not the Vision He, tho' He be not that which He seems?
Dreams are true while they last, and do we not live in dreams?

Earth, these solid stars, this weight of body and limb,
Are they not sign and symbol of thy division from Him?

Dark is the world to thee; thyself art the reason why,
For is He not all but thou, that hast power to feel "I am I"?

Glory about thee, without thee; and thou fulfillest thy doom,
Making Him broken gleams and a stifled splendor and gloom.   10

Speak to Him, thou, for He hears, and Spirit with Spirit can meet—
Closer is He than breathing, and nearer than hands and feet.

God is law, say the wise; O Soul, and let us rejoice,
For if He thunder by law the thunder is yet His voice.

Law is God, say some; no God at all, says the fool,
For all we have power to see is a straight staff bent in a pool;

And the ear of man cannot hear, and the eye of man cannot see;
But if we could see and hear, this Vision—were it not He?

TEARS, IDLE TEARS

Tears, idle tears, I know not what they mean,
Tears from the depth of some divine despair
Rise in the heart, and gather to the eyes,
In looking on the happy autumn-fields,
And thinking of the days that are no more.

Fresh as the first beam glittering on a sail,
That brings our friends up from the underworld,
Sad as the last which reddens over one
That sinks with all we love below the verge;
So sad, so fresh, the days that are no more.   10

Ah, sad and strange as in dark summer dawns
The earliest pipe of half-awaken'd birds
To dying ears, when unto dying eyes
The casement slowly grows a glimmering square;
So sad, so strange, the days that are no more.

Dear as remember'd kisses after death,
And sweet as those by hopeless fancy feign'd
On lips that are for others; deep as love,
Deep as first love, and wild with all regret;
O Death in Life, the days that are no more!   20

THE CHARGE OF
THE LIGHT BRIGADE

Half a league, half a league,
Half a league onward,
All in the valley of Death
   Rode the six hundred.
"Forward the Light Brigade!
Charge for the guns!" he said.
Into the valley of Death
   Rode the six hundred.

"Forward, the Light Brigade!"
Was there a man dismay'd?   10
Not tho' the soldier knew
   Some one had blunder'd.
   Theirs not to make reply,
   Theirs not to reason why,
   Theirs but to do and die.
   Into the valley of Death
      Rode the six hundred.

Cannon to right of them,
Cannon to left of them,
Cannon in front of them   20
   Volley'd and thunder'd;
Storm'd at with shot and shell,
Boldly they rode and well,
Into the jaws of Death,
Into the mouth of hell!
   Rode the six hundred.

Flash'd all their sabres bare,
Flash'd as they turn'd in air
Sabring the gunners there,
Charging an army, while   30
   All the world wonder'd.
Plunged in the battery-smoke
Right thro' the line they broke;
Cossack and Russian
Reel'd from the sabre-stroke
   Shatter'd and sunder'd.

Then they rode back, but not,
  Not the six hundred.

Cannon to right of them,
Cannon to left of them,   40
Cannon behind them
  Volley'd and thunder'd;
Storm'd at with shot and shell,
While horse and hero fell,
They that had fought so well
Came thro' the jaws of Death,
Back from the mouth of hell,
All that was left of them,
  Left of six hundred.

When can their glory fade?   50
O the wild charge they made!
  All the world wonder'd.
Honor the charge they made!
Honor the Light Brigade,
  Noble six hundred!

From IN MEMORIAM

7

Dark house, by which once more I stand
  Here in the long unlovely street,
  Doors, where my heart was used to beat
So quickly, waiting for a hand,

A hand that can be clasp'd no more—
  Behold me, for I cannot sleep,
  And like a guilty thing I creep
At earliest morning to the door.

He is not here; but far away
  The noise of life begins again,
  And ghastly thro' the drizzling rain
On the bald street breaks the blank day.

❧ 27 ❧

I envy not in any moods
   The captive void of noble rage,
   The linnet born within the cage,
That never knew the summer woods;

I envy not the beast that takes
   His license in the field of time,
   Unfetter'd by the sense of crime,
To whom a conscience never wakes;

Nor, what may count itself as blest,
   The heart that never plighted troth
   But stagnates in the weeds of sloth:
Nor any want-begotten rest.

I hold it true, whate'er befall;
   I feel it, when I sorrow most;
   'T is better to have loved and lost
Than never to have loved at all.

❧ 35 ❧

Yet if some voice that man could trust
   Should murmur from the narrow house,
   "The cheeks drop in, the body bows;
Man dies, nor is there hope in dust;"

Might I not say? "Yet even here,
   But for one hour, O Love, I strive
   To keep so sweet a thing alive."
But I should turn mine ears and hear

The moanings of the homeless sea,
   The sound of streams that swift or slow
   Draw down Æonian hills, and sow
The dust of continents to be,

And Love would answer with a sigh,
   "The sound of that forgetful shore
   Will change my sweetness more and more,
Half-dead to know that I shall die."

O me, what profits it to put
   An idle case? If Death were seen
   At first as Death, Love had not been,
Or been in narrowest working shut,

Mere fellowship of sluggish moods,
   Or in his coarsest Satyr-shape
   Had bruised the herb and crush'd the grape,
And bask'd and batten'd in the woods.

❧ 50 ❧

Be near me when my light is low,
   When the blood creeps, and the nerves prick
   And tingle; and the heart is sick,
And all the wheels of Being slow.

Be near me when the sensuous frame
   Is rack'd with pangs that conquer trust;
   And Time, a maniac scattering dust,
And Life, a Fury slinging flame.

Be near me when my faith is dry,
   And men the flies of latter spring,
   That lay their eggs, and sting and sing
And weave their petty cells and die.

Be near me when I fade away,
   To point the term of human strife,
   And on the low dark verge of life
The twilight of eternal day.

❧ 54 ❧

Oh yet we trust that somehow good
   Will be the final goal of ill,
   To pangs of nature, sins of will,
Defects of doubt, and taints of blood;

That nothing walks with aimless feet;
   That not one life shall be destroy'd,
   Or cast as rubbish to the void,
When God hath made the pile complete;

That not a worm is cloven in vain;
 That not a moth with vain desire
 It shrivell'd in a fruitless fire,
Or but subserves another's gain.

Behold, we know not anything;
 I can but trust that good shall fall
 At last—far off—at last, to all,
And every winter change to spring.

So runs my dream: but what am I?
 An infant crying in the night:
 An infant crying for the light:
And with no language but a cry.

   * 108 *

I will not shut me from my kind,
 And, lest I stiffen into stone,
 I will not eat my heart alone,
Nor feed with sighs a passing wind.

What profit lies in barren faith,
 And vacant yearning, tho' with might
 To scale the heaven's highest height,
Or dive below the wells of Death?

What find I in the highest place,
 But mine own phantom chanting hymns?
 And on the depths of death there swims
The reflex of a human face.

I'll rather take what fruit may be
 Of sorrow under human skies:
 'Tis held that sorrow makes us wise,
Whatever wisdom sleep with thee.

   * 124 *

That which we dare invoke to bless;
 Our dearest faith; our ghastliest doubt;
 He, They, One, All; within, without;
The Power in darkness whom we guess;

I found Him not in world or sun,
  Or eagle's wing, or insect's eye;
  Nor thro' the questions men may try,
The petty cobwebs we have spun:

If e'er when faith had fall'n asleep,
  I heard a voice "believe no more"
  And heard an ever-breaking shore
That tumbled in the Godless deep;

A warmth within the breast would melt
  The freezing reason's colder part,
  And like a man in wrath the heart
Stood up and answer'd "I have felt."

No, like a child in doubt and fear:
  But that blind clamour made me wise;
  Then was I as a child that cries,
But, crying, knows his father near;

And what I am beheld again
  What is, and no man understands;
  And out of darkness came the hands
That reach thro' nature, moulding men.

Robert Browning

(1 8 1 2 – 1 8 8 9)

Largely self-educated in his father's library in London, Browning had mixed success as a poet of difficult styles until he found his greatest strength in dramatic monologue: self-revelation by a character out of the ordinary speaking to an unheard listener in a defined situation. The Duke of Ferrara and the artists named in "My Last Duchess" (1842), like the bishop ordering his tomb in Rome (*Dramatic Romances and Lyrics*, 1845), are imagined from Browning's sense of the Renaissance in Italy.

The three shorter poems here, published in 1845, illustrate the particularity and scratchiness of phrase that resurrected Browning's reputation among such Modernists as Pound. One of them, "Home-Thoughts, from Abroad," may be thought to anticipate the poet's return from Florence to London after his wife's death in 1861.

MY LAST DUCHESS

FERRARA

That's my last Duchess painted on the wall,
Looking as if she were alive. I call
That piece a wonder, now: Frà Pandolf's hands
Worked busily a day, and there she stands.
Will't please you sit and look at her? I said
"Frà Pandolf" by design, for never read
Strangers like you that pictured countenance,
The depth and passion of its earnest glance,
But to myself they turned (since none puts by
The curtain I have drawn for you, but I)   10
And seemed as they would ask me, if they durst,
How such a glance came there; so, not the first
Are you to turn and ask thus. Sir, 'twas not
Her husband's presence only, called that spot
Of joy into the Duchess' cheek: perhaps
Frà Pandolf chanced to say "Her mantle laps
Over my lady's wrist too much," or "Paint

601

Must never hope to reproduce the faint
Half-flush that dies along her throat": such stuff
Was courtesy, she thought, and cause enough   20
For calling up that spot of joy. She had
A heart—how shall I say?—too soon made glad,
Too easily impressed; she liked whate'er
She looked on, and her looks went everywhere.
Sir, 'twas all one! My favour at her breast,
The dropping of the daylight in the West,
The bough of cherries some officious fool
Broke in the orchard for her, the white mule
She rode with round the terrace—all and each
Would draw from her alike the approving speech,   30
Or blush, at least. She thanked men,—good! but thanked
Somehow—I know not how—as if she ranked
My gift of a nine-hundred-years-old name
With anybody's gift. Who'd stoop to blame
This sort of trifling? Even had you skill
In speech—(which I have not)—to make your will
Quite clear to such an one, and say, "Just this
Or that in you disgusts me; here you miss,
Or there exceed the mark"—and if she let
Herself be lessoned so, nor plainly set   40
Her wits to yours, forsooth, and made excuse,
—E'en then would be some stooping; and I choose
Never to stoop. Oh sir, she smiled, no doubt,
Whene'er I passed her; but who passed without
Much the same smile? This grew; I gave commands;
Then all smiles stopped together. There she stands
As if alive. Will't please you rise? We'll meet
The company below, then. I repeat,
The Count your master's known munificence
Is ample warrant that no just pretence   50
Of mine for dowry will be disallowed;
Though his fair daughter's self, as I avowed
At starting, is my object. Nay, we'll go
Together down, sir. Notice Neptune, though,
Taming a sea-horse, thought a rarity,
Which Claus of Innsbruck cast in bronze for me!

MEETING AT NIGHT

The grey sea and the long black land;
And the yellow half-moon large and low;
And the startled little waves that leap
In fiery ringlets from their sleep,
As I gain the cove with pushing prow,
And quench its speed i' the slushy sand.

Then a mile of warm sea-scented beach;
Three fields to cross till a farm appears;
A tap at the pane, the quick sharp scratch
And blue spurt of a lighted match,   10
And a voice less loud, through its joys and fears,
Than the two hearts beating each to each!

PARTING AT MORNING

Round the cape of a sudden came the sea,
And the sun looked over the mountain's rim:
And straight was a path of gold for him,
And the need of a world of men for me.

HOME-THOUGHTS,
FROM ABROAD

Oh, to be in England
Now that April's there,
And whoever wakes in England
Sees, some morning, unaware,
That the lowest boughs and the brushwood sheaf
Round the elm-tree bole are in tiny leaf,
While the chaffinch sings on the orchard bough
In England—now!

And after April, when May follows,
And the whitethroat builds, and all the swallows!   10
Hark, where my blossomed pear-tree in the hedge

Leans to the field and scatters on the clover
Blossoms and dewdrops—at the bent spray's edge—
That's the wise thrush; he sings each song twice over,
Lest you should think he never could recapture
The first fine careless rapture!
And though the fields look rough with hoary dew,
All will be gay when noontide wakes anew
The buttercups, the little children's dower
—Far brighter than this gaudy melon-flower!   20

THE BISHOP ORDERS HIS TOMB
AT SAINT PRAXED'S CHURCH
ROME, 15—

Vanity, saith the preacher, vanity!
Draw round my bed: is Anselm keeping back?
Nephews—sons mine . . . ah God, I know not! Well—
She, men would have to be your mother once,
Old Gandolf envied me, so fair she was!
What's done is done, and she is dead beside,
Dead long ago, and I am Bishop since,
And as she died so must we die ourselves,
And thence ye may perceive the world's a dream.
Life, how and what is it? As here I lie   10
In this state-chamber, dying by degrees,
Hours and long hours in the dead night, I ask
"Do I live, am I dead?" Peace, peace seems all.
Saint Praxed's ever was the church for peace;
And so, about this tomb of mine. I fought
With tooth and nail to save my niche, ye know:
—Old Gandolf cozened me, despite my care;
Shrewd was that snatch from out the corner South
He graced his carrion with, God curse the same!
Yet still my niche is not so cramped but thence   20
One sees the pulpit o' the epistle-side,
And somewhat of the choir, those silent seats,
And up into the airy dome where live
The angels, and a sunbeam's sure to lurk:
And I shall fill my slab of basalt there,
And 'neath my tabernacle take my rest,

With those nine columns round me, two and two,
The odd one at my feet where Anselm stands:
Peach-blossom marble all, the rare, the ripe
As fresh-poured red wine of a mighty pulse.   30
—Old Gandolf with his paltry onion-stone,
Put me where I may look at him! True peach,
Rosy and flawless: how I earned the prize!
Draw close: that conflagration of my church
—What then? So much was saved if aught were missed!
My sons, ye would not be my death? Go dig
The white-grape vineyard where the oil-press stood,
Drop water gently till the surface sink,
And if ye find . . . Ah God, I know not, I! . . .
Bedded in store of rotten fig-leaves soft,   40
And corded up in a tight olive-frail,
Some lump, ah God, of *lapis lazuli*,
Big as a Jew's head cut off at the nape,
Blue as a vein o'er the Madonna's breast . . .
Sons, all have I bequeathed you, villas, all,
That brave Frascati villa with its bath,
So, let the blue lump poise between my knees,
Like God the Father's globe on both his hands
Ye worship in the Jesu Church so gay,
For Gandolf shall not choose but see and burst!   50
Swift as a weaver's shuttle fleet our years:
Man goeth to the grave, and where is he?
Did I say basalt for my slab, sons? Black—
'Twas ever antique-black I meant! How else
Shall ye contrast my frieze to come beneath?
The bas-relief in bronze ye promised me,
Those Pans and Nymphs ye wot of, and perchance
Some tripod, thyrsus, with a vase or so,
The Saviour at his sermon on the mount,
Saint Praxed in a glory, and one Pan   60
Ready to twitch the Nymph's last garment off,
And Moses with the tables . . . but I know
Ye mark me not! What do they whisper thee,
Child of my bowels, Anselm? Ah, ye hope
To revel down my villas while I gasp
Bricked o'er with beggar's mouldy travertine
Which Gandolf from his tomb-top chuckles at!
Nay, boys, ye love me—all of jasper, then!
'Tis jasper ye stand pledged to, lest I grieve

My bath must needs be left behind, alas!   70
One block, pure green as a pistachio-nut,
There's plenty jasper somewhere in the world—
And have I not Saint Praxed's ear to pray
Horses for ye, and brown Greek manuscripts,
And mistresses with great smooth marbly limbs?
—That's if ye carve my epitaph aright,
Choice Latin, picked phrase, Tully's every word,
No gaudy ware like Gandolf's second line—
Tully, my masters? Ulpian serves his need!
And then how I shall lie through centuries,   80
And hear the blessed mutter of the mass,
And see God made and eaten all day long,
And feel the steady candle-flame, and taste
Good strong thick stupefying incense-smoke!
For as I lie here, hours of the dead night,
Dying in state and by such slow degrees,
I fold my arms as if they clasped a crook,
And stretch my feet forth straight as stone can point,
And let the bedclothes, for a mortcloth, drop
Into great laps and folds of sculptor's-work: 90
And as yon tapers dwindle, and strange thoughts
Grow, with a certain humming in my ears,
About the life before I lived this life,
And this life too, popes, cardinals and priests,
Saint Praxed at his sermon on the mount,
Your tall pale mother with her talking eyes,
And new-found agate urns as fresh as day,
And marble's language, Latin pure, discreet,
—Aha, ELUCESCEBAT quoth our friend?
No Tully, said I, Ulpian at the best!   100
Evil and brief hath been my pilgrimage.
All *lapis*, all, sons! Else I give the Pope
My villas! Will ye ever eat my heart?
Ever your eyes were as a lizard's quick,
They glitter like your mother's for my soul,
Or ye would heighten my impoverished frieze,
Piece out its starved design, and fill my vase
With grapes, and add a vizor and a Term,
And to the tripod ye would tie a lynx
That in his struggle throws the thyrsus down,   110
To comfort me on my entablature
Whereon I am to lie till I must ask

"Do I live, am I dead?" There, leave me, there!
For ye have stabbed me with ingratitude
To death—ye wish it—God, ye wish it! Stone—
Gritstone, a-crumble! Clammy squares which sweat
As if the corpse they keep were oozing through—
And no more *lapis* to delight the world!
Well go! I bless ye. Fewer tapers there,
But in a row: and, going, turn your backs   120
—Ay, like departing altar-ministrants,
And leave me in my church, the church for peace,
That I may watch at leisure if he leers—
Old Gandolf, at me, from his onion-stone,
As still he envied me, so fair she was!

l. 41. olive-frail = a basket
l. 77. Tully = Cicero
l. 99. ELUCESCEBAT = for Ciceronian *elucebat*, "he was famous"

Edward Lear

(1812 – 1888)

Born in a purlieu of London, a stockbroker's twentieth child, a lonely epileptic with many friends, Lear traveled widely—almost preposterously, to Egypt, India, and beyond—as a watercolor painter of landscapes and birds. He illustrated with comic drawings his nonsense poems, both in his four collective volumes and in impromptu "alphabets" for young friends. Unquestioned master of the limerick in its standard form ("There was an Old Man in a tree"), he often compacted the form without diminishing the illogic. The narratives "The Owl and the Pussy-Cat" and "The Jumblies" (with its yearning for the never-to-be) both appeared in *Nonsense Songs, Stories, Botany, and Alphabets* (1871). Like Lewis Carroll, Lear delighted in the invention of such plausible words as "runcible."

THERE WAS AN OLD MAN
IN A TREE

There was an Old Man in a tree,
Who was horribly bored by a Bee;
When they said, "Does it buzz?" he replied, "Yes, it does!
It's a regular brute of a Bee."

THE OWL AND
THE PUSSY-CAT

The Owl and the Pussy-Cat went to sea
   In a beautiful pea-green boat:
They took some honey, and plenty of money
   Wrapped up in a five-pound note.
The Owl looked up to the stars above,
   And sang to a small guitar,
   "O lovely Pussy, O Pussy, my love,
   What a beautiful Pussy you are,

> You are,
>   You are!   10
> What a beautiful Pussy you are!"

Pussy said to the Owl, "You elegant fowl,
    How charmingly sweet you sing!
Oh! let us be married; too long we have tarried:
    But what shall we do for a ring?"
They sailed away, for a year and a day,
    To the land where the bong-tree grows;
And there in a wood a Piggy-wig stood,
    With a ring at the end of his nose,
                His nose,   20
                His nose,
    With a ring at the end of his nose.

"Dear Pig, are you willing to sell for one shilling
    Your ring?" Said the Piggy, "I will."
So they took it away, and were married next day
    By the Turkey who lives on the hill.
They dined on mince and slices of quince,
    Which they ate with a runcible spoon;
And hand in hand, on the edge of the sand
    They danced by the light of the moon,   30
                The moon,
                The moon,
    They danced by the light of the moon.

THE JUMBLIES

They went to sea in a sieve, they did;
    In a sieve they went to sea:
In spite of all their friends could say,
On a winter's morn, on a stormy day,
    In a sieve they went to sea.
And when the sieve turned round and round,
And every one cried, "You'll all be drowned!"
They called aloud, "Our sieve ain't big;
But we don't care a button, we don't care a fig:
    In a sieve we'll go to sea!"   10
        Far and few, far and few,

Are the lands where the Jumblies live:
Their heads are green, and their hands are blue;
And they went to sea in a sieve.

They sailed away in a sieve, they did,
    In a sieve they sailed so fast,
With only a beautiful pea-green veil
Tied with a ribbon, by way of a sail,
    To a small tobacco-pipe mast.
And every one said who saw them go,   20
"Oh! won't they be soon upset, you know?
For the sky is dark, and the voyage is long;
And, happen what may, it's extremely wrong
    In a sieve to sail so fast."
        Far and few, far and few,
            Are the lands where the Jumblies live:
            Their heads are green, and their hands are blue;
            And they went to sea in a sieve.

The water it soon came in, it did;
    The water it soon came in: 30
So, to keep them dry, they wrapped their feet
In a pinky paper all folded neat;
    And they fastened it down with a pin.
And they passed the night in a crockery-jar;
And each of them said, "How wise we are!
Though the sky be dark, and the voyage be long,
Yet we never can think we were rash or wrong,
    While round in our sieve we spin."
        Far and few, far and few,
            Are the lands where the Jumblies live: 40
            Their heads are green, and their hands are blue;
            And they went to sea in a sieve.

And all night long they sailed away;
    And when the sun went down,
They whistled and warbled a moony song
To the echoing sound of a coppery gong,
    In the shade of the mountains brown.
"O Timballoo! How happy we are
When we live in a sieve and a crockery-jar!
And all night long, in the moonlight pale,   50
We sail away with a pea-green sail

In the shade of the mountains brown."
　　　Far and few, far and few,
　　　　　Are the lands where the Jumblies live:
　　　'Their heads are green, and their hands are blue;
　　　　　And they went to sea in a sieve.

They sailed to the Western Sea, they did,—
　　　To a land all covered with trees:
And they bought an owl, and a useful cart,
And a pound of rice, and a cranberry-tart,　　　　　　　　　60
　　　And a hive of silvery bees;
And they bought a pig, and some green jackdaws,
And a lovely monkey with lollipop paws,
And forty bottles of ring-bo-ree,
　　　And no end of Stilton cheese.
　　　　　Far and few, far and few,
　　　　　　　Are the lands where the Jumblies live:
　　　　　Their heads are green, and their hands are blue;
　　　　　　　And they went to sea in a sieve.

And in twenty years they all came back,—　　　　　　　　70
　　　In twenty years or more;
And every one said, "How tall they've grown!
For they've been to the Lakes, and the Torrible Zone,
　　　And the hills of the Chankly Bore."
And they drank their health, and gave them a feast
Of dumplings made of beautiful yeast;
And every one said, "If we only live,
We, too, will go to sea in a sieve,—
　　　To the hills of the Chankly Bore."
　　　　　Far and few, far and few,　　　　　　　　　　80
　　　　　　　Are the lands where the Jumblies live:
　　　　　Their heads are green, and their hands are blue;
　　　　　　　And they went to sea in a sieve.

Emily Jane Brontë

(1 8 1 8 – 1 8 4 8)

Remaining passionately wedded throughout her short life to the Yorkshire moors of her birth—and of her novel *Wuthering Heights*—Emily continued also the private authorial games begun in childhood with her sisters Charlotte and Anne and their brother Branwell. In the Gondal cycle of these games, the first poem below is a lament addressed by Rosina Alcona to Julius Brenzaida, and the shore of line 6 is of Angora; "Remembrance" is the title assigned to it by Charlotte in *Poems by Currer, Ellis, and Acton Bell* (1846). In the primary manuscript used by Charlotte for that volume, "No Coward Soul" bears the date "Jan. 2, 1846"; Charlotte supplied punctuation and, with other changes, converted the penultimate line to pentameter and conventional piety: "Thou—THOU art Being and Breath."

REMEMBRANCE

Cold in the earth, and the deep snow piled above thee!
Far, far removed, cold in the dreary grave!
Have I forgot, my Only Love, to love thee,
Severed at last by Time's all-wearing wave?

Now, when alone, do my thoughts no longer hover
Over the mountains on that northern shore,
Resting their wings where heath and fern-leaves cover
That noble heart for ever, ever more?

Cold in the earth, and fifteen wild Decembers
From those brown hills have melted into spring—   10
Faithful indeed is the spirit that remembers
After such years of change and suffering!

Sweet Love of youth, forgive if I forget thee
While the World's tide is bearing me along:
Sterner desires and darker hopes beset me,
Hopes which obscure but cannot do thee wrong.

No other Sun has lightened up my heaven;
No other Star has ever shone for me:
All my life's bliss from thy dear life was given—
All my life's bliss is in the grave with thee.   20

But when the days of golden dreams had perished
And even Despair was powerless to destroy,
Then did I learn how existence could be cherished,
Strengthened and fed without the aid of joy;

Then did I check the tears of useless passion,
Weaned my young soul from yearning after thine;
Sternly denied its burning wish to hasten
Down to that tomb already more than mine!

And even yet, I dare not let it languish,
Dare not indulge in Memory's rapturous pain;   30
Once drinking deep of that divinest anguish,
How could I seek the empty world again?

NO COWARD SOUL IS MINE

No coward soul is mine,
No trembler in the world's storm-troubled sphere;
I see Heaven's glories shine,
And Faith shines equal, arming me from Fear.

O God within my breast,
Almighty ever-present Deity!
Life, that in me hast rest,
As I, Undying Life, have power in Thee!

Vain are the thousand creeds
That move men's hearts, unutterably vain,   10
Worthless as withered weeds
Or idlest froth amid the boundless main

To waken doubt in one
Holding so fast by thy infinity;
So surely anchored on
The steadfast rock of Immortality.

With wide-embracing love
Thy spirit animates eternal years,
Pervades and broods above,
Changes, sustains, dissolves, creates and rears.   20

Though Earth and moon were gone
And suns and universes ceased to be,
And thou wert left alone,
Every Existence would exist in thee.

There is not room for Death
Nor atom that his might could render void;
Since thou art Being and Breath
And what thou art may never be destroyed.

Arthur Hugh Clough

(1819–1861)

Unsettled at Oxford after strict Anglican indoctrination at Rugby under Thomas Arnold, Clough resigned from responsibilities to Christian doctrine. He published narrative poems as casual in diction as Byron's satires, but his poems of incisively ruminative doubt were available only to friends. "The Latest Decalogue" appeared in *Poems* (1862); the Faustian dialogue "Dipsychus"—divided soul—appeared first in *Letters and Remains* (1865), edited by the poet's widow, Blanche Smith Clough.

THE LATEST DECALOGUE

Thou shalt have one God only; who
Would be at the expense of two?
No graven images may be
Worshipped, except the currency:
Swear not at all; for for thy curse
Thine enemy is none the worse:
At church on Sunday to attend
Will serve to keep the world thy friend:
Honour thy parents; that is, all
From whom advancement may befall: 10
Thou shalt not kill; but needst not strive
Officiously to keep alive:
Do not adultery commit;
Advantage rarely comes of it:
Thou shalt not steal; an empty feat,
When it's so lucrative to cheat:
Bear not false witness; let the lie
Have time on its own wings to fly:
Thou shalt not covet; but tradition
Approves all forms of competition.   20

The sum of all is, thou shalt love,
If any body, God above:

At any rate shall never labour
More than thyself to love thy neighbour.

From DIPSYCHUS

"There is no God," the wicked saith,
   "And truly it's a blessing,
For what he might have done with us
   It's better only guessing."

"There is no God," a youngster thinks,
   "Or really, if there may be,
He surely didn't mean a man   160
   Always to be a baby."

"There is no God, or if there is,"
   The tradesman thinks, " 'twere funny
If he should take it ill in me
   To make a little money."

"Whether there be," the rich man says,
   "It matters very little,
For I and mine, thank somebody,
   Are not in want of victual."

Some others, also, to themselves   170
   Who scarce so much as doubt it,
Think there is none, when they are well,
   And do not think about it.

But country folks who live beneath
   The shadow of the steeple;
The parson and the parson's wife,
   And mostly married people;

Youths green and happy in first love,
   So thankful for illusion;
And men caught out in what the world   180
   Calls guilt, in first confusion;

And almost every one when age,
   Disease, or sorrows strike him,
Inclines to think there is a God,
   Or something very like Him.

George Eliot

(*pseudonym of Mary Ann Evans, 1 8 1 9 – 1 8 8 0*)

After a brief but intensely Evangelical period, Mary Ann Evans of bucolic Warwickshire became and remained a freethinker dedicated to truth, duty, and moral law. Her lines beginning "O may I join the choir invisible" have been called the hymn of Positivism. She lived from 1854 until his death in 1878 with George Henry Lewes, who encouraged her to become, under the pseudonym George Eliot, the most intellectual, and yet most evenly compassionate, of major Victorian novelists. "A Minor Prophet," written in 1865, published in *The Legend of Jubal, and Other Poems* (1874), treats with affectionate irony the evolutionary hopes of a vegetarian friend (one might compare her treatment of the optimistic Brooke in *Middlemarch*); but then the speaker derives from these excesses her own moral prophecy—leaving the "Minor" of the title still accessible to the reader.

From A MINOR PROPHET

'Tis on this theme—the vegetarian world—
That good Elias willingly expands:
He loves to tell in mildly nasal tones
And vowels stretched to suit the widest views,
The future fortunes of our infant Earth—
When it will be too full of human kind
To have the room for wilder animals.
Saith he, Sahara will be populous
With families of gentlemen retired
From commerce in more Central Africa,   70
Who order coolness as we order coal,
And have a lobe anterior strong enough
To think away the sand-storms. Science thus
Will leave no spot on this terraqueous globe
Unfit to be inhabited by man,
The chief of animals: all meaner brutes
Will have been smoked and elbowed out of life.

       *   *   *

The faith that life on earth is being shaped
To glorious ends, that order, justice, love

Mean man's completeness, mean effect as sure
As roundness in the dew-drop—that great faith
Is but the rushing and expanding stream   290
Of thought, of feeling, fed by all the past.
Our finest hope is finest memory,
As they who love in age think youth is blest
Because it has a life to fill with love.
Full souls are double mirrors, making still
An endless vista of fair things before
Repeating things behind: so faith is strong
Only when we are strong, shrinks when we shrink.
It comes when music stirs us, and the chords
Moving on some grand climax shake our souls   300
With influx new that makes new energies.
It comes in swellings of the heart and tears
That rise at noble and at gentle deeds—
At labours of the master-artist's hand
Which, trembling, touches to a finer end,
Trembling before an image seen within.
It comes in moments of heroic love,
Unjealous joy in joy not made for us—
In conscious triumph of the good within
Making us worship goodness that rebukes.   310
Even our failures are a prophecy,
Even our yearnings and our bitter tears
After that fair and true we cannot grasp;
As patriots who seem to die in vain
Make liberty more sacred by their pangs.

Presentiment of better things on earth
Sweeps in with every force that stirs our souls
To admiration, self-renouncing love,
Or thoughts, like light, that bind the world in one:
Sweeps like the sense of vastness, when at night   320
We hear the roll and dash of waves that break
Nearer and nearer with the rushing tide,
Which rises to the level of the cliff
Because the wide Atlantic rolls behind
Throbbing respondent to the far-off orbs.

Matthew Arnold

(1 8 2 2 – 1 8 8 8)

Arnold was the son of the vigorous headmaster of Rugby, inspector of schools and head of a family from 1851. He was admired as a poet from his undergraduate years at Oxford until he turned increasingly to prose, wherein he called for a poetry of action and for greater breadth in English education, culture, and religion. He seemed unable to avoid in poetry a repeated theme: not even love can overcome the despair of isolation each from each. "To Marguerite" (1852), a continuation of stanzas entitled "Isolation," is one of six love lyrics addressed to a French girl encountered in Switzerland. Arnold began his most famous poem of receding faith, the monologue "Dover Beach," on his honeymoon (1851), but delayed its publication until *New Poems* (1867), when its broken rhythms prophesied later directions in English verse.

The sonnet "In Harmony with Nature" of 1849, denying that Nature can be a moral guide, offers a challenge to the "Memorial Verses" of 1850. That the Arnolds had a summer home near Wordworth's Rydal Mount may account in some degree for the elevation of the poet who laid readers "on the cool flowery lap of earth" above Byron (died 1824) and Goethe (died 1832). Goethe had a place in Arnold's meditations below that of Sophocles but almost even with that of Virgil (whose lines on knowing the causes of things are paraphrased in "Memorial Verses").

DOVER BEACH

The sea is calm to-night.
The tide is full, the moon lies fair
Upon the straits;—on the French coast the light
Gleams and is gone; the cliffs of England stand,
Glimmering and vast, out in the tranquil bay.
Come to the window, sweet is the night-air!

Only, from the long line of spray
Where the sea meets the moon-blanch'd land,
Listen! you hear the grating roar
Of pebbles which the waves draw back, and fling,   10
At their return, up the high strand,

Begin, and cease, and then again begin,
With tremulous cadence slow, and bring
The eternal note of sadness in.

Sophocles long ago
Heard it on the Aegean, and it brought
Into his mind the turbid ebb and flow
Of human misery; we
Find also in the sound a thought,
Hearing it by this distant northern sea.   20

The Sea of Faith
Was once, too, at the full, and round earth's shore
Lay like the folds of a bright girdle furl'd.
But now I only hear
Its melancholy, long, withdrawing roar,
Retreating, to the breath
Of the night-wind, down the vast edges drear
And naked shingles of the world.

Ah, love, let us be true
To one another! for the world, which seems   30
To lie before us like a land of dreams,
So various, so beautiful, so new,
Hath really neither joy, nor love, nor light,
Nor certitude, nor peace, nor help for pain;
And we are here as on a darkling plain
Swept with confused alarms of struggle and flight,
Where ignorant armies clash by night.

TO MARGUERITE

Yes! in the sea of life enisled,
With echoing straits between us thrown,
Dotting the shoreless watery wild,
We mortal millions live *alone*.
The islands feel the enclasping flow,
And then their endless bounds they know.

But when the moon their hollows lights,
And they are swept by balms of spring,

And in their glens, on starry nights,
The nightingales divinely sing;   10
And lovely notes, from shore to shore,
Across the sounds and channels pour—

Oh! then a longing like despair
Is to their farthest caverns sent;
For surely once, they feel, we were
Parts of a single continent!
Now round us spreads the watery plain—
Oh might our marges meet again!

Who order'd, that their longing's fire
Should be, as soon as kindled, cool'd?   20
Who renders vain their deep desire?—
A God, a God their severance ruled!
And bade betwixt their shores to be
The unplumb'd, salt, estranging sea.

IN HARMONY WITH NATURE

To a Preacher

"In harmony with Nature?" Restless fool,
Who with such heat dost preach what were to thee,
When true, the last impossibility—
To be like Nature strong, like Nature cool!

Know, man hath all which Nature hath, but more,
And in that *more* lie all his hopes of good.
Nature is cruel, man is sick of blood;
Nature is stubborn, man would fain adore;

Nature is fickle, man hath need of rest;
Nature forgives no debt, and fears no grave;
Man would be mild, and with safe conscience blest.

Man must begin, know this, where Nature ends;
Nature and man can never be fast friends.
Fool, if thou canst not pass her, rest her slave!

MEMORIAL VERSES

APRIL 1850

Goethe in Weimar sleeps, and Greece,
Long since, saw Byron's struggle cease.
But one such death remain'd to come;
The last poetic voice is dumb—
We stand to-day by Wordsworth's tomb.

When Byron's eyes were shut in death,
We bow'd our head and held our breath.
He taught us little; but our soul
Had *felt* him like the thunder's roll.
With shivering heart the strife we saw   10
Of passion with eternal law;
And yet with reverential awe
We watch'd the fount of fiery life
Which served for that Titanic strife.
    When Goethe's death was told, we said:
Sunk, then, is Europe's sagest head.
Physician of the iron age,
Goethe has done his pilgrimage.
He took the suffering human race,
He read each wound, each weakness clear;   20
And struck his finger on the place,
And said: *Thou ailest here, and here!*
He look'd on Europe's dying hour
Of fitful dream and feverish power;
His eye plunged down the weltering strife,
The turmoil of expiring life—
He said: *The end is everywhere,*
Art still has truth, take refuge there!
And he was happy, if to know
Causes of things, and far below   30
His feet to see the lurid flow
Of terror, and insane distress,
And headlong fate, be happiness.

And Wordsworth!—Ah, pale ghosts, rejoice!
For never has such soothing voice
Been to your shadowy world convey'd,
Since erst, at morn, some wandering shade

Heard the clear song of Orpheus come
Through Hades, and the mournful gloom.
Wordsworth has gone from us—and ye,   40
Ah, may ye feel his voice as we!
He too upon a wintry clime
Had fallen—on this iron time
Of doubts, disputes, distractions, fears.
He found us when the age had bound
Our souls in its benumbing round;
He spoke, and loosed our heart in tears.
He laid us as we lay at birth
On the cool flowery lap of earth,
Smiles broke from us and we had ease;   50
The hills were round us, and the breeze
Went o'er the sun-lit fields again;
Our foreheads felt the wind and rain.
Our youth return'd; for there was shed
On spirits that had long been dead,
Spirits dried up and closely furl'd,
The freshness of the early world.

Ah! since dark days still bring to light
Man's prudence and man's fiery might,
Time may restore us in his course   60
Goethe's sage mind and Byron's force;
But where will Europe's latter hour
Again find Wordsworth's healing power?
Others will teach us how to dare,
And against fear our breast to steel;
Others will strengthen us to bear—
But who, ah! who, will make us feel?
The cloud of mortal destiny,
Others will front it fearlessly—
But who, like him, will put it by?   70

Keep fresh the grass upon his grave
O Rotha, with thy living wave!
Sing him thy best! for few or none
Hears thy voice right, now he is gone.

Coventry Patmore

(1 8 2 3 – 1 8 9 6)

Admired especially by the Pre-Raphaelites and generally praised for his celebra-
tion of married love in *The Angel in the House* (1858; enlarged 1866), Patmore
became a Roman Catholic in 1864 and offended convention even more griev-
ously with such poems in *The Unknown Eros* (1877) as "To the Body," which
justifies adulation of hair and feet by Biblical assurances that these will join in
Heaven the Virgin and the prophet Elijah, who ascended without a death.
Outliving the two wives celebrated in these volumes, Patmore married again
in 1881.

TO THE BODY

Creation's and Creator's crowning good;
Wall of infinitude;
Foundation of the sky,
In Heaven forecast
And long'd for from eternity,
Though laid the last;
Reverberating dome,
Of music cunningly built home
Against the void and indolent disgrace
Of unresponsive space;   10
Little, sequester'd pleasure-house
For God and for His Spouse;
Elaborately, yea, past conceiving, fair,
Since, from the graced decorum of the hair,
Ev'n to the tingling, sweet
Soles of the simple, earth-confiding feet,
And from the inmost heart
Outwards unto the thin
Silk curtains of the skin,
Every least part   20
Astonish'd hears
And sweet replies to some like region of the spheres;
Form'd for a dignity prophets but darkly name,

Lest shameless men cry "Shame!"
So rich with wealth conceal'd
That Heaven and Hell fight chiefly for this field;
Clinging to everything that pleases thee
With indefectible fidelity;
Alas, so true
To all thy friendships that no grace   30
Thee from thy sin can wholly disembrace;
Which thus 'bides with thee as the Jebusite,
That, maugre all God's promises could do,
The chosen People never conquer'd quite;
Who therefore lived with them,
And that by formal truce and as of right,
In metropolitan Jerusalem.
For which false fealty
Thou needs must, for a season, lie
In the grave's arms, foul and unshriven,   40
Albeit, in Heaven,
Thy crimson-throbbing Glow
Into its old abode aye pants to go,
And does with envy see
Enoch, Elijah, and the Lady, she
Who left the roses in her body's lieu.
O, if the pleasures I have known in thee
But my poor faith's poor first-fruits be,
What quintessential, keen, ethereal bliss
Then shall be his   50
Who has thy birth-time's consecrating dew
For death's sweet chrism retain'd,
Quick, tender, virginal, and unprofaned!

George Meredith

(1828–1909)

The son of a Portsmouth tailor and unconventionally educated at a Moravian school in Germany, Meredith by persistence as author became a revered figure to younger Victorians. He married Peacock's daughter, who departed in 1857 with Henry Wallis, for whose painting *The Death of Chatterton* Meredith had served as model. Meredith's rejection as reader (for publishers Chapman & Hall) of Hardy's first novel did not end the admiration for him that Hardy shared with Stevenson and Henry James. Now seen primarily as a novelist who delighted in metaphor, Meredith has been accused of rhyming gnarled language where Tennysonian lyricism was expected and of shaping psychological realism as a novelist would in the autobiographical sequence *Modern Love* (1862), which lays bare the failure of his first marriage. Arthur Symons's phrase "he reasons in pictures" applies equally to "Lucifer in Starlight" (1883), a beacon in Meredith's lifelong campaign against egoism.

LUCIFER IN STARLIGHT

On a starred night Prince Lucifer uprose.
Tired of his dark dominion swung the fiend
Above the rolling ball in cloud part screened,
Where sinners hugged their spectre of repose.
Poor prey to his hot fit of pride were those.
And now upon his western wing he leaned,
Now his huge bulk o'er Afric's sands careened,
Now the black planet shadowed Arctic snows.
Soaring through wider zones that pricked his scars
With memory of the old revolt from Awe,
He reached a middle height, and at the stars,
Which are the brain of heaven, he looked, and sank.
Around the ancient track marched, rank on rank,
The army of unalterable law.

From MODERN LOVE

ॐ 1 ॐ

By this he knew she wept with waking eyes:
That, at his hand's light quiver by her head,
The strange low sobs that shook their common bed
Were called into her with a sharp surprise,
And strangled mute, like little gaping snakes,
Dreadfully venomous to him. She lay
Stone-still, and the long darkness flowed away
With muffled pulses. Then, as midnight makes
Her giant heart of Memory and Tears
Drink the pale drug of silence, and so beat
Sleep's heavy measure, they from head to feet
Were moveless, looking through their dead black years,
By vain regret scrawled over the blank wall.
Like sculptured effigies they might be seen
Upon their marriage-tomb, the sword between;
Each wishing for the sword that severs all.

ॐ 30 ॐ

What are we first? First, animals; and next
Intelligences at a leap; on whom
Pale lies the distant shadow of the tomb,
And all that draweth on the tomb for text.
Into which state comes Love, the crowning sun:
Beneath whose light the shadow loses form.
We are the lords of life, and life is warm.
Intelligence and instinct now are one.
But nature says: "My children most they seem
When they least know me: therefore I decree
That they shall suffer." Swift doth young Love flee,
And we stand wakened, shivering from our dream.
Then if we study Nature we are wise.
Thus do the few who live but with the day:
The scientific animals are they.—
Lady, this is my sonnet to your eyes.

Dante Gabriel Rossetti

(1 8 2 8 – 1 8 8 2)

Gabriel Charles Dante Rossetti, as painter, poet, and personality, became a leader in the Pre-Raphaelite Brotherhood formed in 1848 and sole leader of the second wave, which included William Morris and Swinburne. He and his sister Maria, more distinctly than Christina and their brother William Michael, inherited an addiction to Dante Alighieri from their father, an Italian patriot active in London. After lackadaisical years in King's College School, Gabriel became more attentive, but still unconformable, as a student of drawing and painting and of models with luxuriant hair.

"The Blessed Damozel" (begun 1847; published 1850 in the Pre-Raphaelite Brotherhood periodical *The Germ*, and much revised until 1870) in its final form—especially in the imagining lover's deepest reflections (within parentheses)—reveals the vanity of his hope for "we two" in Heaven. In grief at his wife's suicide in 1862, Gabriel buried with her a sheaf of poems, including "The Woodspurge" and "Sudden Light," that he allowed to be disinterred for publication in *Poems* (1870).

Fifty sonnets of "The House of Life" appeared in 1870; the sequence reached its final 101 in *Ballads and Sonnets* (1881). The "moment's monuments" originally addressed to his wife, Elizabeth Siddal, and descriptive of his own paintings, were absorbed into reflections of his affair with Morris's wife. The sub-sequence "Willowwood" typically turns natural detail into parable and emblems of grief at love's loss. Critics focusing on intention have complained that Rossetti aspired to Dantesque spirituality but remained a "fleshly poet."

THE BLESSED DAMOZEL

The blessed damozel leaned out
    From the gold bar of Heaven;
Her eyes were deeper than the depth
    Of waters stilled at even;
She had three lilies in her hand,
    And the stars in her hair were seven.

Her robe, ungirt from clasp to hem,
    No wrought flowers did adorn,

But a white rose of Mary's gift,
    For service meetly worn;
Her hair that lay along her back
    Was yellow like ripe corn.   10

Herseemed she scarce had been a day
    One of God's choristers;
The wonder was not yet quite gone
    From that still look of hers;
Albeit, to them she left, her day
    Had counted as ten years.

(To one, it is ten years of years.
    . . . Yet now, and in this place,   20
Surely she leaned o'er me—her hair
    Fell all about my face. . . .
Nothing: the autumn-fall of leaves.
    The whole year sets apace.)

It was the rampart of God's house
    That she was standing on;
By God built over the sheer depth
    The which is Space begun;
So high, that looking downward thence
    She scarce could see the sun.   30

It lies in Heaven, across the flood
    Of ether, as a bridge.
Beneath, the tides of day and night
    With flame and darkness ridge
The void, as low as where this earth
    Spins like a fretful midge.

Around her, lovers, newly met
    'Mid deathless love's acclaims,
Spoke evermore among themselves
    Their heart-remembered names;   40
And the souls mounting up to God
    Went by her like thin flames.

And still she bowed herself and stooped
    Out of the circling charm;
Until her bosom must have made

The bar she leaned on warm,
And the lilies lay as if asleep
   Along her bended arm.

From the fixed place of Heaven she saw
   Time like a pulse shake fierce   50
Through all the worlds. Her gaze still strove
   Within the gulf to pierce
Its path; and now she spoke as when
   The stars sang in their spheres.

The sun was gone now; the curled moon
   Was like a little feather
Fluttering far down the gulf; and now
   She spoke through the still weather.
Her voice was like the voice the stars
   Had when they sang together.   60

(Ah sweet! Even now, in that bird's song,
   Strove not her accents there,
Fain to be hearkened? When those bells
   Possessed the mid-day air,
Strove not her steps to reach my side
   Down all the echoing stair?)

"I wish that he were come to me,
   For he will come," she said.
"Have I not prayed in Heaven?—on earth,
   Lord, Lord, has he not pray'd?   70
Are not two prayers a perfect strength?
   And shall I feel afraid?

"When round his head the aureole clings,
   And he is clothed in white,
I'll take his hand and go with him
   To the deep wells of light;
As unto a stream we will step down,
   And bathe there in God's sight.

"We two will stand beside that shrine,
   Occult, withheld, untrod,   80
Whose lamps are stirred continually
   With prayer sent up to God;

And see our old prayers, granted, melt
   Each like a little cloud.

"We two will lie i' the shadow of
   That living mystic tree
Within whose secret growth the Dove
   Is sometimes felt to be,
While every leaf that His plumes touch
   Saith His Name audibly.   90

"And I myself will teach to him,
   I myself, lying so,
The songs I sing here; which his voice
   Shall pause in, hushed and slow,
And find some knowledge at each pause,
   Or some new thing to know."

(Alas! we two, we two, thou say'st!
   Yea, one wast thou with me
That once of old. But shall God lift
   To endless unity   100
The soul whose likeness with thy soul
   Was but its love for thee?)

"We two," she said, "will seek the groves
   Where the lady Mary is,
With her five handmaidens, whose names
   Are five sweet symphonies,
Cecily, Gertrude, Magdalen,
   Margaret and Rosalys.

"Circlewise sit they, with bound locks
   And foreheads garlanded;   110
Into the fine cloth white like flame
   Weaving the golden thread,
To fashion the birth-robes for them
   Who are just born, being dead.

"He shall fear, haply, and be dumb:
   Then will I lay my cheek
To his, and tell about our love,
   Not once abashed or weak:

And the dear Mother will approve
    My pride, and let me speak.   120

"Herself shall bring us, hand in hand,
    To Him round whom all souls
Kneel, the clear-ranged unnumbered heads
    Bowed with their aureoles:
And angels meeting us shall sing
    To their citherns and citoles.

"There will I ask of Christ the Lord
    Thus much for him and me:—
Only to live as once on earth
    With Love,—only to be,   130
As then awhile, for ever now
    Together, I and he."

She gazed and listened and then said,
    Less sad of speech than mild,—
"All this is when he comes." She ceased.
    The light thrilled towards her, fill'd
With angels in strong level flight.
    Her eyes prayed, and she smil'd.

(I saw her smile.) But soon their path
    Was vague in distant spheres: 140
And then she cast her arms along
    The golden barriers,
And laid her face between her hands,
    And wept. (I heard her tears.)

THE WOODSPURGE

The wind flapped loose, the wind was still,
Shaken out dead from tree and hill:
I had walked on at the wind's will,—
I sat now, for the wind was still.

Between my knees my forehead was,—
My lips, drawn in, said not Alas!

My hair was over in the grass,
My naked ears heard the day pass.

My eyes, wide open, had the run
Of some ten weeds to fix upon;   10
Among those few, out of the sun,
The woodspurge flowered, three cups in one.

From perfect grief there need not be
Wisdom or even memory:
One thing then learnt remains to me,—
The woodspurge has a cup of three.

SUDDEN LIGHT

    I have been here before,
        But when or how I cannot tell:
    I know the grass beyond the door,
        The sweet keen smell,
The sighing sound, the lights around the shore.

    You have been mine before,—
        How long ago I may not know:
    But just when at that swallow's soar
        Your neck turned so,
Some veil did fall,—I knew it all of yore.   10

    Has this been thus before?
        And shall not thus time's eddying flight
    Still with our lives our love restore
        In death's despite,
And day and night yield one delight once more?

WILLOWWOOD

    1

I sat with Love upon a woodside well,
    Leaning across the water, I and he;

Nor ever did he speak nor looked at me,
But touched his lute wherein was audible
The certain secret thing he had to tell:
    Only our mirrored eyes met silently
    In the low wave; and that sound came to be
The passionate voice I knew; and my tears fell.

And at their fall, his eyes beneath grew hers;
And with his foot and with his wing-feathers
    He swept the spring that watered my heart's drouth.
Then the dark ripples spread to waving hair,
And as I stooped, her own lips rising there
    Bubbled with brimming kisses at my mouth.

    2

And now Love sang: but his was such a song
    So meshed with half-remembrance hard to free,
    As souls disused in death's sterility
May sing when the new birthday tarries long.
And I was made aware of a dumb throng
    That stood aloof, one form by every tree,
    All mournful forms, for each was I or she,
The shades of those our days that had no tongue.

They looked on us, and knew us and were known;
    While fast together, alive from the abyss,
    Clung the soul-wrung implacable close kiss;
And pity of self through all made broken moan
Which said, "For once, for once, for once alone!"
    And still Love sang, and what he sang was this:—

    3

"O ye, all ye that walk in Willowwood,
    That walk with hollow faces burning white;
What fathom-depth of soul-struck widowhood,
    What long, what longer hours, one lifelong night,
Ere ye again, who so in vain have wooed
    Your last hope lost, who so in vain invite
Your lips to that their unforgotten food,
    Ere ye, ere ye again shall see the light!

Alas! the bitter banks in Willowwood,
   With tear-spurge wan, with blood-wort burning red:
Alas! if ever such a pillow could
   Steep deep the soul in sleep till she were dead,—
Better all life forget her than this thing,
That Willowwood should hold her wandering!"

4

So sang he: and as meeting rose and rose
   Together cling through the wind's wellaway
   Nor change at once, yet near the end of day
The leaves drop loosened where the heart-stain glows,—
So when the song died did the kiss unclose;
   And her face fell back drowned, and was as grey
   As its grey eyes; and if it ever may
Meet mine again I know not if Love knows.

Only I know that I leaned low and drank
A long draught from the water where she sank,
   Her breath and all her tears and all her soul:
And as I leaned, I know I felt Love's face
Pressed on my neck with moan of pity and grace,
   Till both our heads were in his aureole.

Christina Georgina Rossetti

(1830–1894)

Youngest of four talented children of the Italian patriot and Dante scholar Gabriele Rossetti, Christina followed the Anglican faith of her mother with a firm determination that lent to her poems clarity and momentum rare in her brother Gabriel's. "A Birthday," "Uphill," and "Song" appeared in *Goblin Market, and Other Poems* (1862). "Monna Innominata: A Sonnet of Sonnets," in *A Pageant and Other Poems* (1881), includes "Many in aftertimes" (No. 11). In a prefatory note, the poet declares the speaker to be one of "a bevy of 'donne innominate' [unnamed ladies]" preceding Dante's Beatrice and Petrarch's Laura. But Christina's love poems cannot be unrelated to her rejection of two suitors on the grounds of difference in religion, and scholars have sought in the poems and elsewhere for a further amour canceled in pain. Her brother William thought "An Echo from Willow-wood" probably reflected Gabriel's love and loss, but the "echo" may be from Christina's own life. William published "Cobwebs" in Christina's posthumous *New Poems* (1895).

A BIRTHDAY

My heart is like a singing bird
   Whose nest is in a watered shoot;
My heart is like an apple tree
   Whose boughs are bent with thickset fruit;
My heart is like a rainbow shell
   That paddles in a halcyon sea;
My heart is gladder than all these
   Because my love is come to me.

Raise me a dais of silk and down;
   Hang it with vair and purple dyes;   10
Carve it in doves and pomegranates,
   And peacocks with a hundred eyes;
Work it in gold and silver grapes,
   In leaves and silver fleurs-de-lys;
Because the birthday of my life
   Is come, my love is come to me.

SONG

When I am dead, my dearest,
   Sing no sad songs for me;
Plant thou no roses at my head,
   Nor shady cypress tree:
Be the green grass above me
   With showers and dewdrops wet;
And if thou wilt, remember,
   And if thou wilt, forget.

I shall not see the shadows,
   I shall not feel the rain;   10
I shall not hear the nightingale
   Sing on, as if in pain:
And dreaming through the twilight
   That doth not rise nor set,
Haply I may remember,
   And haply may forget.

UPHILL

Does the road wind up-hill all the way?
   Yes, to the very end.
Will the day's journey take the whole long day?
   From morn to night, my friend.

But is there for the night a resting-place?
   A roof for when the slow dark hours begin.
May not the darkness hide it from my face?
   You cannot miss that inn.

Shall I meet other wayfarers at night?
   Those who have gone before.   10
Then must I knock, or call when just in sight?
   They will not keep you standing at that door.

Shall I find comfort, travel-sore and weak?
   Of labour you shall find the sum.
Will there be beds for me and all who seek?
   Yea, beds for all who come.

From *MONNA INNOMINATA*

Many in aftertimes will say of you
"He loved her"—while of me what will they say?
    Not that I loved you more than just in play,
For fashion's sake as idle women do.
Even let them prate; who know not what we knew
    Of love and parting in exceeding pain,
    Of parting hopeless here to meet again,
Hopeless on earth, and heaven is out of view.
But by my heart of love laid bare to you,
    My love that you can make not void nor vain,
Love that foregoes you but to claim anew
        Beyond this passage of the gate of death,
    I charge you at the Judgment make it plain
        My love of you was life and not a breath.

AN ECHO FROM
WILLOW-WOOD

"O ye, all ye that walk in willowwood."
                D. G. Rossetti.

Two gazed into a pool, he gazed and she,
        Not hand in hand, yet heart in heart, I think,
    Pale and reluctant on the water's brink,
As on the brink of parting which must be.
Each eyed the other's aspect, she and he,
    Each felt one hungering heart leap up and sink,
    Each tasted bitterness which both must drink,
There on the brink of life's dividing sea.
Lilies upon the surface, deep below
    Two wistful faces craving each for each,
        Resolute and reluctant without speech:—
A sudden ripple made the faces flow,
    One moment joined, to vanish out of reach:
        So those hearts joined, and ah were parted so.

COBWEBS

It is a land with neither night nor day,
   Nor heat nor cold, nor any wind, nor rain,
   Nor hills nor valleys; but one even plain
Stretches thro' long unbroken miles away:
While thro' the sluggish air a twilight grey
   Broodeth; no moons or seasons wax and wane,
   No ebb and flow are there along the main,
No bud-time, no leaf-falling, there for aye,
No ripple on the sea, no shifting sand,
   No beat of wings to stir the stagnant space,
No pulse of life thro' all the loveless land:
And loveless sea; no trace of days before,
   No guarded home, no toil-won restingplace
No future hope, no fear for evermore.

Charles Stuart Calverley

(1 8 3 1 – 1 8 8 4)

Son of a Worcestershire clergyman who was surnamed Blayds until 1852, Calverley was a Latinist of Harrow, Oxford, Cambridge, and the Inner Temple, limited in practice as a barrister because of an injury in skating. Within the wide range of parodies by Calverley, his "Ballad" deflates the romantic diction of Jean Ingelow and such refrains as D. G. Rossetti's in "Sister Helen," which end each incremental variation with the awesome words *between Hell and Heaven!*

BALLAD

PART I

The auld wife sat at her ivied door,
　(*Butter and eggs and a pound of cheese*)
A thing she had frequently done before;
　　And her spectacles lay on her apron'd knees.

The piper he piped on the hill-top high,
　(*Butter and eggs and a pound of cheese*)
Till the cow said "I die," and the goose ask'd "Why?"
　　And the dog said nothing, but search'd for fleas.

The farmer he strode through the square farmyard;
　(*Butter and eggs and a pound of cheese*)　　　　　　　10
His last brew of ale was a trifle hard—
　　The connexion of which with the plot one sees.

The farmer's daughter hath frank blue eyes;
　(*Butter and eggs and a pound of cheese*)
She hears the rooks caw in the windy skies,
　　As she sits at her lattice and shells her peas.

The farmer's daughter hath ripe red lips;
　(*Butter and eggs and a pound of cheese*)

641

If you try to approach her, away she skips
   Over tables and chairs with apparent ease.   20

The farmer's daughter hath soft brown hair,
   (*Butter and eggs and a pound of cheese*)
And I met with a ballad, I can't say where,
   Which wholly consisted of lines like these.

PART II

She sat with her hands 'neath her dimpled cheeks,
   (*Butter and eggs and a pound of cheese*)
And spake not a word. While a lady speaks
   There is hope, but she didn't even sneeze.

She sat, with her hands 'neath her crimson cheeks;
   (*Butter and eggs and a pound of cheese*)   30
She gave up mending her father's breeks,
   And let the cat roll in her new chemise.

She sat, with her hands 'neath her burning cheeks,
   (*Butter and eggs and a pound of cheese*)
And gazed at the piper for thirteen weeks;
   Then she follow'd him out o'er the misty leas.

Her sheep follow'd her, as their tails did them.
   (*Butter and eggs and a pound of cheese*)
And this song is consider'd a perfect gem,
   And as to the meaning, it's what you please.   40

Lewis Carroll

(pseudonym of Charles Lutwidge Dodgson, 1 8 3 2 – 1 8 9 8)

After childhood in Cheshire and preparation at Rugby School, Dodgson entered
Oxford and remained there. His prestige as a writer and lecturer on mathematics
was followed by fame as author of fantasies for children and a degree of notoriety
as photographer of little girls. The poems here come from *Through the Looking
Glass* (1871), Carroll's sequel to *Alice's Adventures in Wonderland.* "Jabber-
wocky" may be taken as the vocabulary invented for the heroic decapitation of a
fierce monster by a diminutive David-plus-Saint-George. The poem appeared
in reverse until Alice unreversed it with a second mirror. Amoral Tweedledee,
who recites "The Walrus and the Carpenter," thwarts Alice's attempt to sympa-
thize with the Walrus "because he was a *little* sorry for the poor oysters":
nonsense reduces for the reader, but not for Alice, the sting of cruelty.

JABBERWOCKY

'Twas brillig, and the slithy toves
   Did gyre and gimble in the wabe:
All mimsy were the borogoves,
   And the mome raths outgrabe.

"Beware the Jabberwock, my son!
   The jaws that bite, the claws that catch!
Beware the Jubjub bird, and shun
   The frumious Bandersnatch!"

He took his vorpal sword in hand;
   Long time the manxome foe he sought—   10
So rested he by the Tumtum tree,
   And stood awhile in thought.

And, as in uffish thought he stood,
   The Jabberwock, with eyes of flame,
Came whiffling through the tulgey wood,
   And burbled as it came!

One, two! One, two! And through and through
   The vorpal blade went snicker-snack!
He left it dead, and with its head
   He went galumphing back.   20

"And hast thou slain the Jabberwock?
   Come to my arms, my beamish boy!
O frabjous day! Callooh! Callay!"
   He chortled in his joy.

'Twas brillig, and the slithy toves
   Did gyre and gimble in the wabe:
All mimsy were the borogoves,
   And the mome raths outgrabe.

THE WALRUS AND
THE CARPENTER

The sun was shining on the sea,
   Shining with all his might:
He did his very best to make
   The billows smooth and bright—
And this was odd, because it was
   The middle of the night.

The moon was shining sulkily,
   Because she thought the sun
Had got no business to be there
   After the day was done—   10
"It's very rude of him," she said,
   "To come and spoil the fun!"

The sea was wet as wet could be,
   The sands were dry as dry.
You could not see a cloud because
   No cloud was in the sky:
No birds were flying overhead—
   There were no birds to fly.

The Walrus and the Carpenter
   Were walking close at hand: 20

They wept like anything to see
    Such quantities of sand:
"If this were only cleared away,"
    They said, "it *would* be grand!"

"If seven maids with seven mops
    Swept it for half a year,
Do you suppose," the Walrus said,
    "That they could get it clear?"
"I doubt it," said the Carpenter,
    And shed a bitter tear.   30

"O Oysters, come and walk with us!"
    The Walrus did beseech.
"A pleasant walk, a pleasant talk,
    Along the briny beach:
We cannot do with more than four,
    To give a hand to each."

The eldest Oyster looked at him,
    But never a word he said;
The eldest Oyster winked his eye,
    And shook his heavy head—   40
Meaning to say he did not choose
    To leave the oyster-bed.

But four young Oysters hurried up,
    All eager for the treat:
Their coats were brushed, their faces washed,
    Their shoes were clean and neat—
And this was odd, because, you know,
    They hadn't any feet.

Four other Oysters followed them,
    And yet another four;   50
And thick and fast they came at last,
    And more and more and more—
All hopping through the frothy waves,
    And scrambling to the shore.

The Walrus and the Carpenter
    Walked on a mile or so,
And then they rested on a rock

Conveniently low:
And all the little Oysters stood
  And waited in a row.   60

"The time has come," the Walrus said,
  "To talk of many things:
Of shoes—and ships—and sealing-wax—
  Of cabbages—and kings—
And why the sea is boiling hot—
  And whether pigs have wings."

"But wait a bit," the Oysters cried,
  "Before we have our chat;
For some of us are out of breath,
  And all of us are fat!"   70
"No hurry!" said the Carpenter.
  They thanked him much for that.

"A loaf of bread," the Walrus said,
  "Is what we chiefly need:
Pepper and vinegar besides
  Are very good indeed—
Now, if you're ready, Oysters dear,
  We can begin to feed."

"But not on us!" the Oysters cried,
  Turning a little blue.   80
"After such kindness, that would be
  A dismal thing to do!"
"The night is fine," the Walrus said,
  "Do you admire the view?

"It was so kind of you to come!
  And you are very nice!"
The Carpenter said nothing but
  "Cut us another slice.
I wish you were not quite so deaf—
  I've had to ask you twice!"   90

"It seems a shame," the Walrus said,
  "To play them such a trick.
After we've brought them out so far,
  And made them trot so quick!"

The Carpenter said nothing but
　"The butter's spread too thick!"

"I weep for you," the Walrus said:
　"I deeply sympathize."
With sobs and tears he sorted out
　Those of the largest size,   100
Holding his pocket-handkerchief
　Before his streaming eyes.

"O Oysters," said the Carpenter,
　"You've had a pleasant run!
Shall we be trotting home again?"
　But answer came there none—
And this was scarcely odd, because
　They'd eaten every one.

William Morris

(1834 – 1896)

After boyhood in a mansion at the edge of Epping Forest—the money came from copper mines—Morris continued to enjoy a life of comfort. At Oxford, before apprenticeship to the architect G. E. Street, he came under the influence of Gabriel Rossetti, and in later years he was a vigorous socialist. He designed textiles, wallpapers, and furniture for his own manufacturing firm as well as type and typographical ornaments for his Kelmscott Press. He wrote sagas, romances, and utopian narratives in verse and prose. Besides his interest in epic and saga, he may even have journeyed to Iceland in 1871 in the hope that his wife and Rossetti might terminate their affair at Kelmscott, his manor on the Thames. *News from Nowhere* and his socialist lectures on art have remained easily available; his longer poems and tales return at the beck of fashion.

In his first volume of narratives in verse, *The Defence of Guenevere, and Other Poems* (1858), Morris adapted from Froissart's *Chroniques* the fate of Sir Robert de Marny and his mistress after the battle of Poictiers in 1356. Interested equally with Tennyson, Arnold, and Swinburne in Arthurian subjects, only he among eminent Victorians could provide the unromanticized view of medieval cruelty as seen and felt by Jehane.

THE HAYSTACK IN
THE FLOODS

Had she come all the way for this,
To part at last without a kiss?
Yea, had she borne the dirt and rain
That her own eyes might see him slain
Beside the haystack in the floods?

Along the dripping leafless woods,
The stirrup touching either shoe,
She rode astride as troopers do;
With kirtle kilted to her knee,
To which the mud splash'd wretchedly;   10
And the wet dripp'd from every tree

Upon her head and heavy hair,
And on her eyelids broad and fair;
The tears and rain ran down her face.
By fits and starts they rode apace,
And very often was his place
Far off from her; he had to ride
Ahead, to see what might betide
When the roads cross'd; and sometimes, when
There rose a murmuring from his men,   20
Had to turn back with promises;
Ah me! she had but little ease;
And often for pure doubt and dread
She sobb'd, made giddy in the head
By the swift riding; while, for cold,
Her slender fingers scarce could hold
The wet reins; yea, and scarcely, too,
She felt the foot within her shoe
Against the stirrup: all for this,
To part at last without a kiss   30
Beside the haystack in the floods.

For when they near'd that old soak'd hay,
They saw across the only way
That Judas, Godmar, and the three
Red running lions dismally
Grinn'd from his pennon, under which
In one straight line along the ditch,
They counted thirty heads.
              So then,
While Robert turn'd round to his men,
She saw at once the wretched end,   40
And, stooping down, tried hard to rend
Her coif the wrong way from her head,
And hid her eyes; while Robert said:
"Nay, love, 'tis scarcely two to one,
At Poictiers where we made them run
So fast—why, sweet my love, good cheer.
The Gascon frontier is so near,
Nought after this."

        But, "O," she said,
"My God! my God! I have to tread
The long way back without you; then   50

The court at Paris; those six men;
The gratings of the Chatelet;
The swift Seine on some rainy day
Like this, and people standing by,
And laughing, while my weak hands try
To recollect how strong men swim.
All this, or else a life with him,
For which I should be damned at last.
Would God that this next hour were past!"

He answer'd not, but cried his cry,   60
"St. George for Marny!" cheerily;
And laid his hand upon her rein.
Alas! no man of all his train
Gave back that cheery cry again;
And, while for rage his thumb beat fast
Upon his sword-hilt, some one cast
About his neck a kerchief long,
And bound him.
           Then they went along
To Godmar; who said: "Now, Jehane,
Your lover's life is on the wane   70
So fast, that, if this very hour
You yield not as my paramour,
He will not see the rain leave off—
Nay, keep your tongue from gibe and scoff,
Sir Robert, or I slay you now."

She laid her hand upon her brow,
Then gazed upon the palm, as though
She thought her forehead bled, and—"No!"
She said, and turn'd her head away,
As there were nothing else to say,   80
And everything were settled: red
Grew Godmar's face from chin to head:
"Jehane, on yonder hill there stands
My castle, guarding well my lands:
What hinders me from taking you,
And doing that I list to do
To your fair wilful body, while
Your knight lies dead?"
           A wicked smile
Wrinkled her face, her lips grew thin,

A long way out she thrust her chin: 90
"You know that I should strangle you
While you were sleeping; or bite through
Your throat, by God's help—ah!" she said,
"Lord Jesus, pity your poor maid!
For in such wise they hem me in,
I cannot choose but sin and sin,
Whatever happens: yet I think
They could not make me eat or drink,
And so should I just reach my rest."
"Nay, if you do not my behest,   100
O Jehane! though I love you well,"
Said Godmar, "would I fail to tell
All that I know?" "Foul lies," she said.
"Eh? lies my Jehane? by God's head,
At Paris folks would deem them true!
Do you know, Jehane, they cry for you:
'Jehane the brown! Jehane the brown!
Give us Jehane to burn or drown!'—
Eh—gag me Robert!—sweet my friend,
This were indeed a piteous end   110
For those long fingers, and long feet,
And long neck, and smooth shoulders sweet;
An end that few men would forget
That saw it—So, an hour yet:
Consider, Jehane, which to take
Of life or death!"
                    So, scarce awake,
Dismounting, did she leave that place,
And totter some yards: with her face
Turn'd upward to the sky she lay,
Her head on a wet heap of hay,   120
And fell asleep: and while she slept,
And did not dream, the minutes crept
Round to the twelve again; but she,
Being waked at last, sigh'd quietly,
And strangely childlike came, and said:
"I will not." Straightway Godmar's head,
As though it hung on strong wires, turn'd
Most sharply round, and his face burn'd.

For Robert—both his eyes were dry,
He could not weep, but gloomily   130

He seem'd to watch the rain; yea, too,
His lips were firm; he tried once more
To touch her lips; she reach'd out, sore
And vain desire so tortured them,
The poor grey lips, and now the hem
Of his sleeve brush'd them.
                                        With a start
Up Godmar rose, thrust them apart;
From Robert's throat he loosed the bands
Of silk and mail; with empty hands
Held out, she stood and gazed, and saw   140
The long bright blade without a flaw
Glide out from Godmar's sheath, his hand
In Robert's hair; she saw him bend
Back Robert's head; she saw him send
The thin steel down; the blow told well,
Right backward the knight Robert fell,
And moan'd as dogs do, being half dead,
Unwitting, as I deem: so then
Godmar turn'd grinning to his men,
Who ran, some five or six, and beat   150
His head to pieces at their feet.

Then Godmar turn'd again and said:
"So, Jehane, the first fitte is read!
Take note, my lady, that your way
Lies backward to the Chatelet!"
She shook her head and gazed awhile
At her cold hands with a rueful smile,
As though this thing had made her mad.

This was the parting that they had
Beside the haystack in the floods.   160

James Thomson ("B.V.")

(1 8 3 4 – 1 8 8 2)

Thomson—distinguished from his earlier namesake by his pseudonym, "B.V." (an intricate tribute to Shelley and Novalis)—added greatly to late-Victorian pessimism with *The City of Dreadful Night and Other Poems* (1880). Knowledge of Blake's life and symbolic works had been vigorously promoted by the Pre-Raphaelites. Thomson, in 1866, saw Blake as the Romantics saw Chatterton, a martyr to benightedness.

WILLIAM BLAKE

He came to the desert of London town
   Grey miles long;
He wandered up and he wandered down,
   Singing a quiet song.

He came to the desert of London town,
   Mirk miles broad;
He wandered up and he wandered down,
   Ever alone with God.

There were thousands and thousands of human kind
   In this desert of brick and stone: 10
But some were deaf and some were blind,
   And he was there alone.

At length the good hour came; he died
   As he had lived, alone:
He was not missed from the desert wide,
   Perhaps he was found at the Throne.

William Schwenck Gilbert

(1836–1911)

Son of a moderately successful novelist, Gilbert led a busy life as lawyer, illustrator, officer in the militia, clubman, and author of burlesques and burlesque ballads. Most successfully and enduringly, however, as a "kindly cynic," he wrote the comic libretti for the Savoy operas produced by Richard D'Oyly Carte, with music by Arthur Sullivan.

Premature and unnatural death, a staple of balladry, could become overt and unpunished cruelty, on loan from satire, in the grotesquerie of comic ballads. *Punch* rejected as unacceptably cruel the "Yarn of the 'Nancy Bell.'" Reminiscent of the comic verses of Barham and Hood, Gilbert's "Bab Ballads" ran first in the weekly *Fun* and were then collected in 1869. Each of them offered punning relief from Victorian rectitude. Gilbert's ancient mariner of the *Nancy Bell* may possibly be unaware of his own cannibalistic puns, but he knows better than Coleridge's what he has become.

THE YARN OF THE "NANCY BELL"

'Twas on the shores that round our coast
    From Deal to Ramsgate span,
That I found alone on a piece of stone
    An elderly naval man.

His hair was weedy, his beard was long,
    And weedy and long was he,
And I heard this wight on the shore recite,
    In a singular minor key:

"Oh, I am a cook and a captain bold,
    And the mate of the *Nancy* brig,
And a bo'sun tight, and a midshipmite,
    And the crew of the captain's gig."

And he shook his fists and he tore his hair,
    Till I really felt afraid,

10

For I couldn't help thinking the man had been drinking,
    And so I simply said:

"Oh, elderly man, it's little I know
    Of the duties of men of the sea,
But I'll eat my hand if I understand
    How you can possibly be   20

"At once a cook, and a captain bold,
    And the mate of the *Nancy* brig,
And a bo'sun tight, and a midshipmite,
    And the crew of the captain's gig."

Then he gave a hitch to his trousers, which
    Is a trick all seamen larn,
And having got rid of a thumping quid,
    He spun this painful yarn:

" 'Twas in the good ship *Nancy Bell*
    That we sailed to the Indian sea,   30
And there on a reef we come to grief,
    Which has often occurred to me.

"And pretty nigh all o' the crew was drowned
    (There was seventy-seven o' soul),
And only ten of the *Nancy*'s men
    Said 'Here' to the muster-roll.

"There was me and the cook and the captain bold,
    And the mate of the *Nancy* brig,
And the bo'sun tight, and a midshipmite,
    And the crew of the captain's gig.   40

"For a month we'd neither wittles nor drink,
    Till a-hungry we did feel,
So we drawed a lot, and accordin' shot
    The captain for our meal.

"The next lot fell to the *Nancy*'s mate,
    And a delicate dish he made;
Then our appetite with the midshipmite
    We seven survivors stayed.

"And then we murdered the bo'sun tight,
    And he much resembled pig;   50
Then we wittled free, did the cook and me,
    On the crew of the captain's gig.

"Then only the cook and me was left,
    And the delicate question, 'Which
Of us two goes to the kettle?' arose
    And we argued it out as sich.

"For I loved that cook as a brother, I did,
    And the cook he worshipped me;
But we'd both be blowed if we'd either be stowed
    In the other chap's hold, you see.   60

" 'I'll be eat if you dines off me,' says Tom,
    'Yes, that,' says I, 'you'll be,'—
'I'm boiled if I die, my friend,' quoth I,
    And 'Exactly so,' quoth he.

"Says he, 'Dear James, to murder me
    Were a foolish thing to do,
For don't you see that you can't cook *me*,
    While I can—and will—cook *you!*'

"So he boils the water, and takes the salt
    And the pepper in portions true   70
(Which he never forgot), and some chopped shalot,
    And some sage and parsley too.

" 'Come here,' says he, with a proper pride,
    Which his smiling features tell,
''Twill soothing be if I let you see,
    How extremely nice you'll smell.'

"And he stirred it round and round and round,
    And he sniffed at the foaming froth;
When I ups with his heels, and smothers his squeals
    In the scum of the boiling broth.   80

"And I eat that cook in a week or less,
    And—as I eating be

The last of his chops, why, I almost drops,
    For a wessel in sight I see!

———

"And I never larf, and I never smile,
    And I never lark nor play,
But I sit and croak, and a single joke
    I have—which is to say:

"Oh, I am a cook and a captain bold,
    And the mate of the *Nancy* brig,   90
And a bo'sun tight, *and* a midshipmite,
    And the crew of the captain's gig!".

From PATIENCE

BUNTHORNE'S SONG

If you're anxious for to shine in the high aesthetic line as a man of culture rare,
You must get up all the germs of the transcendental terms, and plant them
    everywhere.
You must lie upon the daisies and discourse in novel phrases of your
    complicated state of mind,
The meaning doesn't matter if it's only idle chatter of a transcendental kind.
            And every one will say,
            As you walk your mystic way,
"If this young man expresses himself in terms too deep for *me*,
Why, what a very singularly deep young man this deep young man must be!"
Be eloquent in praise of the very dull old days which have long since passed
    away,
And convince 'em, if you can, that the reign of good Queen Anne was
    Culture's palmiest day.   10
Of course you will pooh-pooh whatever's fresh and new, and declare it's crude
    and mean,
For Art stopped short in the cultivated court of the Empress Josephine.
            And every one will say,
            As you walk your mystic way,
"If that's not good enough for him which is good enough for me,
Why, what a very cultivated kind of youth this kind of youth must be!"
Then a sentimental passion of a vegetable fashion must excite your languid
    spleen,

An attachment *à la* Plato for a bashful young potato, or a not-too-French
    French bean!
Though Philistines may jostle, you will rank as an apostle in the high aesthetic
    band,
If you walk down Piccadilly with a poppy or a lily in your mediaeval hand.   20
                And every one will say,
                As you walk your flowery way,
"If he's content with a vegetable love which would certainly not suit *me*,
Why, what a most particularly pure young man this pure young man must be."

Algernon Charles Swinburne

(1 8 3 7 – 1 9 0 9)

Of good family and poor physique, Swinburne gained from Eton a classical education and interest in flagellation; from Oxford, more Greek and Latin, Pre-Raphaelite friends, and various unorthodoxies; in London, alcohol and sado-masochism; from the wreckage, an incomparable verbal music and wide respect for his range of literary accomplishment. The popular image of an aged imp confined by his friend Watts-Dunton at No. 2, The Pines, in Putney, sinks before the collective but incomplete edition in twenty volumes that includes poems, dramas, critical essays, and approaches to the excluded ribaldry and works of fiction.

Proserpine, abducted by Hades and forced to live as queen of his underworld half of each year, is a prime symbol of the masochism and the rebellion against conventional morality of Swinburne's *Poems and Ballads* (1866). A skillful parodist, even of his own diffuseness, anapests, and alliteration, Swinburne ridiculed in the third poem below (1880) Tennyson's rhetorical assertion of a highest truth in "The Higher Pantheism" (see p. 593).

THE GARDEN OF PROSERPINE

Here, where the world is quiet;
   Here, where all trouble seems
Dead winds' and spent waves' riot
   In doubtful dreams of dreams;
I watch the green field growing
For reaping folk and sowing,
For harvest-time and mowing,
   A sleepy world of streams.

I am tired of tears and laughter,
   And men that laugh and weep;   10
Of what may come hereafter
   For men that sow to reap:
I am weary of days and hours,
Blown buds of barren flowers,

659

Desires and dreams and powers
    And everything but sleep.

Here life has death for neighbour,
    And far from eye or ear
Wan waves and wet winds labour,
    Weak ships and spirits steer;   20
They drive adrift, and whither
They wot not who make thither;
But no such winds blow hither,
    And no such things grow here.

No growth of moor or coppice,
    No heather-flower or vine,
But bloomless buds of poppies,
    Green grapes of Proserpine,
Pale beds of blowing rushes
Where no leaf blooms or blushes   30
Save this whereout she crushes
    For dead men deadly wine.

Pale, without name or number,
    In fruitless fields of corn,
They bow themselves and slumber
    All night till light is born;
And like a soul belated,
In hell and heaven unmated,
By cloud and mist abated
    Comes out of darkness morn.   40

Though one were strong as seven,
    He too with death shall dwell,
Nor wake with wings in heaven,
    Nor weep for pains in hell;
Though one were fair as roses,
His beauty clouds and closes;
And well though love reposes,
    In the end it is not well.

Pale, beyond porch and portal,
    Crowned with calm leaves, she stands   50
Who gathers all things mortal
    With cold immortal hands;

Her languid lips are sweeter
Than love's who fears to greet her
To men that mix and meet her
    From many times and lands.

She waits for each and other,
    She waits for all men born:
Forgets the earth her mother,
    The life of fruits and corn;   60
And spring and seed and swallow
Take wing for her and follow
Where summer song rings hollow
    And flowers are put to scorn.

There go the loves that wither,
    The old loves with wearier wings;
And all dead years draw thither,
    And all disastrous things;
Dead dreams of days forsaken,
Blind buds that snows have shaken,   70
Wild leaves that winds have taken,
    Red strays of ruined springs.

We are not sure of sorrow,
    And joy was never sure;
To-day will die to-morrow;
    Time stoops to no man's lure;
And love, grown faint and fretful,
With lips but half regretful
Sighs, and with eyes forgetful
    Weeps that no loves endure.   80

From too much love of living,
    From hope and fear set free,
We thank with brief thanksgiving
    Whatever gods may be
That no life lives for ever;
That dead men rise up never;
That even the weariest river
    Winds somewhere safe to sea.

Then star nor sun shall waken,
    Nor any change of light: 90

Nor sound of waters shaken,
   Nor any sound or sight:
Nor wintry leaves nor vernal,
Nor days nor things diurnal;
Only the sleep eternal
   In an eternal night.

THE LAKE OF GAUBE

The sun is lord and god, sublime, serene,
   And sovereign on the mountains: earth and air
Lie prone in passion, blind with bliss unseen
   By force of sight and might of rapture, fair
   As dreams that die and know not what they were.
The lawns, the gorges, and the peaks, are one
Glad glory, thrilled with sense of unison
In strong compulsive silence of the sun.

Flowers dense and keen as midnight stars aflame
   And living things of light like flames in flower   10
That glance and flash as though no hand might tame
   Lightnings whose life outshone their stormlit hour
   And played and laughed on earth, with all their power
Gone, and with all their joy of life made long
And harmless as the lightning life of song,
Shine sweet like stars when darkness feels them strong.

The deep mild purple flaked with moonbright gold
   That makes the scales seem flowers of hardened light,
The flamelike tongue, the feet that noon leaves cold,
   The kindly trust in man, when once the sight   20
   Grew less than strange, and faith bade fear take flight,
Outlive the little harmless life that shone
And gladdened eyes that loved it, and was gone
Ere love might fear that fear had looked thereon.

Fear held the bright thing hateful, even as fear,
   Whose name is one with hate and horror, saith
That heaven, the dark deep heaven of water near,
   Is deadly deep as hell and dark as death.
   The rapturous plunge that quickens blood and breath

With pause more sweet than passion, ere they strive   30
To raise again the limbs that yet would dive
Deeper, should there have slain the soul alive.

As the bright salamander in fire of the noonshine exults and is glad of his day,
The spirit that quickens my body rejoices to pass from the sunlight away,
To pass from the glow of the mountainous flowerage, the high multitudinous
    bloom,
Far down through the fathomless night of the water, the gladness of silence
    and gloom.
Death-dark and delicious as death in the dream of a lover and dreamer may be,
It clasps and encompasses body and soul with delight to be living and free:
Free utterly now, though the freedom endure but the space of a perilous breath,
And living, though girdled about with the darkness and coldness and strangeness
    of death: 40

Each limb and each pulse of the body rejoicing, each nerve of the spirit at rest,
All sense of the soul's life rapture, a passionate peace in its blindness blest.
So plunges the downward swimmer, embraced of the water unfathomed of man,
The darkness unplummeted, icier than seas in mid-winter, for blessing or ban;
And swiftly and sweetly, when strength and breath fall short, and the dive
    is done,
Shoots up as a shaft from the dark depth shot, sped straight into sight of the sun;
And sheer through the snow-soft water, more dark than the roof of the pines
    above,
Strikes forth, and is glad as a bird whose flight is impelled and sustained of love.

As a sea-mew's love of the sea-wind breasted and ridden for rapture's sake
Is the love of his body and soul for the darkling delight of the soundless lake: 50
As the silent speed of a dream too living to live for a thought's space more
Is the flight of his limbs through the still strong chill of the darkness from shore
    to shore.
Might life be as this is and death be as life that casts off time as a robe,
The likeness of infinite heaven were a symbol revealed of the lake of Gaube.

   Whose thought has fathomed and measured
     The darkness of life and of death,
   The secret within them treasured,
     The spirit that is not breath?
   Whose vision has yet beholden
     The splendour of death and of life?   60
   Though sunset as dawn be golden,
     Is the word of them peace, not strife?

Deep silence answers: the glory
   We dream of may be but a dream,
And the sun of the soul wax hoary
   As ashes that show not a gleam.
But well shall it be with us ever
   Who drive through the darkness here,
If the soul that we live by never,
   For aught that a lie saith, fear.   70

THE HIGHER PANTHEISM IN A NUTSHELL

One, who is not, we see: but one, whom we see not, is:
Surely this is not that: but that is assuredly this.

What, and wherefore, and whence? for under is over and under:
If thunder could be without lightning, lightning could be without thunder.

Doubt is faith in the main: but faith, on the whole, is doubt:
We cannot believe by proof: but could we believe without?

Why, and whither, and how? for barley and rye are not clover:
Neither are straight lines curves: yet over is under and over.

Two and two may be four: but four and four are not eight:
Fate and God may be twain: but God is the same thing as fate.

Ask a man what he thinks, and get from a man what he feels:
God, once caught in the fact, shows you a fair pair of heels.

Body and spirit are twins: God only knows which is which:
The soul squats down in the flesh like a tinker drunk in a ditch.

More is the whole than a part: but half is more than the whole:
Clearly, the soul is the body: but is not the body the soul?

One and two are not one: but one and nothing is two:
Truth can hardly be false, if falsehood cannot be true.

Once the mastodon was: pterodactyls were common as cocks:
Then the mammoth was God: now is He a prize ox.

Parallels all things are: yet many of these are askew
You are certainly I: but certainly I am not you.

Springs the rock from the plain, shoots the stream from the rock:
Cocks exist for the hen: but hens exist for the cock.

God, whom we see not, is: and God, who is not, we see:
Fiddle, we know, is diddle: and diddle, we take it, is dee.

Thomas Hardy

(1 8 4 0 – 1 9 2 8)

Son of a stonemason and apprenticed to an architect in Dorset (which he called "Wessex," land of West Saxons), Hardy denied that his gloomy rejection of benign providence came from events in his own life. As an architect in London and Dorset for ten years, avidly reading books that challenged belief in the Bible, he began to write fiction. From 1872, with Dorchester as base, he wrote short fiction and novels with increasing success but with steadily mounting charges of bleakness and excessive attention to sex. The carping reviews of *Jude the Obscure* (1895) drove him to a new career as a poet. With the publication of his epic drama *The Dynasts* (1904–1908) he received honorary degrees in both Scotland and England. He assembled his autobiography (published 1928–1930), as if by his second wife, Florence Dugdale.

"Hap"—meaning "chance"—(1866; published 1898), "Shelley's Skylark" (1887), "The Darkling Thrush" (on "31st December 1900," the last day of the century), and "The Oxen" (1915) all reject Romantic faith in Nature and Victorian belief in an omnibenevolent God; but the speaker claims readiness, despite incapacity, to hope. The unconscious, heedless Immanent Will that converges with the SS *Titanic* (published in *Satires of Circumstance*, 1914) had similarly destroyed Napoleon in *The Dynasts*. "Neutral Tones" (1867; 1898) and "Beeny Cliff" (1913) represent passionate efforts to record in disciplined language moments in thirty-odd conflictual years with the poet's first wife, Emma Gifford, who died in 1912. The earthy diction of "Channel Firing" (1914) conveys not only a pitying scorn for war, but also the pervasive cosmic irony of Hardy's novels and poems: war threatens in 1914 prehistoric Stonehenge and legendary Camelot—an overreaching irony enclosed in a modesty of form and integrity of feeling that have impressed younger poets for nearly a century.

HAP

If but some vengeful god would call to me
From up the sky, and laugh: "Thou suffering thing,
Know that thy sorrow is my ecstasy,
That thy love's loss is my hate's profiting!"

Then would I bear it, clench myself, and die,
Steeled by the sense of ire unmerited;
Half-eased in that a Powerfuller than I
Had willed and meted me the tears I shed.

But not so. How arrives it joy lies slain,
And why unblooms the best hope ever sown?
—Crass Casualty obstructs the sun and rain,
And dicing Time for gladness casts a moan. . . .
These purblind Doomsters had as readily strown
Blisses about my pilgrimage as pain.

THE DARKLING THRUSH

I leant upon a coppice gate
    When Frost was spectre-gray,
And Winter's dregs made desolate
    The weakening eye of day.
The tangled bine-stems scored the sky
    Like strings of broken lyres,
And all mankind that haunted nigh
    Had sought their household fires.

The land's sharp features seemed to be
    The Century's corpse outleant,   10
His crypt the cloudy canopy,
    The wind his death-lament.
The ancient pulse of germ and birth
    Was shrunken hard and dry,
And every spirit upon earth
    Seemed fervourless as I.

At once a voice arose among
    The bleak twigs overhead
In a full-hearted evensong
    Of joy illimited;   20
An aged thrush, frail, gaunt, and small,
    In blast-beruffled plume,
Had chosen thus to fling his soul
    Upon the growing gloom.

So little cause for carolings
    Of such ecstatic sound
Was written on terrestrial things
    Afar or nigh around,
That I could think there trembled through
    His happy good-night air   30
Some blessed Hope, whereof he knew
    And I was unaware.

                  31 December 1900

THE OXEN

Christmas Eve, and twelve of the clock,
    "Now they are all on their knees,"
An elder said as we sat in a flock
    By the embers in hearthside ease.

We pictured the meek mild creatures where
    They dwelt in their strawy pen,
Nor did it occur to one of us there
    To doubt they were kneeling then.

So fair a fancy few would weave
    In these years! Yet, I feel,   10
If someone said on Christmas Eve,
    "Come; see the oxen kneel

"In the lonely barton by yonder coomb
    Our childhood used to know,"
I should go with him in the gloom,
    Hoping it might be so.

SHELLEY'S SKYLARK

(THE NEIGHBOURHOOD OF
LEGHORN: MARCH, 1887)

Somewhere afield here something lies
In Earth's oblivious eyeless trust

That moved a poet to prophecies—
A pinch of unseen, unguarded dust:

The dust of the lark that Shelley heard,
And made immortal through times to be;—
Though it only lived like another bird,
And knew not its immortality.

Lived its meek life; then, one day, fell—
A little ball of feather and bone;   10
And how it perished, when piped farewell,
And where it wastes, are alike unknown.

Maybe it rests in the loam I view,
Maybe it throbs in a myrtle's green,
Maybe it sleeps in the coming hue
Of a grape on the slopes of yon inland scene.

Go find it, faeries, go and find
That tiny pinch of priceless dust,
And bring a casket silver-lined,
And framed of gold that gems encrust;   20

And we will lay it safe therein,
And consecrate it to endless time;
For it inspired a bard to win
Ecstatic heights in thought and rhyme.

CHANNEL FIRING

That night your great guns, unawares,
Shook all our coffins as we lay,
And broke the chancel window-squares,
We thought it was the Judgment-day

And sat upright. While drearisome
Arose the howl of wakened hounds:
The mouse let fall the altar-crumb,
The worms drew back into the mounds,

The glebe cow drooled. Till God called, "No;
It's gunnery practice out at sea   10

Just as before you went below;
The world is as it used to be:

"All nations striving strong to make
Red war yet redder. Mad as hatters
They do no more for Christés sake
Than you who are helpless in such matters.

"That this is not the judgment-hour
For some of them's a blessed thing,
For if it were they'd have to scour
Hell's floor for so much threatening. . . .   20

"Ha, ha. It will be warmer when
I blow the trumpet (if indeed
I ever do; for you are men,
And rest eternal sorely need)."

So down we lay again. "I wonder,
Will the world ever saner be,"
Said one, "than when He sent us under
In our indifferent century!"

And many a skeleton shook his head.
"Instead of preaching forty year,"   30
My neighbour Parson Thirdly said,
"I wish I had stuck to pipes and beer."

Again the guns disturbed the hour,
Roaring their readiness to avenge,
As far inland as Stourton Tower,
And Camelot, and starlit Stonehenge.

NEUTRAL TONES

We stood by a pond that winter day,
And the sun was white, as though chidden of God,
And a few leaves lay on the starving sod;
        —They had fallen from an ash, and were gray.

Your eyes on me were as eyes that rove
Over tedious riddles of years ago;
And some words played between us to and fro
    On which lost the more by our love.

The smile on your mouth was the deadest thing
Alive enough to have strength to die;   10
And a grin of bitterness swept thereby
    Like an ominous bird a-wing. . . .

Since then, keen lessons that love deceives,
And wrings with wrong, have shaped to me
Your face, and the God-curst sun, and a tree,
    And a pond edged with grayish leaves.

BEENY CLIFF

MARCH 1870–MARCH 1913

O the opal and the sapphire of that wandering western sea,
And the woman riding high above with bright hair flapping free—
The woman whom I loved so, and who loyally loved me.

The pale mews plained below us, and the waves seemed far away
In a nether sky, engrossed in saying their ceaseless babbling say,
As we laughed light-heartedly aloft on that clear-sunned March day.

A little cloud then cloaked us, and there flew an irised rain,
And the Atlantic dyed its levels with a dull misfeatured stain,
And then the sun burst out again, and purples prinked the main.

—Still in all its chasmal beauty bulks old Beeny to the sky,
And shall she and I not go there once again now March is nigh,
And the sweet things said in that March say anew there by and by?

What if still in chasmal beauty looms that wild weird western shore,
The woman now is—elsewhere—whom the ambling pony bore,
And nor knows nor cares for Beeny, and will laugh there nevermore.

THE CONVERGENCE OF THE TWAIN

(LINES ON THE LOSS OF THE *TITANIC*)

In a solitude of the sea
Deep from human vanity,
And the Pride of Life that planned her, stilly couches she.

Steel chambers, late the pyres
Of her salamandrine fires,
Cold currents thrid, and turn to rhythmic tidal lyres.

Over the mirrors meant
To glass the opulent
The sea-worm crawls—grotesque, slimed, dumb, indifferent.

Jewels in joy designed
To ravish the sensuous mind   10
Lie lightless, all their sparkles bleared and black and blind.

Dim moon-eyed fishes near
Gaze at the gilded gear
And query: "What does this vaingloriousness down here?" . . .

Well: while was fashioning
This creature of cleaving wing,
The Immanent Will that stirs and urges everything

Prepared a sinister mate
For her—so gaily great—   20
A Shape of Ice, for the time far and dissociate.

And as the smart ship grew
In stature, grace, and hue,
In shadowy silent distance grew the Iceberg too.

Alien they seemed to be:
No mortal eye could see
The intimate welding of their later history,

Or sign that they were bent
    By paths coincident
On being anon twin halves of one august event,   30

    Till the Spinner of the Years
    Said "Now!" And each one hears,
And consummation comes, and jars two hemispheres.

Arthur William Edgar O'Shaughnessy

(1 8 4 4 – 1 8 8 1)

Moral in his otherwise aesthetic view of poetry as visionary dreaming—whether expressed in verse, in the magnificent architecture and sculpture of the Assyrian Nineveh ("it seems"), or in the Israelite prophesies by Nahum, Jonah, Isaiah, and Jeremiah that Nineveh would fall—O'Shaughnessy found escape, in the Swinburnian rhythms of the "Ode" and other poems of *Music and Moonlight* (1874), from his mundane occupation as herpetologist in the British Museum.

From ODE

WE ARE THE MUSIC MAKERS

We are the music makers,
    And we are the dreamers of dreams,
Wandering by lone sea-breakers,
    And sitting by desolate streams—
World-losers and world-forsakers,
    On whom the pale moon gleams—
Yet we are the movers and shakers
    Of the world forever, it seems.

With wonderful deathless ditties
We build up the world's great cities,   10
    And out of a fabulous story
    We fashion an empire's glory:
One man with a dream, at pleasure,
    Shall go forth and conquer a crown;
And three with a new song's measure
    Can trample a kingdom down.

We, in the ages lying
    In the buried past of the earth,
Built Nineveh with our sighing,
    And Babel itself in our mirth;   20
And o'erthrew them with prophesying
    To the old of the new world's worth;

For each age is a dream that is dying,
  Or one that is coming to birth.

       *   *   *

For we are afar with the dawning
  And the suns that are not yet high,
And out of the infinite morning
  Intrepid you hear us cry—   60
How, spite of your human scorning,
  Once more God's future draws nigh,
And already goes forth the warning
  That ye of the past must die.

Great hail! we cry to the comers
  From the dazzling unknown shore;
Bring us hither your sun and your summers,
  And renew our world as of yore;
You shall teach us your song's new numbers,
  And things that we dreamed not before—   70
Yea, in spite of a dreamer who slumbers,
  And a singer who sings no more.

Gerard Manley Hopkins

(1 8 4 4 – 1 8 8 9)

As a Jesuit priest, Hopkins took the remark of a superior in 1876 as permitting his revival of the poetry-writing he had enjoyed in freedom as a student at Oxford. A professor of rhetoric and close student of prosody, he regarded what he called "sprung rhythm" as a return to scansion by accent or stress rather than by syllabic feet. Hence his occasional accents to designate unexpected stresses. Most of his poems remained in manuscript until Robert Bridges issued a collective edition in 1918.

The philosophy of Duns Scotus afforded one source of Hopkins's attention to the *thisness* of things, the individual essence and energy that Hopkins called "inscape" and "instress." "God's Grandeur" and "Pied Beauty" smash convention by celebrating the freckled multiplicity of created nature rather than its cohesive unity. One emblem of God's world is farmland divided into plots plowed and planted, plots left fallow, sheep-pens, toolsheds, whatever serves worthy purpose. In some one of several much-debated ways, the concluding sestet of "The Windhover" conveys Christ-counseled renunciation of such pride as the titular falcon evokes. "Felix Randal," eulogizing a muscular blacksmith, perhaps goes in male attachment beyond Hopkins's compassion for the unprivileged and the recognition of universal decay that blazes forth also in "Spring and Fall." "I Wake and Feel the Fell of Dark," with "Carrion Comfort" among several "dark sonnets" of 1885 composed under a conviction of inadequacy, is tempered with the Christian faith that Hell is worse than the pain of his inadequacy.

THE WINDHOVER

To Christ Our Lord

I caught this morning morning's mínion, king-
    dom of daylight's dauphin, dapple-dáwn-drawn Falcon, in his riding
    Of the rólling level úndernéath him steady aír, and stríding
High there, how he rung upon the rein of a wimpling wing
In his écstasy! then off, off forth on swing,
    As a skate's heel sweeps smooth on a bow-bend: the hurl and gliding

Rebuffed the bíg wínd. My heart in hiding
Stírred for a bird,—the achieve of, the mástery of the thing!

Brute beauty and valour and act, oh, air, pride, plúme, here
   Buckle! AND the fire that breaks from thee then, a billion
Tímes told lovelier, more dangerous, O my chevalier!

   No wónder of it: shéer plód makes plough down sillion
Shíne, and blue-bleak embers, ah my dear,
   Fall, gáll themsélves, and gásh góld-vermílion.

l. 12. sillion = ridge shining between two plowed furrows

PIED BEAUTY

Glory be to God for dappled things—
   For skies of couple-colour as a brinded cow;
     For rose-moles all in stipple upon trout that swim;
Fresh-firecoal chestnut-falls; finches' wings;
   Landscape plotted and pieced—fold, fallow, and plough;
     And áll trádes, their gear and tackle and trim.

All things counter, original, spare, strange;
   Whatever is fickle, freckled (who knows how?)
     With swíft, slów; sweet, sóur; adázzle, dím;
He fathers-forth whose beauty is pást chánge:
             Praise him.

SPRING AND FALL

To a Young Child

Márgarét, are you gríeving
Over Goldengrove unleaving?
Leáves, like the thíngs of man, you
With your fresh thoughts care for, can you?
Áh! ás the heart grows older
It will come to such sights colder
By and by, nor spare a sigh

Though worlds of wanwood leafmeal lie;
And yet you will weep and know why.
Now no matter, child, the name: 10
Sórrow's springs áre the same.
Nor mouth had, no nor mind, expressed
What heart heard of, ghost guessed:
It ís the blight man was born for,
It is Margaret you mourn for.

FELIX RANDAL

Felix Randal the farrier, O he is dead then? my duty all ended,
Who have watched his mould of man, big-boned and hardy-handsome
Pining, pining, till time when reason rambled in it and some
Fatal four disorders, fleshed there, all contended?

Sickness broke him. Impatient he cursed at first, but mended
Being anointed and all; though a heavenlier heart began some
Months earlier, since I had our sweet reprieve and ransom
Tendered to him. Ah well, God rest him all road ever he offended!

This seeing the sick endears them to us, us too it endears.
My tongue had taught thee comfort, touch had quenched thy tears,
Thy tears that touched my heart, child, Felix, poor Felix Randal;

How far from then forethought of, all thy more boisterous years,
When thou at the random grim forge, powerful amidst peers,
Didst fettle for the great grey drayhorse his bright and battering sandal!

GOD'S GRANDEUR

The world is charged with the grandeur of God.
    It will flame out, like shining from shook foil;
    It gathers to a greatness, like the ooze of oil
Crushed. Why do men then now not reck his rod?
Generations have trod, have trod, have trod;
    And all is seared with trade; bleared, smeared with toil;
    And wears man's smudge and shares man's smell: the soil
Is bare now, nor can foot feel, being shod.

And for all this, nature is never spent;
  There lives the dearest freshness deep down things;
And though the last lights off the black West went
  Oh, morning, at the brown brink eastward, springs—
Because the Holy Ghost over the bent
  World broods with warm breast and with ah! bright wings.

l. 2. shook foil = shaken goldfoil or other tinsel

DUNS SCOTUS'S OXFORD

Towery city and branchy between towers;
Cuckoo-echoing, bell-swarmèd, lark-charmèd, rook-racked,
        river-rounded;
The dapple-eared lily below thee; that country and town did
Once encounter in, here coped and poisèd powers;

Thou hast a base and brickish skirt there, sours
That neighbour-nature thy grey beauty is grounded
Best in; graceless growth, thou hast confounded
Rúral rural keeping—folk, flocks, and flowers.

Yet ah! this air I gather and I release
He lived on; these weeds and waters, these walls are what
He haunted who of all men most sways my spirits to peace;

Of realty the rarest-veinèd unraveller; a not
Rivalled insight, be rival Italy or Greece;
Who fired France for Mary without spot.

l. 14. fired France = Scotus may have promoted the cult of the Virgin
Mary in Paris

I WAKE AND FEEL THE FELL OF
DARK, NOT DAY

I wake and feel the fell of dark, not day.
What hours, O what black hoürs we have spent
This night! what sights you, heart, saw, ways you went!

And more must, in yet longer light's delay.
    With witness I speak this. But where I say
Hours I mean years, mean life. And my lament
Is cries countless, cries like dead letters sent
To dearest him that lives alas! away.

    I am gall, I am heartburn. God's most deep decree
Bitter would have me taste: my taste was me;
Bones built in me, flesh filled, blood brimmed the curse.
    Selfyeast of spirit a dull dough sours. I see
The lost are like this, and their scourge to be
As I am mine, their sweating selves; but worse.

CARRION COMFORT

Not, I'll not, carrion comfort, Despair, not feast on thee;
Not untwist—slack they may be—these last strands of man
In me ór, most weary, cry *I can no more.* I can;
Can something, hope, wish day come, not choose not to be.
But ah, but O thou terrible, why wouldst thou rude on me
Thy wring-world right foot rock? lay a lionlimb against me? scan
With darksome devouring eyes my bruisèd bones? and fan,
O in turns of tempest, me heaped there; me frantic to avoid thee and flee?

    Why? That my chaff might fly; my grain lie, sheer and clear.
Nay in all that toil, that coil, since (seems) I kissed the rod,
Hand rather, my heart lo! lapped strength, stole joy, would laugh, chéer.
Cheer whom though? the hero whose heaven-handling flung me, fóot tród
Me? or me that fought him? O which one? is it each one? That night, that year
Of now done darkness I wretch lay wrestling with (my God!) my God.

Robert Bridges

(1 8 4 4 – 1 9 3 0)

Born in Kent and some would say overeducated at Eton, Oxford, and St. Bartholomew's Hospital, London, Bridges published his first volume, *Poems*, in 1873. He served as hospital physician through 1881. Dedicated to beauty, the classics, music, Milton, and spelling reform, Poet Laureate from 1913 to 1930, a friend and editor (in 1918) of Hopkins, he could escape his usual placidity as in the protest of "Eros" (in *New Poems*, 1899) and the fierce warning of "Low Barometer" (1921; in *New Verse*, 1926).

EROS

Why hast thou nothing in thy face?
Thou idol of the human race,
Thou tyrant of the human heart,
The flower of lovely youth that art;
Yea, and that standest in thy youth
An image of eternal Truth,
With thy exuberant flesh so fair,
That only Pheidias might compare,
Ere from his chaste marmoreal form
Time had decayed the colours warm;   10
Like to his gods in thy proud dress,
Thy starry sheen of nakedness.

   Surely thy body is thy mind,
For in thy face is nought to find,
Only thy soft unchristen'd smile,
That shadows neither love nor guile,
But shameless will and power immense,
In secret sensuous innocence.

   O king of joy, what is thy thought?
I dream thou knowest it is nought,   20
And wouldst in darkness come, but thou
Makest the light where'er thou go.

Ah yet no victim of thy grace,
None who e'er long'd for thy embrace,
Hath cared to look upon thy face.

LOW BAROMETER

The south-wind strengthens to a gale,
Across the moon the clouds fly fast,
The house is smitten as with a flail,
The chimney shudders to the blast.

On such a night, when Air has loosed
Its guardian grasp on blood and brain,
Old terrors then of god or ghost
Creep from their caves to life again;

And Reason kens he herits in
A haunted house. Tenants unknown   10
Assert their squalid lease of sin
With earlier title than his own.

Unbodied presences, the pack'd
Pollution and remorse of Time,
Slipp'd from oblivion reënact
The horrors of unhouseld crime.

Some men would quell the thing with prayer
Whose sightless footsteps pad the floor,
Whose fearful trespass mounts the stair
Or bursts the lock'd forbidden door.   20

Some have seen corpses long interr'd
Escape from hallowing control,
Pale charnel forms—nay ev'n have heard
The shrilling of a troubled soul,

That wanders till the dawn hath cross'd
The dolorous dark, or Earth hath wound
Closer her storm-spredd cloke, and thrust
The baleful phantoms underground.

Alice Christiana Thompson Meynell

(1847–1922)

Meynell spent most of her childhood on the Continent, where she was educated by her father. In 1868 she converted to Catholicism and seven years later published her first collection of poems, *Preludes*, in which "A Song of Derivations" appeared and for which Meynell was highly praised by Ruskin, Rossetti, and George Eliot. Other volumes of poetry followed, and in 1895 she was nominated for the Poet Laureateship. Meynell, a pacifist and a strong supporter of social reform and women's rights, also published widely as an essayist.

A SONG OF DERIVATIONS

I come from nothing; but from where
Come the undying thoughts I bear?
   Down, through long links of death and birth,
   From the past poets of the earth.
My immortality is there.

I am like the blossom of an hour.
But long, long vanished sun and shower
   Awoke my breath i' the young world's air.
   I track the past back everywhere
Through seed and flower and seed and flower.   10

Or I am like a stream that flows
Full of the cold springs that arose
   In morning lands, in distant hills;
   And down the plain my channel fills
With melting of forgotten snows.

Voices, I have not heard, possessed
My own fresh songs; my thoughts are blessed
   With relics of the far unknown.
   And mixed with memories not my own
The sweet streams throng into my breast.   20

Before this life began to be,
The happy songs that wake in me
    Woke long ago and far apart.
    Heavily on this little heart
Presses this immortality.

THE SHEPHERDESS

She walks—the lady of my delight—
    A shepherdess of sheep.
Her flocks are thoughts. She keeps them white;
    She guards them from the steep;
She feeds them on the fragrant height,
    And folds them in for sleep.

She roams maternal hills and bright,
    Dark valleys safe and deep.
Into that tender breast at night
    The chastest stars may peep.   10
She walks—the lady of my delight—
    A shepherdess of sheep.

She holds her little thoughts in sight,
    Though gay they run and leap.
She is so circumspect and right;
    She has her soul to keep.
She walks—the lady of my delight—
    A shepherdess of sheep.

William Ernest Henley

(1 8 4 9 – 1 9 0 3)

Sharing with his friend Robert Louis Stevenson courage in the face of crippling disease and with Kipling an anti-aesthetic belief in "England, my England," Henley was not always as defiant as in the 1875 "Invictus" (meaning "unconquered"). Son of a bookseller in Gloucester, where he attended grammar school, Henley suffered tubercular arthritis and the consequent amputation of a foot in London. His fortune changed somewhat in an Edinburgh infirmary through treatment by Joseph Lister and by his introduction to Stevenson there. In London after 1890, his influence as editor of the *National Observer* and *New Review* overshadowed his poems and imperialist essays, but his experiments in irregular cadences encouraged later revolt against Tennysonian prosody. The cadenced poem here (written in 1876) was dedicated in 1886 to the memory of his wife's sister Margaret.

INVICTUS

Out of the night that covers me,
  Black as the Pit from pole to pole,
I thank whatever gods may be
  For my unconquerable soul.

In the fell clutch of circumstance
  I have not winced nor cried aloud.
Under the bludgeonings of chance
  My head is bloody, but unbowed.

Beyond this place of wrath and tears
  Looms but the Horror of the shade,
And yet the menace of the years
  Finds, and shall find me, unafraid.

It matters not how strait the gate,
  How charged with punishments the scroll,
I am the master of my fate:
  I am the captain of my soul.

I. M. MARGARITAE SORORI

A late lark twitters from the quiet skies;
And from the west,
Where the sun, his day's work ended,
Lingers as in content,
There falls on the old, grey city
An influence luminous and serene,
A shining peace.

The smoke ascends
In a rosy-and-golden haze.   The spires
Shine, and are changed.   In the valley   10
Shadows rise.   The lark sings on.   The sun,
Closing his benediction,
Sinks, and the darkening air
Thrills with a sense of the triumphing night—
Night with her train of stars
And her great gift of sleep.

So be my passing!
My task accomplished and the long day done,
My wages taken, and in my heart
Some late lark singing,   20
Let me be gathered to the quiet west,
The sundown splendid and serene,
Death.

Robert Louis Stevenson

(1 8 5 0 – 1 8 9 4)

A *Child's Garden of Verses* (1885) and Stevenson's famous novels for and about youth have eclipsed for most readers the keen theorist of romance, the author of such caustic fiction as *The Ebb-Tide*, and the poet for both youth and maturity. The song here records memories of sailing past the Hebrides, off western Scotland, in 1874. In Edinburgh from birth until admission to the bar in 1875, he searched thereafter for an anti-tubercular climate; travel, mostly by sea, took him in 1879 to California (to marry), and later to Samoa, where he built a durable house and continued to write as an acknowledged "master of letters."

SING ME A SONG

Sing me a song of a lad that is gone,
  Say, could that lad be I?
Merry of soul he sailed on a day
  Over the sea to Skye.

Mull was astern, Rum on the port,
  Eigg on the starboard bow;
Glory of youth glowed in his soul—
  Where is that glory now?

Sing me a song of a lad that is gone,
  Say, could that lad be I?   10
Merry of soul he sailed on a day
  Over the sea to Skye.

Give me again all that was there,
  Give me the sun that shone!
Give me the eyes, give me the soul,
  Give me the lad that's gone!

Sing me a song of a lad that is gone,
  Say, could that lad be I?

687

Merry of soul he sailed on a day
　Over the sea to Skye.   20

Billow and breeze, islands and seas,
　Mountains of rain and sun,
All that was good, all that was fair,
　All that was me is gone.

Oscar Wilde

(1854–1900)

Born in Dublin of flamboyant parents, poet and aesthete at Oxford, playwright, novelist, and fabulist, Wilde was a witty essayist, lecturer, talker, and letter-writer. Although he denied moral significance to art and aesthetic value to morality (at his best, as in the comedy *The Importance of Being Earnest*, he circumvented moral issues), his imprisonment on charges of sodomy took from him the psychological values of detachment. Unlike any of his previous poems, the "Ballad," 109 stanzas written in France after his release in 1897 from Reading prison, conveys an earnestness of personal observation—although he wrote of it to Robbie Ross, "I will never again out-Kipling Henley."

From THE BALLAD OF READING GAOL

I

He did not wear his scarlet coat,
   For blood and wine are red,
And blood and wine were on his hands
   When they found him with the dead,
The poor dead woman whom he loved,
   And murdered in her bed.

He walked amongst the Trial Men
   In a suit of shabby grey;
A cricket cap was on his head,
   And his step seemed light and gay;   10
But I never saw a man who looked
   So wistfully at the day.

I never saw a man who looked
   With such a wistful eye
Upon that little tent of blue
   Which prisoners call the sky,
And at every drifting cloud that went
   With sails of silver by.

I walked with other souls in pain,
   Within another ring,   20
And was wondering if the man had done
   A great or little thing,
When a voice behind me whispered low,
   "That fellow's got to swing."

Dear Christ! the very prison walls
   Suddenly seemed to reel,
And the sky above my head became
   Like a casque of scorching steel;
And, though I was a soul in pain,
   My pain I could not feel.   30

I only knew what hunted thought
   Quickened his step, and why
He looked upon the garish day
   With such a wistful eye;
The man had killed the thing he loved,
   And so he had to die.

Yet each man kills the thing he loves,
   By each let this be heard,
Some do it with a bitter look,
   Some with a flattering word.   40
The coward does it with a kiss,
   The brave man with a sword!

Some kill their love when they are young,
   And some when they are old;
Some strangle with the hands of Lust,
   Some with the hands of Gold:
The kindest use a knife, because
   The dead so soon grow cold.

Some love too little, some too long,
   Some sell, and others buy;   50
Some do the deed with many tears,
   And some without a sigh:
For each man kills the thing he loves,
   Yet each man does not die.

He does not die a death of shame
   On a day of dark disgrace,
Nor have a noose about his neck,
   Nor a cloth upon his face,
Nor drop feet foremost through the floor
   Into an empty space.   60

John Davidson

(1857–1909)

A Scot fleeing from straitlaced acceptance and what Lionel Johnson (a fellow member of the Rhymers' Club) called "waterish sentiment," Davidson depicted in *Ballads & Songs* (1894), and in other volumes before and after, persons defeated or nearly so in the "million-peopled lanes and alleys." Before settling in London in 1899 he had served as a schoolmaster for twenty-seven years in Scotland. A selection of his poems in 1961 carried tributes by T. S. Eliot and MacDiarmid acknowledging the influence of his ear for casual speech (Eliot especially noted his indebtedness to Davidson's use of "dingy urban images"). Davidson included "Battle," a lament for the opening of the Boer War, in *The Last Ballad, and Other Poems* (1899).

BATTLE

The war of words is done;
　　The red-lipped cannon speak;
The battle has begun.

The web your speeches spun
　　Tears and blood shall streak;
The war of words is done.

Smoke enshrouds the sun;
　　Earth staggers at the shriek
Of battle new begun.

Poltroons and braggarts run:　　　　　　　　10
　　Woe to the poor, the meek!
The war of words is done.

"And hope not now to shun
　　The doom that dogs the weak,"
Thunders every gun;

"Victory must be won."
   When the red-lipped cannon speak,
The war of words is done,
The slaughter has begun.

THIRTY BOB A WEEK

I couldn't touch a stop and turn a screw,
   And set the blooming world a-work for me,
Like such as cut their teeth—I hope, like you—
   On the handle of a skeleton gold key;
I cut mine on a leek, which I eat it every week:
   I'm a clerk at thirty bob as you can see.

But I don't allow it's luck and all a toss;
   There's no such thing as being starred and crossed;
It's just the power of some to be a boss,
   And the bally power of others to be bossed: 10
I face the music, sir; you bet I ain't a cur;
   Strike me lucky if I don't believe I'm lost!

For like a mole I journey in the dark,
   A-travelling along the underground
From my Pillar'd Halls and broad Suburbean Park,
   To come the daily dull official round;
And home again at night with my pipe all alight,
   A-scheming how to count ten bob a pound.

And it's often very cold and very wet,
   And my missis stitches towels for a hunks;   20
And the Pillar'd Halls is half of it to let—
   Three rooms about the size of travelling trunks.
And we cough, my wife and I, to dislocate a sigh,
   When the noisy little kids are in their bunks.

But you never hear her do a growl or whine,
   For she's made of flint and roses, very odd;
And I've got to cut my meaning rather fine,
   Or I'd blubber, for I'm made of greens and sod:
So p'r'aps we are in Hell for all that I can tell,
   And lost and damn'd and served up hot to God.   30

I ain't blaspheming, Mr. Silver-tongue;
    I'm saying things a bit beyond your art:
Of all the rummy starts you ever sprung,
    Thirty bob a week's the rummiest start!
With your science and your books and your the'ries about spooks,
    Did you ever hear of looking in your heart?

I didn't mean your pocket, Mr., no:
    I mean that having children and a wife,
With thirty bob on which to come and go,
    Isn't dancing to the tabor and the fife: 40
When it doesn't make you drink, by Heaven! it makes you think,
    And notice curious items about life.

I step into my heart and there I meet
    A god-almighty devil singing small,
Who would like to shout and whistle in the street,
    And squelch the passers flat against the wall;
If the whole world was a·cake he had the power to take,
    He would take it, ask for more, and eat it all.

And I meet a sort of simpleton beside,
    The kind that life is always giving beans: 50
With thirty bob a week to keep a bride
    He fell in love and married in his teens:
At thirty bob he stuck; but he knows it isn't luck:
    He knows the seas are deeper than tureens.

And the god-almighty devil and the fool
    That meet me in the High Street on the strike,
When I walk about my heart a-gathering wool,
    Are my good and evil angels if you like.
And both of them together in every kind of weather
    Ride me like a double-seated bike.   60

That's rough a bit and needs its meaning curled.
    But I have a high old hot un in my mind—
A most engrugious notion of the world,
    That leaves your lightning 'rithmetic behind
I give it at a glance when I say "There ain't no chance,
    Nor nothing of the lucky-lottery kind."

And it's this way that I make it out to be:
  No fathers, mothers, countries, climates—none;
Not Adam was responsible for me,
  Nor society, nor systems, nary one: 70
A little sleeping seed, I woke—I did, indeed—
  A million years before the blooming sun.

I woke because I thought the time had come;
  Beyond my will there was no other cause;
And everywhere I found myself at home,
  Because I chose to be the thing I was;
And in whatever shape of mollusc or of ape
  I always went according to the laws.

I was the love that chose my mother out;
  I joined two lives and from the union burst;   80
My weakness and my strength without a doubt
  Are mine alone for ever from the first:
It's just the very same with a difference in the name
  As "Thy will be done." You say it if you durst!

They say it daily up and down the land
  As easy as you take a drink, it's true;
But the difficultest go to understand,
  And the difficultest job a man can do,
Is to come it brave and meek with thirty bob a week,
  And feel that that's the proper thing for you.   90

It's a naked child against a hungry wolf;
  It's playing bowls upon a splitting wreck;
It's walking on a string across a gulf
  With millstones fore-and-aft about your neck;
But the thing is daily done by many and many a one;
  And we fall, face forward, fighting, on the deck.

l. 18. count ten bob a pound = make ten shillings go as far as twenty (one
pound)

James Kenneth Stephen

(1 8 5 9 – 1 8 9 2)

A cousin of Virginia Woolf, and by far the lightest in spirit of an intellectually distinguished family, J. K. Stephen included his close, paraphrasal parody of Wordsworth's "Two Voices" in *Lapsus Calami* (four editions in 1891), along with other keen parodies and hope for the day "When the Rudyards cease from kipling / And the Haggards Ride no more." His promising career was cut short by an accident in 1886 that slowly drove him mad.

A SONNET

Two voices are there: one is of the deep;
It learns the storm-cloud's thunderous melody,
Now roars, now murmurs with the changing sea,
Now bird-like pipes, now closes soft in sleep:
And one is of an old half-witted sheep
Which bleats articulate monotony,
And indicates that two and one are three,
That grass is green, lakes damp, and mountains steep:
And, Wordsworth, both are thine: at certain times
Forth from the heart of thy melodious rhymes,
The form and pressure of high thoughts will burst:
At other times—good Lord! I'd rather be
Quite unacquainted with the A. B. C.
Than write such hopeless rubbish as thy worst.

Alfred Edward Housman

(1 8 5 9 – 1 9 3 6)

Born in Worcestershire, Housman taught and scrupulously edited Latin poetry at University College, London (1892–1911) and (from 1911) at Trinity College, Cambridge. He reviewed with ferocity editions by less meticulous scholars. The enduring popularity of his lyrics of repressed passion suggests that they meet his own test of making a man cut himself when shaving. "Reveille" is almost interchangeable with other ballad-stanza lyrics of A Shropshire Lad (1896) in its melancholy, self-conscious fortitude, hint of the masochistic, and what a contemporary aptly defined as "exquisite simplicity." "Terence, This Is Stupid Stuff" offers an explicit rationale for stoic rejection of Milton and the Romantics. Its hexameter couplets evoke Swift and the Age of Reason. The pessimism of these poems is to serve "luckless lads" who read them as preventive doses of poison (according to Pliny's Natural History) served Mithridates of Pontus (120–63 B.C.).

REVEILLE

Wake: the silver dusk returning
　　Up the beach of darkness brims,
And the ship of sunrise burning
　　Strands upon the eastern rims.

Wake: the vaulted shadow shatters,
　　Trampled to the floor it spanned,
And the tent of night in tatters
　　Straws the sky-pavilioned land.

Up, lad, up, 'tis late for lying:
　　Hear the drums of morning play;　　　　　10
Hark, the empty highways crying
　　"Who'll beyond the hills away?"

Towns and countries woo together,
　　Forelands beacon, belfries call;
Never lad that trod on leather
　　Lived to feast his heart with all.

Up, lad: thews that lie and cumber
   Sunlit pallets never thrive;
Morns abed and daylight slumber
   Were not meant for man alive.   20

Clay lies still, but blood's a rover;
   Breath's a ware that will not keep.
Up, lad: when the journey's over
   There'll be time enough to sleep.

TERENCE, THIS IS STUPID STUFF

   "Terence, this is stupid stuff:
You eat your victuals fast enough;
There can't be much amiss, 'tis clear,
To see the rate you drink your beer.
But oh, good Lord, the verse you make,
It gives a chap the belly-ache.
The cow, the old cow, she is dead;
It sleeps well, the horned head:
We poor lads, 'tis our turn now
To hear such tunes as killed the cow.   10
Pretty friendship 'tis to rhyme
Your friends to death before their time
Moping melancholy mad:
Come, pipe a tune to dance to, lad."

   Why, if 'tis dancing you would be,
There's brisker pipes than poetry.
Say, for what were hop-yards meant,
Or why was Burton built on Trent?
Oh many a peer of England brews
Livelier liquor than the Muse,   20
And malt does more than Milton can
To justify God's ways to man.
Ale, man, ale's the stuff to drink
For fellows whom it hurts to think:
Look into the pewter pot
To see the world as the world's not.

And faith, 'tis pleasant till 'tis past:
The mischief is that 'twill not last.
Oh I have been to Ludlow fair
And left my necktie God knows where,   30
And carried halfway home, or near,
Pints and quarts of Ludlow beer:
Then the world seemed none so bad,
And I myself a sterling lad;
And down in lovely muck I've lain,
Happy till I woke again.
Then I saw the morning sky:
Heigho, the tale was all a lie;
The world, it was the old world yet,
I was I, my things were wet,   40
And nothing now remained to do
But begin the game anew.

   Therefore, since the world has still
Much good, but much less good than ill,
And while the sun and moon endure
Luck's a chance, but trouble's sure,
I'd face it as a wise man would,
And train for ill and not for good.
'Tis true, the stuff I bring for sale
Is not so brisk a brew as ale: 50
Out of a stem that scored the hand
I wrung it in a weary land.
But take it: if the smack is sour,
The better for the embittered hour;
It should do good to heart and head
When your soul is in my soul's stead;
And I will friend you, if I may,
In the dark and cloudy day.

   There was a king reigned in the East:
There, when kings will sit to feast,   60
They get their fill before they think
With poisoned meat and poisoned drink.
He gathered all that springs to birth
From the many-venomed earth;
First a little, thence to more,
He sampled all her killing store;
And easy, smiling, seasoned sound,

Sate the king when healths went round.
They put arsenic in his meat
And stared aghast to watch him eat;   70
They poured strychnine in his cup
And shook to see him drink it up:
They shook, they stared as white's their shirt:
Them it was their poison hurt.
—I tell the tale that I heard told.
Mithridates, he died old.

Francis Thompson

(1859 – 1907)

Thompson grew up in Lancashire and pursued, then abandoned, plans to be a Roman Catholic priest and then a doctor. In 1885 he moved to London, where he was soon destitute and addicted to opium. He was rescued from his plight by Alice and Wilfrid Meynell, who encouraged his literary efforts. Thompson published his first volume of poetry in 1893; it included "The Hound of Heaven," a fervent account of a Catholic fugitive's vain attempt to evade pursuit by God's grace. Patmore and the Meynells could have called Thompson's attention to Crashaw, whose baroque rhetoric evidently influenced him. He never fully recovered his health and died of the combined effects of tuberculosis and opium addiction.

From THE HOUND OF HEAVEN

I fled Him, down the nights and down the days;
   I fled Him, down the arches of the years;
I fled Him, down the labyrinthine ways
   Of my own mind; and in the mist of tears
I hid from Him, and under running laughter.
        Up vistaed hopes I sped;
        And shot, precipitated,
Adown Titanic glooms of chasmèd fears,
  From those strong Feet that followed, followed after.
       But with unhurrying chase,   10
       And unperturbèd pace,
   Deliberate speed, majestic instancy,
      They beat—and a Voice beat
      More instant than the Feet—
"All things betray thee, who betrayest Me."

      I pleaded, outlaw-wise,
By many a hearted casement, curtained red,
   Trellised with intertwining charities;
(For, though I knew His love Who followèd,
      Yet was I sore adread   20
Lest, having Him, I must have naught beside,)

701

But, if one little casement parted wide,
   The gust of His approach would clash it to:
   Fear wist not to evade, as Love wist to pursue.
Across the margent of the world I fled,
      And troubled the gold gateways of the stars,
      Smiting for shelter on their clangèd bars;
        Fretted to dulcet jars
And silvern chatter the pale ports o' the moon.
I said to Dawn: Be sudden—to Eve: Be soon;   30
   With thy young skiey blossoms heap me over
      From this tremendous Lover—
Float thy vague veil about me, lest He see!

        *   *   *

     Now of that long pursuit
     Comes on at hand the bruit;
   That Voice is round me like a bursting sea:
     "And is thy earth so marred,
     Shattered in shard on shard?
   Lo, all things fly thee, for thou fliest Me!   160
   Strange, piteòus, futile thing!
Wherefore should any set thee love apart?
Seeing none but I makes much of naught" (He said),
"And human love needs human meriting:
   How hast thou merited—
Of all man's clotted clay the dingiest clot?
   Alack, thou knowest not
How little worthy of any love thou art!
Whom wilt thou find to love ignoble thee,
   Save Me, save only Me?   170
All which I took from thee I did but take,
   Not for thy harms,
But just that thou might'st seek it in My arms.
   All which thy child's mistake
Fancies as lost, I have stored for thee at home:
   Rise, clasp My hand, and come!"

   Halts by me that footfall:
   Is my gloom, after all,
Shade of His hand, outstretched caressingly?
   "Ah, fondest, blindest, weakest,   180
   I am He Whom thou seekest!
Thou dravest love from thee, who dravest Me."

Mary Elizabeth Coleridge

(1861–1907)

Mary Coleridge was born and lived her entire life in London, where, after 1895, she taught at the Women's Working College and contributed extensively to literary journals, including the *Times Literary Supplement*. In addition to her poetry, which she was reluctant to publish during her lifetime, she also produced several novels.

The folk motif in "The Witch" of lifting a female over a blessed threshold recalls the "Christabel" of the poet's great-great uncle, Samuel Taylor Coleridge, as the flame on the hearth recalls his "Frost at Midnight" (see p. 475). The sense of psychic danger is intensified by the absence of quotation marks to separate the first two stanzas from the third, as if the two speakers have become one witch.

THE WITCH

I have walked a great while over the snow,
And I am not tall nor strong.
My clothes are wet, and my teeth are set,
And the way was hard and long.
I have wandered over the fruitful earth,
But I never came here before.
Oh, lift me over the threshold, and let me in
    at the door!

The cutting wind is a cruel foe;
I dare not stand in the blast.   10
My hands are stone, and my voice a groan,
And the worst of death is past.
I am but a little maiden still;
My little white feet are sore.
Oh, lift me over the threshold, and let me in
    at the door!

Her voice was the voice that women have,
Who plead for their heart's desire.

She came—she came—and the quivering flame
Sank and died in the fire.   20
It never was lit again on my hearth
Since I hurried across the floor,
To lift her over the threshold, and let her in
        at the door!

Amy Levy

(1861 – 1889)

Poet and novelist, Levy attended Newnham College, the first Cambridge establishment for women, where she was the first Jewish student. The "Epitaph" is taken from A *Minor Poet and Other Verse* (1884). A week after correcting proofs for her third and last book, A *London Plane Tree* (1889), Levy committed suicide at the home of her parents in London. Oscar Wilde wrote of Levy in an obituary notice that the ability to "write thus at six-and-twenty is given to very few."

EPITAPH ON A COMMONPLACE PERSON WHO DIED IN BED

This is the end of him, here he lies:
The dust in his throat, the worm in his eyes,
The mould in his mouth, the turf on his breast;
This is the end of him, this is best.
He will never lie on his couch awake,
Wide-eyed, tearless, till dim daybreak.

Never again will he smile and smile
When his heart is breaking all the while.
He will never stretch out his hands in vain
Groping and groping—never again.   10
Never ask for bread, get a stone instead,
Never pretend that the stone is bread.
Never sway and sway 'twixt the false and true,
Weighing and noting the long hours through.
Never ache and ache with the chok'd-up sighs;
This is the end of him, here he lies.

May Kendall

(1861 – 1943?)

Newtonian reliance on the hypothesis of "ether," as a medium for transmitting light and heat, and at the time of Kendall's *Songs from Dreamland* (1894) as a medium for transmitting electromagnetic waves, had long troubled physicists. Einstein's theory of relativity eliminated the need for a transmitting medium but not the human sense of progressive loss of energy (entropy, Kelvin's second law of thermodynamics), which is central to Kendall's "light verse" lament. In addition to her volumes of poetry Kendall also produced satiric essays.

ETHER INSATIABLE

Now Energy's bound to diminish—
   The harder she struggles and moils,
The faster she speeds to the finish,
   The end of her infinite toils.

A million of planets beneath her
   Strong hands she may mould or efface—
'Tis all to the good of the ether,
   That fills circumambient space!

All's quietly caught up and muffled
   By a strange and intangible foe,   10
The ether serene and unruffled,
   The ether we see not nor know.
Life, radiance, in torrents dispelling,
   The universe spins to its goal;
And radiance and life find *one* dwelling—
   This ether's the tomb of the whole.

There is not a hushed malediction,
   There is not a smile or a sigh,
But aids in dispersing, by friction,
   The cosmical heat in the sky;   20
And whether a star falls, or whether

A heart breaks—for stars and for men
Their labour is all for the ether,
   That renders back nothing again.

And we, howsoever we hated
   And feared, or made love, or believed,
For all the opinions we stated,
   The woes and the wars we achieved,
We, too, shall lie idle together,
   In very uncritical case—   30
And no one will win—but the ether,
   That fills circumambient space!

Michael Field

(*pseudonym of Katherine Harris Bradley, 1846–1914, and Edith Cooper, 1862–1913*)

"Michael Field" was the pseudonym adopted in 1884 by Katherine Harris Bradley (1846–1914) and her niece Edith Cooper (1862–1913), who published eight volumes of poetry and collaborated on more than twenty-five verse dramas from 1881 until their deaths. They were inseparable companions. Robert Browning and George Meredith were among their admirers and encouraged them to pursue their collaborative work. Both "La Gioconda," a lyric with a Pater-like view of Leonardo's *Mona Lisa* (from a series on paintings in European galleries), and the "decadent" sonnet "A Dying Viper" illustrate a narrower range from the aesthetic pair than the nine poems—against two by Kipling—chosen by Yeats for *The Oxford Book of Modern Verse, 1892–1935.*

LA GIOCONDA

LEONARDO DA VINCI

THE LOUVRE

Historic, side-long, implicating eyes;
A smile of velvet's lustre on the cheek;
Calm lips the smile leads upward; hand that lies
Glowing and soft, the patience in its rest
Of cruelty that waits and doth not seek
For prey; a dusky forehead and a breast
Where twilight touches ripeness amorously:
Behind her, crystal rocks, a sea and skies
Of evanescent blue on cloud and creek;
Landscape that shines suppressive of its zest
For those vicissitudes by which men die.

A DYING VIPER

The lethargy of evil in her eyes—
As blue snow is the substance of a mere
Where the dead waters of a glacier drear
Stand open and behold—a viper lies.

Brooding upon her hatreds: dying thus
Wounded and broken, helpless with her fangs,
She dies of her sealed curse, yea, of her pangs
At God's first ban that made her infamous.

Yet, by that old curse frozen in her wreath,
She, like a star, hath central gravity
That draws and fascinates the soul to death;

While round her stark and terrible repose,
Vaults for its hour a glittering sapphire fly,
Mocking the charm of death. O God, it knows!

Arthur Symons

(1 8 6 5 – 1 9 4 5)

Born in Wales, but the quintessential Londoner, Symons was prominent in the Decadent movement as poet, essayist, and editor of the *Savoy* (1896). His father was a Methodist minister on circuit from Milford Haven, Wales. The son was educated in various Devonshire schools and later by friendship with prominent men of letters in England and poets in France. In person and through *The Symbolist Movement in Literature* (1899), he introduced the poetry of Verlaine, Rimbaud, Mallarmé, and Laforgue to Yeats and T. S. Eliot and to England and North America. "Nerves" was collected in Symons's third volume, *London Nights* (1895); "Faint Love," which matches the faint colors of the painter Conder, was omitted from *Poems* (1924) but reprinted by A. J. A. Symons in *An Anthology of 'Nineties' Verse* (1928).

FAINT LOVE

(FOR A FAN BY CHARLES CONDER)

Beauty I love, yet more than this I love
Beautiful things; and, more than love, delight;
Colours that faint; dim echo far above
The crystal sound, and shadow beyond sight.

For I am tired with youth and happiness
As other men are tired with age and grief;
This is to me a longer weariness:
Sadly I ask of each sad mask's relief.

For gardens where I know not if I find
Autumn or spring about the shadowy fruit,
And if it is the sighing of the wind
Or if it is the sighing of the lute.

NERVES

The modern malady of love is nerves.
Love, once a simple madness, now observes
The stages of his passionate disease,
And is twice sorrowful because he sees,
Inch by inch entering, the fatal knife.
O health of simple minds, give me your life,
And let me, for one midnight, cease to hear
The clock for ever ticking in my ear,
The clock that tells the minutes in my brain.
It is not love, nor love's despair, this pain
That shoots a witless, keener pang across
The simple agony of love and loss.
Nerves, nerves! O folly of a child who dreams
Of heaven, and, waking in the darkness, screams.

William Butler Yeats

(1 8 6 5 – 1 9 3 9)

Born in County Dublin, son and brother of notable painters, Yeats divided his years from childhood to 1922 between London and Ireland, where he was playwright, co-director of the Abbey Theatre, patriot, and, upon the founding of the Irish Free State, senator (1922–1928). As poet, he soon left behind the romantic rhythms and diction of the Innisfree lyric (written in London; made public by Henley in 1890). Revising constantly, Yeats collected "The Second Coming" in *Michael Robartes and the Dancer* (1921); two year later he was awarded the Nobel Prize in Literature. The years that followed saw "Leda and the Swan," the theological "Among School Children," and the yearning, metaphysical "Sailing to Byzantium" in *The Tower* (1928); "Crazy Jane Talks with the Bishop," with other Crazy Jane poems, appeared in *Words for Music Perhaps* (1932); "Coole Park, 1929" was published in *The Winding Stair* (1933), and "Lapis Lazuli" in *Last Poems* (1939).

The boldness and beauty of Leda and Helen in Yeats's poems characterize in universal myth the Irish revolutionary Maude Gonne, a love unrequited. Byzantium under Justinian was the city, said Yeats, where "religious, aesthetic, and practical life were one." Yeats spent many summers at Coole Park, the home of Lady Gregory, his fellow in directing the Abbey; the playwright Synge, the Gaelic professor and politician Douglas Hyde, and Lady Gregory's nephews Lane and Shawe-Taylor were there. A *Vision* (1925), in prose, gives a systematic exposition of such symbols in the poetry as the gyre, an ascending spiral—the cycles of history, dissipating, alas, in "The Second Coming."

THE LAKE ISLE OF INNISFREE

I will arise and go now, and go to Innisfree,
And a small cabin build there, of clay and wattles made:
Nine bean-rows will I have there, a hive for the honey bee,
And live alone in the bee-loud glade.

And I shall have some peace there, for peace comes dropping slow,
Dropping from the veils of the morning to where the cricket sings;
There midnight's all a glimmer, and noon a purple glow,
And evening full of the linnet's wings.

I will arise and go now, for always night and day
I hear lake water lapping with low sounds by the shore;
While I stand on thc roadway, or on the pavements grey,
I hear it in the deep heart's core.

THE SECOND COMING

Turning and turning in the widening gyre
The falcon cannot hear the falconer;
Things fall apart; the centre cannot hold;
Mere anarchy is loosed upon the world,
The blood-dimmed tide is loosed, and everywhere
The ceremony of innocence is drowned;
The best lack all conviction, while the worst
Are full of passionate intensity.

Surely some revelation is at hand;
Surely the Second Coming is at hand.   10
The Second Coming! Hardly are those words out
When a vast image out of *Spiritus Mundi*
Troubles my sight: somewhere in sands of the desert
A shape with lion body and the head of a man.
A gaze blank and pitiless as the sun,
Is moving its slow thighs, while all about it
Reel shadows of the indignant desert birds.
The darkness drops again; but now I know
That twenty centuries of stony sleep
Were vexed to nightmare by a rocking cradle,   20
And what rough beast, its hour come round at last,
Slouches towards Bethlehem to be born?

SAILING TO BYZANTIUM

That is no country for old men. The young
In one another's arms, birds in the trees
—Those dying generations—at their song,
The salmon-falls, the mackerel-crowded seas,
Fish, flesh, or fowl, commend all summer long
Whatever is begotten, born, and dies.

Caught in that sensual music all neglect
Monuments of unageing intellect.

An aged man is but a paltry thing,
A tattered coat upon a stick, unless　　　　　　　　　　　　10
Soul clap its hands and sing, and louder sing
For every tatter in its mortal dress,
Nor is there singing school but studying
Monuments of its own magnificence;
And therefore I have sailed the seas and come
To the holy city of Byzantium.

O sages standing in God's holy fire
As in the gold mosaic of a wall,
Come from the holy fire, perne in a gyre,
And be the singing-masters of my soul.　　　　　　　　　20
Consume my heart away; sick with desire
And fastened to a dying animal
It knows not what it is; and gather me
Into the artifice of eternity.

Once out of nature I shall never take
My bodily form from any natural thing,
But such a form as Grecian goldsmiths make
Of hammered gold and gold enamelling
To keep a drowsy Emperor awake;
Or set upon a golden bough to sing　　　　　　　　　　　30
To lords and ladies of Byzantium
Of what is past, or passing, or to come.

LEDA AND THE SWAN

A sudden blow: the great wings beating still
Above the staggering girl, her thighs caressed
By the dark webs, her nape caught in his bill,
He holds her helpless breast upon his breast.

How can those terrified vague fingers push
The feathered glory from her loosening thighs?
And how can body, laid in that white rush,
But feel the strange heart beating where it lies?

A shudder in the loins engenders there
The broken wall, the burning roof and tower
And Agamemnon dead.
                          Being so caught up,
So mastered by the brute blood of the air,
Did she put on his knowledge with his power
Before the indifferent beak could let her drop?

AMONG SCHOOL CHILDREN

I walk through the long schoolroom questioning;
A kind old nun in a white hood replies;
The children learn to cipher and to sing,
To study reading-books and history,
To cut and sew, be neat in everything
In the best modern way—the children's eyes
In momentary wonder stare upon
A sixty-year-old smiling public man.

I dream of a Ledaean body, bent
Above a sinking fire, a tale that she   10
Told of a harsh reproof, or trivial event
That changed some childish day to tragedy—
Told, and it seemed that our two natures blent
Into a sphere from youthful sympathy,
Or else, to alter Plato's parable,
Into the yolk and white of the one shell.

And thinking of that fit of grief or rage
I look upon one child or t'other there
And wonder if she stood so at that age—
For even daughters of the swan can share   20
Something of every paddler's heritage—
And had that colour upon cheek or hair,
And thereupon my heart is driven wild:
She stands before me as a living child.

Her present image floats into the mind—
Did Quattrocento finger fashion it
Hollow of cheek as though it drank the wind
And took a mess of shadows for its meat?

And I though never of Ledaean kind
Had pretty plumage once—enough of that,   30
Better to smile on all that smile, and show
There is a comfortable kind of old scarecrow.

What youthful mother, a shape upon her lap
Honey of generation had betrayed,
And that must sleep, shriek, struggle to escape
As recollection or the drug decide,
Would think her son, did she but see that shape
With sixty or more winters on its head,
A compensation for the pang of his birth,
Or the uncertainty of his setting forth?   40

Plato thought nature but a spume that plays
Upon a ghostly paradigm of things;
Solider Aristotle played the taws
Upon the bottom of a king of kings;
World-famous golden-thighed Pythagoras
Fingered upon a fiddle-stick or strings
What a star sang and careless Muses heard:
Old clothes upon old sticks to scare a bird.

Both nuns and mothers worship images,
But those the candles light are not as those   50
That animate a mother's reveries,
But keep a marble or a bronze repose.
And yet they too break hearts—O Presences
That passion, piety or affection knows,
And that all heavenly glory symbolise—
O self-born mockers of man's enterprise;

Labour is blossoming or dancing where
The body is not bruised to pleasure soul,
Nor beauty born out of its own despair,
Nor blear-eyed wisdom out of midnight oil.   60
O chestnut-tree, great-rooted blossomer,
Are you the leaf, the blossom or the bole?
O body swayed to music, O brightening glance,
How can we know the dancer from the dance?

COOLE PARK, 1929

I meditate upon a swallow's flight,
Upon an aged woman and her house,
A sycamore and lime-tree lost in night
Although that western cloud is luminous,
Great works constructed there in nature's spite
For scholars and for poets after us,
Thoughts long knitted into a single thought,
A dance-like glory that those walls begot.

There Hyde before he had beaten into prose
That noble blade the Muses buckled on,   10
There one that ruffled in a manly pose
For all his timid heart, there that slow man,
That meditative man, John Synge, and those
Impetuous men, Shawe-Taylor and Hugh Lane,
Found pride established in humility,
A scene well set and excellent company.

They came like swallows and like swallows went,
And yet a woman's powerful character
Could keep a swallow to its first intent;
And half a dozen in formation there,   20
That seemed to whirl upon a compass-point,
Found certainty upon the dreaming air,
The intellectual sweetness of those lines
That cut through time or cross it withershins.

Here, traveller, scholar, poet, take your stand
When all those rooms and passages are gone,
When nettles wave upon a shapeless mound
And saplings root among the broken stone,
And dedicate—eyes bent upon the ground,
Back turned upon the brightness of the sun   30
And all the sensuality of the shade—
A moment's memory to that laurelled head.

CRAZY JANE TALKS WITH THE BISHOP

I met the Bishop on the road
And much said he and I.
"Those breasts are flat and fallen now,
Those veins must soon be dry;
Live in a heavenly mansion,
Not in some foul sty."

"Fair and foul are near of kin,
And fair needs foul," I cried.
"My friends are gone, but that's a truth
Nor grave nor bed denied,   10
Learned in bodily lowliness
And in the heart's pride.

"A woman can be proud and stiff
When on love intent;
But Love has pitched his mansion in
The place of excrement;
For nothing can be sole or whole
That has not been rent."

LAPIS LAZULI

I have heard that hysterical women say
They are sick of the palette and fiddle-bow,
Of poets that are always gay,
For everybody knows or else should know
That if nothing drastic is done
Aeroplane and Zeppelin will come out,
Pitch like King Billy bomb-balls in
Until the town lie beaten flat.

All perform their tragic play,
There struts Hamlet, there is Lear,   10
That's Ophelia, that Cordelia;
Yet they, should the last scene be there,

The great stage curtain about to drop,
If worthy their prominent part in the play,
Do not break up their lines to weep.
They know that Hamlet and Lear are gay;
Gaiety transfiguring all that dread.
All men have aimed at, found and lost;
Black out; Heaven blazing into the head:
Tragedy wrought to its uttermost.   20
Though Hamlet rambles and Lear rages,
And all the drop-scenes drop at once
Upon a hundred thousand stages,
It cannot grow by an inch or an ounce.

On their own feet they came, or on shipboard,
Camel-back, horse-back, ass-back, mule-back,
Old civilisations put to the sword.
Then they and their wisdom went to rack:
No handiwork of Callimachus,
Who handled marble as if it were bronze,   30
Made draperies that seemed to rise
When sea-wind swept the corner, stands;
His long lamp-chimney shaped like the stem
Of a slender palm, stood but a day;
All things fall and are built again,
And those that build them again are gay.

Two Chinamen, behind them a third,
Are carved in lapis lazuli,
Over them flies a long-legged bird,
A symbol of longevity;   40
The third, doubtless a serving-man,
Carries a musical instrument.

Every discoloration of the stone,
Every accidental crack or dent,
Seems a water-course or an avalanche,
Or lofty slope where it still snows
Though doubtless plum or cherry-branch
Sweetens the little half-way house
Those Chinamen climb towards, and I
Delight to imagine them seated there;   50
There, on the mountain and the sky,

On all the tragic scene they stare.
One asks for mournful melodies;
Accomplished fingers begin to play.
Their eyes mid many wrinkles, their eyes,
Their ancient, glittering eyes, are gay.

Rudyard Kipling

(1865-1936)

Born in Bombay, Kipling was sent to school in England. In India again from 1882 to 1889, he began his prodigious career as journalist, poet, popular novelist, superb teller of tales and the stories in the *Jungle* books, and imperialist. In England again, he composed in rhythms of the music hall such pieces as the complaint of the British soldier, Tommy (published by Henley, 1890; collected in *Barrack-Room Ballads and Other Verses*, 1892). In 1894 he lamented ironically in "The Three-Decker" the demise of sailing ships and long, romantic novels; in "The King," their replacement in the grittier age of steam. In the Jubilee of Victoria's sixtieth year as queen (1897), "Recessional"—meaning procession of withdrawal, or decline—was embraced at once as a national hymn.

TOMMY

I went into a public-'ouse to get a pint o' beer,
The publican 'e up an' sez, "We serve no red-coats here."
The girls be'ind the bar they laughed an' giggled fit to die,
I outs into the street again an' to myself sez I:
 O it's Tommy this, an' Tommy that, an' "Tommy, go away";
 But it's "Thank you, Mister Atkins," when the band begins to play—
 The band begins to play, my boys, the band begins to play,
 O it's "Thank you, Mister Atkins," when the band begins to play.

I went into a theatre as sober as could be,
They gave a drunk civilian room, but 'adn't none for me;   10
They sent me to the gallery or round the music-'alls,
But when it comes to fightin', Lord! they'll shove me in the stalls!
 For it's Tommy this, an' Tommy that, an' "Tommy, wait outside";
 But it's "Special train for Atkins" when the trooper's on the tide—
 The troopship's on the tide, my boys, the troopship's on the tide,
 O it's "Special train for Atkins" when the trooper's on the tide.

Yes, makin' mock o' uniforms that guard you while you sleep
Is cheaper than them uniforms, an' they're starvation cheap;

An' hustlin' drunken soldiers when they're goin' large a bit
Is five times better business than paradin' in full kit.   20
 Then it's Tommy this, an' Tommy that, an' "Tommy, 'ow's yer soul?"
 But it's "Thin red line of 'eroes" when the drums begin to roll—
 The drums begin to roll, my boys, the drums begin to roll,
 O it's "Thin red line of 'eroes" when the drums begin to roll.

We aren't no thin red 'eroes, nor we aren't no blackguards too,
But single men in barricks, most remarkable like you;
An' if sometimes our conduck isn't all your fancy paints,
Why, single men in barricks don't grow into plaster saints;
 While it's Tommy this, an' Tommy that, an' "Tommy, fall be'ind,"
 But it's "Please to walk in front, sir," when there's trouble in the wind— 30
 There's trouble in the wind, my boys, there's trouble in the wind,
 O it's "Please to walk in front, sir," when there's trouble in the wind.

You talk o' better food for us, an' schools, an' fires, an' all:
We'll wait for extry rations if you treat us rational.
Don't mess about the cook-room slops, but prove it to our face
The Widow's Uniform is not the soldier-man's disgrace.
 For it's Tommy this, an' Tommy that, an' "Chuck him out, the brute!"
 But it's "Saviour of 'is country" when the guns begin to shoot;
 An' it's Tommy this, an' Tommy that, an' anything you please;
 An' Tommy ain't a bloomin' fool—you bet that Tommy sees!   40

THE KING

"Farewell, Romance!" the Cave-men said;
 "With bone well carved He went away.
"Flint arms the ignoble arrowhead,
 "And jasper tips the spear to-day.
"Changed are the Gods of Hunt and Dance,
"And He with these. Farewell, Romance!"

"Farewell, Romance!" the Lake-folk sighed;
 "We lift the weight of flatling years;
"The caverns of the mountain-side
 "Hold Him who scorns our hutted piers.   10
"Lost hills whereby we dare not dwell,
"Guard ye His rest. Romance, Farewell!"

"Farewell, Romance!" the Soldier spoke;
  "By sleight of sword we may not win,
"But scuffle 'mid uncleanly smoke
  "Of arquebus and culverin.
"Honour is lost, and none may tell
"Who paid good blows. Romance, farewell!"

"Farewell, Romance!" the Traders cried;
  "Our keels have lain with every sea.   20
"The dull-returning wind and tide
    "Heave up the wharf where we would be;
"The known and noted breezes swell
"Our trudging sails. Romance, farewell!"

"Good-bye, Romance!" the Skipper said;
    "He vanished with the coal we burn.
"Our dial marks full-steam ahead,
    "Our speed is timed to half a turn.
"Sure as the ferried barge we ply
" 'Twixt port and port. Romance, good-bye!"   30

"Romance!" the season-tickets mourn,
  "*He* never ran to catch His train,
"But passed with coach and guard and horn—
  "And left the local—late again!
"Confound Romance!" . . . And all unseen
Romance brought up the nine-fifteen.

His hand was on the lever laid,
  His oil-can soothed the worrying cranks,
His whistle waked the snowbound grade,
  His fog-horn cut the reeking Banks;   40
By dock and deep and mine and mill
The Boy-god reckless laboured still!

Robed, crowned and throned, He wove His spell,
  Where heart-blood beat or hearth-smoke curled,
With unconsidered miracle,
  Hedged in a backward-gazing world:
Then taught His chosen bard to say:
"Our King was with us—yesterday!"

RECESSIONAL

God of our fathers, known of old,
   Lord of our far-flung battle-line,
Beneath whose awful Hand we hold
   Dominion over palm and pine—
Lord God of Hosts, be with us yet,
Lest we forget—lest we forget!

The tumult and the shouting dies;
   The Captains and the Kings depart:
Still stands Thine ancient sacrifice,
   An humble and a contrite heart.   10
Lord God of Hosts, be with us yet,
Lest we forget—lest we forget!

Far-called, our navies melt away;
   On dune and headland sinks the fire:
Lo, all our pomp of yesterday
   Is one with Nineveh and Tyre!
Judge of the Nations, spare us yet,
Lest we forget—lest we forget!

If, drunk with sight of power, we loose
   Wild tongues that have not Thee in awe,   20
Such boastings as the Gentiles use,
   Or lesser breeds without the Law—
Lord God of Hosts, be with us yet,
Lest we forget—lest we forget!

For heathen heart that puts her trust
   In reeking tube and iron shard,
All valiant dust that builds on dust,
   And guarding, calls not Thee to guard,
For frantic boast and foolish word—
Thy mercy on Thy People, Lord!   30

Lionel Johnson

(1 8 6 7 – 1 9 0 2)

Johnson was born in Kent, grew up in Wales, and was educated at Winchester
and Oxford. He was a member in London of the Rhymers' Club and a close
friend of Yeats, who commemorated him as a once-vital alcoholic. Johnson
himself acknowledged his drinking problem in "Mystic and Cavalier" ("Go from
me, I am one of those who fall"). His conversion in 1891 to the Roman
Catholic faith is anticipated in "The Church of a Dream" (1890). After a visit to
Dublin he began to explore his Irish ancestry, and his *Ireland and Other Poems*
appeared in 1897.

THE CHURCH OF A DREAM

Sadly the dead leaves rustle in the whistling wind,
Around the weather-worn, gray church, low down the vale:
The Saints in golden vesture shake before the gale;
The glorious windows shake, where still they dwell enshrined;
Old Saints by long dead, shrivelled hands, long since designed:
There still, although the world autumnal be, and pale,
Still in their golden vesture the old saints prevail;
Alone with Christ, desolate else, left by mankind.

Only one ancient Priest offers the Sacrifice,
Murmuring holy Latin immemorial:
Swaying with tremulous hands the old censer full of spice,
In gray, sweet incense clouds; blue, sweet clouds mystical:
To him, in place of men, for he is old, suffice
Melancholy remembrances and vesperal.

725

Ernest Dowson

(1 8 6 7 – 1 9 0 0)

After leaving Oxford without a degree, Dowson worked at his father's Lime-house docks and joined the Rhymers' Club and similar literary circles of London. A Roman Catholic from 1891, he grew increasingly restless and intemperate. A Polish waitress of twelve may be the original behind "I am not what I was under the reign of gracious Cynara" (Horace *Odes* 4.1). Like his idol Verlaine, Dowson sought in verse a purity of sound, as in the stanzas with their title from Horace *Odes* 1.4: "The brevity of life's span keeps us from entertaining far-off hopes." These poems of 1891 were included in his *Verses* (1896).

NON SUM QUALIS ERAM BONAE
SUB REGNO CYNARAE

Last night, ah, yesternight, betwixt her lips and mine
There fell thy shadow, Cynara! thy breath was shed
Upon my soul between the kisses and the wine;
And I was desolate and sick of an old passion,
    Yea, I was desolate and bowed my head:
I have been faithful to thee, Cynara! in my fashion.

All night upon mine heart I felt her warm heart beat,
Night-long within mine arms in love and sleep she lay;
Surely the kisses of her bought red mouth were sweet;
But I was desolate and sick of an old passion,   10
    When I awoke and found the dawn was gray:
I have been faithful to thee, Cynara! in my fashion.

I have forgot much, Cynara! gone with the wind,
Flung roses, roses riotously with the throng,
Dancing, to put thy pale, lost lilies out of mind;
But I was desolate and sick of an old passion,
    Yea, all the time, because the dance was long:
I have been faithful to thee, Cynara! in my fashion.

I cried for madder music and for stronger wine,
But when the feast is finished and the lamps expire,   20
Then falls thy shadow, Cynara! the night is thine;
And I am desolate and sick of an old passion,
    Yea hungry for the lips of my desire:
I have been faithful to thee, Cynara! in my fashion.

VITAE SUMMA BREVIS
SPEM NOS VETAT
INCOHARE LONGAM

They are not long, the weeping and the laughter,
        Love and desire and hate:
I think they have no portion in us after
            We pass the gate.

They are not long, the days of wine and roses:
        Out of a misty dream
Our path emerges for a while, then closes
            Within a dream.

Laurence Binyon

(1869–1943)

Born in Lancaster, Robert Laurence Binyon won the Newdigate Prize at Oxford in 1890. He published almost annually volumes of poems, poetic dramas, and surveys of art. As ultimately the head of the Department of Prints and Drawings in the British Museum, he achieved expertise in art of the Orient and of Blake and Blake's followers. He held posts as lecturer in the United States, Japan, and Greece. "Harebell and Pansy" was gathered in *The Death of Adam, and Other Poems* in 1904, the year he married Cicely Powell; they had three daughters. "The Unreturning Spring" counts among Binyon's several noble poems of the "Great War" of 1914–1918.

HAREBELL AND PANSY

O'er the round throat her little head
Its gay delight upbuoys:
A harebell in the breeze of June
Hath such melodious poise;
And chiming with her heart, my heart
Is only hers and joy's.

But my heart takes a deeper thrill,
Her cheek a rarer bloom,
When the sad mood comes rich as glow
Of pansies dipped in gloom.
By some far shore she wanders—where?
And her eyes fill—for whom?

THE UNRETURNING SPRING

A leaf on the gray sand-path
Fallen, and fair with rime!

A yellow leaf, a scarlet leaf,
And a green leaf ere its time.

Days rolled in blood, days torn,
Days innocent, days burnt black,
What is it the wind is sighing
As the leaves float, swift or slack?

The year's pale spectre is crying
For beauty invisibly shed,
For the things that never were told
And were killed in the minds of the dead.

Charlotte Mew

(1869–1928)

Three of Mew's siblings died young; two others were institutionalized for insanity. She attended Lucy Harrison's School for Girls and lectures at University College, London, and began writing poetry in her childhood (her first poem, "Passed," was published in 1894). After her father's death in 1898 she lived in Bloomsbury with her mother and remaining sister, Anne, until they died after long illnesses (her mother in 1923, Anne four years later). Shortly thereafter Charlotte Mew committed suicide by drinking disinfectant. "The Farmer's Bride," her most celebrated poem, was the title piece in a collection of 1916 published and promoted by Harold and Alida Monro and admired by Thomas Hardy and many other contemporary poets. The volume was expanded and reprinted in 1921 and expanded yet again in 1929 with a new title, *The Rambling Sailor*.

THE FARMER'S BRIDE

Three Summers since I chose a maid,
    Too young maybe—but more's to do
At harvest-time than bide and woo.
    When us was wed she turned afraid
Of love and me and all things human;
Like the shut of a winter's day
Her smile went out, and 'twadn't a woman—
    More like a little frightened fay.
        One night, in the Fall, she runned away.

"Out 'mong the sheep, her be," they said,   10
'Should properly have been abed;
But sure enough she wadn't there
Lying awake with her wide brown stare.
So over seven-acre field and up-along across the down
We chased her, flying like a hare
Before our lanterns. To Church-Town
    All in a shiver and a scare
We caught her, fetched her home at last
    And turned the key upon her, fast.

She does the work about the house   20
As well as most, but like a mouse:
      Happy enough to chat and play
      With birds and rabbits and such as they,
      So long as men-folk keep away.
"Not near, not near!" her eyes beseech
When one of us comes within reach.
      The women say that beasts in stall
      Look round like children at her call.
      I've hardly heard her speak at all.

Shy as a leveret, swift as he,   30
Straight and slight as a young larch tree,
Sweet as the first wild violets, she,
To her wild self. But what to me?

The short days shorten and the oaks are brown,
      The blue smoke rises to the low grey sky,
One leaf in the still air falls slowly down,
      A magpie's spotted feathers lie
On the black earth spread white with rime,
The berries redden up to Christmas-time.
      What's Christmas-time without there be   40
      Some other in the house than we!

      She sleeps up in the attic there
      Alone, poor maid. 'Tis but a stair
Betwixt us. Oh! my God! the down,
The soft young down of her, the brown,
The brown of her—her eyes, her hair, her hair!

Thomas Sturge Moore

(1870–1944)

Artist and poet, like his friend Binyon author of dramas in verse, the designer of covers for several volumes of Yeats's poems, Sturge Moore—brother of the philosopher G. E. Moore—argued in *Armour for Aphrodite,* and in vigorous correspondence now partly published, that creative beauty requires tension. Moore's lament in response to Rimbaud was among seven poems from his collected *Poems* (4 vols., 1931–1933) included by Yeats in *The Oxford Book of Modern Verse, 1892–1935* (1936). Moore seems to have had in mind Rimbaud's revision of the song beginning "elle est retrouvée / Quoi? l'Éternité" and the revised "Chanson de la plus haute tour."

RESPONSE TO RIMBAUD'S LATER MANNER

The cow eats green grass;
Alas, alas!
Nothing to eat
Surrounds my feet!

Diamond clad
In the stream the naïad
Never sips, dips
All save her lips.

They, they, and not I,
Never ask why   10
The Cathedral tower
Dreams like a flower.

They, they, are healed
From thought congealed

That ploughs up the heart
Which takes its own part.

They, they, have refound
Eternity;
Which is the sun bound
In the arms of the sea.   20

Edward Thomas

(*1878 – 1917*)

After grammar school in Lambeth, Thomas attended St. Paul's School and Lincoln College, Oxford. He married young—while still in his third year at Oxford. For fifteen years a journalist in Kent supporting wife and children, he published topographical and biographical works—until encouraged by Robert Frost in 1914 to take seriously his evident ability as a poet. In 1915 he joined the Artists' Rifles and fought in France. On April 8, 1917, he wrote home to his wife: "You would have laughed to see us dodging shells today." The following day he was killed at Arras. F. R. Leavis subsequently praised Thomas as a "very original poet who devoted great technical subtlety to the expression of a distinctively modern sensibility." At the time of his death at the age of thirty-eight, only a half-dozen of his poems had appeared in print.

AS THE TEAM'S HEAD-BRASS

As the team's head-brass flashed out on the turn
The lovers disappeared into the wood.
I sat among the boughs of the fallen elm
That strewed the angle of the fallow, and
Watched the plough narrowing a yellow square
Of charlock. Every time the horses turned
Instead of treading me down, the ploughman leaned
Upon the handles to say or ask a word,
About the weather, next about the war.
Scraping the share he faced towards the wood,   10
And screwed along the furrow till the brass flashed
Once more.
         The blizzard felled the elm whose crest
I sat in, by a woodpecker's round hole,
The ploughman said. "When will they take it away?"
"When the war's over." So the talk began—
One minute and an interval of ten,
A minute more and the same interval.
"Have you been out?" "No." "And don't want to, perhaps.' "

"If I could only come back again, I should.   20
I could spare an arm. I shouldn't want to lose
A leg. If I should lose my head, why, so,
I should want nothing more. . . . Have many gone
From here?" "Yes." "Many lost?" "Yes, a good few.
Only two teams work on the farm this year.
One of my mates is dead. The second day
In France they killed him. It was back in March,
The very night of the blizzard, too. Now if
He had stayed here we should have moved the tree."
"And I should not have sat here. Everything   30
Would have been different. For it would have been
Another world." "Ay, and a better, though
If we could see all all might seem good." Then
The lovers came out of the wood again:
The horses started and for the last time
I watched the clods crumble and topple over
After the ploughshare and the stumbling team.

OCTOBER

The green elm with the one great bough of gold
Lets leaves into the grass slip, one by one,—
The short hill grass, the mushrooms small, milk-white,
Harebell and scabious and tormentil
That blackberry and gorse, in dew and sun,   5
Bow down to: and the wind travels too light
To shake the fallen birch leaves from the fern;
The gossamers wander at their own will.
At heavier steps than birds' the squirrels scold.
The rich scene has grown fresh again and new   10
As Spring and to the touch is not more cool
Than it is warm to the gaze; and now I might
As happy be as earth is beautiful,
Where I some other or with earth could turn
In alternation of violet and rose,   15
Harebell and snowdrop, at their season due,
And gorse that has no time nor to be gay.
But if this be not happiness,—who knows?

Some day I shall think this a happy day,
And this mood by the name of melancholy   20
Shall no more blackened and obscured be.

l. 4: Varieties of British herbs

John Masefield

(1 8 7 8 – 1 9 6 7)

Born in Ledbury and schooled in Warwick, Masefield served as a merchant seaman in the age of sail and jumped ship for various jobs in New York and London until he became in the new century a superb narrator in verse and prose of tales of sea and country life. After civilian service in World War I, he received almost every available award for literature in English. It is tiring even to count his volumes of poetry, fiction, drama, and "other." "Sea-Fever" and "The West Wind" (an immensely popular poem in galloping anapests) appeared in his first volume, *Salt-Water Ballads* (1902); "Cargoes," a history of shipping written in 1902, appeared in *Ballads and Poems* (1910). Masefield shrugged off complaints that Nineveh was two hundred miles inland.

CARGOES

Quinquireme of Nineveh from distant Ophir,
Rowing home to haven in sunny Palestine,
With a cargo of ivory,
And apes and peacocks,
Sandalwood, cedarwood, and sweet white wine.

Stately Spanish galleon coming from the Isthmus,
Dipping through the Tropics by the palm-green shores,
With a cargo of diamonds,
Emeralds, amethysts,
Topazes, and cinnamon, and gold moidores.　　　　　10

Dirty British coaster with a salt-caked smoke stack,
Butting through the Channel in the mad March days,
With a cargo of Tyne coal,
Road-rails, pig-lead,
Firewood, iron-ware, and cheap tin trays.

SEA-FEVER

I must go down to the seas again, to the lonely sea and the sky,
And all I ask is a tall ship and a star to steer her by,
And the wheel's kick and the wind's song and the white sail's shaking,
And a grey mist on the sea's face and a grey dawn breaking.

I must go down to the seas again, for the call of the running tide
Is a wild call and a clear call that may not be denied;
And all I ask is a windy day with the white clouds flying,
And the flung spray and the blown spume and the sea-gulls crying.

I must go down to the seas again to the vagrant gypsy life,
To the gull's way and the whale's way where the wind's like a whetted knife;
And all I ask is a merry yarn from a laughing fellow-rover,
And quiet sleep and a sweet dream when the long trick's over.

THE WEST WIND

It's a warm wind, the west wind, full of birds' cries;
I never hear the west wind but tears are in my eyes.
For it comes from the west lands, the old brown hills,
And April's in the west wind, and daffodils.

It's a fine land, the west land, for hearts as tired as mine,
Apple orchards blossom there, and the air's like wine.
There is cool green grass there, where men may lie at rest,
And the thrushes are in song there, fluting from the nest.

"Will you not come home, brother? you have been long away,
It's April, and blossom time, and white is the spray;   10
And bright is the sun, brother, and warm is the rain,—
Will you not come home, brother, home to us again?

The young corn is green, brother, where the rabbits run,
It's blue sky, and white clouds, and warm rain and sun.
It's song to a man's soul, brother, fire to a man's brain,
To hear the wild bees and see the merry spring again.

Larks are singing in the west, brother, above the green wheat,
So will ye not come home, brother, and rest your tired feet?

I've a balm for bruised hearts, brother, sleep for aching eyes,"
Says the warm wind, the west wind, full of birds' cries.   20

It's the white road westwards is the road I must tread
To the green grass, the cool grass, and rest for heart and head,
To the violets and the brown brooks and the thrushes' song,
In the fine land, the west land, the land where I belong.

David Herbert Lawrence

(1885 – 1930)

Son of ill-suited parents, a Nottinghamshire miner and a refined mother, Lawrence secured enough training to teach in an elementary school, but began to write verse and fiction in his teens. In 1912 he eloped with Frieda von Richthofen; their stormy, nomadic life gave him material for powerful travel books and novels set in Germany, Ceylon, Australia, Mexico, New Mexico, Italy. "Piano" (1918) is of sweeter memories than his autobiographical *Sons and Lovers* (1913). "Snake" and "Bavarian Gentians" date from 1923. Like Swinburne, Boland, and many others, Lawrence finds resonance in the descent of Persephone (Proserpine) to Dis (Hades). He has few equals, however, in his calls to make women crave masculine dominance, as in his later novels and in "Love on the Farm" (1913). Before *Collected Poems* (1928) that poem bore the title "Cruelty and Love."

PIANO

Softly, in the dusk, a woman is singing to me;
Taking me back down the vista of years, till I see
A child sitting under the piano, in the boom of the tingling strings
And pressing the small, poised feet of a mother who smiles as she sings.

In spite of myself, the insidious mastery of song
Betrays me back, till the heart of me weeps to belong
To the old Sunday evenings at home, with winter outside
And hymns in the cosy parlour, the tinkling piano our guide.

So now it is vain for the singer to burst into clamour
With the great black piano appassionato. The glamour
Of childish days is upon me, my manhood is cast
Down in the flood of remembrance, I weep like a child for the past.

SNAKE

A snake came to my water-trough
On a hot, hot day, and I in pyjamas for the heat,
To drink there.

In the deep, strange-scented shade of the great dark carob-tree
I came down the steps with my pitcher
And must wait, must stand and wait, for there he was at the trough before me.

He reached down from a fissure in the earth-wall in the gloom
And trailed his yellow-brown slackness soft-bellied down, over the edge of the
    stone trough
And rested his throat upon the stone bottom,   10
And where the water had dripped from the tap, in a small clearness,
He sipped with his straight mouth,
Softly drank through his straight gums, into his slack long body,
Silently.

Someone was before me at my water-trough,
And I, like a second comer, waiting.

He lifted his head from his drinking, as cattle do,
And looked at me vaguely, as drinking cattle do,
And flickered his two-forked tongue from his lips, and mused a moment,
And stooped and drank a little more,
Being earth-brown, earth-golden from the burning bowels of the earth   20
On the day of Sicilian July, with Etna smoking.

The voice of my education said to me
He must be killed,
For in Sicily the black, black snakes are innocent, the gold are venomous.

And voices in me said, If you were a man
You would take a stick and break him now, and finish him off.

But must I confess how I liked him,
How glad I was he had come like a guest in quiet, to drink at my water-trough
And depart peaceful, pacified, and thankless,
Into the burning bowels of this earth?   30

Was it cowardice, that I dared not kill him?
Was it perversity, that I longed to talk to him?

Was it humility, to feel so honoured?
I felt so honoured.

And yet those voices:
If you were not afraid, you would kill him!

And truly I was afraid, I was most afraid,
But even so, honoured still more
That he should seek my hospitality
From out the dark door of the secret earth.   40

He drank enough
And lifted his head, dreamily, as one who has drunken,
And flickered his tongue like a forked night on the air, so black;
Seeming to lick his lips,
And looked around like a god, unseeing, into the air,
And slowly turned his head,
And slowly, very slowly, as if thrice adream,
Proceeded to draw his slow length curving round
And climb again the broken bank of my wall-face.

And as he put his head into that dreadful hole,   50
And as he slowly drew up, snake-easing his shoulders, and entered farther,
A sort of horror, a sort of protest against his withdrawing into that horrid
    black hole,
Deliberately going into the blackness, and slowly drawing himself after,
Overcame me now his back was turned.

I looked round, I put down my pitcher,
I picked up a clumsy log
And threw it at the water-trough with a clatter.

I think it did not hit him,
But suddenly that part of him that was left behind convulsed in undignified
    haste,
Writhed like lightning, and was gone   60
Into the black hole, the earth-lipped fissure in the wall-front,
At which, in the intense still noon, I stared with fascination.

And immediately I regretted it.
I thought how paltry, how vulgar, what a mean act!
I despised myself and the voices of my accursed human education.

And I thought of the albatross,
And I wished he would come back, my snake.

For he seemed to me again like a king,
Like a king in exile, uncrowned in the underworld,
Now due to be crowned again.   70

And so, I missed my chance with one of the lords
Of life.
And I have something to expiate;
A pettiness.

BAVARIAN GENTIANS

Not every man has gentians in his house
in Soft September, at slow, sad Michaelmas.

Bavarian gentians, big and dark, only dark
darkening the day-time, torch-like with the smoking blueness of Pluto's gloom,
ribbed and torch-like, with their blaze of darkness spread blue
down flattening into points, flattened under the sweep of white day
torch-flower of the blue-smoking darkness, Pluto's dark-blue daze,
black lamps from the halls of Dis, burning dark blue,
giving off darkness, blue darkness, as Demeter's pale lamps give off light,
lead me then, lead the way.   10

Reach me a gentian, give me a torch!
let me guide myself with the blue, forked torch of this flower
down the darker and darker stairs, where blue is darkened on blueness
even where Persephone goes, just now, from the frosted September
to the sightless realm where darkness is awake upon the dark
and Persephone herself is but a voice
or a darkness invisible enfolded in the deeper dark
of the arms Plutonic, and pierced with the passion of dense gloom,
among the splendour of torches of darkness, shedding darkness on the lost bride
        and her groom.

LOVE ON THE FARM

What large, dark hands are those at the window
Grasping in the golden light
Which weaves its way through the evening wind
    At my heart's delight?

Ah, only the leaves! But in the west
I see a redness suddenly come
Into the evening's anxious breast—
    'Tis the wound of love goes home!

The woodbine creeps abroad
Calling low to her lover: 10
    The sun-lit flirt who all the day
    Has poised above her lips in play
    And stolen kisses, shallow and gay
    Of pollen, now has gone away—
    She woos the moth with her sweet, low word;
And when above her his moth-wings hover
Then her bright breast she will uncover
And yield her honey-drop to her lover.

Into the yellow, evening glow
Saunters a man from the farm below;   20
Leans, and looks in at the low-built shed
Where the swallow has hung her marriage bed.
    The bird lies warm against the wall.
    She glances quick her startled eyes
    Towards him, then she turns away
    Her small head, making warm display
    Of red upon the throat. Her terrors sway
    Her out of the nest's warm, busy ball,
    Whose plaintive cry is heard as she flies
    In one blue stoop from out the sties   30
    Into the twilight's empty hall.

Oh, water-hen, beside the rushes
Hide your quaintly scarlet blushes,
Still your quick tail, lie still as dead,
Till the distance folds over his ominous tread!

The rabbit presses back her ears,
Turns back her liquid, anguished eyes
And crouches low; then with wild spring
Spurts from the terror of *his* oncoming;
To be choked back, the wire ring   40
Her frantic effort throttling:
    Piteous brown ball of quivering fears!
Ah, soon in his large, hard hands she dies,
And swings all loose from the swing of his walk!
Yet calm and kindly are his eyes
And ready to open in brown surprise
Should I not answer to his talk
Or should he my tears surmise.

I hear his hand on the latch, and rise from my chair
Watching the door open; he flashes bare   50
His strong teeth in a smile, and flashes his eyes
In a smile like triumph upon me; then careless-wise
He flings the rabbit soft on the table board
And comes towards me: ah! the uplifted sword
Of his hand against my bosom! and oh, the broad
Blade of his glance that asks me to applaud
His coming! With his hand he turns my face to him
And caresses me with his fingers that still smell grim
Of the rabbit's fur! God, I am caught in a snare!
I know not what fine wire is round my throat;   60
I only know I let him finger there
My pulse of life, and let him nose like a stoat
Who sniffs with joy before he drinks the blood.

And down his mouth comes to my mouth! and down
His bright dark eyes come over me, like a hood
Upon my mind! his lips meet mine, and a flood
Of sweet fire sweeps across me, so I drown
Against him, die, and find death good.

Edwin Muir

(1887–1959)

Born and educated in the Orkney islands of Scotland, Muir, by a prodigious amount of literary work in England, Scotland, and Europe from 1919 until his death, earned prizes, awards, and honorary degrees throughout the 1950s. His wife, Willa, and he translated forty volumes, most notably the novels of Kafka and Broch. "Scotland 1941" laments the decline of romance but questions romanticized virtues; in contrast, "The Horses" lifts mundane change into fantasy.

SCOTLAND 1941

We were a tribe, a family, a people.
Wallace and Bruce guard now a painted field,
And all may read the folio of our fable,
Peruse the sword, the sceptre and the shield.
A simple sky roofed in that rustic day,
The busy corn-fields and the haunted holms,
The green road winding up the ferny brae.
But Knox and Melville clapped their preaching palms
And bundled all the harvesters away,
Hoodicrow Peden in the blighted corn   10
Hacked with his rusty beak the starving haulms.
Out of that desolation we were born.

Courage beyond the point and obdurate pride
Made us a nation, robbed us of a nation.
Defiance absolute and myriad-eyed
That could not pluck the palm plucked our damnation.
We with such courage and the bitter wit
To fell the ancient oak of loyalty,
And strip the peopled hill and the altar bare,
And crush the poet with an iron text,   20
How could we read our souls and learn to be?
Here a dull drove of faces harsh and vexed,
We watch our cities burning in their pit,

746

To salve our souls grinding dull lucre out,
We, fanatics of the frustrate and the half,
Who once set Purgatory Hill in doubt.
Now smoke and dearth and money everywhere,
Mean heirlooms of each fainter generation,
And mummied housegods in their musty niches,
Burns and Scott, sham bards of a sham nation,   30
And spiritual defeat wrapped warm in riches,
No pride but pride of pelf. Long since the young

Fought in great bloody battles to carve out
This towering pulpit of the Golden Calf,
Montrose, Mackail, Argyle, perverse and brave,
Twisted the stream, unhooped the ancestral hill.
Never had Dee or Don or Yarrow or Till
Huddled such thriftless honour in a grave.

Such wasted bravery idle as a song,
Such hard-won ill might prove Time's verdict wrong,   40
And melt to pity the annalist's iron tongue.

THE HORSES

Barely a twelvemonth after
The seven days war that put the world to sleep,
Late in the evening the strange horses came.
By then we had made our covenant with silence,
But in the first few days it was so still
We listened to our breathing and were afraid.
On the second day
The radios failed; we turned the knobs; no answer.
On the third day a warship passed us, heading north,
Dead bodies piled on the deck. On the sixth day   10
A plane plunged over us into the sea. Thereafter
Nothing. The radios dumb;
And still they stand in corners of our kitchens,
And stand, perhaps, turned on, in a million rooms
All over the world. But now if they should speak,
If on a sudden they should speak again,
If on the stroke of noon a voice should speak,
We would not listen, we would not let it bring

That old bad world that swallowed its children quick
At one great gulp. We would not have it again.   20
Sometimes we think of the nations lying asleep,
Curled blindly in impenetrable sorrow,
And then the thought confounds us with its strangeness.
The tractors lie about our fields; at evening
They look like dank sea-monsters couched and waiting.
We leave them where they are and let them rust:
"They'll moulder away and be like other loam."
We make our oxen drag our rusty ploughs,
Long laid aside. We have gone back
Far past our fathers' land.   30
                              And then, that evening
Late in the summer the strange horses came.
We heard a distant tapping on the road,
A deepening drumming; it stopped, went on again
And at the corner changed to hollow thunder.
We saw the heads
Like a wild wave charging and were afraid.
We had sold our horses in our fathers' time
To buy new tractors. Now they were strange to us
As fabulous steeds set on an ancient shield
Or illustrations in a book of knights.   40
We did not dare go near them. Yet they waited,
Stubborn and shy, as if they had been sent
By an old command to find our whereabouts
And that long-lost archaic companionship.
In the first moment we had never a thought
That they were creatures to be owned and used.
Among them were some half-a-dozen colts
Dropped in some wilderness of the broken world,
Yet new as if they had come from their own Eden.
Since then they have pulled our ploughs and borne our loads.   50
But that free servitude still can pierce our hearts.
Our life is changed; their coming our beginning.

Rupert Chawner Brooke

(1 8 8 7 – 1 9 1 5)

Born in Rugby, Brooke attended Rugby School and King's College, Cambridge, where he was noticed for beauty, brains, poems in journals (from 1909), and *Poems* (published 1911). He published letters from wide travel in 1912–1913 before military service in the Royal Navy Volunteer Reserve. He died on the way to the Dardanelles. His range in poems of place, death, and love—including "Jealousy" (1909), about a lover whose marriage will make her tend a "foul sick fumbling dribbling body and old"—is reduced in golden treasuries to one perfect sonnet of innocent patriotism.

THE SOLDIER

If I should die, think only this of me:
    That there's some corner of a foreign field
That is for ever England. There shall be
    In that rich earth a richer dust concealed;
A dust whom England bore, shaped, made aware,
    Gave, once, her flowers to love, her ways to roam,
A body of England's, breathing English air,
    Washed by the rivers, blest by suns of home.

And think, this heart, all evil shed away,
    A pulse in the eternal mind, no less
        Gives somewhere back the thoughts by England given;
Her sights and sounds; dreams happy as her day;
    And laughter, learnt of friends; and gentleness,
        In hearts at peace, under an English heaven.

Edith Sitwell

(1887-1964)

Born in the resort city of Scarborough, Edith, with her brothers Osbert and Sacheverell, set about to astonish and amuse, but each achieved sobriety and distinction in a great variety of works. She began writing poetry at an early age and published her first collection, *The Mother and Other Poems*, in 1915. Among many prizes and honors, she was made Dame Commander of the British Empire in 1954, the first poet honored with this distinction. In the "canticle" here, the horrors of bombing raids on London bring the poet to the Christ who raised Lazarus from death, to the wickedly wealthy Crassus (Dives), and to Faustus, whose repentance in Marlowe's *Doctor Faustus* is quoted in lines 26–27.

STILL FALLS THE RAIN

THE RAIDS, 1940. NIGHT AND DAWN

Still falls the Rain—
Dark as the world of man, black as our loss—
Blind as the nineteen hundred and forty nails
Upon the Cross.

Still falls the Rain
With a sound like the pulse of the heart that is changed to the hammer-beat
In the Potter's Field, and the sound of the impious feet

On the Tomb:
                    Still falls the Rain
In the Field of Blood where the small hopes breed and the human brain   10
Nurtures its greed, that worm with the brow of Cain.

Still falls the Rain
At the feet of the Starved Man hung upon the Cross.
Christ that each day, each night, nails there, have mercy on us—
On Dives and on Lazarus:
Under the Rain the sore and the gold are as one.

Still falls the Rain—
Still falls the Blood from the Starved Man's wounded Side:
Ile bears in Ilis Ileart all wounds—those of the light that died,
The last faint spark   20
In the self-murdered heart, the wounds of the sad uncomprehending dark,
The wounds of the baited bear—
The blind and weeping bear whom the keepers beat
On his helpless flesh . . . the tears of the hunted hare.

Still falls the Rain—
Then—O Ile leape up to my God: who pulles me doune—
See, see where Christ's blood streames in the firmament:
It flows from the Brow we nailed upon the tree
Deep to the dying, to the thirsting heart
That holds the fires of the world—dark-smirched with pain   30
As Caesar's laurel crown.

Then sounds the voice of One who like the heart of man
Was once a child who among beasts has lain—
"Still do I love, still shed my innocent light, my Blood, for thee."

Thomas Stearns Eliot

(1 8 8 8 – 1 9 6 5)

Born in St. Louis, a student of philosophy at Harvard, the Sorbonne, and Oxford, T. S. Eliot worked in London as tutor, clerk, official in Lloyd's Bank (1917–1925), editor and director of the publishing house Faber & Gwyer, later Faber & Faber (1925–1965), and founding editor of *Criterion* (1922–1939), one outlet for his critical essays. A British citizen and Anglican communicant from 1927, he was married to Vivien Haigh-Wood (1915–1947; separated 1933) and to Valerie Fletcher (1957–1965). Of seven verse plays produced on stage, *Murder in the Cathedral* (1935) was also revised as a film. Other honors preceded and many followed his Nobel Prize in Literature and the Order of Merit in 1948.

    The Waste Land (1922), a personal lament revised under persistent advice from Ezra Pound, quickly became a beacon to poets and readers lost in a fragmented world. *Little Gidding* (published separately in 1942) is the last in the *Four Quartets* (1943). The title refers to Nicholas Ferrar's Anglican community of 1625–1647; the whole, set within London's trial by missiles and fire, evokes the tradition of Christian mysticism.

From THE WASTE LAND

"Nam Sibyllam quidem Cumis ego ipse oculis meis vidi in ampulla pendere, et cum illi pueri dicerent: Σίβυλλα τί θέλεις; respondebat illa: ἀποθανεῖν θέλω."

For Ezra Pound
il miglior fabbro.

I

THE BURIAL OF THE DEAD

April is the cruellest month, breeding
Lilacs out of the dead land, mixing
Memory and desire, stirring
Dull roots with spring rain.
Winter kept us warm, covering
Earth in forgetful snow, feeding
A little life with dried tubers.
Summer surprised us, coming over the Starnbergersee

With a shower of rain; we stopped in the colonnade,
And went on in sunlight, into the Hofgarten,   10
And drank coffee, and talked for an hour.
Bin gar keine Russin, stamm' aus Litauen, echt deutsch.
And when we were children, staying at the archduke's,
My cousin's, he took me out on a sled,
And I was frightened. He said, Marie,
Marie, hold on tight. And down we went.
In the mountains, there you feel free.
I read, much of the night, and go south in the winter.

What are the roots that clutch, what branches grow
Out of this stony rubbish? Son of man,   20
You cannot say, or guess, for you know only
A heap of broken images, where the sun beats,
And the dead tree gives no shelter, the cricket no relief,
And the dry stone no sound of water. Only
There is shadow under this red rock,
(Come in under the shadow of this red rock),
And I will show you something different from either
Your shadow at morning striding behind you
Or your shadow at evening rising to meet you;
I will show you fear in a handful of dust.   30
          Frisch weht der Wind
          Der Heimat zu
          Mein Irisch Kind,
          Wo weilest du?
"You gave me hyacinths first a year ago;
"They called me the hyacinth girl."
—Yet when we came back, late, from the Hyacinth garden,
Your arms full, and your hair wet, I could not
Speak, and my eyes failed, I was neither
Living nor dead, and I knew nothing,   40
Looking into the heart of light, the silence.
Oed' und leer das Meer.

Madame Sosostris, famous clairvoyante,
Had a bad cold, nevertheless
Is known to be the wisest woman in Europe,
With a wicked pack of cards. Here, said she,
Is your card, the drowned Phoenician Sailor,
(Those are pearls that were his eyes. Look!)
Here is Belladonna, the Lady of the Rocks,

The lady of situations.   50
Here is the man with three staves, and here the Wheel,
And here is the one-eyed merchant, and this card,
Which is blank, is something he carries on his back,
Which I am forbidden to see. I do not find
The Hanged Man. Fear death by water.
I see crowds of people, walking round in a ring.
Thank you. If you see dear Mrs. Equitone,
Tell her I bring the horoscope myself:
One must be so careful these days.

   Unreal City,   60
Under the brown fog of a winter dawn,
A crowd flowed over London Bridge, so many,
I had not thought death had undone so many.
Sighs, short and infrequent, were exhaled,
And each man fixed his eyes before his feet.
Flowed up the hill and down King William Street,
To where Saint Mary Woolnoth kept the hours
With a dead sound on the final stroke of nine.
There I saw one I knew, and stopped him, crying: "Stetson!
"You who were with me in the ships at Mylae!   70
"That corpse you planted last year in your garden,
"Has it begun to sprout? Will it bloom this year?
"Or has the sudden frost disturbed its bed?
"Oh keep the Dog far hence, that's friend to men,
"Or with his nails he'll dig it up again!
"You! hypocrite lecteur!—mon semblable,—mon frère!"

MARINA

"Quis hic locus, quae regio, quae mundi plaga?"

What seas what shores what grey rocks and what islands
What water lapping the bow
And scent of pine and the woodthrush singing through the fog
What images return
O my daughter.

   Those who sharpen the tooth of the dog, meaning
Death
Those who glitter with the glory of the humming-bird, meaning
Death

Those who sit in the stye of contentment, meaning   10
Death
Those who suffer the ecstasy of the animals, meaning
Death

   Are become unsubstantial, reduced by a wind,
A breath of pine, and the woodsong fog
By this grace dissolved in place

   What is this face, less clear and clearer
The pulse in the arm, less strong and stronger—
Given or lent? more distant than stars and nearer than the eye

   Whispers and small laughter between leaves and hurrying feet   20
Under sleep, where all the waters meet.

   Bowsprit cracked with ice and paint cracked with heat.
I made this, I have forgotten
And remember.
The rigging weak and the canvas rotten
Between one June and another September.
Made this unknowing, half conscious, unknown, my own.
The garboard strake leaks, the seams need caulking.

This form, this face, this life
Living to live in a world of time beyond me; let me   30
Resign my life for this life, my speech for that unspoken,
The awakened, lips parted, the hope, the new ships.

   What seas what shores what granite islands towards my timbers
And woodthrush calling through the fog
My daughter.

From THE FOUR QUARTETS

LITTLE GIDDING

I

Midwinter spring is its own season
Sempiternal though sodden towards sundown,
Suspended in time, between pole and tropic.
When the short day is brightest, with frost and fire,

The brief sun flames the ice, on pond and ditches,
In windless cold that is the heart's heat,
Reflecting in a watery mirror
A glare that is blindness in the early afternoon.
And glow more intense than blaze of branch, or brazier,
Stirs the dumb spirit: no wind, but pentecostal fire   10
In the dark time of the year. Between melting and freezing
The soul's sap quivers. There is no earth smell
Or smell of living thing. This is the spring time
But not in time's covenant. Now the hedgerow
Is blanched for an hour with transitory blossom
Of snow, a bloom more sudden
Than that of summer, neither budding nor fading,
Not in the scheme of generation.
Where is the summer, the unimaginable
Zero summer?   20
                    If you came this way,
Taking the route you would be likely to take
From the place you would be likely to come from,
If you came this way in may time, you would find the hedges
White again, in May, with voluptuary sweetness.
It would be the same at the end of the journey,
If you came at night like a broken king,
If you came by day not knowing what you came for,
It would be the same, when you leave the rough road
And turn behind the pig-sty to the dull façade
And the tombstone. And what you thought you came for   30
Is only a shell, a husk of meaning
From which the purpose breaks only when it is fulfilled
If at all. Either you had no purpose
Or the purpose is beyond the end you figured
And is altered in fulfilment. There are other places
Which also are the world's end, some at the sea jaws,
Or over a dark lake, in a desert or a city—
But this is the nearest, in place and time,
Now and in England.
                            If you came this way,
Taking any route, starting from anywhere,   40
At any time or at any season,
It would always be the same: you would have to put off
Sense and notion. You are not here to verify,
Instruct yourself, or inform curiosity

Or carry report. You are here to kneel
Where prayer has been valid. And prayer is more
Than an order of words, the conscious occupation
Of the praying mind, or the sound of the voice praying.
And what the dead had no speech for, when living,
They can tell you, being dead: the communication   50
Of the dead is tongued with fire beyond the language of the living.
Here, the intersection of the timeless moment
Is England and nowhere. Never and always.

    I I

Ash on an old man's sleeve
Is all the ash the burnt roses leave.
Dust in the air suspended
Marks the place where a story ended.
Dust inbreathed was a house—
The wall, the wainscot and the mouse.
The death of hope and despair,   60
     This is the death of air.

  There are flood and drouth
Over the eyes and in the mouth,
Dead water and dead sand
Contending for the upper hand.
The parched eviscerate soil
Gapes at the vanity of toil,
Laughs without mirth.
    This is the death of earth.

  Water and fire succeed   70
The town, the pasture and the weed.
Water and fire deride
The sacrifice that we denied.
Water and fire shall rot
The marred foundations we forgot,
Of sanctuary and choir.
  This is the death of water and fire.

  In the uncertain hour before the morning
    Near the ending of interminable night
    At the recurrent end of the unending   80

After the dark dove with the flickering tongue
   Had passed below the horizon of his homing
   While the dead leaves still rattled on like tin
Over the asphalt where no other sound was
   Between three districts whence the smoke arose
   I met one walking, loitering and hurried
As if blown towards me like the metal leaves
   Before the urban dawn wind unresisting.
   And as I fixed upon the down-turned face
That pointed scrutiny with which we challenge   90
   The first-met stranger in the waning dusk
   I caught the sudden look of some dead master
Whom I had known, forgotten, half recalled
   Both one and many; in the brown baked features
   The eyes of a familiar compound ghost
Both intimate and unidentifiable.
So I assumed a double part, and cried
And heard another's voice cry: "What! are *you* here?"
Although we were not. I was still the same,
   Knowing myself yet being someone other—   100
   And he a face still forming; yet the words sufficed
To compel the recognition they preceded.
   And so, compliant to the common wind,
   Too strange to each other for misunderstanding,
In concord at this intersection time
   Of meeting nowhere, no before and after,
   We trod the pavement in a dead patrol.
I said: "The wonder that I feel is easy,
   Yet ease is cause of wonder. Therefore speak:
   I may not comprehend, may not remember."   110
And he: "I am not eager to rehearse
   My thought and theory which you have forgotten.
   These things have served their purpose: let them be.
So with your own, and pray they be forgiven
   By others, as I pray you to forgive
   Both bad and good. Last season's fruit is eaten
And the fullfed beast shall kick the empty pail.
   For last year's words belong to last year's language
   And next year's words await another voice.
But, as the passage now presents no hindrance   120
   To the spirit unappeased and peregrine
   Between two worlds become much like each other,
So I find words I never thought to speak

In streets I never thought I should revisit
When I left my body on a distant shore.
Since our concern was speech, and speech impelled us
    To purify the dialect of the tribe
    And urge the mind to aftersight and foresight,
Let me disclose the gifts reserved for age
    To set a crown upon your lifetime's effort.   130
    First, the cold friction of expiring sense
Without enchantment, offering no promise
    But bitter tastelessness of shadow fruit
    As body and soul begin to fall asunder.
Second, the conscious impotence of rage
    At human folly, and the laceration
    Of laughter at what ceases to amuse.
And last, the rending pain of re-enactment
    Of all that you have done, and been; the shame
    Of motives late revealed, and the awareness   140
Of things ill done and done to others' harm
    Which once you took for exercise of virtue.
    Then fools' approval stings, and honour stains.
From wrong to wrong the exasperated spirit
    Proceeds, unless restored by that refining fire
    Where you must move in measure, like a dancer."
The day was breaking. In the disfigured street
    He left me, with a kind of valediction,
    And faded on the blowing of the horn.

   III

There are three conditions which often look alike   150
Yet differ completely, flourish in the same hedgerow:
Attachment to self and to things and to persons, detachment
From self and from things and from persons; and, growing between them,
    indifference
Which resembles the others as death resembles life,
Being between two lives—unflowering, between
The live and the dead nettle. This is the use of memory:
For liberation—not less of love but expanding
Of love beyond desire, and so liberation
From the future as well as the past. Thus, love of a country
Begins as attachment to our own field of action   160
And comes to find that action of little importance
Though never indifferent. History may be servitude,

History may be freedom. See, now they vanish,
The faces and places, with the self which, as it could, loved them,
To become renewed, transfigured, in another pattern.

   Sin is Behovely, but
All shall be well, and
All manner of thing shall be well.
If I think, again, of this place,
And of people, not wholly commendable, 170
Of no immediate kin or kindness,
But some of peculiar genius,
All touched by a common genius,
United in the strife which divided them;
If I think of a king at nightfall,
Of three men, and more, on the scaffold
And a few who died forgotten
In other places, here and abroad,
And of one who died blind and quiet,
Why should we celebrate 180
These dead men more than the dying?
It is not to ring the bell backward
Nor is it an incantation
To summon the spectre of a Rose.
We cannot revive old factions
We cannot restore old policies
Or follow an antique drum.
These men, and those who opposed them
And those whom they opposed
Accept the constitution of silence 190
And are folded in a single party.
Whatever we inherit from the fortunate
We have taken from the defeated
What they had to leave us—a symbol:
A symbol perfected in death.
And all shall be well and
All manner of thing shall be well
By the purification of the motive
In the ground of our beseeching.

   I V

The dove descending breaks the air 200
With flame of incandescent terror

Of which the tongues declare
The one discharge from sin and error.
The only hope, or else despair
   Lies in the choice of pyre or pyre—
   To be redeemed from fire by fire.

   Who then devised the torment? Love.
Love is the unfamiliar Name
Behind the hands that wove
The intolerable shirt of flame   210
Which human power cannot remove.
   We only live, only suspire
   Consumed by either fire or fire.

     V

What we call the beginning is often the end
And to make an end is to make a beginning.
The end is where we start from. And every phrase
And sentence that is right (where every word is at home,
Taking its place to support the others,
The word neither diffident nor ostentatious,
An easy commerce of the old and the new,   220
The common word exact without vulgarity,
The formal word precise but not pedantic,
The complete consort dancing together)
Every phrase and every sentence is an end and a beginning,
Every poem an epitaph. And any action
Is a step to the block, to the fire, down the sea's throat
Or to an illegible stone: and that is where we start.
We die with the dying:
See, they depart, and we go with them.
We are born with the dead: 230
See, they return, and bring us with them.
The moment of the rose and the moment of the yew-tree
Are of equal duration. A people without history
Is not redeemed from time, for history is a pattern
Of timeless moments. So, while the light fails
On a winter's afternoon, in a secluded chapel
History is now and England.

With the drawing of this Love and the voice of this Calling
   We shall not cease from exploration

And the end of all our exploring   240
Will be to arrive where we started
And know the place for the first time.
Through the unknown, remembered gate
When the last of earth left to discover
Is that which was the beginning;
At the source of the longest river
The voice of the hidden waterfall
And the children in the apple-tree
Not known, because not looked for
But heard, half-heard, in the stillness   250
Between two waves of the sea.
Quick now, here, now, always—
A condition of complete simplicity
(Costing not less than everything)
And all shall be well and
All manner of thing shall be well
When the tongues of flame are in-folded
Into the crowned knot of fire
And the fire and the rose are one.

Isaac Rosenberg

(1890–1918)

Born in Bristol to Russian immigrants and taken as a child to the ghetto of East London, Rosenberg studied engraving and lithography in the London County, Birkbeck, and Slade schools of art. After publishing two pamphlets of poetry and spending a year with a sister in South Africa for his health, he entered the army as a foot soldier in 1915 and was killed in action on the Somme on April 1, 1918. His poems are grittier and more vivid than those that survive from officers and noncombatants of 1914–1918.

BREAK OF DAY IN THE TRENCHES

The darkness crumbles away.
It is the same old druid Time as ever,
Only a live thing leaps my hand,
A queer sardonic rat,
As I pull the parapet's poppy
To stick behind my ear.
Droll rat, they would shoot you if they knew
Your cosmopolitan sympathies.
Now you have touched this English hand
You will do the same to a German   10
Soon, no doubt, if it be your pleasure
To cross the sleeping green between.
It seems you inwardly grin as you pass
Strong eyes, fine limbs, haughty athletes,
Less chanced than you for life,
Bonds to the whims of murder,
Sprawled in the bowels of the earth,
The torn fields of France.
What do you see in our eyes
At the shrieking iron and flame   20
Hurled through still heavens?
What quaver—what heart aghast?

763

Poppies whose roots are in man's veins
Drop, and are ever dropping;
But mine in my ear is safe—
Just a little white with the dust.

Hugh MacDiarmid

(pseudonym of Christopher Murray Grieve, 1 8 9 2 – 1 9 7 8)

Born in Langholm, Dumfriesshire, educated there and in Edinburgh, Grieve served in the Royal Army Medical Corps in 1915–1919 and worked as a shipfitter in 1941–1945. He helped found the National Party of Scotland in 1928 (from which he was expelled in 1933) and joined the Communist Party in 1934 (expelled 1938–1956, as at once too nationalist and too independent). He nevertheless accepted a Civil List pension in 1951 and an honorary LL.D. from the University of Edinburgh in 1957.

He had adopted his pseudonym in 1922, at first for poems in Scots. In his last years he wrote in a mix of Joycean polyglot and scientific English. In "Ex Vermibus," collected in *Sangschaw* (1925), superior song results from the conspiracy of a worm with the mother bird feeding her fledgling—declaring perhaps MacDiarmid's refusal to practice the mildness of Burns's imitators or of a lover's assurance to his coy mistress or of salvation through Mary's Jesus. "With the Herring Fishers" is one of the "Shetland Lyrics" in *Stony Limits and Other Poems* (1934). The lament that winter lies "heavy on my heart" appears among the lyrics in *To Circumjack Cencrastus; or, The Curly Snake* (1930).

EX VERMIBUS

Gape, gape, gorlin',
For I ha'e a worm
That'll gi'e ye a slee and sliggy sang
Wi' mony a whuram.

Syne i' the lift
Byous spatrils you'll mak',
For a gorlin' wi' worms like this in its wame
Nae airels sall lack.

But owre the tree-taps
Maun flee like a sperk,   10
Till it hes the haill o' the Heavens alunt
Frae dawin' to derk.

l. 1. gorlin' = nestling
l. 4. whuram = grace note
l. 5. Syne = Then
l. 6. Byous spatrils = Wondrous notes
l. 7. wame = belly
l. 8. airels = reed instruments
l. 11. haill = whole
l. 11. alunt = aflame

WITH THE HERRING FISHERS

"I see herrin'."—I hear the glad cry
And 'gainst the moon see ilka blue jowl
In turn as the fishermen haul on the nets
And sing: "Come, shove in your heids and growl."

"Soom on, bonnie herrin', soom on," they shout,
Or "Come in, O come in, and see me,"
"Come gie the auld man something to dae.
It'll be a braw change frae the sea."

O it's ane o' the bonniest sichts in the warld
To watch the herrin' come walkin' on board   10
In the wee sma' 'oors o' a simmer's mornin'
As if o' their ain accord.

For this is the way that God sees life,
The haill jing-bang o's appearin'
Up owre frae the edge o' naethingness
—It's his happy cries I'm hearin'.

"Left, right—O come in and see me,"
Reid and yellow and black and white
Toddlin' up into Heaven thegither
At peep o' day frae the endless night.   20

"I see herrin'," I hear his glad cry,
And 'gainst the moon see his muckle blue jowl,
As he handles buoy-tow and bush-raip
Singin': "Come, shove in your heids and growl!"

l. 2. ilka = every
l. 5. Soom = Swim

l. 14. haill jing-bang o's = whole crowd of us
l. 22. muckle = large
l. 23. bush-raip = rope attached to net

LOURD ON MY HERT

Lourd on my hert as winter lies
The state that Scotland's in the day.
Spring to the North has aye come slow
But noo dour winter's like to stay
   For guid,
   And no' for guid!

O wae's me on the weary days
When it is scarce grey licht at noon;
It maun be a' the stupid folk
Diffusin' their dullness roon and roon   10
   Like soot,
   That keeps the sunlicht oot.

Nae wonder if I think I see
A lichter shadow than the neist
I'm fain to cry: "The dawn, the dawn!
I see it brakin' in the East."
   But ah
   —It's juist mair snaw!

l. 14. neist = next
l. 18. juist mair snaw = just more snow

Wilfred Owen

(1 8 9 3 – 1 9 1 8)

Owen, of Shropshire, was strongly influenced by Keats's sensuous imagery and patterns of sound. In 1915, after three years as a tutor in English at Bordeaux, he joined the Artists' Rifles. He was hospitalized in 1917 for shellshock, awarded the Military Cross in 1918, and was killed in action a week before the Armistice. His poems were edited by Siegfried Sassoon in 1920, by Edmund Blunden in 1931, by C. Day-Lewis in 1963. His "Anthem for Doomed Youth" is reminiscent of Elizabethan sonnets. In "Dulce et Decorum Est" he mocks Horace's "old lie" that to die for one's country is sweet and proper.

ANTHEM FOR DOOMED YOUTH

What passing-bells for these who die as cattle?
  Only the monstrous anger of the guns.
  Only the stuttering rifles' rapid rattle
Can patter out their hasty orisons.
No mockeries now for them; no prayers nor bells,
  Nor any voice of mourning save the choirs,—
The shrill, demented choirs of wailing shells;
  And bugles calling for them from sad shires.

What candles may be held to speed them all?
  Not in the hands of boys, but in their eyes
Shall shine the holy glimmers of goodbyes.
  The pallor of girls' brows shall be their pall;
Their flowers the tenderness of patient minds,
And each slow dusk a drawing-down of blinds.

DULCE ET DECORUM EST

Bent double, like old beggars under sacks,
Knock-kneed, coughing like hags, we cursed through sludge,
Till on the haunting flares we turned our backs

And towards our distant rest began to trudge.
Men marched asleep. Many had lost their boots
But limped on, blood-shod. All went lame; all blind;
Drunk with fatigue; deaf even to the hoots
Of tired, outstripped Five-Nines that dropped behind.

Gas! Gas! Quick, boys!—An ecstasy of fumbling,
Fitting the clumsy helmets just in time;   10
But someone still was yelling out and stumbling
And flound'ring like a man in fire or lime . . .
Dim, through the misty panes and thick green light,
As under a green sea, I saw him drowning.
In all my dreams, before my helpless sight,
He plunges at me, guttering, choking, drowning.

If in some smothering dreams you too could pace
Behind the wagon that we flung him in,
And watch the white eyes writhing in his face,
His hanging face, like a devil's sick of sin;   20
If you could hear, at every jolt, the blood
Come gargling from the froth-corrupted lungs,
Obscene as cancer, bitter as the cud
Of vile, incurable sores on innocent tongues,—
My friend, you would not tell with such high zest
To children ardent for some desperate glory,
The old Lie: Dulce et decorum est
Pro patria mori.

Robert von Ranke Graves

(1895 – 1985)

Born in London of Irish, English, and German heritage, Graves left Charterhouse School to join the Royal Welch Fusiliers in 1914. Invalided out, he earned a B.Litt. at Oxford and subsequently held positions as lecturer or professor in institutions from Cairo to Massachusetts. After 1929, royalties from his autobiographical *Goodbye to All That* and from his Claudius novels and other prose enabled him to live comfortably, primarily on Majorca. His doctrine of the White Goddess as necessary inspiration cannot be entirely detached from his overlapping relations with his wife's rival of 1959 in "Not at Home" (included in *New Poems*, 1962) and with other women before and after 1959.

THE FACE IN THE MIRROR

Grey haunted eyes, absent-mindedly glaring
From wide, uneven orbits; one brow drooping
Somewhat over the eye
Because of a missile fragment still inhering,
Skin deep, as a foolish record of old-world fighting.

Crookedly broken nose—low tackling caused it;
Cheeks, furrowed; coarse grey hair, flying frenetic;
Forehead, wrinkled and high;
Jowls, prominent; ears, large; jaw, pugilistic;
Teeth, few; lips, full and ruddy; mouth, ascetic.   10

I pause with razor poised, scowling derision
At the mirrored man whose beard needs my attention,
And once more ask him why
He still stands ready, with a boy's presumption,
To court the queen in her high silk pavilion.

NOT AT HOME

Her house loomed at the end of a Berkshire lane,
Tall but retired. She was expecting me;

And I approached with light heart and quick tread,
Having already seen from the garden gate
How bright her knocker shone—in readiness
For my confident rap?—and the steps holystoned.
I ran the last few paces, rapped and listened
Intently for the rustle of her approach. . . .

No reply, no movement. I waited three long minutes,
Then, in surprise, went down the path again   10
To observe the chimney stacks. No smoke from either.
And the curtains: were they drawn against the sun?
Or against what, then? I glanced over a wall
At her well-tended orchard, heavy with bloom
(Easter fell late that year, Spring had come early),
And found the gardener, bent over cold frames.

"Her ladyship is not at home?"
                              "No, sir."
"She was expecting me. My name is Lion.
Did she leave a note?"
                        "No, sir, she left no note."
"I trust nothing has happened. . . ?"
                                      "No, sir, nothing. . . .   20
And yet she seemed preoccupied: we guess
Some family reason."
                      "*Has* she a family?"
"That, sir, I could not say. . . . She seemed distressed—
Not quite herself, if I may venture so."

"But she left no note?"
                        "Only a verbal message:
Her ladyship will be away some weeks
Or months, hopes to return before midsummer,
And, please, you are not to communicate.
There was something else: about the need for patience."

The sun went in, a bleak wind shook the blossom,   30
Dust flew, the windows glared in a blank row. . . .
And yet I felt, when I turned slowly away,
Her eyes boring my back, as it might be posted
Behind a curtain slit, and still in love.

Stevie Smith

(1 9 0 2 – 1 9 7 1)

Florence Margaret Smith, born in Hull, moved in 1905 to Palmers Green in
London and worked for the Newnes Publishing Company (1923–1953), living
with an aunt the quiet life depicted in the film *Stevie*. Noticed first for her
Novel on Yellow Paper (1936), she won devoted admirers by quirky, unillu-
sioned verse. The title poem in her seventh volume of verse, *Not Waving but
Drowning* (1957), has become her widely recognized signature; she attempted
suicide three months after composing it. "Away, Melancholy" was published in
the same volume. A good many of her poems are accompanied by her own,
often comic, drawings.

NOT WAVING BUT DROWNING

Nobody heard him, the dead man,
But still he lay moaning:
I was much further out than you thought
And not waving but drowning.

Poor chap, he always loved larking
And now he's dead
It must have been too cold for him his heart gave way,
They said.

Oh, no no no, it was too cold always
(Still the dead one lay moaning)   10
I was much too far out all my life
And not waving but drowning.

AWAY, MELANCHOLY

Away, melancholy,
Away with it, let it go.

Are not the trees green,
The earth as green?
Does not the wind blow,
Fire leap and the rivers flow?
Away melancholy.

The ant is busy
He carrieth his meat,
All things hurry 10
To be eaten or eat.
Away, melancholy.

Man, too, hurries,
Eats, couples, buries,
He is an animal also
With a hey ho melancholy,
Away with it, let it go.

Man of all creatures
Is superlative
(Away melancholy) 20
He of all creatures alone
Raiseth a stone
(Away melancholy)
Into the stone, the god
Pours what he knows of good
Calling, good, God.
Away melancholy, let it go.

Speak not to me of tears,
Tyranny, pox, wars,
Saying, Can God 30
Stone of man's thought, be good?

Say rather it is enough
That the stuffed
Stone of man's good, growing,
By man's called God.
Away, melancholy, let it go.

Man aspires
To good,

To love
Sighs;   40

Beaten, corrupted, dying
In his own blood lying
Yet heaves up an eye above
Cries, Love, love.
It is his virtue needs explaining,
Not his failing.

Away, melancholy,
Away with it, let it go.

Cecil Day-Lewis

(1904 – 1972)

Taken from Ireland to England in infancy, Cecil Day-Lewis was educated in London, Dorset, and Oxford. A schoolmaster for eight years, he was variously a reader and director in the London publishing world and later a university lecturer, receiving a succession of literary honors on both sides of the Atlantic. A sometime Communist, in 1958 he succeeded Masefield as Poet Laureate. The slant rhymes—for example, "glad," "beds"; "regret," "mute," in this poem from A *Time to Dance* (1935)—belong to the general Modernist revolt against the Romantics and Georgians.

POEM FOR AN ANNIVERSARY

Admit then and be glad
Our volcanic age is over.
A molten rage shook earth from head to toe,
Seas leapt from their beds,
World's bedrock boiling up, the terrible lava.
Now it is not so.

Remember, not regret
Those cloudy dreams that trod on air
How distantly reflecting fire below:
The mating in air, the mute   10
Shuddering electric storms, the foul or fair
Love was used to know.

Admire, no more afraid,
Country made for peace. Earth rent,
Rocks like prayers racked from the heart, are now
Landmarks for us and shade:
Hotfoot to havoc where the lava went,
Cooler rivers flow.

Survey what most survives—
Love's best, climate and contour fine: 20

775

We have trained the giant lightning to lie low
And drive our linked lives;
Those clouds stand not in daydream but for rain,
And earth has grain to grow.

Patrick Kavanagh

(1904–1967)

Poet of the soil and country people of Ireland, Kavanagh was a farmer and maker of shoes who began reading and writing poetry in his birthplace, Inniskeen. His first volume, *Ploughman and Other Poems,* was published in 1936. In 1939 he moved to Dublin, where he was able to earn a living as author, journalist, and editor. "Spraying the Potatoes" was included in *A Soul for Sale* (1947), a self-exploring collection that addresses the issue of failure. The two later poems make his case for the detached and ordinary rather than the ideological: the "common and banal" was preferable to an idealized, Yeatsian vision.

SPRAYING THE POTATOES

The barrels of blue potato-spray
Stood on a headland of July
Beside an orchard wall where roses
Were young girls hanging from the sky.

The flocks of green potato-stalks
Were blossoms spread for sudden flight,
The Kerr's Pinks in a frivelled blue,
The Arran Banners wearing white.

And over that potato-field
A lazy veil of woven sun.   10
Dandelions growing on headlands, showing
Their unloved hearts to everyone.

And I was there with the knapsack sprayer
On the barrel's edge poised. A wasp was floating
Dead on a sunken briar leaf
Over a copper-poisoned ocean.

The axle-roll of a rut-locked cart
Broke the burnt stick of noon in two.

An old man came through a corn field
Remembering his youth and some Ruth he knew.   20

He turned my way. "God further the work."
He echoed an ancient farming prayer.
I thanked him. He eyed the potato-drills.
He said: "You are bound to have good ones there."

We talked and our talk was a theme of kings,
A theme for strings. He hunkered down
In the shade of the orchard wall. O roses
The old man dies in the young girl's frown.

And poet lost to potato-fields,
Remembering the lime and copper smell   30
Of the spraying barrels he is not lost
Or till blossomed stalks cannot weave a spell.

EPIC

I have lived in important places, times
When great events were decided, who owned
That half a rood of rock, a no-man's land
Surrounded by our pitchfork-armed claims.
I heard the Duffys shouting "Damn your soul"
And old McCabe stripped to the waist, seen
Step the plot defying blue cast-steel—
"Here is the march along these iron stones"
That was the year of the Munich bother. Which
Was more important? I inclined
To lose my faith in Ballyrush and Gortin
Till Homer's ghost came whispering to my mind
He said: I made the Iliad from such
A local row. Gods make their own importance.

THE HOSPITAL

A year ago I fell in love with the functional ward
Of a chest hospital: square cubicles in a row

Plain concrete, wash basins—an art lover's woe,
Not counting how the fellow in the next bed snored.
But nothing whatever is by love debarred,
The common and banal her heat can know.
The corridor led to a stairway and below
Was the inexhaustible adventure of a gravelled yard.

This is what love does to things: the Rialto Bridge,
The main gate that was bent by a heavy lorry,
The seat at the back of a shed that was a suntrap.
Naming these things is the love-act and its pledge;
For we must record love's mystery without claptrap,
Snatch out of time the passionate transitory.

Sir John Betjeman

(1906–1984)

Essentially a Londoner who revered the countryside and village life and founder of the Victorian Society, Betjeman attended the Dragon School and Magdalen College in Oxford. During World War II he served in Dublin and Bath and later traversed Britain in the cause of architectural preservation. For his immense popularity as a poet and for accomplishment in the fields of publishing, radio, film, and television, he was made C.B.E. (1960), knighted (1969), and was Poet Laureate (1972 until his death). He chose for models stanzaic lyric or comic poems with a compelling, measured beat, as in "The Licorice Fields at Pontefract." His poems of religious faith and adherence to the Church of England reveal the tensions of doubt, but the anapests of "Huxley Hall," with an ironic thread of Augustinian faith, tread firmly on the complacent agnostics who honor "Darwin's bulldog," T. H. Huxley.

THE LICORICE FIELDS
AT PONTEFRACT

In the licorice fields at Pontefract
   My love and I did meet
And many a burdened licorice bush
   Was blooming round our feet;
Red hair she had and golden skin,
Her sulky lips were shaped for sin,
Her sturdy legs were flannel-slack'd,
The strongest legs in Pontefract.

The light and dangling licorice flowers
   Gave off the sweetest smells;   10
From various black Victorian towers
   The Sunday evening bells
Came pealing over dales and hills
And tanneries and silent mills
And lowly streets where country stops
And little shuttered corner shops.

She cast her blazing eyes on me
   And plucked a licorice leaf;
I was her captive slave and she
   My red-haired robber chief.   20
Oh love! for love I could not speak,
It left me winded, wilting, weak
And held in brown arms strong and bare
And wound with flaming ropes of hair.

HUXLEY HALL

In the Garden City Café with its murals on the wall
Before a talk on "Sex and Civics" I meditated on the Fall.

Deep depression settled on me under that electric glare
While outside the lightsome poplars flanked the rose-beds in the square.

While outside the carefree children sported in the summer haze
And released their inhibitions in a hundred different ways.

She who eats her greasy crumpets snugly in the inglenook
Of some birch-enshrouded homestead, dropping butter on her book

Can she know the deep depression of this bright, hygienic hell?
And her husband, stout free-thinker, can he share in it as well?   10

Not the folk-museum's charting of man's Progress out of slime
Can release me from the painful seeming accident of Time.

Barry smashes Shirley's dolly, Shirley's eyes are crossed with hate,
Comrades plot a Comrade's downfall "in the interests of the State."

Not my vegetarian dinner, not my lime-juice minus gin,
Quite can drown a faint conviction that we may be born in Sin.

Wystan Hugh Auden

(1 9 0 7 – 1 9 7 3)

Born in York, the leader at Oxford of disaffected poets, a traveler geographically and poetically, Auden left England in 1939 for the United States, where he served in the American military as a major in 1945, and where he became a citizen in 1946. After the war, he settled into an almost stable relationship with Chester Kallman (with whom he wrote opera libretti) and received various honors, editorships, and teaching appointments—as he did on occasion in England from 1956 until his death. By 1958 he had decided to omit from the elegy to Yeats the final three stanzas (printed here), which proclaimed that time would forgive Yeats for his retrograde opinions as it had forgiven Kipling and Paul Claudel.

MUSÉE DES BEAUX ARTS

About suffering they were never wrong,
The Old Masters: how well they understood
Its human position; how it takes place
While someone else is eating or opening a window or just walking dully along;
How, when the aged are reverently, passionately waiting
For the miraculous birth, there always must be
Children who did not specially want it to happen, skating
On a pond at the edge of the wood:
They never forgot
That even the dreadful martyrdom must run its course   10
Anyhow in a corner, some untidy spot
Where the dogs go on with their doggy life and the torturer's horse
Scratches its innocent behind on a tree.

In Brueghel's *Icarus*, for instance: how everything turns away
Quite leisurely from the disaster; the ploughman may
Have heard the splash, the forsaken cry,
But for him it was not an important failure; the sun shone
As it had to on the white legs disappearing into the green
Water; and the expensive delicate ship that must have seen
Something amazing, a boy falling out of the sky,   20
Had somewhere to get to and sailed calmly on.

IN MEMORY OF W. B. YEATS

(D. JANUARY 1939)

I

He disappeared in the dead of winter:
The brooks were frozen, the airports almost deserted,
And snow disfigured the public statues;
The mercury sank in the mouth of the dying day.
What instruments we have agree
The day of his death was a dark cold day.

Far from his illness
The wolves ran on through the evergreen forests,
The peasant river was untempted by the fashionable quays;
By mourning tongues   10
The death of the poet was kept from his poems.

But for him it was his last afternoon as himself,
An afternoon of nurses and rumours;
The provinces of his body revolted,
The squares of his mind were empty,
Silence invaded the suburbs,
The current of his feeling failed; he became his admirers.

Now he is scattered among a hundred cities
And wholly given over to unfamiliar affections,
To find his happiness in another kind of wood   20
And be punished under a foreign code of conscience.
The words of a dead man
Are modified in the guts of the living.

But in the importance and noise of to-morrow
When the brokers are roaring like beasts on the floor of the Bourse,
And the poor have the sufferings to which they are fairly accustomed,
And each in the cell of himself is almost convinced of his freedom,
A few thousand will think of this day
As one thinks of a day when one did something slightly unusual.

What instruments we have agree   30
The day of his death was a dark cold day.

I I

You were silly like us; your gift survived it all:
The parish of rich women, physical decay,
Yourself. Mad Ireland hurt you into poetry.
Now Ireland has her madness and her weather still,
For poetry makes nothing happen: it survives
In the valley of its making where executives
Would never want to tamper, flows on south
From ranches of isolation and the busy griefs,
Raw towns that we believe and die in; it survives,   40
A way of happening, a mouth.

I I I

Earth, receive an honoured guest:
William Yeats is laid to rest.
Let the Irish vessel lie
Emptied of its poetry.

In the nightmare of the dark
All the dogs of Europe bark,
And the living nations wait,
Each sequestered in its hate;

Intellectual disgrace   50
Stares from every human face,
And the seas of pity lie
Locked and frozen in each eye.

Follow, poet, follow right
To the bottom of the night,
With your unconstraining voice
Still persuade us to rejoice;

With the farming of a verse
Make a vineyard of the curse,
Sing of human unsuccess   60
In a rapture of distress;

In the deserts of the heart
Let the healing fountain start,

In the prison of his days
Teach the free man how to praise.

Time that is intolerant
Of the brave and innocent,
And indifferent in a week
To a beautiful physique,

Worships language and forgives,   70
Everyone by whom it lives;
Pardons cowardice, conceit,
Lays its honours at their feet.

Time that with this strange excuse
Pardoned Kipling and his views,
And will pardon Paul Claudel,
Pardons him for writing well.

Louis MacNeice

(1 9 0 7 – 1 9 6 3)

Born in Belfast, Frederick Louis MacNeice attended school and college in Dorset and Oxford. In the universities of Birmingham, London, and Cambridge and at Cornell and Sarah Lawrence College he was a lecturer in English and Greek literature. He married twice. He was a writer and producer for the British Broadcasting Corporation (1941–1961) and briefly director of the British School in Athens. "Bagpipe Music" was published in *The Earth Compels* (1938)—the year after his *Letters from Iceland*, with Auden—and looks on Ireland and on such fads as the theosophist Madame Blavatskv (who died in 1891) and perhaps even on Gaelic with an irony usually declared sardonic. Poets in perpetual "minor" limbo could well regard MacNeice's ironic elegy as rhyme royal, with each stanza deprived of its fifth line.

BAGPIPE MUSIC

It's no go the merrygoround, it's no go the rickshaw,
All we want is a limousine and a ticket for the peepshow.
Their knickers are made of crêpe-de-chine, their shoes are made of python,
Their halls are lined with tiger rugs and their walls with heads of bison.

John MacDonald found a corpse, put it under the sofa,
Waited till it came to life and hit it with a poker,
Sold its eyes for souvenirs, sold its blood for whisky,
Kept its bones for dumb-bells to use when he was fifty.

It's no go the Yogi-Man, it's no go Blavatsky,
All we want is a bank balance and a bit of skirt in a taxi.   10

Annie MacDougall went to milk, caught her foot in the heather,
Woke to hear a dance record playing of Old Vienna.
It's no go your maidenheads, it's no go your culture,
All we want is a Dunlop tyre and the devil mend the puncture.

The Laird o' Phelps spent Hogmanay declaring he was sober,
Counted his feet to prove the fact and found he had one foot over.

Mrs. Carmichael had her fifth, looked at the job with repulsion,
Said to the midwife "Take it away; I'm through with overproduction."

It's no go the gossip column, it's no go the ceilidh,
All we want is a mother's help and a sugar-stick for the baby.   20

Willie Murray cut his thumb, couldn't count the damage,
Took the hide of an Ayrshire cow and used it for a bandage.
His brother caught three hundred cran when the seas were lavish,
Threw the bleeders back in the sea and went upon the parish.

It's no go the Herring Board, it's no go the Bible,
All we want is a packet of fags when our hands are idle.

It's no go the picture palace, it's no go the stadium,
It's no go the country cot with a pot of pink geraniums,
It's no go the Government grants, it's no go the elections,
Sit on your arse for fifty years and hang your hat on a pension.   30

It's no go my honey love, it's no go my poppet;
Work your hands from day to day, the winds will blow the profit.
The glass is falling hour by hour, the glass will fall for ever,
But if you break the bloody glass you won't hold up the weather.

l. 15. Hogmanay = New Year's Eve
l. 19. ceilidh = social occasion (Gaelic, pronounced *kaley*)
l. 23. cran = official measure of herrings

ELEGY FOR MINOR POETS

Who often found their way to pleasant meadows
Or maybe once to a peak, who saw the Promised Land,
Who took the correct three strides but tripped their hurdles,
Who had some prompter they barely could understand,
Who were too happy or sad, too soon or late,
I would praise these in company with the Great;

For if not in the same way, they fingered the same language
According to their lights. For them as for us
Chance was a coryphaeus who could be either
An angel or an *ignus fatuus*.   10

Let us keep our mind open, our fingers crossed;
Some who go dancing through dark bogs are lost.

Who were lost in many ways, through comfort, lack of knowledge,
Or between women's breasts, who thought too little, too much,
Who were the world's best talkers, in tone and rhythm
Superb, yet as writers lacked a sense of touch,
So either gave up or just went on and on—
Let us salute them now their chance is gone;

And give the benefit of the doubtful summer
To those who worshipped the sky but stayed indoors   20
Bound to a desk by conscience or by the spirit's
Hayfever. From those office and study floors
Let the sun clamber on to the notebook, shine,
And fill in what they groped for between each line.

Who were too carefree or careful, who were too many
Though always few and alone, who went the pace
But ran in circles, who were lamed by fashion,
Who lived in the wrong time or the wrong place,
Who might have caught fire had only a spark occurred,
Who knew all the words but failed to achieve the Word—   30

Their ghosts are gagged, their books are library flotsam,
Some of their names—not all—we learnt in school
But, life being short, we rarely read their poems,
Mere source-books now to point or except a rule,
While those opinions which rank them high are based
On a wish to be different or on lack of taste.

In spite of and because of which, we later
Suitors to their mistress (who, unlike them, stays young)
Do right to hang on the grave of each a trophy
Such as, if solvent, he would himself have hung   40
Above himself; these debtors preclude our scorn—
Did we not underwrite them when we were born?

John Hewitt

(1907–1987)

Of John Harold Hewitt, a nonconformist Ulsterman who attended the Method-ist College and Queen's University in Belfast, it has been said that he was made native by place and climate. Allied with the Labour Party and the Left Book Club, he served as art director and art critic in Belfast and later in Coventry. Influential as promoter of Northern Irish regionalism, he achieved his widest audience with the poem "Once Alien Here" (1942), included in *No Rebel World* (1948).

ONCE ALIEN HERE

Once alien here my fathers built their house,
claimed, drained, and gave the land the shapes of use,
and for their urgent labour grudged no more
than shuffled pennies from the hoarded store
of well-rubbed words that had left their overtones
in the ripe England of the mounded downs.

The sullen Irish limping to the hills
bore with them the enchantments and the spells
that in the clans' free days hung gay and rich
on every twig of every thorny hedge,   10
and gave the rain-pocked stone a meaning past
the blurred engraving of the fibrous frost.

So, I, because of all the buried men
in Ulster clay, because of rock and glen
and mist and cloud and quality of air
as native in my thought as any here,
who now would seek a native mode to tell
our stubborn wisdom individual,
yet lacking skill in either scale of song,
the graver English, lyric Irish tongue,   20

789

must let this rich earth so enhance the blood
with steady pulse where now is plunging mood
till thought and image may, identified
find easy voice to utter each aright.

Sir Stephen Spender

(1909–1905)

Soon after entering University College, Oxford, Spender, a Londoner, won notice as one of the Marxist "Pylon poets" in the Auden circle. He had published seven volumes of poetry by 1941, the year he married a second time and joined the National Fire Service. Joint editor with Cyril Connolly of *Horizon* (1939–1941), he was co-editor of the equally influential *Encounter* (1953–1966). He was popular as visiting lecturer in a dozen universities in England and the United States but finally settled as professor at University College, London, in 1970. The Queen made him C.B.E. in 1962 and awarded him a knighthood in 1983. Few anthologists since 1933 have been able to resist his stanzas on the integrity of the "truly great," but Thom Gunn's "Lines for a Book" (see p. 818) registers dissent.

THE TRULY GREAT

I think continually of those who were truly great.
Who, from the womb, remembered the soul's history
Through corridors of light where the hours are suns,
Endless and singing. Whose lovely ambition
Was that their lips, still touched with fire,
Should tell of the Spirit, clothed from head to foot in song.
And who hoarded from the Spring branches
The desires falling across their bodies like blossoms.

What is precious is never to forget
The essential delight of the blood drawn from ageless springs   10
Breaking through rocks in worlds before our earth.
Never to deny its pleasure in the morning simple light
Nor its grave evening demand for love.
Never to allow gradually the traffic to smother
With noise and fog, the flowering of the Spirit.

Near the snow, near the sun, in the highest fields,
See how these names are fêted by the waving grass
And by the streamers of white cloud

And whispers of wind in the listening sky.
The names of those who in their lives fought for life,   20
Who wore at their hearts the fire's centre.
Born of the sun, they travelled a short while toward the sun
And left the vivid air signed with their honour.

Norman Alexander MacCaig

(1 9 1 0 –   )

Born and educated in Edinburgh, including Edinburgh University (M.A., 1932), MacCaig has been a schoolmaster, university lecturer, and a poet of distinctive voice honored particularly, but not only, in Scotland. His New Apocalyptic excesses of the 1940s are firmly rejected in "Gone Are the Days," which was published in *The World's Room* (1974) and reprinted with this wee poem on the power of a wee bird in *The Equal Skies* (1980).

BLUE TIT ON A STRING OF PEANUTS

A cubic inch of some stars
weighs a hundred tons—Blue tit,
who could measure the power
of your tiny spark of energy? Your hair-thin legs
(one north-east, one due west) support
a scrap of volcano, four inches
of hurricane: and, seeing me, you make the sound
of a grain of sawdust being sawn
by the minutest of saws.

GONE ARE THE DAYS

Impossible to call a lamb a lambkin
or say eftsoons or spell you ladye.
My shining armour bleeds when it's scratched;
I blow the nose that's part of my visor.

When I go pricking o'er the plain
I say *Eightpence please* to the sad conductress.
The towering landscape you live in has printed
on its portcullis *Bed and breakfast*.

I don't regret it. There are wildernesses
enough in Rose Street or the Grassmarket   10
where dragons' breaths are methylated
and social workers trap the unwary.

So don't expect me, lady with no e,
to look at a lamb and feel lambkin
or give me a down look because I bought
my greaves and cuisses at Marks and Spencers.

Pishtushery's out. But oh, how my heart swells
to see you perched, perjink, on a bar stool.
And though epics are shrunk to epigrams, let me
buy a love potion, a gin, a double.   20

Ronald Stuart Thomas

(1913–   )

Born in Cardiff, a student in classics at the University College of North Wales and of theology at St. Michael's College, Llandaff, Thomas has served the Church (and farmers) as vicar, rector, and questioning poet in a succession of parishes in Wales. He is a poet celebrated both for remarkable use of metaphor and for his evocation of the rough Welsh landscape. "Pisces" is from *Song at the Year's Turning* (1955), "Centuries" from *Later Poems* (1983).

PISCES

Who said to the trout,
You shall die on Good Friday
To be food for a man
And his pretty lady?

It was I, said God,
Who formed the roses
In the delicate flesh
And the tooth that bruises.

CENTURIES

The fifteenth passes with drums and in armour;
the monk watches it through the mind's grating.

The sixteenth puts on its cap and bells
to poach vocabulary from a king's laughter.

The seventeenth wears a collar of lace
at its neck, the flesh running from thought's candle.

The eighteenth has a high fever and hot blood,
but clears its nostrils with the snuff of wit.

The nineteenth emerges from history's cave
rubbing its eyes at the glass prospect.

The twentieth is what it looked forward to
beating its wings at windows that are not there.

Dylan Thomas

(1914–1953)

Born in Glamorganshire, Wales, Dylan Marlais Thomas edited the school magazine in Swansea Grammar School, from which he graduated in 1931 into journalism, filmwriting, and notably as a compelling, mellifluous voice on radio and recordings. He made several reading-talking-tippling tours in the United States, where he died. His pantheistic homage to "the force that . . . drives" was included in his first volume, *18 Poems* (1934); "Fern Hill" came at the peak of his powers in *Deaths and Entrances* (1946). His villanelle of 1951 (five laced tercets ending in a quatrain) protests against the death stalking his father.

THE FORCE THAT THROUGH THE GREEN FUSE DRIVES THE FLOWER

The force that through the green fuse drives the flower
Drives my green age; that blasts the roots of trees
Is my destroyer.
And I am dumb to tell the crooked rose
My youth is bent by the same wintry fever.

The force that drives the water through the rocks
Drives my red blood; that dries the mouthing streams
Turns mine to wax.
And I am dumb to mouth unto my veins
How at the mountain spring the same mouth sucks.

The hand that whirls the water in the pool
Stirs the quicksand; that ropes the blowing wind
Hauls my shroud sail.
And I am dumb to tell the hanging man
How of my clay is made the hangman's lime.

The lips of time leech to the fountain head;
Love drips and gathers, but the fallen blood

Shall calm her sores.
And I am dumb to tell a weather's wind
How time has ticked a heaven round the stars.   20

And I am dumb to tell the lover's tomb
How at my sheet goes the same crooked worm.

FERN HILL

Now as I was young and easy under the apple boughs
About the lilting house and happy as the grass was green,
        The night above the dingle starry,
            Time let me hail and climb
        Golden in the heydays of his eyes,
And honoured among wagons I was prince of the apple towns
And once below a time I lordly had the trees and leaves
            Trail with daisies and barley
        Down the rivers of the windfall light.

And as I was green and carefree, famous among the barns   10
About the happy yard and singing as the farm was home,
        In the sun that is young once only,
            Time let me play and be
        Golden in the mercy of his means,
And green and golden I was huntsman and herdsman, the calves
Sang to my horn, the foxes on the hills barked clear and cold,
            And the sabbath rang slowly
        In the pebbles of the holy streams.

All the sun long it was running, it was lovely, the hay
Fields high as the house, the tunes from the chimneys, it was air   20
        And playing, lovely and watery
            And fire green as grass.
        And nightly under the simple stars
As I rode to sleep the owls were bearing the farm away,
All the moon long I heard, blessed among stables, the night-jars
        Flying with the ricks, and the horses
            Flashing into the dark.

And then to awake, and the farm, like a wanderer white
With the dew, come back, the cock on his shoulder: it was all
        Shining, it was Adam and maiden,   30

The sky gathered again
And the sun grew round that very day.
So it must have been after the birth of the simple light
In the first, spinning place, the spellbound horses walking warm
    Out of the whinnying green stable
        On to the fields of praise.

And honoured among foxes and pheasants by the gay house
Under the new made clouds and happy as the heart was long,
    In the sun born over and over,
        I ran my heedless ways,   40
    My wishes raced through the house high hay
And nothing I cared, at my sky blue trades, that time allows
In all his tuneful turning so few and such morning songs
    Before the children green and golden
        Follow him out of grace,

Nothing I cared, in the lamb white days, that time would take me
Up to the swallow thronged loft by the shadow of my hand,
    In the moon that is always rising,
        Nor that riding to sleep
    I should hear him fly with the high fields   50
And wake to the farm forever fled from the childless land.
Oh as I was young and easy in the mercy of his means,
        Time held me green and dying
    Though I sang in my chains like the sea.

DO NOT GO GENTLE INTO THAT
GOOD NIGHT

Do not go gentle into that good night,
Old age should burn and rave at close of day;
Rage, rage against the dying of the light.

Though wise men at their end know dark is right,
Because their words had forked no lightning they
Do not go gentle into that good night.

Good men, the last wave by, crying how bright
Their frail deeds might have danced in a green bay,
Rage, rage against the dying of the light.

Wild men who caught and sang the sun in flight,   10
And learn, too late, they grieved it on its way,
Do not go gentle into that good night.

Grave men, near death, who see with blinding sight
Blind eyes could blaze like meteors and be gay,
Rage, rage against the dying of the light.

And you, my father, there on the sad height,
Curse, bless, me now with your fierce tears, I pray.
Do not go gentle into that good night.
Rage, rage against the dying of the light.

Donald Davie

(1 9 2 2 –)

Born in Yorkshire, holder of B.A., M.A., and Ph.D. from Cambridge, professor of English and humanities in universities of Britain and in the United States, Donald Alfred Davie has been, as both poet and critic, a strong, continuing influence on other writers. He quotes Coleridge and Donne with authority in "Rejoinder to a Critic" (1955). His poems printed here propound principles he had formed as a leader in the anti-Romantic "Movement" of the 1950s.

REJOINDER TO A CRITIC

You may be right: "How can I dare to feel?"
May be the only question I can pose,
"And haply by abstruse research to steal
From my own nature all the natural man"
My sole resource. And I do not suppose
That others may not have a better plan.

And yet I'll quote again, and gloss it too
(You know by now my liking for collage):
Donne could be daring, but he never knew,
When he inquired, "Who's injured by my love?"   10
Love's radio-active fall-out on a large
Expanse around the point it bursts above.

"Alas, alas, who's injured by my love?"
And recent history answers: Half Japan!
Not love, but hate? Well, both are versions of
The "feeling" that you dare me to . . . Be dumb!
Appear concerned only to make it scan!
How dare we now be anything but numb?

ACROSS THE BAY

A queer thing about those waters: there are no
Birds there, or hardly any.
I did not miss them, I do not remember
Missing them, or thinking it uncanny.

The beach so-called was a blinding splinter of limestone,
A quarry outraged by hulls.
We took pleasure in that: the emptiness, the hardness
Of the light, the silence, and the water's stillness.

But this was the setting for one of our murderous scenes.
This hurt, and goes on hurting: 10
The venomous soft jelly, the undersides.
We could stand the world if it were hard all over.

Philip Larkin

(1922 – 1985)

Born and resident in Coventry until he entered St. John's College, Oxford (M.A. 1947), Philip Arthur Larkin was honored both as poet and as a college librarian (1955–1985) who increased sevenfold the volumes and staff of the Hull University library. He made clear his early rejection of Eliot and his desertion of Yeats in favor of Hardy as model. "Church Going" (1954) and "Next, Please" (1951) have gained both popularity and also acceptance by academic critics. "Aubade" (1977) shows that he could also gaze unflinchingly without the sense of superiority evident in some of his best-known writing.

CHURCH GOING

Once I am sure there's nothing going on
I step inside, letting the door thud shut.
Another church: matting, seats, and stone,
And little books; sprawlings of flowers, cut
For Sunday, brownish now; some brass and stuff
Up at the holy end; the small neat organ;
And a tense, musty, unignorable silence,
Brewed God knows how long. Hatless, I take off
My cycle-clips in awkward reverence,

Move forward, run my hand around the font.   10
From where I stand, the roof looks almost new—
Cleaned, or restored? Someone would know: I don't.
Mounting the lectern, I peruse a few
Hectoring large-scale verses, and pronounce
"Here endeth" much more loudly than I'd meant.
The echoes snigger briefly. Back at the door
I sign the book, donate an Irish sixpence,
Reflect the place was not worth stopping for.

Yet stop I did: in fact I often do,
And always end much at a loss like this,   20
Wondering what to look for; wondering, too,

When churches fall completely out of use
What we shall turn them into, if we shall keep
A few cathedrals chronically on show,
Their parchment, plate and pyx in locked cases,
And let the rest rent-free to rain and sheep.
Shall we avoid them as unlucky places?

Or, after dark, will dubious women come
To make their children touch a particular stone;
Pick simples for a cancer; or on some   30
Advised night see walking a dead one?
Power of some sort or other will go on
In games, in riddles, seemingly at random;
But superstition, like belief, must die,
And what remains when disbelief has gone?
Grass, weedy pavement, brambles, buttress, sky,

A shape less recognisable each week,
A purpose more obscure. I wonder who
Will be the last, the very last, to seek
This place for what it was; one of the crew   40
That tap and jot and know what rood-lofts were?
Some ruin-bibber, randy for antique,
Or Christmas-addict, counting on a whiff
Of gown-and-bands and organ-pipes and myrrh?
Or will he be my representative,

Bored, uninformed, knowing the ghostly silt
Dispersed, yet tending to this cross of ground
Through suburb scrub because it held unspilt
So long and equably what since is found
Only in separation—marriage, and birth,   50
And death, and thoughts of these—for which was built
This special shell? For, though I've no idea
What this accoutred frowsty barn is worth,
It pleases me to stand in silence here;

A serious house on serious earth it is,
In whose blent air all our compulsions meet,
Are recognised, and robed as destinies.
And that much never can be obsolete,
Since someone will forever be surprising

A hunger in himself to be more serious,   60
And gravitating with it to this ground,
Which, he once heard, was proper to grow wise in,
If only that so many dead lie round.

NEXT, PLEASE

Always too eager for the future, we
Pick up bad habits of expectancy.
Something is always approaching; every day
Till then we say,

Watching from a bluff the tiny, clear,
Sparkling armada of promises draw near.
How slow they are! And how much time they waste,
Refusing to make haste!

Yet still they leave us holding wretched stalks
Of disappointment, for, though nothing balks   10
Each big approach, leaning with brasswork prinked,
Each rope distinct,

Flagged, and the figurehead with golden tits
Arching our way, it never anchors; it's
No sooner present than it turns to past.
Right to the last

We think each one will heave to and unload
All good into our lives, all we are owed
For waiting so devoutly and so long.
But we are wrong: 20

Only one ship is seeking us, a black-
Sailed unfamiliar, towing at her back
A huge and birdless silence. In her wake
No waters breed or break.

AUBADE

I work all day, and get half-drunk at night.
Waking at four to soundless dark, I stare.
In time the curtain-edges will grow light.
Till then I see what's really always there:
Unresting death, a whole day nearer now,
Making all thought impossible but how
And where and when I shall myself die.
Arid interrogation: yet the dread
Of dying, and being dead,
Flashes afresh to hold and horrify.   10

The mind blanks at the glare. Not in remorse
—The good not done, the love not given, time
Torn off unused—nor wretchedly because
An only life can take so long to climb
Clear of its wrong beginnings, and may never;
But at the total emptiness for ever,
The sure extinction that we travel to
And shall be lost in always. Not to be here,
Not to be anywhere,
And soon; nothing more terrible, nothing more true.   20

This is a special way of being afraid
No trick dispels. Religion used to try,
That vast moth-eaten musical brocade
Created to pretend we never die,
And specious stuff that says *No rational being*
Can fear a thing it will not feel, not seeing
That this is what we fear—no sight, no sound,
No touch or taste or smell, nothing to think with,
Nothing to love or link with,
The anaesthetic from which none come round.   30

And so it stays just on the edge of vision,
A small unfocused blur, a standing chill
That slows each impulse down to indecision.
Most things may never happen: this one will,
And realisation of it rages out
In furnace-fear when we are caught without
People or drink. Courage is no good:

It means not scaring others. Being brave
Lets no one off the grave.
Death is no different whined at than withstood.   40

Slowly light strengthens, and the room takes shape.
It stands plain as a wardrobe, what we know,
Have always known, know that we can't escape,
Yet can't accept. One side will have to go.
Meanwhile telephones crouch, getting ready to ring
In locked-up offices, and all the uncaring
Intricate rented world begins to rouse.
The sky is white as clay, with no sun.
Work has to be done.
Postmen like doctors go from house to house.   50

Patricia Beer

(1924 –   )

Born in Devon, Patricia Beer was educated at home by her mother (a member of the Plymouth Brethren) and subsequently at grammar school before attending Exeter, London, and Oxford universities. She has enjoyed success as poet, novelist, lecturer, and autobiographer; she recounts the events of her rich life in the autobiographical *Mrs. Beer's House* (1968). A recurring if not obsessive concern in her poetry is death. Much of her published verse (including "Jane Austen") is also concerned with literary or mythic figures. "Lemmings" appears in *Just Like the Resurrection* (1967).

LEMMINGS

Lemmings die every year. Over the cliff
They pour, hot blood into cold sea,
So that you half imagine steam
Will rise. They do not part company
At first, but spread out, a brown team
Like seaweed, undulant and tough.

Light changes, and the wind may veer
As they swim out and on. The sea
May become sleek or shrewish. Foam
May blind them or may let them see   10
The wet horizon. It takes time.
They do not die within an hour.

One by one they leave the air
And drown as individuals.
From minute to minute they blink out
Like aeroplanes or stars or gulls
Whose vanishing is never caught.
All in time will disappear.

And though their vitality
Does not look morbid enough   20

People call it suicide
Which it has some appearance of.
But it may well be that the mood
In which each year these lemmings die

Is nothing worse than restlessness,
The need to change and nothing else.
They have learnt this piece of strand
So thoroughly it now seems false.
They jump, thinking there is land
Beyond them, as indeed there is.   30

JANE AUSTEN

Beautiful in the foregone drawing-room and the dance
The figures of the sum interweave to their answer.
Candles may genuflect, but the exploring wind
Must not unfurl the scrolls of chair and pillar,
Nor, duelling with the trees, transfix
The vulnerable shadow of the sundial.
The road is very short; she does not seek
What lies beyond the bend of the spirit,
What stirs under the feet of lovers.
It is not the bitter roots of grass that pulse   10
Into these fragrant blades, nor the fire at the world's heart
That belches into nosegays above the soil.
The hunting waves throw back their rounded heads,
Curl their bright lips and come no further.
She feels no salt on her mouth nor any taste of how
Canute walked free on the painful beach
After his failure to keep back the sea.

Charles Tomlinson

(*1 9 2 7 –*)

Alfred Charles Tomlinson, born in Stoke-on-Trent, a student of Donald Davie at Cambridge, has sought clean lines both as artist and as poet. William Carlos Williams influenced the form of the poems here that counterpose different encounters during residence in the United States—the first from *The Way of the World* (1969), the second from *American Scenes* (1966). Tomlinson has been a professor of English at the University of Bristol, has translated Spanish-American writers into English, and has collaborated on a sonnet sequence with Octavio Paz titled *Airborn / Hijos del Aire* (1981).

A WORD IN EDGEWAYS

Tell me about yourself they
say and you begin to
tell them about yourself and
that is just the way I
am is their reply: they play
it all back to you in another
key, their key, and then in mid-
narrative they pay you a
compliment as if to say what a good
listener you are I am   10
a good listener my stay
here has developed my faculty I will
say that for me I will not
say that every literate male in
America is a soliloquist, a
ventriloquist, a strategic
egotist, an inveterate
campaigner-explainer over and
back again on the terrain of him-
self—what I will   20
say is they are not un-
interesting: they are simply

unreciprocal and yes it was a
pleasure if not an unmitigated
pleasure and I yes I did enjoy our
conversation goodnightthankyou

A DEATH IN THE DESERT

In Memory of Homer Vance

There are no crosses
on the Hopi graves. They lie
shallowly
under a scattering
of small boulders. The sky
over the desert
with its sand-grain stars
and the immense equality

between
desert and desert sky,   10
seem
a scope and ritual
enough to stem
death and to be its equal.

"Homer
is the name," said
the old Hopi doll-maker.
I met him in summer. He was dead
when I came back that autumn.

He had sat   20
like an Olympian
in his cool room
on the rock-roof of the world,
beyond the snatch
of circumstance
and was to die
beating a burro out of his corn-patch.

"That,"
said his neighbour

"was a week ago." And the week   30
that lay
uncrossably between us
stretched into sand,
into the spread
of the endless
waterless sea-bed beneath
whose space outpacing sight
receded as speechless and as wide as death.

Thomas Kinsella

(1928–   )

Born and educated in Dublin, and a civil servant there until 1965, Kinsella has latterly divided his time between university posts in the United States and residence in Ireland. Among various Irish cultural activities, he has been a director of the Dolmen and Cuala publishing houses and founder of another, Peppercanister. Density of image and complexity of syntax as well as a strong debt to such non-Irish influences as Auden, Eliot, and Pound have distinguished some forty volumes of his poetry. His poems written after 1970 have turned more and more toward origin and myth. "Another September" is the title poem in a highly regarded collection of 1958.

ANOTHER SEPTEMBER

Dreams fled away, this country bedroom, raw
With the touch of the dawn, wrapped in a minor peace,
Hears through an open window the garden draw
Long pitch black breaths, lay bare its apple trees,
Ripe pear trees, brambles, windfall-sweetened soil,
Exhale rough sweetness against the starry slates.
Nearer the river sleeps St. John's, all toil
Locked fast inside a dream with iron gates.

Domestic Autumn, like an animal
Long used to handling by those countrymen,   10
Rubs her kind hide against the bedroom wall
Sensing a fragrant child come back again
—Not this half-tolerated consciousness,
Its own cold season never done,
But that unspeaking daughter, growing less
Familiar where we fell asleep as one.

Wakeful moth-wings blunder near a chair,
Toss their light shell at the glass, and go
To inhabit the living starlight. Stranded hair
Stirs on the still linen. It is as though   20

The black breathing that billows her sleep, her name,
Drugged under judgment, waned and—bearing daggers
And balances—down the lampless darkness they came,
Moving like women: Justice, Truth, such figures.

John Patrick Montague

(1 9 2 9 –   )

Although born in Brooklyn (his father had to leave Ulster in 1925 because of his republican activities), John Montague's education and life have been tilted toward Ireland, and his poetry toward the County Tyrone of his childhood (he was educated at St. Patrick's College, Armagh, before attending University College, Dublin). Montague, who has traveled extensively and lived abroad for many years (especially in the United States and in France), has settled principally in Cork. He has published over a score of volumes of poetry and short stories that explore both autobiographical and Irish concerns.

WILD SPORTS OF THE WEST

The landlord's coat is tulip red,
A beacon on the wine-dark moor;
He turns his well-bred foreign devil's face,
While his bailiff trots before.

His furious hooves drum fire from stone,
A beautiful sight when gone;
Contemplation holds the noble horseman
In his high mould of bone.

Not so beautiful the bandy bailiff,
Churlish servant of an alien will: 10
Behind the hedge a maddened peasant
Poises his shotgun for the kill.

Evening brings the huntsman home,
Blood of pheasants in a bag:
Beside a turfrick the cackling peasant
Cleanses his ancient weapon with a rag.

The fox, evicted from the thicket,
Evades with grace the snuffling hounds:
But a transplanted bailiff, in a feudal paradise,
Patrols for God His private grounds.   20

Thom Gunn

(1 9 2 9 –   )

Born in Kent, Thomson William Gunn was educated in London and Cambridge and as a writing fellow at Stanford University. *Fighting Terms,* his remarkable first collection of verse, was published in 1954, a year after he was graduated from Cambridge. He has lived in London, Paris, New York, San Antonio, Los Angeles, and primarily in San Francisco, where he settled in the 1960s. He also taught at the University of California but resigned full-time tenure in 1966 to focus on his poetry.

The speaker of "Moly" has dreamed he was among Odysseus' sailors, turned by Circe into pigs and searching for the magical redemptive moly. More aggressively, "Lines for a Book" retaliates Spender's best-known poem (see p. 791). In *The Man with Night Sweats* (1992), the title poem confronts the struggles facing gay men in an age of AIDS; the volume offers a series of elegies for "friends who died before their time."

MOLY

Nightmare of beasthood, snorting, how to wake.
I woke. What beasthood skin she made me take?

Leathery toad that ruts for days on end,
Or cringing dribbling dog, man's servile friend,

Or cat that prettily pounces on its meat,
Tortures it hours, then does not care to eat:

Parrot, moth, shark, wolf, crocodile, ass, flea.
What germs, what jostling mobs there were in me.

These seem like bristles, and the hide is tough.
No claw or web here: each foot ends in hoof.   10

Into what bulk has method disappeared?
Like ham, streaked. I am gross—gray, gross, flap-eared.

817

The pale-lashed eyes my only human feature.
My teeth tear, tear. I am the snouted creature

That bites through anything, root, wire, or can.
If I was not afraid I'd eat a man.

Oh a man's flesh already is in mine.
Hand and foot poised for risk. Buried in swine.

    I root and root, you think that it is greed,
It is, but I seek out a plant I need.   20

Direct me, gods, whose changes are all holy,
To where it flickers deep in grass, the moly:

Cool flesh of magic in each leaf and shoot,
From milky flower to the black forked root.

From this fat dungeon I could rise to skin
And human title, putting pig within.

I push my big gray wet snout through the green,
Dreaming the flower I have never seen.

LINES FOR A BOOK

I think of all the toughs through history
And thank heaven they lived, continually.
I praise the overdogs from Alexander
To those who would not play with Stephen Spender.
Their pride exalted some, some overthrew,
But was not vanity at last: they knew
That though the mind has also got a place
It's not in marvelling at its mirrored face
And evident sensibility. It's better
To go and see your friend than write a letter;   10
To be a soldier than to be a cripple;
To take an early weaning from the nipple
Than think your mother is the only girl;
To be insensitive, to steel the will,
Than sit irresolute all day at stool

Inside the heart; and to despise the fool,
Who may not help himself and may not choose,
Than give him pity which he cannot use.
I think of those exclusive by their action,
For whom mere thought could be no satisfaction—   20
The athletes lying under tons of dirt
Or standing gelded so they cannot hurt
The pale curators and the families
By calling up disturbing images.
I think of all the toughs through history
And thank heaven they lived, continually.

THE MAN WITH NIGHT SWEATS

I wake up cold, I who
Prospered through dreams of heat
Wake to their residue,
Sweat, and a clinging sheet.

My flesh was its own shield:
Where it was gashed, it healed.

I grew as I explored
The body I could trust
Even while I adored
The risk that made robust,   10

A world of wonders in
Each challenge to the skin.

I cannot but be sorry
The given shield was cracked,
My mind reduced to hurry,
My flesh reduced and wrecked.

I have to change the bed,
But catch myself instead

Stopped upright where I am
Hugging my body to me   20

As if to shield it from
The pains that will go through me,

As if hands were enough
To hold an avalanche off.

Ted Hughes

(1 9 3 0 –   )

Edward James Hughes was born in western Yorkshire, studied archeology and anthropology at Cambridge, served in the Royal Air Force, and was married to Sylvia Plath from 1956 until her death in 1963. After various odd jobs, he taught in the United States (1957–1959), married Carol Orchard (1970), was awarded the O.B.E. (1977), and was named Poet Laureate in 1984. Among his more than one hundred published volumes are poems and plays for children. "A Modest Proposal" appeared in his first book, *The Hawk in the Rain* (1957), which rejected the urbanity of the reigning Movement. "To Paint a Water Lily" appeared in *Lupercal* (1960); "A Childish Prank" comes from *Crow* (1971), based upon Native American legends of the trickster; "Moon-Hops" comes from *The Earth-Owl and Other Moon People* (1963), one of Hughes's several volumes for children.

A MODEST PROPOSAL

There is no better way to know us
Than as two wolves, come separately to a wood.
Now neither's able to sleep—even at a distance
Distracted by the soft competing pulse
Of the other; nor able to hunt—at every step
Looking backwards and sideways, warying to listen
For the other's slavering rush. Neither can make die
The painful burning of the coal in its heart
Till the other's body and the whole wood is its own.
Then it might sob contentment toward the moon.   10

Each in a thicket, rage hoarse in its labouring
Chest after a skirmish, licks the rents in its hide,
Eyes brighter than is natural under the leaves
(Where the wren, peeping round a leaf, shrieks out
To see a chink so terrifyingly open
Onto the red smelting of hatred) as each
Pictures a mad final satisfaction.

Suddenly they duck and peer.
                      And there rides by
The great lord from hunting. His embroidered
Cloak floats, the tail of his horse pours,   20
And at his stirrup the two great-eyed greyhounds
That day after day bring down the towering stag
Leap like one, making delighted sounds.

TO PAINT A WATER LILY

A green level of lily leaves
Roofs the pond's chamber and paves

The flies' furious arena: study
These, the two minds of this lady.

First observe the air's dragonfly
That eats meat, that bullets by

Or stands in space to take aim;
Others as dangerous comb the hum

Under the trees. There are battle-shouts
And death-cries everywhere hereabouts   10

But inaudible, so the eyes praise
To see the colours of these flies

Rainbow their arcs, spark, or settle
Cooling like beads of molten metal

Through the spectrum. Think what worse
Is the pond-bed's matter of course;

Prehistoric bedragonned times
Crawl that darkness with Latin names,

Have evolved no improvements there,
Jaws for heads, the set stare,   20

Ignorant of age as of hour—
Now paint the long-necked lily-flower

Which, deep in both worlds, can be still
As a painting, trembling hardly at all

Though the dragonfly alight,
Whatever horror nudge her root.

MOON-HOPS

Hops are a menace on the moon, a nuisance crop.
From hilltop to hilltop they hop hopelessly without stop.
Nobody knows what they want to find, they just go on till they drop,
Clip-clop at first, then flip-flop, then slip-slop, till finally they droopily drop
    and all their pods pop.

A CHILDISH PRANK

Man's and woman's bodies lay without souls,
Dully gaping, foolishly staring, inert
On the flowers of Eden.
God pondered.

The problem was so great, it dragged him asleep.

Crow laughed.
He bit the Worm, God's only son,
Into two writhing halves.

He stuffed into man the tail half
With the wounded end hanging out.   10

He stuffed the head half headfirst into woman
And it crept in deeper and up
To peer out through her eyes
Calling its tail-half to join up quickly, quickly
Because O it was painful.

Man awoke being dragged across the grass.
Woman awoke to see him coming.
Neither knew what had happened.

God went on sleeping.

Crow went on laughing.   20

Geoffrey Hill

(1 9 3 2 –   )

Born in Worcestershire, B.A. and M.A. from Keble College, Oxford, lecturer or professor in several universities, including Leeds, Cambridge, and Ibadan, Nigeria (1967), Hill became University Professor at Boston University in 1988. With characteristic revulsion to the brutality of historic event, the "Requiem," in *For the Unfallen* (1959), contemplates both the bloodthirsty Angevin kings who ruled on both sides of the English Channel and the attendant duplicity of language ("They lie; they lie"). "Ovid in the Third Reich" (the first poem in *King Log*, 1968) concerns at one level Ovid, amatory poet and exile who declares in the epigraph that "she only is disgraced who professes her guilt." This Ovid is reborn in the revelation of aesthetic failure to confront fully the Holocaust.

REQUIEM FOR THE PLANTAGENET KINGS

For whom the possessed sea littered, on both shores,
Ruinous arms; being fired, and for good,
To sound the constitution of just wars,
Men, in their eloquent fashion, understood.

Relieved of soul, the dropping-back of dust,
Their usage, pride, admitted within doors;
At home, under caved chantries, set in trust,
With well-dressed alabaster and proved spurs
They lie; they lie; secure in the decay
Of blood, blood-marks, crowns hacked and coveted,
Before the scouring fires of trial-day
Alight on men; before sleeked groin, gored head,
Budge through the clay and gravel, and the sea
Across daubed rock evacuates its dead.

OVID IN THE THIRD REICH

Non peccat, quaecumque potest peccasse negare,
solaque famosam culpa professa facit.

(Amores, III, xiv)

I love my work and my children. God
Is distant, difficult. Things happen.
Too near the ancient troughs of blood
Innocence is no earthly weapon.

I have learned one thing: not to look down
So much upon the damned. They, in their sphere,
Harmonize strangely with the divine
Love. I, in mine, celebrate the love-choir.

Tony Harrison

(1937–   )

Born into a working-class family in Leeds, Harrison won a fellowship to the prestigious Leeds Grammar School, after which he attended Leeds University. Harrison subsequently lived and worked abroad—for much of the next two decades in Nigeria, Czechoslovakia, North and South America, and elsewhere. He has long been active in translation and has produced drama from Greek and French as well as the medieval York mystery plays and opera.

The sardonic "On Not Being Milton," written in the sixteen-line-sonnet form developed by George Meredith in *Modern Love* (1862), was composed after Harrison returned from a conference on colonialism in Tanzania and explores the effects of capitalism on the working people of his native north of England. The Luddites here are both those who smashed new labor-saving machinery in the years just before would-be assassins met in Cato Street (1820) and also all residents of Leeds. The French in line 3 applies also to "Study"—a "memorial of returning to the place of birth."

ON NOT BEING MILTON

Read and committed to the flames, I call
these sixteen lines that go back to my roots
my *Cahier d'un retour au pays natal,*
my growing black enough to fit my boots.

The stutter of the scold out of the branks
of condescension, class and counter-class
thickens with glottals to a lumpen mass
of Ludding morphemes closing up their ranks.
Each swung cast-iron Enoch of Leeds stress
clangs a forged music on the frames of Art,   10
the looms of owned language smashed apart!

Three cheers for mute ingloriousness!

Articulation is the tongue-tied's fighting.
In the silence round all poetry we quote
Tidd the Cato Street conspirator who wrote:

Sir, I Ham a very Bad Hand at Righting.

STUDY

Best clock. Best carpet. Best three chairs.

For deaths, for Christmases, a houseless aunt,
for those too old or sick to manage stairs.

I try to whistle in it but I can't.

Uncle Joe came here to die. His gaping jaws
once plugged in to the power of his stammer
patterned the stuck plosive without pause
like a d-d-damascener's hammer.

Mi aunty's baby still. The dumbstruck mother.
The mirror, tortoise-shell-like celluloid
held to it, passed from one hand to another.
No babble, blubber, breath. The glass won't cloud.

The best clock's only wound for layings out
so the stillness isn't tapped at by its ticks.
The settee's shapeless underneath its shroud.

My mind moves upon silence and *Aeneid* VI.

Ellie McDonald

(1 9 3 7 –   )

Of recent poets employing Scots, McDonald has profited from MacDiarmid's innovations without abandoning the tradition of sentiment from Burns. She lives and works in Dundee. "Itherness" was included in the anthology *Twenty of the Best* (1990). Her *Gangen Fuit* was published in Edinburgh in 1991.

ITHERNESS

Cauld, grey waater heaves on the neap tide,
sweir as the sun i the north east.
Aince, faur back, bairnlik
I wad hae loupt heid first intilt,
had ithers, kennan mair nor me,
no biggit dykes tae haud me siccar.

They fand me a buckie shell
an held it tae my lug.
I saw their een tak pleisur frae my joy,
but Calvin wadnae lat them cry its name,   10
not lat them hear abuin the toun's stramash
the benmaist raxins o the hert.

Yet aye the soun is i my heid.
Ayont kirk bells an carnivals,
hures an guisers, pouder an pent,
ayont the hale stramash
lik a Bach Chorale
sings my stane kist.

Tuim faces at the gless
watch fur the sailor boys   20
skailin frae the boats.
Gang tune the fiddle an licht the lamp,

fur there's maiks fur the guiser
an maiks fur the hure.

Out by, the sea's roar fills the nicht.
Listen, will ye.

l.   2. sweir = unwilling
l.   5. kennan = knowing
l.   6. biggit = builded
l.   6. siccar = sure
l. 11. stramash = row
l. 12. benmaist = innermost
l. 12. raxins = outstretchings
l. 15. guisers = mummers; masqueraders
l. 18. kist = chest
l. 21. skailin = scattering
l. 23. maiks = coppers

Seamus Heaney

(1939–   )

Born in Castledawson raised on a farm in Northern Ireland, and educated at Queen's University, Belfast, Heaney began publishing his influential and widely admired poetry in the 1960s. He also taught at Belfast, Dublin, and (from a home in Ireland) Harvard and Oxford. Heaney has helped draw attention to the problems inherent in locating Northern Irish—and even Irish—identity under the rubric of British. Presented with cultural and political complexity from his early years (in which he studied the Gaelic literature of Ireland as well as English literature), Heaney grew up thinking of himself as Irish in a province that insisted he was British. "Follower" appeared in his early collection, *Death of a Naturalist* (1966), "A New Song" and "The Tollund Man" in *Wintering Out* (1972), and "From the Frontier of Writing" in *The Haw Lantern* (1987).

FOLLOWER

My father worked with a horse-plough,
His shoulders globed like a full sail strung
Between the shafts and the furrow.
The horses strained at his clicking tongue.

An expert. He would set the wing
And fit the bright steel-pointed sock.
The sod rolled over without breaking.
At the headrig, with a single pluck

Of reins, the sweating team turned round
And back into the land. His eye   10
Narrowed and angled at the ground,
Mapping the furrow exactly.

I stumbled in his hobnailed wake,
Fell sometimes on the polished sod;
Sometimes he rode me on his back
Dipping and rising to his plod.

I wanted to grow up and plough,
To close one eye, stiffen my arm.
All I ever did was follow
In his broad shadow round the farm.   20

I was a nuisance, tripping, falling,
Yapping always. But today
It is my father who keeps stumbling
Behind me, and will not go away.

THE TOLLUND MAN

I

Some day I will go to Aarhus
To see his peat-brown head,
The mild pods of his eye-lids,
His pointed skin cap.

In the flat country nearby
Where they dug him out,
His last gruel of winter seeds
Caked in his stomach,

Naked except for
The cap, noose and girdle,
I will stand a long time.   10
Bridegroom to the goddess,

She tightened her torc on him
And opened her fen,
Those dark juices working
Him to a saint's kept body,

Trove of the turfcutters'
Honeycombed workings.
Now his stained face
Reposes at Aarhus.   20

II

I could risk blasphemy,
Consecrate the cauldron bog
Our holy ground and pray
Him to make germinate

The scattered, ambushed
Flesh of labourers,
Stockinged corpses
Laid out in the farmyards,

Tell-tale skin and teeth
Flecking the sleepers   30
Of four young brothers, trailed
For miles along the lines.

III

Something of his sad freedom
As he rode the tumbril
Should come to me, driving,
Saying the names

Tollund, Grauballe, Nebelgard,
Watching the pointing hands
Of country people,
Not knowing their tongue.   40

Out there in Jutland
In the old man-killing parishes
I will feel lost,
Unhappy and at home.

A NEW SONG

I met a girl from Derrygarve
And the name, a lost potent musk,
Recalled the river's long swerve,
A kingfisher's blue bolt at dusk

And stepping stones like black molars
Sunk in the ford, the shifty glaze
Of the whirlpool, the Moyola
Pleasuring beneath alder trees.

And Derrygarve, I thought, was just,
Vanished music, twilit water,   10
A smooth libation of the past
Poured by this chance vestal daughter.

But now our river tongues must rise
From licking deep in native haunts
To flood, with vowelling embrace,
Demesnes staked out in consonants.

And Castledawson we'll enlist
And Upperlands, each planted bawn—
Like bleaching-greens resumed by grass—
A vocable, as rath and bullaun.   20

FROM THE FRONTIER
OF WRITING

The tightness and the nilness round that space
when the car stops in the road, the troops inspect
its make and number and, as one bends his face

towards your window, you catch sight of more
on a hill beyond, eyeing with intent
down cradled guns that hold you under cover

and everything is pure interrogation
until a rifle motions and you move
with guarded unconcerned acceleration—

a little emptier, a little spent   10
as always by that quiver in the self,
subjugated, yes, and obedient.

so you drive on to the frontier of writing
where it happens again. The guns on tripods;
the sergeant with his on-off mike repeating

data about you, waiting for the squawk
of clearance; the marksman training down
out of the sun upon you like a hawk.

And suddenly you're through, arraigned yet freed,
as if you'd passed from behind a waterfall   20
on the black current of a tarmac road

past armor-plated vehicles, out between
the posted soldiers flowing and receding
like tree shadows into the polished windscreen.

Michael Longley

(1 9 3 9 –   )

Before meeting at Trinity College, Dublin, Longley and Derek Mahon had attended the same Protestant grammar school in their native Belfast. The poems of both illustrate the restraints in the wake of Modernism that prevent stanza and sound pattern from returning beyond assonance and half-rhyme to the regulated metrics of previous centuries. "To Derek Mahon," collected in *An Exploded View* (1973), recalls a sudden Protestant recognition of Catholic compatriots. A narrower term for "freeze-up" is "writer's block."

FREEZE-UP

The freeze-up annexes the sea even,
Putting out over the waves its platform.
Let skies fall, the fox's belly cave in—
This catastrophic shortlived reform
Directs to our homes the birds of heaven.
They come on farfetched winds to keep us warm.

Bribing these with bounty, we would rather
Forget our hopes of thaw when spring will clean
The boughs, dust from our sills snow and feather,
Release to its decay and true decline   10
The bittern whom this different weather
Cupboarded in ice like a specimen.

TO DEREK MAHON

And did we come into our own
When, minus muse and lexicon,
We traced in August sixty-nine
Our imaginary Peace Line
Around the burnt-out houses of
The Catholics we'd scarcely loved,

Two Sisyphuses come to budge
The sticks and stones of an old grudge,

Two poetic conservatives
In the city of guns and long knives,   10
Our ears receiving then and there
The stereophonic nightmare
Of the Shankill and the Falls,
Our matches struck on crumbling walls
To light us as we moved at last
Through the back alleys of Belfast?

Why it mattered to have you here
You who journeyed to Inisheer
With me, years back, one Easter when
With MacIntyre and the lone Dane   20
Our footsteps lifted up the larks,
Echoing off those western rocks
And down that darkening arcade
Hung with the failures of our trade,

Will understand. We were tongue-tied
Companions of the island's dead
In the graveyard among the dunes,
Eavesdroppers on conversations
With a Jesus who spoke Irish—
We were strangers in that parish,   30
Black tea with bacon and cabbage
For our sacraments and pottage,

Dank blankets making up our Lent
Till, islanders ourselves, we bent
Our knees and cut the watery sod
From the lazy-bed where slept a God
We couldn't count among our friends,
Although we'd taken in our hands
Splinters of driftwood nailed and stuck
On the rim of the Atlantic.   40

That was Good Friday years ago—
How persistent the undertow
Slapped by currachs ferrying stones,
Moonlight glossing the confusions

Of its each bilingual wave—yes,
We would have lingered there for less. . . .
Six islanders for a ten-bob note
Rowed us out to the anchored boat.

Derek Mahon

(1 9 4 1 –   )

Mahon was born in Belfast, Northern Ireland, and attended Trinity College, Dublin, after which he worked in London as a journalist and reviewer. In the poem on the shed in County Wexford, as throughout his published verse, Mahon is preoccupied with the themes of alienation, loss, and exile. "An Unborn Child" was selected among the choice poems of Heaney and Mahon for inclusion in *In Their Element*, published by the Arts Council of Northern Ireland (1977). Longley has said that Heaney's poems come geologically from the sedimentary process, Mahon's from the igneous.

A DISUSED SHED IN
CO. WEXFORD

Let them not forget us, the weak souls among the asphodels.
—Seferis, *Mythistorema*

Even now there are places where a thought might grow—
Peruvian mines, worked out and abandoned
To a slow clock of condensation,
An echo trapped for ever, and a flutter
Of wildflowers in the lift-shaft,
Indian compounds where the wind dances
And a door bangs with diminished confidence,
Lime crevices behind rippling rainbarrels,
Dog corners for bone burials;
And in a disused shed in Co. Wexford,   10

Deep in the grounds of a burnt-out hotel,
Among the bathtubs and the washbasins
A thousand mushrooms crowd to a keyhole.
This is the one star in their firmament
Or frames a star within a star.
What should they do there but desire?
So many days beyond the rhododendrons

With the world waltzing in its bowl of cloud,
They have learnt patience and silence
Listening to the rooks querulous in the high wood.   20

They have been waiting for us in a foetor
Of vegetable sweat since civil war days,
Since the gravel-crunching, interminable departure
Of the expropriated mycologist.
He never came back, and light since then
Is a keyhole rusting gently after rain.
Spiders have spun, flies dusted to mildew
And once a day, perhaps, they have heard something—
A trickle of masonry, a shout from the blue
Or a lorry changing gear at the end of the lane.   30

There have been deaths, the pale flesh flaking
Into the earth that nourished it;
And nightmares, born of these and the grim
Dominion of stale air and rank moisture.
Those nearest the door grow strong—
"Elbow room! Elbow room!"
The rest, dim in a twilight of crumbling
Utensils and broken flower-pots, groaning
For their deliverance, have been so long
Expectant that there is left only the posture.   40

A half century, without visitors, in the dark—
Poor preparation for the cracking lock
And creak of hinges. Magi, moonmen,
Powdery prisoners of the old regime,
Web-throated, stalked like triffids, racked by drought
And insomnia, only the ghost of a scream
At the flash-bulb firing squad we wake them with
Shows there is life yet in their feverish forms.
Grown beyond nature now, soft food for worms,
They lift frail heads in gravity and good faith.   50

They are begging us, you see, in their wordless way,
To do something, to speak on their behalf
Or at least not to close the door again.
Lost people of Treblinka and Pompeii!
"Save us, save us," they seem to say,

"Let the god not abandon us
Who have come so far in darkness and in pain.
We too had our lives to live.
You with your light meter and relaxed itinerary,
Let not our naive labours have been in vain!"   60

AN UNBORN CHILD

I have already come to the verge of
Departure. A month or so and
I shall be vacating this familiar room.
Its fabric fits me almost like a glove
While leaving latitude for a free hand.
I begin to put on the manners of the world,
Sensing the splitting light above
My head, where in the silence I lie curled.

Certain mysteries are relayed to me
Through the dark network of my mother's body   10
While she sits sewing the white shrouds
Of my apotheosis. I know the twisted
Kitten that lies there sunning itself
Under the bare bulb, the clouds
Of goldfish mooning around upon the shelf—
In me these data are already vested.

I feel them in my bones—bones which embrace
Nothing, for I am completely egocentric.
The pandemonium of encumbrances
Which will absorb me, mind and senses—   20
Intricacies of the box and the rat race—
I imagine only. Though they linger and,
Like fingers, stretch until the knuckles crack,
They cannot dwarf the dimensions of my hand.

I must compose myself in the nerve centre
Of this metropolis, and not fidget—
Although sometimes at night, when the city
Has gone to sleep, I keep in touch with it,
Listening to the warm red water

Racing in the sewers of my mother's body—   30
Or the moths, soft as eyelids, or the rain
Wiping its wet wings on the windowpane.

And sometimes too, in the small hours of the morning
When the dead filament has ceased to ring—
After the goldfish are dissolved in darkness
And the kitten has gathered itself up into a ball
Between the groceries and the sewing,
I slip the trappings of my harness
To range these hollows in discreet rehearsal
And, battering at the concavity of my caul,   40

Produce in my mouth the words *I WANT TO LIVE*—
This my first protest, and shall be my last.
As I am innocent, everything I do
Or say is couched in the affirmative.
I want to see, hear, touch and taste
These things with which I am to be encumbered.
Perhaps I need not worry—give
Or take a day or two, my days are numbered.

Paul Durcan

(1944 –   )

Born in Dublin, Durcan studied archeology and history at University College in Cork. He won the Patrick Kavanagh Award in 1974. The parody here, showing how and why the media entertain with "news," was reprinted from *Teresa's Bar* in *The Selected Paul Durcan* (1982). It may go some way toward explaining why Durcan toured Russia at the invitation of the Union of Soviet Writers in 1983. The surprises in rhythm and perhaps his dramatizing in public readings similarly help explain his invitation to The Frost Place, in New Hampshire, in 1985.

WIFE WHO SMASHED TELEVISION GETS JAIL

"She came home, my Lord, and smashed-in the television;
Me and the kids were peaceably watching Kojak
When she marched into the living-room and declared
That if I didn't turn off the television immediately
She'd put her boot through the screen;
I didn't turn it off, so instead she turned it off
—I remember the moment exactly because Kojak
After shooting a dame with the same name as my wife
Snarled at the corpse—Goodnight, Queen Maeve—
And then she took off her boots and smashed-in the television;   10
I had to bring the kids round to my mother's place;
We got there just before the finish of Kojak;
(My mother has a fondness for Kojak, my Lord);
When I returned home my wife had deposited
What was left of the television into the dustbin,
Saying—I didn't get married to a television
And I don't see why my kids or anybody else's kids
Should have a television for a father or mother,
We'd be much better off all down in the pub talking
Or playing bar-billiards—   20
Whereupon she disappeared off back down again to the pub."
Justice O'Brádaigh said wives who preferred bar-billiards to family television

Were a threat to the family which was the basic unit of society
As indeed the television itself could be said to be a basic unit of the family
And when as in this case wives expressed their preference in forms of violence
Jail was the only place for them. Leave to appeal was refused.

Tom Leonard

(1 9 4 4 –   )

Born in Glasgow, Leonard received the M.A. from Glasgow University in 1971 and continues as a literary force in his native city. With one purpose of shaming readers accustomed to English into the effort of reading verse in Scots, Leonard spells most of his poems in "phonetic urban dialect." His poem "Hangup," on minimalism, ends: "a stull think yi huvty say sumhm." "Fathers and Sons" is the final poem in *Intimate Voices: Selected Work, 1965–1983* (1984).

FATHERS AND SONS

I remember being ashamed of my father
when he whispered the words out loud
reading the newspaper.

"Don't you find
the use of phonetic urban dialect
rather constrictive?"
asks a member of the audience.

The poetry reading is over.
I will go home to my children.

Eavan Boland

(1944–)

Born in Dublin, Boland's mother was a painter, her father a diplomat posted to London in the 1950s. Boland began school in Dublin, but she was moved with her family first to England and then to New York City before returning to her native Ireland. This early separation from Irish culture strengthened a sense of isolation amidst English hostility. Since attending Trinity College, Dublin, she has been active not only as poet but also as critic, journalist, and television figure, as well as wife and mother. Her *Outside History* (1990) is a selection of poems written from 1980 to 1990. "The Pomegranate," with a view of Proserpine neglected by Swinburne, appeared in *The New Yorker* in October 1993.

THE POMEGRANATE

The only legend I have ever loved is
the story of a daughter lost in hell.
And found and rescued there.
Love and blackmail are the gist of it.
Ceres and Persephone the names.
And the best thing about the legend is
I can enter it anywhere. And have.
As a child in exile in
a city of fogs and strange consonants,
I read it first and at first I was   10
an exiled child in the crackling dusk of
the underworld, the stars blighted. Later
I walked out in a summer twilight
searching for my daughter at bed-time.
When she came running I was ready
to make any bargain to keep her.
I carried her back past whitebeams
and wasps and honey-scented buddleias.
But I was Ceres then and I knew
winter was in store for every leaf   20
on every tree on that road.
Was inescapable for each one we passed.

And for me.
        It is winter
and the stars are hidden.
I climb the stairs and stand where I can see
my child asleep beside her teen magazines,
her can of Coke, her plate of uncut fruit.
The pomegranate! How did I forget it?
She could have come home and been safe   30
and ended the story and all
our heart-broken searching but she reached
out a hand and plucked a pomegranate.
She put out her hand and pulled down
the French sound for apple and
the noise of stone and the proof
that even in the place of death,
at the heart of legend, in the midst
of rocks full of unshed tears
ready to be diamonds by the time   40
the story was told, a child can be
hungry. I could warn her. There is still a chance.
The rain is cold. The road is flint-coloured.
The suburb has cars and cable television.
The veiled stars are above ground.
It is another world. But what else
can a mother give her daughter but such
beautiful rifts in time?
If I defer the grief I will diminish the gift.
The legend will be hers as well as mine.   50
She will enter it. As I have.
She will wake up. She will hold
the papery flushed skin in her hand.
And to her lips. I will say nothing.

Liz Lochhead

(1 9 4 7 –   )

Born in Motherwell, near Glasgow, Lochhead studied at the Glasgow School of Art. With Tom Leonard, she leads a Glaswegian school of poets. "The Grim Sisters" (1981) appeared in a volume with an ironically fairy-tale title, *The Grimm Sisters* (1985). Lochhead has also produced revues and screenplays and written a number of plays, including *Mary Queen of Scots Got Her Head Chopped Off* (1989). The sense of dramatic immediacy in her poetry may well owe something to her work as playwright and performer.

THE GRIM SISTERS

And for special things
(weddings, school-
concerts) the grown up girls next door
would do my hair.

Luxembourg announced Amami night.
I sat at peace passing bobbipins
from a marshmallow pink cosmetic purse
embossed with jazzmen,
girls with ponytails and a November
topaz lucky birthstone.   10
They doused my cow's-lick, rollered
and skewered tightly.
I expected that to be lovely
would be worth the hurt.

They read my Stars,
tied chiffon scarves to doorhandles, tried
to teach me tight dancesteps
you'd no guarantee
any partner you might find would ever be able to keep up with
as far as I could see.   20

There were always things to burn
before the men came in.

For each disaster
you were meant to know the handy hint.
Soap at a pinch
but better nailvarnish (clear) for ladders.
For kisscurls, spit.
Those days womanhood was quite a sticky thing
And that was what these grim sisters came to mean.

"You'll know all about it soon enough."   30
But when the clock struck they
stood still, stopped dead.
And they were left there
out in the cold with the wrong skirtlength
and bouffant hair,
dressed to kill,

who'd been
all the rage in fifty eight,
a swish of Persianelle
a slosh of perfume.   40
In those big black mantrap handbags
they snapped shut at any hint of *that*
were hedgehog hairbrushes
cottonwool mice and barbed combs to tease.
Their heels spiked bubblegum, dead leaves.

Wasp waist and cone breast, I see them yet.
I hope, I hope
there's been a change of more than silhouette.

Veronica Forrest-Thomson

(1947–1975)

Forrest-Thomson relates that she was born in Malaya in 1947. After youth in Glasgow, she attended the University of Liverpool and earned a Ph.D. at Cambridge on the topic of science in modern poetry. Her marriage in 1971 did not last, but friends accepted her generally abrupt manner. In April 1975 she was found dead in her home in Cambridge, where she was a lecturer in English. In *Poetic Artifice* (1978) and other expositions of theory, influenced by Wittgenstein, Saussure, Pound, and Empson, she stressed the centrality of language as mediator between reality (whether internal or external) and appearance: poetry—with only an indirect reference to experience—should clash with accepted conventions by innovation in technique and without discarding the heritage of meter and rhyme.

"The Garden of Proserpine" appears in her privately published *Cordelia: or, "A Poem Should Not Mean, but Be"* (1974) and in both the posthumously published *On the Periphery* (1976) and *Collected Poems and Translations* (1990).

THE GARDEN OF PROSERPINE

Th' expense of spirit in a waste of shame
Is lust in action and, till action, lust
Until my last lost taper's end be spent
My sick taper does begin to wink
And, O, many-toned, immortal Aphrodite,
Lend me thy girdle.
You can spare it for an hour or so
Until Zeus has got back his erection.

Here where all trouble seems
Dead winds' and spent waves' riot   10
In doubtful dreams of dreams.
The moon is sinking, and the Pleiades,
Mid Night; and time runs on she said,
I lie alone. I am aweary, aweary,
I would that I were dead.
Be my partner and you'll never regret it.

850

Gods and poets ought to stick together;
They make a strong combination.
So just make him love me again,
You good old triple goddess of tight corners.   20
And leave me to deal with gloomy Dis.

Death never seems a particularly informative topic for poets
Though that doesn't stop them dilating at length upon it.
But then they would dilate on anything.
Love, on the other hand, however trite, is always interesting
At least to those in its clutches
And usually also to their readers.
For, even if the readers be not in its clutches
They think they would like to be
Because they think it is a pleasant experience.   30
I, however, know better.
And so do Sappho, Shakespeare, Swinburne, Tennyson and Eliot.
Not to mention the Greek dramatists:
Sophocles, Euripides, Aeschylos, and Eliot.
We all know better.
Love is hellish.
Which is why Aphrodite is also Persephone,
Queen of love and death.
Love kills people and the police can't do anything to stop it.
Love will: 40
            ravage your beauty
            disrupt your career
            break up your friendships
            squander your energy
            spend every last drop of your self-possession
Even supposing you had such qualities to start with.
The god knows why we bother with it.
It is because it bothers with us.
It won't leave us alone for a minute.
For without us it wouldn't exist.   50
And that is the secret of all human preoccupation
(As others have said before me)
Love, death, time, beauty, the whole bag of tricks.
All our own work including, of course, the gods.
And we let them ride us like the fools we are.
Of all follies that is the penultimate:
To let our own inventions destroy us,
The ultimate folly, of course, is not to let them destroy us.

To pretend a stoic indifference, mask merely of stupidity.
To become ascetic, superior to the pure pleasures of the senses,   60
Arrogant and imbecile senecans, unconscious
Of what is going on even in their own bodies
Old whatsisname stuck up on his pillar,
A laughing stock, the ultimate in insensitivity.

The only thing, contrarily, to do with the problem of love—
As with all other problems—
Is to try to solve it.
You won't succeed but you won't make a fool of yourself, trying
Or, at least, not so much of a fool as those who refuse to try.
So here we go for another trip and hold on to your seat-belt, Persephone. 70

I loved you and you loved me
And then we made a mess.
We still loved each other but
We loved each other less.

I got a job, I wrote a book,
I turned again to play.
However I found out by then
That you had gone away.

My dignity dictated
A restrained farewell.   80
But I love you so much
Dignity can go to hell.

I went to hell with dignity,
For by then, we were three.
And whatever I feel about you,
I certainly hate she.

The god knows what will be the end
And he will never tell.
For I love you and you love me
Although we are in hell.   90

And what death has to do with it
Is always simply this:
If it isn't your arms I'm heading for
It's the arms of gloomy Dis.

Ciaran Carson

(1 9 4 8 –   )

Carson, born in Belfast, attended St. Mary's and Queen's University there. He has continued in his native city as teacher, poet, Irish traditional musician, and Traditional Arts Officer for the Arts Council of Northern Ireland. His first language is Irish. After his *Pocket Guide to Irish Traditional Music* (1986), he gained special attention with the title poem in his *Belfast Confetti* (1989): the phrase refers to metal objects thrown down on Catholics. "Slate Street School" appeared in an earlier collection of poems, *The Irish for No* (1987).

SLATE STREET SCHOOL

Back again. Day one. Fingers blue with cold. I joined the lengthening queue.
Roll-call. Then inside: chalk-dust and iced milk, the smell of watered ink.
Roods, perches, acres, ounces, pounds, tons weighed imponderably in the
    darkening
Air. We had chanted the twelve-times table for the twelfth or thirteenth time.
When it began to snow. Chalky numerals shimmered down; we crowded to the
    window—

These are the countless souls of purgatory, whose numbers constantly diminish
And increase; each flake as it brushes to the ground is yet another soul released.
And I am the avenging Archangel, stooping over mills and factories and
    barracks.
I will bury the dark city of Belfast forever under snow: inches, feet, yards,
    chains, miles.

Tom Paulin

(1949 –   )

Paulin captures with special intensity the unbearable images of revenge that haunt all of Ireland. He was born in Leeds and drawn to Marxism during his education in Belfast, Hull, and Oxford. He has held a lectureship at the University of Nottingham and been a director of the Field Day Theatre Company. "The Impossible Pictures" (from *The Strange Museum*, 1980) evokes the difficulty of spiritual escape from Northern Ireland near the end of the twentieth century.

THE IMPOSSIBLE PICTURES

In this parable of vengeance
There is a grey newsreel
Being shown inside my head.

What happens is that Lenin's brother
(Aleksandr Ulyanov)
Is being led to execution.

He carries a small book
Wrapped in a piece of cloth.
Is it the Bible or a text

His brother will be forced to write?   10
He twists it in his hands.
I think he is frightened.

I am wrong, because suddenly
He strikes an officer on the face—
His gestures now are a jerking

Clockwork anachronism.
He is goosestepped to the scaffold.
The frozen yard of the prison

Is like this dawn of rain showers
And heavy lorries, a gull mewling   20
In its dream of the Atlantic.

Ah, I say, this is Ireland
And my own place, myself.
I see a Georgian rectory

Square in the salt winds
Above a broken coast,
And the sea-birds scattering

Their chill cries: I know
That every revenge is nature,
Always on time, like the waves.   30

Medbh McCaughan McGuckian

(1950–)

Poet and painter, Medbh McCaughan was born in Belfast and attended Queen's University there. Married in 1977 and mother of two sons, she has been a teacher in Belfast. Her first two pamphlets of poems appeared in 1980; the poet Anne Stevenson, reviewing this early work, likened the quality of McGuckian's private, inward-turning poetry to that of a "contemporary, Irish Emily Dickinson." "The Orchid House," like other poems in *The Flower Master* (1982), plays intricately on a woman's blooming sexuality. "The Sitting" was published in *Venus and the Rain* (1984).

THE ORCHID HOUSE

A flower's fragrance is a woman's virtue;
So I tell them underground in pairs,
Or in their fleshy white sleeves, how
Desirable their shapes, how one
Was lost for sixty years, with all
Its arching spikes, its honeyed tessellations,
And how in bloom they will resemble
Moths, the gloss of mirrors, Christmas
Stars, their helmets blushing
Red-brown when they marry.

THE SITTING

My half-sister comes to me to be painted:
She is posing furtively, like a letter being
Pushed under a door, making a tunnel with her
Hands over her dull-rose dress. Yet her coppery
Head is as bright as a net of lemons, I am
Painting it hair by hair as if she had not
Disowned it, or forsaken those unsparkling
Eyes as blue may be sifted from the surface

Of a cloud; and she questions my brisk
Brushwork, the note of positive red   10
In the kissed mouth I have given her,
As a woman's touch makes curtains blossom
Permanently in a house: she calls it
Wishfulness, the failure of the tampering rain
To go right into the mountain, she prefers
My sea-studies, and will not sit for me
Again, something half-opened, rarer
Than railroads, a soiled red-letter day.

Paul Muldoon

(1951–   )

Born into a Catholic family that moved from County Armagh to County Tyrone, Muldoon graduated from Queen's University, Belfast, where his tutor was Seamus Heaney. He has taught at Cambridge, Columbia, and Princeton universities and worked in productions of the BBC in Northern Ireland. The "I" in "Sushi" (published in *Meeting the British*, 1987) is engaged in a creative action epitomized by the rhyme-words of the italicized lines. In *Madoc: A Mystery* (1991), "The Briefcase" is the last of several poems that precede the sequence concerning Southey's Welsh adventurer, Madoc, and philosophers from Anaximander to Jacques Derrida and Julia Kristeva.

SUSHI

"Why do we waste so much time in arguing?"
We were sitting at the sushi-bar
drinking *Kirin* beer
and watching the Master chef
fastidiously shave
salmon, tuna and yellowtail
while a slightly more volatile
apprentice
fanned the rice,
every grain of which was magnetized   10
in one direction—east.
Then came translucent strips
of octopus,
squid and conger,
pickled ginger
and pale-green horseradish . . .
"It's as if you've some kind of death-wish.
You won't even talk . . ."
On the sidewalk
a woman in a leotard   20
with a real leopard

in tow.
For an instant I saw beyond the roe
of sea-urchins,
the erogenous
zones of shad and sea-bream;
I saw, when the steam
cleared, how this apprentice
had scrimshandered a rose's
exquisite petals   30
not from some precious metal
or wood or stone
("I might just as well be eating alone.")
but the tail-end of a carrot:
how when he submitted this work of art
to the Master——
Is it not the height of arrogance
to propose that God's no more arcane
than the smack of oregano,
orgone,   40
the inner organs
of beasts and fowls, the mines of Arigna,
the poems of Louis Aragon?—
it might have been alabaster
or jade
the Master so gravely weighed
from hand to hand
with the look of a man unlikely to confound
Duns Scotus, say, with Scotus Eriugena.

THE BRIEFCASE

FOR SEAMUS HEANEY

I held the briefcase at arm's length from me;
the oxblood or liver
eelskin with which it was covered
had suddenly grown supple.

I'd been waiting in line for the cross-town
bus when an almighty cloudburst
left the sidewalk a raging torrent.

And though it contained only the first
inkling of this poem, I knew I daren't
set the briefcase down
to slap my pockets for an obol—

for fear it might slink into a culvert
and strike out along the East River
for the sea. By which I mean the "open" sea.

l. 11. obol = coin to pay transport of the dead across
the Styx

Nuala Ní Dhomhnaill

(1 9 5 2 –   )

"Labasheedy" ("The Silken Bed") is Nuala Ní Dhomhnaill's own translation in 1986 of her poem in Irish, "Leaba Shíoda," both versions of which are included in her *Selected Poems* / ROGHA DĀNTA (Dublin, 1988). Born in County Kerry, she has lived in Turkey, the Netherlands, and latterly in Dublin, with husband and children. Her recent collection, *Pharoah's Daughter* (1990), includes poems by her in Irish as well as English translations by such leading Irish poets as Heaney, Longley, McGuckian, Mahon, Montague, Muldoon, and Carson.

LEABA SHÍODA

Do chóireoinn leaba duit
i Leaba Shíoda
sa bhféar ard
faoi iomrascáil na gcrann
is bheadh do chraiceann ann
mar shíoda ar shíoda
sa doircheacht
am lonnaithe na leamhan.

Craiceann a shníonn
go gléineach thar do ghéaga   10
mar bhainne á dháil as crúiscíní
am lóin
is tréad gabhar ag gabháil thar chnocáin
do chuid gruaige
cnocáin ar a bhfuil faillte arda
is dhá ghleann atá domhain.

Is bheadh do bheola taise
ar mhilseacht shiúcra
tráthnóna is sinn ag spaisteoireacht
cois abhann   20
is na gaotha meala
ag séideadh thar an Sionna

is na fiúisí ag beannú duit
ceann ar cheann.

Na fiúisí ag ísliú
a gceanna maorga
ag umhlú síos don áilleacht
os a gcomhair
is do phriocfainn péire acu
mar shiogairlíní   30
is do mhaiseoinn do chluasa
mar bhrídeog.

Ó, chóireoinn leaba duit
i Leaba Shíoda
le hamhascarnach an lae
i ndeireadh thall
is ba mhór an pléisiúr dúinn
bheith géaga ar ghéaga
ag iomrascáil
am lonnaithe na leamhan.   40

LABASHEEDY
(THE SILKEN BED)

I'd make a bed for you
in Labasheedy
in the tall grass
under the wrestling trees
where your skin
would be silk upon silk
in the darkness
when the moths are coming down.

Skin which glistens
shining over your limbs   10
like milk being poured
from jugs at dinnertime;
your hair is a herd of goats
moving over rolling hills,
hills that have high cliffs
and two ravines.

And your damp lips
would be as sweet as sugar
at evening and we walking
by the riverside   20
with honeyed breezes
blowing over the Shannon
and the fuchsias bowing down to you
one by one.

The fuchsias bending low
their solemn heads
in obeisance to the beauty
in front of them
I would pick a pair of flowers
as pendant earrings   30
to adorn you
like a bride in shining clothes.

O I'd make a bed for you
in Labasheedy,
in the twilight hour
with evening falling slow
and what a pleasure it would be
to have our limbs entwine
wrestling
while the moths are coming down.   40

ACKNOWLEDGMENTS

For permission to reprint the poems in this book, the publisher gratefully thanks the following poets, copyright holders and publishers. Any omissions or errors are completely unintentional

A. P. WATT LTD.

Kipling, Rudyard: *"Tommy," "The King,"* and *"Recessional,"* from *The Definitive Edition of Rudyard Kipling's Verse.*
Yeats, William Butler: *"The Lake Isle of Innisfree," "The Second Coming," "Sailing to Byzantium," "Leda and the Swan," "Among School Children," "Coole Park, 1929," "Crazy Jane Talks with the Bishop,"* and *"Lapis Lazuli,"* from *The Poems of W. B. Yeats: A New Edition,* edited by Richard J. Finneran. Reprinted by permission of A. P. Watt Ltd.

BLACKSTAFF PRESS

Durcan, Paul: *"Wife Who Smashed Television Gets Jail,"* from *The Selected Paul Durcan,* edited by Edna Longley.
Hewitt, John: *"Once Alien Here,"* from *The Collected Poems of John Hewitt,* edited by Frank Ormsby. Reprinted by permission of The Blackstaff Press.

BROWN UNIVERSITY PRESS

Queen Elizabeth I: *"Written on a Wall at Woodstock"* and *"On Monsieur's Departure,"* from *Poems,* edited by Leicester Bradner. Copyright © 1964. Reprinted by permission of Brown University.

CARCANET

Beer, Patricia: *"Lemmings"* and *"Jane Austen at the Window,"* from *Selected Poems,* by Patricia Beer.
Boland, Eavan: *"The Pomegranate,"* from *In a Time of Violence,* by Eavan Boland.
Davie, Donald: *"Rejoinder to a Critic"* and *"Across the Bay,"* from *Collected Poems, 1950–1970,* by Donald Davie.
Graves, Robert: *"The Face in the Mirror"* and *"Not at Home,"* from *Collected Poems,* by Robert Graves.
MacDiarmid, Hugh: *"Ex Vermibus," "With the Herring Fishers,"* and *"Lourd on My Hert,"* from *Hugh MacDiarmid: Selected Poetry,* edited by Alan Riach and Michael Grieve.
Mew, Charlotte: *"The Farmer's Bride,"* from *Collected Poems of Charlotte Mew,* by Charlotte Mew. Reprinted by permission of Carcanet Press Ltd.

CHAPMAN

McDonald, Ellie: *"Itherness."* Reprinted by permission of Chapman.

CULLER, JONATHAN

Forrest-Thomson, Veronica: *"The Garden of Proserpine,"* from *Collected Poems and Translations,* by Veronica Forrest-Thomson. Copyright © 1990 by Jonathan Culler and The Estate of Veronica Forrest-Thomson. Reprinted by permission of Jonathan Culler.

DAVID HIGHAM ASSOCIATES LTD.

Sitwell, Edith: *"Still Falls the Rain,"* from *The Collected Poems of Edith Sitwell,* by Edith Sitwell.

Thomas, Dylan: *"The force that through the green fuse drives the flower," "Fern Hill,"* and *"Do not go gentle into that good night,"* from *The Collected Poems of Dylan Thomas,* by Dylan Thomas. Reprinted by permission of David Higham Associates Ltd.

DEVIN-ADAIR COMPANY

Kavanagh, Patrick: *"Spraying the Potatoes," "Epic,"* and *"The Hospital,"* from *Collected Poems,* by Patrick Kavanagh. Copyright © 1964 by Patrick Kavanagh. Reprinted by permission of Devin-Adair Company.

DOUBLEDAY

Kipling, Rudyard: *"Tommy," "The King,"* and *"Recessional,"* from *The Definitive Edition of Rudyard Kipling's Verse.* Reprinted by permission of Doubleday, a division of Bantam Doubleday Dell Publishing Group, Inc.

DUFOUR EDITIONS

Hill, Geoffrey: *"Ovid in the Third Reich,"* from *Collected Poems,* by Geoffrey Hill.

Longley, Michael: *"Freeze-Up"* and *"To Derek Mahon,"* from *Poems, 1963–1983,* by Michael Longley. Reprinted by permission of Dufour Editions.

FABER & FABER LTD.

anonymous—Pound, Ezra: *from "The Seafarer,"* from *Collected Shorter Poems,* by Ezra Pound.

Auden, W. H.: *"Musee des Beaux Arts"* and *"In Memory of W. B. Yeats,"* from *Collected Poems,* by W. H. Auden, edited by Edward Mendelson.

Eliot, T. S.: *"The Waste Land I," "Marina,"* and *"Little Gidding,"* from *Collected Poems, 1909–1962,* by T. S. Eliot.

Gunn, Thom: *"Moly,"* from *Moly* by Thom Gunn; *"Lines for a Book,"* from *The Sense of Movement,* by Thom Gunn; *"The Man with Night Sweats,"* from *The Man with Night Sweats,* by Thom Gunn.

Heaney, Seamus: *"Follower," "A New Song," "The Tolland Man,"* and *"From the Frontier of Writing,"* from *Selected Poems, 1966–1987,* by Seamus Heaney.

Hughes, Ted: *"A Modest Proposal,"* from *The Hawk in the Rain,* by Ted Hughes; *"To Paint a Water Lily,"* from *Lupercal,* by Ted Hughes; *"Moon-Hops,"* from *Moon-Whales* by Ted Hughes; *"A Childish Prank,"* from *Crow* by Ted Hughes. Copyright © 1971.

MacNeice, Louis: *"Bagpipe Music"* and *"Elegy for Minor Poets,"* from *The Collected Poems of Louis MacNeice,* edited by E. R. Dodds.

Muir, Edwin: *"Scotland 1941"* and *"The Horses,"* from *Collected Poems,* by Edwin Muir.

Muldoon, Paul: *"Sushi,"* from *Meeting the British,* by Paul Muldoon; *"The Briefcase,"* from *Madoc: A Mystery,* by Paul Muldoon.

Paulin, Tom: *"The Impossible Pictures,"* from *The Strange Museum,* by Tom Paulin.

Spender, Stephen: *"The Truly Great,"* from *Collected Poems, 1928–1985,* by Stephen Spender. Reprinted by permission of Faber & Faber Ltd.

FARRAR, STRAUS & GIROUX

Gunn, Thom: *"Moly," "Lines for a Book,"* and *"The Man with Night Sweats,"* from *Collected Poems,* by Thom Gunn. Copyright © 1994 by Thom Gunn.

Heaney, Seamus: *"Follower," "A New Song," "The Tolland Man,"* and *"From the Froniter of Writing,"* from *Selected Poems, 1966–1987, by Seamus Heaney. Copyright © 1990 by Seamus Heaney.*

Larkin, Philip: *"Aubade,"* from *Collected Poems,* by Philip Larkin. Copyright © 1989 by the Estate of Philip Larkin.

Muldoon, Paul: *"The Briefcase,"* from *Madoc: A Mystery,* by Paul Muldoon. Copyright © 1991 by Paul Muldoon. Reprinted by permission of Farrar, Straus & Giroux, Inc.

GALLERY PRESS

McGuckian, Medbh McCaughan: *"The Orchid House,"* from *The Flower Master and Other Poems,* by Medbh McCaughan McGuckian; *"The Sitting,"* from *Venus and the Rain* by Medbh McCaughan McGuckian. Reprinted by permission of the author and The Gallery Press.

HARCOURT BRACE & COMPANY

Eliot, T.S.: *"The Waste Land I"* and *"Marina,"* from *Collected Poems, 1909–1962,* by T. S. Eliot. Copyright © 1936 by Harcourt Brace & Company, copyright © 1964, 1963 by T. S. Eliot. *"Little Gidding,"* from *Four Quartets,* by T. S. Eliot. Copyright © 1943 by T. S. Eliot and renewed 1971 by Esme Valerie Eliot. Reprinted by permission of Harcourt Brace & Company.

HARPERCOLLINS

Hughes, Ted: *"A Childish Prank,"* from *Crow,* by Ted Hughes. Copyright © 1970 by Ted Hughes. Reprinted by permission of HarperCollins Publishers, Inc.

HARRISON, TONY

Harrison, Tony: *"On Not Being Milton"* and *"Study,"* from *Selected Poems,* by Tony Harrison. Reprinted by permission of Tony Harrison.

HENRY HOLT AND CO., INC.

Housman, A. E.: *"Reveille"* and *"Terence, This is Stupid Stuff,"* from *The Complete Poems of A. E. Housman.* Reprinted by permission of Henry Holt and Co., Inc.

JOHN MURRAY PUBLISHERS, LTD.

Betjeman, Sir John: *"The Licorice Fields at Pontefract"* and *"Huxley Hall,"* from *Collected Poems,* by Sir John Betjeman. Reprinted by permission of John Murray Ltd.

LONGLEY, MICHAEL

Longley, Michael: *"Freeze-Up"* and *"To Derek Mahon,"* from *Poems, 1963–1983,* by Michael Longley. Reprinted by permission of Michael Longley.

MACMILLAN PUBLISHERS LTD.

Hardy, Thomas: *"Hap," "The Darkling Thrush," "The Oxen," "Shelley's Skylark," "Channel Firing," "Neutral Tones," "Beeny Cliff,"* and *"The Convergence of the Twian,"* from *The Complete Poems of Thomas Hardy,* edited by James Gibson.

Moore, T. Sturge: *"Response to Rimbaud's Later Manner,"* from *Collected Poems,* by T. Sturge Moore.

Thomas, Ronald Stuart: *"Pisces"* and *"Centuries,"* from *Experimenting with an Amen,* by Ronald Stuart Thomas. Reprinted by permission of Macmillan General Books.

MARVELL PRESS

Larkin, Philip: *"Church Going"* and *"Next, Please,"* from *The Less Deceived,* by Philip Larkin. Reprinted by permission of Marvell Press.

MCDONALD, ELLIE

McDonald, Ellie: *"Itherness."* Reprinted by permission of the author.

NEW DIRECTIONS

anonymous - Pound, Ezra: *from "The Seafarer,"* from *Personae,* by Ezra Pound. Copyright © 1926.

MacDiarmid, Hugh: *"Ex Vermibus," "With the Herring Fishers,"* and *"Lourd on My Hert,"* from *Selected Poetry,* by Hugh MacDiarmid. Copyright © 1992 by Michael Grieve.

Owen, Wilfred: *"Anthem for Doomed Youth"* and *"Dulce et Decorum Est,"* from *The Collected Poems of Wilfred Owen,* edited by C. Day-Lewis. Copyright © 1963 by Chatto & Windus, Ltd.

Smith, Stevie: *"Not Waving but Drowning"* and *"Away, Melancholy,"* from *Collected Poems of Stevie Smith,* by Stevie Smith. Copyright © 1972.

Thomas, Dylan: *"The force that through the green fuse drives the flower," "Fern Hill,"* and *"Do not go gentle into that good night,"* from *Poems of Dylan Thomas,* by Dylan Thomas. Copyright © 1945 by the Trustees for the Copyrights of Dylan Thomas. Reprinted by permission of New Directions Publishing Corp.

NEW ISLAND BOOKS

Ní Dhomhnaill, Nuala: *"Labysheedy (The Silken Bed),"* from *Nuala Ní Dhomhnaill: Selected Poems, Rogha Danta.* Reprinted by permission of the author and New Island Books.

NÍ DHOMHNAILL

Ní Dhomhnaill, Nuala: *"Leaba Shioda,"* from *Nuala Ní Dhomhnaill: Selected Poems, Rogha Danta.* Reprinted by permission of the author.

ORION PUBLISHING GROUP

Skelton, John: *"Upon a Dead Man's Head"* and *"Knowledge, Acquaintance, Resort, Favor, with Grace,"* from *The Complete Poems of John Skelton,* edited by Philip Henderson. Reprinted by permission of J. M. Dent, publishers.

OXFORD UNIVERSITY PRESS

Hill, Geoffrey: *"Requiem for the Plantagenet Kings,"* from *Collected Poems,* by Geoffrey Hill. Copyright © 1985 by Geoffrey Hill.

Muir, Edwin: *"Scotland 1941"* and *"The Horses,"* from *Collected Poems* by Edwin Muir. Copyright © 1960 by Willa Muir. Reprinted by permission of Oxford University Press.

OXFORD UNIVERSITY PRESS UK

Mahon, Derek: "A Disused Shed in Co. Wexford" and "An Unborn Child," from *Poems, 1962–1978*, by Derek Mahon. Copyright © 1979.

Tomlinson, Charles: "A Word in Edgeways" and "A Death in the Desert," from *Collected Poems*, by Charles Tomlinson. Copyright © 1985. Reprinted by permission of Oxford University Press UK.

PENGUIN LTD.

Hill, Geoffrey: "Requiem for the Plantagenet Kings," from *For the Unfallen*, by Geoffrey Hill; "Ovid in the Third Reich," from *King Log*, by Geoffrey Hill Copyright © 1985 by Penguin Books Ltd. and copyright © 1959, 1968 by Geoffrey Hill. Reprinted by permission of Penguin Books Ltd.

PENGUIN USA

Hughes, Ted: "Moon-Hops," from *Moon-Whales*, by Ted Hughes. Copyright © 1963 by Ted Hughes.

Lawrence, D. H.: "Piano," "Snake," "Bavarian Gentians," and "Love on the Farm," from *The Complete Poems of D. H. Lawrence*, by D. H. Lawrence, edited by V. de Sola Pinto and F. W. Roberts. Copyright © 1964, 1971 by Angelo Ravagli and C. M. Weekley, Executors of the Estate of Frieda Lawrence Ravagli. Reprinted by permission of Viking Penguin, a division of Penguin Books USA Inc.

POLYGON

Lochhead, Liz: "The Grim Sisters," from *Dreaming Frankenstein ("The Grim Sisters")*, by Liz Lochead. Reprinted by permission of Edinburgh University Press, Polygon.

RANDOM HOUSE

Auden, W. H.: "Musee des Beaux Arts" and "In Memory of W. B. Yeats," from *W. H. Auden: Collected Poems*, by W. H. Auden, edited by Edward Mendelson. Copyright © 1940 and renewed 1968 by W. H. Auden.

Spender, Stephen: "The Truly Great," from *Selected Poems*, by Stephen Spender. Copyright © 1934 and 1962 by Stephen Spender. Reprinted by permission of Random House, Inc.

RANDOM HOUSE UK

Leonard, Tom: "Fathers and Sons," from *Intimate Voices*, by Tom Leonard.

MacCaig, Norman: "Blue Tit on a String of Peanuts" and "Gone are the Days," from *Collected Poems of Norman Alexander MacCaig*.

Owen, Wilfred: "Anthem for Doomed Youth" and "Dulce et Decorum Est." from *The Collected Poems of Wilfred Owen*, edited by C. Day-Lewis.

Rosenberg, Isaac: "Break of Day in the Trenches," from *The Collected Works of Isaac Rosenberg*, edited by Ian Parsons (Chatto & Windus). Reprinted by permission of Random House UK.

SIMON & SCHUSTER

Hardy, Thomas: "Hap," "The Darkling Thrush," "The Oxen," "Shelley's Skylark," "Channel Firing," "Neutral Tones," and "Beeny Cliff," "The Convergence of the Twian," from *The Complete Poems of Thomas Hardy*, edited by James Gibson. Copyright © 1978 by The Macmillan Publishing Co.

Yeats, William Butler: "The Lake Isle of Innisfree," copyright © 1983 by The Macmillan Publishing Co., "*The Second Company*," Copyright © 1924 by The Macmillan Company, renewed 1952 by Bertha Georgie Yeats; "*Sailing to Byzantium*," copyright © 1928 by The Macmillan Publishing Company, rewed 1956 by Bertha Georgie Yeats; "*Leda and the Swan*," copyright © 1928 by The Macmillan Publishing Company, renewed 1956 by Bertha Georgie Yeats; "*Among School Children*," copyright © 1928 by The Macmillan Publishing Company, renewed 1956 by Bertha Georgie Yeats; "*Coole Park, 1929*," copyright © 1933 by The Macmillan Publishing Company, renewed 1961 by Bertha Georgie Yeats; "*Crazy Jane Talks with the Bishop*," copyright © 1933 by The Macmillan Publishing Company, renewed 1961 by Bertha Georgie Yeats; "*Lapis Lazuli*," from *The Poems of W. B. Yeats: A New Edition*, edited by Richard J. Finneran. Copyright © 1940 by Georgie Yeats, renewed 1968 by Bertha Georgie Yeats, Michael Butler Yeats, and Anne Yeats. Reprinted with the permission of Simon & Schuster, Inc.

SINCLAIR-STEVENSON LTD.

Day-Lewis, C.: "*Poem for an Anniversary*," from *Collected Poems of C. Day-Lewis*; originally printed in *A Time to Dance*, by C. Day-Lewis. Reprinted by permission of Sinclair-Stevenson Ltd.

STAINER & BELL LTD.

McDonald, Ellie: "*Itherness*." Reprinted by permission of Stainer & Bell Ltd.

THE SOCIETY OF AUTHORS

Binyon, Laurence: "*Harebell and Pansy*" and "*The Unreturning Spring*," from *Collected Poems*, by Laurence Binyon.
Housman, A. E.: "*Reveille*" and "*Terence, This is Stupid Stuff*," from *The Collected Poems of A. E. Housman*, by A. E. Housman.
Masefield, John: "*Cargoes*," "*Sea Fever*," and "*The West Wind*," from *Poems*, by John Masefield. Reprinted by permission of The Society of Authors as the literary representative of the Estate of John Masefield.

THISTLEDOWN PRESS

Durcan, Paul: "*Wife Who Smashed Television Gets Jail*," from *The Selected Paul Durcan*, edited by Edna Longley. Reprinted by permission of the Thistledown Press.

UNIVERSITY OF TEXAS PRESS

"*Beowulf*," from *Beowulf: An Imitative Translation*, by Ruth P. M. Lehmann Copyright © 1988. Reprinted by permission of the author and the University of Texas Press.

UNIVERSITY OF WALES PRESS

Dafydd ap Gwilym: *from "The Month of May*," from *Gwaith Dafydd ap Gwilym*, edited by Thomas Parry. Copyright © 1952. Reprinted by permission of University of Wales Press.

ACKNOWLEDGMENTS   871

W. W. NORTON

Boland, Eavan: *"The Pomegranate,"* from *In a Time of Violence,* by Eavan Boland. Copyright © 1994 by Eavan Boland. Reprinted by permission of W. W. Norton & Company, Inc.

WAKE FOREST UNIVERSITY PRESS

Carson, Ciaran: *"Slate Street School,"* from *The Irish for No,* by Ciaran Carson. Copyright © 1987.

Kinsella, Thomas: *"Another September,"* from *Poems 1956–1973,* by Thomas Kinsella. Copyright © 1979.

Montague, John: *"Wild Sports of the West,"* from *Selected Poems,* by John Montague. Copyright © 1982.

Muldoon, Paul: *"Sushi,"* from *Meeting the British,* by Paul Muldoon. Copyright © 1987 by Paul Muldoon. Reprinted by permission of Wake Forest University Press.

INDEX OF POETS

INDEX OF TITLES AND FIRST LINES

Designer: Teresa Bonner
Text: 10/13 Electra
Compositor: Maple-Vail
Printer: Maple-Vail
Binder: Maple-Vail